Readings to accompany
Experience Humanities

VOLUME I

BEGINNINGS THROUGH THE RENAISSANCE

EDITED BY

Roy T. Matthews & F. DeWitt Platt

Michigan State University

READINGS TO ACCOMPANY EXPERIENCE HUMANITIES:
VOLUME I: BEGINNINGS THROUGH THE RENAISSANCE

ISBN   978-0-07-749472-8
MHID   0-07-749472-5

Senior Vice President, Products & Markets:
    Kurt L. Strand
Vice President, General Manager,
    Products & Markets: *Michael J. Ryan*
Vice President, Content Production & Technology
    Services: *Kimberly Meriwether David*
Director: *Christopher Freitag*
Brand Manager: *Laura Wilk*
Managing Development Editor: *Nancy Crochiere*
Development Editor: *Arthur Pomponio*
Editorial Coordinator: *Jessica Holmes*
Digital Development Editor: *Betty Chen*

Marketing Manager: *Kelly Odom*
Lead Project Manager: *Susan Trentacosti*
Content Project Manager: *Emily Kline*
Senior Buyer: *Carol A. Bielski*
Designer: *Debra Kubiak*
Cover/Interior Designer: *Pam Verros*
Cover Image: *Mona Lisa (or La Gioconda) by Leonardo*
    da Vinci: Photographer's Choice RF/Getty Images
Typeface: *9/11 Palatino*
Compositor: *Thompson Type*
Printer: *Quad/Graphics*

Library of Congress Control Number: 2012955772

For Dixie Leigh

"Many women have done excellently, but you surpassed them all."
—Book of Proverbs 31:29

FDP

———————— ∞ ————————

For Randy and Elizabeth

*We taught them the past, and they have brought us happiness.
Now, they show us the future by making the world a better place.*

RTM

CONTENTS

PREFACE

In this age of e-books, smartphones, social media, and whatever new technology the next news cycle brings—and the printed word seems to be in decline—we are delighted to present this edition of *Readings to accompany Experience Humanities,* called by us affectionately, "the Reader." Since the first edition (1990), both the Reader and our other textbook, *Experience Humanities,* have been widely adopted at universities and colleges across the country. This anthology offers selections from the West's literary and philosophical heritage which, if studied with care, will help students establish vital intellectual linkages to the literary and philosophical achievements of our continually evolving Western tradition.

The Western tradition, originating in about 3000 BCE and developed over five thousand years, consists of a vast, diverse, and complex tapestry of literary and philosophical writings. To keep this anthology to a manageable length, we have followed two principles as we made our selections: (1) include works that have significantly impacted Western culture, and (2) offer as many diverse and representative voices as possible without sacrificing quality. The readings, placed in chronological order, are arranged in twenty-three chapters, echoing the format of *Experience Humanities,* and comprise two volumes. Volume I covers ancient Mesopotamia through the Renaissance; Volume II, the Renaissance through postmodernism.

In Volume I we revised the existing chapter layout by reconfiguring Chapters 4 to 7, in which a new Chapter 5 was inserted, thus bringing the Reader into harmony with *Experience Humanities.* As a result, Volume I now has thirteen chapters. These changes were made by Professor Thomas F. X. Noble, the coauthor of *Experience Humanities,* and they reflect his current thinking about periodization in ancient and medieval history, his academic specialties. In our Chapter 4, we now cover only Greek civilization as part of Hellenistic cultures. We created a new Chapter 5, devoted to Roman civilization, titled Classical Rome: From Republic to Empire. Our new Chapter 6—Judaism and the Rise of Christianity—is our old Chapter 5. Our new Chapter 7—Late Antiquity: The Transformation of the Roman Empire and the Triumph of Christianity—extends from the crisis of the third century to the remaking of the empire into a Christian world. Thereafter, the chapters are renumbered to reflect this new periodization.

In Volume I, besides reformatting Chapters 4 to 7, we added several selections, in response to our surveys and advice from instructors and students. These changes include: in Chapter 4, adding selections from Apollonius of Rhodes, *The Voyage of the Argo,* an ancient adventure tale that still resonates in today's postmodern, global culture; in Chapter 6, adding selections from Tertullian, *The Apparel of Women,* a document that illustrates the early church's complicated views on women and female sexuality; in Chapter 7, adding selections from Eusebius, *The History of the Church,* the earliest surviving history of the early church; in Chapter 8, adding a selection from

Bede, *A History of the English Church and People,* a brief account of the life of Caedmon, the first English poet, along with a window into the mindset of the early middle ages.

*   *   *

For this edition, we express once again our appreciation to the McGraw-Hill editorial and production teams. Things get better with each edition! First, we want to thank Chris Freitag, Director, for his unfaltering support of this project. We also give a shout-out to Nancy Crochiere, Managing Development Editor, for her calm and steady hand during the year and one half required to bring this edition into print. To Art Pomponio, Development Editor, we are grateful for his many helpful suggestions and nudges, when we were falling behind schedule. We especially single out Susan Trentacosti, Lead Project Manager, for her strength and agility in bringing the production to a successful close and on time; and to Jenna Caputo, Permissions Researcher, for her zeal in obtaining permission rights, even of the most difficult sort. We thank the library staffs of Michigan State University, American University, and Georgetown University for their helpful cooperation. To our former humanities students at Michigan State University who served as readers and critics for most of the anthology's selections, we express our thanks; their informed responses helped hone the way we interpret literature and philosophy. If our headnotes and footnotes are clear and apposite, then part of the praise must be shared with those students. And finally, we want to thank LeeAnn and Dixie, our friends and families, especially our grandchildren Clayton, Evan, and Max Matthews, and Victoria Holland Adams; and Martha Burke for their patience, forbearance, and love during this twenty-two-year-long journey—we are eternally in your debt.

1

PREHISTORY AND THE RISE OF CIVILIZATION IN THE NEAR EAST AND EGYPT

Selections from *The Code of Hammurabi*

Hammurabi (?–1750 BCE), who ruled Babylonia from about 1792 to 1750 BCE, is the most famous of the Amorite tribal kings who gained control of the lower Euphrates Valley (modern Iraq) about 2050 BCE. Like most sovereigns of that period, he attended to the welfare of his cities and their inhabitants, attempted to appease the deities, and protected his people through alliances and wars. His reign was relatively peaceful until the last decade of his life, when he fought his enemies and expanded his empire. After his death, the Amorite dynasty declined, and within two centuries the Babylonian kingdom was swept away, but Hammurabi's set of laws, promulgated to unify his diverse subjects, survived and became an enduring legacy.

Known as the Code of Hammurabi, these laws were inscribed on a seven-foot stele—a stone slab or pillar—which was enshrined in the temple of Marduk, the national god of the Babylonians. The stele miraculously survived over the centuries, being rediscovered in 1901 at Susa in southwest Iran, and is on display today in the Louvre. Once thought to be original with Hammurabi, the Code is now considered a summary of a body of long-standing Sumerian laws. Recent discoveries of Sumerian clay tablets, dating from about 2200 BCE and inscribed with laws covering prices, wages, payments of loans, marriage contracts, property, and slaves, indicate that the Code borrowed laws from Hammurabi's predecessors. At one time scholars thought that the Code of Hammurabi influenced the Mosaic laws of the Hebrews (see *The Holy Scriptures* in Chapter 6), but now it appears that the two sets of laws shared a common cultural tradition.

The Code is divided into three parts: the prologue, the laws, and an epilogue. The prologue repeats a message similar to others inscribed on ancient monuments. Hammurabi's achievements are listed and support from the gods is assured. The laws and regulations, usually including the punishments for breaking the law, are conditionally phrased; that is, if a person commits a certain act, he or she will be punished in certain prescribed ways. The extensive list of laws (282 examples) attempts to incorporate every phase of life—commerce, trade, parental and domestic relations, slavery, libel, slander, theft, marriage, adultery, divorce, property rights and ownership, and employer-employee regulations. Punishment for breaking the law is based on the *lex talionis* or the law of retaliation, "an eye for an eye," which most ancient societies imposed on wrongdoers. A long epilogue reiterates that Hammurabi has governed wisely and with the blessings of the deities and, in conclusion, warns future rulers that if they do not follow the laws and obey the gods, they will be cursed.

Reading the Selections

These excerpts illustrate how much the laws, regardless of their nature and types of punishment, were grounded in everyday life and the shared experiences of humans who lived in communities and were willing to accept a set of rules to settle their differences. In their historical context, they reveal how far societies had come from their earlier tribal customs of blood feuds and personal retaliation. Now, a set of laws, with harsh penalties, applied to all members of the kingdom. The selections from the prologue and the epilogue show that the rulers, who had been chosen by the deities to enact and to administer the laws, were totally dependent upon the gods who had originated the laws and would punish those who disobeyed. The Code, so closely related to the society's religious beliefs, meant that doing good or committing evil was what the gods deemed to be right or wrong. Thus, while the laws dealt with ordinary and mundane events, they possessed a moral dimension that bound the society together. Only by following the laws, emphasized the epilogue, would justice be done, peace maintained, and prosperity possible.

∞

Prologue

When the exalted Anum[1] king of the Anunnaki[2] (and) Illil[3] lord of heaven and earth, who allots the destinies of the land, allotted the divine lordship of the multitude of the people unto Marduk[4] the first-born son of Ea,[5] magnified him amongst the Igigi,[6] called Babylon by its exalted name (and) so made it pre-eminent in the (four) quarters of the world, and stablished for him an everlasting kingdom whose foundations are firmly laid like heaven and earth, at that time Anum and Illil for the prosperity of the people called me by name Hammu-rabi, the reverent God-fearing prince, to make justice to appear in the land, to destroy the evil and the wicked that the strong might not oppress the weak, to rise indeed like Shamash[7] over the dark-haired folk to give light to the land.

. . .

When Marduk commanded me to give justice to the people of the land and to let (them) have (good) governance, I set forth truth and justice throughout the land (and) prospered the people.

[1] **Anum** In Akkadian, **Anu;** in Sumerian, **An.** King of the Babylonian gods and guardian of the city of Uruk, dominant from about 4000 to 2500 BCE.
[2] **Anunnaki** Also called **Anunna.** Collective name for the seven gods of the underworld, also called the seven judges of hell. Depending on myth and setting, they are sometimes called the gods of heaven.
[3] **Illil** In Sumerian, **Enlil.** Babylonian god of the air and storms; chief deity of the pantheon and protector of the city of Nippur, dominant from about 2500 to 1500 BCE.
[4] **Marduk** Chief god of the city of Babylon and the national deity of Babylonia.
[5] **Ea** In Sumerian, **Enki.** Babylonian god of water, depicted as half-goat, half-fish in art, the source of the Capricorn astrological sign. Ea, **Anu,** and Enlil were the most important gods of Mesopotamia.
[6] **Igigi** Collective name for the heavenly gods; often portrayed in opposition to the **Anunnaki,** gods of the underworld.

[7] **Shamash** In Sumerian, **Utu.** Babylonian god of the sun, god of justice, and, at night, judge of the underworld.

∞

The Laws

§ 1

If a man has accused a man and has charged him with
manslaughter and then has not proved (it against) him,
his accuser shall be put to death.

§ 2

If a man has charged a man with sorcery and then has not
proved (it against) him, he who is charged with the sorcery shall go to the holy river[8]; he shall leap into the holy
river and, if the holy river overwhelms him, his accuser
shall take and keep his house; if the holy river proves that
man clear (of the offence) and he comes back safe, he who
has charged him with sorcery shall be put to death; he
who leapt into the holy river shall take and keep the house
of his accuser.

§§ 3–4

If a man has come forward in a case to bear witness to a
felony and then has not proved the statement that he has
made, if that case (is) a capital one, that man shall be put
to death.

   If he has come forward to bear witness to (a claim for)
corn or money, he shall remain liable for the penalty for
that suit.

§ 5

If a judge has tried a suit, given a decision, caused a sealed
tablet to be executed, (and) thereafter varies his judgement, they shall convict that judge of varying (his) judgement and he shall pay twelve-fold the claim in that suit;
then they shall remove him from his place on the bench
of judges in the assembly, and he shall not (again) sit in
judgement with the judges.

§ 6

If a man has stolen property belonging to a god or a palace, that man shall be put to death, and he who has received the stolen property from his hand shall be put to
death.

---

[8] **holy river** The Euphrates River.

§ 7

If a man buys silver or gold or slave[9] or slave-girl or ox
or sheep or ass or anything else whatsoever from a (free)
man's son or a (free) man's slave or has received (them) for
safe custody without witnesses or contract, that man is a
thief; he shall be put to death.

§ 127

If a man has caused a finger to be pointed at a high-
priestess or a married lady[10] and has then not proved
(what he has said), they shall flog that man before the
judges and shave half his head.

§ 128

If a man has taken a (woman to) wife and has not drawn
up a contract for her, that woman is not a wife.

§ 129

If a married lady is caught lying with another man, they
shall bind them and cast them into the water; if her husband wishes to let his wife live, then the king shall let his
servant live.

§ 167

If a man has taken a wife and she has borne him sons
(and) that woman goes to (her) fate, (if) after her (death)
he marries another woman and she bears sons, after(!) the
father goes to (his) fate, the sons shall not make a division
according to mothers; they shall take the dowry of their
(respective) mothers and shall divide the property of the
paternal estate in proportion (to their number).

---

[9] **slave** The Code recognized a three-tiered social hierarchy:
(1) free citizens (Amelu), which included government officials,
priests, and soldiers; (2) villeins (Mushkinu), a middle class
of merchants, shop owners, schoolteachers, workers, farmers,
artisans, and craftspeople; and (3) slaves. Criminal law penalties were set according to one's place in the social hierarchy; no
distinctions were made in issues of property.
[10] **married lady** The Code treated monogamy as the standard
practice for families in Babylonian society, though concubines
were tolerated.

§§ 168–169

If a man sets his face to disinherit his son (and) states to the judges "I will disinherit my son," the judges shall determine the facts of his case and, if he has not deserved the heavy penalty of disinheritance, the father may not disinherit his son.

If he deserves the heavy penalty of disinheritance at the hands of his father, a first time they shall pardon him; if he deserves the (same) heavy penalty a second time, his father may disinherit his son.

§§ 196–205

If a man has put out the eye of a free man, they shall put out his eye.

If he breaks the bone of a (free) man, they shall break ₁₅ his bone.

If he puts out the eye of a villein or breaks the bone of a villein, he shall pay 1 maneh of silver.

If he puts out the eye of a (free) man's slave or breaks the bone of a (free) man's slave, he shall pay half his price.

If a man knocks out the tooth of a (free) man equal (in rank) to him(self), they shall knock out his tooth.

If he knocks out the tooth of a villein, he shall pay ⅓ maneh of silver.

If a man strikes the cheek of a (free) man who is su- ₂₀ perior (in rank) to him(self), he shall be beaten with sixty stripes with a whip of ox-hide in the assembly.

If the man strikes the cheek of a free man equal to him(self in rank), he shall pay 1 maneh of silver.

If a villein strikes the cheek of a villein, he shall pay 10 shekels of silver.

If the slave of a (free) man strikes the cheek of a free man, they shall cut off his ear.

.   .   .

Epilogue

(These are) the just laws which Hammurabi the able king ₁ has stablished and (thereby) has enabled the land to enjoy stable governance and good rule.

I Hammu-rabi, the gracious king, have not been careless nor been slack on behalf of the dark-haired folk whom Illil has granted to me (and) whose shepherding Marduk has given to me; I seek out peaceful places for them (and) have relieved their cruel distresses, (and) I make light to rise upon them. With the mighty weapon which Ilbaba[11] and Ishtar[12] have bestowed upon me, with the wisdom which Ea has allotted to me, with the ability which Marduk has given to me, I have plucked up (my) enemies from north to south, extinguished wars (and) prospered the land; I have made the people of the towns to lie down in safety (and) have left them none to affright them.

.   .   .

If that man has not heeded my words which I have inscribed on my monument, has despised my curses and has not feared the curses of the gods and so has razed the judgment which I have judged, revoked my commandments (and) altered my carved figures, has erased my name inscribed (thereon) and has then inscribed his (own) name (in its place), (or if) in fear of those curses he suborns another indeed (to do so), may the great Anum the father of the gods who has called me to reign deprive that man, whether king or lord or governor or any of mankind that bears a name, of royal splendour, break his sceptre (and) curse his destiny; may the lord Illil who allots the destinies (of mankind), whose word then is unalterable, the magnifier of my kingdom, kindle disorder that cannot be put down (and) despair to be the ruin of him in his habitation, may he allot unto him as (his) destiny a reign of sighs, days of scarcity (and) years of famine, thick darkness (and) death in the twinkling of an eye; may he by his honoured mouth ordain the ruin of his city, the scattering of his people, the overthrow of his kingdom, the extinction of his name and of his fame in the land.

.   .   .

May Ishtar, the lady of battle and conflict who unsheathes my weapon, my favouring guardian spirit (and) the lover of my reign, curse his kingdom in her great rage from her wrathful heart, turn his good fortune into ill fortune, break his weapons in field battle and conflict, raise disorder (and) rebellion against him, strike down his heroes (and) let the earth drink their blood, (and) let his armies be left a heap of corpses on the plain, let no quarter be given to his soldiers, deliver that man into the hand of his enemies and lead him in bonds to a land at enmity with him.

May Nergal,[13] mighty amongst the gods, the warrior ₅ whom none can resist, who has fulfilled my eager desire, by his great power consume his people like a fire raging amongst rushes, may he cleave him asunder with his mighty weapon and shatter his limbs as of a statue of clay.

---

[11] **Ilbaba** Also called **Zamama**. Babylonian god of war and protector of the city of Kish.
[12] **Ishtar** In Sumerian, **Inanna**. Babylonian goddess of love, fertility, and fighting. Said to be the daughter of various gods, including **Anu.**

---

[13] **Nergal** An underworld deity, the god of war and sudden death.

May Nintu,[14] the exalted lady of the lands, the mother my creatress, bereave him of an heir and let him have no name, let him create no seed of mankind in the midst of his people.

May Ninkarrak,[15] the daughter of Anum, who speaks in my favour in Ekur,[16] bring upon his limbs a grievous sore, an evil plague, a sore wound which none can assuage (and) of which no physician knows the nature (and)

cannot relieve it with dressings, (and which) like the sting of death cannot be plucked out, so that he may then bewail his (lost) manhood until his life is extinguished.

May the great gods of heaven and earth, the Anunnaki all together, and the protecting deity of the house, the brick-god of Ebabbar,[17] curse that (man), his seed, his land, his soldiers, his people and his army, with a baleful curse.

May Illil with his word which shall then be unalterable curse him with clear curses, and may they quickly overtake him!

---

[14] **Nintu** Babylonian mother goddess.
[15] **Ninkarrak** Perhaps a minor mother goddess.
[16] **Ekur** Heaven.

[17] **Ebabbar** Temple of the sun god **Shamash**.

Questions for Critical Thinking

1. In what ways does the Code of Hammurabi reflect its historical period? Give three examples.

2. Compare three examples of different crimes and punishments described in the Code of Hammurabi with similar crimes and punishments in today's United States legal system.

Selections from *The Epic of Gilgamesh*

The Epic of Gilgamesh is now considered by most scholars to be the oldest known epic in Western literature. This work predates Homer's *Iliad* and *Odyssey* by some fifteen hundred years, appearing about 2200 BCE.

Like other epics, *The Epic of Gilgamesh* went through several variations before reaching its final form. It is based on a historical figure who quickly passed over into folklore. Gilgamesh reigned as king of the Sumerian city of Uruk around 2700 BCE, and soon after his death, his ordinary experiences were turned into stories of heroic deeds and dangerous journeys. Civilizations that succeeded the Sumerians infused into the epic new episodes and characters, different sets of deities, and issues reflecting the concerns of their own time. Despite its evolution through various civilizations, this epic recalls similar events that appear in other cultures' histories. In *The Epic of Gilgamesh*, the tale of a devastating flood that killed all animals and humans except those who took refuge in a boat resembles stories from other societies, in particular the biblical narrative of Noah, his family, and God.

Another reason *The Epic of Gilgamesh* evolved from its original form was that it, like all epics, was sung long before it was written, and storytellers adapted the episodes and characters to fit their new audiences. The earliest written form of *The Epic of Gilgamesh* uncovered by archaeologists dates from about 600 BCE, a time when many Middle Eastern societies were disappearing and just before many others would fall under the influence of Greek civilization, later to become provinces of the Roman Empire.

Reading the Selections

These excerpts deal with two themes: (1) that mortals cannot insult the gods and goddesses without punishment and (2) that humans are destined to die. Ishtar, the goddess of love, attempts to seduce Gilgamesh, who spurns her overtures by recalling how she ruined other humans. Furious at Gilgamesh, Ishtar asks her father to send the Bull of Heaven to kill Gilgamesh. Gilgamesh and Enkidu, the former wildman who had become civilized and had fought Gilgamesh before becoming his close companion, kill the bull. The gods and goddesses decide that Enkidu must die for this transgression. As Enkidu lies dying, he dreams of walking through the "house of dust," where he encounters dead kings and priests and various deities. Homer and many other writers later copy this device of transporting their heroes into the world of the dead to speak with the great men and, sometimes, women of history, as a way to glorify the past and allow the characters to be told of future events by the dead.

Touched by Enkidu's death, Gilgamesh recognizes his own mortal nature but refuses to accept his final fate. He sets out to find Utnapishtim, to whom the gods have given everlasting life and who, Gilgamesh hopes, will answer his questions about immortality. Gilgamesh, on his journey, has many adventures, among them meeting Siduri, who keeps a vineyard and advises Gilgamesh to enjoy life now, for he is destined to die. When Gilgamesh finally meets Utnapishtim, he is told that nothing is permanent; thus life is not everlasting. Gilgamesh asks Utnapishtim why the gods gave him immortality, and the old man replies that he will reveal a secret about the gods and proceeds to tell The Story of the Flood.

Ishtar and Gilgamesh, and the Death of Enkidu

Gilgamesh washed out his long locks and cleaned his weapons; he flung back his hair from his shoulders; he threw off his stained clothes and changed them for new. He put on his royal robes and made them fast. When Gilgamesh had put on the crown, glorious Ishtar[18] lifted her eyes, seeing the beauty of Gilgamesh. She said, "Come to me Gilgamesh, and be my bridegroom; grant me seed of your body, let me be your bride and you shall be my husband. I will harness for you a chariot of lapis lazuli[19] and of gold, with wheels of gold and horns of copper; and you shall have mighty demons of the storm for draft-mules. When you enter our house in the fragrance of cedar-wood, threshold and throne will kiss your feet. Kings, rulers, and princes will bow down before you; they shall bring you tribute from the mountains and the plain. Your ewes shall drop twins and your goats triplets; your pack-ass shall outrun mules; your oxen shall have no rivals, and your chariot horses shall be famous far-off for their swiftness."

Gilgamesh opened his mouth and answered glorious Ishtar, "If I take you in marriage, what gifts can I give in return? What ointments and clothing for your body? I would gladly give you bread and all sorts of food fit for a god. I would give you wine to drink fit for a queen. I would pour out barley to stuff your granary; but as for

making you my wife—that I will not. How would it go with me? Your lovers have found you like a brazier which smoulders in the cold, a backdoor which keeps out neither squall of wind nor storm, a castle which crushes the garrison, pitch that blackens the bearer, a water-skin that chafes the carrier, a stone which falls from the parapet, a battering-ram turned back from the enemy, a sandal that trips the wearer. Which of your lovers did you ever love for ever? What shepherd of yours has pleased you for all time? Listen to me while I tell the tale of your lovers. There was Tammuz,[20] the lover of your youth, for him you decreed wailing, year after year. You loved the many-coloured roller,[21] but still you struck and broke his wing; now in the grove he sits and cries, 'Kappi,[22] kappi, my wing, my wing.' You have loved the lion tremendous in strength: seven pits you dug for him, and seven. You have loved the stallion magnificent in battle, and for him you decreed whip and spur and a thong, to gallop seven leagues by force and to muddy the water before he drinks; and for his mother Silili[23] lamentations. You have loved the shepherd of the flock; he made meal-cake for you day after day, he killed kids for your sake. You struck and turned him into a wolf; now his own herd-boys chase him

---

[18] **Ishtar** Also called **Inanna.** The goddess of love, fertility, and war. Identified with the planet Venus. Daughter of **Anu,** king of the gods, and **Antum.**
[19] **lapis lazuli** A semiprecious stone that is usually azure blue; greatly valued in Mesopotamia.

[20] **Tammuz** Also called **Dumuzi** ("true son"). The shepherd god. In the myth titled "Inanna's Journey to Hell," the goddess Ishtar abandons her husband Dumuzi in Hell.
[21] **roller** A bird that symbolized a lover of the goddess **Ishtar.**
[22] **kappi** A bird sound.
[23] **Silili** The divine mare, the mother of all horses.

away, his own hounds worry his flanks. And did you not love Ishullanu,[24] the gardener of your father's palm-grove? He brought you baskets filled with dates without end; every day he loaded your table. Then you turned your eyes on him and said, 'Dearest Ishullanu, come here to me, let us enjoy your manhood, come forward and take me, I am yours.' Ishullanu answered, 'What are you asking from me? My mother has baked and I have eaten; why should I come to such as you for food that is tainted and rotten? For when was a screen of rushes sufficient protection from frosts?' But when you had heard his answer you struck him. He was changed to a blind mole deep in the earth, one whose desire is always beyond his reach. And if you and I should be lovers, should not I be served in the same fashion as all these others whom you loved once?"

When Ishtar heard this she fell into a bitter rage, she went up to high heaven. Her tears poured down in front of her father Anu,[25] and Antum[26] her mother. She said, "My father, Gilgamesh has heaped insults on me, he has told over all my abominable behaviour, my foul and hideous acts." Anu opened his mouth and said, "Are you a father of gods? Did not you quarrel with Gilgamesh the king, so now he has related your abominable behaviour, your foul and hideous acts?"

Ishtar opened her mouth and said again, "My father, give me the Bull of Heaven[27] to destroy Gilgamesh. Fill Gilgamesh, I say, with arrogance to his destruction; but if you refuse to give me the Bull of Heaven I will break in the doors of hell and smash the bolts; there will be confusion of people, those above with those from the lower depths. I shall bring up the dead to eat food like the living; and the hosts of dead will outnumber the living." Anu said to great Ishtar, "If I do what you desire there will be seven years of drought throughout Uruk when corn will be seedless husks. Have you saved grain enough for the people and grass for the cattle?" Ishtar replied, "I have saved grain for the people, grass for the cattle; for seven years of seedless husks there is grain and there is grass enough."

When Anu heard what Ishtar had said he gave her the Bull of Heaven to lead by the halter down to Uruk. When they reached the gates of Uruk the Bull went to the river; with his first snort cracks opened in the earth and a hundred young men fell down to death. With his second snort cracks opened and two hundred fell down to death. With his third snort cracks opened, Enkidu doubled over but instantly recovered, he dodged aside and leapt on the Bull and seized it by the horns. The Bull of Heaven foamed in his face, it brushed him with the thick of its tail. Enkidu cried to Gilgamesh, "My friend, we boasted that we would leave enduring names behind us. Now thrust in your sword between the nape and the horns." So Gilgamesh followed the Bull, he seized the thick of its tail, he thrust the sword between the nape and the horns and slew the Bull.

When they had killed the Bull of Heaven they cut out its heart and gave it to Shamash, and the brothers rested.

But Ishtar rose up and mounted the great wall of Uruk; she sprang on to the tower and uttered a curse: "Woe to Gilgamesh, for he has scorned me in killing the Bull of Heaven." When Enkidu heard these words he tore out the Bull's right thigh and tossed it in her face saying, "If I could lay my hands on you, it is this I should do to you, and lash the entrails to your side." Then Ishtar called together her people, the dancing and singing girls, the prostitutes of the temple, the courtesans. Over the thigh of the Bull of Heaven she set up lamentation.

But Gilgamesh called the smiths and the armourers, all of them together. They admired the immensity of the horns. They were plated with lapis lazuli two fingers thick. They were thirty pounds each in weight, and their capacity in oil was six measures, which he gave to his guardian god, Lugulbanda.[28] But he carried the horns into the palace and hung them on the wall. Then they washed their hands in Euphrates, they embraced each other and went away. They drove through the streets of Uruk where the heroes were gathered to see them, and Gilgamesh called to the singing girls, "Who is most glorious of the heroes, who is most eminent among men?" "Gilgamesh is the most glorious of heroes, Gilgamesh is most eminent among men." And now there was feasting, and celebrations and joy in the palace, till the heroes lay down saying, "Now we will rest for the night."

When the daylight came Enkidu got up and cried to Gilgamesh, "Oh my brother, such a dream I had last night. Anu, Enlil,[29] Ea[30] and heavenly Shamash[31] took counsel together, and Anu said to Enlil, 'Because they have killed the Bull of Heaven, and because they have killed Humbaba[32] who guarded the Cedar Mountain one of the two must die.' Then glorious Shamash answered the hero Enlil, 'It was by your command they killed the Bull of Heaven, and killed Humbaba, and must Enkidu die although innocent?' Enlil flung round in rage at glorious Shamash, 'You dare to say this, you who went about with them every day like one of themselves!'"

So Enkidu lay stretched out before Gilgamesh; his tears ran down in streams and he said to Gilgamesh, "O my brother, so dear as you are to me, brother, yet they will take me from you." Again he said, "I must sit down on the threshold of the dead and never again will I see my dear brother with my eyes."

While Enkidu lay alone in his sickness he cursed the gate as though it was living flesh, "You there, wood of the gate, dull and insensible, witless, I searched for you over twenty leagues until I saw the towering cedar. There is no wood like you in our land. Seventy-two cubits high and twenty-four wide, the pivot and the ferrule[33] and the

---

[24] **Ishullanu** The gardener of **Anu,** king of the Mesopotamian gods.
[25] **Anu** King of the Mesopotamian gods and father of **Ishtar.**
[26] **Antum** From Sumerian, "the earth." Mother of **Ishtar** and consort of **Anu.**
[27] **Bull of Heaven** Monster created by **Anu** and given to **Ishtar** to be used against Gilgamesh.

[28] **Lugulbanda** God-king of the city of Uruk and perhaps Gilgamesh's father. Gilgamesh worshiped him as a god.
[29] **Enlil** Babylonian god of air and storms.
[30] **Ea** In Sumerian, **Enki.** Babylonian god of water.
[31] **Shamash** Babylonian god of the sun.
[32] **Humbaba** Also called **Huwawa.** A nature god assigned to protect the cedar forest.
[33] **ferrule** A metal brace to keep a gate from splitting.

jambs[34] are perfect. A master craftsman from Nippur has made you; but O, if I had known the conclusion! If I had known that this was all the good that would come of it, I would have raised the axe and split you into little pieces and set up here a gate of wattle instead. Ah, if only some future king had brought you here, or some god had fashioned you. Let him obliterate my name and write his own, and the curse fall on him instead of on Enkidu."

With the first brightening of dawn Enkidu raised his head and wept before the Sun God,[35] in the brilliance of the sunlight his tears streamed down. "Sun God, I beseech you, about that vile Trapper, that Trapper of nothing because of whom I was to catch less than my comrade; let him catch least; make his game scarce, make him feeble, taking the smaller of every share, let his quarry escape from his nets."

When he had cursed the Trapper to his heart's content he turned on the harlot. He was roused to curse her also. "As for you, woman, with a great curse I curse you! I will promise you a destiny to all eternity. My curse shall come on you soon and sudden. You shall be without a roof for your commerce, for you shall not keep house with other girls in the tavern, but do your business in places fouled by the vomit of the drunkard. Your hire will be potter's earth,[36] your thievings will be flung into the hovel, you will sit at the cross-roads in the dust of the potter's quarter, you will make your bed on the dunghill at night, and by day take your stand in the wall's shadow. Brambles and thorns will tear your feet, the drunk and the dry will strike your cheek and your mouth will ache. Let you be stripped of your purple[37] dyes, for I too once in the wilderness with my wife had all the treasure I wished."

When Shamash heard the words of Enkidu he called to him from heaven: "Enkidu, why are you cursing the woman, the mistress who taught you to eat bread fit for gods and drink wine of kings? She who put upon you a magnificent garment, did she not give you glorious Gilgamesh for your companion, and has not Gilgamesh, your own brother, made you rest on a royal bed and recline on a couch at his left hand? He has made the princes of the earth kiss your feet, and now all the people of Uruk lament and wail over you. When you are dead he will let his hair grow long for your sake, he will wear a lion's pelt and wander through the desert."

When Enkidu heard glorious Shamash his angry heart grew quiet, he called back the curse and said, "Woman, I promise you another destiny. The mouth which cursed you shall bless you! Kings, princes and nobles shall adore you. On your account a man though twelve miles off will clap his hand to his thigh and his hair will twitch. For you he will undo his belt and open his treasure and you shall have your desire; lapis lazuli, gold and carnelian[38] from the heap in the treasury. A ring for your hand and a robe shall be yours. The priest will lead you into the presence of the gods. On your account a wife, a mother of seven, was forsaken."

As Enkidu slept alone in his sickness, in bitterness of 15 spirit he poured out his heart to his friend. "It was I who cut down the cedar, I who levelled the forest, I who slew Humbaba and now see what has become of me. Listen, my friend, this is the dream I dreamed last night. The heavens roared, and earth rumbled back an answer; between them stood I before an awful being, the somber-faced man-bird; he had directed on me his purpose. His was a vampire face, his foot was a lion's foot, his hand was an eagle's talon. He fell on me and his claws were in my hair, he held me fast and I smothered; then he transformed me so that my arms became wings covered with feathers. He turned his stare towards me, and he led me away to the palace of Irkalla,[39] the Queen of Darkness, to the house from which none who enters ever returns, down the road from which there is no coming back.

"There is the house whose people sit in darkness; dust is their food and clay their meat. They are clothed like birds with wings for covering, they see no light, they sit in darkness. I entered the house of dust and I saw the kings of the earth, their crowns put away for ever; rulers and princes, all those who once wore kingly crowns and ruled the world in the days of old. They who had stood in the place of the gods like Anu and Enlil, stood now like servants to fetch baked meats in the house of dust, to carry cooked meat and cold water from the water-skin. In the house of dust which I entered were high priests and acolytes, priests of the incantation and of ecstasy; there were servers of the temple, and there was Etana,[40] that King of Kish whom the eagle carried to heaven in the days of old. I saw also Samuqan,[41] god of cattle, and there was Ereshkigal[42] The Queen of the Underworld; and Belit-Sheri[43] squatted in front of her, she who is recorder of the gods and keeps the book of death. She held a tablet from which she read. She raised her head, she saw me and spoke: "Who has brought this one here?" Then I awoke like a man drained of blood who wanders alone in a waste of rushes; like one whom the bailiff has seized and his heart pounds with terror."

Gilgamesh had peeled off his clothes, he listened to his words and wept quick tears, Gilgamesh listened and his tears flowed. He opened his mouth and spoke to Enkidu: "Who is there in strong-walled Uruk who has wisdom like this? Strange things have been spoken, why does your heart speak strangely? The dream was marvellous but the terror was great; we must treasure the dream whatever the terror; for the dream has shown that misery comes at last to the healthy man, the end of life is sorrow."

---

[34] **jamb** An upright piece forming the side of a door opening.
[35] **Sun God Shamash** (see footnote 31).
[36] **potter's earth** Dirt for a graveyard.
[37] **purple** Tyrian purple, an expensive dye available only from a mollusk at Tyre (in modern Lebanon), a color falling between red and blue; usually reserved for royalty or other high rank in ancient times.
[38] **carnelian** A hard, reddish stone used in jewelry.

[39] **Irkalla** Another name for **Ereshkigal,** the queen of the underworld.
[40] **Etana** Legendary king of Kish and a great friend of Gilgamesh.
[41] **Samuqan** Mesopotamian god of cattle; a member of **Ereshkigal's** court in the underworld.
[42] **Ereshkigal** Mesopotamian queen of the underworld.
[43] **Belit-Sheri** Female scribe in the underworld; works for **Ereshkigal.**

And Gilgamesh lamented, "Now I will pray to the great gods, for my friend had an ominous dream."

This day on which Enkidu dreamed came to an end and he lay stricken with sickness. One whole day he lay on his bed and his suffering increased. He said to Gilgamesh, the friend on whose account he had left the wilderness, "Once I ran for you, for the water of life, and I now have nothing." A second day he lay on his bed and Gilgamesh watched over him but the sickness increased. A third day he lay on his bed, he called out to Gilgamesh, rousing him up. Now he was weak and his eyes were blind with weeping. Ten days he lay and his suffering increased, eleven and twelve days he lay on his bed of pain. Then he called to Gilgamesh, "My friend, the great goddess cursed me and I must die in shame. I shall not die like a man fallen in battle; I feared to fall, but happy is the man who falls in the battle, for I must die in shame." And Gilgamesh wept over Enkidu. . . .

He touched his heart but it did not beat, nor did he lift his eyes again. When Gilgamesh touched his heart it did not beat. So Gilgamesh laid a veil, as one veils the bride, over his friend. He began to rage like a lion, like a lioness robbed of her whelps. This way and that he paced round the bed, he tore out his hair and strewed it around. He dragged off his splendid robes and flung them down as though they were abominations.

In the first light of dawn Gilgamesh cried out, "I made ₂₀ you rest on a royal bed, you reclined on a couch at my left hand, the princes of the earth kissed your feet. I will cause all the people of Uruk to weep over you and raise the dirge of the dead. The joyful people will stoop with sorrow; and when you have gone to the earth I will let my hair grow long for your sake, I will wander through the wilderness in the skin of a lion." The next day also, in the first light, Gilgamesh lamented; seven days and seven nights he wept for Enkidu, until the worm fastened on him. Only then he gave him up to the earth, for the Anunnaki, the judges, had seized him.

Then Gilgamesh issued a proclamation through the land, he summoned them all, the coppersmiths, the goldsmiths, the stone-workers, and commanded them, "Make a statue of my friend." The statue was fashioned with a great weight of lapis lazuli for the breast and of gold for the body. A table of hard-wood was set out, and on it a bowl of carnelian filled with honey, and a bowl of lapis lazuli filled with butter. These he exposed and offered to the Sun; and weeping he went away.

∽

The Search for Everlasting Life

Bitterly Gilgamesh wept for his friend Enkidu; he wan- ₁ dered over the wilderness as a hunter, he roamed over the plains; in his bitterness he cried, "How can I rest, how can I be at peace? Despair is in my heart. What my brother is now, that shall I be when I am dead. Because I am afraid of death I will go as best I can to find Utnapishtim[44] whom they call the Faraway, for he has entered the assembly of the gods." So Gilgamesh travelled over the wilderness, he wandered over the grasslands, a long journey, in search of Utnapishtim, whom the gods took after the deluge; and they set him to live in the land of Dilmun,[45] in the garden of the sun; and to him alone of men they gave everlasting life.

At night when he came to the mountain passes Gilgamesh prayed: "In these mountain passes long ago I saw lions, I was afraid and I lifted my eyes to the moon; I prayed and my prayers went up to the gods, so now, O moon god Sin,[46] protect me." When he had prayed he lay down to sleep, until he was woken from out of a dream.

He saw the lions round him glorying in life; then he took his axe in his hand, he drew his sword from his belt, and he fell upon them like an arrow from the string, and struck and destroyed and scattered them.

. . .

There was the garden of the gods; all round him stood bushes bearing gems. Seeing it he went down at once, for there was fruit of carnelian with the vine hanging from it, beautiful to look at; lapis lazuli leaves hung thick with fruit, sweet to see. For thorns and thistles there were haematite[47] and rare stones, agate, and pearls from out of the sea. While Gilgamesh walked in the garden by the edge of the sea Shamash saw him, and he saw that he was dressed in the skins of animals and ate their flesh. He was distressed, and he spoke and said, "No mortal man has gone this way before, nor will, as long as the winds drive over the sea." And to Gilgamesh he said, "You will never find the life for which you are searching." Gilgamesh said to glorious Shamash, "Now that I have toiled and strayed so far over the wilderness, am I to sleep, and let the earth cover my head for ever? Let my eyes see the sun until they are dazzled with looking. Although I am no better than a dead man, still let me see the light of the sun."

---

[44] **Utnapishtim** Son of **Ubara-Tutu.** Often called the Babylonian Noah (see The Holy Scriptures in Chapter 6). Utnapishtim and his wife are made immortal after the flood.
[45] **Dilmun** The heavenly paradise of the immortal **Utnapishtim** and his wife. Historic Dilmun was an ancient kingdom on the island known today as al-Bahrain in the Persian Gulf, which flourished about 2000 BCE.
[46] **Sin** Also called **Su-en** or **Suen;** in Sumerian, **Nanna.** Babylonian moon god.

[47] **haematite, or hematite** Iron ore occurring in two forms: crystals and reddish earth.

Beside the sea she lives, the woman of the vine, the maker of wine; Siduri[48] sits in the garden at the edge of the sea, with the golden bowl and the golden vats that the gods gave her. She is covered with a veil; and where she sits she sees Gilgamesh coming towards her, wearing skins, the flesh of the gods in his body, but despair in his heart, and his face like the face of one who has made a long journey. She looked, and as she scanned the distance she said in her own heart, "Surely this is some felon; where is he going now?" And she barred her gate against him with the cross-bar and shot home the bolt. But Gilgamesh, hearing the sound of the bolt, threw up his head and lodged his foot in the gate; he called to her, "Young woman, maker of wine, why do you bolt your door; what did you see that made you bar your gate? I will break in your door and burst in your gate, for I am Gilgamesh who seized and killed the Bull of Heaven, I killed the watchman of the cedar forest, I overthrew Humbaba who lived in the forest, and I killed the lions in the passes of the mountain."

Then Siduri said to him, "If you are that Gilgamesh 5 who seized and killed the Bull of Heaven, who killed the watchman of the cedar forest, who overthrew Humbaba that lived in the forest, and killed the lions in the passes of the mountain, why are your cheeks so starved and why is your face so drawn? Why is despair in your heart and your face like the face of one who has made a long journey? Yes, why is your face burned from heat and cold, and why do you come here wandering over the pastures in search of the wind?"

Gilgamesh answered her, "And why should not my cheeks be starved and my face drawn? Despair is in my heart and my face is the face of one who has made a long journey, it was burned with heat and with cold. Why should I not wander over the pastures in search of the wind? My friend, my younger brother, he who hunted the wild ass of the wilderness and the panther of the plains, my friend, my younger brother who seized and killed the Bull of Heaven and overthrew Humbaba in the cedar forest, my friend who was very dear to me and who endured dangers beside me, Enkidu my brother, whom I loved, the end of mortality has overtaken him. I wept for him seven days and nights till the worm fastened on him. Because of my brother I am afraid of death, because of my brother I stray through the wilderness and cannot rest. But now, young woman, maker of wine, since I have seen your face do not let me see the face of death which I dread so much."

She answered, "Gilgamesh, where are you hurrying to? You will never find that life for which you are looking. When the gods created man they allotted to him death, but life they retained in their own keeping. As for you, Gilgamesh, fill your belly with good things; day and night, night and day, dance and be merry, feast and rejoice. Let your clothes be fresh, bathe yourself in water, cherish the little child that holds your hand, and make your wife happy in your embrace; for this too is the lot of man."

But Gilgamesh said to Siduri, the young woman, "How can I be silent, how can I rest, when Enkidu whom I

love is dust, and I too shall die and be laid in the earth. You live by the sea-shore and look into the heart of it; young woman, tell me now, which is the way to Utnapishtim, the son of Ubara-Tutu[49]? What directions are there for the passage; give me, oh, give me directions. I will cross the Ocean if it is possible; if it is not I will wander still farther in the wilderness." The wine-maker said to him, "Gilgamesh, there is no crossing the Ocean; whoever has come, since the days of old, has not been able to pass that sea. The Sun in his glory crosses the Ocean, but who beside Shamash has ever crossed it? The place and the passage are difficult, and the waters of death are deep which flow between. Gilgamesh, how will you cross the Ocean? When you come to the waters of death what will you do? But Gilgamesh, down in the woods you will find Urshanabi,[50] the ferryman of Utnapishtim; with him are the holy things, the things of stone. He is fashioning the serpent prow of the boat. Look at him well, and if it is possible, perhaps you will cross the waters with him; but if it is not possible, then you must go back."

When Gilgamesh heard this he was seized with anger. He took his axe in his hand, and his dagger from his belt. He crept forward and he fell on them like a javelin. Then he went into the forest and sat down. Urshanabi saw the dagger flash and heard the axe, and he beat his head, for Gilgamesh had shattered the tackle of the boat in his rage. Urshanabi said to him, "Tell me, what is your name? I am Urshanabi, the ferryman of Utnapishtim the Faraway." He replied to him, "Gilgamesh is my name, I am from Uruk, from the house of Anu." Then Urshanabi said to him, "Why are your cheeks so starved and your face drawn? Why is despair in your heart and your face like the face of one who has made a long journey; yes, why is your face burned with heat and with cold, and why do you come here wandering over the pastures in search of the wind?"

Gilgamesh said to him, "Why should not my cheeks 10 be starved and my face drawn? Despair is in my heart, and my face is the face of one who has made a long journey. I was burned with heat and with cold. Why should I not wander over the pastures? My friend, my younger brother who seized and killed the Bull of Heaven, and overthrew Humbaba in the cedar forest, my friend who was very dear to me, and who endured dangers beside me, Enkidu my brother whom I loved, the end of mortality has overtaken him. I wept for him seven days and nights till the worm fastened on him. Because of my brother I am afraid of death, because of my brother I stray through the wilderness. His fate lies heavy upon me. How can I be silent, how can I rest? He is dust and I too shall die and be laid in the earth for ever. I am afraid of death, therefore, Urshanabi, tell me which is the road to Utnapishtim? If it is possible I will cross the waters of death; if not I will wander still farther through the wilderness."

Urshanabi said to him, "Gilgamesh, your own hands have prevented you from crossing the Ocean; when you

---

[48] **Siduri** A young woman who makes wine and counsels Gilgamesh to seek pleasure instead of immortality.

[49] **Ubara-Tutu** Father of **Utnapishtim.**
[50] **Urshanabi** The ferryman and sailor god who crosses the water daily between the garden of the sun and the paradise where the immortal **Utnapishtim** and his wife live.

destroyed the tackle of the boat you destroyed its safety."
Then the two of them talked it over and Gilgamesh said,
"Why are you so angry with me, Urshanabi, for you yourself cross the sea by day and night, at all seasons you cross
it." "Gilgamesh, those things you destroyed, their property is to carry me over the water, to prevent the waters
of death from touching me. It was for this reason that I
preserved them, but you have destroyed them, and the
urnu snakes[51] with them. But now, go into the forest, Gilgamesh; with your axe cut poles, one hundred and twenty,
cut them sixty cubits long, paint them with bitumen,[52] set
on them ferrules and bring them back."

When Gilgamesh heard this he went into the forest,
he cut poles one hundred and twenty; he cut them sixty
cubits long, he painted them with bitumen, he set on them
ferrules, and he brought them to Urshanabi. Then they
boarded the boat, Gilgamesh and Urshanabi together,
launching it out on the waves of Ocean. For three days
they ran on as it were a journey of a month and fifteen
days, and at last Urshanabi brought the boat to the waters
of death. Then Urshanabi said to Gilgamesh, "Press on,
take a pole and thrust it in, but do not let your hands touch
the waters. Gilgamesh, take a second pole, take a third,
take a fourth pole. Now, Gilgamesh, take a fifth, take a
sixth and seventh pole. Gilgamesh, take an eighth, and
ninth, a tenth pole. Gilgamesh, take an eleventh, take a
twelfth pole." After one hundred and twenty thrusts Gilgamesh had used the last pole. Then he stripped himself,
he held up his arms for a mast and his covering for a sail.
So Urshanabi the ferryman brought Gilgamesh to Utnapishtim, whom they call the Faraway, who lives in Dilmun
at the place of the sun's transit, eastward of the mountain.
To him alone of men the gods had given everlasting life.

Now Utnapishtim, where he lay at ease, looked into
the distance and he said in his heart, musing to himself,
"Why does the boat sail here without tackle and mast;
why are the sacred stones[53] destroyed, and why does the
master not sail the boat? That man who comes is none of
mine; where I look I see a man whose body is covered
with skins of beasts. Who is this who walks up the shore
behind Urshanabi, for surely he is no man of mine?" So
Utnapishtim looked at him and said, "What is your name,
you who come here wearing the skins of beasts, with your
cheeks starved and your face drawn? Where are you hurrying to now? For what reason have you made this great
journey, crossing the seas whose passage is difficult? Tell
me the reason for your coming."

He replied, "Gilgamesh is my name. I am from Uruk,
from the house of Anu." Then Utnapishtim said to him,
"If you are Gilgamesh, why are your cheeks so starved and
your face drawn? Why is despair in your heart and
your face like the face of one who has made a long journey? Yes, why is your face burned with heat and cold; and

why do you come here, wandering over the wilderness in
search of the wind?"

Gilgamesh said to him, "Why should not my cheeks
be starved and my face drawn? Despair is in my heart
and my face is the face of one who has made a long journey. It was burned with heat and with cold. Why should
I not wander over the pastures? My friend, my younger
brother who seized and killed the Bull of Heaven and
overthrew Humbaba in the cedar forest, my friend who
was very dear to me and endured dangers beside me, Enkidu, my brother whom I loved, the end of mortality has
overtaken him. I wept for him seven days and nights till
the worm fastened on him. Because of my brother I am
afraid of death; because of my brother I stray through the
wilderness. His fate lies heavy upon me. How can I be silent, how can I rest? He is dust and I shall die also and be
laid in the earth for ever." Again Gilgamesh said, speaking to Utnapishtim, "It is to see Utnapishtim whom we
call the Faraway that I have come this journey. For this
I have wandered over the world, I have crossed many
difficult ranges, I have crossed the seas, I have wearied
myself with travelling; my joints are aching, and I have
lost acquaintance with sleep which is sweet. My clothes
were worn out before I came to the house of Siduri. I have
killed the bear and hyena, the lion and panther, the tiger,
the stag and the ibex, all sorts of wild game and the small
creatures of the pastures. I ate their flesh and I wore their
skins; and that was how I came to the gate of the young
woman, the maker of wine, who barred her gate of pitch
and bitumen against me. But from her I had news of the
journey; so then I came to Urshanabi the ferryman, and
with him I crossed over the waters of death. Oh, father
Utnapishtim, you who have entered the assembly of the
gods, I wish to question you concerning the living and the
dead, how shall I find the life for which I am searching?"

Utnapishtim said, "There is no permanence. Do we
build a house to stand for ever, do we seal a contract to
hold for all time? Do brothers divide an inheritance to
keep for ever, does the flood-time of rivers endure? It is
only the nymph[54] of the dragon-fly who sheds her larva
and sees the sun in his glory. From the days of old there is
no permanence. The sleeping and the dead, how alike they
are, they are like a painted death. What is there between
the master and the servant when both have fulfilled their
doom? When the Anunnaki, the judges, come together,
and Mammetun[55] the mother of destinies, together they
decree the fates of men. Life and death they allot but the
day of death they do not disclose."

Then Gilgamesh said to Utnapishtim the Faraway, "I
look at you now, Utnapishtim, and your appearance is no
different from mine; there is nothing strange in your features. I thought I should find you like a hero prepared for
battle, but you lie here taking your ease on your back. Tell
me truly, how was it that you came to enter the company
of the gods and to possess everlasting life?" Utnapishtim
said to Gilgamesh, "I will reveal to you a mystery, I will
tell you a secret of the gods."

---

[51] *urnu* **snakes** Unclear, but the references to sacred stones and
urnu snakes are to somethingnecessary for a ferry crossing; various conjectures have been made, including idols, magical amulets, and shore pylons to hold a crossing rope. See footnote 53.
[52] **bitumen** Mineral pitch or tar.
[53] **sacred stones** Unclear; perhaps idols or magical amulets. See
footnote 51.

[54] **nymph** The larval form of an insect.
[55] **Mammetun** The goddess who makes fate.

∞

The Story of the Flood

"You know the city Shurrupak,[56] it stands on the banks of
Euphrates? That city grew old and the gods that were in
it were old. There was Anu, lord of the firmament, their
father, and warrior Enlil their counsellor, Ninurta[57] the
helper, and Ennugi[58] watcher over canals; and with them
also was Ea. In those days the world teemed, the people
multiplied, the world bellowed like a wild bull, and the
great god was aroused by the clamour. Enlil heard the
clamour and he said to the gods in council, 'The uproar of
mankind is intolerable and sleep is no longer possible by
reason of the babel.'[59] So the gods agreed to exterminate
mankind. Enlil did this, but Ea because of his oath warned
me in a dream. He whispered their words to my house
of reeds, 'Reed-house, reed-house! Wall, O wall, hearken
reed-house, wall reflect; O man of Shurrupak, son of Ubara-
Tutu; tear down your house and build a boat, abandon
possessions and look for life, despise worldly goods and
save your soul alive. Tear down your house, I say, and
build a boat. These are the measurements of the barque as
you shall build her: let her beam equal her length, let her
deck be roofed like the vault that covers the abyss; then
take up into the boat the seed of all living creatures.'

"When I had understood I said to my lord, 'Behold,
what you have commanded I will honour and perform,
but how shall I answer the people, the city, the elders?'
Then Ea opened his mouth and said to me, his servant,
'Tell them this: I have learnt that Enlil is wrathful against
me, I dare no longer walk in his land nor live in his city;
I will go down to the Gulf to dwell with Ea my lord. But
on you he will rain down abundance, rare fish and shy
wildfowl, a rich harvest-tide. In the evening the rider of
the storm[60] will bring you wheat in torrents.'

"In the first light of dawn all my household gathered
round me, the children brought pitch and the men whatever was necessary. On the fifth day I laid the keel and
the ribs, then I made fast the planking. The ground-space
was one acre, each side of the deck measured one hundred and twenty cubits, making a square. I built six decks
below, seven in all, I divided them into nine sections with
bulkheads between. I drove in wedges where needed, I
saw to the punt-poles,[61] and laid in supplies. The carri-
ers brought oil in baskets, I poured pitch into the furnace

and asphalt and oil; more oil was consumed in caulking, and more again the master of the board took into his
stores. I slaughtered bullocks[62] for the people and every
day I killed sheep. I gave the shipwrights wine to drink
as though it were river water, raw wine and red wine and
oil and white wine. There was feasting then as there is at
the time of the New Year's festival[63]; I myself anointed my
head. On the seventh day the boat was complete.

"Then was the launching full of difficulty; there was
shifting of ballast[64] above and below till two thirds was
submerged. I loaded into her all that I had of gold and
of living things, my family, my kin, the beast of the field
both wild and tame, and all the craftsmen. I sent them on
board, for the time that Shamash had ordained was already fulfilled when he said, 'In the evening, when the
rider of the storm sends down the destroying rain, enter
the boat and batten her down.' The time was fulfilled, the
evening came, the rider of the storm sent down the rain.
I looked out at the weather and it was terrible, so I too
boarded the boat and battened[65] her down. All was now
complete, the battening and the caulking; so I handed the
tiller to Puzur-Amurri[66] the steersman, with the navigation and the care of the whole boat.

"With the first light of dawn a black cloud came from
the horizon; it thundered within where Adad,[67] lord of
the storm was riding. In front over hill and plain Shullat[68] and Hanish,[69] heralds of the storm, led on. Then the
gods of the abyss rose up; Nergal[70] pulled out the dams of
the nether waters, Ninurta the war-lord threw down the
dykes, and the seven judges of hell, the Anunnaki, raised
their torches, lighting the land with their livid flame. A
stupor of despair went up to heaven when the god of the
storm turned daylight to darkness, when he smashed the
land like a cup. One whole day the tempest raged, gathering fury as it went, it poured over the people like the tides
of battle; a man could not see his brother nor the people
be seen from heaven. Even the gods were terrified at the
flood, they fled to the highest heaven, the firmament of

---

[56] **Shurrupak** A city in Mesopotamia. One of the five cities that,
according to the Sumerian King List, were founded before the
Flood (see The Epic of Gilgamesh).
[57] **Ninurta** The rain god and a war god, son of **Enlil.**
[58] **Ennugi** An underworld god who guards canals for the
Anunnaki. Son of **Enlil,** he is called Lord Who Returns Not.
[59] **babel** A confusion of sounds or voices. The Hebrew Bible
(Gen. 11:1–9) describes the Tower of Babel and its destruction—
a warning against human ambition.
[60] **rider of the storm** The Mesopotamian weather god **Adad,** the
son of **Anu.**
[61] **punt-poles** Poles used to propel a punt, a flat-bottomed boat
with square ends.

[62] **bullocks** Young bulls.
[63] **New Year's festival** Akitu, the chief festival of the Babylonian
religious calendar. It was celebrated over an eleven-day period,
during the spring equinox, in the month of Nisan (our April).
Also, a second festival, the Autumn New Year, was sometimes
observed after the gathering of last fruits and before the winter
plowing.
[64] **ballast** Heavy material placed in a boat to ensure stability.
[65] **batten** To ready a boat for a storm, by securing open hatches
and placing wooden strips in pockets at the edges of sails to
keep them flat.
[66] **Puzur-Amurri** The steersman for **Utnapishtim's** boat.
[67] **Adad** In Sumerian, **Ishkur.** The Mesopotamian weather god,
the son of **Anu.**
[68] **Shullat** A divine herald of storms and bad weather.
[69] **Hanish** A divine herald of storms and bad weather.
[70] **Nergal** The Mesopotamian god of war and sudden death; an
underworld god. Son of **Enlil.**

Anu; they crouched against the walls, cowering like curs. Then Ishtar the sweet-voiced Queen of Heaven cried out like a woman in travail: 'Alas the days of old are turned to dust because I commanded evil; why did I command this evil in the council of all the gods? I commanded wars to destroy the people, but are they not my people, for I brought them forth? Now like the spawn[71] of fish they float in the ocean.' The great gods of heaven and of hell wept, they covered their mouths.

"For six days and six nights the winds blew, torrent and tempest and flood overwhelmed the world, tempest and flood raged together like warring hosts. When the seventh day dawned the storm from the south subsided, the sea grew calm, the flood was stilled; I looked at the face of the world and there was silence, all mankind was turned to clay. The surface of the sea stretched as flat as a rooftop; I opened a hatch and the light fell on my face. Then I bowed low, I sat down and I wept, the tears streamed down my face, for on every side was the waste of water. I looked for land in vain, but fourteen leagues distant there appeared a mountain, and there the boat grounded; on the mountain of Nisir[72] the boat held fast, she held fast and did not budge. One day she held, and a second day on the mountain of Nisir she held fast and did not budge. A third day, and a fourth day she held fast on the mountain and did not budge; a fifth day and a sixth day she held fast on the mountain. When the seventh day dawned I loosed a dove and let her go. She flew away, but finding no resting-place she returned. Then I loosed a swallow, and she flew away but finding no resting-place she returned. I loosed a raven, she saw that the waters had retreated, she ate, she flew around, she cawed, and she did not come back. Then I threw everything open to the four winds, I made a sacrifice and poured out a libation[73] on the mountain top. Seven and again seven cauldrons I set up on their stands, I heaped up wood and cane and cedar and myrtle. When the gods smelled the sweet savour, they gathered like flies over the sacrifice. Then, at last, Ishtar also came, she lifted her necklace with the jewels of heaven that once Anu had made to please her. 'O you gods here present, by the lapis lazuli round my neck I shall remember these days as I remember the jewels of my throat; these last days I shall not forget. Let all the gods gather round the sacrifice, except Enlil. He shall not approach this offering, for without reflection he brought the flood; he consigned my people to destruction.'

"When Enlil had come, when he saw the boat, he was wrath and swelled with anger at the gods, the host of heaven, 'Has any of these mortals escaped? Not one was to have survived the destruction.' Then the god of the wells and canals Ninurta opened his mouth and said to the warrior Enlil, 'Who is there of the gods that can devise without Ea? It is Ea alone who knows all things.' Then Ea opened his mouth and spoke to warrior Enlil, 'Wisest of gods, hero Enlil, how could you so senselessly bring down the flood?

> Lay upon the sinner his sin,
> Lay upon the transgressor his transgression,
> Punish him a little when he breaks loose,
> Do not drive him too hard or he perishes;
> Would that a lion had ravaged mankind
> Rather than the flood,
> Would that a wolf had ravaged mankind
> Rather than the flood,
> Would that famine had wasted the world
> Rather than the flood
> Would that pestilence had wasted mankind
> Rather than the flood.

It was not I that revealed the secret of the gods; the wise man learned it in a dream. Now take your counsel what shall be done with him.'

"Then Enlil went up into the boat, he took me by the hand and my wife and made us enter the boat and kneel down on either side, he standing between us. He touched our foreheads to bless us saying, 'In time past Utnapishtim was a mortal man; henceforth he and his wife shall live in the distance at the mouth of the rivers.'[74] Thus it was that the gods took me and placed me here to live in the distance, at the mouth of the rivers."

---

[71] **spawn** Fish eggs.
[72] **Nisir** The mountain on whose top **Utnapishtim's** boat finally reached land. Called Ararat in the Genesis story of the flood in the Bible (see The Holy Scriptures in Chapter 6).
[73] **libation** The pouring of a liquid offering on the ground, as part of a religious ritual.

---

[74] **the mouth of the rivers** Dilmun, the paradise of **Utnapishtim** and his wife. Historic **Dilmun** was an ancient kingdom on the island known today as al-Bahrain in the Persian Gulf. The rivers are the Tigris and Euphrates, whose waters empty into the Persian Gulf.

∞

Questions for Critical Thinking

1. How does Gilgamesh honor his friend? In what ways is this typical of ancient societies?

2. Summarize the Gilgamesh version of The Story of the Flood and compare it to that of Noah in the Bible.

The Dispute of a Man with His Soul

The Dispute of a Man with His Soul is probably Egypt's most philosophical work. Surviving in one manuscript found in about 1843, this complex text has aroused a great deal of curiosity and has provoked much controversy. Its text combines prose and poetry, a hybrid style of writing that also flourished in medieval Europe (see Boethius's *The Consolation of Philosophy* in Chapter 8).

This work dates from the Middle Kingdom (ca. 2050–1800 BCE), a period characterized by a significant shift in the social system. The old ruling elite of high-ranking royal officials now had to make room for lower officials. Mildly "democratic," this step resulted in revised funeral customs, as nobles claimed the right to immortality enjoyed by rulers; those with sufficient wealth to afford monuments began to build private funeral chapels. *The Dispute of a Man with His Soul* provides evidence of these changes because it was found in a tomb dating from about 1850 BCE, deposited there as reading matter for the deceased in eternity.

The Dispute is one of the outstanding achievements of the Middle Kingdom, Egypt's classical age, a period marked by an outpouring of literary works in many genres and with a complete mastery of forms. This work belongs to the wisdom literature genre, which began in the Old Kingdom and now reached its zenith. Wisdom literature is didactic writing that ponders a problem of life and offers a solution. The wisdom literature of the Egyptians (and the Mesopotamians) contributed mightily to the subsequent flowering of this genre among the Hebrews, as in the book of Job (see *The Holy Scriptures* in Chapter 6).

The wisdom literature of the Middle Kingdom was dominated by the theme of "national distress," which portrayed the state as threatened by civil war and social upheaval, although no evidence has been unearthed to support this gloomy outlook. *The Dispute* shared the age's general pessimism, but its topic, unlike other Middle Kingdom writing, was personal and not social.

Reading the Selection

The theme of *The Dispute of a Man with His Soul* is whether death is a blessing, given the sorrows of this life. It is written in the form of a dialogue between a man ["I"] and the mysterious life force that Egyptians called the *ba* [the "soul"]. The *ba* was the inner power that guided human life, escaped from the body at death, and played a vital but ill-defined role in one's afterlife. Presented as an internal conflict without any specific references to a real person, the text is thus universally applicable to humankind. Beyond this exists very little agreement about the nature of the dispute and the positions of the two opponents.

Some well-regarded interpretations of *The Dispute* describe it as a clash between (1) the traditional belief in funerary rites (the man) and the skeptical view of those without financial means for proper burial (the *ba*); (2) a conservative, idealistic outlook (the man) and a materialistic, hedonistic view (the *ba*); (3) Osirian beliefs (the *ba*) and the solar theology of Ra (the man).

Regardless of its final meaning, the problem presented in *The Dispute of a Man with His Soul* is resolved through four poems, each marked by a repeated first line. In these poems the man laments the pain of human life and celebrates the promised joys of death and resurrection. After listening to the poems, the *ba* agrees to abide with the man—a conservative ending typical of the wisdom literature of the times.

∞

... Then[75] I opened my mouth to my soul,[76] that I might answer what it had said: "This is too much for me now, that my soul does not speak with me. My soul goes forth; let it stand and wait for me!

"Behold, my soul disobeys me because I did not hearken to it, and drag myself to death ere I have come to it, to cast myself upon the fire in order to consume myself. Rather, let it be near to me on this day of misfortune, and wait on the other side!

"My soul is foolish to hold back one wretched over life and delay me from death before I have come to it. Rather, make the West[77] pleasant for me! Is it something bad? The period of life is limited in any case: even the trees must fall! Thoth,[78] who contents the gods, he will judge me! Khonsu,[79] the Scribe in Truth, he will defend me! Ra,[80] who guides the Solar Bark,[81] he will hear my words! My distress is heavy, and he bears it for me!"

And this is what my soul said to me: "And are you not a plain man? Yet you are as concerned as if you were a possessor of wealth!"

I said: "If my soul will hearken to me, and its heart agrees with me, it will be happy. I will cause it to reach the West, like one who is in his pyramid,[82] and at whose burial there has stood a survivor. I shall drink from the river whose water is drawn, and look down on the souls that are unsatisfied!"

Then my soul opened its mouth to me, to answer what I had said: "If you are calling burial to mind, that is a distress of the heart; it is a bringing of tears, it is making a man sorrowful. It is hauling a man from his house and throwing him upon the hill. Never shall you go up above to behold the sun. They who built in granite and fashioned pyramids—fine things of good work—when the builders have become gods, their offering tables[83] are as empty as those of the wretches who die on the riverbank—part of their bodies held by the water and part by the heat of the sun, and the fish of the bank hold converse with them! Listen, then, to me; lo, it is good to listen to people! Follow the happy day and forget care!

"Take the case of a poor man who plows his field and then loads his harvest on to a boat, and hurries to tow the boat since his feast day approaches. He sees a flood coming on in the night, and keeps vigil when Ra goes down. He comes forth with his wife, but his children perish upon the water, dangerous with crocodiles in the night. At last he sits down, when he can regain his voice, and says: 'I do not weep for that girl; there is no coming forth into the West for her. I am troubled for her children that are broken in the egg, that behold the face of the crocodile-god[84] before they had lived.'"

Then I opened my mouth to my soul, that I might answer what it had said:

"Behold, you make my name reek,
lo, more than the stench of carrion
on days in summer, when the sky is hot.

"Behold, you make my name reek
lo, more than a fisherman
on the day of the catch, when the sky is hot.

"Behold, you make my name reek
lo, more than the stench of bird droppings,
more than the hill of willows with the geese.

"Behold, you make my name reek
lo, more than the odor of fishermen,
more than the shores of the swamps when they have
    fished.

"Behold, you make my name reek
lo, more than the stench of crocodiles,
more than sitting among crocodiles.

"Behold, you make my name reek
lo, more than that of a woman
when lies are told about her to her man.

"Behold, you make my name reek
lo, more than that of a lusty boy
against whom it is said, 'He belongs to his hated
    one!'

---

[75] **Then** The poem begins in the midst of a dispute; the first part has not survived. The man seemingly has threatened suicide, a crime in the Egyptian religion, and the soul, failing to dissuade him, has ceased speaking. The man speaks first.

[76] **my soul** In Egyptian thought, the soul has three parts: the ka, the perishable body; the ba, the manifestation of the spirit that can take different forms, mainly in the afterlife; and the akh, the transformed spirit after death. In this work, soul refers to the ba, which typically manifests itself at the moment of death.

[77] **the West** The domain of the dead.

[78] **Thoth** The Egyptian god of the moon and of writing. Thoth also weighed the hearts of the dead at their final judgment and reported the results to **Osiris,** king of the underworld.

[79] **Khonsu** An Egyptian moon god, who was sometimes identified with the god **Thoth.**

[80] **Ra** Also spelled **Re.** The sun god, who headed Egypt's solar religion. As father of Ma'at, the goddess of cosmic order, he was ultimately responsible for justice and right.

[81] **Solar Bark** The boat in which **Ra,** the sun god, traveled across the sky during the day. At night, **Ra** sailed through the underworld in a second boat, to be reborn at dawn of day.

[82] **in his pyramid** An allusion to the burial arrangement, which, because of its great cost, was available only to the wealthiest Egyptians.

[83] **offering tables** Tables for ritual offerings, such as food, wine, and beer, for the dead.

[84] **crocodile-god** The Egyptian god **Sobek,** who was associated with death and burial.

"Behold, you make my name reek
   lo, more than a treacherous city,
   more than a traitor who turns his back.

"To whom shall I speak today?
   One's fellows are evil;
   the friends of today do not love.

"To whom shall I speak today?
   Men are rapacious;
   every one seizes his neighbor's goods.

"To whom shall I speak today?
   Gentleness has perished;
   insolence has access to all men.

"To whom shall I speak today?   20
   The evil have a contented countenance;
   good is rejected in every place.

"To whom shall I speak today?
   He who by his evil deeds should arouse wrath
   moves all men to laughter, though his iniquity is
      grievous.

"To whom shall I speak today?
   Men rob;
   Every man seizes his neighbor's goods.

"To whom shall I speak today?
   The foul man is trusted,
   but one who was a brother to him has become an
      enemy.

"To whom shall I speak today?
   No one remembers yesterday;
   no one now requites good to him who has done it.

"To whom shall I speak today?   25
   Brothers are evil;
   a man is treated as an enemy for his uprightness.

"To whom shall I speak today?
   Faces are not seen;
   every man's face is downcast toward his brethren.

"To whom shall I speak today?
   Hearts are greedy;
   the man on whom men rely has no heart.

"To whom shall I speak today?
   There are no righteous ones;
   the land is given over to the doers of evil.

"To whom shall I speak today?
   There is lack of a trusty friend;
   one must go to an unknown in order to complain.

"To whom shall I speak today?   30
   There is none that is peaceable;
   the one with whom one went no longer exists.

"To whom shall I speak today?
   I am laden with misery,
   and lack a trusted friend.

"To whom shall I speak today?
   The evil which treads the earth,
   it has no end.

"Death is in my sight today
   as when a sick man becomes whole,
   as when one goes out after an illness.

"Death is in my sight today
   as the odor of myrrh,[85]
   as when sitting under sail on a breezy day.

"Death is in my sight today   35
   as the odor of lotus flowers,[86]
   as when sitting on the riverbank getting drunk.

"Death is in my sight today
   as a well-trodden path,
   as when a man returns home to his house from war.

"Death is in my sight today
   as a clearing of the sky,
   as a man discerning what he knew not.

"Death is in my sight today
   as when a man longs to see his home again
   after he has spent many years in captivity.

"Nay, but he who is Yonder[87]
   will be as a living god,
   inflicting punishment for evil upon him who does it.

"Nay, but he who is Yonder   40
   will stand in the bark of the Sun-god
   and will assign the choicest things therein to the
      temples.

"Nay, but he who is Yonder
   will be a man of knowledge,
   not hindered from petitioning Ra when he speaks."

---

[85] **myrrh** From Arabic, "bitter." An aromatic, resinous gum from a flowering tree. It was used to make incense, perfume, cosmetics, and medicines and in embalming.
[86] **lotus flower** The white water lily, sacred to **Isis,** the mother goddess who was a central figure in the cult of the underworld. The lotus blooms in the day and closes at night and, thus, is a fitting symbol of rebirth and the promise of everlasting life.
[87] **Yonder** The Eastern Kingdom, the place of rebirth, where souls go to be reincarnated.

This is what my soul said to me: "Set aside lamentation, you who are mine, my brother! Although offered up on the brazier, still you shall cling to life, as you say. Whether I remain here if you reject the West, or whether you reach the West and your body is joined with the earth, I will alight after you go to rest. Then we shall make an abode together!"

Questions for Critical Thinking

1. Define wisdom literature and note how *The Dispute of a Man with His Soul* is an example of this genre.

2. List three examples of the pains of life and three examples of the description of death. Are these examples relevant to humans alive today? If so, how and why?

The Story of Sinuhe the Egyptian

Egyptian literature, although not noted for fiction, gave birth to one great work of the imagination, *The Story of Sinuhe the Egyptian,* a short narrative that ranks among the classics of world literature. Several manuscripts and many fragments of this work are extant, thus attesting to its ancient popularity. A model of style and a masterpiece of the storyteller's art, it was assigned as a "set text" for teaching Egypt's classical language to aspiring scribes. In modern times, Sinuhe's story proved its lasting appeal when it became the basis of a historical novel and a popular movie. The original tale was written in a mix of prose and poetry, the typical style of Middle Kingdom literature (see *The Dispute of a Man with His Soul*).

Like most Egyptian writing, *The Story of Sinuhe* owes its form to the cult of the dead; it is an autobiography composed for a tomb. It may be a true account, but the original tomb-text has not been discovered. Whether true or not, the work reflects an actual event: the death of Amenemhat I [Amen-em-Hat] around 1908 BCE and the onset of the reign of his coregent, Senwosret I [Sen-Wesret] (ca. 1918–1875 BCE).

Reading the Selection

Senwosret's abrupt change of status set in motion *The Story of Sinuhe's* simple plot. Hearing of Amenemhat's death, Sinuhe—an attendant of Senwosret's wife—is seized by uncontrollable shaking and rushes from the scene. Why should a high official who stood to gain from the royal changes bolt and run? In his defense, Sinuhe blames his hasty retreat on anxiety over "civil strife" and fear for his safety. The words "civil strife" echo the Middle Kingdom theme of "national distress" (see *The Dispute of a Man with His Soul*), but nothing else in the tale enlarges on his fears. This opening episode appears to be simply a pretext to throw the hero into foreign lands, where, as time passes, his beloved Egypt becomes all the more precious.

The middle part of the story concerns Sinuhe's flight to and success in Palestine, where he founds a family and acquires fabled riches among the local tribes. With the patronage of a local chief, he proves his worth as a chieftain and a warrior. Most memorable is the episode in which Sinuhe conquers a boastful Syrian warrior, much as David did Goliath in the Old Testament.

Running through these adventures is the theme that contrasts the ideal order of Egyptian life with the unstructured existence of the Palestinian tribes. The story's turning point occurs in the middle of Sinuhe's rejoicing at his worldly success, when he breaks down and bemoans the futility of his life. He prays: "O whichever God ordained this flight, show mercy and return me to the Palace! Surely you will grant that I see the place where dwells my heart!" For Sinuhe, life is meaningful and lasting only within the Egyptian state, as symbolized by the king and courtly ritual.

The story concludes with the hero's homecoming and reception into Egyptian court society. Welcomed by King Senwosret, the aged Sinuhe rids himself of foreign clothing, puts on court dress, and looks forward to the day of his own burial in a "pyramid-tomb of stone," a gift from the king.

∞

The Hereditary Prince and Chief,[88] Treasurer of the King, and Unique Courtier, Administrative Dignitary of the districts and estates of the Sovereign in the lands of the Syrians, Actual Acquaintance of the King and beloved of him, the King's Retainer Sinuhe says:

I was a retainer who followed his lord, a servant of the Royal Harem and of the Princess great of praise, the wife of King Sen-Wesret and daughter of King Amen-em-Hat, namely, Neferu, Lady of Reverence.

In the year 30 of his reign, in the third month of the season of Inundation,[89] the god ascended unto his horizon,[90] the King of Upper and Lower Egypt,[91] Amen-em-Hat, was taken up to heaven and united with the sun. The body of the god was united with him who made him. The city of royal residence was silent, all hearts were in grief, and the great Double Gates were sealed. The courtiers sat with heads bent down upon their laps, and the people were in mourning.

Now His Majesty had sent a great army to the land of the Libyans,[92] with his eldest son in command of it, namely, the beautiful god Sen-Wesret. He had been sent to smite the foreign lands, to strike down the dwellers in Libya. Indeed, even now was he returning, bringing living prisoners from among the Libyans and all kinds of cattle without limit.

The courtiers of the palace sent to the western border, advising the King's son of what had come about in the Palace. The messengers found him on the road, having reached him at the time of evening. Not a moment at all did he delay: The Falcon[93] flew with his attendants, not letting his army know what had happened.

Now those others of the King's sons who were following him in this expedition were sought out, and one of them was called aside. And lo, I happened to be standing near by, and heard his voice as he was speaking. My heart was distraught, my arms flung apart, and trembling seized all my limbs. I sprang bounding away to seek myself a place to hide. I placed myself between two bushes to hide from the passers-by. I certainly had no intention of returning to the Residence, for I expected civil strife to break out, and I did not think I would live after the King's death.

I crossed Lake Maati[94] near Nehet[95] and landed at the island of Senefru.[96] I passed the day at the edge of the fields, and at dawn the next morning I set forth again. I met a man standing on the road. He was frightened of me, and stood in awe. When it was time for supper, I reached the town of Negau.[97] I crossed the river on a barge without a rudder, with the aid of a westerly wind. I passed eastward of the quarry, above the temple of Hathor,[98] Lady of the Red Hill.[99] I gave road to my legs and went northward.

I arrived at the Walls of the Ruler,[100] which were made to repel the Syrians[101] and to defeat the Sand-crossers.[102] I took up a crouching position under a bush, in fear lest the

---

[88] **The Hereditary Prince and Chief** The grandiose titles of courtiers, such as these of **Sinuhe,** were typical of the Egyptian court where rulers were worshiped as divine beings.
[89] **the season of Inundation** Egypt's agricultural calendar had three phases: the season of Inundation, when the Nile River overflowed; the Going Forth, the planting season, when the Nile receded to its banks; and the Deficiency, the harvest season, when the Nile was at low level.
[90] **god . . . horizon Horus,** the Egyptian god of the horizon, depicted as a falcon with his eyes as the sun and the moon. The ruler was believed to be a manifestation of **Horus.**
[91] **Upper and Lower Egypt** Egypt became the Double Land in 3100 BCE, when Menes, its legendary first king, united the South (Upper Egypt) and the North (Lower Egypt).
[92] **Libyans** North African nomads, living west of the Nile Valley, but not limited to modern Libya.

[93] **The Falcon** The new king, Sen-Wesret, who was identified with **Horus,** the falcon god.
[94] **Maati** Unidentified. The name derives from the Hall of Maati, a temple associated with the cult of the underworld.
[95] **Nehet** Unidentified. The name means sycamore, from sycamore tree. The rulers grew these trees, using them for water wheels, farming tools, shade, wind shields, and fuel.
[96] **island of Senefru** Unidentified island in the Nile. **Senefru** (ca. 2613–ca. 2589 BCE) founded the Fourth Dynasty and built the first true pyramid at Dahshur.
[97] **Negau** Neg is Egyptian for "ox"; perhaps a town devoted to the cattle trade.
[98] **Hathor** The Egyptian goddess associated with the royal queens; patroness of the sky, of women, and of fertility and love. Depicted either as a cow or as a woman with horns.
[99] **Lady of the Red Hill** Title of the goddess **Hathor.** Red is **Hathor's** color, because of the red earth of Lower Egypt, her original home, and the vengeful side of her nature.
[100] **Walls of the Ruler** A royal fortress on Egypt's eastern border.
[101] **Syrians** A collective name for people from the region embracing the modern states of Syria, Lebanon, Jordan, and Israel.
[102] **Sand-crossers** Bedouins.

watch of the day standing on the wall would see me. At the time of late evening I journeyed on, and when the sun came forth again I reached Peten,[103] and halted at the island of Kem-Wer.[104] A great attack of thirst overtook me. My throat was hot and dry, and I said, "This is the taste of death."

Then I lifted up my heart and pulled my limbs together, for I heard the sound of the lowing of cattle and I spied some Syrians. A distinguished chieftain among them, who had been in Egypt, recognized me. Then he gave me water and cooked milk for me. I proceeded with him to his tribe, and they treated me well.

Land gave me to land. I went forth to Byblos,[105] and 10 then I turned back to Kedem.[106] There I spent a year and a half. Then Amu-nenshi, a ruler in Palestine,[107] fetched me. He said to me, "You will fare well with me; here you will hear the speech of Egypt." He said this since he knew my character and had heard of my capacities. The Egyptians who were there with him bore witness for me.

He said to me, "For what reason have you come to this place? What is it? Has something happened at the Residence?"

Then I said to him, "King Amen-em-Hat has proceeded to the Horizon.[108] No one knows what can happen because of it." But I added, untruthfully:

"I was returning from an expedition to the land of the Libyans when it was reported to me. My mind became unquiet. My heart was not in my body, and it drew me to the desert roads. I had not been accused of anything, no one had spat in my face, and no wretched remarks had been heard about me. My name had not been heard in the mouth of the herald. I do not know what brought me to this land. It is like the dispensation of some god; or like a dream in which a man of the Delta might see himself in Nubia!"[109]

Then he said to me, "What, then, will the land be without him, that excellent god, the fear of whom pervaded the foreign lands like Sekhmet[110] in a year of pestilence?"

I spoke to him in reply, "Indeed his son has entered 15 into the Palace and has assumed the heritage of his father.

For he[111] is a god; there is none his equal,
    and there is none other who surpasses him.
He is a master of understanding, excellent in plans and
        beneficent of decrees;
    and going and coming are according to his commands.

He it was who subdued the foreign lands while his father
        was within the palace;
    and he reported to him that what he was ordered had
        been done.
Mighty indeed is he, achieving with his strong arm;
    a valiant one, and there is not his equal!
He slakes his wrath by smashing skulls;
    and no one can stand up about him.
He is robust of heart at the moment of attack;
    and does not let sloth rest upon his heart.
Bold of countenance is he when sees the mêlée;
    to attack the barbarian is his joy.
He girds his shield and crushes the foe;
    and does not strike twice in order to kill!
But he is lord of charm and great of sweetness;
    and through love has he conquered!
His city loves him more than itself;
    it rejoices in him more than in its god;
    men and women salute and rejoice with him now that
        he is King!
He conquered while still in the egg,
    and his face was turned to royal deeds since he was born.
He makes multiply those who were born with him;
    he is unique, the gift of the god.
He is one who makes wide the boundaries;
    he will seize the southern countries, and the northern
        ones with ease,
    having been created to smite the Syrians and to crush
        the Sand-crossers.
How this land rejoices now that he is come to rule!

Send to him, cause him to know your name as an inquirer far from His Majesty. He will not cease to make happy a land which will be loyal to him!"

Then he said to me, "Well, assuredly then, Egypt is happy, knowing that he flourishes. Behold, you are here, and you shall stay with me. I will treat you well."

He placed me at the head of his children, and he married me to his eldest daughter. He let me choose for myself from his land, from the choicest that he had, on his boundary adjoining another territory. It was a good land, and Yaa[112] was its name. There were figs in it, together with grapes. It had more wine than water; great was its honey and abundant its olives. Every fruit was on its trees. There was barley there, and emmer wheat,[113] and all kinds of cattle without limit.

And much, indeed, accrued to me as a result of the love of me. He appointed me as ruler of a tribe of the choicest of his country. Provisions were assigned for me daily, and wine for each day's needs; cooked meat and roasted fowl besides desert game. They used to snare for me and set aside game for me over and above what my hounds caught. Much wine was made for me, and milk was used in every kind of cooking.

Thus I spent many years. My children became strong men, each man in control of a tribe. The couriers who

---

[103] **Peten** Probably a foreign settlement east of Egypt.
[104] **Kem-Wer** One of the Bitter Lakes, on the Suez Isthmus.
[105] **Byblos** Jubayl in modern Lebanon.
[106] **Kedem** A city inland from Byblos.
[107] **Palestine** In Egyptian, Retenu, meaning variously Canaan, north Palestine, or south Syria.
[108] **Horizon** The domain of the dead.
[109] **a man of the Delta . . . in Nubia** As out of place as a man from Lower Egypt (the Nile's Delta region) in Upper Egypt (Nubia began at the Nile's first cataract).
[110] **Sekhmet** The "eye of **Ra.**" Egyptian goddess of war and of disease and the destroyer of the enemies of the sun god **Ra.**
[111] **he** King Sen-Wesret. This poem praising the ruling king establishes that **Sinuhe's** tale is basically a work of royal propaganda.

[112] **Yaa** Unidentified.
[113] **emmer wheat** A type of hardy wheat.

went north or south to the Palace would tarry because of me, and I made all travelers tarry. I gave water to the thirsty; I put on the road those who had become lost, and I rescued those who were plundered.

When the Bedouin became so bold as to oppose the "Chiefs of the Foreign Lands," I advised them how to proceed. This ruler of the Syrians caused me to spend many years as commander of his army. Every foreign territory against which I went forth, I attacked and it was driven away from its pasturage and its wells. I plundered its cattle, I carried away its inhabitants, and seized their food. I slew people thereof with my strong arm, and by my movements and my excellent devices, I found favor in the ruler's heart, and he loved me. He recognized my valor, and placed me even before his children, since he saw that my arms flourished.

There came a powerful man of the Syrians to taunt me with challenges in my tent. He was a hero without peer, and he had beaten all the Syrians. He said he would fight with me. He expected to despoil me and plunder my cattle, being so counseled by his tribe.

The ruler discussed the matter with me, and I said, "I do not know him, and I certainly am not an associate of his going about in his camp. Is it that I have opened his gate, or thrown down his fence? It is envy, because he sees me carrying out your orders. Assuredly, I am like a bull who has wandered into the herd, and whom the long-horned steer of the herd attacks. Is there any man of humble origin who is loved when he becomes a superior? Well, if he wants to fight, let him speak out what he has in mind. Is a god ignorant of the fact that the nature of whatever he has ordained will eventually be known?"

During the night I strung my bow and practised my shooting. I made my dagger loose and free and polished my weapons. At dawn all Syria came, its tribes stirred up and half its peoples assembled; this fight had been planned.

Then he came toward me as I waited, and I placed myself in position near him. Every heart burned for me, and the women and even the men were murmuring. Every heart was sick for me as they said, "Is there another strong enough to fight him?"

But I escaped his missiles and made his arrows pass me by until none remained, and his shield, his ax, and his armful of spears fell down before me. Then he charged at me. I shot him; my arrow stuck in his neck. He shrieked and fell on his nose. I killed him with his own battle-ax. I gave forth my shout of victory on his back while every Syrian roared. I gave jubilant praise to Montu[114] while his partisans mourned him.

This ruler Amu-nenshi took me in his embrace. Then I carried away my enemy's goods, and I plundered his cattle. What he had planned to do to me, this I did to him. I seized all that was in his tent, and stripped his encampment. Thus I widened my possessions and became numerous in cattle. I became great there. Thus has the god done, in being gracious unto one against whom he had been angered, and whom he had sent astray into another land. Today is his heart appeased.

> *A fugitive has fled in his straitened moment;*
>   *now my good report is in the Palace.*
> *A lingerer lingered because of hunger;*
>   *now I give bread to my neighbor.*
> *A man left his land because of nakedness;*
>   *now I am bright of raiment and of linen.*
> *A man ran for lack of someone to send;*
>   *now I am rich in slaves.*
> *My house is beautiful, and broad is my abode.*
>   *The memory of me is in the Palace.*

O whichever God ordained this flight, show mercy and return me to the Palace! Surely you will grant that I see the place where dwells my heart!

What is more important than that my body be buried in Egypt, the land where I was born? O come to my aid!

That which has occurred is a fortunate event—the god has shown mercy. May he do the like to bring to a good end him whom he has afflicted!

May his heart be sick for him whom he has cast out to live in a foreign land. Is it true that today he is appeased? Then let him hear the prayer of one who is afar! Let him turn his hand toward him who trod the earth, leading him back to the place whence he drew him forth!

May the King of Egypt be gracious unto me, who lives in his grace! May I hail the Lady of the Land, who is in his Palace, and may I hear word of his children! Then might my limbs flourish, since old age has befallen me, and infirmity has overtaken me.

My arms are weak, and my legs have slackened. My heart is weary; I am near to departure, and they will take me away to the City of Eternity!

Might I once more serve the Lady of All! Then will she tell me that it is well with her children! May she spend eternity over me!

Now, it was told to the Majesty of the King of Upper and Lower Egypt, Kheper-Ka-Ra [Senusret I], regarding the circumstances under which I was living. And His Majesty kept sending to me bearers of gifts of the royal bounty, that he might gladden the heart of this his servant like the ruler of any foreign land. And the children of the King, who were in the Palace, let me hear word from them.

[Here Sinuhe inserts the text of the message sent by King Senusret inviting him to return to Egypt:]

Copy of the decree brought to this servant about bringing him back to Egypt:

"The Horus Living-of-Births,[115] the Two Ladies Living-of-Births, the King of Upper and Lower Egypt, Kheper-KaRa, Son of Ra, Senusret, Living forever unto eternity!

"A decree of the King to the Retainer Sinuhe:

---

[114] **Montu** Old Egyptian god of war and of the sun, first worshiped in Upper Egypt.

[115] **The Horus Living-of-Births** Here begin the various titles of King Sen-Wesret.

"Behold, this decree of the King is brought to you to advise you as follows: You have wandered about foreign lands—you have gone from Kedem to Tenu.[116] Under the counsel of your own heart, land gave you to land! What have you done, that anything should be done against you? You have not blasphemed, that your words should be reproved. Your words have not been evil in the Council of the Nobles, that your utterances should be opposed. This plan of yours carried away your heart. It was not in my heart against you.

"This your 'Heaven,' who is in the Palace, today prospers and flourishes. Her head is covered with the royalty of the land. Her children are in the Residence; you shall heap up precious things of what they will give you, and you shall live by their largesse.

"Do you return to Egypt, that you may see the Residence wherein you grew up. You shall kiss the earth at the Great Double Door, and you shall join the courtiers.

"For today indeed you have begun to grow old, and have lost your virile powers. Be mindful of the day of burial, of passing to a revered state! A night will be assigned for you for oils and wrappings from the hands of Tayit.[117] A funeral cortege will be made for you on the day of interment, a mummy case of gold with a headpiece of lapis lazuli[118] and a heaven canopy above you. You will be placed upon a bier, with oxen drawing you and singers going before you, and the mortuary dances will be performed at the door of your tomb. The lists of the offering-table shall be invoked for you, sacrifices shall be made before your tomb stelae, and your tomb columns shall be built of white limestone amidst the tombs of the royal children.

"You must not die in a foreign land! The Asiatics[119] shall not escort you to burial. You shall not be put in a sheepskin and a mound[120] made over you!

"This is too long to tread the earth. Be mindful of illness, and come back!"

This decree reached me as I was standing in the midst of my tribe. It was recited to me; I placed myself on my belly. I touched the earth and scattered it upon my hair. I went about my camp rejoicing and saying, "How can such things be done to a servant whom his heart led astray to foreign and barbarous lands? Good indeed is the clemency which rescued me from the hand of death! Your Divine Essence[121] will allow me to make my end with my body in the Residence!"

[Sinuhe now gives the text of his reply:]

Copy of the answer to this decree:

"The Servant of the Palace, Sinuhe, says:

"In very good peace! It is known to your Divine Essence, this flight made by your servant in his ignorance, O good God, Lord of the Two Lands, Beloved of Ra, Favored of Montu, Lord of Thebes!

"Amen,[122] Lord of the Thrones of the Two Lands, Sebek,[123] Ra, Horus, Hathor, Atum[124] with his Ennead,[125] Soped,[126] Nefer-Bau,[127] Semseru,[128] the Eastern Horus,[129] the Lady of Yemet[130]—The Serpent-goddess,[131] may she continue to enfold your head—the Council over the Nile waters, Min-Horus,[132] amidst the foreign lands, Wereret Lady of Punt,[133] Nut,[134] Ra-Horus[135] the Elder, and all the Gods of Egypt and the Islands of the Sea, may they give life and strength to your nostrils, may they endow you with their bounty, may they give you eternity without bound and everlasting without limit! May the fear of you be repeated in the lowlands and the highlands, when you have subdued all that the sun encircles! This is the prayer of your servant for his Lord, who saves from the West!

"The lord of perception who perceives his people, he perceives in the Majesty of his Palace that which your servant feared to say, and which is a grave thing to repeat. O great God, likeness of Ra, make prudent one who is laboring on his own behalf! Your servant is in the hand of one who takes counsel concerning him, and verily am I placed under his guidance. Your Majesty is Horus the Conqueror; your arms are mighty over all lands.

"Lo, this flight your servant made, I did not plan it; it was not in my heart, I did not devise it. I do not know what separated me from my place. It was like some sort of dream, as when a man of the Delta marshes sees himself in Elephantine,[136] or a man of the northern swamps in Nubia. I did not take fright, no one was pursuing me, I had

---

[116] **Tenu** In Egyptian, [Re]tenu, meaning variously Canaan, north Palestine, or south Syria.
[117] **Tayit** Alternative spelling, **Tait.** Goddess of weaving, who wove the threads of fate.
[118] **lapis lazuli** A semiprecious stone, usually azure blue, greatly valued in Egypt.
[119] **Asiatics** A collective name for the Near Eastern peoples east of Egypt.
[120] **a sheepskin and a mound** A pejorative Egyptian notion of a foreign burial practice.
[121] **Divine Essence** The ka, the perishable part of the soul.

[122] **Amen** Also spelled **Amon** and **Ammon.** Creator god from Thebes; during the Middle Kingdom, he became a national deity, **Amen-Re,** king of the gods.
[123] **Sebek** Also spelled **Sobek.** Egyptian crocodile god; associated with death and burial.
[124] **Atum Atum-Re,** god of the setting sun and head of the **Ennead** cult at Heliopolis.
[125] **Ennead** From Greek, "nine." The nine deities worshiped at Heliopolis.
[126] **Soped** Hawk god and personification of Egypt's eastern frontier.
[127] **Nefer-Bau** Unclear epithet describing **Soped.**
[128] **Semseru** Unclear epithet describing **Soped.**
[129] **the Eastern Horus** The god **Horus,** in his manifestation as ruler of the East.
[130] **the Lady of Yemet** Uncertain; perhaps goddess of floodwaters.
[131] **the Serpent-goddess** A title of the **Lady of Yemet.**
[132] **Min-Horus** A fusion of **Min,** the god of male virility, with **Horus,** the falcon god. The worship of **Min-Horus** flourished in the Middle Kingdom.
[133] **Wereret Lady of Punt** Uncertain; perhaps **Ipy,** also called **Taweret,** the goddess of childbirth. **Punt** is an unidentified land, located south of Egypt, the source of **myrrh.**
[134] **Nut** Egyptian goddess of the sky, portrayed with her body arched over the Earth and her star-studded belly representing the Night Sky.
[135] **Ra-Horus** A fusion of **Ra,** the sun god, and **Horus,** the falcon god.
[136] **Elephantine** An island in the Nile River in Upper Egypt, opposite modern Aswan.

heard no reviling word. My name had not been heard in the mouth of the herald.

"However, my limbs began to quiver, and my legs began to tremble. My heart led me away. The god who ordained this flight[137] drew me, although I had not been rebellious.

"Any man who knows his land stands in awe, for Ra [50] has set the fear of you throughout the earth, and the dread of you in every foreign land. Whether I am at the Palace or whether I am in this place, it is you, indeed, who clothes this horizon. The sun shines at your pleasure; the water in the rivers, it is drunk at your desire; the air is in the heaven, it is breathed when you so say.

"This your servant will resign the vizierhip which he has exercised in this place; it was a function they had requested your servant to perform. Your Majesty will act as he pleases; one lives by the breath which you bestow. Ra, Horus, and Hathor love this thy noble nose, which Montu, Lord of Thebes, desires shall live for ever!"

They came for me. I was allowed to spend a day in Yaa for transferring my possessions to my children, my eldest son having charge of my tribe—my tribe and all my property in his hands, my serfs and all my cattle, my stores of fruit and every pleasant tree of mine.

Then this servant went southward. I halted at the Roads of Horus. The commander there who was in charge of the frontier patrol sent a message to the Palace to make it known. Then His Majesty sent a capable overseer of the peasants who belonged to the Palace, followed by ships laden with gifts of the King for the Syrians who had come escorting me to the Roads of Horus. I introduced each of them by his name. Every servant was at his task when I set out and hoisted sail. They kneaded and strained before me, until I reached the vicinity of Yetchet-Tawy.[138]

And when it dawned, very early, they came to call me, ten men coming and ten men going, to conduct me to the Palace. I touched my forehead to the ground beneath the sphinxes. The King's children were standing in the gateway to meet me. The courtiers who had been led into the Great Hall took me on the way to the royal chambers.

I found His Majesty on a great throne in a gilded [55] niche. Then when I was stretched out on my belly, I lost consciousness before him. This god addressed me joyfully, but I was like a man overcome by dusk. My soul departed; my limbs were powerless, my heart, it was not in my body, that I should know life from death.

Then His Majesty said to one of the courtiers, "Raise him, and let him speak to me."

And His Majesty said, "Behold, you have returned! You have trodden foreign lands; you fled away. Now infirmity has seized you, and you have reached old age. It is of no little importance for your body to be buried, that you

should not be interred by the Bedouin. Come, do not behave thus, not to speak when your name is pronounced!"

But I still feared punishment, and I answered with the response of one afraid, "What does my Lord say to me? I should answer, but I can do nothing. It is indeed the hand of a god. There is a terror in my belly, like that which brought about that destined flight. Behold me before you; life is yours; may Your Majesty do as he desires!"

Then they had the King's children brought in, and His Majesty said to the Queen, "Behold Sinuhe, come as a Bedouin, as if born a Syrian!"

She uttered a very great cry, and the King's children [60] all shouted together. And they said to His Majesty, "Is it not he, in truth, O King, My Lord?"

And His Majesty said, "It is he, in truth!"

Now they had brought with them their *menit* collars[139] and their rattles[140] and sistra[141] of Hathor, and they presented them before His Majesty, saying:

"Put forth your hands to these beautiful things.
    O enduring King,
    the adornments of the Lady of Heaven![142]
May the Golden One[143] give life to your nostrils;
    may she join with you, The Lady of the Stars![144]
May the Crown-goddess of Upper Egypt sail northward
    and the Crown-goddess of Lower Egypt sail
        southward,
    joined and united by the utterance of Your Majesty!
The Cobra-goddess[145] is set upon your brow,
    and you have removed your subjects from evil.
May Ra, Lord of the Two Lands, be gracious unto you;
    hail to you, as to the Lady of All!
Slacken your bow, make loose your arrow,
    give breath to him who is stifling!
Give us as good festal gift this sheik, son of the North,
    a barbarian born in Egypt!
He made flight through fear of you,
    he left the land through dread of you!
May the face of him who has seen your face not be afraid;
    may the eye which has looked at you not be terrified!"

Then said His Majesty, "Let him not fear, and let him not fall into dread. He shall be a courtier among the nobles, and he shall be placed in the midst of the courtiers. Proceed you to the Morning-chamber, and wait upon him!"

And so I went forth from the royal chambers, the King's children giving me their hands. We proceeded afterward to the Great Double Door. I was placed in the house of a son of the King, which had fine things in it;

---

[137] **the god who ordained this flight Sinuhe** is being evasive; he now blames an unspecified god for his flight from Egypt.
[138] **Yetchet-Tawy** Probably Itj-Tawy, meaning "Seizer of Two Lands," located on the border between Upper and Lower Egypt, made capital of Egypt by Amenemhet I.

[139] *menit* **collars** Necklaces.
[141] **rattle** A noisemaker, or **sistrum** (pl. **sistra**), associated with the goddess **Hathor**.
[14] **sistra** (sing. **sistrum**) Noisemakers, associated with the goddess **Hathor**.
[142] **Lady of Heaven** A title of **Hathor**.
[143] **the Golden One** A title of **Hathor**.
[144] **Lady of the Stars** A title of **Hathor**.
[145] **Cobra-goddess** The goddess **Wadjet**, the patroness of Lower Egypt, and one of "the Two Ladies," an ancient title of the ruler.

there was a cooling room in it, and landscape decoration. There were valuables of the Treasury in it, and in every room was clothing of royal linen, and myrrh,[146] and the best oil of the King, and of the courtiers, whom he loves. Every serving-man was at his task.

The years were made to pass away from my limbs 65 as I was shaved and my hair was combed. A load of dirt was given back to the desert, and their clothes to the sand farers. I was clothed in fine linen, and anointed with fine oil. I slept upon a bed. I gave back the sand to those who live in it, and tree oil to those who rub themselves with it.

There was given to me a house with grounds, which had belonged to a courtier. Many craftsmen restored it, and all its trees made to flourish anew. Meals from the Palace were brought to me three or four times a day besides what the King's children kept on giving me.

There was built for me a pyramid-tomb of stone, in the midst of the pyramids. The chief pyramid mason took charge of its ground, the chief draftsman designed it, the chief sculptor carved in it, and the chief builders of the necropolis concerned themselves with it. All the equipment which is placed in a tomb, those were supplied therein. Ka-priests[147] were assigned to me. A funerary domain was made for me with fields in it, as is done for a foremost courtier. My statue was overlaid with gold, its kilt with fine gold.

By His Majesty was it caused to be done. There is no commoner for whom the like has been done. I was bestowed the favors of the King until there came the day of mooring.

IT HAS COME FROM ITS BEGINNING TO ITS END, AS WAS FOUND IN THE WRITING.

---

[146] **myrrh** From Arabic, "bitter." An aromatic, resinous gum from a flowering tree. It was used to make incense, perfume, cosmetics, and medicines and in embalming.

[147] **Ka-priests** Mortuary priests who prepare the body (the ka) for embalming.

Questions for Critical Thinking

1. Discuss and give examples of how Sinuhe places his own personal life within the context of events occurring around him in Egypt and in Palestine.

2. Why does Sinuhe yearn to return to Egypt, and how does his yearning reflect attitudes that Egyptians had about non-Egyptians?

The Great Hymn to the Aten

In Egyptian culture, hymns to deities were simply part of the state religion and only incidentally expressions of literary art. Hymns functioned as a kind of metalanguage, a "language" beyond ordinary speech and writing, used by the elite to understand the universe. (The religious beliefs of the majority are virtually unknown.) Because the deities were never arranged into a logical structure, hymns (as well as rituals and figurative art) helped to shape theology, to the extent that it could be defined. Hymns offer information on ancient myths and beliefs and ritual, and over time, show the shifting "pecking order" among the deities. Recited during funerary rituals, hymns give evidence of the common belief that the divine coexists with the earthly, the eternal with the transient.

One of the most famous hymns is *The Great Hymn to the Aten*, dating from the New Kingdom (ca. 1552–1079 BCE). This hymn is well known because of its association with King Akhenaten ("the glory of Aten") (ca. 1369–1353 BCE). This king changed his name from Amenhotep ("Amen is content") IV as part of a campaign to make the Aten—the god of the solar disk—the head of the state religion. He ordered this change to downgrade the influence of the rich priests of Amen-Re, the local deity from Thebes who rose to national prominence in the New Kingdom and became Re (the sun god).

Abandoning Thebes, Akhenaten founded a new capital called Aket-Aten ("the horizon of the Aten"), today known by its Arabic name, Tel el Amarna, or simply Amarna, from which he launched a religious and an artistic revolution. (In Amarna art, the Aten is always represented as the sun disk, emitting rays that end in tiny hands, that bless the royal family and hold the *ankh,* the symbol of eternal life.) His innovations angered the political elite and the priests of Amen-Re, who got their revenge after Akhenaten's death by restoring Amen-Re to supremacy and trying to erase the heretic's memory from history. However, knowledge of Akhenaten's reign survives in inscriptions, artworks, and *The Great Hymn to the Aten.*

Reading the Selection

The Great Hymn to the Aten, perhaps written by Akhenaten himself, was inscribed in the tomb of King Ay, a brief successor to Akhenaten who ruled before the restoration of Amen-Re. The hymn is framed within a complex literary form that includes a list of the Aten's titles and a similar list, repeated at the beginning and the end, of the titles of Akhenaten and Queen Nefertiti.

This hymn's major theme is universalism, the idea that there is one god (the Aten) who is the lord of the entire creation, as in, for example: "You [the Aten] have created the earth according to your desire, while you were alone, / With men, cattle, and wild beasts, all that is upon earth and goes upon feet, and all that soars above and flies with its wings." Paralleling a similar theme in Psalm 104 of the Old Testament, this hymn is an example of the strong influence of Egypt on Hebrew culture over the centuries.

A second theme of the hymn is the mediating role played by the king in interpreting the divine world to humankind—a theme as old as *The Story of Sinuhe.* To the elite, who composed its literature, Egypt is a cosmic stage with the king as the sole actor, performing its history through his actions. The hymn expresses this idea in these words: "[T]here is no one who knows you [the Aten] save your son [Akhenaten]."

∞

Praise of the Living Ra,[148] Horus of the Double Horizon,[149] Rejoicing on the Horizon, in His Name of Shu Who is in the Aten,[150] living forever unto eternity; Aten living and great, He who is in the Jubilee Festival,[151] Lord of all that the Aten encircles, Lord of the Heavens and Lord of the Earth, Lord of the House of Aten in Akhet-Aten.[152] The King of Upper and Lower Egypt,[153] Living in Truth, the Lord of the Two Lands, Nefer-Kheperu-Ra Wa-en-Ra,[154]

Son of Ra,[155] Living in Truth, Lord of Diadems, Akh-en-Aten, Great in His Duration, and the Great Wife of the King,[156] His Beloved, the Lady of the Two Lands, Nefer-Neferu-Aten Nefert-Iti,[157] living, healthy, and youthful forever unto eternity. He[158] says:

Beautiful is your shining forth on the horizon,
  O living Aten, beginning of life!
When you arise on the eastern horizon,
  you fill every land with your beauty.
You are bright and great and gleaming,
  and are high above every land.
Your rays envelop the lands,
  as far as all you have created.
You are Ra, and you reach unto their end,
  and subdue them all for your beloved son.

---

[148] **the Living Ra** Hereafter follow a list of names of King Akhenaten. These are not simply royal titles. Kings are gods in their own right, and various other deities manifest themselves in the king's person. **Ra,** also spelled **Re,** the sun god and creator god.
[149] **Horus of the Double Horizon** The falcon god.
[150] **in His Name of Shu . . . Aten** A fusion of **Shu,** the primordial Egyptian god of the air and supporter of the sky, with **Aten,** the god of the solar disk.
[151] **Jubilee Festival** Sed-Festival, a repetition of the coronation ritual, in which the vows of kingship are renewed; usually held after thirty years of a reign, but sometimes after three.
[152] **Akhet-Aten** Also called **Aket-Aten.** "The horizon of the Aten." The capital of Akhenaten's kingdom.
[153] **The King of Upper and Lower Egypt** An old title, dating from 3100 BCE, when Menes united Egypt into one country. It precedes the Throne Name (see footnote 154).
[154] **Nefer-Kheperu-Ra Wa-en-Ra** Throne name of Akhenaten.

---

[155] **Son of Ra** Epithet that accompanies the king's name. The ruler's divinity arises from the belief that he or she is the offspring of the sun god **Ra,** also known as **Re.**
[156] **the Great Wife of the King** Here follow a list of divine names of Queen Nefertiti, Akhenaten's consort.
[157] **Nefer-Neferu-Aten Nefert-Iti** Throne name of Nefertiti.
[158] **He** King Akhenaten.

You are afar, yet are your rays upon earth;
  you are before their face, yet one knows not their going!
When you go down in the western horizon,
  the earth is in darkness, as if it were dead.
They sleep in their chamber, their heads enwrapped,
  and no eye sees the other.
Though all their things were taken while under their
    heads,
  yet would they not perceive it.   20
Every lion comes forth from his den,
  and all serpents that bite.

Darkness is without and the earth is silent,
  for he who created it rests in his horizon.
When the earth brightens and you rise on the horizon,
  and shine as the Aten in the day,
When you scatter the darkness and offer your beams,
  the Two Lands are in festival,
They are awake and they stand on their feet,
  for you have raised them up.
They wash their bodies, and they take their garments,   30
  and their hands praise your arising.
    The whole land, it performs its work!

All beasts are content upon their pasture,
  and the trees and herbs are verdant.
The birds fly out of their nests,
  and their wings praise your Divine Essence.[159]
All wild beasts prance upon their feet,
  and all that fly and alight.
They live when you shine forth for them!
The ships voyage downstream and upstream likewise,   40
  and every way is open, since you have arisen.
The fish in the river leap up before your face,
  and your rays are in the midst of the Great Green.[160]

You who bring children into being in women,
  and make fluid[161] into mankind,
Who nourishes the son in the womb of his mother,
  who soothes him so that he weeps not,
  O nurse in the womb!
Who gives breath in order to keep alive
  all that he has made;   50

When he comes forth from the womb on the day of his
    birth,
  you open his mouth in speech, and give all that he
    needs.
The chick in the egg chirps in the shell
  for you give it breath therein to sustain its life.
You make its completion for it in the egg in order to
    break it;
It comes forth from the egg at its completion,
  and walks on its feet when it comes forth therefrom.

How manifold are the things which you have made,
  and they are hidden from before man!   60
    O unique god, who has no second to him!
You have created the earth according to your desire,
  while you were alone,
With men, cattle, and wild beasts,
  all that is upon earth and goes upon feet,
    and all that soars above and flies with its wings.

The lands of Syria[162] and Kush,[163]
  and the land of Egypt,
You put every man in his place,
  and supply their needs.
Each one has provision   70
  and his lifetime is reckoned.
Their tongues are diverse in speech,
  and their form likewise;
Their skins are distinguished,
  for you distinguish the peoples of foreign lands.

You make the Nile in the Other World,[164]
  and bring it whither you wish,
In order to sustain the people,
  even as you have made them.
For you are lord of them all,   80
  who weary yourself on their behalf,
The lord of every land, who arises for them,
  O Aten of the day, great of majesty!

All strange foreign lands,
  you make that whereon they live.
You have put a Nile in the sky,
  that it may come down for them,
And make waves on the hills like the sea,
  to water their fields in their townships.
How excellently made are your designs, O Lord of   90
    Eternity!
  the Nile in heaven, you appoint it for foreign peoples,
    and all beasts of the wilderness which walk upon
      feet;
The Nile upon earth,
  it proceeds from the Other World for the Beloved Land.

Your rays suckle every field,
  and when you shine forth
    they live and flourish for you.
You make the seasons
  to cause to continue all you have created:
The winter to cool them,   100
  and the warmth that they may taste of you.
You have made the sky afar off to shine therein,
  in order to behold all you have made.

---

[159] **Divine Essence** The perishable part of **Aten's** soul, the ka.
[160] **Great Green** The sea.
[161] **fluid** Semen.

[162] **Syria** Retenu, identified variously as Canaan, north Palestine, and south Syria.
[163] **Kush** Nubia, the land on Egypt's southern border.
[164] **Nile in the Other World** The god **Aten** is praised for making a Nile River in heaven, for those foreigners who cannot enjoy the Nile River in this world.

You are alone, shining in your forms as living Aten,
   appearing, shining, withdrawing, returning, you make
     millions of forms of yourself alone!
Cities, townships, fields, road, and river,
   all eyes behold you against them. O Aten of the day
     above the earth!

You are in my heart,   110
   and there is no one who knows you save your son,
Nefer-Kheperu-Ra Wa-en-Ra,
   whom you made understanding of your designs and
     your might.
The earth came into being by your hand,
   even as you have created them.
When you arise they live,
   and when you set they die.
But you have eternity in your members,
   and all creatures live in you.

The eyes look on your beauty until you set;   120
   all work is laid aside when you set in the west.
When you rise you make all to flourish for the King,
   you who made the foundations of the earth.
You raise them up for your son,
   he who came forth from your body,
the King of Upper and Lower Egypt, Living in Truth, the
Lord of the Two Lands, Nefer-Kheperu-Ra Wa-en-Ra, Son
of Ra, Living in Truth, Lord of Diadems, Akh-en-Aten,
Great in His Duration, and for the Great Wife of the King,
His Beloved, the Lady of the Two Lands, Nefer-Neferu-
Aten Nefert-Iti, living and youthful forever unto eternity.

∞

Questions for Critical Thinking

1. What were some of the political and religious issues surrounding Akhenaten's reforms? Are they similar to "church-state" issues in the United States? If so, how?

2. List at least three powers Aten possesses that make him a "universal" deity, and give examples of how they are evident in everyday life for the Egyptians.

2

THE AEGEAN

The Minoans, the Mycenaeans, and the Greeks of the Archaic Age

---

HOMER
Selections from the *Iliad*

The two Greek epics, the *Iliad* and the *Odyssey* (see the following selection), have never lost their appeal, though they were composed nearly three thousand years ago. Homer, with his strong grasp of the human psyche, expressed his characters' sorrow and happiness, hopes and fears, and most especially, their love of life and certainty of death. Performed as oral poetry accompanied by music, these works electrified his first audiences because they represented the basic human condition as his listeners had experienced it. In later periods, after the works were written down, readers were equally thrilled because they recognized the timeless truths contained in his words. Contributing to the epics' enduring appeal were the similes and metaphors that invoked images from Homer's world and remain memorable today as sublime expressions of poetic beauty. It is a measure of Homer's classic status that ever since his day, writers have reworked his two stories of war and travel, respectively, giving their own versions of his heroes and heroines and updating the plots to reflect their own times.

The *Iliad* focuses on the climactic year of the Greeks' nine-year siege of Ilium, or Troy (though it stops short of the fall of Troy). Composed in about the middle of the eighth century BCE, Homer's works are his own reworking of tales that previously had been circulating orally for about three hundred years. The oral tales reflected an earlier civilization, the Mycenaean (1900–1100 BCE); thus, the Homeric heroes and the Olympian deities, who are considered the quintessence of Greek culture, are in reality Mycenaean in origin. The popularity of both the *Iliad* and the *Odyssey* resulted in their becoming moral guidebooks, offering to Greek youths models of behavior both on and off the battlefield. The works were also treated as religious scripture, providing insight into the personalities and motives of the Olympian deities.

Reading the Selections

These four selections from the *Iliad* illustrate Homer's talents as a storyteller and as a teacher of moral lessons. In the selection from Book 1, Homer's genius is evident in the opening line that announces his theme: "the anger of Achilles son of Peleus, that accursed anger, which brought the Greeks endless sufferings. . . ." This theme becomes the thread that holds together the epic, despite the convoluted plot and its "cast of thousands." The Trojan War—the battle between the Greeks (Achaeans) and the Trojans—always forms the backdrop and sometimes the temporary foreground to the story. Further complicating the plot are the adventures of the Olympic deities, who allow nothing to happen on earth without their consent.

The first selection also details the quarrel between Achilles and Agamemnon, the king, over their claims to a captured woman. Their quarrel creates dissension in the ranks of the Greek soldiers and angers Achilles to the point that he withdraws himself and his men from battling the Trojans. The consequences of this private dispute become clearer when many men are slaughtered as the two sides fight back and forth.

The selection from Book 6 shows how war touches the lives of everyone, especially wives and children. The conversation between Hector, the leading warrior for the Trojans, and his wife Andromache is one of the most moving scenes in literature. In a brief exchange, the husband and wife discuss why men fight wars and how women and children are the victims. The desire to live, so evident in this scene, is then contrasted in the selection from Book 22, where Hector and Achilles finally face each other. Homer shows that in the heat of battle, men, driven by revenge and the will to survive, kill their enemies and mutilate their bodies. He underscores both the glory and gore of war—themes that writers over the centuries will address to the present day.

The selection from Book 24, the climax of the *Iliad*, begins with Achilles out of control, intent on humiliating the corpse of Hector by dragging it behind his chariot. Confronted by Hector's grieving father, King Priam of Troy, Achilles is able to let go of his all-consuming rage only when the two men weep for their loved ones and for their own fate as mortals. Achilles yields up Hector's body to Priam, and the epic ends with Hector's funeral (not included here).

∞

Book 1, Plague and Wrath

Anger[1]—sing, goddess,[2] the anger of Achilles son of Peleus,[3] that 1
accursed anger, which brought the Greeks[4] endless sufferings
and sent the mighty souls of many warriors to Hades,[5] leaving
their bodies as carrion for the dogs and a feast for the birds; and
Zeus'[6] purpose was fulfilled. It all began when Agamemnon[7]
lord of men and godlike Achilles quarreled and parted.

Which of the gods[8] was it that made them quarrel? It was
Apollo,[9] son of Zeus and Leto,[10] who started the feud because he was furious with Agamemnon for not respecting
his priest[11] Chryses. So Apollo inflicted a deadly plague   10
on Agamemnon's army and destroyed his men.

Chryses[12] had come to the Greeks' swift ships to recover his captured daughter.[13] He brought with him an immense ransom and carried the emblems of the Archergod[14] Apollo on a golden staff in his hands. He spoke in supplication to the whole Greek army and most of all its two commanders, Agamemnon and Menelaus,[15] the sons of Atreus:[16]

"Sons of Atreus and you other Greek men-at-arms; you hope to sack Priam's town[17] and get home in safety. 20
May the gods that live on Olympus[18] grant your wish. Now respect the Archer-god Apollo son of Zeus, accept this ransom and release my beloved daughter."

Then all the other Greeks shouted in agreement. They wanted to see the priest respected and the splendid ransom taken. But this was not at all to Agamemnon's liking. He cruelly and bluntly dismissed the priests:

"Old man, don't let me catch you loitering by the hollow ships today or coming back again in the future, 30
or you may find the god's staff and emblems a very poor defence. That girl I will not release. She will grow old in

---

[1] **Anger . . . of Achilles** The theme of the *Iliad*.
[2] **goddess** Calliope, the music of epic poetry.
[3] **Peleus** Father of Achilles, by the sea goddess **Thetis**. King of **Phthia**, in Thessaly.
[4] **Greeks** Mainland Greece contained many kingdoms, but its people were known collectively as the Greeks.
[5] **Hades** The underworld.
[6] **Zeus** Son of **Cronos** and **Rhea**. King and father of the Olympic deities; god of the sky, of the weather, of hospitality, and of guests.
[7] **Agamemnon** King of Mycenae and overall leader of the Greek army; son of **Atreus**, husband of **Clytaemnestra**, brother of **Menelaus**.
[8] **Which . . . gods** The Greeks thought the gods controlled human behavior.
[9] **Apollo** Son of Zeus, by Leto. Patron of the arts, leader of the muses. He fights for the Trojans.
[10] **Leto** A goddess, mother of **Apollo** and **Artemis**, by **Zeus**.
[11] **not respecting his priest** When humans humiliate a priest, a god's representative, they are guilty of impiety, a sin for which they will be punished severely.

---

[12] **Chryses** A priest of **Apollo**.
[13] **daughter** Chryseis, daughter of the priest **Chryses**.
[14] **Archer-god** Apollo, who also was god of archery and sudden death in men.
[15] **Menelaus** King of **Lacedaemon**, a city on the Peloponnesus; husband of **Helen** and brother of **Agamemnon**.
[16] **Atreus** Father of **Agamemnon** and **Menelaus**.
[17] **Priam's town** Troy, ruled by King **Priam**. Priam is son of **Laomedon**, husband of **Hecuba**, father of **Hector** and **Paris**.
[18] **Olympus** The home of the Greek gods; an actual mountain in Thessaly.

Argos,[19] in my household, a long way from her country, working at the loom,[20] sharing my bed. Now get out and don't provoke me, if you want to save your skin."

So he spoke, and the old man was afraid and did as he was told. He went off without a word along the shore of the sounding sea. But when he had gone some distance, the old man poured out prayers to lord Apollo, son of lovely-haired Leto:

"Hear me, Apollo, lord of the silver bow, protector of Chryse and holy Cilla,[21] and mighty ruler over Tenedos![22] Plague-god,[23] if ever I built a temple that pleased you, if ever I burnt you offerings of the fat thighs of bulls or goats, grant me this wish. Make the Greeks pay with your arrows for my tears." 40

So he spoke in prayer, and Phoebus[24] Apollo heard him and came down in fury from the heights of Olympus, his bow and covered quiver on his back. With every movement of the furious god, the arrows rattled on his shoulders, and his descent was like nightfall. He settled down some way from the ships and shot an arrow, with a terrifying twang from his silver bow. He attacked the mules first and the swift dogs; then he aimed his sharp arrows at the men, and struck again and again. Day and night, packed funeral pyres[25] burned. 50

For nine days the god's arrows rained down on the camp. On the tenth, Achilles had the men summoned to assembly, an idea the goddess white-armed Hera[26] gave him in her concern for the Greeks whose destruction she was witnessing. When everyone had arrived and the gathering was complete, swift-footed Achilles rose and spoke to them: 60

"Agamemnon son of Atreus, what with the ravages of the fighting and the plague, any of us that are not dead by then will soon, I think, have to sail for home. Come, let us consult some prophet or priest or some interpreter of dreams (dreams, as you know, are sent by Zeus) and find out from him why Phoebus Apollo is so angry with us. He may be offended at some broken vow or failure in our rites. If so, he may be willing to accept an offering of unblemished sheep and goats and save us from the plague." 70

With these words Achilles sat down, and Calchas son of Thestor rose to his feet. As a prophet, Calchas had no rival in the camp. Past, present and future held no secrets from him; and it was his second sight[27]—a gift he owed

to Apollo—that had guided the Greek ships to Ilium. He had their interests at heart as he rose and addressed them:

"Achilles dear to Zeus, you have instructed me to account for the anger of lord Apollo the Archer-god; and I will do so. But listen to me first and swear an oath to use all your eloquence and strength to look after me and protect me. I ask this of you, being well aware that I am about to infuriate a man whose authority is great among us and whose word is law to all the Greeks. An ordinary mortal is no match for anyone in authority he angers. Even if his superior swallows his anger for the moment, he will still nurse his grievance till the day when he can settle the account. Consider, then, whether you can guarantee my safety." 80

Swift-footed Achilles replied and said: 90

"Put your mind at rest and tell us everything you have learnt from the god. For by Apollo son of Zeus, the very god to whom you pray, Calchas, when you reveal your prophecies—I swear that as long as I am alive and look on the earth, not one of all the Greeks here by the hollow ships will raise a fist against you, not even if the man you mean is Agamemnon, who now claims to be far the best of all."

Then the matchless prophet took heart and said:

"Apollo has found no fault with any broken vows or failures in our rites. Agamemnon insulted his priest, did not free his daughter and refused the ransom—that is why Apollo made us suffer and will continue to do so. He will not release us from this loathsome plague till we give the dark-eyed girl back to her father, without recompense or ransom, and send a sacred offering to the priest's town of Chryse. Appease him like that, and we might persuade him to relent." 100

With these words Calchas sat down, and the warrior son of Atreus, wide-ruling Agamemnon, leapt up, enraged. His heart seethed with fury, and his eyes were like flames of fire. With a menacing look he spoke first to Calchas: 110

"Prophet of evil, never yet have you said a word to my advantage. It's always trouble you revel in predicting. Not once have you delivered a positive prophecy—not once! And now you hold forth as the army's prophet, telling the Greeks that the Archer-god Apollo is persecuting them because I refused the splendid ransom for the girl Chryseis. And why? Because I wanted to have her at home myself. Indeed, I like her better than my wife Clytaemnestra.[28] Chryseis is quite as beautiful and no less clever or skilful with her hands. 120

"Still, I am willing to give her up, if that appears the better course. I want my army alive and well, not dead or dying. But give me another prize at once or I will be the only one of us without one. That cannot be right. You can all see for yourselves that the prize I was given is on its way elsewhere."

Swift-footed godlike Achilles replied:

"Most glorious Agamemnon, unequalled in your greed, where will the great-hearted Greeks find you a fresh prize? I have yet to hear of any store of common property we have laid by. The plunder we took from captured 130

---

[19] **Argos** (1) A city on the Peloponnesus, ruled by **Diomedes;** (2) another name for mainland Greece; (3) another name for the kingdom of **Agamemnon;** (4) Pelasgian **Argos,** in northern Greece, the kingdom of **Achilles.**

[20] **working . . . loom** Women had two basic roles: to be beautiful and to weave at the loom.

[21] **Chryse . . . Cilla** Two cities in the Trojan lands; **Chryse** was the home of **Chryses.**

[22] **Tenedos** An island in the Aegean Sea, off the coast of **Troy.**

[23] **Plague-god** **Apollo,** whose arrows were thought to bring on the plague.

[24] **Phoebus** Epithet for **Apollo.**

[25] **funeral pyres** Both the Greeks and the Trojans honored the dead by burning their corpses on funeral pyres.

[26] **Hera** Daughter of **Cronos** and **Rhea,** sister and long-suffering wife of **Zeus.** She fights for the Greeks.

[27] **second sight** Since **Calchas** was blind, it was believed that **Apollo** had given him "second sight," the gift of prophecy.

[28] **Clytaemnestra** Wife of **Agamemnon** and sister of **Helen.**

towns has been distributed. It cannot be right to ask the men to reassemble that. No: give the girl back now, as the god demands, and we will compensate you three, four times over, if Zeus ever allows us to sack this Trojan town with its fine walls."

Lord Agamemnon replied and said:

"You are a great warrior, godlike Achilles, but don't 140 imagine you can trick me into that. I am not going to be outmanoeuvred or persuaded by you. 'Give up the girl,' you say, in order to keep your own prize safe. Do you expect me to sit tamely by, while I am robbed? No: if the army is prepared to give me a fresh prize, they must choose one to my taste to make up for my loss. If not, I shall come and help myself to your prize, or Ajax's,[29] or maybe I shall walk off with Odysseus'.[30] And what an angry man I shall leave behind me!

"However, we can deal with all that later. For the 150 moment, let us run a black ship down into the bright sea, carefully select her crew, load the animals for sacrifice and put the girl herself, fair-cheeked Chryseis, on board. And let some adviser be in charge, Ajax, Idomeneus,[31] godlike Odysseus, or you yourself, Achilles, most impetuous of all Greeks, to offer the sacrifice and win us back Apollo's favour."

Swift-footed Achilles gave him a black look and replied:

"You shameless, self-centered . . . ! How can you ex- 160 pect any of the men to comply with you willingly when you send them on a raid or into battle? It was no quarrel with Trojan warriors that brought *me* here to fight. They have never done *me* any harm. They have never lifted oxen or horses of mine, nor ravaged my crops back home in fertile Phthia,[32] nurse of warriors. The roaring seas and many a dark range of mountains lie between us.

"We joined your expedition, you shameless swine, to please you, to get satisfaction from the Trojans for Menelaus and yourself, dog-face—a fact you utterly ignore. 170 And now comes this threat from you, of all people, to rob me of my prize, in person, my hard-earned prize which was a tribute from the army. It's not as though I am ever given a prize equal to yours when the Greeks sack some prosperous Trojan town. The heat and burden of the fighting fall on me, but when it comes to dealing out the spoils, it is you that takes the lion's share, leaving me to return to my ships, exhausted from battle, with some pathetic portion to call my own.

"So, I shall now go back home to Phthia. That is the 180 best thing I can do—to sail home with my beaked ships. I can see no point in staying here to be insulted, while I pile up wealth and luxuries for you."

Agamemnon lord of men replied:

"Run for it, then, by all means, if that's the way you feel. I am not going down on bended knees to entreat you to stay here on my account. There are others with me who will treat me with respect, and Zeus wise in counsel is first among them. Of all the Olympian-bred lords here, you are the most hateful to me. Rivalry, war, fighting—these are 190 the breath of life to you. If you *are* a great warrior, it is because the god made you so. Go home now with your ships and your men-at-arms and rule your Myrmidons.[33] I have no interest in you whatsoever. Your resentment leaves me cold.

"But here is a threat: in the same way as Phoebus Apollo is robbing me of Chryseis, whom I propose to send off in my ship with my crew, I will come in person to your hut and take away fair-cheeked Briseis,[34] your prize, Achilles, to let you know how far I am your superior and 200 to teach others to shrink from claiming parity with me and playing the equal to my face."

So he spoke, and his words infuriated Achilles. In his manly chest, his heart was torn whether to draw the sharp sword from his side, thrust his way through the crowd and disembowel Agamemnon, or control himself and check his angry impulse. These thoughts were racing through his mind, and he was just drawing his great sword from his sheath when Athene[35] came down from the skies. The goddess white-armed Hera had sent her 210 because she felt equally close to both men and was concerned for them.

Athene stood behind Achilles and seized him by his auburn hair. No one but Achilles was aware of her; the rest saw nothing. Achilles was amazed. He swung round, recognized Pallas[36] Athene at once—so wonderful was the light from her eyes—and spoke winged words:

"Why have you come here this time, daughter of Zeus who drives the storm-cloud? Is it to witness Agamemnon's humiliating affront? I tell you bluntly and, believe me, I 220 mean it: he stands to pay for this insolence with his life."

The goddess grey-eyed Athene replied:

"I came from the skies to cool your fury, if you will listen to me. The goddess white-armed Hera sent me because she feels equally close to both of you and is concerned for you. Come now, give up this quarrel and take your hand from your sword. Insult him with words instead and tell him what you mean to do. I tell you bluntly and I *do* mean it: the day shall come when splendid gifts three times as valuable as what you have now lost will be 230 laid at your feet because of that humiliating affront. Hold your hand, then, and do as we tell you."

Swift-footed Achilles replied and said:

"Goddess, a man must respect what you and Hera say, however angry he may be. Better for him if he does. The gods listen to the man who goes along with them."

He spoke, placed his heavy hand on the silver hilt, drove the long sword back into its scabbard and complied

---

[29] **Ajax** Greek warlord; son of **Telamon.** Called **Telamonian** or **Great Ajax;** led the troops from **Salamis.**

[30] **Odysseus** Greek warlord; son of **Laertes** and father of **Telemachus;** king of **Ithaca.**

[31] **Idomeneus** Greek warlord; son of **Deucalion;** leader of the troops from **Crete.**

[32] **Phthia** A region in Thessaly; home of **Peleus** and **Achilles.**

[33] **Myrmidons** The troops from **Phthia** in Thessaly, the followers of **Achilles.**

[34] **Briseis** A woman loved by **Achilles;** daughter of **Briseus,** a captive of **Achilles.**

[35] **Athene** Goddess of wisdom, of warfare; patron of the city of Athens. She sprang full-grown from **Zeus's** head, after a headache. She fought for the Greeks.

[36] **Pallas** Epithet for **Athene.**

with Athene, who then set out for Olympus and the palace of Zeus who drives the storm-cloud, where she rejoined the other gods. 240

Not that Achilles curbed his anger. He rounded bitterly on Agamemnon and said:

"You drunkard, you, with your eyes of a dog and heart of a doe! You never have the courage to arm yourself and go into battle with the men, let alone join the pick of the Greeks in an ambush—you'd sooner die. It suits you better to remain in camp, walking off with the prizes of anyone who contradicts you—a leader who grows fat on his own people! But then, you rule over nobodies: other- 250 wise, son of Atreus,[37] this outrage would prove your last.

"But I tell you bluntly, and I am going to take a solemn oath on that staff in my hands. Once cut from its stem in the hills, it can never put out leaves or twigs again. The bronze axe stripped it of its bark and foliage: it will sprout no more. The men who in the name of Zeus safeguard our traditions now hold it when they give judgement. By this I solemnly swear that the day is coming when the Greeks one and all will miss Achilles badly, and you in your despair will be powerless to help them as they fall in their multitudes to 260 man-slaying Hector. Then you will tear your heart out in remorse for giving no respect to the best of the Greeks."

So spoke the son of Peleus, flung down the staff with its golden studs and resumed his seat, leaving Agamemnon thundering at him from the other side. But Nestor now leapt up, eloquent Nestor,[38] the clear-voiced orator from Pylos[39] whose speech flowed sweeter than honey off his tongue. He had already seen two generations of men born, grow up and die in sacred Pylos, and now he ruled the third. He had their interests at heart as he rose and addressed them: 270

"What can I say? This is indeed enough to make Greece weep! How happy Priam and his sons would be, how all the Trojans would rejoice, if they could hear you at each other's throats, you, the two best Greeks when it comes to giving advice and fighting!

"Now listen to me. You are both my juniors. What's more, I have mixed in the past with even better men than you and never failed to carry conviction with them, the finest men I have ever seen or shall see, men like Peirithous and Dryas shepherd of the people, Caeneus, Exadius, god- 280 like Polyphemus and Aegeus' son Theseus, a man like the gods. These Lapiths[40] were the strongest men that earth has bred, the strongest men who pitted themselves against the strongest enemies—the mountain-dwelling Centaurs,[41]

whom they violently destroyed. These were the men I left my home in Pylos to join. I traveled far to meet them—they invited me, personally—and I fought my own campaign. Not a soul on earth today could live with those men in battle—and they listened to what I said and followed my advice. You two do the same. It's for your own good to go 290 along with what I tell you.

"You, Agamemnon, though you have the authority, do not rob him of his girl. The Greek army gave her to him first. Let him keep his prize. And you, Achilles, give up your desire to cross swords with your leader. Through the authority he derives from Zeus, a leader who holds the sceptre of power has more claim to our respect than anyone else. Even if you, with a goddess for mother, are the better fighter, yet Agamemnon is your superior since he rules more people. Agamemnon, cool your fury; I, Nestor, 300 entreat you to put aside your anger against Achilles who is a mighty tower of strength for every Greek in the hell of battle."

Lord Agamemnon replied and said:

"Venerable sir, all that is very true. But this man here wants no superiors: he wants to dominate everyone, to lord it over everyone and to give us each our orders, though I know one person who is not going to stand for that. What if the everlasting gods did make a spearman of him? Does that entitle him to hurl insults—?" 310

Abruptly, godlike Achilles replied:

"A pathetic little nonentity I shall be called, for sure, if I give in to you at every point, no matter what you say. Issue your commands to the rest. Don't tell me what to do. I have done with taking your orders. And I'll tell you something else, and you bear it in mind. I am not going to fight you, or anyone else, with my bare hands for this girl's sake. You Greeks gave her to me, and now you take her back. But there's much else by my swift black ship that is mine, and you will take none of that against my 320 will. Come on, just try, so that everyone here can see what happens. Your black blood will soon be flowing down my spear."

The war of words was over. The two stood up and dismissed the assembly by the Greek ships. Achilles, with Menoetius' son Patroclus[42] and his Myrmidon troops, made off to his hut and ships; while Agamemnon launched a swift ship into the water, chose twenty rowers, loaded the offering of cattle for sacrifice to the god and seated fair-cheeked Chryseis on board. Quick-thinking 330 Odysseus went as their leader and, when everyone was aboard, they set off along the highways of the sea.

Meanwhile Agamemnon ordered the army to purify itself by bathing. When they had done this and thrown the dirty water into the waves, they offered perfect sacrifices of bulls and goats to Apollo on the shore of the murmuring sea. The smell of sacrifice, mixed with the curling smoke, went up into the sky.

· · ·

---

[37] **son of Atreus** Patronymic of **Agamemnon** and **Menelaus**.
[38] **Nestor** The oldest Greek warlord. Son of **Neleus,** king of **Pylos.**
[39] **Pylos** A city and region in the Peloponnesus; home to **Nestor.**
[40] **Peirithous . . . Lapiths** **Nestor** describes here the legendary tribe of **Lapiths,** in Thessaly. Their king, **Peirithous,** was a son of **Zeus,** and his warlords included **Dryas, Caeneus, Exadius, Polyphemus,** and **Theseus. Theseus** was also the son of **Aegeus,** king of Athens, and **Aegeus** was the eponymous source for the **Aegean** Sea.
[41] **Centaurs** Legendary creatures, half-man and half-horse. The battle between the **Lapiths** and **Centaurs**—a frequent subject in Greek art—became a symbol of the struggle between civilization and barbarism.

---

[42] **Patroclus** Greek warrior; son of **Menoetius;** companion of **Achilles.**

∞

Book 6, Hector and Andromache

Hector of the flashing helmet took his leave and soon ₁
reached his own welcoming house. But he did not find his
white-armed wife Andromache[43] at home. She had gone
up to a tower on the wall with her child[44] and well-robed
waiting-woman and was standing there crying her heart
out. Failing to find his matchless wife in the house, Hector
went to the threshold and said to the serving-women:

"Women, tell me what's happened. Where has white-
armed Andromache gone to from the house? Is she visit- ₁₀
ing one of my sisters or my brothers' well-robed wives?
Or has she gone to Athene's shrine where the rest of the
Trojan women with their lovely hair are interceding with
that august goddess?"

A busy serving-woman replied:

"Hector, since you order me to tell the truth, she is not
visiting your sisters or your brothers' well-robed wives
and she has not gone to Athene's shrine with the rest of
the women to pray to that august goddess. She has gone
to the great tower of Ilium.[45] She had heard that our men ₂₀
were being ground down, and the Greeks were well on
top. So she rushed out like a woman possessed and must
have arrived at the walls. The nurse followed her with the
baby in her arms."

So spoke the serving-woman, and Hector raced out
of the house and retraced his steps down the well-built
streets. He had crossed the great town and reached the
Scaean gate[46]—his route out on to the plain—when Andromache herself, who married him with a rich dowry, came
running up to meet him. Andromache was the daughter
of great-hearted Eëtion, the Cilician ruler who lived be- ₃₀
low the woods of Mount Placus in Thebe-under-Placus.[47]
It was his daughter that the warrior Hector had married.

Andromache came to meet him, and her waiting-
woman carried the little boy in her arms, their baby son
and Hector's darling, lovely as a star, whom Hector called
Scamandrius, but everyone else called Astyanax,[48] "Town-
lord," because his father was the one defence of Ilium.

Hector looked at his son and smiled, but said nothing. Andromache, bursting into tears, went up to him, put
her hand in his and said: ₄₀

"Hector, you are possessed! This determination of
yours will be the death of you. You have no pity on your little boy or your luckless wife, who will soon be your widow,
when the Greeks kill you in a massed attack. And when I
lose you, I might as well be dead. There will be no comfort
left when you have met your end—nothing but grief.

"And I have no father or lady mother either. My father Eëtion fell to godlike Achilles when he sacked our
welcoming town, Cilician Thebe[49] with its high gates. But
though Achilles killed Eëtion, he did not think it right ₅₀
to strip the body. He cremated him in his ornate arms
and built a grave-mound above him; and the mountain
Nymphs, daughters of Zeus who drives the storm-cloud,
planted elms around it.

"I had seven brothers too at home. In one day, all of
them went down into Hades. Godlike swift-footed Achilles killed them all while they were looking after their
shambling cattle and white sheep. As for my mother, who
ruled in Thebe under the one man who might have kept
you free. But may the earth be piled high over my dead ₆₀
body before I hear your cries as they drag you off."

With these words glorious Hector reached out for his
boy. But the child shrank back with a cry to the bosom of
his girdled nurse, alarmed by his father's appearance, terrified by his bronze helmet with its horsehair plume that
he saw nodding frighteningly from the top. His father and
lady mother burst out laughing. Glorious Hector quickly
took his helmet off and put it, all shining, on the ground.
Then he kissed his dear son, dandled him in his arms and
prayed to Zeus and the other gods: ₇₀

"Zeus and you other gods, grant that this boy of mine
becomes, like me, pre-eminent among the Trojans; as
strong and brave as I; a mighty ruler of Ilium. May people
say, when he comes back from battle, 'Here is a man much
better than his father.' Let him bring home the bloodstained armour of the enemy he has killed and delight his
mother's heart."

With these words Hector handed the boy into the arms
of his wife, who took him to her fragrant bosom, laughing
through her tears. When her husband saw this, pity over- ₈₀
came him. He stroked her with his hand and said:

"Dear heart, I beg you, don't distress yourself too
much. No one is going to send me down to Hades before
my time, though death itself, I think, is something no
man, coward or hero, can escape, once he has come into
this world. You go home now and attend to your work, the
loom and the spindle, and tell the waiting-women to get
on with theirs. War is men's business; and this war will
be the business of every man in Ilium, myself above all."

With these words glorious Hector picked up his hel- ₉₀
met with its horsehair plume. His wife set out for home,
weeping profusely and with many a backward look. She
soon reached the welcoming palace of man-slaying Hector, found many of her waiting-women inside and stirred
them all to lamentation. They mourned for Hector in his
own house, though he was still alive, thinking he would
never survive the fury of the Greeks' assault and come
home from the battle.

· · ·

---

[43] **Andromache** Trojan princess; daughter of **Eetion;** wife of
Hector.
[44] **her child Astyanax,** a young Trojan prince; son of **Andromache** and **Hector.**
[45] **Ilium** Troy, hence the title of the epic, **Iliad.**
[46] **Scaean gate** The main gates of Troy.
[47] **Eëtion ... Thebe-under-Plaucus** Eëtion was king of the **Cili-
cians** in **Thebe,** in the Trojan lands; father of **Andromache.**
[48] **Scamandrius ... Astyanax** Hector's pet name for his son,
Scamandrius, derives from the Trojan river, **Scamander.**

---

[49] **Cilician Thebe** Trojan city ruled by **Eetion.**

∞

Book 22, The Death of Hector

Athene treacherously led him forward. When Hector and   1
Achilles came within range of each other, great Hector of
the flashing helmet spoke first:

"Achilles, I'm not going to run from you any more. I
have already been chased by you three times round Priam's great town without daring to stop and let you come
near. But now I have made up my mind to fight you man
to man and kill you or be killed.

"But let us call on the gods to witness an agreement:
no compact could have better guarantors. If Zeus grants   10
me staying-power and I kill you, I will not violently mal-
treat you. All I shall do, Achilles, is to strip you of your famous armour. Then I will give up your body to the Greeks.
You do the same."

Swift-footed Achilles gave him a black look and
replied:

"Hector, I'm never going to forgive you. So don't talk
to me about agreements. Lions don't come to terms with
men, the wolf doesn't see eye to eye with the lamb—they
are enemies to the end. It's the same with you and me.   20
Friendship between us is impossible, and there will be no
truce of any kind till one of us has fallen and glutted the
shield-bearing god of battles[50] with his blood.

"So summon up all the courage you possess. This
is the time to show your bravery and ability as a fighter.
Not that anything is going to save you now, when Pallas
Athene is waiting to bring you down with my spear. This
moment you are going to pay the full price for all the sufferings of my companions you killed on your rampage
with your spear."   30

He spoke, balanced his long-shadowed spear and
hurled it. But glorious Hector was on the lookout and
avoided the bronze spear. He crouched, his eye on the
weapon, and it flew over him and stuck in the ground.
But Pallas Athene snatched it up and brought it back to
Achilles without Hector shepherd of the people noticing.
Hector spoke to the matchless son of Peleus:

"You missed! So, godlike Achilles, Zeus gave you the
wrong date for my death after all! You thought you knew
everything. But then you're so glib, so clever with your   40
tongue—trying to frighten me and undermine my determination and courage. But you won't make me run and
then hit me in the back with your spear. Drive it through
my chest as I charge—if the god lets you. But first you will
have to avoid this one of mine. May the whole length of
it find a home in your body! This war would be an easier business for the Trojans if you, their greatest scourge,
were dead."

He spoke, balanced his long-shadowed spear and
hurled it. He hit the center of Achilles' shield and did not   50
miss, but the spear rebounded from it. Hector was frus-
trated that the swift spear had left his hand to no purpose
and stood there dismayed, since he had no other one. He
shouted aloud to Deiphobus[51] of the white shield, asking
him for a long spear. But Deiphobus was nowhere near
him. Hector realized what had happened and said:

"It's over. So the gods did, after all, summon me to
my death. I thought the warrior Deiphobus was at my side.
But he is behind the wall, and Athene has deceived me.
Evil death is no longer far away; it is staring me in the face   60
and there is no escape. Zeus and his Archer son must long
have been resolved on this, for all their earlier goodwill
and help.

"So now my destiny confronts me. Let me at least
sell my life dearly and not without glory, after some great
deed for future generations to hear of."

With these words Hector draw the sharp, long, heavy
sword hanging down at his side. He gathered himself
and swooped like a high-flying eagle that drops to earth
through black clouds to pounce on a tender lamb or cow-   70
ering hare. So Hector swooped, brandishing his sharp
sword.

Achilles sprang to meet him, his heart filled with
savage determination. He kept his chest covered with
his fine, ornate shield; his glittering helmet with its four
plates nodded, and above it danced the lovely plumes that
Hephaestus[52] had lavished on the crest. Like a star moving with others through the night, Hesperus,[53] the loveliest star set in the skies—such was the gleam from his
spear's sharp point as he weighed it in his right hand with   80
murder in his heart for godlike Hector, searching that
handsome body for its most vulnerable spot.

Hector's body was completely covered by the fine
bronze armour he had taken from great Patroclus when
he killed him, except for the flesh that could be seen at
the windpipe, where the collar bones hold the neck from
the shoulders, the easiest place to kill a man. As Hector
charged him, godlike Achilles drove at this spot with his
spear, and the point went right through Hector's soft neck,
though the heavy bronze head did not cut his windpipe   90
and left him still able to speak. Hector crashed in the dust,
and godlike Achilles triumphed over him:

"Hector, no doubt you imagined, as you stripped Patroclus, that you would be safe. You never thought of me: I
was too far away. You innocent. Down by the hollow ships
a man much better than Patroclus had been left behind.
It was I, and I have brought you down. So now the dogs
and birds of prey are going to mangle you foully, while
we Greeks will give Patroclus full burial honours."

Fading fast, Hector of the flashing helmet replied: 100

"I entreat you, by your knees, by your own life, and
by your parents, do not throw my body to the dogs by the
Greek ships but take a ransom for me. My father and my

---

[50] **shield-bearing . . . battles Ares,** the god of war.

[51] **Deiphobus** Trojan warrior; son of King **Priam.**
[52] **Hephaestus** Smith god, who fashioned all the weaponry
for the deities. Achilles, as befitting the son of the sea goddess,
Thetis, has been outfitted by **Hephaestus.**
[53] **Hesperus** The evening star, the planet Venus.

lady mother will give you bronze and gold in plenty. Give up my body to be brought home, so that the Trojans and their wives can cremate it properly."

Swift-footed Achilles gave him a black look and replied:

"You dog, don't entreat me by my knees or my parents. I only wish I could summon up the will to carve and eat you raw myself, for what you have done to me. But this at least is certain: nobody is going to keep the dogs off your head, not even if the Trojans bring here and weigh out a ransom ten or twenty times your worth, and promise more besides; not even if Dardanian Priam[54] tells them to offer your weight in gold—not even so shall your lady mother lay you on a bier to mourn the son she bore, but the dogs and birds of prey will divide you up, leaving nothing." 110

Dying, Hector of the flashing helmet said: 120

"How well I know you and see you for what you are! Your heart is hard as iron. I have been wasting my breath. But reflect now before you act, in case angry gods remember how you treated me, on the day Paris and Phoebus Apollo bring you down in all your greatness at the Scaean gate."

As he spoke, the end that is death enveloped him. Life left his limbs and took wing for the house of Hades, bewailing its lot and the youth and the manhood it had left behind. But godlike Achilles spoke to him again, though he was gone: 130

"Die! As for my death, I will welcome it when Zeus and the other immortal gods wish it to be."

He spoke, withdrew his bronze spear from the body and put it on one side. As he removed the bloodstained arms from Hector's shoulders, other Greeks came running

up and gathered round. They gazed in wonder at the stature and marvelous good looks of Hector. As each went in and stabbed the body, they looked at each other and said as one man: 140

"Well, well! Hector's certainly softer to handle now than when he set the ships on fire!"

So they spoke, as they stood by, stabbing him. After stripping Hector, swift-footed godlike Achilles stood up among the Greeks and spoke winged words:

"My friends, rulers and leaders of the Greeks, now that the gods have let us get the better of this man, who did more damage than all the rest together, let's make a circuit of the town under arms and find out what the Trojans mean to do next, whether they will abandon their town now that Hector is fallen, or make up their minds to hold it without his help . . . 150

"But why talk to myself like this? Lying by my ships is a dead man, unburied, unwept—Patroclus, whom I shall never forget as long as I am among the living and can walk the earth, my own dear comrade, whom I shall still remember even though the dead forget their dead, even in Hades' halls. So come now, young Greeks, let us go back to the hollow ships carrying this body and singing a song of triumph. We have won great glory. We have killed godlike Hector, who was treated like a god in Ilium." 160

He spoke and foully maltreated godlike Hector. He sliced into the tendons at the back of both his feet between the heel and ankle, inserted leather straps and tied them to his chariot, leaving the head to drag. Then he lifted his famous armour into the chariot, got in himself, and lashed the horses with the whip to get them moving. The willing pair flew off. Dust rose from the body they dragged behind them; Hector's sable hair streamed out on either side and his whole head, so graceful once, lay in the dirt. Zeus now let his enemies disfigure him in the very own land of his fathers. 170

. . .

[54] **Dardanian Priam** From Dardania, the kingdom of Dardanus, a predecessor to Troy. Thus, **Priam's Ilium** is the successor kingdom to Dardanus.

∞

Book 24, Priam and Achilles

[Under cover of night, the Trojan King Priam, accompanied by a herald, approaches the place where the Greeks are encamped.]

Hermes[55] the runner spoke and leapt into the chariot, seized the whip and reins in his hands and put fresh heart into the horses and mules. When they came to the ditch and the wall round the ships, they found the sentries just beginning to prepare a meal. But the guide and slayer of Argus put them all to sleep, unfastened the gates, thrust 1

[55] **Hermes** God of merchants and thieves; messenger for the deities. Wore a broad-brimmed traveler's hat and winged sandals.

back the bars and ushered Priam in with his waggon-load of precious gifts.

They went on to the lofty hut of Peleus' son Achilles. The Myrmidons had built it for their master with planks of deal cut by themselves and roofed it over with a rough thatch of reeds gathered in the meadows. It stood in the large enclosure they made for their master surrounded by a close-set fence, and the gate was fastened by a single pine-wood bar. It took three men to drive this mighty bolt home and three to draw it back; three ordinary men, of course—Achilles could work it by himself. Now Hermes the runner opened it up for the old man, drove in with the splendid presents for swift-footed Achilles, dismounted from the chariot and said to Priam: 10 20

"Venerable sir, an immortal god has been accompanying you. I am Hermes and my father sent me as your escort. But I shall leave you now, as I do not intend to enter into Achilles' presence. It would be reprehensible for mortals to entertain an immortal god face to face in that way. But go inside yourself, clasp Achilles' knees and, as you supplicate him, invoke his father and his lovely-haired mother and his son, if you want your words to go straight to his heart."

With these words Hermes went off to high Olympus. Priam leapt from his chariot to the ground and, leaving Idaeus[56] there to look after the horses and mules, walked straight into the hut where Achilles dear to Zeus usually sat. He found him inside. Most of his men were sitting some way off, but two of them, the warrior Automedon and Alcimedon[57] ally of the War-god, were waiting on him busily, as he had just finished eating and drinking and the table had not yet been removed. Great Priam came in unobserved by them, went up to Achilles, grasped his knees and kissed his hands, those terrible, man-slaying hands that had killed so many of his sons. As a thick cloud of delusion possesses a man who, after murdering someone in his own country, seeks refuge abroad in the home of a wealthy man, and the onlookers are astounded, so Achilles was astounded when he saw godlike Priam. The others were astounded too and exchanged glances.

Supplicating Achilles, Priam addressed him:

"Remember your own father, godlike Achilles, who is the same age as I am and on the threshold of miserable old age. No doubt his neighbours are tormenting him and there is nobody to protect him from the harm and damage they cause. Yet, while he knows you are still alive, he can rejoice in spirit and look forward day by day to seeing his beloved son come back from Troy.

"But my life has been dogged by calamity. I had the best sons in the whole of this broad realm and now not one, not one I say, is left. There were fifty when the Greek army arrived. Nineteen of them were borne by one mother and the rest to other women in my palace. Most of them have fallen in action, and the only one I could still count on, the mainstay of Ilium and its inhabitants—you killed him a short while ago, fighting for his native land. Hector. It is to get him back from you that I have now come to the Greek ships, bringing an immense ransom with me.

"Achilles, respect the gods and have pity on me, remembering your own father. I am even more entitled to pity, since I have brought myself to do something no one else on earth has done—I have raised to my lips the hands of the man who killed my sons."

With these words he awoke in Achilles a longing to weep for his own father. Taking the old man's hand, Achilles gently put him from him, and they were both overcome by their memories: Priam, huddled at Achilles' feet, wept aloud for man-slaying Hector, and Achilles wept for his father, and then again for Patroclus. The house was filled with the sounds of their lamentation. But when godlike Achilles had had enough of tears and the longing had ebbed from mind and body, he leapt at once from his chair and in compassion for the old man's grey head and grey beard took him by the arm and raised him. Then he spoke winged words:

"Unhappy man of sorrows, you have indeed suffered much. How could you bring yourself to come alone to the Greek ships into the presence of a man who had killed so many of your fine sons? You must have a heart of iron. Here now, be seated on this chair and, for all our grief, let us leave our sorrows locked up in our hearts, for weeping is cold comfort and does little good. We men are wretched creatures and the gods have woven grief into our lives: but they themselves are free from care.

"Zeus who delights in thunder has two jars standing on the floor of his palace in which he keeps his gifts, evils in one and blessings in the other. People who receive from him a mixture of the two enjoy varying fortunes, sometimes good and sometimes bad. But when Zeus serves a man from the jar of evil only, he debases him; ruinous hunger drives him over the bright earth and he goes his way respected by no one, god or man.

"Look at my father Peleus. From the moment he was born, the gods showered splendid gifts on him, fortune and wealth unparalleled among men, lordship over the Myrmidons and, though he was a man, a goddess[58] for his wife. But the god also gave him his share of evil—no children in his palace to follow in his steps, only a single son and he destined for an untimely death. What is more, even though he is growing old, he gets no care from me because I am sitting around here in Troy far from the land of my fathers, seeing to you and your children.

"Now we have heard, venerable sir, there was a time when fortune smiled on you. They say there was no one to compare with you for wealth and sons in all the lands that are enclosed between Lesbos out to sea where Macar reigned,[59] Phrygia[60] inland and the vast Hellespont.[61] But ever since the Sky-gods brought me here to be your scourge, there has been nothing but warfare and carnage round your city.

"Endure and do not mourn without end. Lamenting for your son will do no good at all. You will not bring him back to life before you are dead yourself."

The old man godlike Priam replied:

"Do not ask me to sit down, Olympian-born Achilles, while Hector lies neglected in your huts, but give him back to me without delay and let me set my eyes on him.

---

[56] **Idaeus** The herald of King **Priam**.
[57] **Automedon and Alcimedon Myrmidons**, from **Achilles'** army. **Automedon**, the son of Diores, was **Achilles'** charioteer, and **Alcimedon**, the son of Laerces, was a troop commander.
[58] **a goddess** The sea goddess **Thetis**.
[59] **Lesbos . . . reigned Lesbos** was an island in the **Aegean** Sea, south of Troy. **Macar** founded a kingdom there.
[60] **Phrygia** A region in Asia Minor, east of Troy.
[61] **Hellespont** Greek, "Greek Bridge." Modern **Dardanelles**. Narrow strait between Europe (Gallipoli peninsula) and Turkey in Asia; connects Sea of Marmara with **Aegean** Sea.

Accept the great ransom I bring. May you enjoy it and return safely to the land of your fathers, since from the very
first you spared my life."
  Looking blackly at him swift-footed Achilles replied:

"Now don't push me too far, venerable sir. I have made
my mind up without your help to give Hector back to you.   130
A messenger from Zeus came to me—my very own mother
that bore me, daughter to the Old Man of the Sea."

Questions for Critical Thinking

1. In what ways do the acts of the warriors on and off the
    battlefield serve as models of behavior for the Greeks?
    How do you think today's soldiers serve as models for
    Americans?

2. Discuss and give examples from the *Iliad* that show
    how the work has influenced books about wars.

HOMER
Selections from the *Odyssey*

The *Odyssey* is the story of the ten years of wandering by the Greek warrior Odysseus, after the
Greeks' triumph over the Trojans in the Trojan War. He is trying to return to his island kingdom of Ithaca and be reunited with his faithful wife, Penelope. His odyssey, or long voyage
marked by many challenges and changes of fortune, is in fact a divine punishment meted out
by Poseidon, the god of the sea and creator of the waters and earthquakes. Supportive of the
Greeks during the Trojan War, he now turns against Odysseus and tries to thwart his voyage
home. Poseidon is the father of the Cyclops, the one-eyed giant whom Odysseus outwits and
blinds, as recounted in one of the following selections. After the adventure with Polyphemus,
the Cyclops, Odysseus experiences numerous other adventures and narrowly escapes death
several times, as Poseidon uses his supernatural powers to try to destroy his mortal enemy.
Athena, the goddess of war and wisdom, supports Odysseus in his many struggles against
Poseidon. Thus, the deities, through favor or ill will, affect the daily lives and determine the
fate of humankind.

Reading the Selections

The first eight books of the *Odyssey* set the stage for the succeeding sixteen books. They introduce the deities, show how they control the lives of mortals, and describe Odysseus's plight
and his family's problems. Several of these books narrate the adventures of Telemachus, the
son of Odysseus, who seeks information about his father's fate from some of the Greek warriors who have returned from the Trojan War. Other books note how Odysseus, through the
intervention of the gods and goddesses, eventually finds himself on the island of Scheria, the
home of the Phaeacians.
  Book 9 of the *Odyssey* contains the first flashback in Western literature. In it, Odysseus
tells his story from the time he left Troy until he arrived in the land of the Phaeacians, where
he is welcomed by King Alcinous. The excerpt from Book 9 opens at a banquet with Odysseus
thanking his host, King Alcinous, for the opportunity to recall his travels. The banqueters
appreciate a lively story and, full of wine and good food, are eager to hear a tale of adventure.

Odysseus first identifies himself, his lineage, and his kingdom. In passages omitted here, Odysseus talks about his men plundering the Cicones and, next, escaping the lures of the land of the lotus-eaters. They then arrive on the island of the Cyclops, the one-eyed giant. Odysseus, in outmaneuvering the Cyclops, displays his cunning and his bravery, the two talents that aided him in all of his travels. In Books 10–12, Homer has Odysseus finish the stories of his adventures. In Books 13–24, the author follows Odysseus's schemes and fights to win back his kingdom.

Homer writes more than an adventure story. He makes Odysseus, for all his faults, into a hero blessed with *arete,* or leadership qualities, including physical bravery, a keen wit, and a high regard for his servants. Above all, he possesses a deep resolve, come what may, to return to his devoted wife. Among the world's literary classics, the *Odyssey* is one of the few that celebrates the love of a husband and wife, as illustrated by the selection from Book 23, the reconciliation scene between Odysseus and Penelope. Faced with a stranger, who, at first, says he is a beggar and then throws off his rags and claims to be Odysseus, Penelope is initially skeptical of his true identity. Hence, she requires that the stranger pass a test known only to herself and her husband: explain the secret design of their marriage bed. Odysseus passes the test without missing a beat, and only then does faithful Penelope welcome him as her long-lost husband.

Book 9, The Cyclops

This is how Odysseus, the man of many resources, began his tale:

"King Alcinous,[62] most illustrious of all your people, it is indeed a lovely thing to hear a bard such as this, with a voice like the voice of the gods. I myself feel that there is nothing more delightful than when the festive mood reigns in the hearts of all the people and the banqueters listen to a minstrel from their seats in the hall, while the tables before them are laden with bread and meat, and a steward carries round the wine he has drawn from the bowl and fills their cups. This, to my way of thinking, is perfection.

"However, your heart has prompted you to ask me about my troubles, and that intensified my grief. Well, where shall I begin, where end, my tale? For the list of woes which the gods in heaven have sent me is a long one. I shall start by giving you my name: I wish you all to know it so that in times to come, if I escape the evil day, I may always be your friend, though my home is far from here.

"I am Odysseus,[63] Laertes'[64] son. The whole world talks of my stratagems, and my fame has reached the heavens. My home is under the clear skies of Ithaca.[65] Our landmark is Mount Neriton[66] with its quivering leaves. Other islands are clustered round it, Dulichium and Same and wooded Zacynthus.[67] But Ithaca, the farthest out to sea,

lies slanting to the west, whereas the others face the dawn and rising sun. It is a rough land, but nurtures fine men. And I, for one, know of no sweeter sight for a man's eyes than his own country. The divine Calypso[68] was certainly for keeping me in her cavern home because she yearned for me to be her husband and with the same object Circe, the Aeaean[69] witch, detained me in her palace; but never for a moment did they win my heart. So true it is that a man's fatherland and his parents are what he holds sweetest, even though he has settled far away from his people in some rich home in foreign lands. However, let me tell you of the disastrous voyage Zeus[70] inflicted on me when I started back from Troy.[71]

.   .   .

"At this point, I told the rest of my loyal companions to stay there on guard by the ship, but I myself picked out the twelve best men in the company and advanced. I took with me in a goatskin some dark and mellow wine which had been given to me by Maron[72] son of Euanthes,[73] the

---

[62] **Alcinous** King of the **Phaeacians.**
[63] **Odysseus** King of **Ithaca.** Son of **Laertes** and **Anticleia;** husband of **Penelope;** father of **Telemachus.**
[64] **Laertes** Son of **Arcesius;** father of **Odysseus.**
[65] **Ithaca** Island in the Ionian Sea, off the west coast of Greece; home of **Odysseus.**
[66] **Neriton** A mountain on the island of **Ithaca.**
[67] **Dulichium . . . Same . . . Zacynthus** Islands in the Ionian Sea, south of **Ithaca.**

[68] **Calypso** Goddess daughter of **Atlas;** lived on the island of Ogygia.
[69] **Circe . . . Aeaean** Goddess, living on the island of Aeaean, whose magic turned men into swine.
[70] **Zeus** Son of **Cronos** and **Rhea.** King and father of the Olympic deities' god of the sky, of the weather, of hospitality, and of guests.
[71] **Troy** Also called **Ilium.** City besieged by the Greeks in the *Iliad* and destroyed later, according to legends. **Odysseus,** in the *Odyssey,* is returning home from **Troy.**
[72] **Maron** Son of **Euanthes.**
[73] **Euanthes** Priest of **Apollo.**

priest of Apollo,[74] the tutelary god of Ismarus,[75] because we had protected him and his child and wife out of respect for his office. He lived in a wooded grove sacred to Phoebus[76] Apollo. This man had given me some fine presents: seven talents of wrought gold, with a mixing-bowl of solid silver, and he drew off for me a dozen jars of mellow unmixed wine as well. It was a wonderful drink. It had been kept secret from all his serving-men and maids, in fact from everyone in the house but himself, his good wife and a housekeeper. To drink this red and honeyed vintage, he would pour one cupful of wine into twenty of water,[77] and the bouquet that rose from the bowl was pure heaven—those were occasions when abstinence would have no charms.

"Well, I filled a big goatskin with this wine and also took some food in a bag with me; for I had no instant foreboding that we were going to find ourselves face to face with some barbarous being of colossal strength[78] and ferocity, uncivilized and unprincipled. It took us very little time to reach the cave, but we did not find its owner at home: he was tending his fat sheep in the pastures. So we went inside and looked in amazement at everything. There were baskets laden with cheeses, and the folds were thronged with lambs and kids, each group—the spring ones, the summer ones, and the new-born ones—being separately penned. All his well-made vessels, the pails and bowls he used for milking, were swimming with whey.[79]

"To start with my men begged me to let them take away some of the cheeses, then come back, drive the kids and lambs quickly out of the pens down to the good ship, and so set sail across the salt water. But though it would have been far better so, I was not to be persuaded. I wished to see the owner of the cave and had hopes of some friendly gifts from my host. But when he did appear, my men were not going to find him a very likeable character.

"We lit a fire, made an offering to the gods, helped ourselves to some of the cheeses, and when we had eaten, sat down in the cave to await his arrival. At last he came up, shepherding his flocks and carrying a huge bundle of dry wood to burn at supper-time. With a great crash he threw this down inside the cavern, giving us such a fright that we hastily retreated to an inner recess. Meanwhile he drove some of his fat flock into the wider part of the cave—all the ones he was milking—the rams and he-goats he left out of doors in the walled yard. He then picked up a huge stone, with which he closed the entrance. It was a mighty slab; twenty-two four-wheeled waggons could not shift such a massive stone from the entrance, such was the monstrous size of the rock with which he

closed the cave. Next he sat down to milk his ewes and his bleating goats, which he did methodically, putting her young to each mother as he finished. He then curdled half the white milk, collected the whey, and stored it in wicker cheese-baskets; the remainder he left standing in pails, so that it would be handy at supper-time when he wanted a drink. When he had efficiently finished all his tasks, he re-lit the fire and spied us.

"'Strangers!' he cried. 'And who are you? Where do you come from over the watery ways? Is yours a trading venture; or are you cruising the main on chance, like roving pirates, who risk their lives to ruin other people?'

"Our hearts sank. The booming voice and the very sight of the monster filled us with panic. Still, I managed to find words to answer him. 'We are Achaeans,'[80] I said, 'on our way back from Troy—driven astray by contrary winds across a vast expanse of sea—we're making our way home but took the wrong way—the wrong route—as Zeus, I suppose, intended that we should. We are proud to say that we belong to the forces of Agamemnon, Atreus' son,[81] who by sacking the great city of Ilium and destroying all its armies has made himself the most famous man in the world today. We find ourselves here as suppliants at your knees, in the hope that you may give us hospitality, or even give us the kind of gifts that hosts customarily give their guests. Good sir, remember your duty to the gods; we are your suppliants, and Zeus is the champion of suppliants and guests. He is the god of guests: guests are sacred to him, and he goes alongside them.'

"That is what I said, and he answered me proudly out of his pitiless heart: 'Stranger, you must be a fool, or must have come from very far afield, to order me to fear or reverence the gods. We Cyclopes[82] care nothing for Zeus with his aegis,[83] nor for the rest of the blessed gods, since we are much stronger than they are. I would never spare you or your men for fear of incurring Zeus' enmity, unless I felt like it. But tell me where you moored your good ship when you came. Was it somewhere along the coast, or nearby? I'd like to know.'

"His words were designed to get the better of me, but he could not outwit someone with my knowledge of the world. I answered with plausible words: 'As for my ship, it was wrecked by the Earthshaker Poseidon[84] on the borders of your land. The wind had carried us on to a lee shore. He drove the ship up to a headland and hurled it on the rocks. But I and my friends here managed to escape with our lives.'

---

[74] **Apollo** Son of **Zeus** and **Leto**. Patron of the arts, leader of the muses; god of archery and sudden death in men.
[75] **Ismarus** Town in Thrace.
[76] **Phoebus** An epithet for **Apollo**.
[77] **one cupful . . . water** The Greeks usually watered their wine for drinking.
[78] **being . . . strength** Here begins the episode of the **Cyclops,** the one-eyed monster.
[79] **whey** Watery by-product of cheese-making.

[80] **Achaeans** Greeks. The Greek mainland was known as **Achaea.**
[81] **Agamemnon . . . son** King of Mycenae, the son of Atreus. Also, husband of Clytemnestra and brother of **Menelaus. Agamemnon's** homecoming from Troy contrasts starkly with that of **Odysseus. Agamemnon** is killed by the unfaithful **Clytemnestra,** whereas **Odysseus** is welcomed home by the faithful **Penelope,** who has kept his property intact.
[82] **Cyclopes** Plural of **Cyclops.** A race of one-eyed giants.
[83] **aegis** Protection. **Zeus's** protective powers stemmed from his status as king of the Olympians.
[84] **Earthshaker Poseidon** Son of **Cronos** and **Rhea;** brother of **Zeus;** god of the sea and of earthquakes. Father of **Polyphemus,** the **Cyclops;** enemy of **Odysseus** in the *Odyssey.*

"To this the cruel brute made no reply. Instead, he jumped up, and reaching out towards my men, seized a couple and dashed their heads against the floor as though they had been puppies. Their brains ran out on the ground and soaked the earth. Limb by limb he tore them to pieces to make his meal, which he devoured like a mountain lion, leaving nothing, neither entrails nor flesh, marrow nor bones, while we, weeping, lifted up our hands to Zeus in horror at the ghastly sight. We felt completely helpless. When the Cyclops had filled his great belly with this meal of human flesh, which he washed down with unwatered milk, he stretched himself out for sleep among his flocks inside the cave.

"On first thoughts I planned to summon my courage, draw my sharp sword from the scabbard at my side, creep up to him, feel for the right place with my hand and stab him in the breast where the liver is supported by the midriff. But on second thoughts I refrained, realizing that we would seal our own fate as well as his, because we would have found it impossible with our unaided hands to push aside the huge rock with which he had closed the great mouth of the cave. So with sighs and groans we waited for the blessed light of day.

"As soon as Dawn[85] appeared, fresh and rosy-fingered, the Cyclops re-lit the fire and milked his splendid ewes and goats, all in their proper order, putting her young to each. Having efficiently completed all these tasks, he once more snatched up a couple of my men and prepared his meal. When he had eaten, he turned his plump flocks out of the cave, removing the great doorstone without an effort. But he replaced it once more, as though he were putting the lid on a quiver. Then, with frequent whistles, he drove his plump flocks off towards the mountain, and I was left, with murder in my heart, scheming how to pay him out if only Athene[86] would grant me my prayer. The best plan I could think of was this.

"Lying by the pen the Cyclops had a huge staff of green olive-wood, which he had cut to carry in his hand when it was seasoned. To us it looked more like the mast of some black ship of twenty oars, a broad-bottomed merchantman such as makes long sea-voyages. That was the impression which its length and thickness made on us. Standing beside this piece of timber I cut off a fathom's length, which I handed over to my men and told them to smooth it down. When they had done this I stood and sharpened it to a point. Then I hardened it in the fire, and finally I carefully hid it under the dung, of which there were great heaps scattered throughout the cave. I then told my company to cast lots for the dangerous task of helping me to lift the pole and twist it in the Cyclops' eye when he was sound asleep. The lot fell on the very men that I myself would have chosen, four of them, so that counting myself we made a party of five.

"Evening came, and with it the Cyclops, shepherding his plump flocks, every one of which he herded into the broad cave, leaving none out in the walled yard, either because he suspected something or because a god had ordered him to. He lifted the great doorstone, set it in its place, and then sat down to milk his ewes and bleating goats, which he did methodically, giving each mother its young ones in due course. When he had efficiently completed all these tasks, he once more snatched two of us and prepared his supper. Then with an olive-wood bowl of my dark wine in my hands, I went up to him and said: 'Here, Cyclops, have some wine to wash down that meal of human flesh, and find out for yourself what kind of vintage was stored away in our ship's hold. I brought it for you as an offering in the hope that you would take pity on me and help me on my homeward way. But your savagery is more than we can bear. Hard-hearted man, how can you expect ever to have a visitor again from the world of men? You have not behaved rightly.'

"The Cyclops took the wine and drank it up. And the delicious drink gave him such exquisite pleasure that he asked me for another bowlful. 'Give me more, please, and tell me your name, here and now—I would like to make you a gift that will please you. We Cyclopes have wine of our own made from the grapes that our rich soil and rains from Zeus produce. But this vintage of yours is a drop of the real nectar and ambrosia.[87]'

"So said the Cyclops, and I handed him another bowlful of the sparkling wine. Three times I filled it for him; and three times the fool drained the bowl to the dregs. At last, when the wine had fuddled his wits, I addressed him with soothing words.

"'Cyclops,' I said, 'you ask me my name. I'll tell it to you; and in return give me the gift you promised me. My name is Nobody. That is what I am called by my mother and father and by all my friends.'

"The Cyclops answered me from his cruel heart. 'Of all his company I will eat Nobody last, and the rest before him. That shall be your gift.'

"He had hardly spoken before he toppled over and fell face upwards on the floor, where he lay with his great neck twisted to one side, and all-compelling sleep overpowered him. In his drunken stupor he vomited, and a stream of wine mixed with morsels of men's flesh poured from his throat. I went at once and thrust our pole deep under the ashes of the fire to make it hot, and meanwhile gave a word of encouragement to all my men, to make sure that no one would hang back through fear. When the fierce glow from the olive stake warned me that it was about to catch alight in the flames, green as it was, I withdrew it from the fire and my men gathered round. A god now inspired them with tremendous courage. Seizing the olive pole, they drove its sharpened end into the Cyclops' eye, while I used my weight from above to twist it home, like a man boring a ship's timber with a drill which his mates below him twirl with a strap they hold at either end, so that it spins continuously. In much the same way we handled our pole with its red-hot point and twisted it in his eye till the blood boiled up round the burning wood. The scorching heat singed his lids and brow all

---

[85] **Dawn** Goddess of the morning.
[86] **Athene** Goddess of wisdom, of warfare; patron of the city of Athens. She sprang full-grown from **Zeus's** head, after a headache.

---

[87] **ambrosia** Food for the gods.

round, while his eyeball blazed and the very roots crackled in the flame. The Cyclops' eye hissed round the olive stake in the same way that an axe or adze hisses when a smith plunges it into cold water to quench and strengthen the iron. He gave a dreadful shriek, which echoed round the rocky walls, and we backed away from him in terror, while he pulled the stake from his eye, streaming with blood. Then he hurled it away from him with frenzied hands and raised a great shout to the other Cyclopes who lived in neighbouring caves along the windy heights. Hearing his screams they came up from every quarter, and gathering outside the cave asked him what the matter was.

"'What on earth is wrong with you, Polyphemus?[88] Why must you disturb the peaceful night and spoil our sleep with all this shouting? Is a robber driving off your sheep, or is somebody trying by treachery or violence to kill you?'

"Out of the cave came mighty Polyphemus' voice in reply: 'O my friends, it's Nobody's treachery, not violence, that is doing me to death.'

"'Well then,' came the immediate reply, 'if you are alone and nobody is assaulting you, you must be sick and sickness comes from almighty Zeus and cannot be helped. All you can do is to pray to your father, the Lord Poseidon.'

"And off they went, while I laughed to myself at the way in which my cunning *notion*[89] of a false name had taken them in. The Cyclops, still moaning in agonies of pain, groped around with his hands and pushed the rock away from the mouth of the cave. Then he sat himself down in the doorway and stretched out both arms in the hope of catching us in the act of slipping out among the sheep. What a fool he must have thought me! Meanwhile I was cudgeling my brains for the best possible course, trying to hit on some way of saving my friends as well as myself. I thought up plan after plan, scheme after scheme. It was a matter of life or death: we were in mortal peril.

"This was the scheme that eventually seemed best. The rams of the flock were of good stock, thick-fleeced, fine, big animals in their coats of black wool. These I quietly lashed together with the plaited willow twigs which the inhuman monster used for his bed. I took them in threes. The middle one was to carry one of my followers, with its fellows on either side to protect him. Each of my men thus had three rams to bear him. But for myself I chose a full-grown ram who was the pick of the whole flock. Seizing him by the back, I curled myself up under his shaggy belly and lay there upside down, with a firm grip on his wonderful fleece and with patience in my heart. In this way, with sighs and groans, we waited for the blessed Dawn.

"As soon as she arrived, fresh and rosy-fingered, the he-goats and the rams began to scramble out and make for the pastures, but the females, unmilked as they were and with udders full to bursting, stood bleating by the pens. Their master, though tortured and in terrible agony, passed his hands along the backs of all the animals as they stopped in front of him; but the idiot never noticed that my men were tied under the chests of his own woolly rams. The last of the flock to come up to the doorway was the big ram, burdened by his own fleece and by me with my thoughts racing. As he felt him with his hands the great Polyphemus broke into speech:

"'Sweet ram,' he said, 'why are you the last of the flock to pass out of the cave like this? You have never before lagged behind the others, but always step so proudly out and are the first of them to crop the lush shoots of the grass, first to make your way to the flowing stream, and first to want to return to the fold when evening falls. Yet today you are the last of all. You must be grieved for your master's eye, blinded by a wicked man and his accursed friends, when he had robbed me of my wits with wine. Nobody was his name; and I swear that he has not yet saved his skin! Ah, if only you could feel as I do and find a voice to tell me where he's hiding from my fury! I'd hammer him and splash his brains all over the floor of the cave, and my heart would find some relief from the suffering which that nothing, that Nobody, has caused me!'

"So he let the ram pass through the entrance and when we had put a little distance between ourselves and the courtyard of the cave, I first let go my ram and then untied my men. Then, quickly, though with many a backward look, we drove out long-striding sheep and goats—a rich, fat flock—right down to the ship. My dear companions were overjoyed when they caught sight of us survivors, but broke into loud lamentations for the others. With nods and frowns I indicated silently that they should stop their weeping and hurry to bundle the fleecy sheep and goats on board and put to sea. So they went on board at once, took their places at the oars, and all together struck the white water with the blades.

"But before we were out of earshot, I shouted out derisive words at Polyphemus. 'Cyclops! So he was not such a weakling after all, the man whose friends you meant to overpower and eat in your hollow cave! And your crimes were bound to catch up with you, you brute, who did not shrink from devouring your guests. Now Zeus and all the other gods have paid you out.'

"My words so enraged the Cyclops that he tore the top off a great pinnacle of rock and hurled it at us. The rock fell just ahead of our blue-painted bows. As it plunged in, the water surged up and the backwash, like a swell from the open sea, swept us landward and nearly drove us on to the beach. Seizing a long pole, I pushed the ship off, at the same time commanding my crew with urgent nods to bend to their oars and save us from disaster. They leant forward and rowed with a will; but when they had taken us across the water to twice our previous distance I was about to shout something else to the Cyclops, but from all parts of the ship my men called out, trying to restrain and pacify me.

"'Why do you want to provoke the savage in this obstinate way? The rock he threw into the sea just now drove the ship back to the land, and we thought it was all up with us. Had he heard a cry, or so much as a word,

---

[88] **Polyphemus** One of the **Cyclops**; son of **Poseidon**.
[89] *notion* The "cunning" consists of an untranslatable Greek pun. The translator conveys this notion by having Polyphemus refer to himself as *Nobody,* a ploy that effectively tricks Polyphemus.

from a single man, he'd have smashed in our heads and the ship's timbers with another jagged boulder from his hand. We're within easy range for him!' 370

"But my temper was up; their words did not dissuade me, and in my rage I shouted back at him once more: 'Cyclops, if anyone ever asks you how you came by your blindness, tell him your eye was put out by Odysseus, sacker of cities, the son of Laertes, who lives in Ithaca.'

"The Cyclops gave a groan. 'Alas!' he cried. 'Those ancient prophecies have come back to me now! We had a prophet living with us once, a great and mighty man, Eurymus' son Telemus,[90] the best of soothsayers, who grew old 380 as a seer among us Cyclopes. All that has now happened he foretold, when he warned me that a man called Odysseus would rob me of my sight. But I always expected some big handsome man of tremendous strength to come along. And now, a puny, feeble good-for-nothing fuddles me with wine and then puts out my eye! But come here, Odysseus, so that I can give you some friendly gifts and prevail on the great Earthshaker, Poseidon, to see you safely home. For I am his son, and he is proud to call himself my father. He is the one who will heal me if he's willing—a thing no other 390 blessed god nor any man on earth could do.'

"To which I shouted in reply: 'I only wish I could make as sure of robbing you of life and breath and sending you to Hell, as I am certain that not even the Earthshaker will ever heal your eye.'

"At this the Cyclops lifted up his hands to the starry heavens and prayed to the Lord Poseidon: 'Hear me, Poseidon, Sustainer of the Earth, god of the sable locks. If I am yours indeed and you claim me as your son, grant that Odysseus, sacker of cities and son of Laertes, may 400 never reach his home in Ithaca. But if he is destined to see his friends again, to come once more to his own house

and reach his native land, let him come late, in wretched plight, having lost all his comrades, in a foreign ship, and let him find trouble in his home.'

"So Polyphemus prayed; and the god of the sable locks heard his prayer. Once again the Cyclops picked up a boulder—bigger, by far, this time—and hurled it with a swing, putting such tremendous force into his throw that the rock fell only just astern of our blue-painted ship, nar- 410 rowly missing the tip of the rudder. The water heaved up as it plunged into the sea; but the wave that it raised carried us on towards the further shore.

"And so we reached our island, where the rest of our good ships were all waiting for us, their crews sitting round disconsolate and keeping a constant watch for our return. Once there, we beached our ship, jumped out on the shore, and unloaded the Cyclops' flocks from the hold. We then divided our spoil so that no one, as far as I could help it, should go short of his proper share. But my 420 comrades-in-arms did me the special honour, when the sheep and goats were distributed, of presenting me with the big ram in addition. Him I sacrificed on the beach, burning slices from his thighs as an offering to Zeus of the Black Clouds, the Son of Cronos, who is lord of us all. But Zeus took no notice of my sacrifice; his mind must already have been full of plans for the destruction of all my fine ships and of my loyal band.

"So the whole day long till sundown we sat and feasted on our rich supply of meat and mellow wine. 430 When the sun set and darkness fell, we lay down to sleep on the sea-shore. As soon as Dawn appeared, fresh and rosy- fingered, I roused my men and ordered them to go on board and cast off. They climbed on board at once, took their places at the oars and all together struck the white surf with the blades. Thus we left the island and sailed on with heavy hearts, grieving for the dear friends we had lost but glad at our own escape from death."

. . .

---

[90] **Eurymus' son Telemus** One of the **Cyclops,** who was a prophet.

Book 23, Odysseus and Penelope

The lion-hearted Odysseus, in his own home again, was 1 bathed and rubbed with oil by the housekeeper Eurynome,[91] and clothed by her in a beautiful cloak and tunic. Then Athene enhanced his comeliness from head to foot. She made him look taller and sturdier, and she caused the bushy locks to hang from his head thick as the petals of a hyacinth in bloom. Just as a craftsman trained by Hephaestus[92] and herself in the secrets of his art takes pains to put a graceful finish to his work by overlaying silver-ware with gold, she endowed his head and 10

shoulders with an added beauty. He came out from the bath looking like one of the everlasting gods, and went and sat down once more in the chair opposite his wife.

"What a strange woman you are!" he exclaimed. "The gods of Olympus gave you a harder heart than any other woman. No other wife could have steeled herself to keep so long out of the arms of a husband who had just returned to her in his native land after twenty wearisome years. Well, nurse,[93] make a bed for me to sleep in alone. For my wife's heart is as hard as iron." 20

---

[91] **Eurynome** Maid to **Penelope,** in **Ithaca.**
[92] **Hephaestus** Smith god, who fashioned weaponry and tools for the deities.

[93] **nurse Eurycleia,** the old nurse who had tended **Odysseus;** servant to **Penelope.**

"What a strange man *you* are," said the cautious Penelope. "I am not being haughty or contemptuous of you, though I'm not surprised that you think I am. But I have too clear a picture of you in my mind as you were when you sailed from Ithaca in your long-oared ship. Come, Eurycleia, move the great bed outside the bedroom that he himself built and make it up with fleeces and blankets and brightly coloured rugs."

This was her way of putting her husband to the test. But Odysseus flared up at once and rounded on his loyal wife. "Lady," he cried, "your words are a knife in my heart! Who has moved my bed? That would be hard even for a skilled workman, though for a god who took it into his head to come and move it somewhere else it would be quite easy. No man alive, not even one in his prime, would find it easy to shift. A great secret went into the making of that complicated bed; and it was my work and mine alone. Inside the court there was a long-leaved olive-tree, which had grown to full height with a trunk as thick as a pillar. Round this I built my room of compact stonework, and when that was finished, I roofed it over carefully, and put in a solid, neatly fitted, double door. Next I lopped all the branches off the olive, trimmed the trunk from the root up, rounded it smoothly and carefully with my adze and trued it to the line, to be my bedpost. I drilled holes in it, and using it as the first bedpost I constructed the rest of the bed. Then I finished it off with an inlay of gold, silver and ivory, and fixed a set of gleaming purple straps across the frame. So I have shown you the secret. What I don't know, lady, is whether my bedstead stands where it did, or whether someone has cut the tree-trunk through and moved it."

At his words her knees began to tremble and her heart melted as she realized that he had given her infallible proof. Bursting into tears she ran up to Odysseus, threw her arms round his neck and kissed his head. "Odysseus," she cried, "do not be angry with me, you who were always the most understanding of men. All our unhappiness is due to the gods, who couldn't bear to see us share the joys of youth and reach the threshold of old age together. But don't be cross with me now, or hurt because I did not give you this loving welcome the moment I first saw you. For I had always had the cold fear in my heart that somebody might come here and deceive me with his talk. There are many who think up wicked selfish schemes. Helen of Argos,[94] born of Zeus, would never have slept in her foreign lover's arms had she known that her countrymen would go to war to fetch her back to Argos. It was the god who drove her to do this shameful deed, though not until that moment had her heart contemplated that fatal madness, the madness which was the cause of her woes and ours. But now you have faithfully described the secret of our bed, which no one ever saw but you and I and one maid, Actoris,[95] who was my father's gift when first I came to

you, and was the keeper of our bedroom door. You have convinced my unbelieving heart."

Her words stirred a great longing for tears in Odysseus' heart, and he wept as he held his dear and loyal wife in his arms. It was like the moment when the blissful land is seen by struggling sailors, whose fine ship Poseidon has battered with wind and wave and smashed on the high seas. A few swim safely to the mainland out of the foaming surf, their bodies caked with brine; and blissfully they tread on solid land, saved from disaster. It was bliss like that for Penelope to see her husband once again. Her white arms round his neck never quite let go. Rosy-fingered Dawn would have found them still weeping, had not Athene of the flashing eyes had other ideas. She held the night lingering at the western horizon and in the East at Ocean's[96] Stream she kept golden-throned Dawn waiting and would not let her yoke the nimble steeds who bring us light, Lampus and Phaethon,[97] the colts that draw the chariot of Day.

At last the shrewd Odysseus said to his wife, "Dear wife, we have not yet come to the end of our trials. There lies before me still a great and hazardous adventure, which I must see through to the very end. That was what Teiresias' soul predicted for me when I went down to the House of Hades to find a way home for my followers and myself. So come to bed now, dear wife, and let us at last enjoy a sweet sleep in each other's arms."

Thoughtful Penelope answered, "Your bed shall be ready the moment you wish, not that the gods have brought you back to your own country and your lovely home. But since you have mentioned it—since a god put it in your heart—tell me all about this new ordeal; I suppose I shall hear about it sooner or later, so I might as well learn about it at once."

"What a strange woman you are!" said the quick-witted Odysseus. "Why press me so insistently? However, I will tell you all, holding nothing back. Not that you will find it to your liking, any more than I do! Teiresias[98] told me to carry a well-balanced oar and wander on from city to city, till I came to a people who know nothing of the sea, and never use salt with their food, so that crimson-painted ships and the long oars that serve those ships as wings are quite beyond their experience. He gave me this infallible sign (which I now reveal to you)—when I met some other traveller who referred to the oar I was carrying on my shoulder as a 'winnowing-fan,' then, he said, the time would have come for me to plant my oar in the earth and offer the Lord Poseidon the rich sacrifice of a ram, a bull and a breeding boar. After that I was to go back home and make ceremonial sacrifices to the everlasting gods who live in the far-flung heavens, to all of them this time, in due precedence. As for my end, he said that Death would come to me away from the sea, and that I would die

[94] **Helen of Argos** Another name for **Helen of Troy.** She was daughter of **Zeus** and the mortal woman **Leda;** wife of **Menelaus;** and lover of **Paris.**
[95] **Actoris** The maid to **Penelope.**

[96] **Ocean** In Greek mythology, the great river that encircles the world and the god who controls the waters.
[97] **Lampus and Phaethon** Two horses that pull the chariot of the goddess **Dawn.**
[98] **Teiresias** Blind prophet from **Thebes,** who remained a seer in the underworld.

peacefully in old age, surrounded by a prosperous people. He assured me that all this would come true."

"If the gods make your old age a happier time," the sagacious Penelope replied, "there is a hope of an end to your troubles."

While they were talking, Eurynome and the nurse, by the light of torches, were putting soft bedclothes on their bed. When the work was done and the bed comfortably made, the old woman went back to her own quarters for the night, and the housekeeper Eurynome, with a torch in her hands, lit them on their way to bed, taking her leave when she had brought them to their room. And blissfully they lay down on their own familiar bed.

130

140

Questions for Critical Thinking

1. In what ways does Odysseus use his cunning and bravery in dealing with the Cyclops? How has this episode become an inspiration for stories of other adventures and heroes?

2. What are the major themes of the *Odyssey*, and how are they manifested in the work?

SAPPHO

Poems

Sappho is unquestionably Greece's finest composer of lyric poetry, which originally meant verses sung to the music of a lyre (a stringed instrument) but later was applied to poetry characterized by musical qualities, subjectivism, and sensual words. Ancient writers, including Plato (see *The Republic* and *Phaedo* in Chapter 3), hailed her as the master of lyric poetry; modern critics tend to do the same. Unlike epic poetry, in which the author speaks for an entire community (see Homer's *Iliad* and *Odyssey*, and Virgil's *Aeneid* in Chapter 5), lyric poetry focuses on the speaker's personal, private thoughts. Sappho's autobiographical works helped to make lyric verse popular in her day, and this genre has dominated Western poetry ever since.

Lyric poetry flowered during Greece's Archaic Age (800–480 BCE), a tumultuous period of change on many fronts. Coming after three centuries of cultural breakdown, the Archaic Age was a time of rebirth, marked by the growth of trade and the spread of Greek peoples around the shores of the Mediterranean and Black seas. The old hereditary kingships gave way to independent city-states ruled by landed aristocrats, in which the invention of money permitted the rise of a monied class, a group of savers and lenders who both challenged the power of the aristocrats and enslaved poorer debtors. These events embittered social relations and sparked class warfare, which led to new types of regimes, such as tyranny, and expansion of voting rights to ordinary male citizens. The shift from epic to lyric poetry in the sixth century BCE coincided with these changes in the city-states, where the rising democratic spirit encouraged a variety of voices to be heard.

The meager facts of Sappho's life (ca. 600 BCE) reflect this turbulent age. Her home was the island of Lesbos in the Aegean, an Archaic cultural center that produced two well-known lyric poets before her birth. An aristocrat, she experienced exile twice—the penalty for being related to the landed elite who were overthrown by a coalition of merchants and poor citizens. Eventually, she opened a school on Lesbos for aristocratic young women, to whom she taught poetry, music, and dancing.

Reading the Selections

These poems (actually sections taken from extant works, which are fragmented in the extreme and number only about six hundred lines) show that love was never far from Sappho's thoughts. Addressed to her circle, this poetry is private, filled with intimate expression. Poem I offers a burning description of erotic feelings and thus gives a glimpse into this world. Speaking of her young friend Anactoria, who is "far away," Sappho proclaims: "I would rather watch her moving in her lovely way (than any other beautiful thing on earth)."

In "Let's Not Pretend," Sappho speaks of love and old age. Gray and wrinkled, she likens herself to Tithonos, the mythic hero whom the gods gave eternal life but not eternal youth; just as Tithonos, ever older and feebler, makes love to the goddess Dawn each day, so does Sappho, grown old herself, continue to seek beauty and light.

In "Very Well, Charaxus," Sappho speaks of another form of love, family love, in which she offers sisterly advice to her brother Charaxus, a successful wine merchant on Lesbos. As the poem shows, she believes her brother has forgotten his roots and has let his wealth go to his head.

Sappho's poetic legacy lives on in today's confessional verses and most especially in popular love songs.

∞

I

There are those who say
an array of horsemen,
and others of marching men,
and others of ships, is
the most beautiful thing on the dark earth.

But I say it is whatever one loves.

It is very easy
to show this to all:
for Helen,[99]
by far the most beautiful of mortals,
left her husband

and sailed to Troy
giving no thought at all
to her child nor dear parents,
but was led . . .
[by her love alone.]

Now, far away, Anactoria[100]
comes to my mind.
For I would rather watch her
moving in her lovely way,
and see her face, flashing radiant,
than all the force of Lydian[101] chariots,
and their infantry in full display of arms.

---

[99] **Helen** Daughter of **Zeus** and the mortal woman **Leda**; wife of **Menelaus**, and lover of **Paris**.

[100] **Anactoria** The name of Sappho's beloved.
[101] **Lydia** Ancient country in western part of Asia Minor (modern Turkey).

∞

Let's Not Pretend

No, Children, do not delude me.
You mock the good gifts of the Muses[102]

When you say: "Dear Sappho we'll crown you,
Resonant player,
First on the clear sweet lyre. . . ."
Do you not see how I alter:
My skin with its aging,
My black hair gone white,

---

[102] **Muses** The nine goddesses who inspired creativity in the arts and sciences.

My legs scarcely carrying
Me, who went dancing
More neatly than fawns once
(Neatest of creatures)?
No, no one can cure it; keep beauty from going,
And *I* cannot help it.
God himself cannot do what cannot be done.
So age follows after and catches
Everything living.
Even rosy-armed Eos,[103] the Dawn,
Who ushers in morning to the ends of the earth,
Could not save from the grasp of old age

Her lover immortal Tithonus. [104]
And I too, I know, must waste away.
Yet for me—listen well—
My delight is the exquisite.
Yes, for me,
Glitter and sunlight and love
Are one society.
So I shall not go creeping away
To die in the dark:
I shall go on living with you,
Loving and loved.

[103] **Eos** The Greek goddess of **Dawn.**

[104] **Tithonos** Lover of the goddess **Dawn;** he was granted eternal life but not eternal youth.

Very Well, Charaxus

If you must flutter around the steps of the great and
Not of the noble and true, and say good-bye to
All your friends and get so swollen-headed
You hurt me and say I am

Only a nuisance—well, enjoy it up to the
Hilt; but I am not soft-minded enough to
Pay attention to childish tantrums

Make no mistake, for the trick won't catch an
Old bird who has put two and two together and
Understands to the core the cad you were before
And what she is up against.

Better reform and take advice, for I know
I am not a difficult person, so have
On *my* side the angels.

Questions for Critical Thinking

1. What are Sappho's fears about the effect of aging upon her ability to love? Would her outlook be out of place in today's world?

2. How does Sappho view her successful brother Charaxus? Summarize her advice to him.

3

CLASSICAL GREECE
The Hellenic Age

SOPHOCLES
Oedipus the King

Sophocles' *Oedipus the King* is the most famous tragedy of antiquity. When first staged (about 430 BCE) in Athens, it was awarded first prize—the civic honor voted by judges for reasons as political and social as they were aesthetic. In the fourth century BCE it was used by Aristotle as the ground for his analysis of tragedy in the *Poetics*, the West's earliest book of literary criticism. In modern times, it has come to mean the perfect tragedy.

Tragedy (Greek, "goat song") developed from the choral odes sung to the rural god Dionysus. In sixth-century BCE Athens, a tyrant introduced this god's cult to the city and made the staging of tragedies part of the Great Dionysia. The coming of democracy to Athens (after 508 BCE) made these plays even more popular, as people of all classes formed the audience (though it is uncertain if women were present). The Hellenic Age—with Persia in retreat and Athens as the center of Greece—saw the flowering of this genre in the works of three native Athenians: Aeschylus (ca. 525–456 BCE), Sophocles (ca. 496–406 BCE), and Euripides (ca. 480–406 BCE).

Tragedy was basically political in that it addressed the city-state, or its metaphorical equivalent in the audience at the Great Dionysia. Tragedians wrote for this community, speaking as citizens to citizens. A city leader chose three dramatists to present four plays each, and other officials appointed wealthy citizens to pay production costs. The spectators were seated according to tribes, thus mapping the city's political structure. A panel of ten judges was chosen, one from each tribe. Before the plays, the city scored propaganda points by parading orphans of soldiers killed in service and welcoming foreign emissaries. In sum, the drama was the centerpiece of a rite devoted to reinforcing community cohesion.

At first, tragedy (like comedy) had two distinct elements, the actors and the chorus, symbolic of opposing forces in the city-state. In political terms, the actors symbolized individualism (a democratic idea), and the chorus stood for community values (an aristocratic idea). As tragedy evolved, the chorus waned in importance until it disappeared in the fourth century BCE, leaving the actors supreme. This event paralleled the decline of both the city-state and tragic drama.

Reading the Selection

Oedipus the King is typical of what became known as Sophoclean tragedy in that it has two themes: the relation between humans and gods and the hero's moral dilemmas. These themes converge in the character Oedipus, a king destroyed by the gods as he tries to act morally. Highly ironic, the plot shows Oedipus unleashing new catastrophes despite good intentions. Warned by an oracle that he will kill his father and marry his mother, the well-meaning Oedipus flees from Corinth to Thebes, only to learn that his efforts to escape his dread fate have been in vain. Oedipus's downfall is the result of good motives, for he discovers his true identity after ordering an investigation into the old king's murder, so that a plague may be driven from the city.

Above all else, this tragedy is about the unbridgeable gulf between gods and humans. Oedipus repeatedly shows arrogance in his desire to credit himself and deny the truth of oracles ("the world knows my fame"; "I count myself the son of Chance"). Struck down, he finally recognizes that humans, even kings, are fated to suffer. The chorus makes this harsh vision the moral of the tragedy: "[L]ook on Oedipus. . . . [C]ount no man happy till he dies, free of pain at last."

∞

Characters

OEDIPUS *king of Thebes*
PRIEST *of Zeus*
KREON *Oedipus' brother-in-law*
CHORUS *of Theban elders*
LEADER *of the chorus*
TEIRESIAS *prophet, servant to Apollo*
JOCASTA *wife of Oedipus*
MESSENGER *from Corinth*
SHEPHERD *member of Laios' household*
SERVANT *household slave of Oedipus*

Delegation of Thebans, servants to lead Teiresias and Oedipus; attendants to Oedipus, Kreon, Jocasta; and Antigone and Ismene, the daughters of Oedipus.

Dawn. Silence. The royal palace of Thebes. The altar of Apollo to the left of the central palace. A delegation of Thebans—old men, boys, young children—enters the orchestra by the steps below the altar, assembles, and waits. They carry suppliant boughs—olive branches tied with strips of wool. Some climb the steps between the orchestra and the altar, place their branches on the altar, and return to the orchestra. A PRIEST stands apart from the suppliants at the foot of one of the two stairs. Silence. Waiting. The central doors open. From inside the palace, limping, OEDIPUS comes through the palace doors and stands at the top of the steps leading down into the orchestra. He is dressed in gold and wears a golden crown.

OEDIPUS: Why, children,   1
  why are you here, why
  are you holding those branches tied with wool,
  begging me for help? Children,
  the whole city smolders with incense.
  Wherever I go I hear sobbing, praying. Groans fill
    the air.
  Rumors, news from messengers, they are not enough
    for me.
  Others cannot tell me what you need.
  I am king, I had to come. As king,
  I had to know. Know for myself, know for me.   10
  Everybody everywhere knows who I am: Oedipus.
    King.

Priest of Zeus, we respect your age, your high office.
  Speak.
  Why are you kneeling? Are you afraid, old man?
  What can I give you?
  How can I help? Ask.
  Ask me anything. Anything at all.
  My heart would be a stone
  if I felt no pity for these poor shattered people of mine
  kneeling here, at my feet.   20
PRIEST: Oedipus, lord of Thebes, you see us, the people of
    Thebes, your people,
  crowding in prayer around your altar,
  these small children here, old men bent with age,
    priests, and I, the priest of Zeus,[1]
  and our noblest young men, the pride and strength
    of Thebes.
  And there are more of us, lord Oedipus, more—
    gathered in the city, stunned,
  kneeling, offering their branches, praying before the
    two great temples of Athena[2]
  or staring into the ashes of burnt offerings, staring,
  waiting, waiting for the god[3] to speak.
  Look,
  look at it,   30
  lord Oedipus—right there,
  in front of your eyes—this city—
  it reels under a wild storm of blood, wave after wave
    battering Thebes.
  We cannot breathe or stand.
  We hunger, our world shivers with hunger. A
    disease hungers,
  nothing grows, wheat, fruit, nothing grows bigger
    than a seed.
  Our women bear
  dead things,

---

[1] **Zeus** Chief deity and keeper of order on Mount Olympos, where the gods and goddesses live.
[2] **Athena** Goddess of wisdom and warfare.
[3] **the god** Apollo, god of wisdom and moderation. Also god of prophecy, with a shrine at Delphi.

all they can do is grieve,
our cattle wither, stumble, drop to the ground,   40
flies simmer on their bloated tongues,
the plague spreads everywhere, a stain seeping
        through our streets, our fields, our houses,
look—god's fire eating everyone, everything,
stroke after stroke of lightning, the god stabbing it
        alive—
it can't be put out, it can't be stopped,
its heat thickens the air, it glows like smoking metal,
this god of plague guts our city and fills the black
        world under us where the dead go
with the shrieks of women,
living women, wailing.
You are a man, not a god—I know.   50
We all know this, the young kneeling here before
        you know it, too,
but we know how great you are, Oedipus, greater
        than any man.
When crisis struck, you saved us here in Thebes,
you faced the mysterious, strange disasters
        hammered against us by the gods.
This is our history—
we paid our own flesh to the Sphinx[4] until you set
        us free.
You knew no more than anyone, but you knew.
There was a god in it, a god in you.

                        The PRIEST kneels.

Help us. Oedipus, we beg you, we all turn to you,
        kneeling to your greatness.
Advice from the gods or advice from human   60
        beings—you will know which is needed.
But help us. Power and experience are yours, all
        yours.
Between thought and action, between
our plans and their results a distance opens.
Only a man like you, Oedipus, tested by experience,
can make them one. That much I know.
Oedipus, more like a god than any man alive,
deliver us, raise us to our feet. Remember who you are.
Remember your love for Thebes. Your skill was our
        salvation once before.
For this Thebes calls you savior.
Don't let us remember you as the king—godlike in   70
        power—
who gave us back our life, then let us die.
Steady us forever. You broke the riddle for us then.
It was a sign. A god was in it. Be the man you were—
rule now as you ruled before.
Oh Oedipus,
how much better to rule a city of men than be king
        of empty earth.

A city is nothing, a ship is nothing
where no men live together, where no men work
        together.
OED.: Children, poor helpless children,
I know what brings you here, I know.   80
You suffer, this plague is agony for each of you,
but none of you, not one suffers as I do.
Each of you suffers for himself, only himself.
My whole being wails and breaks
for this city, for myself, for all of you,
old man, all of you.
Everything ends here, with me. I am the man.
You have not wakened me from some kind of sleep.
I have wept, struggled, wandered in this maze of
        thought,
tried every road, searched hard—   90
finally I found one cure, only one:
I sent my wife's brother, Kreon, to great Apollo's
        shrine at Delphi;
I sent him to learn what I must say or do to save
        Thebes.
But his long absence troubles me. Why isn't he here?
        Where is he?
When he returns, what kind of man would I be
if I failed to do everything the god reveals?

*Some of the suppliants by the steps to the orchestra stand to
announce* KREON's *arrival to the* PRIEST. KREON *comes in by
the entrance to the audience's left with a garland on his head.*

PRIEST: You speak of Kreon, and Kreon is here.

OED.: (*turning to the altar of Apollo, then to* KREON)

Lord Apollo, look at him—his head is crowned with
        laurel, his eyes glitter.
Let his words blaze, blaze like his eyes, and save us.
PRIEST: He looks calm, radiant, like a god. If he brought   100
        bad news,
would he be wearing that crown of sparkling leaves?
OED.: At last we will know.
Lord Kreon, what did the god Apollo say?
KREON: His words are hopeful.
Once everything is clear, exposed to the light,
we will see our suffering is blessing. All we need is
        luck.
OED.: What do you mean? What did Apollo say? What
        should we do?
Speak.
KREON: Here? Now? In front of all these people?
Or inside, privately?   110

                        KREON *moves toward the palace.*

OED.: Stop. Say it. Say it to the whole city.
I grieve for them, for their sorrow and loss, far more
        than I grieve for myself.
KREON: This is what I heard—there was no mistaking the
        god's meaning—
Apollo commands us:
Cleanse the city of Thebes, cleanse the plague from
        that city,
destroy the black stain spreading everywhere,
        spreading,
poisoning the earth, touching each house, each citizen,

---

[4] **Sphinx** The winged monster, with the body of a lion and
the head and breasts of a woman, who, from her lair outside
Thebes, asked each traveler a riddle. She killed everyone who
could not answer the riddle: "What is it that walks on four legs
in the morning, on two at noon, and on three in the evening?"
Oedipus answered correctly that it was *man.* The Sphinx then
leapt from a rock and destroyed herself.

sickening the hearts of the people of Thebes!
Cure this disease that wastes all of you, spreading,
      spreading,
before it grows so vast nothing can cure it.   120
OED.: What is this plague?
   How can we purify the city?
KREON: A man must be banished. Banished or killed.
   Blood for blood. The plague is blood,
   blood, breaking over Thebes.
OED.: *Who* is the man? *Who* is Apollo's victim?
KREON: My lord, before you came to Thebes, before you
      came to power,
   Laios was our king.
OED.: I know. But I never saw Laios.
KREON: Laios was murdered. Apollo's command was   130
      very clear:
   Avenge the murderers of Laios. Whoever they are.
OED.: But where *are* his murderers?
   The crime is old. How will we find their tracks?
   The killers could be anywhere.
KREON: Apollo said the killers are still here, here in
      Thebes.
   Pursue a thing, and you may catch it;
   ignored, it slips away.
OED.: And Laios—where was he murdered?
   At home? Or was he away from Thebes?
KREON: He told us before he left—he was on a mission to 140
      Delphi,
   his last trip away from Thebes. He never returned.
OED.: Wasn't there a witness, someone with Laios who
      saw what happened?
KREON: They were all killed, except for one man. He
      escaped.
   But he was so terrified he remembered only one thing.
OED.: What was it? One small clue might lead to others.
KREON: This is what he said: bandits ambushed Laios,
      not one man.
   They attacked him like hail crushing a stalk of wheat.
OED.: How could a single bandit dare attack a king unless
   he had supporters, people with money, here, here in
      Thebes?   150
KREON: There were suspicions. But after Laios died we
      had no leader, no king.
   Our life was turmoil, uncertainty.
OED.: But once the throne was empty,
   what threw you off the track, what kept you from
      searching
   until you uncovered everything, knew every detail?
KREON: The intricate, hard song of the Sphinx
   persuaded us the crime was not important, not then.
   It seemed to say we should focus on what lay at our
      feet, in front of us,
   ignore what we could not see.
OED.: Now *I* am here.   160
   I will begin the search again, I
   will reveal the truth, expose everything, let it all be
      seen.
   Apollo and you were right to make us wonder about
      the dead man.
   Like Apollo, I am your ally.
   Justice and vengeance are what I want,

for Thebes, for the god.
Family, friends—I won't rid myself of this stain, this
      disease, for them—
they're far from here. I'll do it for myself, for me.
The man who killed Laios might take revenge on me
just as violently.   170
So by avenging Laios' death, I protect myself.

(*turning to the suppliants*) Rise, children,

pick up your branches,
let someone announce my decision to the whole city
      of Thebes.

(*to the* PRIEST) I will do everything. Everything.

And, with the god's help, we will be saved.
Bright Apollo, let your light help us see.
Our happiness is yours to give, our failure and ruin
      yours.
PRIEST: Rise. We have the help we came for, children.   180
   The king himself has promised.
   May Apollo, who gave these oracles, come as our
      savior now.
   Apollo, heal us, save us from this plague!

OEDIPUS *enters the palace. Its doors close.* KREON *leaves by a door to the right on the wing of the stage. The* PRIEST *and suppliants go down into the orchestra and leave by the entrance to the left as a chorus of fifteen Theban elders files into the orchestra by the entrance on the right, preceded by a flute player.*

CHORUS: voice voice voice
   voice who knows everything o god
   glorious voice of Zeus
   how have you come from Delphi bathed in gold
   what are you telling our bright city Thebes
   what are you bringing me
   health death fear
   I know nothing   190
   so frightened rooted here
   awed by you
   healer what have you sent
   is it the sudden doom of grief
   or the old curse the darkness
   looming in the turning season

   o holy immortal voice
   hope golden seed of the future
   listen be with me speak
   these cries of mine rise   200
   tell me
   I call to you reach out to you first
   holy Athena god's daughter who lives forever
   and your sister Artemis[5]
   who cradles the earth our earth
   who sits on her great throne at the hub of the market
      place
   and I call to Apollo who hurls light
   from deep in the sky

---

[5] **Artemis** Virgin goddess who aided women. Huntress of wild creatures and patroness of chastity. Sister of Athena and twin sister of Apollo.

o gods be with us now
shine on us your three shields   210
blazing against the darkness
come in our suffering as you came once before
to Thebes o bright divinities
and threw your saving light against the god of grief
o gods
be with us now

pain pain my sorrows have no sound
no name no word no pain like this
plague sears my people everywhere
everyone army citizens no one escapes   220
no spear of strong anxious thought protects us
great Thebes grows nothing
seeds rot in the ground
our women when they labor
cry Apollo Apollo but their children die
and lives one after another split the air
birds taking off
wingrush hungrier than fire
souls leaping away they fly
to the shore   230
of the cold god of evening
west

the death stain spreads
so many corpses lie in the streets everywhere
nobody grieves for them
the city dies and young wives
and mothers gray-haired mothers wail
sob on the altar steps
they come from the city everywhere mourning their
     bitter days
prayers blaze to the Healer   240
grief cries a flute mingling
daughter of Zeus o shining daughter show us
the warm bright face of peace of help
of our salvation

The doors of the palace open. OEDIPUS *enters.*

and turn back the huge raging jaws of the death god
     Ares[6]
drive him back drive him away
his flames lash at me
this is his war these are his shields
shouts pierce us on all sides
turn him back lift him on a strong wind   250
rush him away
to the two seas at the world's edge
the sea where the waters boil
the sea where no traveler can land
because if night leaves anything alive
day destroys it
o Zeus
god beyond all other gods
handler of the fire

father   260
make the god of our sickness
ashes

Apollo
great bowman of light draw back your bow
fire arrow after arrow
make them a wall circling us
shoot into our enemy's eyes
draw the string twined with gold
come goddess
who dances on the mountains   270
sowing light where your feet brush the ground
blind our enemy come
god of golden hair
piled under your golden cap Bacchus[7]
your face blazing like the sea when the sun falls on it
like sunlight on wine
god whose name is our name Bacchus
god of joy god of terror
be with us now your bright face
like a pine torch roaring   280
thrust into the face of the slaughtering war god
blind him
drive him down from Olympos
drive him away from Thebes
forever

OED.: Every word of your prayers has touched me.
    Listen. Follow me. Join me in fighting this sickness,
         this plague,
    and all your sufferings may end, like a dark sky,
    clear suddenly, blue, after a week of storms,
    soothing the torn face of the sea,   290
    soothing our fears.
    Your fate looms in my words—
    I heard nothing about Laios' death,
    I know nothing about the murder,
    I was alone, how could I have tracked the killer,
         without a clue,
    I came to Thebes after the crime was done,
    I was made a Theban after Laios' death. Listen
         carefully—
    these words come from an innocent man.

                              Addressing the CHORUS.

    One of you knows who killed Laios.
    Where is that man?   300
    Speak.
    I command it. Fear is no excuse.
    He must clear himself of the dangerous charge.
    Who did this thing?
    Was it a stranger?
    Speak.
    I will not harm him. The worst he will suffer is exile.
    I will pay him well. He will have a king's thanks.
    But if he will not speak because he fears me,

---

[6] **Ares** God of war.

[7] **Bacchus** God of the vine, who often represented the irrational
side of Greek character. Also known as Dionysus.

if he fears what I will do to him or to those he loves,   310
if he will not obey me,
I say to him:
My power is absolute in Thebes, my rule reaches
     everywhere,
my words will drive the guilty man, the man who
     knows,
out of this city, away from Thebes, forever.
Nothing.
My word for him is nothing.
Let him *be* nothing.
Give him nothing.
Let him touch nothing of yours, he is nothing to you.   320
Lock your doors when he approaches.
Say nothing to him, do not speak.
No prayers with him, no offerings with him.
No purifying water.
Nothing.
Drive him from your homes. Let him have no home,
     nothing.
No words, no food, shelter, warmth of hand, shared
     worship.
Let him have nothing. Drive him out, let him die.
He is our disease.
                         I know.   330
                    Apollo has made it clear.
Nothing can stop me, nothing can change my words.
I fight for Apollo, I fight for the dead man.
You see me, you hear me, moving against the killer.
My words are his doom.
Whether he did it alone, and escaped unseen,
whether others helped him kill, it makes no
     difference—
let my hatred burn out his life, hatred, always.
Make him an ember of suffering.
Make all his happiness   340
ashes.
If he eats at my side, sits at my sacred hearth, and I
     know these things,
let every curse I spit out against him find *me*,
come home to *me*.
Carry out my orders. You must,
for me, for Apollo, and for Thebes, Thebes,
this poor wasted city,
deserted by its gods.
I know—the gods have given us this disease.
That makes no difference. You should have acted,   350
you should have done something long ago to purge
     our guilt.
The victim was noble, a king—
you should have done everything to track his
     murderer down.
And so,
because I rule now where he ruled;
because I share his bed, his wife;
because the same woman who mothered my
     children might have mothered his;
because fate swooped out of nowhere and cut him
     down;
because of all these things   360

I will fight for him as I would fight for my own
     murdered father.
Nothing will stop me.
No man, no place, nothing will escape my gaze. I
     will not stop
until I know it all, all, until everything is clear.
For every king, every king's son and his sons,
for every royal generation of Thebes, *my* Thebes,
I will expose the killer, I will reveal him
to the light.
Oh gods, gods,
destroy all those who will not listen, will not obey.   370
Freeze the ground until they starve.
Make their wives barren as stone.
Let this disease that shakes Thebes to its roots—
or any worse disease, if there is any worse than
     this—waste them,
crush everything they have, everything they are.
But you men of Thebes—
you, who know my words are right, who obey me—
may justice and the gods defend you, bless you,
graciously, forever.

LEADER: Your curse forces me to speak, Master.   380
     I cannot escape it.
     I did not murder the king, I cannot show you the
          man who did.
     Apollo told us to search for the killer.
     Apollo must name him.
OED.: No man can force the gods to speak.
LEADER: Then I will say the next best thing.
OED.: If there's a third best thing, say that too.
LEADER: Teiresias sees what the god Apollo sees.
     Truth, truth.
     If you heard the god speaking, heard his voice,   390
     you might see more, more, and more.
OED.: Teiresias? I have seen to that already.
     Kreon spoke of Teiresias, and I sent for him. Twice.
     I find it strange he still hasn't come.
LEADER: And there's an old story, almost forgotten, a
     dark, faded rumor.
OED.: What rumor? I must sift each story, see it,
     understand it.
LEADER: Laios was killed by bandits.
OED.: I have heard that story: but who can show me the   400
     man who saw the murderer?
     Has anyone seen him?
LEADER: If he knows the meaning of fear,
     if he heard those curses you spoke against him,
     those words still scorching the air,
     you won't find him now, not in Thebes.
OED.: The man *murdered*. Why would words frighten him?

TEIRESIAS *has appeared from the stage entrance to the right of
the audience. He walks with a staff and is helped by a slave boy
and attendants. He stops at some distance from center stage.*

LEADER: Here is the man who can catch the criminal.
     They're bringing him now—
     the godlike prophet who speaks with the voice of god.
     He, only he, knows truth.   410
     The truth is rooted in his soul.

OED.: Teiresias, you understand all things,
   what can be taught, what is locked in silence,
   the distant things of heaven, and things that crawl
      the earth.
   You cannot see, yet you know the nature of this
      plague infesting our city.
   Only you, my lord, can save us, only you can defend
      us.
   Apollo told our messenger—did you hear?—
   that we could be saved only by tracking down Laios'
      killers,
   only by killing them, or sending them into exile.
   Help us, Teiresias.   420
   Study the cries of birds, study their wild paths,
   ponder the signs of fire, use all your skills of
      prophecy.
   Rescue us, preserve us.
   Rescue yourself, rescue Thebes, rescue me.
   Cleanse every trace of the growing stain left by the
      dead man's blood.
   We are in your hands, Teiresias.
   No work is more nobly human than helping others,
   helping with all the strength and skill we possess.
TEIRESIAS: Wisdom is a curse
   when wisdom does nothing for the man who has it.   430
   Once I knew this well, but I forgot.
   I never should have come.
OED.: Never should have come? Why this reluctance,
      prophet?
TEI.: Let me go home.
   That way is best, for you, for me.
   Let me live my life, and you live yours.
OED.: Strange words, Teiresias, cruel to the city that gave
      you life.
   Your holy knowledge could save Thebes. How can
      you keep silent?
TEI.: What have *you* said that helps Thebes? Your words
      are wasted.
   I would rather be silent than waste my words.   440

OED.: Look at us,   (OEDIPUS *stands, the* CHORUS *kneel*)

   kneeling to you, Teiresias, imploring you.
   In the name of the gods, if you know—
   help us, tell us what you know.
TEI.: You kneel because you do not understand.
   But I will never let you see my grief. Never.
   My grief is yours.
OED.: What? You know and won't speak?
   You'd betray us all, you'd destroy the city of Thebes?
TEI.: I will do nothing to hurt myself, or you. Why insist? 450
   I will not speak.
OED.: Stubborn old fool, you'd make a rock angry!
   Tell me what you know! Say it!
   Where are your feelings? Won't you ever speak?
TEI.: You call me cold, stubborn, unfeeling, you insult
      me. But *you,*
   Oedipus, what do you know about yourself,
   about your real feelings?
   You don't see how much alike we are.
OED.: How can *I* restrain my anger when I see how little
      you care for Thebes.

TEI.: The truth will come, by itself,   460
   the truth will come
   no matter how I shroud it in silence.
OED.: All the more reason why you should speak.
TEI.: Not another word.
   Rage away. You will never make me speak.
OED.: I'll rage, prophet, I'll give you all my anger.
   I'll say it all—
   Listen: I think you were involved in the murder of
      Laios,
   you helped plan it, I think you
   did everything in your power to kill Laios,   470
   everything but strike him with your own hands,
   and if you weren't blind, if you still had eyes to see
      with,
   I'd say you, and *you* alone, did it all.
TEI.: Do you think so? Then obey your own words, obey
   the curse everyone heard break from your own lips:
   Never speak again to these men of Thebes,
   never speak again to me.
                              You, it's
   you.   480
   What plagues the city is *you.*
   The plague is *you.*
OED.: Do you know what you're saying?
   Do you think I'll let you get away with these vile
      accusations?
TEI.: I am safe.
   Truth lives in me, and the truth is strong.
OED.: Who taught you this truth of yours? Not your
      prophet's craft.
TEI.: *You* taught me. You forced me to speak.
OED.: Speak what? Explain. Teach me.
TEI.: Didn't you understand?
   Are you trying to make me say the word?   490
OED.: What word? Say it. Spit it out.
TEI.: Murderer.
   I say *you,*
   you are the killer you're searching for.
OED.: You won't say *that* again to me and get away
      with it.
TEI.: Do you want more? Shall I make you really angry?
OED.: Say anything you like. Your words are wasted.
TEI.: I say you live in shame, and you do not know it,
   do not know that you
   and those you love most   500
   wallow in shame,
   you do not know
   in what shame you live.
OED.: You'll pay for these insults, I swear it.
TEI.: Not if the truth is strong.
OED.: The truth *is* strong, but not your truth.
   You have no truth. You're blind.
   Blind in your eyes. Blind in your ears. Blind in your
      mind.
TEI.: And I pity you for mocking my blindness.
   Soon everyone in Thebes will mock you, Oedipus.   510
      They'll mock you
   as you have mocked me.
OED.: One endless night swaddles you in its unbroken
      black sky.

You can't hurt me, you can't hurt anyone who sees
the light of day.

TEI.: True. Nothing I do will harm you. You, you and
your fate belong to Apollo.
Apollo will see to *you.*

OED.: Are these your own lies, prophet—or Kreon's?

TEI.: Kreon? Your plague is *you,* not Kreon.

OED.: Money, power, one great skill surpassing another,
if a man has these things, other men's envy grows   520
and grows,
their greed and hunger are insatiable.
Most men would lust for a life like mine—but I did
not demand my life,
Thebes gave me my life, and from the beginning, my
good friend Kreon,
loyal, trusted Kreon,
was reaching for my power, wanted to ambush me,
get rid of me by hiring this cheap wizard,
this crass, conniving priest, who sees nothing but
profit,
whose prophecy is simple profit. *You,*
what did *you* ever do that proves you a real seer?
What did you ever *see,* prophet?
And when the Sphinx who sang mysteriously   530
imprisoned us
why didn't you speak and set us free?
No ordinary man could have solved her riddle,
it took prophecy, prophecy and skill you clearly
never had.
Even the paths of birds, even the gods' voices were
useless.
But I showed up, I, Oedipus,
stupid, untutored Oedipus,
I silenced her, I destroyed her, I used my wits, not
omens,
to sift the meaning of her song.
And this is the man you want to kill so you can get   540
close to King Kreon,
weigh his affairs for him, advise him, influence him.
No, I think you and your master, Kreon, who
contrived this plot,
will be whipped out of Thebes.
Look at you.
If you weren't so old, and weak, oh
I'd make you pay
for this conspiracy of yours.

LEADER: Oedipus, both of you spoke in anger.
Anger is not what we need.
We need all our wits, all our energy to interpret   550
Apollo's words.
Then we will know what to do.

TEI.: Oedipus, you are king, but you must hear my reply.
My right to speak is just as valid as yours.
I am not your slave. Kreon is not my patron.
My master is Apollo. I can say what I please.
You insulted me. You mocked me. You called me
blind.
Now hear *me* speak, Oedipus.
You have eyes to see with,
but you do not see yourself, you do not see
the horror shadowing every step of your life,   560

the blind shame in which you live,
you do not see where you live and who lives with you,
lives always at your side.
Tell me, Oedipus, who are your parents?
Do you know?
You do not even know
the shame and grief you have brought your family,
those still alive, those buried beneath the earth.
But the curse of your mother, the curse of your father
will whip you, whip you again and again, wherever   570
you turn,
it will whip you out of Thebes forever,
your clear eyes flooded with darkness.
That day will come.
And then what scoured, homeless plain, what
leafless tree,
what place on Kithairon,[8]
where no other humans are or ever will be,
where the wind is the only thing that moves,
what raw track of thorns and stones, what rock, gulley,
or blind hill won't echo your screams, your howls of
anguish
when you find out that the marriage song,   580
sung when you came to Thebes, heard in your house,
guided you to *this* shore, this wilderness
you thought was home, *your* home?
And you do not see
all the other awful things
that will show you who you really are, show you
to your children, face to face.
Go ahead! Call me quack, abuse Kreon, insult
Apollo, the god
who speaks through me, whose words move on my
lips.
No man will ever know worse suffering than you,   590
your life, your flesh, your happiness an ember of
pain. Ashes.

OED.: (*to the* CHORUS) Must I stand here and listen to these
attacks?

TEI.: (*beginning to move away*) I am here, Oedipus, because
you sent for me.

OED.: You old fool,
I'd have thought twice before asking you to come
if I had known you'd spew out such idiocy.

TEI.: Call me fool, if you like, but your parents,
who gave you life, they respected my judgment.

OED.: Parents?
What do you mean?   600
Who are my mother and father?

TEI.: This day is your mother and father—this day will
give you your birth.
It will destroy you too.

---

[8] **Kithairon** Also called Cithaeron. A mountain on the frontier of Boeotia, the isthmus of Corinth, and Attica. Oedipus was abandoned here when a baby, according to legend. Sophocles' use of this particular mountain is an example of his irony, and the audience most likely knew the legend and could appreciate the playwright's ironical references.

OED.: How you love mysterious, twisted words.

TEI.: Aren't you the great solver of riddles?
Aren't you Oedipus?

OED.: Taunt me for the gift of my brilliant mind.
That gift is what makes me great.

TEI.: That gift is your destiny. It made you everything
you are,
and it has ruined you.   610

OED.: But if this gift of mine saved Thebes, who cares
what happens to me?

TEI.: I'm leaving. Boy, take me home.

OED.: Good. Take him home. Here
I keep stumbling over you, here you're in my way.
Scuttle home, and leave us in peace!

TEI.: I'm going. I said what I came to say,
and that scowl, darkening your face, doesn't frighten
me. How can you hurt me?
I tell you again:
the man you've been trying to expose—
with all your threats, with your inquest into Laios'   620
murder—
that man is here, in Thebes.
Now people think he comes from Corinth, but later
they will see he was born in Thebes.
When they know, he'll have no pleasure in that news.
Now he has eyes to see with, but they will be slashed
out;
rich and powerful now, he will be a beggar,
poking his way with a stick, feeling his way to a
strange country.
And his children—the children he lives with—
will see him at last, see what he is, see who he
really is:
their brother and their father; his wife's son, his   630
mother's husband;
the lover who slept with his father's wife; the man
who murdered his father—
the man whose hands still drip with his father's
blood.
These truths will be revealed.

Go inside and ponder *that* riddle, and if you find
I've lied,
then call me a prophet who cannot see.

OEDIPUS *turns and enters the palace.* TEIRESIAS *is led out
through the stage entrance on the right.*

CHORUS: who did crimes unnameable things
things words cringe at
which man did the rock of prophecy at Delphi say
did these things
his hands dripping with blood   640
he should run now flee
his strong feet swallowing the air
stronger than the horses of storm winds
their hooves slicing the air
now in his armor
Apollo lunges at him
his infinite branching fire reaches out

and the steady dread death-hungry Fates[9] follow and
never stop
their quick scissors seeking the cloth of his life

just now   650
from high snowy Parnassus[10]
the god's voice exploded its blazing message
follow his track find the man
no one knows
a bull loose under wild bushes and trees
among caves and gray rocks
cut from the herd he runs and runs but runs nowhere
zigzagging desperate to get away
birds of prophecy birds of death circling his head
forever   660
voices forged at the white stone core of the earth
they go where he goes always

terror's in me flooding me
how can I judge
what the god Apollo says
trapped hoping confused
I do not see what is here now
when I look to the past I see nothing
I know nothing about a feud
wounding the families of Laios or Oedipus   670
no clue to the truth then or now
nothing to blacken his golden fame in Thebes
and help Laios' family
solve the mystery of his death

Zeus and Apollo know
they understand
only they see
the dark threads crossing beneath our life
but no man can say a prophet sees more than I
one man surpasses another   680
wisdom against wisdom skill against skill
but I will not blame Oedipus
whatever anyone says
until words are as real as things

one thing is clear
years back the Sphinx tested him
his answer was true
he was wise and sweet to the city
so he can never be evil
not to me   690

KREON *enters through the stage entrance at right, and
addresses the* CHORUS.

---

[9] **Fates** The Furies. The goddesses who avenge murder, perjury, and other crimes, who chase and madden those who have committed such crimes. They are winged maidens with snakes in their hair and blood dripping from their eyes. Sometimes called the Erinyes or the Eumenides.
[10] **Parnassus** A Greek mountain sacred to Apollo and the nine muses who are the goddesses of literature, music, dance, and other artistic and creative pursuits.

KREON: Men of Thebes, I hear Oedipus, our king and
    master,
  has brought terrible charges against me.
  I have come to face those charges. I resent them
    bitterly.
  If he imagines I have hurt him, spoken or acted
    against him
  while our city dies, believe me—I have nothing left
    to live for.
  His accusations pierce me, wound me mortally—
  nothing they touch is trivial, private—
  if you, my family and friends,
  think I'm a traitor, if all Thebes believes it, says it.
LEADER: Perhaps he spoke in anger, without thinking,   700
  perhaps his anger made him accuse you.
KREON: Did he really say I persuaded Teiresias to lie?
LEADER: I heard him say these things,
  but I don't know what they mean.
KREON: Did he look you in the eye when he accused me?
  Was he in his right mind?
LEADER: I do not know or see what great men do.

(turning to OEDIPUS, *who has emerged from the palace*)

  But here he is—Oedipus.
OED.: What? *You* here? Murderer!
  You dare come here, to my palace, when it's clear   710
  you've been plotting to murder me and seize the
    throne of Thebes?
  You're the bandit, *you're* the killer.
                                 Answer me—
  Did you think I was cowardly or stupid?
  Is that why you betrayed me?
  Did you really think I wouldn't see what you were
    plotting,
  how you crept up on me like a cloud inching across
    the sun?
  Did you think I wouldn't defend myself against you?
  You thought I was a fool, but the fool was *you*, Kreon.
  Thrones are won with money and men, you fool!   720
KREON: You have said enough, Oedipus. Now let me reply.
  Weigh my words against your charges, then judge
    for yourself.
OED.: Eloquent, Kreon. But you won't convince me now.
  Now that I know your hatred, your malice.
KREON: Let me explain.
OED.: Explain?
  What could explain your treachery?
KREON: If you think this stubborn anger of yours, this
    perversity,
  is something to be proud of, you're mad.
OED.: And if you think you can injure your sister's   730
    husband,
  and not pay for it, *you're* mad.
KREON: I would be mad to hurt you. How have I hurt
    you?
OED.: Was it you who advised me to send for that great
    holy prophet?
KREON: Yes, and I'd do it again.
OED.: How long has it been since Laios disappeared?
KREON: Disappeared?

OED.: Died. Was murdered. . . .
KREON: Many, many years.
OED.: And this prophet of yours—was he practicing his
    trade at the time?
KREON: With as much skill, wisdom and honor as ever.   740
OED.: Did he ever mention my name?
KREON: Not in my presence.
OED.: Was there an inquest? A formal inquiry?
KREON: Of course. Nothing was ever discovered.
OED.: Then why didn't our wonderful prophet, our
    Theban wizard,
  denounce me as the murderer then?
KREON: I don't know. And when I don't know, I don't speak.
OED.: But you know this. You know it with perfect certainty.
KREON: What do you mean?
OED.: This: if you and Teiresias were not conspiring   750
    against me,
  Teiresias would never have charged *me* with Laios'
    murder.
KREON: If he said that, you should know.
  But now, Oedipus, it's my right, my turn to question
    you.
OED.: Ask anything. You'll never prove I killed Laios.
KREON: Did you marry my sister, Jocasta?
OED.: I married Jocasta.
KREON: And you gave her an equal share of the power in
    Thebes?
OED.: Whatever she wants is hers.
KREON: And I share that power equally with you and her?
OED.: Equally.   760
  And that's precisely why it's clear you're false,
    treacherous.
KREON: No, Oedipus.
  Consider it rationally, as I have. Reflect:
  What man, what sane man, would prefer a king's
    power
  with all its dangers and anxieties,
  when he could enjoy that same power, without its
    cares,
  and sleep in peace each night? Power?
  I have no instinct for power, no hunger for it either.
  It isn't royal power I want, but its advantages.
  And any sensible man would want the same.   770
  Look at the life I lead. Whatever I want, I get from you,
  with your goodwill and blessing. I have nothing
    to fear.
  If I were king, my life would be constant duty and
    constraint.
  Why would I want your power or the throne of Thebes
  more than what I enjoy now—the privilege of power
  without its dangers? I would be a fool to want more
  than what I have—the substance, not the show, of
    power.
  As matters stand, no man envies me, I am courted
  and admired by all. Men wear no smiling masks for
    Kreon.
  And those who want something from you come to me   780
  because the way to royal favor lies through me.
  Tell me, Oedipus, why should I give these blessings up
  to seize your throne and all the dangers it confers?

A man like me, who knows his mortal limits and
    accepts them,
cannot be vicious or treacherous by nature.
The love of power is not my nature, nor is treason
or the thoughts of treason that go with love of power.
I would never dare conspire against your life.

Do you want to test the truth of what I say?
Go to Delphi, put the question to the oracle,   790
ask if I have told you exactly what Apollo said.
Then if you find that Teiresias and I have plotted
    against you,
seize me and put me to death. Convict me
not by one vote alone, but two—yours *and* mine,
    Oedipus.
But don't convict me on the strength of your suspicions,
don't confuse friends with traitors, traitors with
    friends.
There's no justice in that.
To throw away a good and loyal friend
is to destroy what you love most—
your own life, and what makes life worth living.   800
Someday you will know the truth:
time, only time reveals the good man;
one day's light reveals the evil man.

LEADER: Good words
    for someone careful, afraid he'll fall.
    But a mind like lightning
    stumbles.

OED.: When a clever man plots against me and moves
    swiftly
    I must move just as swiftly, I must plan.
    But if I wait, if I do nothing, he will win, win   810
      everything,
    and I will lose.

KREON: What do you want? My exile?

OED.: No. Your death.

KREON: You won't change your mind? You won't believe
    me?

OED.: I'll believe you when you teach me the meaning of
    envy.

KREON: Envy? You talk about envy. You don't know what
    sense is.
    Can't you listen to me?

OED.: I *am* listening. To my own good sense.

KREON: Listen to *me*. I have sense on my side too.

OED.: You? You were born devious.   820

KREON: And if you're wrong?

OED.: I still must govern.

KREON: Not if you govern badly.

OED.: Oh Thebes, Thebes . . .

KREON: Thebes is mine too.

LEADER: (*turning to* JOCASTA, *who has entered from the
    palace, accompanied by a woman attendant*)

    Stop. I see
    Jocasta coming from the palace
    just in time, my lords, to help you
    settle this deep, bitter feud raging between you.
    Listen to what she says.   830

JOCASTA: Oedipus! Kreon! Why this insane quarreling?
    You should be ashamed, both of you. Forget
      yourselves.
    This is no time for petty personal bickering.
    Thebes is sick, dying.
                 —Come inside, Oedipus
    —And you, Kreon, leave us.
    Must you create all this misery over nothing, nothing?

KREON: Jocasta,
    Oedipus has given me two impossible choices:
    Either I must be banished from Thebes, my city, my   840
      home,
    or be arrested and put to death.

OED.: That's right.
    I caught him plotting against me, Jocasta.
    Viciously, cunningly plotting against the king of
      Thebes.

KREON: Take every pleasure I have in life, curse me, let
    me die,
    if I've done what you accuse me of, let the gods
    destroy everything I have, let them do anything to
      me.
    I stand here, exposed to their infinite power.

JOC.: Oedipus, in the name of the gods, believe him.
    His prayer has made him holy, naked to the mysterious   850
    whims of the gods, has taken him beyond what is
      human.
    Respect his words, respect me, respect these men
      standing at your side.

CHORUS: (*beginning a dirge-like appeal to* OEDIPUS)

    listen to her
    think yield
    we implore you

OED.: What do you want?

CHORUS: be generous to Kreon give him respect
    he was never foolish before
    now his prayer to the gods has made him great
    great and frightening   860

OED.: Do you know what you're asking?

CHORUS: I know

OED.: Then say it.

CHORUS: don't ever cut him off
    without rights or honor
    blood binds you both
    his prayer has made him sacred
    don't accuse him
    because some blind suspicion hounds you

OED.: Understand me: 870
    when you ask for these things
    you ask for my death or exile.

CHORUS: no
    by the sun
    the god who bathes us in his light
    who sees all
    I will die godless no family no friends
    if what I ask means that
    it is Thebes
    Thebes dying wasting away life by life   880
    this is the misery

that breaks my heart
and now this quarrel raging between you and Kreon
is more more than I can bear

OED.: Then let him go, even if it means I must die
or be forced out of Thebes forever, stripped of all my
rights, all my honors.
Your grief, *your* words touch me. Not his.
I pity you. But him,
my hatred will reach him wherever he goes.

KREON: It's clear you hate to yield, clear   890
you yield only under pressure, only
when you've worn out the fierceness of your anger.
Then all you can do is sit, and brood.
Natures like yours are a torment to themselves.

OED.: Leave. Go!

KREON: I'm going. Now I know
you do not know me.
But these men know I am the man I seem to be, a just
man,
not devious, not a traitor.

KREON *leaves.*

CHORUS: woman why are you waiting   900
lead him inside comfort him

JOC.: Not before I know what has happened here.

CHORUS: blind ignorant words suspicion without proof
the injustice of it
gnaws at us

JOC.: From both men?

CHORUS: yes

JOC.: What caused it?

CHORUS: enough enough
no more words   910
Thebes is so tormented now
let it rest where it ended.

OED.: Look where cooling my rage,
where all your decent, practical thoughts have led you.

CHORUS: Oedipus I have said this many times
I would be mad helpless to give advice
if I turned against you now
once
you took our city in her storm of pain
straightened her course found fair weather   920
o lead her to safety now
if you can

JOC.: If you love the gods, tell me, too, Oedipus—I
implore you—
why are you still so angry, why can't you let it go?

OED.: I will tell you, Jocasta.
You mean more, far more to me than these men here.
Jocasta, it is Kreon—Kreon and his plots against me.

JOC.: What started your quarrel?

OED.: He said I murdered Laios.

JOC.: Does he know something? Or is it pure hearsay?   930

OED.: He sent me a vicious, trouble-making prophet
to avoid implicating himself. He did not say it to my
face.

JOC.: Oedipus, forget all this. Listen to me:
no mortal can practise the art of prophecy, no man
can see the future.

One experience of mine will show you why.
Long ago an oracle came to Laios.
It came not from Apollo himself but from his priests.
It said Laios was doomed to be murdered by a son,
his son and mine.
But Laios, from what we heard, was murdered by
bandits from a foreign country,
cut down at a crossroads. My poor baby   940
was only three days old when Laios had his feet
pierced together behind the ankles
and gave orders to abandon our child on a mountain,
leave him alone to die
in a wilderness of rocks and bare gray trees
where there were no roads, no people.
So you see—Apollo didn't make that child his
father's killer,
Laios wasn't murdered by his son. That dreadful act
which so terrified Laios—
it never happened.

All those oracular voices meant was nothing, nothing.
Ignore them.
Apollo creates. Apollo reveals. He needs no help   950
from men.

OED.: (*who has been very still*)

While you were speaking, Jocasta, it flashed through
my mind
like wind suddenly ruffling a stretch of calm sea.
It stuns me. I can almost see it—some memory, some
image.
My heart races and swells—

JOC.: Why are you so strangely excited, Oedipus?

OED.: You said Laios was cut down *near* a crossroads?

JOC.: That was the story. It hasn't changed.

OED.: Where did it happen? Tell me. Where?

JOC.: In Phokis.[11] Where the roads from Delphi and
Daulia meet.

OED.: When?   960

JOC.: Just before you came to Thebes and assumed power.
Just before you were proclaimed King.

OED.: O Zeus, Zeus,
what are you doing with my life?

JOC.: Why are you so disturbed, Oedipus?

OED.: Don't ask me. Not yet.
Tell me about Laios.
How old was he? What did he look like?

JOC.: Streaks of gray were beginning to show in his black
hair.
He was tall, strong—built something like you.   970

OED.: No! O gods, o
it seems each hard, arrogant curse
I spit out
was meant for me, and I
didn't
know it!

---

[11] **Phokis** The territory in which the towns Daulia and Delphi
were located. Apollo's temple was in Delphi.

JOC.: Oedipus, what do you mean? Your face is so strange.
You frighten me.

OED.: It *is* frightening—can the blind prophet see, can he
really see?
I would know if you told me . . . 980

JOC.: I'm afraid to ask, Oedipus.
Told you what?

OED.: Was Laios traveling with a small escort
or with many armed men, like a king?

JOC.: There were five, including a herald.
Laios was riding in his chariot.

OED.: Light, o light, light
now everything, everything is clear. All of it.
Who told you this? Who was it?

JOC.: A household slave. The only survivor. 990

OED.: Is he here, in Thebes?

JOC.: No. When he returned and saw that you were king
and learned Laios was dead, he came to me and
clutched my hand,
begged me to send him to the mountains
where shepherds graze their flocks, far from the city,
so he could never see Thebes again.
I sent him, of course. He deserved that much, for a
slave, and more.

OED.: Can he be called back? Now?

JOC.: Easily. But why?

OED.: I am afraid I may have said too much— 1000
I *must* see him.
Now.

JOC.: Then he will come.
But surely I have a right to know what disturbs you,
Oedipus.

OED.: Now that I've come this far, Jocasta,
hope torturing me, each step of mine heavy with fear,
I won't keep anything from you.
Wandering through the mazes of a fate like this,
how could I confide in anyone but you?

My father was Polybos, of Corinth. 1010
My mother, Merope, was Dorian.
Everyone in Corinth saw me as its first citizen,
but one day something happened,
something strange, puzzling. Puzzling, but nothing
more.
Still, it worried me.
One night, I was at a banquet,
and a man—he was very drunk—said I wasn't my
father's son,
called me "bastard." That stung me, I was shocked.
I could barely control my anger, I lay awake all night.
The next day I went to my father and mother, 1020
I questioned them about the man and what he said.
They were furious with him, outraged by his insult,
and I was reassured. But I kept hearing the word
"bastard" "bastard"—
I couldn't get it out of my head.
Without my parents' knowledge, I went to Delphi: I
wanted the truth,
but Apollo refused to answer me.
And yet he did reveal other things, he did show me

a future dark with torment, evil, horror,
he made me *see*—
see myself, doomed to sleep with my own mother, 1030
doomed
to bring children into this world where the sun
pours down,
children no one could bear to see, doomed
to murder the man who gave me life, whose blood is
my blood. My father.
And after I heard all this, I fled Corinth,
measuring my progress by the stars, searching for a
place
where I would never see those words, those dreadful
predictions
come true. And on my way
I came to the place where you say King Laios was
murdered.

Jocasta, the story I'm about to tell you is the truth:
I was on the road, near the crossroads you 1040
mentioned,
when I met a herald, with an old man, just as you
described him.
The man was riding in a chariot
and his driver tried to push me off the road
and when he shoved me I hit him. I hit him.
The old man stood quiet in the chariot until I passed
under him,
then he leaned out and caught me on the head with
an ugly goad—
its two teeth wounded me—and with this hand of
mine,
this hand clenched around my staff,
I struck him back even harder—so hard, so quick he
couldn't dodge it,
and he toppled out of the chariot and hit the ground, 1050
face up.
I killed them. Every one of them. I still see them.

(to the CHORUS*)*

If this stranger and Laios
are somehow linked by blood,
tell me what man's torment equals mine?

Citizens, hear my curse again—
Give this man nothing. Let him touch nothing of
yours.
Lock your doors when he approaches.
Say nothing to him when he approaches.
And these, these curses,
with my own mouth I 1060
spoke these monstrous curses against myself.

*(*OEDIPUS *turns back to* JOCASTA*)*

These hands, these bloodstained hands made love to
you in your dead husband's bed,
these hands murdered him.

If I must be exiled, never to see my family,
never to walk the soil of my country

so I will not sleep with my mother
and kill Polybos, my father, who raised me—his
    son!—
wasn't I born evil—answer me!—isn't every part of
    me
unclean? Oh
some unknown god, some savage venomous demon   1070
    must have done this,
raging, swollen with hatred. Hatred
for me.

Holiness, pure, radiant powers, o gods
don't let me see that day,
don't let it come, take me away
from men, men with their eyes, hide me
before I see
the filthy black stain reaching down over me, into me.

(The CHORUS *have moved away from the stage)*

LEADER: Your words make us shudder, Oedipus,
    but hope, hope   1080
    until you hear more from the man who witnessed
      the murder.
OED.: That is the only hope I have. Waiting.
    Waiting for that man to come from the pastures.
JOC.: And when he finally comes, what do you hope to
    learn?
OED.: If his story matches yours, I am saved.
JOC.: What makes you say that?
OED.: Bandits—you said he told you bandits killed Laios.
    So if he still talks about bandits,
    more than one, I couldn't have killed Laios.
    One man is not the same as many men.   1090
    But if he speaks of one man, traveling alone,
    then all the evidence points to me.
JOC.: Believe me, Oedipus, those were his words.
    And he can't take them back: the whole city heard
      him, not only me.
    And if he changes only the smallest detail of his story,
    that still won't prove Laios was murdered as the
      oracle foretold.
    Apollo was clear—it was Laios' fate to be killed by
      my son,
    but my poor child died before his father died.
    The future has no shape. The shapes of prophecy lie.
    I see nothing in them, they are all illusions.   1100
OED.: Even so, I want that shepherd summoned here.
    Now. Do it now.
JOC.: I'll send for him immediately. But come inside.
    My only wish is to please you.

JOCASTA *dispatches a servant.*

CHORUS: fate
    be here let what I say be pure
    let all my acts be pure
    laws forged in the huge clear fields of heaven
    rove the sky
    shaping my words limiting what I do   1110
    Olympos made those laws not men who live and die
    nothing lulls those laws to sleep

they cannot die
and the infinite god in them never ages

arrogance insatiable pride
breed the tyrant
feed him on thing after thing blindly
at the wrong time uselessly
and he grows reaches so high
nothing can stop his fall   1120
his feet thrashing the air standing on nothing
and nowhere to stand he plunges down
o god shatter the tyrant
but let men compete let self-perfection grow
let men sharpen their skills
soldiers citizens building the good city
Apollo
protect me always
always the god I will honor   1130
if a man walks through his life arrogant
strutting proud
says anything does anything
does not fear justice
fear the gods bow to their shining presences
let fate make him stumble in his tracks
for all his lecheries and headlong greed
if he takes whatever he wants right or wrong
if he touches forbidden things
what man who acts like this would boast   1140
he can escape the anger of the gods
why should I join these sacred public dances
if such acts are honored

no
I will never go to the holy untouchable stone
navel of the earth at Delphi
never again
go to the temples at Olympia at Abai[12]
if all these things are not joined
if past present future are not made one   1150
made clear to mortal eyes
o Zeus if that is your name
power above all immortal king
see these things look
those great prophecies are fading
men say they're nothing
nobody prays to the god of light no one believes
nothing of the gods stays

JOCASTA *enters from the palace, carrying a branch tied with
strands of wool, and a jar of incense. She is accompanied by a
servant woman. She addresses the* CHORUS.

JOC.: Lords of Thebes, I come to the temples of the god
    with offerings—this incense and this branch.   1160
    So many thoughts torture Oedipus. He never rests.
    He acts without reason. He is like a man
    who has lost everything he knows—the past
    is useless to him; strange, new things baffle him.

---

[12] **Abai** A town in **Phokis,** where an oracle of Apollo resided.

And if someone talks disaster, it stuns him: he
  listens, he is afraid.
I have tried to reassure him, but nothing helps.
So I have come to you—
Apollo, close to my life, close to this house,

listen to my prayers: (*she kneels*)

        help us purify ourselves of this disease, 1170
help us survive the long night of our suffering,
protect us. We are afraid when we see Oedipus
  confused
and frightened—Oedipus, the only man who can
  pilot Thebes
to safety.

A MESSENGER *from Corinth has arrived by the entrance to the*
orchestra on the audience's left. He sees JOCASTA *praying, then*
turns to address the CHORUS.

MESSENGER: Friends,
  can you tell me where King Oedipus lives
  or better still, where I can find him?
LEADER: Here, in this house.
  This lady is his wife and mother
  of his children. 1180
MESS.: May you and your family prosper.
  May you be happy always under this great roof.
JOC.: Happiness and prosperity to you, too, for your kind
  words.
  But why are you here? Do you bring news?
MESS.: Good news for your house, good news for King
  Oedipus.
JOC.: What is your news? Who sent you?
MESS.: I come from Corinth, and what I have to say I
  know will bring you joy.
  And pain perhaps. . . . I do not know.
JOC.: Both joy and pain? What news could do that?
MESS.: The people of Corinth want Oedipus as their 1190
  king.
  That's what they're saying.
JOC.: But isn't old Polybos still king of Corinth?
MESS.: His kingdom is his grave.
JOC.: Polybos is *dead*?
MESS.: If I'm lying, my lady, let me die for it.
JOC.: You. (*to a servant*) Go in and tell Oedipus.
  O oracles of the gods, where are you now!
  This man, the man Oedipus was afraid he would
  murder,
  the man he feared, the man he fled from has died a
  natural death.
  Oedipus didn't kill him, it was luck, luck. 1200

She turns to greet OEDIPUS *as he comes out of the palace.*

OED.: Jocasta, why did you send for me? (*taking her gently*
  by the arm)
JOC.: Oedipus,
  listen to this man, see what those ominous, holy
  predictions of Apollo mean now.
OED.: Who is this man? What does he say?
JOC.: He comes from Corinth.
  Your father is dead. Polybos is dead!

OED.: What?
  Let me hear those words from your own mouth,
  stranger.
  Tell me yourself, in your own words.
MESS.: If it's what you want to hear first, then I'll say it: 1210
  Polybos is dead.
OED.: How did he die? Assassination? Illness? How?
MESS.: An old man's life hangs by a fragile thread.
  Anything can snap it.
OED.: That poor old man. It was illness then?
MESS.: Illness and old age.
OED.: Why, Jocasta,
  why should men look to the great hearth at Delphi
  or listen to birds shrieking and wheeling overhead—
  cries meaning I was doomed to kill my father? 1220
  He is dead, gone, covered by the earth.
  And here I am—my hands never even touched a
  spear—
  I did not kill him,
  unless he died from wanting me to come home.
  No. Polybos has bundled up all these oracles
  and taken them with him to the world below.
  They are only words now, lost in the air.
JOC.: Isn't that what I predicted?
OED.: You were right. My fears confused me.
JOC.: You have nothing to fear. Not now. Not ever. 1230
OED.: But the oracle said I am doomed to sleep with my
  mother.
  How can I live with that and not be afraid?
JOC.: Why should men be afraid of anything? Fortune
  rules our lives.
  Luck is everything. Things happen. The future is
  darkness.
  No human mind can know it.
  It's best to live in the moment, live for today,
  Oedipus.
  Why should the thought of marrying your mother
  make you so afraid?
  Many men have slept with their mothers in their
  dreams.
  Why worry? See your dreams for what they are—
  nothing, nothing at all.
  Be happy, Oedipus. 1240
OED.: All that you say is right, Jocasta. I know it.
  I should be happy,
  but my mother is still living. As long as she's alive,
  I live in fear. This fear is necessary.
  I have no choice.
JOC.: But Oedipus, your father's death is a sign, a great
  sign—
  the sky has cleared, the sun's gaze holds us in its
  warm, hopeful light.
OED.: A great sign, I agree. But so long as my mother is
  alive,
  my fear lives too.
MESS.: Who is this woman you fear so much? 1250
OED.: Merope, King Polybos' wife.
MESS.: Why does Merope frighten you so much?
OED.: A harrowing oracle hurled down upon us by some
  great god.

MESS.: Can you tell me? Or did the god seal your lips?

OED.: I can.

Long ago, Apollo told me I was doomed to sleep with my mother

and spill my father's blood, murder him

with these two hands of mine.

That's why I never returned to Corinth. Luckily, it would seem.

Still, nothing on earth is sweeter to a man's eyes   1260

than the sight of his father and mother.

MESS.: And you left Corinth because of this prophecy?

OED.: Yes. And because of my father. To avoid killing my father.

MESS.: But didn't my news prove you have nothing to fear?

I brought good news.

OED.: And I will reward you for your kindness.

MESS.: That's why I came, my lord. I knew you'd remember me

when you returned to Corinth.

OED.: I will never return, never live with my parents again.

MESS.: Son, it's clear you don't know what you're doing.   1270

OED.: What do you mean? In the name of the gods, speak.

MESS.: If you're afraid to go home because of your parents.

OED.: I *am* afraid, afraid

Apollo's prediction will come true, all of it.

as god's sunlight grows brighter on a man's face at dawn

when he's in bed, still sleeping,

and reaches into his eyes and wakes him.

MESS.: Afraid of murdering your father, of having his blood

on your hands?

OED.: Yes. His blood. The stain of his blood. That terror   1280

never leaves me.

MESS.: But Oedipus, then you have no reason to be afraid.

OED.: I'm their son, they're my parents, aren't they?

MESS.: Polybos is nothing to you.

OED.: Polybos is not my father?

MESS.: No more than I am.

OED.: But you are nothing to me. Nothing.

MESS.: And Polybos is nothing to you either.

OED.: They why did he call me his son?

MESS.: Because I gave you to him. With these hands

I gave you to him.   1290

OED.: How could he have loved me like a father if I am not his son?

MESS.: He had no children. That opened his heart.

OED.: And what about you?

Did you buy me from someone? Or did you find me?

MESS.: I found you squawling, left alone to die in the thickets of Kithairon.

OED.: Kithairon? What were you doing on Kithairon?

MESS.: Herding sheep in the high summer pastures.

OED.: You were a shepherd, a drifter looking for work?

MESS.: A drifter, yes, but it was I who saved you.

OED.: Saved me? Was I hurt when you picked me up?   1300

MESS.: Ask your feet.

OED.: Why,

why did you bring up that childhood pain?

MESS.: I cut you free. Your feet were pierced, tied together at the ankles

with leather thongs strung between the tendons and the bone.

OED.: That mark of my shame—I've worn it from the cradle.

MESS.: That mark is the meaning of your name:

Oedipus, Swollenfoot, Oedipus.

OED.: Oh gods

who did this to me?   1310

My mother?

My father?

MESS.: I don't know. The man I took you from—he would know.

OED.: So you didn't find me? Somebody else gave me to you?

MESS.: I got you from another shepherd.

OED.: What shepherd? Who was he? Do you know?

MESS.: As I recall, he worked for Laios.

OED.: The same Laios who was king of Thebes?

MESS.: The same Laios. The man was one of Laios' shepherds.

OED.: Is he still alive? I want to see this man.   1320

MESS.: (*pointing to the* CHORUS) These people would know that better than I do.

OED.: Do any of you know this shepherd he's talking about?

Have you ever noticed him in the fields or in the city?

Answer, if you have.

It is time everything came out, time everything was made clear.

Everything.

LEADER: I think he's the shepherd you sent for.

But Jocasta, she would know.

OED.: (*to* JOCASTA)

Jocasta, do you know this man?

Is he the man this shepherd here says worked for   1330
Laios?

JOC.: What man? Forget about him. Forget what was said.

It's not worth talking about.

OED.: How can I forget

with clues like these in my hands?

With the secret of my birth staring me in the face?

JOC.: *No*, Oedipus!

No more questions.

For god's sake, for the sake of your own life!

Isn't my anguish enough—more than enough?

OED.: You have nothing to fear, Jocasta.   1340

Even if my mother

and her mother before her were both slaves,

that doesn't make *you* the daughter of slaves.

JOC.: Oedipus, you *must* stop.

I beg you—stop!

OED.: Nothing can stop me now. I must know everything.

Everything!

JOC.: I implore you, Oedipus. For your own good.

OED.: Damn my own good!

JOC.: Oh, Oedipus, Oedipus,   1350
   I pray to god you never see who you are!

OED.: (*to one of the attendants, who hurries off through the exit
      stage left*)

   You there, go find that shepherd, bring him here.
   Let that woman bask in the glory of her noble birth.
JOC.: God help you, Oedipus—
   you were born to suffer, born
   to misery and grief.
   These are the last last words I will ever speak, ever
   Oedipus.

(JOCASTA *rushes offstage into the palace. Long silence.*)

LEADER: Why did Jocasta rush away,
   Oedipus, fleeing is such pain?   1360
   I fear disaster, or worse,
   Will break from this silence of hers.
OED.: Let it break! Let everything break!
   I must discover who I am, know the secret of my birth,
   no matter how humble, how vile.
   Perhaps Jocasta is ashamed of my low birth,
      ashamed to be my wife
   Like all women she's proud.
   But Luck, goddess who gives men all that is good,
      made *me*,
   and I won't be cheated of what is mine, nothing can
      dishonor me, ever.
   I am like the months, my brothers the months—they   1370
      shaped me
   when I was a baby in the cold hills of Kithairon,
   they guided me, carved out my times of greatness,
   and they still move their hands over my life.
   I am the man I am. I will not stop
   until I discover who my parents are.
CHORUS: if I know if I see
   if the dark force of prophecy is mine
   Kithairon
   when the full moon
   rides over us tomorrow   1380
   listen listen to us sing to you
   dance worship praise you
   mountain where Oedipus was found
   know Oedipus will praise you
   praise his nurse country and mother
   who blessed our king
   I call on you Apollo
   let these visions please you
   god Apollo
   healer   1390

   Oedipus son
   who was your mother
   which of the deathless mountain nymphs who lay
   with the great god Pan[13]

on the high peaks he runs across
or with Apollo
who loves the high green pastures above
which one bore you
did the god of the bare windy peaks Hermes[14]
or the wild, dervish Dionysos   1400
living in the cool air of the hills
take you
a foundling
from one of the nymphs he plays with
joyously lift you hold you in his arms
OED.: Old men, I think the man coming toward us now
   must be the shepherd we are looking for.
   I have never seen him, but the years, chalking his
      face and hair, tell me
   he's the man. And my men are with him. But you
      probably know him.
LEADER: I do know him. If Laios ever had a man he   1410
      trusted,
   this was the man.

OED.: (*to the* MESSENGER)

   You—is this the man you told me about?
MESS.: That's him. You're looking at the man.

OED.: (*to the* SHEPHERD *who has been waiting, hanging back*)

   You there, come closer.
                           Answer me, old man.
   Did you work for Laios?
SHEPHERD: I was born his slave, and grew up in his
      household.
OED.: What was your work?
SHEP.: Herding sheep, all my life.
OED.: Where?   1420
SHEP.: Kithairon, mostly. And the country around
      Kithairon.
OED.: Do you remember seeing this man?
MESS.: Which man?

OED.: (*pointing to the* MESSENGER)

   This man standing here. Have you ever seen him
      before?
SHEP.: Not that I remember.
MESS.: No wonder, master. But I'll make him remember.
   He knows who I am. We used to graze our flocks
      together
   in the pastures around Kithairon.
   Every year, for six whole months, three years running.
   From March until September, when the Dipper rose,   1430
      signaling the harvest.
   I had one flock, he had two.
   And when the frost came, I drove my sheep back to
      their winter pens
   and he drove his back to Laios' fold.
   Remember, old man? Isn't that how it was?
SHEP.: Yes. But it was all so long ago.

---
[13] **Pan** Nature and fertility deity, who was god of goat herds and flocks. He wandered in hills pursuing nymphs and playing his musical instrument, a set of reed pipes cut in various lengths and fastened together. Pan is considered to be a son of **Hermes.**

---
[14] **Hermes** God of merchants and thieves. Messenger for the deities. Wore a broad-brimmed traveler's hat and winged sandals. Also known as an early Greek fertility god.

MESS.: And do you remember giving me a baby boy at
the time—
    to raise as my own son?
SHEP.: What if I do? Why all these questions?
MESS.: That boy became King Oedipus, friend.
SHEP.: Damn you, can't you keep quiet.   1440
OED.: Don't scold him, old man.
    It's you who deserve to be punished, not him.
SHEP.: What did I say, good master?
OED.: You haven't answered his question about the boy.
SHEP.: He's making trouble, master. He doesn't know a
    thing.

(OEDIPUS *takes the* SHEPHERD *by the cloak*)

OED.: Tell me or you'll be sorry.
SHEP.: For god's sake, don't hurt me, I'm an old man.

OED.: (*to one of his men*) You there, hold him. We'll make
    him talk.

(*The attendant pins the* SHEPHERD'S *arms behind his back*)

SHEP.: Oedipus, Oedipus,
    god knows I pity you.   1450
    What more do you want to know?
OED.: Did you give the child to this man?
                        Speak.   Yes or no?
SHEP.: Yes.
    And I wish to god I'd died that day.
OED.: You *will* be dead unless you tell me the whole truth.
SHEP.: And worse than dead, if I do.
OED.: It seems our man won't answer.
SHEP.: No. I told you already. I gave him the boy.
OED.: Where did you get him? From Laios' household? Or
    where?
SHEP.: He wasn't *my* child. He was given to me.   1460

OED.: (*turning to the* CHORUS *and the audience*)

    By whom? Someone here in Thebes?
SHEP.: Master, please, in god's name, no more questions.
OED.: You're a dead man if I have to ask you once more.
SHEP.: He was one
    of the children
    from Laios'
    household.
OED.: A slave child? Or Laios' own?
SHEP.: I can't say it . . . it's
    awful, the words   1470
    are awful . . . awful.
OED.: And I,
    I am afraid to hear them . . .
    but I must.
SHEP.: He was Laios' own child.
    Your wife, inside the palace, she can explain it all.
OED.: *She* gave you the child?
SHEP.: My lord . . . yes.
OED.: Why?
SHEP.: She wanted me to abandon the child on a   1480
    mountain.
OED.: His own mother?
SHEP.: Yes. There were prophecies, horrible oracles. She
    was afraid.

OED.: What oracles?
SHEP.: Oracles predicting he would murder his own father.
OED.: But why did you give the boy to this old man?
SHEP.: Because I pitied him, master, because I
    thought the man would take the child away, take
        him to another country.
    Instead he saved him. Saved him for—oh gods,
    a fate so horrible, so awful, words can't describe it.
    If you were the baby that man took from me, Oedipus, 1490
    what misery, what grief is yours!

OED.: (*looking up at the sun*)

    LIGHT   LIGHT   LIGHT
    never again flood these eyes with your white
        radiance, oh gods, my eyes. All, all
    the oracles have proven true. I, Oedipus, I
    am the child
    of parents who should never have been mine—
        doomed, doomed!
    Now everything is clear—I
    lived with a woman, she was my mother, I slept in
        my mother's bed, and I
    murdered, murdered my father,
    the man whose blood flows in these veins of mine,   1500
    whose blood stains these two hands red.

OEDIPUS *raises his hands to the sun, then turns and walks into
the palace.*

CHORUS: man after man after man
    o mortal generations
    here once
    almost not here
    what are we
    dust ghosts images a rustling of air
    nothing nothing
    we breathe on the abyss
    we are the abyss   1510
    our happiness no more than traces of a dream
    the high noon sun sinking into the sea
    the red spume of its wake raining behind it
    we are you
    we are you Oedipus
    dragging your maimed foot
    in agony
    and now that I see your life finally revealed
    your life fused with the god
    blazing out of the black nothingness of all we know   1520
    I say
    no happiness lasts nothing human lasts

    wherever you aimed you hit
    no archer had your skill
    you grew rich powerful great
    everything came falling to your feet
    o Zeus
    after he killed the Sphinx
    whose claws curled under
    whose weird song of the future baffled and   1530
        destroyed
    he stood like a tower high above our country
    warding off death

and from then on Oedipus we called you
king our king
draped you in gold
our highest honors were yours
and you ruled this shining city
Thebes   Thebes

now
your story is pain pity no story is worse   1540
than yours Oedipus
ruined savage blind
as you struggle with your life
as your life changes
and breaks and shows you who you are
Oedipus   Oedipus
son father you harbored in the selfsame place
the same place sheltered you both
bridegroom
how could the furrow your father plowed   1550
not have cried out all this time
while you lay there unknowing
and saw the truth too late

time like the sun sees all things
and it sees you
you cannot hide from that light
your own life opening itself to you
to all
married unmarried father son
for so long   1560
justice comes like the dawn
always
and it shows the world your marriage now

I wish
o child of Laios
I wish I had never seen you
I grieve for you
wail after wail fills me and pours out
because of you my breath came flowing back
but now   1570
the darkness of your life
floods my eyes

The palace doors open. A SERVANT *enters and approaches the* CHORUS *and audience.*

SERVANT: Noble citizens, honored above all others in
    Thebes,
  if you still care for the house of Laios,
  if you still can feel the spirit of those who ruled
      before, now
  the horrors you will hear, the horrors you will see,
      will shake your hearts and shatter you with
      grief beyond enduring.
  Not even the waters of those great rivers Ister and
      Phasis
  could wash away the blood
  that now darkens every stone of this shining house,   1580
  this house that will reveal, soon, soon
  the misery and evil two mortals,

both masters of this house, have brought upon
    themselves.

  The griefs we cause ourselves cut deepest of all.
LEADER: What we already know
    has hurt us enough,
    has made us cry out in pain.
  What more can you say?
SERV.: This:
    Jocasta is dead. The queen is dead.   1590
LEADER: Ah, poor
    unhappy Jocasta,
    how did she die?
SERV.: She killed herself. She did it.
  But you did not see what happened there,
  you were not there, in the palace. You did not see it.
  I did.
  I will tell you how Queen Jocasta died,
  the whole story, all of it. All I can remember.
  After her last words to Oedipus   1600
  she rushed past us through the entrance hall,
      screaming,
  raking her hair with both hands, and flew into the
      bedroom, *their* bedroom,
  and slammed the doors shut as she lunged at her
      bridal bed,
  crying "Laios" "Laios"—dead all these years—
  remembering Laios—how his own son years ago
  grew up and then killed him, leaving her to
  sleep with her own son, to have his children, *their*
      children,
  children—not sons, not daughters, something else,
      monsters. . . .
  Then she collapsed, sobbing, cursing the bed where
      she held both men in her arms,
  got husband from husband, children from her child.   1610
  We heard it all, but suddenly, I couldn't tell what was
      happening.
  Oedipus came crashing in, he was howling,
  stalking up and down—we couldn't take our eyes off
      him—
  and we stopped listening to her pitiful cries.
  We stood there, watching him move like a bull,
      lurching, charging,
  shouting at each of us to give him a sword,
      demanding we tell him
  where his wife was, that woman whose womb
      carried him,
  him and his children, that wife who gave him birth.
  Some god, some demon, led him to her, and he
      knew—
  none of us showed him—   1620
  suddenly a mad, inhuman cry burst from his mouth
  as if the wind rushed through his tortured body,
  and he heaved against those bedroom doors so the
      hinges whined
  and bent from their sockets and the bolts snapped,
  and he stood in the room.
  There she was—
  we could see her—his wife

dangling by her neck from a noose of braided, silken
    cords
tied to a rafter, still swaying.
And when he saw her he bellowed and stretched up   1630
    and loosened the rope,
cradling her in one arm,
and slowly laid her body on the ground.

That's when it happened—he
ripped off the gold
brooches she was wearing—one on each shoulder of
    her gown—
and raised them over his head—you could see them
    flashing—
and tilted his face up and
brought them right down into his eyes
and the long pins sank deep, all the way back into
    the sockets,
and he shouted at his eyes: 1640
"Now you won't see me, you won't see
my agonies or my crimes,
but in endless darkness, always, there you'll see
those I never should have seen.
And those I should have known were my parents,
    father and mother—
these eyes will never see their faces in the light.
These eyes will never see the light again, never."
Cursing his two blind eyes over and over, he
lifted the brooches again and drove their pins
    through his eyeballs up
to the hilts until they were pulp, until the blood   1650
    streamed out
soaking his beard and cheeks,
a black storm splashing its hail across his face.

Two mortals acted. Now grief tears their lives apart
as if that pain sprang from a single, sorrowing root
to curse each one, man and wife. For all those years
their happiness was truly happiness, but now, now
wailing, madness, shame and death,
every evil men have given a name,
everything criminal and vile
that mankind suffers they suffer. Not one evil is   1660
    missing.
LEADER: But now
    does this torn, anguished man
    have any rest from his pain?
SERV.: No, no—
    then he shouted at us to open the doors and show
        everyone in Thebes
    his father's killer, his mother's—I cannot say it.
    Once we have seen him as he is
    he will leave Thebes, lift the curse from his city—
    banish himself, cursed by his own curses.
    But his strength is gone, his whole life is pain,   1670
    more pain than any man can bear.
    He needs help, someone to guide him.
    He is alone, and blind. Look,
    look—the palace doors are opening—now
    a thing

so horrible will stand before you
you will shudder with disgust and try to turn away
while your hearts will swell with pity for what you see.

The central doors open. OEDIPUS *enters, led by his household
servants. His mask is covered with blood. The* CHORUS *begin a
dirge to which* OEDIPUS *responds antiphonally.*

CHORUS: horror horror o what suffering
    men see   1680
    but none is worse than this
    Oedipus o
    how could you have slashed out your eyes
    what god leaped on you
    from beyond the last border of space
    what madness entered you
    clawing even more misery into you
    I cannot look at you

    but there are questions
    so much I would know   1690
    so much that I would see
    no no
    the shape of your life makes me shudder
OED.: I   I
    this voice of agony
    I am what place am I
    where? Not here, nowhere I know!
    What force, what tide breaks over my life?
    Pain, demon stabbing into me
    leaving nothing, nothing, no man I know, not human,   1700
    fate howling out of nowhere what am I
    fire a voice where where
    is it being taken?
LEADER: Beyond everything to a place
    so terrible nothing is seen there, nothing is heard.

OED.: *(reaching out, groping)*

    Thing   thing   darkness
    spilling into me, my
    black cloud smothering me forever,
    nothing can stop you, nothing can escape,
    I cannot push you away.   1710

    I am
    nothing but my own cries breaking
    again and again
    the agony of those gold pins
    the memory of what I did
    stab me
    again
    again.
LEADER: What can you feel but pain.
    It all comes back, pain in remorse,   1720
    remorse in pain, to tear you apart with grief.
OED.: Dear, loyal friend
    you, only you, are still there with me, still care
    for this blind, tortured man.
    Oh,
    I know you are there, I know you, friend,
    even in this darkness, friend, touched by your voice.

LEADER: What you did was horrible,
    but how could you quench the fire of your eyes,
    what demon lifted your hands?   1730
OED.: Apollo   Apollo
    it was Apollo, always Apollo,
    who brought each of my agonies to birth,
    but I,
    nobody else, *I*,
    I raised these two hands of mine, held them above
        my head,
    and plunged them down,
    I stabbed out these eyes.
    Why should I have eyes? Why,
    when nothing I saw was worth seeing?   1740
    Nothing.
LEADER: Nothing. Nothing.
OED.: Oh friends. Nothing.
    No one to see, no one to love,
    no one to speak to, no one to hear!
            Friends, friends, lead me away now.
    Lead me away from Thebes—Oedipus,
    destroyer and destroyed,
    the man whose life is hell
    for others and for himself, the man   1750
    more hated by the gods than any other man, ever.
LEADER: Oh I pity you,
    I weep for your fate
    and for your mind,
    for what it is to be you, Oedipus.
    I wish you had never seen the man you are.
OED.: I hate
    the man who found me, cut the thongs from my
        feet,
    snatched me from death, cared for me—
    I wish he were dead!   1760
    I should have died up there on those wild, desolate
        slopes of Kithairon.
    Then my pain and the pain
    those I love suffer now
    never would have been.
LEADER: These are my wishes too.
OED.: Then I never would have murdered my father,
    never heard men call me my mother's husband.

    Now
    I am
    Oedipus!   1770
    Oedipus, who lay in that loathsome bed, made love
        there in that bed,
    his father's and mother's bed, the bed
    where he was born.
    No gods anywhere now, not for me, now,
    unholy, broken man.
    What man ever suffered grief like this?
LEADER: How can I say that what you did was right?
    Better to be dead than live blind.
OED.: I did what I had to do. No more advice.
    How could *my* eyes,   1780
    when I went down into that black, sightless place
        beneath the earth,

the place where the dead go down, how,
how could I have looked at anything,
with what human eyes could I have gazed
on my father, on my mother—
oh gods, my mother!
What I did against those two
not even strangling could punish.

And my children, how would the sight of them, born
    as they were born,
be sweet? Not to these eyes of mine, never to these   1790
    eyes.
Nothing, nothing is left me now—no city with its
    high walls,
no shining statues of the gods. I stripped all these
    things from myself—
I, Oedipus, fallen lower than any man now, born
    nobler than the best,
born the king of Thebes! Cursed with my own
    curses, I
commanded Thebes to drive out the killer.
I banished the royal son of Laios, the man the gods
    revealed
is stained with the awful stain. The secret stain
that I myself revealed is *my* stain. And now, revealed
    at last,
how could I ever look men in the eyes?
Never. Never.   1800

If I could, I would have walled my ears so they heard
    nothing,
I would have made this body of mine a wall.
I would have heard nothing, tasted nothing, smelled
    nothing, seen
nothing.
No thought. No feeling. Nothing. Nothing.
So pain would never reach me any more.

O Kithairon,
why did you shelter me and take me in?
Why did you let me live? Better to have died on that
    bare slope of yours
where no man would ever have seen me or known   1810
    the secret of my birth!

Polybos, Corinth, that house I thought was my
    father's home,
how beautiful I was when you sheltered me as a
    child
and oh what disease festered beneath that beauty.
Now everyone knows the secret of my birth, knows
how vile I am.
O roads, secret valley, cluster of oaks,
O narrow place where two roads join a third,
roads that drank my blood as it streamed from my
    hands,
flowing from my dead father's body,
do you remember me now?   1820
Do you remember what I did with my own two
    hands, there in your presence,

and what I did after that, when I came here to
    Thebes?
O marriage, marriage, you gave me my life, and then
from the same seed, *my* seed, spewed out
fathers, brothers, sisters, children, brides, wives—
nothing, no words can express the shame.
No more words. Men should not name what men
    should never do.

(*To the* CHORUS)

    Gods, oh gods, gods,
    hide me, hide me
    now   1830
    far away from Thebes,
    kill me,
    cast me into the sea,
    drive me where you will never see me—never again.

(*Reaching out to the* CHORUS, *who back away*)

    Touch this poor man, touch me,
    don't be afraid to touch me. Believe me, nobody,
    nobody but me can bear
    this fire of anguish.
    It is mine. Mine.
LEADER: Kreon has come.   1840
    Now he, not you, is the sole guardian of Thebes,
    and only he can grant you what you ask.

OED.: (*turning toward the palace*)

    What can I say to him, how can anything I say
    make him listen now?
    I wronged him. I accused him, and now everything
        I said
    proves I am vile.

KREON: (*enters from the entrance to the right. He is
    accompanied by men who gather around* OEDIPUS)

    I have not come to mock you, Oedipus; I have not
    come to blame you for the past.

(*To attendants*)

    You men, standing there, if you have no respect for
        human dignity,
    at least revere the master of life,
    the all-seeing sun whose light nourishes   1850
    every living thing on earth.
    Come, cover this cursed, naked, holy thing, hide him
    from the earth and the sacred rain and the light,
    you powers who cringe from his touch.
    Take him. Do it now. Be reverent.
    Only his family should see and hear his grief.
    Their grief.
OED.: I beg you, Kreon, if you love the gods,
    grant me what I ask.
    I have been vile to you, worse than vile.   1860
    I have hurt you, terribly, and yet
    you have treated me with kindness, with nobility.
    You have calmed my fear, you did not turn away
        from me.
    Do what I ask. Do it for yourself, not for me.

KREON: What do you want from me, Oedipus?
OED.: Drive me out of Thebes, do it now, now—
    drive me someplace where no man can speak to me,
    where no man can see me anymore.
KREON: Believe me, Oedipus, I would have done it long
        ago.
    But I refuse to act until I know precisely what the   1870
        god desires.
OED.: Apollo has revealed what he desires. Everything is
    clear.
    I killed my father, I am polluted and unclean.
    I must die.
KREON: That is what the god commanded, Oedipus.
    But there are no precedents for what has happened.
    We need to *know* before we act.
OED.: Do you care so much for me, enough to ask Apollo?
    For *me*, Oedipus?
KREON: Now even you will trust the god, I think.
OED.: I will. And I turn to you, I implore you, Kreon—   1880
    the woman lying dead inside, your sister,
    give her whatever burial you think best.
                               As for me,
    never let this city of my fathers see me here in
        Thebes.
    Let me go and live on the mountain, on Kithairon—
        the mountain
    my parents intended for my grave.
    Let me die the way they wanted me to die: slowly,
        alone—
    die *their* way.
    And yet this much I know—
                           no sickness,   1890
    no ordinary, natural death is mine.
    I have been saved, preserved, kept alive
    for some strange fate, for something far more awful
        still.
    When that thing comes, let it take me
    where it will.

(OEDIPUS *turns, looking for something, waiting*)

    As for my sons, Kreon,
    they are grown men, they can look out for
        themselves.
    But my daughters, those two poor girls of mine,
    who have never left their home before, never left
        their father's side,
    who ate at my side every day, who shared whatever   1900
        was mine,
    I beg you, Kreon,
    care for them, love them.
    But more than anything, Kreon,
    I want to touch them,

(*he begins to lift his hands*)

    let me touch them with these hands of mine,
    let them come to me so we can grieve together.
    My noble lord, if only I could touch them with my
        hands,
    they would still be mine just as they were
    when I had eyes that could still see.

(OEDIPUS' *two small daughters are brought out of the palace*)

O gods, gods, is it possible? Do I hear   1910
my two daughters crying? Has Kreon pitied me and
    brought me
what I love more than my life—
my daughters?

KREON: I brought them to you, knowing how much you
    love them, Oedipus,
knowing the joy you would feel if they were here.

OED.: May the gods who watch over the path of your life,
    Kreon,
prove kinder to you than they were to me.
Where are you, children?
Come, come to your brother's hands—

(*taking his daughters into his arms*)

his mother was your mother, too,   1920
come to these hands which made these eyes, bright
    clear eyes once,
sockets seeing nothing, the eyes
of the man who fathered you. Look . . . your father's
    eyes,
your father—
who knew nothing until now, saw nothing until
    now, and became
the husband of the woman who gave him birth.
                              I weep for you
when I think how men will treat you, how bitter
    your lives will be.
What festivals will you attend, whose homes will
    you visit
and not be assailed by whispers, and people's stares?   1930
Where will you go and not leave in tears?
And when the time comes for you to marry,
what men will take you as their brides, and risk the
    shame of marrying
the daughters of Oedipus?
What sorrow will not be yours?
Your father killed his father, made love
to the woman who gave birth to him. And he
    fathered you
in the same place where he was fathered.
That is what you will hear; that is what they will say.
Who will marry you then? You will never marry,   1940
but grow hard and dry like wheat so far beyond
    harvest
that the wind blows its white flakes into the winter
    sky.
Oh Kreon,
now you are the only father my daughters have.
Jocasta and I, their parents, are lost to them forever.
These poor girls are yours. Your blood.
Don't let them wander all their lives.
begging, alone, unmarried, helpless.

Don't let them suffer as their father has. Pity them,
    Kreon,
pity these girls, so young and helpless except for you.   1950
Promise me this. Noble Kreon,
touch me with your hand, give me a sign.

(KREON *takes his hands*)

    Daughters,
daughters, if you were older, if you could
    understand,
there is so much more I would say to you.
But for now, I give you this prayer—
                              Live,
live your lives, live each day as best you can,
may your lives be happier than your father's was.

KREON: No more grief. Come in.   1960
OED.: I must. But obedience comes hard.
KREON: Everything has its time.
OED.: First, promise me this.
KREON: Name it.
OED.: Banish me from Thebes.
KREON: I cannot. Ask the gods for that.
OED.: The gods hate me.
KREON: Then you will have your wish.
OED.: You promise?
KREON: I say only what I mean.   1970
OED.: Then lead me in.

(OEDIPUS *reaches out and touches his daughters, trying to take
them with him*)

KREON: Oedipus, come with me. Let your daughters go.
    Come.
OED.: No. You will not take my daughters. I forbid it.
KREON: You *forbid* me?
    You have no power any more.
    All the great power you once had is gone, gone
        forever.

The CHORUS *turn to face the audience.* KREON *leads* OEDIPUS
*toward the palace. His daughters follow. He moves slowly, and
disappears into the palace as the* CHORUS *ends.*

CHORUS: O citizens of Thebes, this is Oedipus,
    who solved the famous riddle, who held more power
        than any mortal.
    See what he is: all men gazed on his fortunate life,   1980
    all men envied him, but look at him, look.
    All he had, all this man was,
    pulled down and swallowed by the storm of his own
        life,
    and by the god.
    Keep your eyes on that last day, on your dying.
    Happiness and peace, they were not yours
    unless at death you can look back on your life and
        say
    I lived, I did not suffer.

Questions for Critical Thinking

1. What is the role and purpose of Teiresias, and how does he interact with Oedipus? Discuss the scenes between Teiresias and Oedipus as examples of how Sophocles explores the relationships between humans.

2. Was it Oedipus's arrogance or ignorance that brought him down? Should his behavior and his fate be an example to all of us, and what can we learn from this Greek play?

HERODOTUS
Selections from the *Histories*

Herodotus (he-ROD-uh-tuhs) (ca. 484–430 BCE), the Greek historian who is known as the "Father of History," was born in Halicarnassus (modern Bodrum, Turkey), a seaport on the Aegean Sea, then under Persian rule. While there is little record of his family, education, and early years, it is known that he departed Halicarnassus in about 457 BCE and traveled throughout Asia Minor, including most of the Persian Empire; made side trips to Libya and Egypt; and crossed the Black Sea into what is now Ukraine and southern Russia. He also visited northern Greece and spent several years in Samos and Athens before settling in southern Italy in a Greek colony.

The *Histories,* whose narrative ends in about 430 BCE, were published soon after Herodotus's death. Scholars at the Library in Alexandria, around the middle of the third century BCE, probably divided the original work into its nine books—the format still used today. The first six books provide the background leading up to the series of wars between Persia and Greece (499–479 BCE), usually known as the Persian Wars, and the final three books detail the history of the wars, including the invasion of Greece, the major battles, and the wars' turning points. The first six books also set forth the customs, traditions, legends, and histories of several societies, including those of the Egyptians, Medes, Assyrians, and Persians. Herodotus's accounts and assessments of these cultures and their histories allow him to compare and contrast societies, to speculate on why empires rise and fall, and to comment upon and analyze human behavior. In particular, his extensive coverage of the Persian Empire over several chapters—its geography, history, dynasties, and social structure—sets the stage for the historic conflict between the Persians and the Greeks.

Western scholars have debated the content and importance of the *Histories.* They concede that Herodotus was the first to practice historical writing in the modern sense and to write a prose work of such great length. Nevertheless, Herodotus was influenced by Greece's older poetic tradition associated with Homer, which was oral and grew out of storytelling rituals (see the *Iliad* and the *Odyssey* in Chapter 2). Herodotus also accepted myths and folklore as part of a society's history, though he often qualified them, mixing his own observations, interviews, and evidence in his descriptions. Because he sometimes included myths and folktales, some critics charge he was naive and gullible, while others argue that Herodotus understood and appreciated their role in uncovering and revealing a civilization's past, mores, and values. Most scholars agree that Herodotus tried to be impartial and attempted to understand other societies and be tolerant of their patterns of life and values. Indeed, by so doing, he represented the Persians as fellow humans who shared many characteristics with the Greeks. He also recognized that the Persian Wars symbolized a titanic struggle between two contrasting ways of life—what may today be called the East and the West—and that their outcome would determine the future of much of human history. Herodotus knew that if Persia defeated the Greeks, a military-based dynasty would replace Greek democracy and an open society that honored the individual and respected rationality would be lost forever.

Students of history also agree that Herodotus was the first historian to show that human behavior, often driven by greed, arrogance, and folly, explains the rise and fall of most societies. For example, the overreaching of a ruler's power—expressed through vanity, or *hubris*—could bring defeat, disgrace, and an ignoble end, as he illustrated in his depiction of the Persian kings. Finally, most historians concede that Herodotus, as a humanist, liberated the mind from its enthrallment to religious forces by showing that good fortune and bad fortune, or fate, chance, and human choices—not the gods—determine the lives of individuals and the destiny of societies.

Reading the Selections

In the first selection, from Book One, Herodotus recounts four myths or stories about the origins of the conflicts between the Greeks and the Persians, concluding with his version of why and how both sides went to war. The second selection, from Book Two, typifies Herodotus's impartiality and detailed explanations of another culture, in this case, the Egyptians. The third selection, from Book Six, begins the narrative of the Persian Wars, dramatizing the uncertainties before battle and the heroics of the Greeks at Marathon, when their outnumbered army defeated the Persians. The fourth selection, from Book Seven, demonstrates Herodotus's attention to detail. In it, he reveals the character of the Persian king Xerxes (ca. 519–465 BCE), showing the ruler's reaction to the collapse of the bridge his troops built over the Hellespont.

∞

Book One, Introduction and Myths

Herodotus of Halicarnassus,[15] his *Researches* are here set down to preserve the memory of the past by putting on record the astonishing achievements both of our own and of other peoples; and more particularly, to show how they came into conflict.

Learned Persians put the responsibility for the quarrel on the Phoenicians.[16] These people came originally from the so called Red Sea,[17] and as soon as they had penetrated to the Mediterranean and settled in the country where they are to-day, they took to making long trading voyages. Loaded with Egyptian and Assyrian goods, they called at various places along the coast, including Argos, in those days the most important place in the land, now called Hellas.[18]

Here in Argos they displayed their wares, and five or six days later when they were nearly sold out, a number of women came down to the beach to see the fair. Amongst these was the king's daughter, whom Greek and Persian writers agree in calling Io, daughter of Inachus. These women were standing about near the vessel's stern, buying what they fancied, when suddenly the Phoenician sailors passed the word along and made a rush at them. The greater number got away; but Io and some others were caught and bundled aboard the ship, which cleared at once and made off for Egypt.

This, according to the Persian account (the Greeks have a different story), was how Io came to Egypt; and this was the first in a series of provocative acts.

Later on some Greeks, whose name the Persians fail to record—they were probably Cretans[19]—put into the Phoenician port of Tyre and carried off the king's daughter Europa, thus giving them tit for tat.

For the next outrage it was the Greeks again who were responsible. They sailed in an armed merchantman to Aea in Colchis on the river Phasis,[20] and, not content

---

[15] **Halicarnassus** Modern city of Bodrum, Turkey, on the southeast coast of the peninsula on the Aegean Sea. Earlier a Greek colony, but occupied by the Persians when Herodotus was born.
[16] **Phoenicians** Inhabitants from Phoenicia, which was a maritime country in the eastern Mediterranean and is now part of modern Lebanon.
[17] **Red Sea** The Persian Gulf is what Herodotus means. The Greeks used this term for what is the southern Indian Ocean.
[18] **Hellas** The Greeks called their land Hellas and themselves, Hellenes.

[19] **Cretans** Inhabitants from the island of Crete in the eastern Mediterranean.
[20] **Aea, Colchis, Phasis** Ancient names for the modern-day city of Kutaisi located in the Republic of Georgia (Colchis) and on the Rioni (Phasis) River. Georgia is on the east coast of the Black Sea, south of the Caucasus Mountains.

with the regular business which had brought them there, they abducted the king's daughter Medea.[21] The king sent to Greece demanding reparations and his daughter's return; but the only answer he got was that the Greeks had no intention of offering reparation, having received none themselves for the abduction of Io from Argos.

The accounts go on to say that some forty or fifty years afterwards Paris, the son of Priam, was inspired by these stories to steal a wife for himself out of Greece, being confident that he would not have to pay for the venture any more than the Greeks had done. And that was how he came to carry off Helen.[22]

The first idea of the Greeks after the rape was to send a demand for satisfaction and for Helen's return. The demand was met by a reference to the seizure of Medea and the injustice of expecting satisfaction from people to whom they themselves had refused it, not to mention the fact that they had kept the girl.

Thus far there had been nothing worse than woman-stealing on both sides; but for what happened next the Greeks, they say, were seriously to blame; for it was the Greeks who were, in a military sense, the aggressors. Abducting young women, in their opinion, is not, indeed, a

lawful act; but it is stupid after the event to make a fuss about it. The only sensible thing is to take no notice; for it is obvious that no young woman allows herself to be abducted if she does not wish to be. The Asiatics, according to the Persians, took the seizure of the women lightly enough, but not so the Greeks: the Greeks, merely on account of a girl from Sparta, raised a big army, invaded Asia and destroyed the empire of Priam. From that root sprang their belief in the perpetual enmity of the Grecian world towards them—Asia with its various foreign-speaking peoples belonging to the Persians, Europe and the Greek states being, in their opinion, quite separate and distinct from them.

Such then is the Persian story. In their view it was the capture of Troy that first made them enemies of the Greeks. 10

As to Io, the Phoenicians do not accept the Persians' account; they deny that they took her to Egypt by force. On the contrary, the girl while she was still in Argos went to bed with the ship's captain, found herself pregnant, and, ashamed to face her parents, sailed away voluntarily to escape exposure.

So much for what Persians and Phoenicians say; and I have no intention of passing judgement on its truth or falsity. I prefer to rely on my own knowledge, and to point out who it was in actual fact that first injured the Greeks; then I will proceed with my history, telling the story as I go along of small cities no less than of great. For most of those which were great once are small to-day; and those which used to be small were great in my own time. Knowing, therefore, that human prosperity never abides long in the same place, I shall pay attention to both alike.

---

[21] **Medea** This is part of the story of Jason and the Argonauts when he abducted Medea. She later helped him obtain the Golden Fleece and became his wife for a short time.
[22] **Helen** This paragraph refers to the story of Paris abducting Helen, the wife of Menelaus, the event that set off the Trojan War, which Homer recorded in the *Iliad*.

Book Two, Description of the Egyptians

About Egypt I shall have a great deal more to relate because of the number of remarkable things which the country contains, and because of the fact that more monuments which beggar description are to be found there than anywhere else in the world. That is reason enough for my dwelling on it at greater length. Not only is the Egyptian climate peculiar to that country, and the Nile different in its behaviour from other rivers elsewhere, but the Egyptians themselves in their manners and customs seem to have reversed the ordinary practices of mankind. For instance, women attend market and are employed in trade, while men stay at home and do the weaving. In weaving the normal way is to work the threads of the weft upwards, but the Egyptians work them downwards. Men in Egypt carry loads on their heads, women on their shoulders; women pass water standing up, men sitting down. To ease themselves they go indoors, but eat outside in the streets, on the theory that what is unseemly but necessary should be done in private, and what is not un-seemly should be done openly. No woman holds priestly office, either in the service of goddess or god; only men are priests in both cases. Sons are under no compulsion to support

their parents if they do not wish to do so, but daughters must, whether they wish it or not. Elsewhere priests grow their hair long, in Egypt they shave their heads. In other nations the relatives of the deceased in time of mourning cut their hair, but the Egyptians, who shave at all other times, mark a death by letting the hair grow both on head and chin. They live with their animals—unlike the rest of the world, who live apart from them. Other men live on wheat and barley, but any Egyptian who does so is blamed for it, their bread being made from spelt, or *Zea* as some call it. Dough they knead with their feet, but clay with their hands—and even handle dung. They practise circumcision, while men of other nations—except those who have learnt from Egypt—leave their private parts as nature made them. Men in Egypt have two garments each, women only one. The ordinary practice at sea is to make sheets fast to ring-bolts fitted outboard; the Egyptians fit them inboard. In writing or calculating, instead of going, like the Greeks, from left to right, the Egyptians go from right to left—and obstinately maintain that theirs is the dexterous method, ours being left-handed and awkward. They have two sorts of writing, the sacred and the common. They are religious to excess, beyond any other nation in the world, and here are some of the customs which illustrate the fact; they drink from brazen cups which they scour every day—everyone, without exception. They wear linen clothes which they make a special point of continually washing. They circumcise themselves for cleanliness' sake, preferring to be clean rather than comely. The priests shave their bodies all over every other day to guard against the presence of lice, or anything else equally unpleasant, while they are about their religious duties; the priests, too, wear linen only, and shoes made from the papyrus plant—these materials, for dress and shoes, being the only ones allowed them. They bath in cold water twice a day and twice every night—and observe innumerable other ceremonies besides. Their life, however, is not by any means all hardship, for they enjoy advantages too: for instance, they are free from all personal expense, having bread made for them out of the sacred grain, and a plentiful daily supply of goose-meat and beef, with wine in addition. Fish they are forbidden to touch; and as for beans they cannot even bear to look at them, because they imagine they are unclean (in point of fact the Egyptians never sow beans, and even if any happen to grow wild, they will not eat them, either raw or boiled). They do not have a single priest for each god, but a number, of which one is chief-priest, and when a chief-priest dies his son is appointed to succeed him.

Book Six, Battle of Marathon

Amongst the Athenian commanders opinion was divided: some were against risking a battle, on the ground that the Athenian force was too small to stand a chance of success; others—and amongst them Miltiades[23]—urged it. It seemed for a time as if the more faint-hearted policy would be adopted—and so it would have been but for the action of Miltiades. In addition to the ten generals, there was another person entitled to a vote, namely the polemarch, or War Archon, appointed by lot.[24] This office (which formerly carried an equal vote in military decisions with the generals) was held at this time by Callimachus of Aphidnae.[25] To Callimachus, therefore, Miltiades turned. 'It is now in your hands, Callimachus,' he said, 'either to enslave Athens, or to make her free and to leave behind you for all future generations a memory more glorious than even Harmodius and Aristogeiton[26] left. Never in our history have we Athenians been in such peril as now. If we submit to the Persians, Hippias[27] will be restored to power—and there is little doubt what misery must then ensue: but if we fight and win, then this city of ours may well grow to pre-eminence amongst all the cities of Greece. If you ask me how this can be, and how the decision rests with you, I will tell you: we commanders are ten in number, and we are not agreed upon what action to take; half of us are for a battle, half against it. If we refuse to fight, I have little doubt that the result will be bitter dissension; our purpose will be shaken, and we shall submit to Persia. But if we fight before the rot can show itself in any of us, then, if God gives us fair play, we can not only fight but win. Yours is the decision; all hangs upon you; vote on my side, and our country will be free—yes, and the mistress of Greece. But if you support those who have voted against fighting, that happiness will be denied you—you will get the opposite.'

Miltiades' words prevailed, and by the vote of Callimachus the War Archon the decision to fight was made.

The generals held the presiding position in succession, each for a day; and those of them who had voted with Miltiades, offered when their turn for duty came to surrender it to him. Miltiades accepted the offer, but would not fight until the day came when he would in any case have presided. When it did come, the Athenian army moved into position for the coming struggle. The right wing was commanded by Callimachus—for it was the regular practice at that time in Athens that the War Archon should lead the right wing; then followed the tribes, in their regular order; and, finally, on the left wing, were the Plataeans.[28] Ever since the battle of Marathon, when the Athenians offer sacrifice at their quadrennial festival, the herald links the names of Athens and Plataea in the prayer for God's blessing.

One result of the disposition of Athenian troops before the battle was the weakening of their centre by the

[23] **Miltiades** Leader of the Chersonese ("peninsula"), allies of the Athenians, who were from the modern peninsula of Gallipoli in Turkey.
[24] **polemarch, or War Archon** This office, by the time of Herodotus, was mainly ceremonial, but he reverts back to earlier times when the War Archon did have a vote in matters of war and thus the parentheses in the next sentence.
[25] **Callimachus of Aphidnae** A Greek official from the small settlement, or deme, of Aphidnae, north of Athens, which was part of the Athenian democratic government.
[26] **Harmodius and Aristogeiton** The two Athenians who killed a political leader who was trying to set up a dictatorship; thus, they had helped save Athens in the past. Apparently both were from Aphidnae, which made **Miltiades'** appeal more attractive to **Callimachus.**
[27] **Hippias** An Athenian who had been expelled from the city because he was a threat to the democratic government and had joined the Persians. Thus, if the Athenians lost, he would return to rule them.

[28] **Plataeans** Citizens from the city of Plataea, which was located in central Greece and near the border of Attica, the land of Athens. They fought with the Athenians during the entire Persian War.

effort to extend the line sufficiently to cover the whole Persian front; the two wings were strong, but the line in the centre was only a few ranks deep. The dispositions made, and the preliminary sacrifice promising success, the word was given to move, and the Athenians advanced at a run towards the enemy, not less than a mile away. The Persians, seeing the attack developing at the double, prepared to meet it, thinking it suicidal madness for the Athenians to risk an assault with so small a force—rushing in with no support from either cavalry or archers. Well, that was what they imagined; nevertheless, the Athenians came on, closed with the enemy all along the line, and fought in a way not to be forgotten. They were the first Greeks, so far as I know, to charge at a run, and the first who dared to look without flinching at Persian dress and the men who wore it; for until that day came, no Greek could hear even the word Persian without terror.

The struggle at Marathon was long drawn out. In the centre, held by the Persians themselves and the Sacae,[29] the advantage was with the foreigners, who were so far successful as to break the Greek line and pursue the fugitives inland from the sea; but the Athenians on one wing and the Plataeans on the other were both victorious. Having got the upper hand, they left the defeated enemy to make their escape, and then, drawing the two wings together into a single unit, they turned their attention to the Persians who had broken through in the centre. Here again they were triumphant, chasing the routed enemy, and cutting them down until they came to the sea, and men were calling for fire and taking hold of the ships.

---

[29] **Sacae** The name Herodotus gave to the nomadic tribes living to the northeast of the Persian Empire, which today would include southern Russia and Ukraine.

Book Seven, Xerxes at the Hellespont

In Sardis[30] Xerxes' first act was to send representatives to every place in Greece except Athens and Sparta with a demand for earth and water and a further order to prepare entertainment for him against his coming. This renewed demand for submission was due to his confident belief that the Greeks who had previously refused to comply with the demand of Darius[31] would now be frightened into complying with his own. It was to prove whether or not he was right that he took this step.

He then prepared to move forward to Abydos,[32] where a bridge had already been constructed across the Hellespont from Asia to Europe. Between Sestos and Madytus in the Chersonese[33] there is a rocky headland running out into the water opposite Abydos. It was here not long afterwards that the Greeks under Xanthippus the son of Ariphron took Artaÿctes the Persian governor of Sestos, and nailed him alive to a plank—he was the man who collected women in the temple of Protesilaus at Elaeus and committed various acts of sacrilege. This headland was the point to which Xerxes' engineers carried their two bridges from Abydos—a distance of seven furlongs.[34] One was constructed by the Phoenicians using flax cables, the other by the Egyptians with papyrus cables. The work was successfully completed, but a subsequent storm of great violence smashed it up and carried everything away.

Xerxes was very angry when he learned of the disaster, and gave orders that the Hellespont should receive three hundred lashes and have a pair of fetters thrown into it. I have heard before now that he also sent people to brand it with hot irons. He certainly instructed the men with the whips to utter, as they wielded them, the barbarous and presumptuous words: 'You salt and bitter stream, your master lays this punishment upon you for injuring him, who never injured you. But Xerxes the King will cross you, with or without your permission. No man sacrifices to you, and you deserve the neglect by your acid and muddy waters.' In addition to punishing the Hellespont Xerxes gave orders that the men responsible for building the bridges should have their heads cut off. The men who received these invidious orders duly carried them out, and other engineers completed the work. The method employed was as follows: galleys and triremes[35] were lashed together to support the bridges—360 vessels for the one on the Black Sea side, and 314 for the other. They were moored slantwise to the Black Sea and at right angles to the Hellespont, in order to lessen the strain on the cables. Specially heavy anchors were laid out both upstream and downstream—those to the eastward to hold the vessels against winds blowing down the straits from the direction of the Black Sea, those on the other side, to the westward and towards the Aegean, to take the strain when it blew from the west and south. Gaps were left in three places to allow any boats that might wish to do so to pass in or out of the Black Sea.

Once the vessels were in position, the cables were hauled taut by wooden winches ashore. This time the two sorts of cable were not used separately for each bridge, but

---

[30] **Sardis** Capital city of Lydia, in the western part of modern Turkey.
[31] **Darius** (r. 522–486 BCE), Persian king, father of Xerxes. Defeated at the Battle of Marathon.
[32] **Abydos** Town on the east side of the Hellespont in northwest Turkey.
[33] **Sestos, Madytus, Chersonese** Sestos and Madytus, in the land of the Chersonese, lay on the west side of the Hellespont, opposite Abydos, which was on the east side. See fn. 23.
[34] **furlong** A distance equal to 220 yards.

[35] **galleys and triremes** Two types of ancient war ships. The trireme was a galley with three rows of oars, as opposed to one.

both bridges had two flax cables and four papyrus ones. The flax and papyrus cables were of the same thickness and quality, but the flax was the heavier—half a fathom of it weighed 114 lb. The next operation was to cut planks equal in length to the width of the floats, lay them edge to edge over the taut cables, and then bind them together on their upper surface. That done, brushwood was put on top and spread evenly, with a layer of soil, trodden hard, over all. Finally a paling was constructed along each side, high enough to prevent horses and mules from seeing over and taking fright at the water.

The bridges were now ready; and when news came from Athos[36] that work on the canal was finished, includ-

ing the breakwaters at its two ends, which had been built to prevent the surf from silting up the entrances, the army, after wintering at Sardis and completing its preparations, started the following spring on its march to Abydos.

No sooner had the troops begun to move than the sun vanished from his place in the sky and it grew dark as night, though the weather was perfectly clear and cloudless. Xerxes, deeply troubled, asked the Magi[37] to interpret the significance of this strange phenomenon, and was given to understand that God meant to foretell to the Greeks the eclipse of their cities—for it was the sun which gave warning of the future to Greece, just as the moon did to Persia. Having heard this Xerxes continued the march in high spirits.

---

[36] **Athos** Located on the Chalcidice peninsula jutting out in the Aegean Sea from the land of Macedonia, in northern Greece.

[37] **Magi** Plural for magus. The hereditary priestly class of the Persians who advised the rulers on omens and other matters.

Questions for Critical Thinking

1. Discuss the various accounts offered by Herodotus as to the causes of the Persian Wars, note his response to these accounts, and summarize his plans to explain the origins of the conflict.

2. Compare and contrast Herodotus's explanation of the Egyptians as a people and society and his description of Xerxes' thoughts and reactions at the Hellespont as a study in human behavior.

THUCYDIDES
Selections from *History of the Peloponnesian War*

In about 450 BCE Athens was at the height of its political and cultural accomplishments; however, its towering position came at a high cost to other Greek city-states and, ultimately, to itself. Its decades of greatness were bracketed by two costly wars—the first against the Persians, which Athens won, at the beginning of the century (see Herodotus's *Histories*); and the second against a coalition of other Greek city-states, which Athens lost, at the century's end.

In the second war—known as the Peloponnesian War—Athens, with a group of like-minded allies, attempted to impose its will on neighboring city-states. Alarmed at Athenian imperialism, these city-states turned to Sparta, which, responding to their pleas, formed a military alliance that overran Athens in 404 BCE. The events of this struggle were recorded by Thucydides, an Athenian general who fought in the war until he was forced into exile for his inability to raise a siege during the war.

In his history, Thucydides set standards of scholarship that have seldom been equaled. He interviewed eyewitnesses, read the sources, and attempted to verify evidence. Although he left the work unfinished, stopping in about 410 BCE, he detailed events so vividly that the narrative still holds the attention of today's readers. He displayed a dramatic flair by inserting speeches that were attributed to generals and politicians whose decisions affected the war's outcome. Of special note is his distinction as the first writer to interpret war in purely human terms, rather than searching for divine causes. He also presented his history as "philosophy teaching by example"; that is, he used the events of the war to speculate about human nature and behavior.

Reading the Selections

In these two selections from Book II, Thucydides displays his talents as a writer and an analyst. His prose reaches poetic heights in the funeral oration, the first selection. In his chapter on the plague, the second selection, the author provides a clinical account of the disease and then assesses its impact on the populace and on Athenian society.

Pericles, the Athenian general, delivered this funeral oration during the first year of the war (430 BCE) to honor the young men who had died in battle. (Pericles himself was carried off by the plague in the next year.) In a brief introduction, Thucydides sets the scene before Pericles gives his memorial speech to the mourners.

Pericles' speech has two themes: praise for Athens and the Athenian way of life and the traditional argument that the soldiers have not died in vain. Pericles envisions Athens as a place where the individual is honored in a free and open society. Tolerance and respect for others in their private lives is matched by respect for the law on the part of those engaged in public affairs. He praises Athenian education because it emphasizes natural rather than "state-induced" courage—a dig at Sparta. He has praise for the Athenian business community, pointing out that it, like other segments of society, is committed to the general welfare. In sum, Athens is "an education to Greece."

Following Pericles' funeral oration Thucydides wrote about the plague, which swept through Athens during the second year of the Peloponnesian War. He details how the disease attacked the individual and manifested itself in body sores, high fevers, and spasms that nearly always resulted in a painful death—descriptions similar to other accounts of the plague (see Boccaccio's *The Decameron* in Chapter 10). During such times of crisis, Thucydides notes, humans turn to oracles and the supernatural for answers, and he quotes an oracle that might offer an explanation of the plague.

∞

Book II

Pericles' Funeral Oration

. . .

"Many of those who have spoken here in the past have ₁ praised the institution of this speech at the close of our ceremony. It seemed to them a mark of honour to our soldiers who have fallen in war that a speech should be made over them. I do not agree. These men have shown themselves valiant in action, and it would be enough, I think, for their glories to be proclaimed in action, as you have just seen it done at this funeral organized by the state. Our belief in the courage and manliness of so many should not be hazarded on the goodness or badness of one man's speech. Then it is not easy to speak with a proper sense of balance, when a man's listeners find it difficult to believe in the truth of what one is saying. The man who knows the facts and loves the dead may well think that an oration tells less than what he knows and what he would like to hear: others who do not know so much may feel envy for

the dead, and think the orator over-praises them, when he speaks of exploits that are beyond their own capacities. Praise of other people is tolerable only up to a certain point, the point where one still believes that one could do oneself some of the things one is hearing about. Once you get beyond this point, you will find people becoming jealous and incredulous. However, the fact is that this institution was set up and approved by our forefathers, and it is my duty to follow the tradition and do my best to meet the wishes and the expectations of every one of you.

"I shall begin by speaking about our ancestors, since it is only right and proper on such an occasion to pay them the honour of recalling what they did. In this land of ours there have always been the same people living from generation to generation up till now, and they, by their courage and their virtues, have handed it on to us, a free country. They certainly deserve our praise. Even more so do our fathers deserve it. For to the inheritance they had received they added all the empire we have now, and it was not without blood and toil that they handed it down to us of the present generation. And then we ourselves, assembled here today, who are mostly in the prime of life, have, in most directions, added to the power of our empire and have organized our State in such a way that it is perfectly well able to look after itself both in peace and in war.

"I have no wish to make a long speech on subjects familiar to you all: so I shall say nothing about the warlike deeds by which we acquired our power or the battles in which we or our fathers gallantly resisted our enemies, Greek or foreign. What I want to do is, in the first place, to discuss the spirit in which we faced our trials and also our constitution and the way of life which has made us great. After that I shall speak in praise of the dead, believing that this kind of speech is not inappropriate to the present occasion, and that this whole assembly, of citizens and foreigners, may listen to it with advantage.

"Let me say that our system of government does not copy the institutions of our neighbours. It is more the case of our being a model to others, than of our imitating anyone else. Our constitution is called a democracy because power is in the hands not of a minority but of the whole people. When it is a question of settling private disputes, everyone is equal before the law; when it is a question of putting one person before another in positions of public responsibility, what counts is not membership of a particular class, but the actual ability which the man possesses. No one, so long as he has it in him to be of service to the state, is kept in political obscurity because of poverty. And, just as our political life is free and open, so is our day-to-day life in our relations with each other. We do not get into a state with our next-door neighbour if he enjoys himself in his own way, nor do we give him the kind of black looks which, though they do no real harm, still do hurt people's feelings. We are free and tolerant in our private lives; but in public affairs we keep to the law. This is because it commands our deep respect.

"We give our obedience to those whom we put in 5 positions of authority, and we obey the laws themselves, especially those which are for the protection of the oppressed, and those unwritten laws which it is an acknowledged shame to break.

"And here is another point. When our work is over, we are in a position to enjoy all kinds of recreation for our spirits. There are various kinds of contests and sacrifices regularly throughout the year; in our own homes we find a beauty and a good taste which delight us every day and which drive away our cares. Then the greatness of our city brings it about that all the good things from all over the world flow in to us, so that to us it seems just as natural to enjoy foreign goods as our own local products.

"Then there is a great difference between us and our opponents, in our attitude towards military security. Here are some examples: Our city is open to the world, and we have no periodical deportations in order to prevent people observing or finding out secrets which might be of military advantage to the enemy. This is because we rely, not on secret weapons, but on our own real courage and loyalty. There is a difference, too, in our educational systems. The Spartans, from their earliest boyhood, are submitted to the most laborious training in courage; we pass our lives without all these restrictions, and yet are just as ready to face the same dangers as they are. Here is a proof of this: When the Spartans invade our land, they do not come by themselves, but bring all their allies with them; whereas we, when we launch an attack abroad, do the job by ourselves, and, though fighting on foreign soil, do not often fail to defeat opponents who are fighting for their own hearths and homes. As a matter of fact none of our enemies has ever yet been confronted with our total strength, because we have to divide our attention between our navy and the many missions on which our troops are sent on land. Yet, if our enemies engage a detachment of our forces and defeat it, they give themselves credit for having thrown back our entire army; or, if they lose, they claim that they were beaten by us in full strength. There are certain advantages, I think, in our way of meeting danger voluntarily, with an easy mind, instead of with a laborious training, with natural rather than with state-induced courage. We do not have to spend our time practising to meet sufferings which are still in the future; and when they are actually upon us we show ourselves just as brave as these others who are always in strict training. This is one point in which, I think, our city deserves to be admired. There are also others:

"Our love of what is beautiful does not lead to extravagance; our love of the things of the mind does not make us soft. We regard wealth as something to be properly used, rather than as something to boast about. As for poverty, no one need be ashamed to admit it: the real shame is in not taking practical measures to escape from it. Here each individual is interested not only in his own affairs but in the affairs of the state as well: even those who are mostly occupied with their own business are extremely well informed on general politics—this is a peculiarity of ours: we do not say that a man who takes no interest in politics is a man who minds his own business; we say that he has no business here at all. We Athenians, in our own persons, make our decisions on policy or submit them to proper discussions: for we do not think that there is an incompatibility between words and deeds; the worst thing is to rush into action before the consequences have been properly debated. And this is another point where we differ from other people. We are capable at the same time of taking risks and of estimating them beforehand. Others are brave out of ignorance; and, when they stop to think, they begin to fear. But the man who can most truly be accounted brave is he who best knows the meaning of what is sweet in life and of what is terrible, and then goes out undeterred to meet what is to come.

"Again, in questions of general good feeling there is a great contrast between us and most other people. We make friends by doing good to others, not by receiving good from them. This makes our friendship all the more reliable, since we want to keep alive the gratitude of those who are in our debt by showing continued goodwill to them: whereas the feelings of one who owes us something lack the same enthusiasm, since he knows that, when he repays our kindness, it will be more like paying back a debt than giving something spontaneously. We are unique in this. When we do kindnesses to others, we do not do them out of any calculations of profit or loss: we do them without afterthought, relying on our free liberality. Taking everything together then, I declare that our city is an education to Greece, and I declare that in my opinion each single one of our citizens, in all the manifold aspects of life, is able to show himself the rightful lord and owner of his own person, and do this, moreover, with exceptional grace and exceptional versatility. And to show that this is no empty boasting for the present occasion, but real tangible fact, you have only to consider the power which our city possesses and which has been won by those very qualities which I have mentioned. Athens, alone of the states we know, comes to her testing time in a greatness that surpasses what was imagined of her. In her case, and in her case alone, no invading enemy is ashamed at being defeated, and no subject can complain of being governed by people unfit for their responsibilities. Mighty indeed are the marks and monuments of our empire which we have left. Future ages will wonder at us, as the present age wonders at us now. We do not need the praises of a Homer, or of anyone else whose words may delight us for the moment, but whose estimation of facts will fall short of what is really true. For our adventurous spirit has forced an entry into every sea and into every land; and everywhere we have left behind us everlasting memorials of good done to our friends or suffering inflicted on our enemies.

"This, then, is the kind of city for which these men, 10 who could not bear the thought of losing her, nobly fought and nobly died. It is only natural that every one of us who survive them should be willing to undergo hardships in her service. And it was for this reason that I have spoken at such length about our city, because I wanted to make it clear that for us there is more at stake than there is for others who lack our advantages; also I wanted my words of praise for the dead to be set in the bright light of evidence. And now the most important of these words has been spoken. I have sung the praises of our city; but it was the courage and gallantry of these men, and of people like them, which made her splendid. Nor would you find it true in the case of many of the Greeks, as it is true of them, that no words can do more than justice to their deeds.

"To me it seems that the consummation which has overtaken these men shows us the meaning of manliness in its first revelation and in its final proof. Some of them, no doubt, had their faults; but what we ought to remember first is their gallant conduct against the enemy in defence of their native land. They have blotted out evil with good, and done more service to the commonwealth than

they ever did harm in their private lives. No one of these men weakened because he wanted to go on enjoying his wealth: no one put off the awful day in the hope that he might live to escape his poverty and grow rich. More to be desired than such things, they chose to check the enemy's pride. This, to them, was a risk most glorious, and they accepted it, willing to strike down the enemy and relinquish everything else. As for success or failure, they left that in the doubtful hands of Hope, and when the reality of battle was before their faces, they put their trust in their own selves. In the fighting, they thought it more honourable to stand their ground and suffer death than to give in and save their lives. So they fled from the reproaches of men, abiding with life and limb the brunt of battle; and, in a small moment of time, the climax of their lives, a culmination of glory, not of fear, were swept away from us.

"So and such they were, these men—worthy of their city. We who remain behind may hope to be spared their fate, but must resolve to keep the same daring spirit against the foe. It is not simply a question of estimating the advantages in theory. I could tell you a long story (and you know it as well as I do) about what is to be gained by beating the enemy back. What I would prefer is that you should fix your eyes every day on the greatness of Athens as she really is, and should fall in love with her. When you realize her greatness, then reflect that what made her great was men with a spirit of adventure, men who knew their duty, men who were ashamed to fall below a certain standard. If they ever failed in an enterprise, they made up their minds that at any rate the city should not find their courage lacking to her, and they gave to her the best contribution that they could. They gave her their lives, to her and to all of us, and for their own selves they won praises that never grow old, the most splendid of sepulchres—not the sepulchre in which their bodies are laid, but where their glory remains eternal in men's minds, always there on the right occasion to stir others to speech or to action. For famous men have the whole earth as their memorial: it is not only the inscriptions on their graves in their own country that mark them out; no, in foreign lands also, not in any visible form but in people's hearts, their memory abides and grows. It is for you to try to be like them. Make up your minds that happiness depends on being free, and freedom depends on being courageous. Let there be no relaxation in face of the perils of the war. The people who have most excuse for despising death are not the wretched and unfortunate, who have no hope of doing well for themselves, but those who run the risk of a complete reversal in their lives, and who would feel the difference most intensely, if things went wrong for them. Any intelligent man would find a humiliation caused by his own slackness more painful to bear than death, when death comes to him unperceived, in battle, and in the confidence of his patriotism."

⚭

Book II

Second Year of the War. The Plague and Its Effects

In this way the public funeral was conducted in the winter   1
that came at the end of the first year of the war. At the beginning of the following summer the Peloponnesians and
their allies, with two-thirds of their total forces as before,
invaded Attica, again under the command of the Spartan
King Archidamus, the son of Zeuxidamus. Taking up their
positions, they set about the devastation of the country.

They had not been many days in Attica before the
plague first broke out among the Athenians. Previously
attacks of the plague had been reported from many other
places in the neighbourhood of Lemnos[38] and elsewhere,
but there was no record of the disease being so virulent
anywhere else or causing so many deaths as it did in Athens. At the beginning the doctors were quite incapable of
treating the disease because of their ignorance of the right
methods. In fact mortality among the doctors was the
highest of all, since they came more frequently in contact
with the sick. Nor was any other human art or science of
any help at all. Equally useless were prayers made in the
temples, consultation of oracles, and so forth; indeed, in
the end people were so overcome by their sufferings that
they paid no further attention to such things.

The plague originated, so they say, in Ethiopia in upper Egypt, and spread from there into Egypt itself and
Libya and much of the territory of the King of Persia. In
the city of Athens it appeared suddenly, and the first cases
were among the population of Piraeus, so that it was supposed by them that the Peloponnesians had poisoned the
reservoirs.[39] Later, however, it appeared also in the upper
city, and by this time the deaths were greatly increasing in
number. As to the question of how it could first have come
about or what causes can be found adequate to explain its
powerful effect on nature, I must leave that to be considered by other writers, with or without medical experience.
I myself shall merely describe what it was like, and set
down the symptoms, knowledge of which will enable it to
be recognized, if it should ever break out again. I had the
disease myself and saw others suffering from it.

That year, as is generally admitted, was particularly
free from all other kinds of illness, though those who did
have any illness previously all caught the plague in the
end. In other cases, however, there seemed to be no reason
for the attacks. People in perfect health suddenly began to
have burning feelings in the head; their eyes became red
and inflamed; inside their mouths there was bleeding from
the throat and tongue, and the breath became unnatural

and unpleasant. The next symptoms were sneezing and
hoarseness of voice, and before long the pain settled on the
chest and was accompanied by coughing. Next the stomach was affected with stomach-aches and with vomitings
of every kind of bile that has been given a name by the
medical profession, all this being accompanied by great
pain and difficulty. In most cases there were attacks of
ineffectual retching, producing violent spasms; this sometimes ended with this stage of the disease, but sometimes
continued long afterwards. Externally the body was not
very hot to the touch, nor was there any pallor: the skin
was rather reddish and livid, breaking out into small pus-
tules and ulcers. But inside there was a feeling of burning,
so that people could not bear the touch even of the lightest linen clothing, but wanted to be completely naked, and
indeed most of all would have liked to plunge into cold
water. Many of the sick who were uncared for actually did
so, plunging into the water-tanks in an effort to relieve a
thirst which was unquenchable; for it was just the same
with them whether they drank much or little. Then all the
time they were afflicted with insomnia and the desperate
feeling of not being able to keep still.

In the period when the disease was at its height, the   5
body, so far from wasting away, showed surprising powers of resistance to all the agony, so that there was still
some strength left on the seventh or eighth day, which was
the time when, in most cases, death came from the internal fever. But if people survived this critical period, then
the disease descended to the bowels, producing violent
ulceration and uncontrollable diarrhoea, so that most of
them died later as a result of the weakness caused by this.
For the disease, first settling in the head, went on to affect every part of the body in turn, and even when people
escaped its worst effects, it still left its traces on them by
fastening upon the extremities of the body. It affected the
genitals, the fingers, and the toes, and many of those who
recovered lost the use of these members; some, too, went
blind. There were some also who, when they first began to
get better, suffered from a total loss of memory, not knowing who they were themselves and being unable to recognize their friends.

Words indeed fail one when one tries to give a general picture of this disease; and as for the sufferings of
individuals, they seemed almost beyond the capacity of
human nature to endure. Here in particular is a point
where this plague showed itself to be something quite different from ordinary diseases: though there were many
dead bodies lying about unburied, the birds and animals
that eat human flesh either did not come near them or, if
they did taste the flesh, died of it afterwards. Evidence for
this may be found in the fact that there was a complete
disappearance of all birds of prey: they were not to be
seen either round the bodies or anywhere else. But dogs,

---

[38] **Lemnos** An island in the northeastern Aegean Sea. Athens
sent to the island many of its poor inhabitants, who were given
land and expected to serve in the Athenian army. These exiles
also kept the islanders under control.

[39] **Piraeus** The port that served Athens. There were no wells in
Piraeus at this time.

being domestic animals, provided the best opportunity of observing this effect of the plague.

These, then, were the general features of the disease, though I have omitted all kinds of peculiarities which occurred in various individual cases. Meanwhile, during all this time there was no serious outbreak of any of the usual kinds of illness; if any such cases did occur, they ended in the plague. Some died in neglect, some in spite of every possible care being taken of them. As for a recognized method of treatment, it would be true to say that no such thing existed: what did good in some cases did harm in others. Those with naturally strong constitutions were no better able than the weak to resist the disease, which carried away all alike, even those who were treated and dieted with the greatest care. The most terrible thing of all was the despair into which people fell when they realized that they had caught the plague; for they would immediately adopt an attitude of utter hopelessness, and, by giving in this way, would lose their powers of resistance. Terrible, too, was the sight of people dying like sheep through having caught the disease as a result of nursing others. This indeed caused more deaths than anything else. For when people were afraid to visit the sick, then they died with no one to look after them; indeed, there were many houses in which all the inhabitants perished through lack of any attention. When, on the other hand, they did visit the sick, they lost their own lives, and this was particularly true of those who made it a point of honour to act properly. Such people felt ashamed to think of their own safety and went into their friends' houses at times when even the members of the household were so overwhelmed by the weight of their calamities that they had actually given up the usual practice of making laments for the dead. Yet still the ones who felt most pity for the sick and the dying were those who had had the plague themselves and had recovered from it. They knew what it was like and at the same time felt themselves to be safe, for no one caught the disease twice, or, if he did, the second attack was never fatal. Such people were congratulated on all sides, and they themselves were so elated at the time of their recovery that they fondly imagined that they could never die of any other disease in the future.

A factor which made matters much worse than they were already was the removal of people from the country into the city, and this particularly affected the incomers. There were no houses for them, and, living as they did during the hot season in badly ventilated huts, they died like flies. The bodies of the dying were heaped one on top of the other, and half-dead creatures could be seen staggering about in the streets or flocking around the fountains in their desire for water. The temples in which they took up their quarters were full of the dead bodies of people who had died inside them. For the catastrophe was so overwhelming that men, not knowing what would happen next to them, became indifferent to every rule of religion or of law. All the funeral ceremonies which used to be observed were now disorganized, and they buried

the dead as best they could. Many people, lacking the necessary means of burial because so many deaths had already occurred in their households, adopted the most shameless methods. They would arrive first at a funeral pyre that had been made by others, put their own dead upon it and set it alight; or, finding another pyre burning, they would throw the corpse that they were carrying on top of the other one and go away.

In other respects also Athens owed to the plague the beginnings of a state of unprecedented lawlessness. Seeing how quick and abrupt were the changes of fortune which came to the rich who suddenly died and to those who had previously been penniless but now inherited their wealth, people now began openly to venture on acts of self-indulgence which before then they used to keep dark. Thus they resolved to spend their money quickly and to spend it on pleasure, since money and life alike seemed equally ephemeral. As for what is called honour, no one showed himself willing to abide by its laws, so doubtful was it whether one would survive to enjoy the name for it. It was generally agreed that what was both honourable and valuable was the pleasure of the moment and everything that might conceivably contribute to that pleasure. No fear of god or law of man had a restraining influence. As for the gods, it seemed to be the same thing whether one worshipped them or not, when one saw the good and the bad dying indiscriminately. As for offences against human law, no one expected to live long enough to be brought to trial and punished: instead everyone felt that already a far heavier sentence had been passed on him and was hanging over him, and that before the time for its execution arrived it was only natural to get some pleasure out of life.

This, then, was the calamity which fell upon Athens, and the times were hard indeed, with men dying inside the city and the land outside being laid waste. At this time of distress people naturally recalled old oracles, and among them was a verse which the old men claimed had been delivered in the past and which said:

War with the Dorians comes, and a death will come at the same time.[40]

There had been a controversy as to whether the word in this ancient verse was 'dearth' rather than 'death'; but in the present state of affairs the view that the word was 'death' naturally prevailed; it was a case of people adapting their memories to suit their sufferings. Certainly I think that if there is ever another war with the Dorians after this one, and if a dearth results from it, then in all probability people will quote the other version.

---

[40] **Dorians** The last of the Hellenic tribes who settled in Greece around the eleventh century BCE. They infiltrated the peninsula over several centuries and destroyed the Mycenaean culture. Their reputation as brutal warriors was passed down in folklore and popular sayings.

Questions for Critical Thinking

1. Give examples from Pericles' Funeral Oration where he is both idealistic and pragmatic in describing Athenian democracy.

2. Describe how the plague in Athens affected the civic and political structure of Athens and personal relationships among its citizens.

PLATO
Selections from *The Republic*

Plato (ca. 427–347 BCE), who was Socrates' (ca. 470–399 BCE) best-known student, dedicated his life to explaining his master's methods of learning and his ideas. According to Plato, whose writings constitute the most authentic source for Socrates' life, the older philosopher saw himself as a "gadfly" whose mission was to annoy others by questioning their knowledge. Rather than being concerned with such issues as the nature of matter or the structure of the universe, the only topics being studied by philosophers at the time, Socrates caused an intellectual revolution by turning to more human interests such as Justice, Beauty, Love, and Wisdom. By recording in dialogue form the discussions between Socrates and others (sometimes a pupil, sometimes a critic), Plato illustrated Socrates' method of discourse, which reflected the belief that admitting one's ignorance is the first step toward wisdom. The Socratic method has three steps: First, Socrates encouraged his students to express opinions on a topic; second, he analyzed these opinions, pointing out faulty premises (what was taken for granted) and weak arguments; third, through a series of questions, he led them not to a new truth but to a recognition of the rational steps needed to attain enlightenment. The Socratic method became a standard mode of inquiry that is still practiced today, formally in classroom settings and informally in personal discussions.

Plato taught in the Academy, the school he founded in Athens after 400 BCE for the instruction of would-be political leaders. Its curriculum was mathematics and philosophy, ideal subjects for philosophers and kings—a reflection of Plato's anti-democratic beliefs. In his classes he put into practice his and Socrates' learning ideal—to lead students to ever higher levels of abstract thought, concluding with the ultimate truth. Plato's students, upon graduation, spread the tenets of Platonism, as his philosophy is called, across the ancient world. Platonism helped shape Hellenistic (see Epicurus's "Letter to Menoeceus" in Chapter 4), Roman, and early Christian (see St. Augustine's *Confessions* in Chapter 7) thought. Athens became the intellectual center of the classical world, and Plato's Academy taught generations of thinkers until the Christians closed it in the sixth century CE.

Reading the Selections

Plato was perhaps the first feminist in Western culture. Women as well as men were taught in his school, the Academy, thus contradicting the basic norm of Greek life—to keep women fully separate from men in public. In *The Republic,* the West's first text in political theory, Plato made the case for equality between the sexes to be achieved through equal educational opportunity.

"The Allegory of the Cave," taken from Book VII, is the most famous episode in *The Republic.* An allegory is a parable meant to clarify an idea too complex to understand on its own. In this selection, Socrates uses an allegory to explain his method of learning, introduced earlier in the book. For Socrates, the learning process is of prime concern, because he believed that only when rulers ("philosopher-kings") are well versed in the meaning of Justice can a state be said to be well regulated. Defining Justice and determining how it can be taught to future leaders is thus *The Republic*'s purpose, constituting, in effect, a textbook to be studied in the Academy.

Socrates' words about the nature of the learning process leave his audience puzzled, so he offers "The Allegory of the Cave" by way of explanation. The allegorical journey symbolizes the intellectual journey that Socrates thought all students must undergo if they were to reach the ultimate truth.

∞

Book V

. . .

The men have fully played their part on our stage and made their exit; and now perhaps it would be right to call in the women, especially since you invite me to do it.

"For people then, born and educated as we explained, the only right way, in my opinion, for them to get and use children and women is the way we started them to go. You remember we tried in our discourse to establish the men as it were guardians of a herd."

"Yes."

"Then let us follow up by giving the women birth and training like theirs, and see if it is proper for us or not."

"How?" he asked.

"Thus; do we think that the females of the guardian dogs ought to share in the guard which the males keep? Ought they to join in the hunt and whatever else they do? Or should the females keep kennel indoors, as being unable because of the birth and training of pups, and should the males do the hard work and have all the care of the flocks?"

"They ought to do everything together," he said, "except that we treat the males as stronger and the females as weaker."

"But is it possible," I said, "to use animals for the same things, if you do not give them the same training and education?"

"Impossible."

"Then if we are to use the women for the same things as the men, we must teach them the same things."

"Yes."

"Now music and gymnastic were taught to the men."

"Yes."

"So we must teach the women those same two arts, and matters of war too, and use them in the same way."

"That seems fair from what you say," he replied.

"Well then," said I, "perhaps much in our present proposals would appear funny in contrast with usual custom, if they were done in the way we say."

"Likely enough," he said.

"And what will be the biggest joke of all?" I asked. "Surely to see naked women in the wrestling schools exercising with the men—not only the young women, but even the older ones too? Like old men in the gymnasium, all over wrinkles and not pleasant to look at, who still fancy the game!"

"You are right, upon my word!" said he; "it would seem funny as things are now!"

"Very well," said I, "since we have set out to speak, let us not fear the jests of refined people. Let them talk how they like and say what they like of such an upheaval, about gymnastic and music, and not least about wearing armour and riding on horseback."

"Quite right," said he.

"But since we have begun let us march on to the rough part of our law. We will entreat these wits to leave their usual business and be serious for once; we will remind them that it is not so very long since Hellenes[41] thought it ugly and funny, as most barbarians do still, to see men naked; and when the Cretan[42] began naked athletics, and the Lacedaimonians[43] followed, the clever people then were able to make fun of the thing. Don't you agree?"

"Yes, I do."

"But we found by experience that it was better to strip than to hide all such things; and soon the seeming funny to the eyes melted away before that which was revealed in the light of reason to be the best. It showed also that he is a vain fool who thinks anything ridiculous but what is evil; and he is a fool who tries to raise laughter against any sight, as being that of something funny, other than the sight of folly and evil; or in earnest sets up any other mark to aim at than what is honourable and good."

"By all manner of means," he said.

"Then surely we must decide first whether this is possible or not. Next, we must open the debate to all, whether a man chooses to argue in jest or in earnest; and let them discuss whether the female nature in mankind allows women to share the same work with men in everything, or in nothing, or only in some things, and if in some, to

---

[41] **Hellenes** Another name for the Greeks.
[42] **Cretan** An inhabitant of the island of Crete.
[43] **Lacedaimonians** Another name for the Spartans who lived in Sparta, which was the ancient city of Laconia on the Peloponnesian peninsula.

which class war belongs. Would not this be the best beginning which would lead most likely to the best end?"

"Much the best," he said.

"Are you willing, then," said I, "that we should defend the others against ourselves, and not take the fort of the counterargument undefended?"

"There's nothing to hinder that," he replied.

"Then let us say on their behalf, 'You need no others ₃₀ to dispute with you, Socrates and Glaucon; you yourselves at the first foundation of your city admitted that each single person must do his own one business according to nature.' 'We admitted it, I think; of course.' 'Is there not all the difference in the world between man and woman according to nature?' 'There is a difference, certainly.' 'Then further, is it not proper to appoint work for each according to the nature of each?' 'What then?' 'Then you are mistaken surely, and contradict yourselves, when you say now that men and women must do the same things, although their natures are very different!' Come on now, answer me that and I will thank you!"

"What! all of a sudden!" he said. "That's not altogether easy; but I beg and pray you to interpret our argument for us, whatever that may be."

"That is what I expected, my dear Glaucon," said I, "and there are many other such objections, which I foresaw long ago; that is why I feared and shrank to touch the law about getting and training women and children."

"No, by heaven, it does not look like an easy thing," said he.

"And it is not," said I, "but it's like this: If anyone tumbles into a small swimming pool, or if into the middle of the broad sea, he has to swim all the same."

"Certainly." ₃₅

"Then we must swim too, and try to save ourselves out of the argument; we may hope for some dolphin to take us on his back, or some other desperate salvation."

"So it seems," he said.

"Come along then," said I, "see if we can find the way out anywhere. We agreed, you know, that a different nature ought to practise a different work, and that man and woman have different natures; now we say that these different natures must do the same work. Is that the accusation against us?"

"Exactly."

"How noble is the power, my dear Glaucon," said I, ₄₀ "of the art of word controversy!"

"How so?" he said.

"Because," I said, "so many seem unable to help falling into it; they think they are arguing, when they are only striving quarrelsomely. The reason is that they don't know how to split up a given utterance into its different divisions, but pursue simply a verbal opposition to what is uttered. They bandy words with each other, instead of using reasoned discussion."

"That certainly does happen," he said, "in many cases; but surely it does not apply to us in this case?"

"It does, by all manner of means," I said; "at any rate we appear to have got into a word controversy without meaning to."

"How?" ₄₅

"That *different* natures ought not to engage in the *same* practices; we have been chasing the words about with plenty of courage and eristic wrangling, and never thought of enquiring in any way what was the sense of 'different nature' and what was the sense of 'same nature,' and what we were aiming at in our definition when we allotted to a different nature different practices, and to the same nature the same."

"True, we did not," said he.

"It seems we might just as well ask ourselves," I said, "whether the natures of bald men and hairy men are the same or opposite; and in case we agree that they are opposite, we might forbid long-haired men to make shoes if bald men do, and forbid bald men if long-haired men do."

"That would be ridiculous," he said.

"Yes, ridiculous," I said, "but only because we did ₅₀ not then mean the words 'different' and 'same nature' absolutely; we were thinking only of that kind of sameness or difference which had to do with their actual callings. Thus we meant that a man and a woman who have a physician's mind have the same nature, didn't we?"

"Yes."

"But a man physician and a man carpenter different natures?"

"Yes, I suppose so."

"Now," said I, "take the male and the female sex; if either is found to be better as regards any art or other practice, we shall say that this ought to be assigned to it. But if we find that they differ only in one thing, that the male begets and the female bears the child, we shall not take that difference as having proved any more clearly that a woman differs from a man for what we are speaking of; but we shall still believe that our guardians and their wives should practise the same things."

"And rightly so," he said. ₅₅

. . .

"My friend, no practice or calling in the life of the city belongs to woman as woman, or to man as man, but the various natures are dispersed among both sexes alike; by nature the woman has a share in all practices, and so has man, but in all, woman is rather weaker than man."

"Certainly."

"Then shall we assign all to man and none to woman?"

"Why, how can we?"

"No, for as I believe, we shall say one woman is musi- ₆₀ cal by nature, one not, one is medical by nature, one not."

"Of course."

"But are we not to add—one woman is athletic or warlike, and another is unwarlike and unathletic?"

"Indeed we are."

"Shall we not say the same of philosophy and misosophy, one loves wisdom and one hates it? One has high spirit, one no spirit?"

"That is so also." ₆₅

"Then there may be a woman fit to be a guardian, although another is not; for such was the nature we chose for our guardian men also?"

"Yes, it was."

"Then both woman and man may have the same nature fit for guarding the city, only one is weaker and one stronger."

"So it seems."

"Such women, then, must be chosen for such men, to live with them and to guard with them, since they are fit for it and akin to them by nature."

"Certainly."

"Practice and calling must be assigned to both sexes, the same for the same natures?"

"Just the same."

"So we have come round to where we began, and we agree that it is not against nature to assign music and gymnastic to the wives of the guardians."

"By all means."

"Then our law was not impossible, not only like a pious dream; the law we laid down was natural. But rather, it seems, what happens now, the other way of doing things, is unnatural."

"So it seems."

"Our question then was: Is our proposal possible, and is it best?"

"Yes, that was it."

"It is possible, we are both agreed, aren't we?"

"Yes."

"Then the next thing is to agree if it is best."

"Clearly."

"Well, for a woman to become fit to be a guardian, we shall not need one education to make men fit and a different one to make women fit, especially as it will be dealing with the same nature in both?"

"No; the same education."

"Then what is your opinion about the following?"

"What?"

"About the notion in your mind that one man is better, another is worse. Or do you think all men are alike?"

"Not by any means."

"In the city that we were founding, then, which do you think we formed into better men, the guardians educated as we described, or the cobblers educated in cobbling?"

"A ridiculous question," said he.

"I understand," said I, "but tell me—are not the guardians the best of all the citizens?"

"Much the best."

"Very well, will not these women be the best of the women?"

"Again the very best," he said.

"And is there anything better for a city than that both women and men in it should be as good as they can be?"

"There is not."

"But this will be brought about by the aid of music and gymnastic, as we have described?"

"Of course."

"Then the plan we proposed is not only possible, but best for the city?"

"Just so."

"So the women of the guardians must strip, since naked they will be clothed in virtue for gowns; they must share in war and in all the guarding of the city, and that shall be their only work. But in these same things lighter parts will be given to women than men because of the weakness of their sex. And the man who laughs at naked women, exercising for the greatest good, plucks an unripe fruit of wisdom from his laughter; he apparently does not know what he laughs at or what he is doing. For it is and will be the best thing ever said, that the useful is beautiful and the harmful is ugly."

"Assuredly so."

Book VII
The Allegory of the Cave

"Next, then," I said, "take the following parable of education and ignorance as a picture of the condition of our nature. Imagine mankind as dwelling in an underground cave with a long entrance open to the light across the whole width of the cave; in this they have been from childhood, with necks and legs fettered, so they have to stay where they are. They cannot move their heads round because of the fetters, and they can only look forward, but light comes to them from fire burning behind them higher up at a distance. Between the fire and the prisoners is a road above their level, and along it imagine a low wall has been built, as puppet showmen have screens in front of their people over which they work their puppets."

"I see," he said.

"See, then, bearers carrying along this wall all sorts of articles which they hold projecting above the wall, statues of men and other living things, made of stone or wood and all kinds of stuff, some of the bearers speaking and some silent, as you might expect."

"What a remarkable image," he said, "and what remarkable prisoners!"

"Just like ourselves," I said. "For, first of all, tell me this: What do you think such people would have seen of themselves and each other except their shadows, which the fire cast on the opposite wall of the cave?"

"I don't see how they could see anything else," said he, "if they were compelled to keep their heads unmoving all their lives!"

"Very well, what of the things being carried along? Would not this be the same?"

"Of course it would."

"Suppose the prisoners were able to talk together, don't you think that when they named the shadows which they saw passing they would believe they were naming things?"

"Necessarily."   10

"Then if their prison had an echo from the opposite wall, whenever one of the passing bearers uttered a sound, would they not suppose that the passing shadow must be making the sound? Don't you think so?"

"Indeed I do," he said.

"If so," said I, "such persons would certainly believe that there were no realities except those shadows of handmade things."

"So it must be," said he.

"Now consider," said I, "what their release would be   15
like, and their cure from these fetters and their folly; let us imagine whether it might naturally be something like this. One might be released, and compelled suddenly to stand up and turn his neck round, and to walk and look towards the firelight; all this would hurt him, and he would be too much dazzled to see distinctly those things whose shadows he had seen before. What do you think he would say, if someone told him that what he saw before was foolery, but now he saw more rightly, being a bit nearer reality and turned towards what was a little more real? What if he were shown each of the passing things, and compelled by questions to answer what each one was? Don't you think he would be puzzled, and believe what he saw before was more true than what was shown to him now?"

"Far more," he said.

"Then suppose he were compelled to look towards the real light, it would hurt his eyes, and he would escape by turning them away to the things which he was able to look at, and these he would believe to be clearer than what was being shown to him."

"Just so," said he.

"Suppose, now," said I, "that someone should drag him thence by force, up the rough ascent, the steep way up, and never stop until he could drag him out into the light of the sun, would he not be distressed and furious at being dragged; and when he came into the light, the brilliance would fill his eyes and he would not be able to see even one of the things now called real?"

"That he would not," said he, "all of a sudden."   20

"He would have to get used to it, surely, I think, if he is to see the things above. First he would most easily look at shadows, after that images of mankind and the rest in water, lastly the things themselves. After this he would find it easier to survey by night the heavens themselves and all that is in them, gazing at the light of the stars and moon, rather than by day the sun and the sun's light."

"Of course."

"Last of all, I suppose, the sun; he could look on the sun itself by itself in its own place, and see what it is like, not reflections of it in water or as it appears in some alien setting."

"Necessarily," said he.

"And only after all this he might reason about it, how   25
this is he who provides seasons and years, and is set over all there is in the visible region, and he is in a manner the cause of all things which they saw."

"Yes, it is clear," said he, "that after all that, he would come to this last."

"Very good. Let him be reminded of his first habitation, and what was wisdom in that place, and of his fellow prisoners there; don't you think he would bless himself for the change, and pity them?"

"Yes, indeed."

"And if there were honours and praises among them and prizes for the one who saw the passing things most sharply and remembered best which of them used to come before and which after and which together, and from these was best able to prophesy accordingly what was going to come—do you believe he would set his desire on that, and envy those who were honoured men or potentates among them? Would he not feel as Homer says, and heartily desire rather to be serf of some landless man on earth and to endure anything in the world, rather than to opine as they did and to live in that way?"

"Yes, indeed," said he, "he would rather accept any-   30
thing than live like that."

"Then again," I said, "just consider, if such a one should go down again and sit on his old seat, would he not get his eyes full of darkness coming in suddenly out of the sun?"

"Very much so," said he.

"And if he should have to compete with those who had been always prisoners, by laying down the law about those shadows while he was blinking before his eyes were settled down—and it would take a good long time to get used to things—wouldn't they all laugh at him and say he had spoiled his eyesight by going up there, and it was not worth-while so much as to try to go up? And would they not kill anyone who tried to release them and take them up, if they could somehow lay hands on him and kill him?"

"That they would!" said he.

"Then we must apply this image, my dear Glaucon,"   35
said I, "to all we have been saying. The world of our sight is like the habitation in prison, the firelight there to the sunlight here, the ascent and the view of the upper world is the rising of the soul into the world of mind; put it so and you will not be far from my own surmise, since that is what you want to hear; but God knows if it is really true. At least, what appears to me is, that in the world of the known, last of all, is the idea of the good, and with what toil to be seen! And seen, this must be inferred to be the cause of all right and beautiful things for all, which gives birth to light and the king of light in the world of sight, and, in the world of mind, herself the queen produces truth and reason; and she must be seen by one who is to act with reason publicly or privately."

Questions for Critical Thinking

1. Discuss the arguments put forth to justify female equality in Plato's ideal state.

2. Describe the setting within the cave, how the individual moves out of the cave, and what he sees once out of the cave. How do you get out of the caves in which you live?

PLATO
Selection from *Phaedo*

Reading the Selection

Plato's dialogue titled *Phaedo* lovingly recounts the last hours of Socrates: Having been convicted of impiety against the gods and corrupting Athenian youth, Socrates awaits execution. During these hours, he is shown talking with family and friends, drinking hemlock, as required by law, and quietly dying—an exemplary death. This setting enabled Plato to discourse on life's meaning, death's role in shaping life, and his belief in the soul's immortality.

Since Plato was not present, he made Phaedo, who was there, the narrator of these events. Phaedo first names those present and then describes their anguished reactions to Socrates' impending death, thus setting the stage for a discussion on immortality. Not merely a philosophical discussion, the *Phaedo* resembles a stage drama, through such dramatically realistic details as the jailer's comings and goings and Socrates' friends referring to the passage of time. These details, while heightening the tension in the dialogue, also build toward one of the most poignant and memorable death scenes ever written in Western literature.

[Socrates is speaking.] "Now then, I want to give the proof at once, to you as my judges, why I think it likely that one who has spent his life in philosophy should be confident when he is going to die, and have good hopes that he will win the greatest blessings in the next world when he has ended: so Simmias and Cebes my judges, I will try to show how this could be true.

"The fact is, those who tackle philosophy aright are simply and solely practising dying, practising death, all the time, but nobody sees it. If this is true, then it would surely be unreasonable that they should earnestly do this and nothing else all their lives, yet when death comes they should object to what they had been so long earnestly practising."

Simmias laughed at this, and said, "I don't feel like laughing just now, Socrates, but you have made me laugh. I think that many if they heard that would say, 'That's a good one for the philosophers!' And other people in my city would heartily agree that philosophers are really suffering from a wish to die, and now they have found them out, that they richly deserve it!"

"That would be true, Simmias," said Socrates, "except the words 'found out.' For they have not found out in what sense the real philosophers wish to die and deserve to die, and what kind of death it is. Let us say good-bye to them," he went on, "and ask ourselves: Do we think there is such a thing as death?"

"Certainly," Simmias put in.

"Is it anything more than the separation of the soul from the body?" said Socrates. "Death is, that the body separates from the soul, and remains by itself apart from the soul, and the soul, separated from the body, exists by itself apart from the body. Is death anything but that?"

"No," he said, "that is what death is."

"Then consider, my good friend, if you agree with me here, for I think this is the best way to understand the question we are examining. Do you think it the part of a philosopher to be earnestly concerned with what are called pleasures, such as these—eating and drinking, for example?"

"Not at all," said Simmias.

"The pleasures of love, then?" 10

"Oh no."

"Well, do you suppose a man like that regards the other bodily indulgences as precious? Getting fine clothes and shoes and other bodily adornments—ought he to price them high or low, beyond whatever share of them it is absolutely necessary to have?"

"Low, I think," he said, "if he is a true philosopher."

"Then in general," he said, "do you think that such a man's concern is not for the body, but as far as he can he stands aloof from that and turns towards the soul?"

"I do." 15

"Then firstly, is it not clear that in such things the philosopher as much as possible sets free the soul from communion with the body, more than other men?"

"So it appears."

"And I suppose, Simmias, it must seem to most men that he who has no pleasure in such things and takes no share in them does not deserve to live, but he is getting pretty close to death if he does not care about pleasures which he has by means of the body."

"Quite true, indeed."

"Well then, what about the actual getting of wisdom? 20 Is the body in the way or not, if a man takes it with him as companion in the search? I mean, for example, is there any truth for men in their sight and hearing? Or as poets are forever dinning into our ears, do we hear nothing and see nothing exactly? Yet if these of our bodily senses are not exact and clear, the others will hardly be, for they are all inferior to these, don't you think so?"

"Certainly," he said.

"Then," said he, "when does the soul get hold of the truth? For whenever the soul tries to examine anything in company with the body, it is plain that it is deceived by it."

"Quite true."

"Then is it not clear that in reasoning, if anywhere, something of the realities becomes visible to it?"

"Yes." 25

"And I suppose it reasons best when none of these senses disturbs it, hearing or sight, or pain, or pleasure indeed, but when it is completely by itself and says good-bye to the body, and so far as possible has no dealings with it, when it reaches out and grasps that which really is."

"That is true."

"And is it not then that the philosopher's soul chiefly holds the body cheap and escapes from it, while it seeks to be by itself?"

"So it seems."

"Let us pass on, Simmias. Do we say there is such a 30 thing as justice by itself, or not?"

"We do say so, certainly!"

"Such a thing as the good and beautiful?"

"Of course!"

"And did you ever see one of them with your eyes?"

"Never," said he. 35

"By any other sense of those the body has did you ever grasp them? I mean all such things, greatness, health, strength, in short everything that really is the nature of things whatever they are: Is it through the body that the real truth is perceived? Or is this better—whoever of us prepares himself most completely and most exactly to comprehend each thing which he examines would come nearest to knowing each one?"

"Certainly."

"And would he do that most purely who should approach each with his intelligence alone, not adding sight to intelligence, or dragging in any other sense along with reasoning, but using the intelligence uncontaminated alone by itself, while he tries to hunt out each essence uncontaminated, keeping clear of eyes and ears and, one might say, of the whole body, because he thinks the body disturbs him and hinders the soul from getting possession of truth and wisdom when body and soul are companions—is not this the man, Simmias, if anyone, who will hit reality?"

"Nothing could be more true, Socrates," said Simmias.

"Then from all this," said Socrates, "genuine philoso- 40 phers must come to some such opinion as follows, so as to make to one another statements such as these: 'A sort of direct path, so to speak, seems to take us to the conclusion that so long as we have the body with us in our enquiry, and our soul is mixed up with so great an evil, we shall never attain sufficiently what we desire, and that, we say, is the truth. For the body provides thousands of busy distractions because of its necessary food; besides, if diseases fall upon us, they hinder us from the pursuit of the real. With loves and desires and fears and all kinds of fancies and much rubbish, it infects us, and really and truly makes us, as they say, unable to think one little bit about anything at any time. Indeed, wars and factions and battles all come from the body and its desires, and from nothing else. For the desire of getting wealth causes all wars, and we are compelled to desire wealth by the body, being slaves to its culture; therefore we have no leisure for philosophy, from all these reasons. Chief of all is that if we do have some leisure, and turn away from the body to speculate on something, in our searches it is everywhere interfering, it causes confusion and disturbance, and dazzles us so that it will not let us see the truth; so in fact we see that if we are ever to know anything purely we must get rid of it, and examine the real things by the soul alone; and then, it seems, after we are dead, as the reasoning shows, not while we live, we shall possess that which we desire, lovers of which we say we are, namely wisdom. For if it is impossible in company with the body to know anything purely, one thing of two follows: either knowledge is possible nowhere, or only after death; for then alone the soul will be quite by itself apart from the body, but not before. And while we are alive, we shall be nearest to knowing, as it seems, if as far as possible we have no commerce or communion with the body which is not absolutely necessary, and if we are not infected with its nature, but keep ourselves pure from it, until God himself shall set us free. And so, pure and rid of the body's foolishness, we shall probably be in the company of those like ourselves, and shall know through our own selves complete incontamination, and that is perhaps the truth. But for the impure to grasp the pure is not, it seems, allowed.' So we must think, Simmias, and so we must say to one another, all who are rightly lovers of learning; don't you agree?"

"Assuredly, Socrates."

"Then," said Socrates, "if this is true, my comrade, there is great hope that when I arrive where I am travelling, there if anywhere I shall sufficiently possess that for which all our study has been pursued in this past life. So the journey which has been commanded for me is made with good hope, and the same for any other man who believes he has got his mind purified, as I may call it."

"Certainly," replied Simmias.

"And is not purification really that which has been mentioned so often in our discussion, to separate as far as possible the soul from the body, and to accustom it to collect itself together out of the body in every part, and to dwell alone by itself as far as it can, both at this present and in the future, being freed from the body as if from a prison?"

"By all means," said he.

"Then is not this called death—a freeing and separation of soul from body?"

"Not a doubt of that," said he.

"But to set it free, as we say, is the chief endeavour of those who rightly love wisdom, nay of those alone, and the very care and practice of the philosophers is nothing but the freeing and separation of soul from body, don't you think so?"

"It appears to be so."

"Then, as I said at first, it would be absurd for a man preparing himself in his life to be as near as possible to death, so to live, and then when death came, to object?"

"Of course."

"Then in fact, Simmias," he said, "those who rightly love wisdom are practising dying, and death to them is the least terrible thing in the world. Look at it in this way: If they are everywhere at enmity with the body, and desire the soul to be alone by itself, and if, when this very thing happens, they shall fear and object—would not that be wholly unreasonable? Should they not willingly go to a place where there is good hope of finding what they were in love with all through life (and they loved wisdom), and of ridding themselves of the companion which they hated? When human favourites and wives and sons have died, many have been willing to go down to the grave, drawn by the hope of seeing there those they used to desire, and of being with them; but one who is really in love with wisdom and holds firm to this same hope, that he will find it in the grave, and nowhere else worth speaking of—will he then fret at dying and not go thither rejoicing? We must surely think, my comrade, that he will go rejoicing, if he is really a philosopher; he will surely believe that he will find wisdom in its purity there and there alone. If this is true, would it not be most unreasonable, as I said just now, if such a one feared death?"

"Unreasonable, I do declare," said he. . . .

With these words, he got up and retired into another room for the bath, and Criton went after him, telling us to wait. So we waited discussing and talking together about what had been said, or sometimes speaking of the great misfortune which had befallen us, for we felt really as if we had lost a father and had to spend the rest of our lives as orphans. When he had bathed, and his children had been brought to see him—for he had two little sons, and one big—and when the women of his family had come, he talked to them before Criton and gave what instructions he wished. Then he asked the women and children to go, and came back to us. It was now near sunset, for he had spent a long time within. He came and sat down after his bath, and he had not talked long after this when the servant of the Eleven came in, and standing by him said, "O Socrates! I have not to complain of you as I do of others, that they are angry with me, and curse me, because I bring them word to drink their potion, which my officers make me do! But I have always found you in this time most generous and gentle, and the best man who ever came here. And now too, I know well you are not angry with me, for you know who are responsible, and you keep it for them. Now you know what I came to tell you, so farewell, and try to bear as well as you can what can't be helped."

Then he turned and was going out, with tears running down his cheeks. And Socrates looked up at him and said, "Farewell to you also, I will do so." Then, at the same time turning to us, "What a nice fellow!" he said. "All the time he has been coming and talking to me, a real good sort, and now how generously he sheds tears for me! Come along, Criton, let's obey him. Someone bring the potion, if the stuff has been ground; if not, let the fellow grind it."

Then Criton said, "But Socrates, I think the sun is still over the hills, it has not set yet. Yes, and I know of others who, having been told to drink the poison, have done it very late; they had dinner first and a good one, and some enjoyed the company of any they wanted. Please don't be in a hurry, there is time to spare."

But Socrates said, "Those you speak of have very good reason for doing that, for they think they will gain by doing it; and I have good reasons why I won't do it. For I think I shall gain nothing by drinking a little later, only that I shall think myself a fool for clinging to life and sparing when the cask's empty. Come along," he said, "do what I tell you, if you please."

And Criton, hearing this, nodded to the boy who stood near. The boy went out, and after spending a long time, came in with the man who was to give the poison carrying it ground ready in a cup. Socrates caught sight of the man and said, "Here, my good man, you know about these things; what must I do?"

"Just drink it," he said, "and walk about till your legs get heavy, then lie down. In that way the drug will act of itself."

At the same time, he held out the cup to Socrates, and he took it quite cheerfully, Echecrates, not a tremble, not a change in colour or looks; but looking full at the man under his brows, as he used to do, he asked him, "What do you say about this drink? What of a libation to someone? Is that allowed, or not?"

He said, "We only grind so much as we think enough for a moderate potion."

"I understand," he said, "but at least, I suppose, it is allowed to offer a prayer to the gods and that must be done, for good luck in the migration from here to there. Then that is my prayer, and so may it be!"

With these words he put the cup to his lips and, quite easy and contented, drank it up. So far most of us had been able to hold back our tears pretty well; but when we saw him begin drinking and end drinking, we could no longer. I burst into a flood of tears for all I could do, so I wrapped up my face and cried myself out; not for him indeed, but for my own misfortune in losing such a man and such a comrade. Criton had got up and gone out even before I did, for he could not hold the tears in. Apollodoros had never ceased weeping all this time, and now he burst out into loud sobs, and by his weeping and lamentations completely broke down every man there except Socrates himself. He only said, "What a scene! You amaze me. That's just why I sent the women away, to keep them from making a scene like this. I've heard that one ought to make an end in decent silence. Quiet yourselves and endure."

When we heard him we felt ashamed and restrained our tears. He walked about, and when he said that his legs were feeling heavy, he lay down on his back, as the man told him to do; at the same time the one who gave him the potion felt him, and after a while examined his feet and legs; then pinching a foot hard, he asked if he felt any-thing; he said no. After this, again, he pressed the shins; and, moving up like this, he showed us that he was growing cold and stiff. Again he felt him, and told us that when it came to his heart, he would be gone. Already the cold had come nearly as far as the abdomen, when Socrates threw off the covering from his face—for he had covered it over—and said, the last words he uttered, "Criton," he said, "we owe a cock to Asclepios[44]; pay it without fail."

"That indeed shall be done," said Criton. "Have you anything more to say?"   65

When Criton had asked this, Socrates gave no further answer, but after a little time, he stirred, and the man uncovered him, and his eyes were still. Criton, seeing this, closed the mouth and eyelids.

This was the end of our comrade, Echecrates, a man, as we would say, of all then living we had ever met, the noblest and the wisest and most just.

---

[44] **Asclepios** A legendary Greek physician who became the god of healing. His temple was at Epidaurus in Greece. Serpents and cocks were sacred to him. Individuals would make an offering to the cock in the hope that the person would awake in the morning, to the cock's crowing, having survived the night. Socrates is probably referring to this ritual, but with his usual wit and as a paradox—that is, the thank-offering is to be made because death is the cure for life.

Questions for Critical Thinking

1. As a true philosopher, why does Socrates not fear death? Cite examples of his arguments as to why one should not fear death.

2. Describe the last few moments of Socrates' life, and compare this scene to death scenes of other famous teachers or thinkers.

ARISTOTLE
Selections from *Poetics* and *Politics*

In many ways Aristotle (384–322 BCE) has had a more far-reaching effect on Western thought than Plato (see *The Republic, Phaedo*). Aristotle wrote on many topics that Plato never addressed, notably in the natural and physical sciences; thus, Aristotle was considered the greater authority. Western thinkers have tended to favor Aristotle's empirical approach, with its reliance on the senses, rather than Plato's deductive method based on abstract reasoning and mathematics. Westerners have also preferred Aristotle's focus on what exists to Plato's imaginings about an ideal world, beyond the here and now.

Reading the Selections

In the *Poetics*—the first extant work of literary criticism and thus the one that established this genre—Aristotle addressed the topic of "poetry." At the time, poetry included tragedy, comedy, and the epic. Over the centuries Aristotle's section on comedy disappeared, and the part discussing the epic grew so mutilated that it is generally ignored today. The result is that the portion dealing with tragedy is all that effectively survives from Aristotle's original essay.

The section on tragedy shows Aristotle's empirical method in action, as he tries to define the rules to guide an author working in this genre. Typical of his method, he gathered scripts of existing tragedies on which to base his theory. From his studies of playscripts, he isolated the six cardinal features of tragedy—plot, character, diction, thought, spectacle, and song— gave definitions of each, and showed the part each played in making tragedy work. Aristotle's terms and definitions are still used by modern literary critics. This treatise itself has had tremendous influence on Western literature as a whole and in particular on seventeenth-century French classical drama.

Aristotle was at his most original when he claimed that tragedy was cathartic ("purgative"). Though under fire from today's critics, who believe that violence breeds violence, Aristotle's claim for tragedy as catharsis has had tremendous significance for Western drama.

In the *Politics* Aristotle discusses what constitutes good and bad governments, what are the purposes of government, and how to achieve the best forms of government. As in the *Poetics* and his other works, he takes the empirical approach. That is, he examines political systems as they exist or operate, not as they might be imagined in a utopian state. Aristotle believes that since a government is no better than its citizens, the training of those who will participate in the government is essential to the well-being of the political system. Citizenship, therefore, must be taught and practiced by those who aspire to rule. As in his *Ethics,* so in his *Politics,* humans learn what is virtue—or the good—not by seeking knowledge or debating terms but by practicing virtue. The state has to train its youth to be worthwhile citizens so that they can create a government that is based on justice and equality and that will bring the greatest happiness to the largest number of its inhabitants.

The selection from Book I of the *Politics* begins with some general observations on the relationships between those who rule and those who are ruled. Aristotle then turns to the basic units of any society. The state becomes a necessity because "man," who by nature is a political animal, cannot live alone. From this discussion of the most basic units in society, he proceeds to examine all aspects of the political system and proposes practical ways to make it work.

Poetics

A Description of Tragedy

Tragedy . . . , is a representation of an action that is worth 1 serious attention, complete in itself, and of some amplitude; in language enriched by a variety of artistic devices appropriate to the several parts of the play; presented in the form of action, not narration; by means of pity and fear bringing about the purgation of such emotions. By language that is enriched I refer to language possessing rhythm, and music or song; and by artistic devices appropriate to the several parts I mean that some are produced by the medium of verse alone, and others again with the help of song.

Now since the representation is carried out by men performing the actions, it follows, in the first place, that spectacle is an essential part of tragedy, and secondly that there must be song and diction, these being the medium of representation. By diction I mean here the arrangement of the verses; song is a term whose sense is obvious to everyone.

In tragedy it is action that is imitated, and this action is brought about by agents who necessarily display certain distinctive qualities both of character and of thought, according to which we also define the nature of the actions. Thought and character are, then, the two natural causes of actions, and it is on them that all men depend for success or failure. The representation of the action is the plot of the tragedy; for the ordered arrangement of the incidents is what I mean by plot. Character, on the other hand, is that which enables us to define the nature of the participants, and thought comes out in what they say when they are proving a point or expressing an opinion.

Necessarily, then, every tragedy has six constituents, which will determine its quality. They are plot, character, diction, thought, spectacle, and song. Of these, two represent the media in which the action is represented, one involves the manner of representation, and three are connected with the objects of the representation; beyond them nothing further is required. These, it may be said, are the dramatic elements that have been used by practically all playwrights; for all plays alike possess spectacle, character, plot, diction, song, and thought.

Of these elements the most important is the plot, the ordering of the incidents; for tragedy is a representation, not of men, but of action and life, of happiness and unhappiness—and happiness and unhappiness are bound up with action. The purpose of living is an end which is a kind of activity, not a quality; it is their characters, indeed, that make men what they are, but it is by reason of their actions that they are happy or the reverse. Tragedies are not performed, therefore, in order to represent character, although character is involved for the sake of the action. Thus the incidents and the plot are the end aimed at in tragedy, and as always, the end is everything. Furthermore, there could not be a tragedy without action, but there could be without character; indeed the tragedies of most of our recent playwrights fail to present character, and the same might be said of many playwrights of other periods. A similar contrast could be drawn between Zeuxis and Polygnotus as painters, for Polygnotus represents character well, whereas Zeuxis is not concerned with it in his painting.[45] Again, if someone writes a series of speeches expressive of character, and well composed as far as thought and diction are concerned, he will still not achieve the proper effect of tragedy; this will be done much better by a tragedy which is less successful in its use

of these elements, but which has a plot giving an ordered combination of incidents. Another point to note is that the two most important means by which tragedy plays on our feelings, that is, "reversals" and "recognitions," are both constituents of the plot. A further proof is that beginners can achieve accuracy in diction and the portrayal of character before they can construct a plot out of the incidents, and this could be said of almost all the earliest dramatic poets.

The plot, then, is the first essential of tragedy, its lifeblood, so to speak, and character takes the second place. It is much the same in painting; for if an artist were to daub his canvas with the most beautiful colours laid on at random, he would not give the same pleasure as he would by drawing a recognizable portrait in black and white. Tragedy is the representation of an action, and it is chiefly on account of the action that it is also a representation of persons.

The third property of tragedy is thought. This is the ability to say what is possible and appropriate in any given circumstances; it is what, in the speeches in the play, is related to the arts of politics and rhetoric. The older dramatic poets made their characters talk like statesmen, whereas those of today make them talk like rhetoricians. Character is that which reveals personal choice, the kinds of thing a man chooses or rejects when that is not obvious. Thus there is no revelation of character in speeches in which the speaker shows no preferences or aversions whatever. Thought, on the other hand, is present in speeches where something is being shown to be true or untrue, or where some general opinions is being expressed.

Fourth comes the diction of the speeches. By diction I mean, as I have already explained, the expressive use of words, and this has the same force in verse and in prose.

Of the remaining elements, the music is the most important of the pleasurable additions to the play. Spectacle, or stage-effect, is an attraction, of course, but it has the least to do with the playwright's craft or with the art of poetry. For the power of tragedy is independent both of performance and of actors, and besides, the production of spectacular effects is more the province of the property-man than of the playwright.

---

[45] **Zeuxis and Polygnotus** Two famous artists who lived in the fifth century. Their frescoes and paintings were greatly admired and influenced other artists, but none of their works has survived.

<hr/>

Reversal, Discovery, and Calamity

As has already been noted, a reversal is a change from one state of affairs to its opposite, one which conforms, as I have said, to probability or necessity. In *Oedipus*,[46] for example, the Messenger who came to cheer Oedipus and relieve him of his fear about his mother did the very

opposite by revealing to him who he was. In the *Lynceus*,[47] again, Lynceus is being led off to execution, followed by Danaus who is to kill him, when, as a result of events that

---

[46] **Oedipus** Sophocles' play, *Oedipus Rex*, which Aristotle admired as an example of how a play should be constructed.

[47] **Lynceus** A play by Theodectes, who was a playwright and friend of Aristotle. Lynceus was a mythological figure who was king of Argos. Aristotle's reference is to an episode in Lynceus's life when he is about to be killed and the reversal takes place. Danaus, his father-in-law, by a quick turn of events, is the victim. Theodectes probably invented this incident.

occurred earlier, it comes about that he is saved and it is Danaus who is put to death.

As the word itself indicates, a discovery is a change from ignorance to knowledge, and it leads either to love or to hatred between persons destined for good or ill fortune. The most effective form of discovery is that which is accompanied by reversals, like the one in *Oedipus*. There are of course other forms of discovery, for what I have described may happen in relation to inanimate and trifling objects, and moreover it is possible to discover whether a person has done something or not. But the form of discovery most essentially related to the plot and action of the play is the one described above, for a discovery of this kind in combination with a reversal will carry with it either pity or fear, and it is such actions as these that, according to my definition, tragedy represents; and further, such a combination is likely to lead to a happy or an unhappy ending.

As it is persons who are involved in the discovery, it may be that only one person's identity is revealed to another, that of the second being already known. Sometimes, however, a natural recognition of two parties is necessary, as for example, when the identity of Iphigenia was made known to Orestes by the sending of the letter, and a second discovery was required to make him known to Iphigenia.[48]

Two elements of plot, then, reversal and discovery, turn upon such incidents as these. A third is suffering, or calamity. Of these three, reversal and discovery have already been defined. A calamity is an action of a destructive or painful nature, such as death openly represented, excessive suffering, wounding, and the like. . . .

---

[48] **Orestes and Iphigenia** Brother and sister who appeared in several plays by Greek playwrights. Aristotle is referring to a scene from Euripides' *Iphigenia in Tauris*.

∞

Tragic Action

Following upon the points I have already made, I must go on to say what is to be aimed at and what guarded against in the construction of plots, and what are the sources of the tragic effect.

We saw that the structure of tragedy at its best should be complex, not simple, and that it should represent actions capable of awakening fear and pity—for this is a characteristic function of representations of this type. It follows in the first place that good men should not be shown passing from prosperity to misery, for this does not inspire fear or pity, it merely disgusts us. Nor should evil men be shown progressing from misery to prosperity. This is the most untragic of all plots, for it has none of the requisites of tragedy; it does not appeal to our humanity, or awaken pity or fear in us. Nor again should an utterly worthless man be seen falling from prosperity into misery. Such a course might indeed play upon our humane feelings, but it would not arouse either pity or fear; for our pity is awakened by undeserved misfortune, and our fear by that of someone just like ourselves—pity for the undeserving sufferer and fear for the man like ourselves—so that the situation in question would have nothing in it either pitiful or fearful.

There remains a mean between these extremes. This is the sort of man who is not conspicuous for virtue and justice, and whose fall into misery is not due to vice and depravity, but rather to some error, a man who enjoys prosperity and a high reputation, like Oedipus and Thyestes[49] and other famous members of families like theirs.

Inevitably, then, the well-conceived plot will have a single interest, and not, as some say, a double. The change in fortune will be, not from misery to prosperity, but the reverse, from prosperity to misery, and it will be due, not to depravity, but to some great error either in such a man as I have described or in one better than this, but not worse. This is borne out by existing practice. For at first the poets treated any stories that came to hand, but nowadays the best tragedies are written about a handful of families, those of Alcmaeon, for example, and Oedipus and Orestes and Meleager and Thyestes and Telephus, and others whom it has befallen to suffer or inflict terrible experiences.[50]

---

[49] **Oedipus and Thyestes** Both were powerful rulers who then committed horrendous crimes that haunted them for the rest of their lives and affected their own children.
[50] **Alcmaeon, Oedipus, Orestes, Meleager, Thyestes, Telephus** According to various Greek myths, each person killed a member or several members of his family.

∞

Fear and Pity

Fear and pity may be excited by means of spectacle; but they can also take their rise from the very structure of the action, which is the preferable method and the mark of a better dramatic poet. For the plot should be so ordered that even without seeing it performed anyone merely hearing what is afoot will shudder with fear and pity as a result of what is happening—as indeed would be the experience of anyone hearing the story of Oedipus. To produce this effect by means of stage-spectacle is less artistic, and requires the cooperation of the producer. Those who employ spectacle to produce an effect, not of fear, but of something merely monstrous, have nothing to do with tragedy, for not every kind of pleasure should be demanded of tragedy, but only that which is proper to it; and since the dramatic poet has by means of his representation to produce the tragic pleasure that is associated with pity and fear, it is obvious that this effect is bound up with the events of the plot.

Let us now consider what kinds of incident are to be regarded as fearful or pitiable. Deeds that fit this description must of course involve people who are either friends to one another, or enemies, or neither. Now if a man injures his enemy, there is nothing pitiable either in his act or in his intention, except in so far as suffering is inflicted; nor is there if they are indifferent to each other. But when the sufferings involve those who are near and dear to one another, when for example brother kills brother, son father, mother son, or son mother, or if such a deed is contemplated, or something else of the kind is actually done, then we have a situation of the kind to be aimed at. Thus it will not do to tamper with the traditional stories, the murder of Clytemnestra by Orestes, for instance, and that of Eriphyle by Alcmaeon[51]; on the other hand, the poet must use his imagination and handle the traditional material effectively.

I must explain more clearly what I mean by "effectively." The deed may be done by characters acting consciously and in full knowledge of the facts, as was the way of the early dramatic poets, when for instance Euripides made Medea kill her children. Or they may do it without realizing the horror of the deed until later, when they

discover the truth; this is what Sophocles did with Oedipus. Here indeed the relevant incident occurs outside the action of the play; but it may be a part of the tragedy, as with Alcmaeon in Astydamas's play, or Telegonus in *The Wounded Odysseus*.[52] A third alternative is for someone who is about to do a terrible deed in ignorance of the relationship to discover the truth before he does it. These are the only possibilities, for the deed must either be done or not done, and by someone either with or without knowledge of the facts.

The least acceptable of these alternatives is when someone in possession of the facts is on the point of acting but fails to do so, for this merely shocks us, and, since no suffering is involved, it is not tragic. Hence nobody is allowed to behave like this, or only seldom, as when Haemon fails to kill Creon in the *Antigone*.[53] Next in order of effectiveness is when the deed is actually done, and here it is better that the character should act in ignorance and only learn the truth afterwards, for there is nothing in this to outrage our feelings, and the revelation comes as a surprise. However, the best method is the last, when, for example, in the *Cresphontes* Merope intends to kill her son, but recognizes him and does not do so; or when the same thing happens with brother and sister in *Iphigenia in Tauris*; or when, in the *Helle*,[54] the son recognizes his mother when he is just about to betray her.

This then is the reason why, as I said before, our tragedies keep to a few families. For in their search for dramatic material it was by chance rather than by technical knowledge that the poets discovered how to gain tragic effects in their plots. And they are still obliged to have recourse to those families in which sufferings of the kind I have described have been experienced.

I have said enough now about the arrangement of the incidents in a tragedy and the type of plot it ought to have.

---

[51] **Clytemnestra and Orestes; Eriphyle and Alcmaeon** Orestes and Alcmaeon murdered their respective mothers, Clytemnestra and Eriphyle, to avenge the killings of their fathers by their mothers.

[52] **Astydamas, Telegonus** Astydamas was a fourth-century Athenian playwright who wrote a play about Alcmaeon killing his mother. Telegonus, the illegitimate son of Odysseus, accidentally killed his father in Sophocles' lost play *The Wounded Odysseus*.
[53] **Haemon and Creon** Haemon was Creon's son and engaged to marry Antigone, the daughter of Oedipus and for whom Sophocles named his play.
[54] **Cresphontes, Iphigenia in Tauris, Helle** *Cresphontes* is one of Euripides' lost plays; *Iphigenia in Tauris* is one of Euripides' extant plays; *Helle* is the title of an unknown tragedy.

The Characters of Tragedy

In characterization there are four things to aim at. First [1] and foremost, the characters should be good. Now character will be displayed, as I have pointed out, if some preference is revealed in speech or action, and if it is a preference for what is good the character will be good. There can be goodness in every class of person; for instance, a woman or a slave may be good, though the one is possibly an inferior being and the other in general an insignificant one.

In the second place the portrayal should be appropriate. For example, a character may possess manly qualities, but it is not appropriate that a female character should be given manliness or cleverness.

Thirdly, the characters should be lifelike. This is not the same thing as making them good, or appropriate in the sense in which I have used the word.

And fourthly, they should be consistent. Even if the person who is being represented is inconsistent, and this trait is the basis of his character, he must nevertheless be portrayed as consistently inconsistent.

As an example of unnecessary badness of charac- [5] ter, there is Menelaus in the *Orestes*. The character who behaves in an unsuitable and inappropriate way is exemplified in Odysseus' lament in the *Scylla*,[55] and in Melanippe's speech.[56] An inconsistent character is shown in *Iphigenia at Aulis*, for Iphigenia as a suppliant is quite unlike what she is later.

As in the arrangement of the incidents, so too in characterization one must always bear in mind what will be either necessary or probable; in other words, it should be necessary or probable that such and such a person should say or do such and such a thing, and similarly that this particular incident should follow on that.

Furthermore, it is obvious that the unravelling of the plot should arise from the circumstances of the plot itself, and not be brought about *ex machina*, as is done in the *Medea* and in the episode of the embarkation in the *Iliad*. The *deus ex machina*[57] should be used only for matters outside the play proper, either for things that happened before it and that cannot be known by the human characters, or for things that are yet to come and that require to be foretold prophetically—for we allow to the gods the power to see all things. However, there should be nothing inexplicable about what happens, or if there must be, it should be kept outside the tragedy, as is done in Sophocles's *Oedipus*.

Since tragedy is a representation of people who are better than average, we must copy the good portrait-painters. These, while reproducing the distinctive appearance of their sitters and making likenesses, paint them better-looking than they are. In the same way the poet, in portraying men who are hot-tempered, or phlegmatic, or who have other defects of character, must bring out these qualities in them, and at the same time show them as decent people, as Agathon[58] and Homer have portrayed Achilles.

These points must be carefully watched, as too must those means used to appeal to the eye, which are necessarily dependent on the poet's art; for here too it is often possible to make mistakes. However, enough has been said about these matters in my published works.

---

[55] **Scylla** A dithyramb written by Timotheus, a fourth-century poet. The dithyramb is a type of lyric poem, often performed by large choruses. Aristotle believes that Odysseus overreacted when Scylla, the sea monster, swallowed his companions. Timotheus was inspired by one of Odysseus's adventures from the *Odyssey*.
[56] **Melanippe** A mythological figure and the subject of one of Euripides' lost plays, *Melanippe the Wise*.

[57] **deus ex machina** Literally, "a god from a machine." Can be a person or a thing suddenly introduced in a play to provide a contrived solution to a seemingly insoluble problem.
[58] **Agathon** Athenian playwright and poet active in the later part of the fifth century.

Questions for Critical Thinking

1. Define Aristotle's six cardinal features of tragedy, and give examples of three of these features you have seen in a recent film.

2. According to Aristotle, how can fear and pity be aroused in a play, and in which plays does he give examples of fear and pity? Why do you think the playwright wants the audience to have this experience?

∞

Politics
Book I

Every state is a community of some kind, and every community is established with a view to some good; for mankind always act in order to obtain that which they think good. But, if all communities aim at some good, the state or political community, which is the highest of all, and which embraces all the rest, aims at good in a greater degree than any other, and at the highest good.

Some people think that the qualifications of a statesman, king, householder, and master are the same, and that they differ, not in kind, but only in the number of their subjects. For example, the ruler over a few is called a master; over more, the manager of a household; over a still larger number, a statesman or king, as if there were no difference between a great household and a small state. The distinction which is made between the king and the statesman is as follows: When the government is personal, the ruler is a king; when, according to the rules of the political science, the citizens rule and are ruled in turn, then he is called a statesman.

But all this is a mistake; for governments differ in kind, as will be evident to anyone who considers the matter according to the method which has hitherto guided us. As in other departments of science, so in politics, the compound should always be resolved into the simple elements or least parts of the whole. We must therefore look at the elements of which the state is composed, in order that we may see in what the different kinds of rule differ from one another, and whether any scientific result can be attained about each one of them.

He who thus considers things in their first growth and origin, whether a state or anything else, will obtain the clearest view of them. In the first place there must be a union of those who cannot exist without each other; namely, of male and female, that the race may continue (and this is a union which is formed, not of deliberate purpose, but because, in common with other animals and with plants, mankind have a natural desire to leave behind them an image of themselves), and of natural ruler and subject, that both may be preserved. For that which can foresee by the exercise of mind is by nature intended to be lord and master, and that which can with its body give effect to such foresight is a subject, and by nature a slave; hence master and slave have the same interest. Now nature has distinguished between the female and the slave. For she is not niggardly, like the smith who fashions the Delphian knife for many uses; she makes each thing for a single use, and every instrument is best made when intended for one and not for many uses. But among barbarians no distinction is made between women and slaves, because there is no natural ruler among them: they are a community of slaves, male and female. Wherefore the poets say—

"It is meet that Hellenes should rule over barbarians";

as if they thought that the barbarian and the slave were by nature one.

Out of these two relationships between man and woman, master and slave, the first thing to arise is the family, and Hesiod[59] is right when he says—

"First house and wife and an ox for the plough,"

for the ox is the poor man's slave. The family is the association established by nature for the supply of men's everyday wants, and the members of it are called by Charondas[60] "companions of the cupboard," and by Epimenides the Cretan,[61] "companions of the manger." But when several families are united, and the association aims at something more than the supply of daily needs, the first society to be formed is the village. And the most natural form of the village appears to be that of a colony from the family, composed of the children and grandchildren, who are said to be "suckled with the same milk." And this is the reason why Hellenic states were originally governed by kings; because the Hellenes were under royal rule before they came together, as the barbarians still are. Every family is ruled by the eldest, and therefore in the colonies of the family the kingly form of government prevailed because they were of the same blood. As Homer[62] says:

"Each one gives law to his children and to his wives."

For they lived dispersedly, as was the manner in ancient times. Wherefore men say that the Gods have a king, because they themselves either are or were in ancient times under the rule of a king. For they imagine, not only the forms of the Gods, but their ways of life to be like their own.

When several villages are united in a single complete community, large enough to be nearly or quite self-sufficing, the state comes into existence, originating in the bare needs of life, and continuing in existence for the sake of a good life. And therefore, if the earlier forms of society are natural, so is the state, for it is the end of them, and the nature of a thing is its end. For what each thing is when fully developed, we call its nature, whether we are speaking of a man, a horse, or a family. Besides, the final cause and end of a thing is the best, and to be self-sufficing is the end and the best.

----

[59] **Hesiod** Eighth-century BCE Greek poet who wrote *Works and Days,* a collection of stories and advice on such matters as running a farm, navigating the seas, and living by moral codes.
[60] **Charondas** Sixth-century BCE Greek lawgiver who made special laws for families.
[61] **Epimenides** Sixth-century BCE philosopher, poet, and prophet from the island of Crete who wrote religious and poetical works. Subject of many legends.
[62] **Homer** Eighth-century BCE poet and author of the *Iliad* and the *Odyssey.*

Thence it is evident that the state is a creation of nature, and that man is by nature a political animal. And he who by nature and not by mere accident is without a state, is either a bad man or above humanity; he is like the

"Tribeless, lawless, heartless one,"

whom Homer denounces—the natural outcast is forthwith a lover of war; he may be compared to an isolated piece at draughts.

Now, that man is more of a political animal than bees or any other gregarious animals is evident. Nature, as we often say, makes nothing in vain, and man is the only animal whom she has endowed with the gift of speech. And whereas mere voice is but an indication of pleasure or pain, and is therefore found in other animals (for their nature attains to the perception of pleasure and pain and the intimation of them to one another, and no further), the power of speech is intended to set forth the expedient and inexpedient, and therefore likewise the just and the unjust. And it is a characteristic of man that he alone has any sense of good and evil, of just and unjust, and the like, and the association of living beings who have this sense makes a family and a state.

Further, the state is by nature clearly prior to the family 10 and to the individual, since the whole is of necessity prior to the part; for example, if the whole body be destroyed, there will be no foot or hand, except in an equivocal sense, as we might speak of a stone hand; for when destroyed the hand will be no better than that. But things are defined by their working and power; and we ought not to say that they are the same when they no longer have their proper quality, but only that they have the same name. The proof that the state is a creation of nature and prior to the individual is that the individual, when isolated, is not self-sufficing; and therefore he is like a part in relation to the whole. But he who is unable to live in society, or who has no need because he is sufficient for himself, must be either a beast or a god: he is no part of a state. A social instinct is implanted in all men by nature, and yet he who first founded the state was the greatest of benefactors. For man, when perfected, is the best of animals, but, when separated from law and justice, he is the worst of all; since armed injustice is the more dangerous, and he is equipped at birth with arms, meant to be used by intelligence and virtue, which he may use for the worst ends. Wherefore, if he have not virtue, he is the most unholy and the most savage of animals, and the most full of lust and gluttony. But justice is the bond of men in states, for the administration of justice, which is the determination of what is just, is the principle of order in political society.

Questions for Critical Thinking

1. What are the basic units in a society, and how do they then evolve into a state?

2. Show how man is a "political animal" and note why he should live in the state. What does this tell us about Aristotle's view of human nature?

4

THE HELLENISTIC WORLD

THEOCRITUS
Selection from the *Idylls*

During the Hellenistic Age, original creative literature hardly existed; most writers either imitated the forms and styles of their Hellenic predecessors or, following the lead of Aristotle, turned to literary criticism. These authors, often working from manuscripts on deposit at the library in Egypt's port city of Alexandria, perfected a literary style known as Alexandrianism. What distinguished these writers were their wide knowledge of details of Greek myths and history, their understanding of exotic literary figures and references, and their masterful command of the Greek language. They polished the Greek styles until their own works only faintly echoed the robustness of the originals. The Alexandrians owed their success, in part, to Egypt's Ptolemaic rulers, who built the great library in Alexandria, stocking it with ancient manuscripts either through purchase or as spoils of war, and providing financial subsidies for scholars. Alexandrianism eventually spread across the Hellenistic world, affecting local literary styles and influencing Roman culture.

In the cosmopolitan Hellenistic world, educated readers turned to scientific essays or to biographies; the writers based in Alexandria tended to serve the mass market, who demanded updated copies of Greek works. Among the popular but mediocre writers who catered to this market, only one or two, such as Theocritus, were able to establish reputations beyond their lifetime.

Theocritus (ca. 310–250 BCE) was more original than his contemporaries for he pioneered two literary forms: the pastoral and the idyll. The pastoral focuses on the lives of shepherds in the wilds; it became a popular genre in this period because it had special appeal to those who had moved from the countryside to newly founded Hellenistic cities. Theocritus's sensitive descriptions of unspoiled nature, lowing cattle, and lovesick shepherds resulted in charming, though artificial, poems. However, Theocritus's reputation rests on his idylls—small portraits or vignettes of Hellenistic life, dating from the 270s. These poems evoked a simpler past or addressed themselves to familiar human traits such as love and jealousy.

Reading the Selection

Of Theocritus's thirty surviving idylls, the best is perhaps Idyll 14, "Aeschines and Thyonichus," which offers a rare glimpse of daily life in Hellenistic Egypt. Written in the form of a conversation, the idyll recounts a chance meeting between two old friends, the slightly disheveled Aeschines and the empathetic Thyonichus. The conversation ends with Thyonichus advising his friend to forget his troubles and join the army—that is, become a mercenary soldier for King Ptolemy, Egypt's ruler.

This idyll provides a window into Egypt's Greek community, populated by colonists who settled there after Alexander's conquest and the founding of the city of Alexandria in 332 BCE. According to scholars, the Egyptian Greeks maintained a distinct identity, living apart from the native population. In the poem, all the named characters have Greek names, there are references to a Greek city—Athens—and to two Greek-speaking regions, Thessaly and Thrace. The expression "Seen a wolf?" is a bit of Greek folklore, the equivalent of the English saying, "Has the cat got your tongue?"

Aeschines and Thyonichus

AESCHINES: Good to see you, Thyonichus.   1
THYONICHUS: And you, Aeschines.
     It's been some time.
AESCHINES: It has.
THYONICHUS: What's up with you?
AESCHINES: Trouble, Thyonichus.
THYONICHUS: Look how thin you've got;
     Unshaved moustache, long straggly hair! You're like
     That pasty-faced barefoot "philosopher"[1]
     Who came by the other day. "From Athens," he said.   10
AESCHINES: Was he in love too?
THYONICHUS: Pining . . . for a square meal.
AESCHINES: You can joke! It's driven me nearly crazy,
     The way Cynisca's been messing me about.
THYONICHUS: You could never take things easy,
          Aeschines.
     You want everything "just right." . . .
                              Tell me the worst.
AESCHINES: The Argive[2] and Agis, the trainer[3] from
          Thessaly,
     And me and the soldier, Cleunicus—we were drinking
     At my country place. I'd killed a sucking pig   20
     And a pair of chickens, opened a jar of old wine
     —It smelt as good, almost, as the day it was pressed—
     Got onions and snails. It was a proper party.
     When things were going nicely we offered a toast
     "To the one I love," and we had to say the name.
We all spoke up and the toast went round. But *she*
Went quiet. And me right there! You can guess my
          feelings.
"Seen a wolf?" quipped someone. "That's right," she said,
Then blushed. You could have lit a lamp at her cheeks.[4]

There *is* a wolf—a wolf at the door, you might say.   30
My neighbour Labas's son. That's her great lover!
Handsome they call him. Skinny and overgrown!
A whisper about it had reached my ears, it's true,
But I took no notice. Trusting as a babe, I was.
Well, the four of us had had a few by this time,
And the man from Thessaly sang "Little Red
          Ridinghood"[5]
Right through from the beginning, which didn't help.
Cynisca burst into tears like a girl of six
Sobbing to be taken up on her mother's lap.
So I let her have it, Thyonichus—you know me—   40
I smacked[6] her about the head a couple of times,
"Not good enough for you, am I?" She picked herself up
And ran. "Don't hang around, dear. That boyfriend of
          yours
Will be catching cold. I hope he makes you cry."
A swallow, bringing a scrap to its young in the eaves,
Darts out a split-second later to fetch more food:
That's how she was, one moment stretched in a chair,
The next, flying down the passage and out of the house.
Talk about the stable door and the bolting horse!
Twenty days . . . then eight . . . nine . . . then ten more . . .   50
Eleven till today. Plus two makes two whole months[7]
Since we split up. If I spiked my hair like a Thracian
She'd never notice the change. The Wolf's her man now,
She has him in at nights.
                    I'm out in the cold,
No room for a poor Yahoo like me in her life.
If I could stop thinking about her, well and good.
But as it is . . . I'm like a mouse in a trap.
What the doctor orders to treat a lover's pangs

---

[1] **barefoot "philosopher"** Perhaps a reference to the Cynics, a philosophic school that flourished in the Hellenistic period; the Cynics practiced a life of self-denial.
[2] **Argive** A person from Argos, a city and region in the Peloponnesus.
[3] **trainer** A person who helps athletes prepare for the games.
[4] **lit a lamp at her cheeks** She was blushing red.

[5] **"Little Red Ridinghood"** A song with a wolf-theme, meant to make Cynisca uneasy about her dalliance with the neighbor's "wolfish" son.
[6] **smacked** Aeschines shows no remorse for his physical abuse of Cynisca.
[7] **two whole months** The days add up to sixty—two whole months.

I don't know. But when my old friend Simus fell   60
For that brassy girl, a sea-voyage did the trick.
I'll cross the sea too, and enlist as a soldier—
Not the best life, perhaps, but it could be worse.
THYONICHUS: I only wish that things had gone as you
        wanted,
    Aeschines. But if serving abroad's your answer,
    King Ptolemy gives a free man honest terms.
AESCHINES: Tell me more.
THYONICHUS: Ptolemy's one of the best!
Warm-hearted, loves his mistresses, loves learning,

Never forgets a friend—or an enemy.   70
He's generous to a fault, as a great prince should be,
But be careful not to push your luck in asking,
Aeschines. If you're ready to sling a soldier's
Cloak about your shoulders and bear the brunt
Of an enemy charge without budging from your place,
Hurry to Egypt.
                    A touch of grey at the temples
Creeps outward, hair by hair, and before we know it
Our time has gone. Act now, while the sap runs green.

Questions for Critical Thinking

1. How would you describe the relationship between Aeschines and Cynisca, and what does the relationship tell us about love?

2. Cite examples of how this idyll reveals the ways Greek and Egyptian cultures are part of the Hellenistic world.

EPICURUS
"Letter to Menoeceus"

The Greek philosopher Epicurus (ca. 342–270 BCE) is the founder of a type of hedonism that identifies the good with pleasure and the bad with pain—epicureanism. Born on the island of Samos, he moved to Athens, where he founded a school. Most of his writings have been lost; only scattered fragments survive. His disciples, including the Roman thinker Lucretius, wrote extensively on his teachings, preserving their basic ideas. Consequently, Epicurus's personal letter (early third century BCE) to Menoeceus is a treasured document because it records both the philosopher's observations, in his own words, on what is needed to gain happiness and his view of the "good life."

Epicurus apparently practiced what he preached, living a simple and frugal, almost monastic, existence in the company of his pupils. Among them, he expounded his simple rules for becoming happy and avoiding fear and pain. He pointed out that death should not be feared, since dying has little meaning to a person who understands the workings of nature. Building on the ideas of the Greek thinker Democritus (ca. 460 BCE–?), the founder of the atomic theory, Epicurus argued that death is simply the loss of a few atoms from the body. He believed that everything, including soul and body, is composed of atoms, or particles of matter. That being the case, humans should shut their ears to priests who try to put fear of death into their hearts. Many educated people in his day, and later in Roman times, found satisfaction in this teaching about calmness in the face of death; thus, Epicurus came to be known as a "savior of souls."

Reading the Selection

In this letter to a pupil, Menoeceus, Epicurus offers advice on happiness, the final goal of most philosophies and religions. For Epicurus, the beginning of happiness lies in accepting that the gods exist but, at the same time, rejecting the common notion that the deities have any interest in mortals.

Having offered his preconditions of happiness, Epicurus explains the meaning of the good life. He maintains that the human ability to differentiate between "natural" and "unnecessary" desires will help bring us happiness. In his final observations, Epicurus turns to a question that is central to many philosophies and religions, that of free will versus predestination.

∞

No one should postpone the study of philosophy when he is young, nor should he weary of it when he becomes mature, because the search for mental health is never untimely or out of season. To say that the time to study philosophy has not yet arrived or that it is past is like saying that the time for happiness is not yet at hand or is no longer present. Thus both the young and the mature should pursue philosophy, the latter in order to be rejuvenated as they age by the blessings that accrue from pleasurable past experience, and the youthful in order to become mature immediately through having no fear of the future. Hence we should make a practice of the things that make for happiness, for assuredly when we have this, we have everything, and we do everything we can to get it when we don't have it.

The Preconditions of Happiness

[1. You should do and practice all the things I constantly recommended to you, with the knowledge that they are the fundamentals of the good life. First of all, you should think of deity as imperishable and blessed being (as delineated in the universal conception of it common to all men), and you should not attribute to it anything foreign to its immortality or inconsistent with its blessedness. On the contrary, you should hold every doctrine that is capable of safeguarding its blessedness in common with its imperishability. The gods do indeed exist, since our knowledge of them is a matter of clear and distinct perception; but they are not like what the masses suppose them to be, because most people do not maintain the pure conception of the gods. The irreligious man is not the person who destroys the gods of the masses but the person who imposes the ideas of the masses on the gods. The opinions held by most people about the gods are not true conceptions of them but fallacious notions, according to which awful penalties are meted out to the evil and the greatest of blessings to the good. The masses, by assimilating the gods in every respect to their own moral qualities, accept deities similar to themselves and regard anything not of this sort as alien.

Second, you should accustom yourself to believing that death means nothing to us, since every good and every evil lies in sensation; but death is the privation of sensation.[8] Hence a correct comprehension of the fact that death means nothing to us makes the mortal aspect of life pleasurable, not by conferring on us a boundless period of time but by removing the yearning for deathlessness. There is nothing fearful in living for the person who has really laid hold of the fact that there is nothing fearful in not living. So it is silly for a person to say that he dreads death—not because it will be painful when it arrives but because it pains him now as a future certainty; for that which makes no trouble for us when it arrives is a meaningless pain when we await it. This, the most horrifying of evils, means nothing to us, then, because so long as we are existent death is not present and whenever it is present we are nonexistent. Thus it is of no concern either to the living or to those who have completed their lives. For the former it is nonexistent, and the latter are themselves nonexistent.

Most people, however, recoil from death as though it were the greatest of evils; at other times they welcome it as the end-all of life's ills. The sophisticated person, on the other hand, neither begs off from living nor dreads not living. Life is not a stumbling block to him, nor does he regard not being alive as any sort of evil. As in the case of food he prefers the most savory dish to merely the larger portion, so in the case of time, he garners to himself the most agreeable moments rather than the longest span.

Anyone who urges the youth to lead a good life but counsels the older man to end his life in good style is silly, not merely because of the welcome character of life but because of the fact that living well and dying well are one and the same discipline. Much worse off, however, is the person[9] who says it were well not to have been born "but once born to pass Hades' portals as swiftly as may be." Now if he says such a thing from inner persuasion why does he not withdraw from life? Everything is in readiness for him once he has firmly resolved on this course. But if he speaks facetiously he is a trifler standing in the midst of men who do not welcome him.

It should be borne in mind, then, that the time to come is neither ours nor altogether not ours. In this way we shall neither expect the future outright as something destined to be, nor despair of it as something absolutely not destined to be.

The Good Life

[2. It should be recognized that within the category of desire certain desires are natural, certain others unnecessary and trivial; that in the case of the natural desires

_____

[8] **sensation** Sense impressions, a belief based on the atomic theory.

[9] **the person** Theognis (fl. sixth–fifth-century BCE); Greek poet.

certain ones are necessary, certain others merely natural; and that in the case of necessary desires certain ones are necessary for happiness, others to promote freedom from bodily discomfort, others for the maintenance of life itself. A steady view of these matters shows us how to refer all moral choice and aversion to bodily health and imperturbability of mind, these being the twin goals of happy living. It is on this account that we do everything we do—to achieve freedom from pain and freedom from fear. When once we come to this, the tumult in the soul is calmed and the human being does not have to go about looking for something that is lacking or to search for something additional with which to supplement the welfare of soul and body. Accordingly we have need of pleasure only when we feel pain because of the absence of pleasure, but whenever we do not feel pain we no longer stand in need of pleasure. And so we speak of pleasure as the starting point[10] and the goal of the happy life because we realize that it is our primary native good, because every act of choice and aversion originates with it, and because we come back to it when we judge every good by using the pleasure feeling as our criterion.

Because of the very fact that pleasure is our primary and congenital good we do not select every pleasure; there are times when we forego certain pleasures, particularly when they are followed by too much unpleasantness. Furthermore, we regard certain states of pain as preferable to pleasures, particularly when greater satisfaction results from our having submitted to discomforts for a long period of time. Thus every pleasure is a good by reason of its having a nature akin to our own, but not every pleasure is desirable. In like manner every state of pain is an evil, but not all pains are uniformly to be rejected. At any rate, it is our duty to judge all such cases by measuring pleasures against pains, with a view to their respective assets and liabilities, inasmuch as we do experience the good as being bad at times and, contrariwise, the bad as being good.

In addition, we consider limitation of the appetites[11] a major good, and we recommend this practice not for the purpose of enjoying just a few things and no more but rather for the purpose of enjoying those few in case we do not have much. We are firmly convinced that those who need expensive fare least are the ones who relish it most keenly and that a natural way of life is easily procured, while trivialities are hard to come by. Plain foods afford pleasure equivalent to that of a sumptuous diet, provided that the pains of penury are wholly eliminated. Barley bread and water yield the peak of pleasure whenever a person who needs them sets them in front of himself. Hence becoming habituated to a simple rather than a lavish way of life provides us with the full complement of health; it makes a person ready for the necessary business of life; it puts us in a position of advantage when we happen upon sumptuous fare at intervals and prepares us to be fearless in facing fortune.

Thus when I say that pleasure is the goal of living I [10] do not mean the pleasures of libertines or the pleasures inherent in positive enjoyment, as is supposed by certain persons who are ignorant of our doctrine or who are not in agreement with it or who interpret it perversely. I mean, on the contrary, the pleasure that consists in freedom from bodily pain and mental agitation. The pleasant life is not the product of one drinking party after another or of sexual intercourse with women and boys or of the sea food and other delicacies afforded by a luxurious table. On the contrary, it is the result of sober thinking—namely, investigation of the reasons for every act of choice and aversion and elimination of those false ideas about the gods and death which are the chief source of mental disturbances.

The starting point of this whole scheme and the most important of its values is good judgment, which consequently is more highly esteemed even than philosophy. All the other virtues stem from sound judgment, which shows us that it is impossible to live the pleasant Epicurean life without also living sensibly, nobly, and justly and, vice versa, that it is impossible to live sensibly, nobly, and justly without living pleasantly. The traditional virtues grow up together with the pleasant life; they are indivisible. Can you think of anyone more moral than the person who has devout beliefs about the gods, who is consistently without fears about death, and who has pondered man's natural end? Or who realizes that the goal of the good life is easily gained and achieved and that the term of evil is brief, both in extent of time and duration of pain? Or the man who laughs at the "decrees of Fate," a deity[12] whom some people have set up as sovereign of all?

The good Epicurean believes that certain events occur deterministically, that others are chance events, and that still others are in our own hands. He sees also that necessity cannot be held morally responsible and that chance is an unpredictable thing, but that what is in our own hands, since it has no master, is naturally associated with blameworthiness and the opposite. (Actually it would be better to subscribe to the popular mythology than to become a slave by accepting the determinism of the natural philosophers, because popular religion underwrites the hope of supplicating the gods by offerings but determinism contains an element of necessity, which is inexorable.) As for chance, the Epicurean does not assume that it is a deity (as in popular belief) because a god does nothing irregular; nor does he regard it as an unpredictable cause of all events. It is his belief that good and evil are not the chance contributions of a deity, donated to mankind for the happy life, but rather that the initial circumstances for great good and evil are sometimes provided by chance. He thinks it preferable to have bad luck rationally than good luck irrationally. In other words, in human action it is better for a rational choice to be unsuccessful than for an irrational choice to succeed through the agency of chance.

---

[10] **pleasure as the starting point** The basic doctrine of hedonism.
[11] **limitation of the appetites** Here Epicurus makes the case for simple living.

---

[12] **Fate, a deity** The worship of Fate as a deity began in Babylonia and spread to the Hellenistic states, flourishing there and later in the Roman world.

Think about these and related matters day and night, by yourself and in company with someone like yourself. If you do, you will never experience anxiety, waking or sleeping, but you will live like a god among men. For a human being who lives in the midst of immortal blessings is in no way like mortal man!

Questions for Critical Thinking

1. What does Epicurus mean by "the good life," and how, according to him, is it achieved?

2. Discuss the Epicurean's position in the debate of free will versus predestination. Is this debate relevant to life in the twenty-first century?

APOLLONIUS OF RHODES
Selections from *The Voyage of Argo* or *Argonautica*

The Voyage of Argo—also known as *Argonautica*—manifests many traits of Hellenistic literature, namely, imitative of Hellenic genres and styles, but less creative, and often artificial. Typical of Hellenistic writers, Apollonius of Rhodes wrote about Greek heroes and deities, employed similes and metaphors, and described exotic and faraway places. Hellenistic literature is called Alexandrianism, a name that memorializes Alexandria, in Egypt—the largest city of the time. Alexandrianism appealed to the period's educated and well-traveled classes and became the defining literary style, which influenced later Roman writers, including Virgil (see Chapter 5).

Little is known of the life of Apollonius of Rhodes, who flourished in the first half of the third century BCE. He was probably born in Egypt. He may have been the student of Callimachus (ca. 305–ca. 240 BCE), a well-known poet and scholar. A few questionable sources state that Apollonius was head of the fabled Library of Alexandria. Early on, he made a name for himself with "foundation poems"—poetic tributes to cities across the Hellenistic world that were being founded or discovered by sailors and tradespeople. Apollonius's connection to the island of Rhodes remains a mystery. Some scholars argue that he fled to Rhodes after a feud with his mentor, Callimachus, while others claim he was there because of the poor reception of *The Voyage of the Argo*—his only complete surviving work.

Apollonius's epic poem exhibits the influences of Greek literature, including the plays of Sophocles (see Chapter 3) and Euripides and, above all, the epics of Homer (see Chapter 2). Like Homer's *Iliad*, *The Voyage of Argo* opens with a list of heroes, and, like Homer's *Odyssey*, the heroes encounter strange and wonderful characters, are tempted by women and goddesses, suffer hardships, and are threatened with death and destruction. But, unlike either Homeric epic, Apollonius of Rhodes interjects a passionate and ill-fated love story—that of Jason and Medea—into his adventurous tale and makes the lovers more human as their relationship grows. Jason, at first, is timid, torn by his own self-doubts, but he evolves into a clever and resolute leader. Medea, who possesses magical powers, is divided between loyalty to her family and love for Jason.

The complex plot of Apollonius's epic involves the myth of the Golden Fleece. The Golden Fleece was the sole surviving remnant of a flying, golden-haired ram, whose oral story was already ancient in Apollonius's day. When the epic opens, Jason is a would-be king. His uncle Pelias has usurped the throne of Iolcus in Thessaly, a region in northwest Greece, along the

Aegean Sea. When challenged, Pelias agrees to hand over the reins of power if Jason will perform a seemingly impossible task: to bring back the Golden Fleece from its secluded hideaway in the kingdom of Colchis. The adventures of Jason and his loyal followers, along with the budding love story between Jason and Medea, and the triumphant return home of Jason make up the narrative of this epic poem.

Reading the Selections

In Book I, Preparation and Departure, Jason and his fellow warriors meet numerous characters. Among the most intriguing and seductive people are the women who live on the island of Lemnos, in the Aegean Sea. In this selection, the queen of Lemnos, Hypsipyle, weaves a false tale to explain why there are no men on the island.

In Book II, Onward to Colchis, the perils of the voyage are recorded in a breathtaking scene as the crew passes through the straits of the Clashing Rocks, which no ship had ever before survived. The conversation between Tiphys, the helmsman, and Jason reveals another side of their leader.

In Book III, Jason and Medea, the hero and Medea, the daughter of the king of Colchis, meet and fall in love. Jason also learns the nature of the tasks he must perform if he is to bring the Golden Fleece back to Iolcus. Against overwhelming odds, Jason exhibits strength and bravery—qualities that mark a man as a hero.

In Book IV, Homeward Bound, Jason and Medea visit and receive a blessing from the goddess Circe, who is both Medea's aunt and the sister of the king of Colchis.

∞

Book I, Preparation and Departure

... [Hypsipyle is speaking:] "So I invite you all to stay here and settle with us. If you yourself accept and the prospect pleases you, my royal father's scepter shall certainly be yours. And I have no fear that you may think poorly of our land. It has the richest soil of any isle in the Aegean Sea. But first go to your ship and tell your comrades what I say. And pray do not avoid the city any more."

Thus she glossed over the massacre and what had really happened to the men.

"Hypsipyle," Jason replied, "we need your help, and all you may give us will indeed be welcome. I shall come back to the city when I have told my people everything. But I must leave this island and its sovereignty to you. I refuse, not through indifference, but because a hazardous adventure calls me on."

As he finished, he touched her right hand; then quickly turned and went. Countless young girls ran up from every side and danced round him in their joy, till he had passed through the city-gates. Then, when he had reported to his friends all that Hypsipyle had summoned him to hear, the girls drove down to the beach in smooth-running wagons laden with gifts. And they did not find it difficult to make the Argonauts come home with them for entertainment. Cypris,[13] the goddess of desire, had done her sweet work in their hearts. She wished to please

Hephaestus,[14] the great Artificer, and save his isle of Lemnos from ever lacking men again.

Jason himself set out for Hypsipyle's royal home, and the rest scattered as chance took them—all but Heracles,[15] who chose to stay by the ship with a few select companions. Soon the whole city was alive with dance and banquet. The scent of burnt-offerings filled the air; and of all the immortals, it was Here's[16] glorious son Hephaestus and Cypris herself whom their songs and sacrifices were designed to please. Day followed day, and still they did not sail. Indeed there is no knowing when they would have left if Heracles had not summoned a meeting, from which the women were excluded, and sharply admonished his friends.

"My good sirs," he began, not without irony. "Are we exiled for manslaughter? Cast out for killing relatives at home? Or have we come here for brides, not fancying

---

[13] **Cypris** Another name for Aphrodite.

[14] **Hephaestus** God of metalwork and of fire, who was born lame and weak. His wife, Aphrodite, was often unfaithful. He was the butt of many jokes, played by the other deities.
[15] **Heracles** Also called Hercules. One of the Argonauts; the son of Zeus and a mortal mother—hence, a demi-god. On the way to Colchis, Heracles is left behind on an island. A god explains that this is part of the deities' plan, so that Heracles later will perform the Twelve Labors and, thus, win immortality.
[16] **Here** Also called Hera. The wife and consort of Zeus. She and Zeus quarrel and often plot against one another.

our own women there? Are we really content to stay and cultivate the soil of Lemnos? We shall get no credit, I assure you, by shutting ourselves up with a set of foreign women all this time. And it is no good praying for a miracle. Fleeces do not come to people of their own accord. We might as well go home, leaving this captain of ours to spend all day in Hypsipyle's arms till he has won the admiration of the world by repopulating Lemnos."

Such was the force of his rebuke that not a man could look him in the eye or answer him. With no more said, the meeting broke up and they hurried off to make ready for departure. But when the women got wind of their intention, they came running down and swarmed round them, moaning for grief, as bees come pouring out from their rocky hive when the meadows are gay with dew, and buzz about the lilies, flitting to and fro to take their sweet toll from the flowers. There was a loving hand and a kind word for every man, with many a prayer to the happy gods for his safe return. Hypsipyle took Jason's hands in hers and prayed in tears for the lover she was losing.

"Go," she said, "and may the gods bring you and all your comrades home with the golden fleece for the king, since that is what you have set your heart on. This island and my father's scepter will be waiting for you if you ever choose to come again when you are back in Hellas.[17] You

could easily collect a host of emigrants from other towns. But that is not what you will wish; something tells me that it will not happen. Nevertheless, remember Hypsipyle when you are far away and when you are at home. But tell me what I am to do if the gods allow me to become a mother; and I will gladly do it."

Jason was moved. "Hypsipyle," he said, "may the happy gods grant all the prayers you made on my behalf. But I hope that you will not think ill of me if I elect, with Pelias'[18] permission, to live in my own country. Release from toil is all I ask of Heaven. But if I am not destined to return to Hellas from my travels, and you bear me a son, send him when he is old enough to Pelasgian Iolcus.[19] I should like him to console my father and mother in their grief if he finds them still alive, and to care for them as their own fireside at home with no interference from the king."

With that, Jason led the way on board. The other chieftains followed him, went to their seats and manned the oars; Argus[20] loosed the stern-cable from its sea-beaten rock; and they struck the water lustily with their long blades of pine. . . .

---

[17] **Hellas** Another name for the Greek lands.

[18] **Pelias** King of **Iolcus** who promised Jason the kingdom, if he returned with the golden fleece.
[19] **Pelasgian Iolcus** Another way to describe **Pelias'** kingdom. **Iolcus** was the capital city.
[20] **Argus** Son of **Chalciope**, grandson of King **Aeetes.** Jason will return him to his homeland.

Book II, Onward to Colchis

. . . *Argo*'s departure did not escape Athene's[21] eye. She promptly took her stand on a cloud which, though light, could bear her formidable weight, and swept down to the sea, filled with concern for the oarsmen in the ship. There comes a moment to the patient traveler (and there are many such that wander far afield) when the road ahead of him is clear and the distance so foreshortened that he has a vision of his home, he sees his way to it over land and sea, and in his fancy travels there and back so quickly that it seems to stand before his eager eyes. Such was Athene's speed as she darted down to set foot on the inhospitable coast of Thynia.[22]

In due course they found themselves entering the narrowest part of the winding straits. Rugged cliffs hemmed them in on either side, and *Argo* as she advanced began to feel a swirling undercurrent. They moved ahead in fear, for now the clash of the colliding Rocks and the

thunder of surf on the shores fell ceaselessly on their ears. Euphemus[23] seized the dove and climbed on to the prow, while the oarsmen, at Tiphys' orders, made a special effort, hoping by their own strength of arm to drive *Argo* through the Rocks forthwith. They rounded a bend and saw a thing that no one after them has seen—the Rocks were moving apart. Their hearts sank; but now Euphemus launched the dove on her flight and the eyes of all were raised to watch her as she passed between the Rocks.

Once more the Rocks met face to face with a resounding crash, flinging a great cloud of spray into the air. The sea gave a terrific roar and the broad sky rang again. Caverns underneath the crags bellowed as the sea came surging in. A great wave broke against the cliffs and the white foam swept high above them. *Argo* was spun round as the flood reached her.

But the dove got through, unscathed but for the tips of her tail-feathers, which were nipped off by the Rocks. The oarsmen gave a cry of triumph and Tiphys shouted at them to row with all their might, for the Rocks were

---

[21] **Athene** Also known as Athena. Daughter of Zeus, goddess of wisdom and of war, patron of the arts and crafts. She watches over and protects Jason and the Argonauts on their journey.
[22] **Thynia** Exact location uncertain; probably off the coast of the Bosporus Strait, which connect the Sea of Marmora with the Black Sea.

[23] **Euphemus. Tiphys** Two leading Argonauts. **Tiphys** is the steersman for the Argo.

opening again. So they rowed on full of dread, till the backwash, overtaking them, thrust *Argo* in between the Rocks. Then the fears of all were turned to panic. Sheer destruction hung above their heads.

They had already reached a point where they could 5 see the vast sea opening out on either side, when they were suddenly faced by a tremendous billow arched like an overhanging rock. They bent their heads down at the sight, for it seemed about to fall and overwhelm the ship. But Tiphys just in time checked her as she plunged forward, and the great wave slid under her keel. Indeed it raised her stern so high in the air that she was carried clear of the Rocks. Euphemus ran along shouting to all his friends to put their backs into their rowing, and with answering shouts they struck the water. Yet for every foot that *Argo* made she lost two, though the oars bent like curved bows as the men put out their strength.

Just now another overhanging wave came rushing down on them, and when *Argo* had shot end-on like a rolling-pin through the hollow lap of this terrific sea, she found herself held back by the swirling tide just in the place where the Rocks met. To right and left they shook and rumbled; but *Argo* could not budge.

This was the moment when Athene intervened. Holding on to the hard rock with her left hand, she pushed the ship through with the other; and *Argo* clove the air like a winged arrow, though even so the Rocks, clashing in their accustomed way, sheared off the tip of the mascot on the stern. When the men had thus got through unhurt, Athene soared up to Olympus. But the Rocks were now rooted for ever in one spot close to one another. It had been decided by the happy gods that this should be their fate when a human being had seen them and sailed through. The Argonauts, freed from the cold grip of panic, breathed again when they saw the sky once more and the vast ocean stretching out ahead. They felt that they had come through Hell alive.

Tiphys was the first to speak. "I think," he said, "that we can say all's well. *Argo* is safe and so are we. And for that, to whom are we indebted but Athene, who endowed

the ship with supernatural strength when Argus drove the bolts home in her planks? *Argo* shall not be caught; that seems to be a law. And so, Lord Jason, now that Heaven has allowed us to pass safely through the Rocks, I beg you not to dread so much the duty that your king assigned you. Has not Phineus[24] told us that from now on we shall meet no obstacle we cannot easily surmount?"

Tiphys, with that, steered straight across the open sea along the Bithynian coast. But Jason, for his own purposes, took him gently to task. "Tiphys," he said, "why do you try to comfort me in my distress? I was blind and made a fatal error. When Pelias ordered me to undertake this mission, I ought to have refused outright, even though he would have torn me limb from limb without compunction. But as things are, I am obsessed by fears and intolerable anxiety, hating the thought of the cruel sea that we must cross and of what may happen when we land and find the natives hostile, as we are sure to do at every point. Ever since you all rallied to my side these cares have occupied my mind, and when each day is done I spend the night in misery. It is easy for you, Tiphys, to talk in a cheerful vein. You are only concerned for your own life, whereas I care nothing for mine, but *am* concerned for each and all alike, you and the rest of my friends. How can I tell whether I shall bring you safely back to Hellas?"

Jason's speech, which was designed to put his noble 10 comrades to the test, met with acclamation. His heart was warmed by their reassuring cries and he spoke again, this time with greater candour. "My friends, your courage fills me with fresh confidence. The resolution that you show in face of awful perils makes me feel that I could go through Hell itself and fear nothing. However, now that we have left the Clashing Rocks behind us I have no reason to expect another such ordeal, provided that we keep to the course laid down for us by Phineus." . . .

---

[24] **Phineus** Blind prophet, who predicted Jason's adventure; gave advice about navigating the Clashing Rocks.

∞

Book III, Jason and Medea

· · ·

. . . When Chalciope[25] saw her sons among the strangers, 1 she lifted up her hands for joy. They greeted her in the same fashion and then in their happiness embraced her. But she had her moan to make. "So after all," she said, "you were not allowed to roam so very far from your neglected mother: Fate turned you back. But how I have suffered!

This mad desire of yours for Hellas! This blind obedience to your dying father's wishes! What misery, what heartache, they brought me! Why should you go to the city of Orchomenus,[26] whoever he may be, abandoning your widowed mother for the sake of your grandfather's estate?"

Last of all, Aeetes[27] with his queen, Eidyia, who had heard Chalciope speaking, came out of the house. And at

---

[25] **Chalciope** Daughter of King **Aeetes** of Colchis and mother of the shipwrecked sons brought back to Colchis by Jason and the Argonauts.

[26] **Orchomenus** King of the city of Orchomenus, located in Boeotia, or central Greece.
[27] **Aeetes and Eidyia** King and queen of Colchis, parents of **Chalciope** and Medea.

once the whole courtyard was astir. A number of his men busied themselves over the carcass of a large bull; others chopped firewood; others heated water for the baths. Not one of them took a rest: they were working for the king.

Meanwhile Eros,[28] passing through the clear air, had arrived unseen and bent on mischief, like a gadfly setting out to plague the grazing heifers, the fly that cowherds call the breese. In the porch, under the lintel of the door, he quickly strung his bow and from his quiver took a new arrow, fraught with pain. Still unobserved, he ran across the threshold glancing around him sharply. Then he crouched low at Jason's feet, fitted the notch to the middle of the string, and drawing the bow as far as his hands would stretch, shot at Medea. And her heart stood still.

With a happy laugh Eros sped out of the high-roofed hall on his way back, leaving his shaft deep in the girl's breast, hot as fire. Time and again she darted a bright glance at Jason. All else was forgotten. Her heart, brimful of this new agony, throbbed within her and overflowed with the sweetness of the pain.

A working woman, rising before dawn to spin and needing light in her cottage room, piles brushwood on a smouldering log, and the whole heap kindled by the little brand goes up in a mighty blaze. Such was the fire of Love, stealthy but all consuming, that swept through Medea's heart. In the turmoil of her soul, her soft cheeks turned from rose to white and white to rose. 5

By now the servants had prepared a banquet for the newcomers, who gladly sat down to it after refreshing themselves in warm baths. When they had enjoyed the food and drink, Aeetes put some questions to his grandsons:

"Sons of my daughter and of Phrixus,[29] the most deserving guest I have ever entertained, how is it that you are back in Aea[30]? Did some misadventure cut your journey short? You refused to listen when I told you what a long way you had to go. But I knew; for I myself was whirled along it in the chariot of my father Helios,[31] when he took my sister Circe[32] to the Western Land and we reached the coast of Tyrrhenia, where she still lives, far, far indeed from Colchis. But enough of that. Tell me plainly what befell you, who your companions are, and where you disembarked."

To answer these questions, Argus stepped out in front of his brothers, being the eldest of the four. His heart misgave him for Jason and his mission; but he did his best to conciliate the king. "My lord," he said, "that ship of ours soon fell to pieces in a storm. We hung on to one of her planks and were cast ashore on the Island of Ares[33] in the pitch-dark night. But Providence looked after us: there was not a sign of the War-god's birds, who used to haunt the desert isle. They were driven off by these men, who had landed on the previous day and been detained there by the will of Zeus in pity for ourselves—or was it only chance? In any case, they gave us plenty of food and clothing directly they heard the illustrious name of Phrixus, and your own, my lord, since it was your city they were bound for. As to their purpose, I will be frank with you. A certain king, wishing to banish and dispossess this man because he is the most powerful of the Aeolids, has sent him here on a desperate venture, maintaining that the House of Aeolus will not escape the inexorable wrath of Zeus, the heavy burden of their guilt, and vengeance for the sufferings of Phrixus, till the fleece returns to Hellas. The ship that brought him was built by Pallas Athene on altogether different lines from the Colchian craft, the rottenest of which, as luck would have it, fell to us. For *she* was smashed to pieces by the wind and waves, whereas the bolts of *Argo* hold her together in any gale that blows, and she runs as sweetly when the crew are tugging at the oars as she does before the wind. This ship he manned with the pick of all Achaea, and in her he has come to your city, touching at many ports and crossing formidable seas, in the hope that you will let him have the fleece. But it must be as you wish. He has not come here to force your hand. On the contrary, he is willing to repay you simply for the gift by reducing for you your bitter enemies, the Sauromatae, of whom I told him. But now you may wish to know the names and lineage of your visitors. Let me tell you. Here is the man to whom the others rallied from all parts of Hellas, Jason son of Aeson, Cretheus' son. He must be a kinsman of our own on the father's side, if he is a grandson of Cretheus, for Cretheus and Athamas were both sons of Aeolus, and our father Phrixus was a son of Athamas. Next, and in case you have heard that we have a son of Helios with us, behold the man, Augeias. And this is Telamon, son of the illustrious Aeacus, a son of Zeus himself. Much the same is true of all the rest of Jason's followers. They are all sons or grandsons of immortal gods."

The king was filled with rage as he listened to Argus. And now, in a towering passion, he gave vent to his displeasure, the brunt of which fell on the sons of Chalciope, whom he held responsible for the presence of the rest. His eyes blazed with fury as he burst into speech:

"You scoundrels! Get out of my sight at once. Get out of my country, you and your knavish tricks, before you meet a Phrixus and a fleece you will not relish. It was no fleece that brought you and your confederates from Hellas, but a plot to seize my sceptre and my royal power. If you had not eaten at my table first, I would tear your tongues out and chop off your hands, both of them, and send you back with nothing but your feet, to teach you to think twice before starting on another expedition. As for all that about the blessed gods, it is nothing but a pack of lies." 10

---

[28] **Eros** The young god of love, son of Aphrodite. Called Cupido by the Romans.
[29] **Phrixus** Husband of **Chalciope**. He escaped to Colchis on the back of the a flying ram. Welcomed by King **Aeetes**, he offered the ram as a sacrifice to Zeus. He then hung the golden fleece in King **Aeetes'** garden, where it was protected by a monster.
[30] **Aea** Name of the capital city of Colchis, ruled by King **Aeetes**. Port on the Tyrrhenian Sea, which is on the west coast of Italy. Also the home of **Circe**, sister of King **Aeetes** and aunt of Medea.
[31] **Helios** The sun god and father of **Aeetes** and Circe and many other mythic characters.
[32] **Circe** Sister to King **Aeetes** and aunt to Medea. Medea and Jason visit her on their return to **Iolcus**.

---

[33] **Ares** The god of war; known as Mars by the Romans.

Telamon's gorge rose at this outburst from the angry king, and he was on the point of flinging back defiance, to his own undoing, when he was checked by Jason, who forestalled him with a more politic reply.

"My lord," he said, "pray overlook our show of arms. We have not come to your city and palace with any such designs as you suspect. Nor have we predatory aims. Who of his own accord would brave so vast a sea to lay his hands on other people's goods? No; it was Destiny and the cruel orders of a brutal king that sent me here. Be generous to your suppliants, and I will make all Hellas ring with the glory of your name. And by way of more immediate recompense, we are prepared to take the field in your behalf against the Sauromatae or any other tribe you may wish to subdue."

Jason's obsequious address had no effect. The king was plunged in sullen cogitation, wondering whether to leap up and kill them on the spot or to put their powers to the proof. He ended by deciding for a test and said to Jason:

"Sir, there is no need for me to hear you out. If you are really children of the gods or have other grounds for approaching me as equals in the course of your piratical adventure, I will let you have the golden fleece—that is, if you still want it when I have put you to the proof. For I am not like your overlord in Hellas, as you describe him; I am not inclined to be ungenerous to men of rank.

"I propose to test your courage and abilities by set- 15 ting you a task which, though formidable, is not beyond the strength of my two hands. Grazing on the plain of Ares, I have a pair of bronze-footed and fire-breathing bulls. These I yoke and drive over the hard fallow of the plain, quickly ploughing a four-acre field up to the ridge at either end. Then I sow the furrows, not with corn, but with the teeth of a monstrous serpent, which presently come up in the form of armed men, whom I cut down and kill with my spear as they rise up against me on all sides. It is morning when I yoke my team and by evening I have done my harvesting. That is what I do. If you, sir, can do as well, you may carry off the fleece to your king's palace on the very same day. If not, you shall not have it—do not deceive yourself. It would be wrong for a brave man to truckle to a coward."

Jason listened to this with his eyes fixed on the floor; and when the king had finished, he sat there just as he was, without a word, resourceless in the face of his dilemma. For a long time he turned the matter over in his mind, unable boldly to accept a task so clearly fraught with peril. But at last he gave the king an answer which he thought would serve:

"Your Majesty, right is on your side and you leave me no escape whatever. Therefore I will take up your challenge, in spite of its preposterous terms, and though I may be courting death. Men serve no harsher mistress than Necessity, who drives me now and forced me to come here at another king's behest."

He spoke in desperation and was little comforted by Aeetes' sinister reply: "Go now and join your company: you have shown your relish for the task. But if you hesitate to yoke the bulls or shirk the deadly harvesting, I will take the matter up myself in a manner calculated to make others shrink from coming here and pestering their betters."

He had made his meaning clear, and Jason rose from his chair. Augeias and Telamon followed him at once, and so did Argus, but without his brothers, whom he had warned by a nod to stay there for the time being. As the party went out of the hall, Jason's comeliness and charm singled him out from all the rest: and Medea, plucking her bright veil aside, turned wondering eyes upon him. Her heart smouldered with pain and as he passed from sight her soul crept out of her, as in a dream, and fluttered in his steps.

They left the palace with heavy hearts. Meanwhile 20 Chalciope, to save herself from Aeetes' wrath, had hastily withdrawn to her own room together with her sons. Medea too retired, a prey to all the inquietude that Love awakens. The whole scene was still before her eyes—how Jason looked, the clothes he wore, the things he said, the way he sat, and how he walked to the door. It seemed to her, as she reviewed these images, that there was nobody like Jason. His voice and the honey-sweet words that he had used still rang in her ears. But she feared for him. She was afraid that the bulls or Aeetes with his own hands might kill him; and she mourned him as one already dead. The pity of it overwhelmed her; a round tear ran down her cheek; and weeping quietly she voiced her woes:

"What is the meaning of this grief? Hero or villain (and why should I care which?) the man is going to his death. Well, let him go! And yet I wish he had been spared. Yes, Sovran Lady Hecate, this is my prayer. Let him live to reach his home. But if he must be conquered by the bulls, may he first learn that I for one do not rejoice in his cruel fate."

While Medea thus tormented herself, Jason was listening to some advice from Argus, who had waited to address him till the people and the town were left behind and the party were retracing their steps across the plain.

"My lord," he said, "I have a plan to suggest. You will not like it; but in a crisis no expedient should be left untried. You have heard me speak of a young woman who practices witchcraft under the tutelage of the goddess Hecate. If we could win her over, we might banish from our minds all fear of your defeat in the ordeal. I am only afraid that my mother may not support me in this scheme. Nevertheless, since we all stand to lose our lives together, I will go back and sound her."

"My friend," said Jason, responding to the good will shown by Argus, "if you are satisfied, then I have no objections. Go back at once and seek your mother's aid, feeling your way with care. But oh, how bleak the prospect is, with our one hope of seeing home again in women's hands!"

Soon after this they reached the marsh. Their com- 25 rades, when they saw them coming up, greeted them with cheerful enquiries, which Jason answered in a gloomy vein. "Friends," he said, "if I were to answer all your questions, we should never finish; but the cruel king has definitely set his face against us. He said he had a couple of bronze-footed and fire-breathing bulls grazing on the plain of Ares, and told me to plough a four-acre field with these.

He will give me seed from a serpent's jaws which will produce a crop of earthborn men in panoplies of bronze. And I have got to kill them before the day is done. That is my task. I straightway undertook it, for I had no choice."

The task, as Jason had described it, seemed so impossible to all of them that for a while they stood there without a sound or word, looking at one another in impotent despair. But at last Peleus[34] took heart and spoke out to his fellow chieftains: "The time has come. We must confer and settle what to do. Not that debate will help us much: I would rather trust to strength of arm. Jason, my lord, if you fancy the adventure and mean to yoke Aeetes' bulls you will naturally keep your promise and prepare. But if you have the slightest fear that your nerve may fail you, do not force yourself. And you need not sit there looking round for someone else. I, for one, am willing. The worst that I shall suffer will be death."

So said the son of Aeacus. Telamon too was stirred and eagerly leapt up; next Idas, full of lofty thoughts; then Castor and Polydeuces; and with them one who was already numbered with the men of might though the down was scarcely showing on his cheeks, Meleager son of Oeneus, his heart uplifted by the courage that dares all. But the others made no move, leaving it to these; and Argus addressed the six devoted men[35]:

"My friends, you certainly provide us with a last resource. But I have some hopes of timely help that may be coming from my mother. So I advise you, keen as you are, to do as you did earlier and wait here in the ship for a little while—it is always better to think twice before one throws away one's life for nothing. There is a girl living in Aeetes' palace whom the goddess Hecate has taught to handle with extraordinary skill all the magic herbs that grow on dry land or in running water. With these she can put out a raging fire, she can stop rivers as they roar in spate, arrest a star, and check the movement of the sacred moon. We thought of her as we made our way down here from the palace. My mother, her own sister, might persuade her to be our ally in the hour of trial; and with your approval I am prepared to go back to Aeetes' palace this very day and see what I can do. Who knows? Some friendly Power may come to my assistance." . . .

---

[34] **Peleus** A leading Argonaut; father of the warrior Achilles in Homer's *Iliad* (see Chapter 2).

[35] **six devoted men** The six Argonauts who pledge their loyalty to death for Jason (above, each gives a testimonial).

∞

Book IV, Homeward Bound

. . . Passing swiftly over the Ausonian Sea, with the Tyrrhenian coast in sight, they came to the famous haven of Aea, took *Argo* close in, and tied up to the shore.

Here they found Circe bathing her head in the salt water. She had been terrified by a nightmare in which she saw all the rooms and walls of her house streaming with blood, and fire devouring all the magic drugs with which she used to bewitch her visitors. But she managed to put out the red flames with the blood of a murdered man, gathering it up in her hands; and so the horror passed. When morning came she rose from bed, and now she was washing her hair and clothes in the sea.

A number of creatures whose ill-assorted limbs declared them to be neither man nor beast had gathered round her like a great flock of sheep following their shepherd from the fold. Nondescript monsters such as these, fitted with miscellaneous limbs, were once produced spontaneously by Earth out of the primeval mud, when she had not yet solidified under a rainless sky and was deriving no moisture from the blazing sun. But Time, combining this with that, brought the animal creation into order. The Argonauts were dumbfounded by the scene. But a glance at Circe's form and eyes convinced them all that she was the sister of Aeetes.

As soon as she had dismissed the fears engendered by her dream, Circe set out for home, but as she left she invited the young men to come with her, beckoning them on in her own seductive way. Jason told them to take no notice, and they all stayed where they were. But he himself, bringing Medea with him, followed in Circe's steps till they reached her house. Circe, at a loss to know why they had come, invited them to sit in polished chairs; but without a word they made for the hearth and sat down there after the manner of suppliants in distress. Medea hid her face in her hands, Jason fixed in the ground the great hilted sword with which he had killed Apsyrtus,[36] and neither of them looked her in the face. So she knew at once that these were fugitives with murder on their hands and took the course laid down by Zeus, the god of suppliants, who heartily abhors the killing of a man, and yet as heartily befriends the killer. She set about the rites by which a ruthless slayer is absolved when he seeks asylum at the hearth. First, to atone for the unexpiated murder, she took a suckling pig from a sow with dugs still swollen after littering. Holding it over them, she cut its throat and let the blood fall on their hands. Next she propitiated Zeus with other libations, calling on him as the Cleanser, who listens to a murderer's prayer with friendly ears. Then the attendant naiads who did her housework carried all the refuse out of doors. But she herself stayed by the hearth,

---

[36] **Apsyrtus** Half brother of Medea. He chased Medea and Jason as they fled Colchis. They plotted to murder him

burning cakes and other wineless offerings with prayers to Zeus, in the hope that she might cause the loathsome Furies[37] to relent, and that he himself might once more smile upon this pair, whether the hands they lifted up to him were stained with a kinsman's or a stranger's blood.

When all was done she raised them up, seated them ⁵ in polished chairs and taking a seat near by, where she could watch their faces, she began by asking them to tell her what had brought them overseas, from what port they had sailed to visit her and why they had sought asylum at her hearth. Horrible memories of her dream came back to her as she wondered what was coming; and she waited eagerly to hear a kinswoman's voice, as soon as the girl had looked up from the ground and she noticed her eyes. For all Children of the Sun[38] were easy to recognize, even from a distance, by their flashing eyes, which shot out rays of golden light.

----

[37] **Furies** The avenging goddesses of guilt; they relentlessly pursue those who commit murder and other violent crimes. These winged maidens had serpents in their hair and blood oozing from their eyes.
[38] **Children of the Sun** Offspring of Perse, daughter of Ocean and **Helios**, the sun god. Medea's father, **Aeetes**, and his sister **Circe** are products of this union.

Medea, daughter of Aeetes the black-hearted king, answered all her aunt's questions, speaking quietly in the Colchian tongue. She told her of the quest and voyage of the Argonauts, of their stern ordeal, and how she herself had been induced to sin by her unhappy sister and had fled from her father's tyranny with Phrixus' sons; but she said nothing of the murder of Apsyrtus. Not that Circe was deceived. Nevertheless she felt some pity for her weeping niece.

"Poor girl," she said, "you have indeed contrived for yourself a shameful and unhappy home-coming; for I am sure you will not long be able to escape your father's wrath. The wrongs you have done him are intolerable, and he will soon be in Hellas itself to avenge his son's murder. However, since you are my suppliant and kinswoman, I will not add to your afflictions now that you are here. But I do demand that you should leave my house, you that have linked yourself to this foreigner, whoever he may be, this man of mystery whom you have chosen without your father's consent. And do not kneel to me at my hearth, for I never will approve your conduct and disgraceful flight."

Medea's grief, when she heard this, was more than she could bear. She drew her robe across her eyes and wailed till Jason took her by the hand and led her out of doors shivering with fear. Thus they left Circe's house. . . .

❧

Questions for Critical Thinking

1. Compare and contrast this Hellenistic epic with Homer's Greek epic, giving examples from each work.

2. In what ways does Apollonius humanize Jason and Medea?

5

CLASSICAL ROME
From Republic to Empire

CICERO
Selection from *On the Republic*

For more than two thousand years Cicero (106–43 BCE) has been one of the West's guiding spirits. The impact of his writings first on Rome and later on Europe cannot be overestimated. Within his vast works, the most famous passage is perhaps "The Dream of Scipio" from *On the Republic,* a study of the ideal polity. Its popularity stems largely from its lofty theme: The joys of heaven are greater than the glories of earth. Romans heard in this theme an echo of Plato; later, Christians thought it signaled that Cicero was one of them, even if he did live before Christ.

Cicero was both a man of action and a man of letters. When in power, he worked to heal the social ills of late republican Rome (133–31 BCE), a period racked by civil wars. When in eclipse, he wrote prodigiously and quickly, advocating constitutionalism and opposing autocracy. In the end he failed as a statesman and, though not a conspirator, was killed in the fallout from the plot to murder Julius Caesar.

Cicero wrote from the vantage point of an eclectic thinker, one who knew philosophy but was not a true philosopher. He was open to criticism and claimed the right to change his mind. In his letters he describes his method of reaching a decision—by debating both sides of a problem. For his treatises, such as *On the Republic,* he favored the dialogue form because its "give-and-take" format enabled readers to make up their minds based on opposing viewpoints.

Two traits characterized Cicero's world: it was civilized and tolerant. To express this ideal, Cicero coined the term *humanitas* (humanity), meaning devotion to books, language, and art. He gave *humanitas* a social face in his dialogues, setting them in a courteous society free of rudeness. He himself lived this ideal, being well read in Greek and Roman letters, philosophy, history, and law. His learning, though highly valued, still could not compete with his love of politics. When called to office, he welcomed the chance to be a "man of the world." Hence, the claim in "The Dream" that contemplation is superior to action must be doubted, reflecting instead Cicero's exile from politics when he wrote it.

Reading the Selection

"The Dream of Scipio" offers a cosmic perspective on human affairs. Not original in outlook, it is a Romanized synthesis of Greek thought on the soul and the afterlife; it is drawn largely from sixth-century thinker Pythagoras, whose ideas were passed on to Plato (see *Phaedo* in Chapter 3). Expressive of *humanitas* and his love of Rome, Cicero's "The Dream" claims that there is a life beyond the grave for deserving politicians and philosophers.

Cicero's choice of Publius Cornelius Scipio (the younger) (ca. 184–129 BCE) as his mouthpiece reflects Cicero's patriotism and Hellenism (love of Greek culture), the bedrock of his ideals. Deeply aware of his status as a "new man" (the first in his family to achieve the consulship), Cicero adopted as spiritual ancestors the younger Scipio and his friends. The grandson of Scipio Africanus (the elder) (237–183 BCE), Rome's savior during the Second Punic War, Scipio the younger was, in his own right, a great statesman and the leader of a highly educated literary circle. It was this circle that introduced to Rome the Stoic ideas that Cicero quoted in "The Dream," such as the stress on virtue and duty.

∞

The Dream of Scipio

As you know, I was military tribune in the Fourth Legion in Africa under the command of the consul Manius Manilius.[1] When I arrived there I was particularly eager to meet King Masinissa,[2] who for good reason was a close friend of my family. When I came into his presence the old man embraced me and wept. Then, after a moment, he lifted his eyes to heaven and uttered these words.

"Most glorious Sun and other heavenly beings, I offer you my thanks! For before I depart from this life, I am now seeing with my own eyes, within this kingdom of mine and beneath my roof, Publius Cornelius Scipio. The very sound of his name revives my strength. For never a moment has the recollection of his glorious, invincible forbear faded from my memory."

Then I began asking him questions about his kingdom, and he in turn interrogated me about Rome; and so we spent the whole day in conversation. Afterwards, he entertained me in regal splendour, and we continued our discussion far into the night, as the aged king wanted nothing better than to talk of Africanus. He had not forgotten a single deed the great man had ever done, or a single word he had ever uttered.

When we finally parted and retired to bed, my journey and the lateness of the hour had made me tired, and I fell into a deeper sleep than usual. As I slept I had a dream, prompted no doubt by what we had been talking about. For it frequently happens that the subjects of our meditations and discussions reappear in our dreams. This happened for example to the poet Ennius[3]; he writes of his dream about Homer, who was naturally the constant subject of his thoughts and conversations when he

was awake. And so I dreamt that Africanus was with me; his appearance recalled his portrait busts rather than his actual living self.

. . .

I recognized him—and trembled with fear. But he spoke to me; and this is what he said.

"Calm yourself, Scipio. Do not be afraid. But remember carefully the things I am about to tell you. Do you see that city there? It was I who made its people submit to Rome. But now they are starting up the old conflicts once again; they refuse to remain at peace!" And from where he stood amid the bright illumination of radiant stars, he pointed down at Carthage, and began speaking once more. "This," he declared, "is the city you have come to attack. At present you are not much more than an ordinary soldier. But within the space of two years you will have been elected consul, and then you will overthrow the place utterly. Thereafter the surname, which you now bear as an inheritance from myself, will be yours by your own right. Later on, after you have destroyed Carthage and celebrated a Triumph, after you have held the office of censor and undertaken missions to Egypt, Syria, Asia and Greece, you will be elected to the consulship for the second time, while you are absent, and you will win a very great war and raze Numantia[4] to the ground. But at the time when you yourself are proceeding in Triumph to the Capitol, you will find the government in a state of confusion: for which the machinations of my grandson will be responsible.

"After that, Africanus, it will be your duty to devote to your people the full splendid benefit of all your integrity, talent and wisdom. But at that juncture I see two divergent paths of destiny opening up before you. For when your life has completed seven times eight circuitous revolutions of

[1] **Manius Manilius** Consul in 149 BCE who commanded the Roman army that besieged Carthage, in North Africa, during the Third Punic War.
[2] **King Masinissa** King of Numidia, which was located in modern-day Algeria. He helped start the Third Punic War.
[3] **Ennius** Third-century BCE Roman poet and playwright who is considered to be the founder of Latin literature. Only fragments of his works remain.

[4] **Numantia** Ancient city in Spain, captured by the Romans in 133 BCE. This victory marked the triumph of the Romans in Spain.

the sun, and when these two numbers, each of which for a different reason is regarded as possessing some quality of perfection, have in their natural course brought you to your supreme moment of destiny, that is the time when the entire Roman State will turn to you and all that you stand for: the Senate, every right-minded citizen, our subject allies, the entire Latin people. The fate of the whole country, at that juncture, will depend on you and you alone. In other words, it will be your duty to assume the role of dictator, and restore order to our commonwealth—provided only that death does not overtake you at the criminal hands of your own kinsmen!"

At this, Laelius[5] cried out aloud, and a deep groan was heard from all. But the younger Scipio smiled serenely, and went on: "Hush! Do not, I beg you, awaken me from my sleep. Listen a little longer, and take heed of what my ancestor went on to say next."

For then he continued speaking. "But consider this, Africanus," he said, "and the thought will make your determination to defend your homeland even greater than it is already. Every man who has preserved or helped his country, or has made its greatness even greater, is reserved a special place in heaven, where he may enjoy an eternal life of happiness. For all things that are done on earth nothing is more acceptable to the Supreme God, who rules the whole universe, than those gatherings and assemblages of men who are bound together by law, the communities which are known as states. Indeed, it is from here in heaven that the rulers and preservers of those states once came; and it is to here that they eventually return."

By now I was thoroughly alarmed. It was not the idea of death that frightened me so much, but the thought of treachery inside my own family. Nevertheless, I managed to ask Africanus a question. Was he, was my father Paullus, were the other men we think of as having died, really dead? Or were they still alive?

"To be sure they are still living," he replied, "seeing that they have escaped from the prison-house of their bodies—that is to say from 'life,' as you call it, which is, in fact, death. Look: do you not see your father Paullus coming towards you?"

Indeed I now saw him approaching; and I burst into a flood of tears. But my father put his arms round me and kissed me, and told me not to weep. So when I had suppressed my tears and felt able to speak, I cried out, "Since this, most revered and best of fathers, is true life, as I hear Africanus declare, why must I stay any longer upon earth? Why should I not come and join you, with the utmost possible speed?"

"That must not be," replied Paullus. "For unless God, whose sacred domain is all that you see around you here, has freed you from your confinement in the body, you cannot be admitted to this place. For men were brought into existence in order that they should inhabit the globe known as the earth, which you see here at the centre of this holy space. They have been endowed with souls made out of the everlasting fires called stars and constellations, consisting of globular, spherical bodies which are animated by the divine mind and move with marvellous speed, each in its own orbit and cycle. Therefore it is destined that you, Publius, and all other righteous men, shall suffer your souls to stay in the custody of the body. You must not abandon human life except at the command of him who gave it to you. For otherwise you would have failed in the duty which you, like the rest of humanity, have to fulfil.

"Instead, then, Scipio, do upon earth as your grandfather has done. Do as I have done, who begot you. Cherish justice and devotion. These qualities in abundance are owed to parents and kinsmen; and most of all they are owed to one's country.

"That is the life which leads to heaven, and to the company of those who, having completed their lives in the world, are now released from their bodies and dwell in that region you see over there, which the Greeks have taught you people on earth to call the Milky Way." And he pointed to a circle of light, blazing brilliantly among all other fires.

As I gazed out from where I stood, first in one direction and then another, the whole prospect looked marvellously beautiful. There were stars we never see from the earth, and they were larger than we could possibly have imagined. The smallest was the luminary which is farthest away from heaven and nearest to the earth, and shines with reflected light. These starry spheres were much larger than the earth. Indeed the earth now seemed to me so small that I began to think less of this empire of ours, which only amounts to a pinpoint on its surface.

· · ·

While I looked more and more intently down at the earth Africanus checked me. "How long," he asked, "do you propose to keep your eyes fastened down there upon that world of yours? Look up, instead, and look round at the sacred region into which you have now entered.

"The universe is held together by nine concentric spheres. The outermost sphere is heaven itself, and it includes and embraces all the rest. For it is the Supreme God in person, enclosing and comprehending everything that exists, that is to say all the stars which are fixed in the sky yet rotate upon their eternal courses. Within this outermost sphere are eight others. Seven of them contain the planets—a single one in each sphere, all moving in the contrary direction to the great movement of heaven itself. The next sphere to the outermost is occupied by the orb which people on earth name after Saturn. Below Saturn shines the brilliant light of Jupiter, which is benign and healthful to mankind. Then comes the star we call Mars, red and terrible to men upon earth.

"Next, almost midway between heaven and earth, blazes the Sun. He is the prince, lord and ruler of all the other worlds, the mind and guiding principle of the entire universe, so gigantic in size that everything, everywhere, is pervaded and drenched by his light. In attendance upon the Sun are Venus and Mercury, each in its own orbit; and the lowest sphere of all contains the Moon, which takes

---
[5] **Laelius** Gaius Laelius was one of the characters who appeared in several of Cicero's writing as a voice or foil in the dialogues.

its light, as it revolves, from the rays of the sun. Above the Moon there is nothing which is not eternal, but beneath that level everything is moral and transient (except only for the souls in human beings, which are a gift to mankind from the gods). For there below the Moon is the earth, the ninth and lowest of the spheres, lying at the centre of the universe. The earth remains fixed and without motion; all things are drawn to it, because the natural force of gravity pulls them down."

I surveyed the scene in a stupor. But finally I recovered enough to ask: "What is this sound, so strong and so sweet, which fills my ears?"

"That," he replied, "is the music of the spheres. They create it by their own motion as they rush upon their way. The intervals between them, although differing in length, are all measured according to a fixed scheme of proportions; and this arrangement produces a melodious blend of high and low notes, from which emerges a varied harmony. For it cannot be that these vast movements should take place in silence, and nature has ordained that the spheres utter music, those at the summit giving forth high sounds, whereas the sounds of those beneath are low and deep. That is to say, the spheres containing the uppermost stars, comprising those regions of the sky where the movements are speediest, give out a high and piercing sound, whereas the Moon, which lies beneath all the others, sends forth the lowest note.

"The ninth of the spheres, the earth, fixed at the centre of the universe, is motionless and silent. But the other eight spheres produce seven different sounds on the scale—not eight, since two of these orbs move at identical speeds, but seven, a number which is the key to almost all things that exist. Clever men, by imitating these musical effects with their stringed instruments and voices, have given themselves the possibility of eventually returning to this place; and the same chance exists for others too, who during their earthly lives have devoted their outstanding talents to heavenly activities.

"The ears of mankind are filled with this music all the time. But they have become completely deaf to its melody; no other human faculty has become so atrophied as this. The same thing happens where the Nile rushes down from high mountains to the place known as Catadupa. For the sound there is so loud that the people who live nearby have entirely lost their sense of hearing. And that, too, is why the mighty music of the spheres, created by the immeasurably fast rotations of the whole universe, cannot be apprehended by the human ears—any more than you can look at the light of the Sun, which is so intense it blots out your power of vision altogether."

The scene filled me with awe and delight. And yet all the time I still could not help riveting my eyes upon our own world there below. Africanus noticed this, and spoke again. "I see," he said, "that your gaze is still fastened, even now, upon the places where mortals dwell upon the earth. But can you not understand that the earth is totally insignificant? Contemplate these heavenly regions instead! Scorn what is mortal!

"For the lips of mankind can give you no fame or glory worth the seeking. Note how few and minute are 25

the inhabited portions of the earth, and look upon the vast deserts that divide each one of these patches from the next. See, the inhabitants of the world are so cut off from one another that their different centres cannot even communicate with each other. The place where you yourself dwell, for example, is far removed from certain of the other populated areas, both in latitude and longitude; and some people live in regions that are at the very opposite end of the world from yours. Surely you cannot expect *them* to honour your name.

"Furthermore, you will observe that the surface of the earth is girdled and encompassed by a number of different zones; and that the two which are most widely separated from one another, and lie beneath opposite poles of the heavens, are rigid with icy cold, while the central, broadest zone is burnt up with the heat of the sun. Two others, situated between the hot zones and the cold, are habitable. The zone which lies towards the south has no connexion with yours at all; it represents your antipodes. As to its northern counterpart, where you yourselves live, you will realize, if you look, what a diminutive section of this region can really be regarded as your property. For the territory you occupy is nothing more than a small island, narrow from north to south, somewhat less narrow from east to west, and surrounded by the sea which is known on earth as the Atlantic, or the Great Sea, or the Ocean. In spite of the grand name this stretch of water bears, you can tell from here how tiny it really is.

"And I must disabuse you of any idea that your own fame, or the fame of any one of us, could ever be great enough to extend beyond these known and settled lands. It could never scale the Caucasus mountains (you see them down there); it could never swim the river Ganges. Not one of the inhabitants of all those eastern tracts, or the remote west either, or the far off north and south, will ever so much as hear the sound of your name! And once you leave all these hosts of people out of account, you will have to conclude that the area over which your glory is so eager to extend itself is really of the most trifling dimensions.

"And now about the people who *do* know and speak about us. The point is, how long will this go on? Assume, if you like, that future generations, having inherited our praises from their fathers, will indeed retain the desire to hand them down to their children as well. Even so the deluges and conflagrations which inevitably descend upon the earth at fixed intervals will make it impossible for any glory we may gain in this way to be eternal—or even to last for any length of time. But in any case why do you regard it as so important to be talked about by people who have not yet been born? After all, you were never spoken of by all the multitudes who lived before you—and they were every bit as numerous, and were better men.

"It is also necessary to remind ourselves that even the people who may in fact hear our names mentioned will not retain the recollection even for as much as the space of one year. I am not referring to the year as it is commonly understood, which is measured according to the revolution of the sun, that is to say according to the movements of one single star. But when *all* the stars return to the places where they started from, so that after an immense interval has elapsed the entire heavens finally resume their original configuration, then that great period of rotation can truly be called a year—but how many generations of human life it comprises, I should not venture to say.

"Long ago, when the spirit of Romulus ascended into 30 these sacred expanses, it seemed to those living at the time that a shadow suddenly passed over the sun, and its light was blotted out. When, once again, the sun shall go into eclipse in the very same position and at the very same hour, that will signify that all the constellations and stars have returned to their original positions: and then you will know that the Year has been completed. But you must understand that, up to now, not one twentieth part of its course has been run.

. . .

"As for yourself, do not abandon hope of coming back here one day. For this is the place which offers great and eminent men their authentic reward—and, after all, such fame as you are able to win among mere human beings can evidently be disregarded, seeing that it is scarcely capable of enduring even for a small part of one single year. Look upwards, then! Contemplate this place which is a habitation for all eternity! Then you will not need any longer to be at the mercy of what the multitude says about you: then you will not have to put your trust in whatever human rewards your achievements may earn.

"Instead let Virtue herself, by her own unaided allurements, summon you to a glory that is genuine and real. Feel no concern about what other people may say about you. They will say it in any case. Besides, whatever words they may choose to utter will not pass beyond the narrow limits you now see below you. No utterance of man about his fellowmen has ever been lasting. When a person dies his words die with him. Posterity forgets them; and they pass into annihilation."

He stopped speaking, and I cried out my assent. "Even when I was only a boy, Africanus," I declared, "I was already exerting myself to the utmost to follow in your footsteps, and in those of my father. I longed to be not unworthy of your fame! And if there is really a path leading right to the entrance of heaven for those who have served their country well, the knowledge of this great goal before me will inspire me to redouble my endeavours."

"Strive on," he replied. "And rest assured that it is only your body that is mortal; your true self is nothing of the kind. For the man you outwardly appear to be is not yourself at all. Your real self is not that corporeal, palpable shape, but the spirit inside. *Understand that you are god.* You have a god's capacity of aliveness and sensation and memory and foresight; a god's power to rule and govern and direct the body that is your servant, in the same way as God himself, who reigns over us, directs the entire universe. And this rule exercised by eternal God is mirrored in the dominance of your frail body by your immortal soul.

. . .

"That which is always in motion is eternal; yet that which 35 communicates motion to something else, but is itself moved by another force, must necessarily cease to live when the transmission of this motion to it has ceased. Consequently the only thing that never ceases to move is something which has the power of starting up motion all *on its own*—it can go on moving because its power to achieve motion depends on itself and itself alone. This, therefore, it must be concluded, is the source and first principle of motion for all things that move.

"Being the first principle, it never had a beginning: since the first principle is what everything else has originated from, it cannot possibly have originated from anything else. For if it owed its origin to something else, it could not be described as the first principle.

"And since it never had a beginning it will never have an end. For if the first principle were destroyed it could never be reborn from any other source and would no longer be able to create things on its own account—which is obviously what the first principle has to do.

"The beginning of all movement, then, comes from that which has set itself in motion: which can neither be born nor die. For if that were not so, one would have to envisage the entire heavens and all things that have ever been created crashing down and coming to an end—for that is what would happen if the force generating their motion were taken away from them.

"Since, therefore, it is plain that the self-moving principle is eternal, the same must evidently apply to the human soul. For unlike lifeless objects which can only be set in motion from outside, the soul, by its very essence and nature, is a living thing such as can only derive its life and motion from within itself. And since, uniquely, it possesses this characteristic of self-impulsion, surely it has no beginning, and lives for ever.

. . .

"Use this eternal force, therefore, for the most splendid 40 deeds it is in you to achieve! And the very best deeds are those which serve your country. A soul devoted to such pursuits will find it easiest of all to soar upwards to this place, which is its proper habitation and home. And its flight will be all the more rapid if already during the period of its confinement within the body it has ranged freely abroad, and, by contemplating what lies outside itself, has contrived to detach itself from the body to the greatest possible degree.

"When, on the other hand, a man has failed to do this, and has abandoned himself instead to bodily indulgence and become its slave, letting the passions which serve pleasure impel him to flout the laws both of gods and of men, his soul, after departing from his body, hovers about close to the earth. Nor does it return to this place until many ages of torment have been undergone."

Then Africanus vanished; and I awoke from my sleep.

Questions for Critical Thinking

1. Discuss the music of the spheres of the universe as explained by Africanus, and note his description of earth and its inhabitants.

2. What did Africanus mean when he told Scipio that "you are god," and what was the lesson that Africanus wanted Scipio to learn from that statement?

CATULLUS
Poems

Born into a wealthy and distinguished Italian family, Catullus (ca. 84–57 BCE) enjoyed a short, bittersweet life during the turbulent last years of the Roman Republic. Indeed, his life seemed to mirror the unsettled times of political intrigue and the scramble for power as he suffered through torrid love affairs, experienced fickle friendships, and endured life's capriciousness.

Often rebuffed by his manipulative mistress, Clodia, the wife of a Roman consul, whom he immortalized in his love poetry as "Lesbia" (named for Sappho; see the selection of her extant poetry in Chapter 2), Catullus chose to spend much of his time in travel. While away from Rome, he was intent on trying to heal his wounded heart and restore his fortune. During one long voyage to the eastern Mediterranean, he wrote a series of poems setting forth his adventures, as he tried to put his life in perspective. This poetry survived his own short life to leave a personal testament; it transcends the times and reminds readers that sometimes the best way to survive calamity is to turn inward and commune with one's soul.

Catullus's poems, closely linked with the Alexandrian style (see Theocritus's *Idylls* in Chapter 4), fall into three categories: the "small" or short epic, epigrams or elegies, and love poetry. In his short epics, he exhibits his vast knowledge of Greek myth. His epigrams, short and diverse, range across the spectrum of human life—from mourning a friend's death to attacking Julius Caesar. His love poems—his best-known works—express his innermost feelings, from raw lust to calculated betrayals and total rejection that break the heart.

Reading the Selections

Poems 5, 51, 72, and 75 treat of Catullus's love for his beloved Lesbia, though in contradictory ways. Poem 22 reveals his sharp insight into the human condition. What Catullus wrote regarding the human tendency to self-delusion still rings true after more than two thousand years.

∞

Poems

5

Lesbia
  live with me
& love me so
we'll laugh at all
the sour-faced strict-
ures of the wise.
This sun once set
will rise again,
when our sun sets
follows night &
an endless sleep.
Kiss me now a
thousand times &
now a hundred
more & then a

1 hundred & a
thousand more again
till with so many
hundred thousand
kisses you & I   20
shall both lose count
nor any can
from envy of
so much of kissing
10 put his finger
on the number
of sweet kisses
you of me &
I of you,
darling, have had.   30

22

I must, Varus, tell you:
  Suffenus, known to us both as
a man of elegance, wit
    & sophistication
is also a poet
  who turns out verse by the yard.
No palimpsest copies
  but new books with new ivories
inscribed on Augustan Royal,
  the lines lead-ruled,
red tabs & red wrappers,
  the ends shaved with pumice.
But unwind the scroll
  & Suffenus
the well-known diner-out
  disappears.
A goatherd
  a country bumpkin

1 looks at us—
  strangely transmogrified.   20
What should one think?
  The envy of wits
becomes
  at the touch of the Muses
a bundle of gaucheries. . . .
  and he likes nothing better
fancies himself
10   in the role of a poet. . . .
Yet who,
  in his own way,
is not a Suffenus?
  Each has his blind spot.   30
The mote & the beam.
  As Aesop says,
the pack on our own back
  that we don't see.

51

Godlike the man who
sits at her side, who
watches and catches
   that laughter
which (softly) tears me
to tatters: nothing is
left of me, each time
   I see her,
. . . tongue numbed; arms, legs
melting, on fire; drum
drumming in ears; headlights gone black.
	1
	
	10

1   **Coda**

Her ease is your sloth, Catullus
you itch & roll in her ease:

former kings and cities
lost in the valley of her arm.

72

There was a time, Lesbia, when   1
you confessed only to Catullus in love:
you would set me above Jupiter himself.
I loved you then
   not as men love their women
but as a father his children—his family.
Today I know you too well
   and desire burns deeper in me

and you are more coarse   10
   more frivolous in my thought.
"How," you may ask, "can this be?"
Such actions as yours excite
   increased violence of love,
Lesbia, but with friendless intention.

75

Reason blinded by sin, Lesbia,   1
a mind drowned in its own devotion:
come clothed in your excellences—

I cannot think tenderly of you,
sink to what acts you dare—
I can never cut this love.

∞

Questions for Critical Thinking

1. Discuss the varied types of love and feelings that Catullus expresses in his poems written for Lesbia.

2. What does Catullus think of his fellow poet, Suffenus, and what is the lesson about life that should be drawn from Aesop?

VIRGIL
Selections from the *Aeneid*

Virgil (70–19 BCE), from a modest rural family of northern Italy, studied, as part of his education, the Greek and Alexandrian poets and writers. Homer, his chief inspiration, would guide him through much of his literary career. Returning to his family farm upon completing his education, Virgil worked the land and began to compose poetry. By a series of chance circumstances, he met Octavian, the future Caesar Augustus (ruled 31 BCE–14 CE), to whom he dedicated his first collection of poems. Virgil, upon moving to Rome, was introduced to the wealthy and powerful who became his patrons. His two books of poems, *Eclogues* and *Georgics*, reminded the Romans of the simple rural values that had made them masters of the Mediterranean and the envy of all nations; these poems established Virgil as the leading voice of the Golden Age of Roman literature. Virgil drew on his earlier years as a farmer to argue that the plain life of the early Romans had prepared them for their mission and responsibility as world leaders, but he warned his readers to return to the good old days and to reject the temptation to amass wealth and live in cities.

As Virgil's fame grew, he decided to write an epic that would portray Rome's glorious past down to the triumph of Augustus. His tale was to be a sweeping story of symbolic events built around the adventures of Aeneas, the Trojan prince, who escaped from Troy at the time of its fall with his son, father, and loyal band of soldiers. Driven by fate and his own sense of duty, Aeneas overcame one obstacle after another to fulfill his destiny to found Rome. In laying the foundation of this great nation, Aeneas was foreshadowing Augustus; under his wise and just leadership, Rome was prepared to play a dominant role in history. By today's standards, Virgil's praise for Augustus flatters his hero too much; for the Romans, however, the *Aeneid* inspired generations of young men to take their place among those who served Rome.

Reading the Selections

Book I introduces the major characters in the *Aeneid* and sets the stage for the doomed love affair between Aeneas and Dido that will have repercussions throughout the epic and represents the larger themes Virgil is addressing in his work. Aeneas, after the sack of Troy, sails for Italy, where he and his followers will settle and eventually establish a colony that will one day become Rome. En route, a storm drives his ships to the coast of Africa and Carthage. He and his men are welcomed by Dido, the queen of Carthage. Venus, who is Aeneas's mother, seeks to protect him from Juno, the goddess who is determined to thwart Aeneas's mission to get to Italy.

In this selection from Book I, Dido sees Aeneas for the first time. Dido entertains her new guests at a banquet where, with food and wine, she becomes infatuated with the Trojan prince. Dido asks him to tell about the fall of Troy and his wanderings. Aeneas, in a flashback similar to Odysseus's recounting of his wanderings (see Homer's *Odyssey* in Chapter 2), recounts his adventures from the fall of Troy to arriving in Carthage.

Book VI records Aeneas's journey through the underworld with the aid of a sibyl (a female prophet). Along the way, they encounter many of Aeneas's friends and a few enemies. As Aeneas and the sibyl pass from one hideous scene in the underworld to the next, she explains to him why the dead souls behave as they do.

In the *Aeneid*, Virgil is heavily indebted to Homer, his literary hero; indeed, he modeled his epic's first six books on the *Odyssey* and imitated the *Iliad* in the last six books. Although Virgil's style and method (using invocations, digressions, and similes) recall Homer's, Virgil is a more "civilized" poet, a more self-conscious artist who has an intense feeling for and sense of the past.

∞

Book I

While Trojan Aeneas stood gazing, rooted to the spot and lost in amazement at what he saw, queen Dido in all her beauty arrived at the temple with a great crowd of warriors around her. She was like Diana leading the dance on the banks of the Eurotas or along the ridges of Mount Cynthus with a thousand mountain nymphs thronging behind her on either side.[6] She carries her quiver on her shoulder, and as she walks, she is the tallest of all the goddesses. Her mother Latona does not speak, but a great joy stirs her heart at the sight of her. Dido was like Diana, and like Diana she bore herself joyfully among her people, urging on their work for the kingdom that was to be. Then she sat on her high throne under the coffered roof, in the middle of the temple before the doors of the shrine of the goddess. There, as she was giving laws and rules of conduct to her people, and dividing the work that had to be done in equal parts or allocating it by lot, Aeneas suddenly saw a great throng approaching, Antheus, Sergestus, brave Cloanthus and the other Trojans who had been scattered over the sea by the dark storm and swept away to distant shores. He was astounded, and Achates, too, was stunned with joy and fear. They burned with longing to clasp the hands of their comrades, but were at a loss because they did not understand what they saw. They did nothing, but stayed hidden in their cloak of cloud, waiting to learn how Fortune had dealt with their comrades. On what shore had they left their fleet? Why were they here? For these were picked men coming from each of the ships to plead their case, and they were now walking to the temple with shouting all about them.

They came in and were allowed to address the queen. Ilioneus, the oldest of them, made this appeal: "You are a queen whom Jupiter[7] has allowed to found a new city and curb proud peoples with your justice; we are the unhappy men of Troy, blown by the winds over all the oceans of the world, and we come to you as suppliants. Save our ships from the impious threat of fire. We are god-fearing men. Take pity on us. Look more closely at us—we have not come to Libya to pillage your homes and their gods, to take plunder and drive it down to the shore. Such violence and arrogance are not to be found in the hearts of the defeated.

"There is a place which Greeks know by the name Hesperia.[8] It is an ancient land, strong in war and rich in the fertility of its soil. It was once tilled by Oenotrians,[9] but now we believe their descendants have called themselves Italians after their king Italus. This is where we were steering when suddenly Orion[10] rose in cloud and tempest and drove us on to hidden shallows, the sea overwhelmed us and fierce southerly squalls scattered us far and wide among breakers and uncharted rocks. A few of us drifted ashore here to your land. What manner of men are these? Is this a country of barbarians that allows its people to act in this way? Sailors have a right to the shore and we are refused it. They make war on us and will not let us set foot on land. You may be no respecters of men. You may fear no men's arms, but think of the gods, who see right and wrong and do not forget. Our king was Aeneas. He had no equal for his piety and his care for justice, and no equal in the field of battle. If the Fates still protect him, if he still breathes the air of heaven, if he is not even now laid low among the merciless shades, you would have nothing to fear or to regret by taking the lead in a contest of kindness. In the land of Sicily we have arms and cities and the great Acestes, sprung from Trojan blood. Allow us to draw up our storm-battered ships, to hew timbers in your woods and shape new oars, so that we can make for Italy and Latium with joy in our hearts, if indeed we go to Italy with our comrades and our king; but if they are lost, if you, great Father of the Trojans, are drowned in the sea off Libya, and there are no hopes left in Iulus, then we can at least go back to where we came from across the Sicilian sea, to the place that is prepared for us, and return to king Acestes."[11] So spoke Ilioneus and all the Trojans to a man murmured in agreement.

Then Dido looked down at them and made a brief answer: "Have no fear, men of Troy. Put every anxious thought out of your hearts. This is a new kingdom, and it is harsh necessity that forces me to take these precautions and to post guards on all our frontiers. But who could fail to know about the people of Aeneas and his ancestry, or the city of Troy, the valour of its men and the flames of war that engulfed it? We here in Carthage are not so dull in mind as that. The sun does spare a glance for our Tyrian city when he yokes his horses in the morning. Whether you choose to go to great Hesperia and the fields of Saturn, or to the land of Eryx[12] and king Acestes, you will leave here safe under my protection, and I shall give you supplies to help you on your way. Or do you wish to settle here with me on an equal footing, even here in this kingdom of

---

[6] **Diana, Eurotas, Mount Cynthus** Diana, the Roman goddess (Artemis in the Greek Olympian system) is playing one of her major roles—that of the maiden huntress. She is described as being either along the shores of the Eurotas River, located in Greece near Sparta, or on Mount Cynthus, her alleged birthplace on the island of Delos in the Aegean Sea.
[7] **Jupiter** The original Italian sky-god who was later linked to Zeus, the chief god of the Greek Olympian system. Jupiter was associated with storms and thunder. The Romans placed his temple in Rome at the center of their state religion.
[8] **Hesperia** A Greek name for Italy and Sicily; it means "Land of the Evening." To the Greeks, these lands were to the west.

[9] **Oenotrians** The inhabitants of Oenotria; another name for a region of Italy.
[10] **Orion** Originally, he was a legendary giant hunter. **Diana** then made him into a constellation.
[11] **king Acestes** An earlier Trojan chieftain who had settled in Sicily before the time of Aeneas.
[12] **Eryx** Both a city and a mountain in Sicily. Eryx was a mythical Sicilian hero whose mother was Venus.

Carthage? The city which I am founding is yours. Draw up your ships on the beach. Trojan and Tyrian shall be as one in my eyes. I wish only that your king Aeneas had been driven by the same south wind, and were here with you now. But what I can, I shall do. I shall send men whom I can trust all along the coast, and order them to cover every furthest corner of Libya, in case he has been shipwrecked and is wandering in any of the woods or cities."

The brave Achates and Father Aeneas had long been impatient to break out of the cloud, and at Dido's words their eagerness increased. "Aeneas," said Achates, "son of the goddess, what thoughts are now rising in your heart? You see there is no danger. Our ships are safe. Our comrades are rescued. Only one of them is missing, and we saw him with our own eyes founder in mid-ocean. Everything else is as your mother Venus said it would be."

He had scarcely finished speaking when the cloud that was all about them suddenly parted and dissolved into the clear sky. Aeneas stood there resplendent in the bright light of day with the head and shoulders of a god. His own mother had breathed upon her son and given beauty to his hair and the sparkle of joy to his eyes, and the glow of youth shone all about him. It was as though skilled hands had added embellishments to ivory or applied gilding to silver or Parian marble. Then suddenly, to the surprise of all, he addressed the queen: "The man you are looking for is standing before you. I am Aeneas the Trojan, saved from the Libyan sea. And you, Dido, alone have pitied the unspeakable griefs of Troy. We are the remnants left by the Greeks. We have suffered every calamity that land and sea could inflict upon us. We have lost everything. And now you offer to share your city and your home with us. It is not within our power to repay you as you deserve, nor could whatever survives of the Trojan race, scattered as it is over the face of the wide earth. May the gods bring you the reward you deserve, if there are any gods who have regard for goodness, if there is any justice in the world, if their minds have any sense of right. What happy age has brought you to the light of life? What manner of parents have produced such a daughter? While rivers run into the sea, while shadows of mountains move in procession round the curves of valleys, while the sky feeds the stars, your honour, your name, and your praise will remain for ever in every land to which I am called." As he spoke, he put out his right hand to his friend Ilioneus and his left to Serestus, then greeted the others, brave Gyas, and brave Cloanthus.

Dido of Sidon was amazed at her first sight of him and then at the thought of the ill fortune he had endured. "What sort of chance is this," she exclaimed, "that hounds the son of a goddess through all these dangers? What power has driven you to these wild shores? Are you that Aeneas whom the loving goddess Venus bore to Dardanian Anchises in Phrygia by the river waters of the Simois? I myself remember the Greek Teucer coming to Sidon after being exiled from his native Salamis. He was looking to found a new kingdom, and was helped by my father Belus, who in those days was laying waste the wealth of Cyprus. He had conquered the island and it was under his control. From that day on I knew all the misfortunes of the city of Troy. I knew your name and the names of the Greek kings. Teucer himself, your enemy, held the Teucrians, the people of Troy, in highest respect and claimed descent from an ancient Teucrian family. This is why I now invite your warriors to come into my house. I, too, have known ill fortune like yours and been tossed from one wretchedness to another until at last I have been allowed to settle in this land. Through my own suffering, I am learning to help those who suffer."

With these words she led Aeneas into her royal palace, and as she went she appointed sacrifices to be offered in the temples of the gods. Nor at that moment did she forget Aeneas' comrades on the shore, but sent down to them twenty bulls, a hundred great bristling hogs' backs and a hundred fat lambs with their mothers, rich gifts to celebrate the day. Meanwhile the inside of her palace was being prepared with all royal luxury and splendour. They were laying out a banquet in the central hall and the draperies were of proud purple, richly worked. The silver was massive on the tables, with the brave deeds of their ancestors embossed in gold, a long tradition of feats of arms traced through many heroes from the ancient origins of the race.

But a father's love allowed Aeneas' mind no rest, and he asked Achates to go quickly ahead to the ships to take the news to Ascanius and bring him back to the city. All his thoughts were on his dear son Ascanius. He also told Achates to bring back with him as gifts for Dido some of the treasures that had been rescued from the ruins of Troy, a cloak stiff with gold-embroidered figures and a dress with a border woven of yellow acanthus flowers. These miracles of workmanship had been given to Helen of Argos by her mother Leda, and she had taken them from Mycenae when she came to Troy for her illicit marriage with Paris. There was also the sceptre which had once been carried by Ilione, the eldest daughter of Priam, a necklace of pearls and a double gold coronet set with jewels. Achates set off for the ships in great haste to carry out his instructions.

Venus meanwhile was turning over new schemes in her mind and devising new plans. She decided to change the form and features of Cupid, and send him in place of the lovely young Ascanius to inflame the heart of the queen, driving her to madness by the gifts and winding the fire of passion round her bones. For Venus was afraid of the treacherous house of Carthage and the double-tongued people of Tyre. The thought of the bitterness of Juno's hatred burned in her heart, and as night began to fall and her anxiety kept returning, she spoke to the winged god of love in these words: "My dear son, you are the source of my power. You are my great strength. Only you, my son, can laugh at the thunderbolts which my father, highest Jupiter, hurled against the Giant Typhoeus.[13] To you I come for help. I am your suppliant, begging the aid of your divine power. You well know how Juno's bitter hatred is tossing your own brother from shore to shore round all the seas of the world

---

[13] **Giant Typhoeus** A mythical fire-eating creature who was supposed to live under a volcano.

and you have often grieved to see me grieving. Now he is in the hands of the Phoenician Dido, who is delaying him with honeyed words, and I am afraid of Juno's hospitality and what it may bring. She will not stand idle when the gate of the future is turning. That is why I am resolved to act first, taking possession of the queen by a stratagem and surrounding her with fire. No power in heaven will change her. I shall grapple her to myself in love for Aeneas. As for how you are to achieve this, listen now and I shall tell you my mind. Aeneas has sent for his son, whom I so love, and the young prince is preparing to go to the city of Carthage, bringing gifts which have survived the burning of Troy and the hazards of the sea. I shall put him into a deep sleep and hide him in one of my sacred shrines on Mount Idalium or on the heights of Cythera,[14] so that he will not know of my scheme or suddenly arrive to interrupt it. You will have to use your cunning and take on his appearance for just one night. He is a boy like yourself and you know him, so put on his features, and when the royal table is flowing with wine that brings release, and Dido takes you happily on to her lap and gives you sweet kisses, you can then breathe fire and poison into her and she will not know."

Cupid obeyed his beloved mother. He took off his wings and strutted about copying Iulus' walk and laughing. But the goddess poured quiet and rest into all the limbs of Ascanius, and holding him to the warmth of her breast, she lifted him into the high Idalian woods, where the soft amaracus breathed its fragrant shade and twined its flowers around him.

Now Cupid was obeying his instructions and taking the royal gifts, amused to be escorted by Achates. When he came in, the queen was already sitting under a rich awning on a golden couch in the middle of the palace. Presently Father Aeneas and after him the men of Troy arrived and reclined on purple coverlets. Attendants gave them water for their hands, plied them with bread from baskets and brought them fine woollen napkins with close-cut nap. Inside were fifty serving-women, whose task it was to lay out the food in order in long lines and honour the Penates[15] by tending their fires. There were a hundred other female slaves and a hundred men, all of the same age, to load the tables for the banquet and set out the drinking cups. The Tyrians, too, came thronging through the doors, and the palace was full of joy as they took their appointed places on the embroidered couches. They admired the gifts Aeneas had given. They admired Iulus, the glowing face of the god and his false words, the cloak and the dress embroidered with yellow acanthus flowers. But most of all the unfortunate Dido, doomed to be the victim of a plague that was yet to come, could not have

her fill of gazing, and as she gazed, moved by the boy as much as by the gifts, the fire within her grew. After he had embraced Aeneas and hung on his neck to satisfy the great love of his father who was not his father, he went to the queen. She fixed her eyes and her whole heart on him and sometimes dandled him on her knee, without knowing what a great god was sitting there marking her out to suffer. But he was remembering his mother, the goddess of the Acidalian spring, and he began gradually to erase the memory of Sychaeus,[16] trying to turn towards a living love, a heart that had long been at peace and long unused to passion.

As soon as the first pause came in the feasting and the tables were cleared away, they set up great mixing bowls full of wine and garlanded them with flowers. The palace was ringing with noise and their voices swelled through the spacious hall. Lamps were lit and hung from the gold-coffered ceilings and the flame of torches routed the darkness. The queen now asked for a golden bowl heavy with jewels, and filled it with wine unmixed with water. From this bowl Belus had drunk, and all the royal line descended from Belus. They called for silence in the great chamber as Dido spoke: "Jupiter, to you we pray, since men say that you ordain the laws of hospitality. Grant that this day may be a day of happiness for the Tyrians and the men from Troy, and may our descendants long remember it. Let Bacchus, giver of good cheer, be among us, and kindly Juno, and you, Tyrians, celebrate this gathering with welcome in your hearts."

At these words she poured a libation of wine on the table to honour the gods, and having poured it, she took it first and just touched it to her lips. She then passed it to Bitias with a smile and a challenge. Nothing loth, he took a great draught from the golden bowl foaming to the brim, and bathed himself in wine. The other leaders of the Carthaginians did the same after him. Long-haired Iopas, the pupil of mighty Atlas, then sang to his gilded lyre of the wanderings of the moon and the labours of the sun, the origin of the human race and of the animals, the causes of rain and of the fires of heaven, of Arcturus, of the Hyades, bringers of rain, of the two Triones, the oxen of the Plough; why the winter suns are so eager to immerse themselves in the ocean, and what it is that slows down the passage of the nights. The Tyrians applauded again and again and the Trojans followed their lead.

So the doomed Dido was drawing out the night with all manner of talk, drinking long draughts of love as she asked question after question about Priam and Hector, what armour Memnon, son of the Dawn, was wearing when he came, what kind of horses did Diomede have, how tall was Achilles. "But no," she said, "come tell your hosts from the beginning about the treachery of the Greeks, the sufferings of your people and your own wanderings, for this is now the seventh summer that has carried you as a wanderer over every land and sea."

---

[14] **Mount Idalium and Cythera** Two places sacred to Venus where she was worshiped. Mount Idalium was on the island of Cyprus, and Cythera was an island off the southeast coast of Greece.

[15] **Penates** Roman household gods that watched over the goods and the pantry of the home. Probably originated with ancient Roman kings but, according to legend, Aeneas bought them from Troy. Virgil repeats this story in the *Aeneid*.

---

[16] **Sychaeus** Dido's husband, who was murdered in Tyre. She and her fellow Tyrians escaped to Carthage soon after his death.

∞

Book VI

. . .

You gods who rule the world of the spirits, you silent ₁
shades, and Chaos, and Phlegethon,[17] you dark and silent
wastes, let it be right for me to tell what I have been told,
let it be with your divine blessing that I reveal what is hidden deep in the mists beneath the earth.

They walked in the darkness of that lonely night with
shadows all about them, through the empty halls of Dis
and his desolate kingdom, as men walk in a wood by the
sinister light of a fitful moon when Jupiter has buried the
sky in shade and black night has robbed all things of their
colour. Before the entrance hall of Orcus,[18] in the very
throat of hell, Grief and Revenge have made their beds
and Old Age lives there in despair, with white faced Diseases and Fear and Hunger, corrupter of men, and squalid
Poverty, things dreadful to look upon, and Death and
Drudgery besides. Then there are Sleep, Death's sister,
perverted Pleasures, murderous War astride the threshold, the iron chambers of the Furies and raving Discord
with blood-soaked ribbons binding her viperous hair. In
the middle a huge dark elm spreads out its ancient arms,
the resting-place, so they say, of flocks of idle dreams, one
clinging under every leaf. Here too are all manner of monstrous beasts, Centaurs stabling inside the gate, Scyllas—
half dogs, half women—Briareus with his hundred heads,
the Hydra of Lerna hissing fiercely, the Chimaera armed
in fire, Gorgons and Harpies and the triple phantom of
Geryon. Now Aeneas drew his sword in sudden alarm
to meet them with naked steel as they came at him, and
if his wise companion had not warned him that this was
the fluttering of disembodied spirits, a mere semblance of
living substance, he would have rushed upon them and
parted empty shadows with steel.

Here begins the road that leads to the rolling waters
of Acheron, the river of Tartarus. Here is a vast quagmire
of boiling whirlpools which belches sand and slime into
Cocytus, and these are the rivers and waters guarded by
the terrible Charon in his filthy rags. On his chin there
grows a thick grey beard, never trimmed. His glaring
eyes are lit with fire and a foul cloak hangs from a knot
at his shoulder. With his own hands he plies the pole and
sees to the sails as he ferries the dead in a boat the colour
of burnt iron. He is no longer young but, being a god, enjoys rude strength and a green old age. The whole throng
of the dead was rushing to this part of the bank, mothers,
men, great-hearted heroes whose lives were ended, boys,
unmarried girls and young men laid on the pyre before
the faces of their parents, as many as are the leaves that

fall in the forest at the first chill of autumn, as many as
the birds that flock to land from deep ocean when the cold
season of the year drives them over the sea to lands bathed
in sun. There they stood begging to be allowed to be the
first to cross and stretching out their arms in longing for
the further shore. But the grim boatman takes some here
and some there, and others he pushes away far back from
the sandy shore.

Aeneas, amazed and distressed by all this tumult,
cried out: "Tell me, virgin priestess, what is the meaning of this crowding to the river? What do the spirits
want? Why are some pushed away from the bank while
others sweep the livid water with their oars?" The aged
Sibyl made this brief reply: "Son of Anchises, beyond all
doubt the offspring of the gods, what you are seeing is the
deep pools of the Cocytus and the swamp of the Styx, by
whose divine power the gods are afraid to swear and lie.
The throng you see on this side are the helpless souls of
the unburied. The ferryman there is Charon. Those sail-
ing the waters of the Styx have all been buried. No man
may be ferried from fearful bank to fearful bank of this
roaring current until his bones are laid to rest. Instead
they wander for a hundred years, fluttering round these
shores until they are at last allowed to return to the pools
they have so longed for." The son of Anchises checked his
stride and stood stock still with many thoughts coursing through his mind as he pitied their cruel fate, when
there among the sufferers, lacking all honour in death,
he caught sight of Leucaspis, and Orontes, the captain
of the Lycian fleet, men who had started with him from
Troy, sailed the wind-torn seas and been overwhelmed by
gales from the south that rolled them in the ocean, ships
and crews. . . .

And so they carried on to the end of the road on ₅
which they had started, and at last came near the river.
When the boatman, now in mid-stream, looked ashore
from the waves of the Styx and saw them coming through
the silent wood towards the bank, he called out to them
and challenged them: "You there, whoever you are, making for our river with a sword by your side, come tell us
why you are here. Speak to us from where you stand. Take
not another step. This place belongs to the shades, to Sleep
and to Night, the bringer of Sleep. Living bodies may not
be carried on the boat that plies the Styx. It gave me little
enough pleasure to take even Hercules aboard when he
came, or Theseus, or Pirithous,[19] although they said they
were born of gods and their strength was irresistible. It
was Hercules whose hand put chains on the watchdog of
Tartarus and dragged him shivering from the very throne

---

[17] **Chaos and Phlegethon** The vast abysmal deep that existed
before the universe or the deities, and a river of fire located in
Hades. They symbolize powers or forces deep in the earth—
images of impending evil and frightening events to come.
[18] **Orcus** A Roman name for Hades.

---

[19] **Theseus and Pirithous** Theseus, legendary king of Athens,
and his companion, Pirithous, attempted to carry off Proserpina, who was queen of the dead, from the underworld.

of our king. The others had taken it upon themselves to steal the queen, my mistress, from the chamber of Dis." The answer of the Amphrysian Sibyl was brief: "Here there are no such designs. You have no need for alarm. These weapons of his bring no violence. The monstrous keeper of the gate can bark in his cave and frighten the bloodless shades till the end of time and Proserpina can stay chaste behind her uncle's doors. Trojan Aeneas, famous for his devotion and his feats of arms, is going down to his father in the darkest depths of Erebus. If the sight of such devotion does not move you, then look at this branch," she said, showing the branch that had been hidden in her robes, "and realize what it is." At this the swelling anger subsided in his heart. No more words were needed. Seeing it again after a long age, and marvelling at the fateful branch, the holy offering, he turned his dark boat and steered towards the bank. He then drove off the souls who were on board with him sitting all along the cross benches, and cleared the gangways. In the same moment he took the huge Aeneas into the hull of his little boat. Being only sewn together, it groaned under his weight, shipping great volumes of stagnant water through the seams, but in the end it carried priestess and hero safely over and landed them on the foul slime among the grey-green reeds.

The kingdom on this side resounded with barking from the three throats of the huge monster Cerberus lying in a cave in front of them. When the priestess was close enough to see the snakes writhing on his neck, she threw him a honey cake steeped in soporific drugs. He opened his three jaws, each of them rabid with hunger, and snapped it up where it fell. The massive back relaxed and he sprawled full length on the ground, filling his cave. The sentry now sunk in sleep, Aeneas leapt to take command of the entrance and was soon free of the bank of that river which no man may recross.

In that instant they heard voices, a great weeping and wailing of the souls of infants who had lost their share of the sweetness of life on its very threshold, torn from the breast on some black day and drowned in the bitterness of death. Next to them were those who had been condemned to death on false charges, but they did not receive their places without the casting of lots and the appointment of juries. Minos, the president of the court, shakes the lots in the urn, summoning the silent dead to act as jurymen, and holds inquiry into the lives of the accused and the charges against them. Next to them were those unhappy people who had raised their innocent hands against themselves, who had so loathed the light that they had thrown away their own lives. But now how they would wish to be under high heaven, enduring poverty and drudgery, however hard! That cannot be, for they are bound in the coils of the hateful swamp of the waters of death, trapped in the ninefold windings of the river Styx. Not far from here could be seen what they call the Mourning Plains, stretching away in every direction. Here are the victims of unhappy love, consumed by that cruel wasting sickness, hidden in the lonely byways of an encircling wood of myrtle trees, and their suffering does not leave them even in death. Here Aeneas saw Phaedra, and Procris, and

Eriphyle[20] in tears as she displayed the wounds her cruel son had given her. Here he saw Evadne and Pasiphae with Laodamia[21] walking by their side, and Caeneus,[22] once a young man, but now a woman restored by destiny to her former shape.

Wandering among them in that great wood was Phoenician Dido with her wound still fresh. When the Trojan hero stopped beside her, recognizing her dim form in the darkness, like a man who sees or thinks he has seen the new moon rising through the clouds at the beginning of the month, in that instant he wept and spoke sweet words of love to her: "So the news they brought me was true, unhappy Dido? They told me you were dead and had ended your life with the sword. Alas! Alas! Was I the cause of your dying? I swear by the stars, by the gods above, by whatever there is to swear by in the depths of the earth, it was against my will, O queen, that I left your shore. It was the stern authority of the commands of the gods that drove me on, as it drives me now through the shades of this dark night in this foul and mouldering place. I could not have believed that my leaving would cause you such sorrow. Do not move away. Do not leave my sight. Who are you running from? Fate has decreed that I shall not speak to you again." With these words Aeneas, shedding tears, tried to comfort that burning spirit, but grim-faced she kept her eyes upon the ground and did not look at him. Her features moved no more when he began to speak than if she had been a block of flint or Parian marble quarried on Mount Marpessus. Then at last she rushed away, hating him, into the shadows of the wood where Sychaeus, who had been her husband, answered her grief with grief and her love with love. Aeneas was no less stricken by the injustice of her fate and long did he gaze after her, pitying her as she went.

From here they continued on their appointed road and they were soon on the most distant of these fields, the place set apart for brave warriors. Here Tydeus came to meet him, and Parthenopaeus, famous for his feats of arms, and the pale phantom of Adrastus.[23] Here he saw and groaned to see standing in their long ranks all the sons of Dardanus who had fallen in battle and been bitterly lamented in the upper world, Glaucus, Medon and Thersilochus, the three sons of Antenor, and Polyboetes, the consecrated priest of Ceres, and Idaeus still keeping hold of Priam's chariot, still keeping hold of his armour. The shades crowded round him on the right and on the

---

[20] **Phaedra, Procris, and Eriphyle** Three women who either killed or betrayed their husbands or sons.
[21] **Evadne, Pasiphae, Laodamia** Evadne and Laodamia committed suicide. Pasiphae was the wife of King Minos of Crete and the mother of the monster the Minotaur, who lived in the Labyrinth and ate the prisoners sent into the Labyrinth.
[22] **Caeneus** A mythological character who was first a nymph, then changed into a man by Neptune, the sea god, and then to a woman.
[23] **Tydeus, Parthenopaeus, and Adrastus** Tydeus was the father of Diomede, who was a Greek warrior in the *Iliad*. Parthenopaeus was a member of the "seven against Thebes" band that laid siege to the city. Adrastus, the mythical king of Argos, lost two sons-in-law in the battle of Thebes.

left and it was not enough just to see him, they wished to delay him, to walk with him, to learn the reasons for his coming. But when the Greek leaders and the soldiers of Agamemnon in their phalanxes saw the hero and his armour gleaming through the shadows, a wild panic seized them. Some turned and ran as they had run once before to get back to their ships, while others lifted up their voices and raised a tiny cry, which started as a shout from mouth wide open, but no shout came.[24]

Here too he saw Deiphobus, son of Priam, his whole body mutilated and his face cruelly torn. The face and both hands were in shreds. The ears had been ripped from the head. He was noseless and hideous. Aeneas, barely recognizing him as he tried frantically to hide the fearsome punishment he had received, went up to him and spoke in the voice he knew so well: "Deiphobus, mighty warrior, descended from the noble blood of Teucer, who could have wished to inflict such a punishment upon you? And who was able to do this? I was told that on that last night you wore yourself out killing the enemy and fell on a huge pile of Greek and Trojan dead. At that time I did all I could do, raising an empty tomb for you on the shore of Cape Rhoeteum and lifting up my voice to call three times upon your shade. Your name and your arms mark the place but you I could not find, my friend, to bury your body in our native land as I was leaving it."

To this the son of Priam answered: "You, my friend, have left nothing undone. You have paid all that is owed to Deiphobus and to his dead shade. It is my own destiny and the crimes of the murderess from Sparta that have brought me to this. These are reminders of Helen. You know how we spent that last night in false joy. It is our lot to remember it only too well. When the horse that was the instrument of Fate, heavy with the brood of armed men in its belly, leapt over the high walls of Pergamum, Helen was pretending to be worshipping Bacchus, leading the women of Phrygia around the city, dancing and shrieking their ritual cries. There she was in the middle of them with a huge torch, signalling to the Greeks from the top of the citadel, and all the time I was sleeping soundly in our accursed bed, worn out by all I had suffered and sunk in a sleep that was sweet and deep and like the peace of death. Meanwhile this excellent wife of mine, after moving all my armour out of the house and taking the good sword from under my head, called in Menelaus and threw open the doors, hoping no doubt that her loving husband would take this as a great favour to wipe out the memory of her past sins. You can guess the rest. They burst into the room, taking with them the man who had incited them to their crimes, their comrade Ulixes—they say he is descended from Aeolus. You gods, if the punishment I ask is just, grant that a fate like mine should strike again and strike Greeks. But come, it is now time for you to tell me what chance has brought you here alive. Is it your sea

wanderings that have taken you here? Are you under the instructions of the gods? What fortune is dogging you, that you should come here to our sad and sunless homes in this troubled place?"

While they were speaking to one another, Dawn's rosy chariot had already run its heavenly course past the midpoint of the vault of the sky, and they might have spent all the allotted time in talking but for Aeneas' companion. The Sibyl gave her warning in few words: "Night is running quickly by, Aeneas, and we waste the hours in weeping. This is where the way divides. On the right it leads up to the walls of great Dis. This is the road we take for Elysium. On the left is the road of punishment for evildoers, leading to Tartarus,[25] the place of the damned." "There is no need for anger, great priestess," replied Deiphobus. "I shall go to take my place among the dead and return to darkness. Go, Aeneas, go, great glory of our Troy, and enjoy a better fate than mine." These were his only words, and as he spoke he turned on his heel and strode away.

Aeneas looked back suddenly and saw under a cliff on his left a broad city encircled by a triple wall and washed all round by Phlegethon, one of the rivers of Tartarus, a torrent of fire and flame, rolling and grinding great boulders in its current. There before him stood a huge gate with columns of solid adamant so strong that neither the violence of men nor of the heavenly gods themselves could ever uproot them in war, and an iron tower rose into the air where Tisiphone[26] sat with her blood-soaked dress girt up, guarding the entrance and never sleeping, night or day. They could hear the groans from the city, the cruel crack of the lash, the dragging and clanking of iron chains. Aeneas stood in terror, listening to the noise. "What kinds of criminal are here? Tell me, virgin priestess, what punishments are inflicted on them? What is this wild lamentation in the air?" The Sibyl replied: "Great leader of the Trojans, the chaste may not set foot upon the threshold of that evil place, but when Hecate put me in charge of the groves of Avernus,[27] she herself explained the punishments the gods had imposed and showed me them all. Here Rhadamanthus, king of Cnossus, holds sway with his unbending laws, chastising men, hearing all the frauds they have practised and forcing them to confess the undiscovered crimes they have gloated over in the upper world—foolishly, for they have only delayed the day of atonement till after death. Immediately the avenging Tisiphone leaps upon the guilty and flogs them till they writhe, waving fearful serpents over them in her left hand and calling up the cohorts of her savage sisters,

---

[24] **Dardanus, Glaucus, Medon, Thersilochus, Antenor, Polyboetes, Idaeus, Priam, and Agamemnon** All these characters were warriors or leaders on both sides of the Trojan War and were in the *Iliad*.

[25] **Dis, Elysium, Tartarus** Three regions in the underworld. Dis was another name for Hades. Elysium was where the souls of the blessed dead dwelled. Tartarus was an abyss under Hades where some of the most heinous offenders were kept, including the Titans, who were a family of mythical giants who came before the Roman deities and were put here by Jupiter when he became the chief god.
[26] **Tisiphone** A goddess of the underworld, whose name means "Avenger of Blood."
[27] **Hecate, Avernus** Hecate was a goddess of the underworld. Avernus is a lake near Naples, thought to be an entrance to the underworld.

the Furies. Then at last the gates sacred to the gods below shriek in their sockets and open wide. You see what a watch she keeps, sitting in the entrance? What a sight she is guarding the threshold? Inside, more savage still, the huge, black-throated, fifty-headed Hydra has its lair. And then there is Tartarus itself, stretching sheer down into its dark chasm twice as far as we look up to the ethereal Olympus in the sky. Here, rolling in the bottom of the abyss, is the ancient brood of Earth, the army of Titans, hurled down by the thunderbolt. Here too I saw the huge bodies of the twin sons of Aloeus who laid violent hands on the immeasurable sky to wrench it from its place and tear down Jupiter from his heavenly kingdom. I saw too Salmoneus suffering cruel punishment, still miming the flames of Jupiter and the rumblings of Olympus. He it was who, riding his four-horse chariot and brandishing a torch, used to go in glory through the peoples of Greece and the city of Olympia in the heart of Elis, laying claim to divine honours for himself—fool that he was to copy the storm and the inimitable thunderbolt with the rattle of the horn of his horses' hooves on bronze. Through the thick clouds the All-powerful Father hurled his lightning—no smoky light from pitchy torches for him—and sent him spinning deep into the abyss. Tityos too I could see, the nurseling of Earth, mother of all, his body sprawling over nine whole acres while a huge vulture with hooked beak cropped his immortal liver and the flesh that was such a rich supplier of punishment. Deep in his breast it roosts and forages for its dinners, while the filaments of his liver know no rest but are restored as soon as they are consumed. I do not need to speak of the Lapiths, of Ixion or Pirithous, over whose heads the boulder of black flint is always slipping, always seeming to be falling. The gold gleams on the high supports of festal couches and a feast is laid in regal splendour before the eyes of the guilty, but the greatest of the Furies is reclining at table and allows no hand to touch the food, but leaps up brandishing a torch and shouting with a voice of thunder. Immured in this place and waiting for punishment are those who in life hated their brothers, beat their fathers, defrauded their dependants, found wealth and brooded over it alone without setting aside a share for their kinsmen—these are most numerous of all—men caught and killed in adultery, men who took up arms against their own people and did not shrink from abusing their masters' trust. Do not ask to know what their punishments are, what form of pain or what misfortune has engulfed them. Some are rolling huge rocks, or hang spreadeagled on the spokes of wheels. Theseus is sitting there dejected, and there he will sit until the end of time, while Phlegyas,[28] most wretched of them all, shouts this lesson for all men at the top of his voice in the darkness: 'Learn to be just and not to slight the gods. You have been warned.' Here is the man who has sold his native land for gold, and set a tyrant over it, putting up tablets with new laws for a price and for a price removing them. Here is the man who forced his way into his daughter's bed and a forbidden union. They have all dared to attempt some monstrous crime against the gods and have succeeded in their attempt. If I had a hundred tongues, a hundred mouths and a voice of iron, I could not encompass all their different crimes or speak the names of all their different punishments."

When the aged priestess of Apollo had finished her answer, she added these words: "But come now, you must take the road and complete the task you have begun. Let us hasten. I can see the high walls forged in the furnaces of the Cyclopes[29] and the gates there in front of us in the arch. This is where we have been told to lay the gift that is required of us." After these words they walked the dark road together, soon covering the distance and coming close to the doors. There Aeneas leapt on the threshold, sprinkled his body with fresh water and fixed the bough full in the doorway.

When this rite was at last performed and his duty to 15
the goddess was done, they entered the land of joy, the lovely glades of the fortunate woods and the home of the blest. Here a broader sky clothes the plains in glowing light, and the spirits have their own sun and their own stars. Some take exercise on grassy wrestling-grounds and hold athletic contests and wrestling bouts on the golden sand. Others pound the earth with dancing feet and sing their songs while Orpheus, the priest of Thrace, accompanies their measures on his seven-stringed lyre, plucking the notes sometimes with his fingers, sometimes with his ivory plectrum. Here was the ancient line of Teucer, the fairest of all families, great-hearted heroes born in a better time, Ilus, Assaracus and Dardanus,[30] the founder of Troy. Aeneas admired from a distance their armour and empty chariots. Their swords were planted in the ground and their horses wandered free on the plain cropping the grass. Reposing there below the earth, they took the same joy in their chariots and their armour as when alive, and the same care to feed their sleek horses. Then suddenly he saw others on both sides of him feasting on the grass, singing in a joyful choir their paean to Apollo all through a grove of fragrant laurels where the mighty river Eridanus rolls through the forest to the upper world. Here were armies of men bearing wounds received while fighting for their native land, priests who had been chaste unto death and true prophets whose words were worthy of Apollo; then those who have raised human life to new heights by the skills they have discovered and those whom men remember for what they have done for men. All these with sacred ribbons of white round their foreheads gathered round Aeneas and the Sibyl, and she addressed these words to them, especially to Musaeus,[31] for the whole great throng looked up to him as he stood there

---

[28] **Phlegyas** Mythical king of the Lapiths, who supposedly burnt Apollo's temple at Delphi and was punished in the underworld by having to sit under a rock that could fall on him at any moment.

---

[29] **Cyclopes** The giants with one eye in the middle of their foreheads. One legend claims that they were thrown into Hades by Kronos, the Titan god who was the father of Zeus. They were also associated with working around forges.
[30] **Teucer, Ilus, Assaracus, Dardanus** All these characters were identified with the city of Troy.
[31] **Musaeus** Ancient mythical poet, considered to be the successor to Orpheus, the first poet.

in the middle, head and shoulders above them all: "Tell me, blessed spirits, and you, best of poets, which part of this world holds Anchises? Where is he to be found? It is because of Anchises that we have come here and crossed the great rivers of Erebus." The hero returned a short answer. "None of us has a fixed home. We live in these densely wooded groves and rest on the soft couches of the river bank and in the fresh water-meadows. But if that is the desire of your hearts, come climb this ridge and I shall soon set you on an easy path." So saying, he walked on in front of them to a place from where they could see the plains below them bathed in light, and from that point Aeneas and the Sibyl came down from the mountain tops.

Father Anchises was deep in a green valley, walking among the souls who were enclosed there and eagerly surveying them as they waited to rise into the upper light. It so happened that at that moment he was counting the number of his people, reviewing his dear descendants, their fates and their fortunes, their characters and their courage in war. When he saw Aeneas coming towards him over the grass, he stretched out both hands in eager welcome, with the tears streaming down his cheeks, and these were the words that broke from his mouth: "You have come at last," he cried. "I knew your devotion would prevail over all the rigour of the journey and bring you to your father. Am I to be allowed to look upon your face, my son, to hear the voice I know so well and answer it with my own? I never doubted it. I counted the hours, knowing you would come, and my love has not deceived me. I understand how many lands you have travelled and how many seas you have sailed to come to me here. I know the dangers that have beset you. I so feared the kingdom of Libya would do you harm." "It was my vision of you," replied Aeneas, "always before my eyes and always stricken with sorrow, that drove me to the threshold of this place. The fleet is moored in the Tyrrhenian sea on the shores of Italy. Give me your right hand, father. Give it me. Do not avoid my embrace." As he spoke these words his cheeks were washed with tears and three times he tried to put his arms around his father's neck. Three times the phantom melted in his hands, as weightless as the wind, as light as the flight of sleep.

And now Aeneas saw in a side valley a secluded grove with copses of rustling trees where the river Lethe glided along past peaceful dwelling houses. Around it fluttered numberless races and tribes of men, like bees in a meadow on a clear summer day, settling on all the many-coloured flowers and crowding round the gleaming white lilies while the whole plain is loud with their buzzing. Not

understanding what he saw, Aeneas shuddered at the sudden sight of them and asked why this was, what was that river in the distance and who were all those companies of men crowding its banks. "These are the souls to whom Fate owes a second body," replied Anchises. "They come to the waves of the river Lethe and drink the waters of serenity and draughts of long oblivion. I have long been eager to tell you who they are, to show them to you face to face and count the generations of my people to you so that you could rejoice the more with me at the finding of Italy." "But are we to believe," replied Aeneas to his dear father, "that there are some souls who rise from here to go back under the sky and return to sluggish bodies? Why do the poor wretches have this terrible longing for the light?" "I shall tell you, my son, and leave you no longer in doubt," replied Anchises, and he began to explain all things in due order.

"In the beginning Spirit fed all things from within, the sky and the earth, the level waters, the shining globe of the moon and the Titan's star, the sun. It was Mind that set all this matter in motion. Infused through all the limbs, it mingled with that great body, and from the union there sprang the families of men and of animals, the living things of the air and the strange creatures born beneath the marble surface of the sea. The living force within them is of fire and its seeds have their source in heaven, but their guilt-ridden bodies make them slow and they are dulled by earthly limbs and dying flesh. It is this that gives them their fears and desires, their griefs and joys. Closed in the blind darkness of this prison they do not see out to the winds of air. Even when life leaves them on their last day of light, they are not wholly freed from all the many ills and miseries of the body which must harden in them over the long years and become ingrained in ways we cannot understand. And so they are put to punishment, to pay the penalty for all their ancient sins. Some are stretched and hung out empty to dry in the winds. Some have the stain of evil washed out of them under a vast tide of water or scorched out by fire. Each of us suffers his own fate in the after-life. From here we are sent over the broad plains of Elysium and some few of us possess these fields of joy until the circle of time is completed and the length of days has removed ingrained corruption and left us pure ethereal sense, the fire of elemental air. All these others whom you see, when they have rolled the wheel for a thousand years, are called out by God to come in great columns to the river of Lethe, so that they may duly go back and see the vault of heaven again remembering nothing, and begin to be willing to return to bodies.". . .

Questions for Critical Thinking

1. Give examples from Book I of how the goddesses Venus and Juno conspire and interfere in the lives of Aeneas and Dido to carry out their own plans.

2. From Book VI, describe the underworld that Aeneas visits, note some of the inhabitants they meet, and explain the types of punishments they must endure. Why is the image of the underworld such a useful and compelling device in literature?

HORACE
Selections from *Odes*

Horace's *Odes* (Books I–III, 23 BCE; Book IV, ca. 13 BCE) were a milestone in ancient literature. They signal the beginning of Latin lyric poetry and are also its zenith. They confirmed Horace's literary reputation and brought him favor from Augustus, Rome's first emperor. Ignored in medieval Europe, Horace's works came into their own during the Renaissance and enjoyed their finest hour in the classical revival of the seventeenth and eighteenth centuries. The poems' tact and good taste are traits of the Augustan Age (31 BCE–14 CE), which gave them birth.

Horace (65–8 BCE) and the Greek poet Pindar (522–442 BCE) are usually credited with begetting the ode, a lyric poem expressing lofty feelings and ideas in a stately tone. Pindar's odes were written for public occasions, such as honoring victors in the games. In contrast, Horace's odes were private and personal, speaking of love and wine, religion and the state, life and death, and praise for his patron, Maecenas. Their variety reflects Horace's love of Greek literature and his experiences as a man of both city and countryside.

In the *Odes*, Horace adapted Greek verse forms, borrowing largely from Sappho and Alcaeus (fl. ca. 611–580 BCE). Following them, he grew into a master of poetic subtlety and tightly compressed lyrics. He delighted in finding the exact word to convey a precise shade of meaning: "If a clever combination makes a familiar word new, that is distinguished writing." One feature, however, made his odes distinctive—unlike Alcaeus's and Sappho's lyrics, his odes were not composed for musical performance.

The *Odes* are normally called his greatest work, but Horace also wrote poetic epistles, epodes ("refrains"), and satires (see Juvenal's *Satire III*), the latter of which he pioneered. He also wrote the *Art of Poetry*, a book of literary advice whose focus on decorum undergirded the classicism of seventeenth- and eighteenth-century literature.

Horace was the son of an ex-slave. Partly because of the paradox that freedmen were second-class citizens whereas their sons had full rights, he had a keen eye for social slights. Even at the height of his fame, he detected traces of resentment. Nevertheless, he experienced the best of his world. Paternal wealth enabled him to study at an aristocratic school in Rome and at the Academy in Athens, and his literary works won the esteem of the imperial court.

Reading the Selections

Horace's theme in Ode II.16 is peace of mind and how to achieve it. Addressed to a rich man named Grosphus, the ode gently chides as it gives advice. The reference to "a little farm" is Horace's Sabine farm, a gift from Maecenas.

Ode III.6 is a public ode, reflecting Horace's critique of Rome written before Augustus's reign. The ode concludes with a chilling forecast. A highlight of this lyric is that, near the end, it conveys the poet's love of nature.

∞

Ode II.16

Otium divos (Restiveness)

Peace, Grosphus, is what the man on the open
Aegean requires of the Gods when black cloud
obscures the moon and no fixed star can flash for the
sailors.

Peace for the Thracians[32] enraged with war,
peace for the Medes[33] with their stylish quivers,
is not to be bought with gems or gold or gleaming fabrics.

Neither Persian treasure nor the consul's
lictor can disperse the wretched mob
of the mind or the cares that flit about your coffered
ceilings.

He lives well on a little whose family
salt-cellar shines amid a modest
table, whose gentle sleep is not dispelled by fear or base
greed.

Why do we aim so high, so bravely,

so briefly? Why hanker for countries scorched
by an alien sun? What exile from home can avoid
himself?

Care clambers aboard the armoured ships,
keeps pace with the cavalry squadrons, comes
swift as East-Wind-driven rain, comes swift as any stag.

The soul content with the present
is not concerned with the future and tempers
dismay with an easy laugh. No blessing is unmixed.

An early death snatched bright Achilles;
long senility reduced Tithonus:[34]
this hour will offer to me, maybe, the good it denies
to you.

For you a hundred herds of Sicilian
cattle moo; for you are bred
neighing mares apt for the chariot; you dress in
twice-dyed

Tyrian purple wool: to me honest Fate
has given a little farm, the delicate breath
of the Grecian Muse, and disdain for the jealous mob.

[32] **Thracians** Inhabitants of Thrace, which was located east of Macedonia and north of the Aegean Sea. They were often at war and subject to various conquerors. The Roman emperor Claudius subdued Thrace in 26 BCE, during Horace's lifetime.
[33] **Medes** Inhabitants of Media, which was located in western Asia or in modern western Iran. The Medes conquered the Persians in the eighth century BCE and then were overrun by the Assyrians, from whom they gained their independence. Later conquered by the Persians, then the Parthians, and, finally, the Romans.

[34] **Tithonus** A legendary Trojan who was loved by Eos, the goddess of the dawn. She granted him immortality but not eternal youth, so he grew very decrepit and, by some accounts, turned into a grasshopper.

∞

Ode III.6

Delicta maiorum (How we are fallen!)

Though innocent you shall atone for the crimes
of your fathers, Roman, until you have restored
the temples and crumbling shrines of the Gods
and their statues grimy with smoke.

Acknowledge the rule of the Gods—and rule:
hence all things begin, to this ascribe the outcome.
Contemned, the Gods have visited many
evils on grieving Hesperia.[35]

Already twice Monaeses and Pacorus'[36] band
have crushed our ill-starred offensive
and preen themselves on having added
Roman spoils to their paltry gauds.

Our city busied with sedition has almost
suffered destruction by Egypt allied to Dacia,
the former renowned for her fleet, the latter
rather for hurtling arrows.

[35] **Hesperia** The Greek name for the western or evening land, that is, Italy.

[36] **Monaeses and Pacorus** Two Parthian commanders who defeated the Romans during Horace's lifetime.

Teeming with sin, the times have sullied
first marriage, our children, our homes:
sprung from that source disaster has whelmed
our fatherland and our people.   20

The grown girl loves to be taught to be
artful and dance oriental dances,
obsessed to her dainty fingernails
with illicit amours.

She sniffs out young philand'rers at her
husband's feast, nor is she nice to choose
to whom she (hurriedly) grants her favours
when the lamps are removed,

but brazenly stands when called—with her
husband's assent—though some travelling   30
salesman or Spanish ship's captain
may be the agent of Shame.

The generation that dyed the Punic
sea with blood and laid low Pyrrhus,
Antiochus and Hannibal[37] was not born
of parents such as these,

but of manly comrades, yeoman soldiers
taught to turn the soil with Sabine[38] hoes
and carry cut firewood at a strict
mother's bidding when the Sun   40

advanced the shadows of the hills
and lifted the yokes from weary steers,
his departing chariot leading in
the hours of comfort.

What does corrupting time not diminish?
Our grandparents brought forth feebler heirs;
we are further degen'rate; and soon will beget
progeny yet more wicked.

---

[37] **Pyrrhus, Antiochus, Hannibal** Three generals who tried to conquer Rome but failed.
[38] **Sabine** The Sabines were an ancient tribe north of Rome that was conquered in the early years of the third century BCE. The Romans adopted many religious traditions from the Sabines.

Questions for Critical Thinking

1. What is Horace's advice in Ode II.16 on how to achieve peace of mind? Do you agree that this is the way to achieve peace of mind? Why or why not?

2. Discuss the reasons Horace gives in Ode III.6 for the decline of Rome. Do you think these are valid reasons why nations and societies decline? Why or why not?

OVID
Selections from *Metamorphoses*

Ovid (43 BCE–17 CE), like Horace (see *Odes*), was a great Latin writer who was not a native Roman. From Sulmo (central Italy), Ovid came to Rome to study in an aristocratic school. Trained for politics, he turned to poetry and became the epitome of the worldly set that dominated Roman fashion in his day.

Ovid's *Metamorphoses* has delighted readers since it first circulated (8 CE) in Rome's Augustan Age; few works from any period have had such a lasting impact on later culture. Since the Middle Ages, poets and artists have mined it for subjects and plots from the collection of Roman and mainly Greek myths and legends—the intellectual stock-in-trade of Ovid's day.

A long poem, the *Metamorphoses* consists of more than two hundred stories divided into fifteen "books" and organized around a simple theme: All are tales of shape-shifting, or magical changes of form. They are about people, usually legendary, changed into stone, trees, animals, birds, and stars. The poet's tone toward these shape-shiftings is lighthearted, even tongue-in-cheek.

The poem's subject touched on a growing trend in Rome: the worship of rulers as gods—an inheritance from the Middle East as new peoples joined the empire. Ovid welcomed this trend, for he made the poem's climax (Book XV) the transformation of Julius Caesar into a blazing comet, with the added prediction that Augustus too would "make his way to heaven. . . ." Here Ovid showed his patriotism, because the Senate had voted Caesar divine status, and plans were afoot to do the same for Augustus.

The *Metamorphoses* is ironic in that Ovid's praise for Augustus did not save him from the emperor's wrath. As the poet was finishing this work, Augustus banished him to a remote frontier-post of the empire, Tomis (Constanta, in Rumania). He was never granted permission to return. Why Ovid was banished is not clear. Perhaps it was the flippant *Art of Love,* a handbook on seduction, which offended propriety and thus damaged Augustus's efforts to reform Roman morals. Perhaps he knew too much about a sex scandal involving the emperor's granddaughter Julia. Whatever the reason, Ovid saw his exile as a spiritual death. He nevertheless continued to write, sustained by the thought that his poetry would make him immortal. "I shall live to all eternity, immortalized by fame."

Reading the Selections

The story of Daphne and Apollo (Book I of the *Metamorphoses*) is Ovid's account of the star-crossed love of the god Apollo (called Phoebus) for the nymph Daphne. Its premise is that the gods have absolute power but lack moral scruples. Apollo, pierced by Cupid's arrow, is overcome with lust, so that his prophetic powers are useless. To win Daphne, he first tries to woo her; when that fails, he decides on rape. Apollo is depicted as the slave of his passions. Daphne ultimately escapes rape by being changed into a laurel tree. True "happy endings" are rare in this poem.

Ovid's lighthearted style sugarcoats his basic cynicism. He wrote to entertain, not to improve. Not religious in any ordinary sense, Ovid did not shrink from depicting the gods in indecent roles. His world was conspicuously amoral and, as with humans, the gods were victims of their emotions and liable to be swept away by fate.

Ovid's tone in the *Metamorphoses* was not completely cynical, however, as may be seen in the story of Pyramus, "the most handsome of young men," and Thisbe, "the fairest beauty of the East" (Book IV). Ovid's is the first known account of this tale and, later writers, finding it attractive, composed their own versions. Shakespeare used the Pyramus and Thisbe episode as a subject for comedy, in *A Midsummer Night's Dream.*

∞

Book I, Daphne and Apollo

. . .

Daphne, the daughter of Peneus,[39] was Phoebus'[40] first love, and it was not blind chance which brought this about, but Cupid's savage spite. Not long before, the Delian god, still exultant over his slaying of the serpent, had seen Cupid[41] bending his taut bow, and had said:

"You naughty boy, what have you to do with a warrior's arms? Weapons such as these are suited to my shoulders: for I can aim my shafts unerringly, to wound wild beast or human foe, as I lately slew the bloated Python with my countless arrows, though it covered so many acres with its pestilential coils. You be content with your torch to excite love, whatever that may be, and do not aspire to praises that are my prerogative." But Venus' son replied: "Your bow may pierce everything else, Phoebus, but mine will pierce *you:* and as all animals are inferior to the gods, your glory is to that extent less than mine."

---

[39] **Peneus** A river in Thessaly, a country in northeastern Greece, and the name of the god of the river.
[40] **Phoebus** Another name for Apollo.
[41] **Cupid** The Roman god of love; son of Venus, the Roman goddess of love.

With these words he swiftly winged his way through the air, till he alighted on the shady summit of Parnassus.[42] From his quiver, full of arrows, he drew two darts, with different properties. The one puts love to flight, the other kindles it. That which kindles love is golden, and shining, sharp-tipped; but that which puts it to flight is blunt, its shaft tipped with lead. With this arrow the god pierced the nymph, Peneus' daughter, but Apollo he wounded with the other, shooting it into the marrow of his bones. Immediately the one fell in love; the other, fleeing the very word "lover," took her delight in woodland haunts and in the spoils of captured beasts, emulating Diana,[43] the maiden goddess, with her hair carelessly caught back by a single ribbon.

Many a suitor wooed her but, turning away from their entreaties, she roamed the pathless woods, knowing nothing of men, and caring nothing for them, heedless of what marriage or love or wedded life might be. Again and again her father said: "It is your duty to marry and give me a son-in-law, my child." Often he repeated: "My child, it is your duty to give me grandchildren." But she blushed, hating the thought of marriage as if it were some crime. The modest colour crimsoned her fair face and, throwing her arms round her father's neck, she cried imploringly: "My dear, dear father let me enjoy this state of maiden bliss for ever! Diana's father granted her such a boon in days gone by!" Her father did, indeed, yield to her request, but her very loveliness prevented her from being what she desired, and her beauty defeated her own wishes.

As soon as Phoebus saw Daphne, he fell in love with her, and wanted to marry her. His own prophetic powers deceived him and he hoped to achieve his desire. As the light stubble blazes up in a harvested field, or as the hedge is set alight, if a traveller chance to kindle a fire too close, or leaves one smouldering when he goes off at daybreak, so the god was all on fire, his whole heart was aflame, and he nourished his fruitless love on hope. He eyed her hair as it hung carelessly about her neck, and sighed: "What if it were properly arranged!" He looked at her eyes, sparkling bright as stars, he looked at her lips, and wanted to do more than look at them. He praised her fingers, her hands and arms, bare almost to the shoulder. Her hidden charms he imagined lovelier still.

But Daphne ran off, swifter than the wind's breath, and did not stop to hear his words, though he called her back: "I implore you, nymph, daughter of Peneus, do not run away! Though I pursue you, I am no enemy. Stay, sweet nymph! You flee as a lamb flees the wolf, or the deer the lion, as doves on fluttering wings fly from an eagle, as all creatures flee their natural foes! But it is love that drives me to follow you. Alas, how I fear lest you trip and fall, lest briars scratch your innocent legs, and I be the cause of your hurting yourself. These are rough places through which you are running—go less swiftly, I beg of you, slow your flight, and I in turn shall pursue less swiftly!

"Yet stay to inquire whose heart you have charmed. I am no peasant, living in a mountain hut, nor am I a shepherd or boorish herdsman who tends his flocks and cattle in these regions. Silly girl, you do not know from whom you are fleeing: indeed, you do not, or else you would not flee. I am lord of Delphi, Claros, and Tenedos, and of the realms of Patara[44] too. I am the son of Jupiter.[45] By my skill, the past, the present, and the future are revealed; thanks to me, the lyre strings thrill with music. My arrow is sure, though there is one surer still, which has wounded my carefree heart. The art of medicine is my invention, and men the world over give me the name of healer. All the properties of herbs are known to me: but alas, there are no herbs to cure love, and the skill which helps others cannot help its master."

He would have said more, but the frightened maiden fled from him, leaving him with his words unfinished; even then, she was graceful to see, as the wind bared her limbs and its gusts stirred her garments, blowing them out behind her. Her hair streamed in the light breeze, and her beauty was enhanced by her flight. But the youthful god could not endure to waste his time on further blandishments and, as love itself prompted, sped swiftly after her. Even so, when a Gallic hound spies a hare in some open meadow he tries by his swiftness to secure his prey, while the hare, by her swiftness, seeks safety: the dog, seeming just about to fasten on his quarry, hopes at every moment that he has her, and grazes her hind quarters with outstretched muzzle, but the hare, uncertain whether she has not already been caught, snatches herself out of his very jaws, and escapes the teeth which almost touch her.

Thus the god and the nymph sped on, one made swift by hope and one by fear; but he who pursued was swifter, for he was assisted by love's wings. He gave the fleeing maiden no respite, but followed close on her heels, and his breath touched the locks that lay scattered on her neck, till Daphne's strength was spent, and she grew pale and weary with the effort of her swift flight. Then she saw the waters of the Peneus: "O father," she cried, "help me! If your rivers really have divine powers, work some transformation, and destroy this beauty which makes me please all too well!" Her prayer was scarcely ended when a deep languor took hold on her limbs, her soft breast was enclosed in thin bark, her hair grew into leaves, her arms into branches, and her feet that were lately so swift were held fast by sluggish roots, while her face became the tree-top. Nothing of her was left, except her shining loveliness.

Even as a tree, Phoebus loved her. He placed his hand against the trunk, and felt her heart still beating under the new bark. Embracing the branches as if they were limbs he kissed the wood: but, even as a tree, she shrank from his kisses. Then the god said: "Since you cannot be my bride, surely you will at least be my tree. My hair, my lyre, my quivers will always display the laurel. You will accompany the generals of Rome, when the Capitol

---

[42] **Parnassus** A mountain near Delphi in Greece, sacred to Apollo and the Muses.
[43] **Diana** Twin sister of Apollo and the virgin huntress goddess.

[44] **Delphi, Claros, Tenedos, Patara** Locations, around the Mediterranean area, of temples to Apollo.
[45] **Jupiter** Chief god of the Romans.

beholds their long triumphal processions, when joyful voices raise the song of victory. You will stand by Augustus' gateposts too, faithfully guarding his doors, and keeping watch from either side over the wreath of oak leaves that will hang there. Further, as my head is ever young, my tresses never shorn, so do you also, at all times, wear the crowning glory of never-fading foliage." Paean, the healer, had done: the laurel tree inclined her newmade branches, and seemed to nod her leafy top, as if it were a head, in consent. . . .

∞

Book IV, Pyramus and Thisbe

"Pyramus and Thisbe lived next door to each other, in the lofty city whose walls of brick are said to have been built by Semiramis.[46] Pyramus was the most handsome of young men, and Thisbe the fairest beauty of the East. Living so near, they came to know one another, and a friendship was begun; in time, love grew up between them, and they would have been married, but their parents forbade it. None the less—for this their parents could not forbid—both their hearts were caught in love's snare, and both burned with equal passion. No one shared their secret: they communicated by nods and signs, and the more it was concealed, the more their hidden love blazed up.

"There was a crack, a slender chink, that had developed in the party wall between their two houses, when it was being built. This fault had gone unnoticed for long years, and the lovers were the first to find it: nothing can escape a lover's eyes! They used it as a channel for their voices, and by this means their endearments were safely conveyed to one another, in the gentlest of whispers. Often when Pyramus stood on this side, Thisbe on that, when in turn they felt each other's breath, they used to exclaim: 'Jealous wall, why do you stand in the way of lovers? How little it would be to ask that you should let us embrace or, if that is too much, that you should at least open wide enough for us to exchange kisses! Not that we are ungrateful—we admit that it is thanks to you that we have any way at all by which our words can reach our true love's ears.' So they talked, in vain, on their opposite sides. At nightfall, they said good-bye, and though they could not reach each other with their kisses, they kissed their own side of the wall.

"Next day, when Aurora[47] had put out night's starry fires and the sun's rays had dried the frosty grass, they came to their usual meeting place. At first, softly sighing, they lamented their sad lot. Then they determined that, at dead of night, they would try to slip past the watchmen and steal out of doors; once outside their homes, they would make their way out of the city too; and in case they should miss each other, wandering aimlessly in the open country, they agreed to meet at Ninus' tomb, and to hide in the shade of its tree. For a tree grew there, a tall mulberry, hung thick with snowy fruits; it stood close by a cool spring. They were enraptured with their plan. The daylight seemed slow to depart, but at last the sun plunged into the waters, and from those waters came forth the night. Stealthily Thisbe turned the door on its hinges, and slipped out into the darkness, unseen by any. Her face hidden by her veil, she came to the tomb, and sat down under the appointed tree. Love made her bold. But suddenly a lioness, fresh from the kill, her slavering jaws dripping with the blood of her victims, came to slake her thirst at the neighbouring spring. While the animal was still some distance off, Thisbe saw her in the moonlight. Frightened, she fled into the darkness of a cave, and as she ran her veil slipped from her shoulders, and was left behind.

"When the savage lioness had drunk her fill, and was returning to the woods, she found the garment, though not the girl, and tore its fine fabric to shreds, ripping it with bloodstained jaws.

"Pyramus came out of the city a little later. He saw the prints of the wild beast, clearly outlined in the deep dust, and the colour drained from his face. Worse still, he found the veil, all stained with blood. Then he cried out: 'This night will bring about the death of two fond lovers, and of the two she deserved to live far more than I. 'Tis I who am to blame: poor girl, it was I who killed you! I told you to come, by night, to a place that was full of danger, and did not arrive first myself. Come, all you lions who live beneath this cliff, come and tear me limb from limb! With your fierce jaws, devour my guilty person. But it is a coward's trick, only to pray for death!' He picked up Thisbe's veil, and carried it into the shade of the tree where they should have met. Weeping and kissing the garment he knew so well, he said: 'Drink deep, now, of my blood too.' And as he spoke he took the sword which hung at his waist, and thrust it into his side: then, with a dying effort, pulled it out of the warm wound. As he lay, fallen back upon the ground, his blood spouted forth, just as when a water pipe bursts, if there is some flaw in the lead, and through the narrow hissing crack a long stream of water shoots out, and beats on the air. The fruits of the tree were sprinkled with his blood, and changed to a dark purple hue. The roots, soaked in his gore, tinged the hanging berries with the same rich colour.

"Now, though Thisbe had not yet quite recovered from her fear, she came back; for she was anxious not to disappoint her lover. She looked about for the youth with eager eyes and heart, impatient to tell him of the perils she had escaped. But although she recognized the spot,

---

[46] **Semiramis** Queen of Babylon, the home of Pyramus and Thisbe.
[47] **Aurora** Goddess of the dawn.

and the shape of the tree, yet the colour of its fruit made her uncertain; she was unable to decide whether this was the place or not. As she stood in doubt, she saw the quivering limbs writhing on the bloodstained ground, and started back. Her cheeks grew paler than boxwood, and she trembled as the sea shivers when a soft breeze ripples its surface. After a moment's pause, she recognized her love. Wailing aloud, she beat her innocent arms, tore her hair, and embracing his beloved form, bathed his wound with her tears, mingling the salt drops with his blood, and passionately kissing his cold cheeks. 'Pyramus,' she cried, 'What mischance has taken you from me? Pyramus, speak to me! It is your own dear Thisbe who is calling you! Hear me, and raise your drooping head!' At Thisbe's name, Pyramus opened his eyes, which were already heavy with death's stupor; then, with one last look, closed them for ever. Thisbe, when she recognized her veil, and saw the ivory scabbard empty of its sword, exclaimed: 'Alas, your own hand and your love have destroyed you. I, too, have a hand resolute for this one deed; my love, as great as yours, will give me strength to deal the wound. I shall follow you in death, and men will speak of me as at once the unhappy cause and the companion of your fate. Only death could have separated you from me, but not even death will part us. Most wretched parents, mine and his, I beg this one boon for us both: since our steadfast love and the hour of our death have united us, do not grudge that we be laid together in a single tomb. And you, O tree, already sheltering one hapless body, soon to shelter two, bear for ever the marks of our death: always have fruit of a dark and mournful hue, to make men remember the blood we two have shed!' As she spoke, she placed the sword blade beneath her breast, and fell forward on the steel, which was still warm from Pyramus' death. Her prayers touched the gods, and they touched the parents also: for the berry of the tree, when ripe, is a dark purple colour, and the remains of the two lovers, gathered from the funeral fires, rest together in a single urn."

Questions for Critical Thinking

1. How did Phoebus or Apollo pursue Daphne, and what was her fate? How did her fate become a symbol for Rome?

2. Describe the signs for first love between Pyramus and Thisbe. How did the outcome of their love affair compare with that of Daphne and Apollo?

JUVENAL
Satire III

Much of Juvenal's life (ca. 60–140 CE) remains a mystery. He is seldom mentioned by his contemporaries, and his satires contain very little autobiographical material. Some events in his satires can be dated, which aid scholars in determining when and where Juvenal wrote. Evidence indicates that he was the son of a fairly prosperous Spanish freedman and that he served in the Roman army. Upon returning from a campaign in Britain, he became mayor of his hometown but failed to launch a political career. Meanwhile, Juvenal started to write satirical works. He soon displeased the Emperor Domitian, who exiled him to Egypt and stripped him of his property and civil rights. Emperor Nerva, Domitian's successor, permitted Juvenal to return to Rome; however, being poor and without patrons, he was forced to live the life of a hanger-on, one who survived only by flattering those in power. This experience led him to write many embittered and vindictive poems. Only in his later years, when he received patronage from influential Romans, including the Emperor Hadrian, did his satires lose their coarse tone and become nostalgic. When he died, he was not well known, and for two hundred years Juvenal was a forgotten poet. In about 400 CE, he was rediscovered, and his reputation has remained high ever since.

Many of Juvenal's satires reflected his contempt for his age. He was highly critical of its literature. He singled out the Greeks, whom he denounced for undermining Roman values. Looking at the Rome of his day, he saw only the decline of those values that he believed still survived in small villages among simple folk who appreciated the old ways.

Reading the Selection

Satire III contains most of Juvenal's major complaints and popular targets against contemporary Rome. In the opening lines he confesses his admiration for an old friend, Umbricius, who was leaving Rome for good to live in a provincial town. As they walked from one familiar site to another and observed the changes—all for the worse—Umbricius blamed his own lowered standard of living on the corrupt engineers and flattering hypocrites who dominated society. Juvenal saved his richest invective for the Jews and Greeks, who seemed to have overrun Rome. As a result of this deterioration, the city was under siege and its inhabitants afraid to leave their homes. In closing, Umbricius bade final farewell, asking Juvenal to visit him when he tired of the city. Rome, in Juvenal's eyes, had become the symbol of all that was evil in his day.

Despite the wrench of parting, I applaud my old friend's   1
Decision to make his home in lonely Cumae[48]—the poor
Sibyl[49] will get at least *one* fellow-citizen now!
It's a charming coastal retreat, and just across the point
From our smartest watering-spot. Myself, I would value
A barren offshore island more than Rome's urban heart:
Squalor and isolation are minor evils compared
To this endless nightmare of fires and collapsing houses,
The cruel city's myriad perils—and poets reciting
Their work in *August!*   10
                          While his goods were being loaded
On one small waggon, my old friend lingered a while
By the ancient dripping arches of the Capuan Gate,[50]
        where once
King Numa[51] had nightly meetings with his mistress.
        (But today
Egeria's[52] grove and shrine and sacred spring are rented
To Jewish squatters, their sole possession a Sabbath
        haybox.[53]
Each tree must show a profit, the Muses have been evicted,
The wood's aswarm with beggars.)
                          From here we strolled down
To the nymph's new, modernized grotto. (What a gain in   20
        sanctity

And atmosphere there would be if grassy banks
Surrounded the pool, if no flash marble affronted
Our native limestone!) Here Umbricius[54] stood, and
Opened his heart to me.
                          "There's no room in this city,"
He said, "for the decent professions: they don't show any
        profit.
My resources have shrunk since yesterday, and tomorrow
Will eat away more of what's left. So I am going
Where Daedalus[55] put off his weary wings, while as yet
I'm in vigorous middle age, while active years are left me,   30
While my white hairs are still few, and I need no stick
To guide my tottering feet. So farewell Rome, I leave you
To sanitary engineers and municipal architects, men
Who by swearing black is white land all the juicy
        contracts
Just like that—a new temple, swamp-drainage,
        harbour-works,
River-clearance, undertaking, the lot—then pocket
        the cash
And fraudulently file their petition in bankruptcy.
Once these fellows were horn-players, stumping the
        provinces
In road-shows, their puffed-out cheeks a familiar sight
To every country village. But now they stage shows   40
        themselves,
Of the gladiatorial sort, and at the mob's thumbs-down
Will butcher a loser for popularity's sake, and
Pass on from that to erecting public privies. Why not?
These are such men as Fortune, by way of a joke,

[48] **Cumae** A seacoast town on the western Italian coast. The first Greek settlement was here. By Juvenal's time it was a sleepy and forgotten place but near more-fashionable resorts.
[49] **Sibyl** Cumae was known for a famous prophetess who resided there in a grotto.
[50] **Capuan Gate** A gate on the Appian Way, a road leading to Rome. An aqueduct passed over the gate, thus the dripping arches.
[51] **King Numa** A semimythical king of Rome.
[52] **Egeria** A nymph through whom King Numa received the laws for the kingdom.
[53] **Sabbath haybox** A container for keeping food hot on a day when cooking was prohibited, the Sabbath.

[54] **Umbricius** Juvenal's friend, who may have been a real or an imaginary person.
[55] **Daedalus** The legendary inventor and hero who flew with wax wings from Crete to Cumae.

Will sometimes raise from the gutter and make Top
    People.
What can I do in Rome? I never learnt how
To lie. If a book is bad, I cannot puff it, or bother
To ask around for a copy; astrological clap-trap
Is not in my stars. I cannot and will not promise
To encompass any man's death by way of obliging his son.   50
I have never meddled with frogs' guts; the task of
    carrying
Letters and presents between adulterous lovers
I resign to those who know it. I refuse to become
An accomplice in theft—which means that no governor
Will accept me on his staff. It's like being a cripple
With a paralysed right hand. Yet who today is favoured
Above the conspirator, his head externally seething
With confidential matters, never to be revealed?
Harmless secrets carry no obligations, and he
Who shares them with you feels no great call thereafter   60
To keep you sweet. But if Verres[56] promotes a man
You can safely assume that man has the screws on Verres
And could turn him in tomorrow. Not all the gold
Washed seaward with the silt of tree-lined Tagus[57]
Is worth the price you pay, racked by insomnia, seeing
Your high-placed friends all cringe at your
    approach—and
For what? Too-transient prizes, unwillingly resigned.
"Now let me turn to that race which goes down so well
With our millionaires, but remains *my* special pet
    aversion,
And not mince my words. I cannot, citizens, stomach   70
A Greek-struck Rome. Yet what fraction of these
    sweepings
Derives, in fact, from Greece? For years now Syrian
Orontes[58] has poured its sewerage into our native Tiber—
Its lingo and manners, its flutes, its outlandish harps
With their transverse strings, its native tambourines,
And the whores who hang out round the race-course.
    (That's where to go
If you fancy a foreign piece in one of those saucy
    toques.[59])
Our beloved Founder should see how his homespun
    rustics
Behave today, with their dinner-pumps—*trechedipna*
They call them—not to mention their *niceteria*   80
(Decorations to you) hung round their *ceromatic*[60] (that's
Well-greased) wrestlers' necks. Here's one from Sicyon,
Another from Macedonia, two from Aegean islands—
Andros, say, or Samos—two more from Caria,[61]

All of them lighting out for the City's classiest districts
And burrowing into great houses, with a long-term plan
For taking them over. Quick wit, unlimited nerve, a gift
Of the gab that outsmarts a professional public speaker—
These are their characteristics. What do you take
That fellow's profession to be? He has brought a whole   90
    bundle
Of personalities with him—schoolmaster, rhetorician,
Surveyor, artist, masseur, diviner, tightrope-walker,
Magician or quack, your versatile hungry Greekling
Is all by turns. Tell him to fly—he's airborne.
The inventor of wings was no Moor or Slav, remember,
Or Thracian, but born in the very heart of Athens.
    "When such men as these wear the purple, when some
      creature
Blown into Rome along with the figs and damsons
Precedes me at dinner-parties, or for the witnessing
Of manumissions and wills—*me*, who drew my first   100
    breath
On these Roman hills, and was nourished on Sabine[62]
    olives!—
Things have reached a pretty pass. What's more, their
    talent
For flattery is unmatched. They praise the conversation
Of their dimmest friends; the ugly they call handsome,
So that your scrag-necked weakling finds himself
    compared
To Hercules holding the giant Antaeus[63] aloft
Way off the earth. They go into ecstasies over
Some shrill and scrannel voice that sounds like a hen
When the cock gets at her. We can make the same
    compliments, but
It's they who convince. On the stage they remain   110
    supreme
In female parts, courtesan, matron or slave-girl,
With no concealing cloak: you'd swear it was a genuine
Woman you saw, and not a masked performer.
Look there, beneath that belly: no bulge, all smooth, a
    neat
Nothingness—even a hint of the Great Divide. Yet back
    home
These queens and dames[64] pass unnoticed. Greece is a
    nation
Of actors. Laugh, and they split their sides. At the sight
Of a friend's tears, they weep too—though quite
    unmoved.
If you ask for a fire in winter, the Greek puts on his cloak;
If you say "I'm hot," *he* starts sweating. So you see   120
We are not on an equal footing: he has the great advantage

---

[56] **Verres** A governor of the island of Sicily who was corrupt and extorted money from the public.
[57] **Tagus** A river in Spain that flows from central Spain to the Atlantic Ocean; longest river in the Iberian peninsula.
[58] **Orontes** A river in Syria. The reference is not to the river itself but to the Syrians who have polluted the Tiber River with their way of life.
[59] **toques** A woman's hat, brimless and close fitting.
[60] *trechedipna, niceteria, ceromatic* Juvenal is mocking Romans who use Greek words to impress others. Thus, *niceteria* are decorations and *ceromatic* is the mud in wrestling pits.
[61] **Sicyon, Macedonia, Andros, Samos, Caria** Greek islands and towns whose inhabitants are taking over Rome.

[62] **Sabine** Territory northeast of Rome, conquered by the Romans in the early third century BCE. Juvenal is being nostalgic about his youth and remembering food grown in the Sabine region.
[63] **Antaeus** The giant wrestler who murdered his defeated opponents. Hercules killed Antaeus by crushing him in the air and keeping him off the ground, which was the source of Antaeus's strength.
[64] **queens and dames** Juvenal, in lines 107–116, comments on Greek male actors playing female parts so well that one would believe them to be women. He then proceeds to condemn Greeks who flatter Romans in order to seduce their females.

Of being able on all occasions, night and day,
To take his cue, his mask, from others. He's always ready
To throw up his hands and applaud when a friend
    delivers
A really resounding belch, or pisses right on the mark,
With a splendid drumming sound from the upturned
    golden basin.
    "Besides, he holds nothing sacred, not a soul is safe
From his randy urges, the lady of the house, her
Virgin daughter, her daughter's still unbearded
Husband-to-be, her hitherto virtuous son—   130
And if none of these are to hand, he'll cheerfully lay
His best friend's grandmother. (Anything to ferret
Domestic secrets out, and get a hold over people.)
    "And while we are on the subject of Greeks, let us
    consider
Academics and their vices—not the gymnasium crowd
But big philosophical wheels, like that Stoic greybeard[65]
Who narked on his friend and pupil, and got him
    liquidated.
He was brought up in Tarsus, by the banks of that river
Where Bellerophon fell to earth from the Gorgon's flying
    nag.
No room for honest Romans when Rome's ruled by a   140
    junta
Of Greek-born secret agents, who—like all their race—
Never share friends or patrons. One small dose of venom
(Half Greek, half personal) dropped in that ready ear
And I'm out, shown the back-door, my years of
    obsequious
Service all gone for nothing. Where can a hanger-on
Be ditched with less fuss than in Rome? Besides (not to
    flatter ourselves)
What use are our poor efforts, where does it all get us,
Dressing up while it's dark still, hurrying along
To pay our morning respects to a couple of wealthy
Maiden aunts? But the praetor's really worked up, his   150
Colleague may get there before him, the ladies have been
    awake
For hours already, the minions catch it—"Get
A *move* on there, can't you?" Here a citizen, free-born,
Must stand aside on the pavement for some wealthy
    tycoon's slave:
He can afford to squander a senior officer's income
On classy amateur harlots, just for the privilege
Of laying them once or twice. But when *you* fancy
A common-or-garden tart, you dither and hesitate:
Can I afford to accost her? With witnesses in court
The same applies. Their morals may be beyond cavil,   160
    and yet
If Scipio took the stand (and he was selected
To escort the Mother Goddess on her journey to Rome) or
    Metellus

Who rescued Minerva's image from her blazing shrine,
    or even
King Numa[66] himself, still the first and foremost question
Would be: *"What's he worth?"* His character would
    command
Little if any respect. "How many slaves does he keep?
What's his acreage? What sort of dinner-service
Appears on his table—how many pieces, how big?"
Each man's word is as good as his bond—or rather,
The number of bonds in his strong-box. A pauper can   170
    swear by every
Altar, and every god between Rome and Samothrace,[67]
    still
(Though the gods themselves forgive them) he'll pass for
    a perjuror
Defying the wrath of heaven. The poor man's an eternal
Butt for bad jokes, with his torn and dirt-caked top-coat,
His grubby toga, one shoe agape where the leather's
Split—those clumsy patches, that coarse and tell-tale
    stitching
Only a day or two old. The hardest thing to bear
In poverty is the fact that it makes us ridiculous.
"Out of those front-row seats," we're told. "You ought to be
Ashamed of yourselves—your incomes are far too small,   180
    and
The law's the law. Make way for some pander's son,
Spawned in an unknown brothel, let your place be
    occupied
By that natty auctioneer's offspring, with his high-class
    companions
The trainer's brat and the son of the gladiator
Applauding beside him." Such were the fruits of that
    pinhead
Otho's Reserved Seat Act.[68] What prospective son-in-law
Ever passed muster here if he was short on cash
To match the girl's dowry? What poor man ever inherits
A legacy, or is granted that meanest of sinecures—
A job with the Office of Works? All lower-income citizens 190
Should have marched out of town, in a body, years ago.
Nobody finds it easy to get to the top if meagre
Resources cripple his talent. But in Rome the problem's
    worse
Than anywhere else. Inflation hits the rental
Of your miserable apartment, inflation distends
The ravenous maws of your slaves; your humble dinner
Suffers inflation too. You feel ashamed to eat
Off earthenware dishes—yet if you were transported
To some rural village, you'd be content enough
And happily wear a cloak of coarse blue broadcloth   200
Complete with hood. Throughout most of Italy—we
Might as well admit it—no one is seen in a toga
Till the day he dies. Even on public holidays,

---

[65] **that Stoic greybeard** Stoicism, the Greek philosophy, was very popular in Rome. The Stoic greybeard was Publius Egnatius Celer, who betrayed his friend and his own daughter to Roman authorities. Juvenal identified Celer's home as Tarsus (in modern Turkey), which had been annexed by Rome in the first century BCE. Juvenal linked the city to the myth of Bellerophon, who fell from Pegasus, the winged horse, at this spot.

[66] **Scipio, Metellus, King Numa** Scipio and Metellus helped save some of Rome's sacred objects. **King Numa,** as noted in footnote 51, was a semimythical ruler of Rome.
[67] **Samothrace** A Greek island in the Aegean Sea, off the coast of Thrace.
[68] **Otho's Reserved Seat Act** Otho, an official in Rome, established the seating arrangements in Roman theaters, whereby the rich always had the best seats.

When the same old shows as last year are cheerfully
    staged
In the grassgrown theatre, when peasant children, sitting
On their mothers' laps, shrink back in terror at the sight
Of those gaping, whitened masks, you will still find the
    whole
Audience—top row or bottom—dressed exactly alike;
Even the magistrates need no better badge of status
Than a plain white tunic. But here in Rome we must toe   210
The line of fashion, living beyond our means, and
Often on borrowed credit: every man jack of us
Is keeping up with his neighbours. To cut a long story
    short,
Nothing's for free in Rome. How much does it cost you
To salute our noble Cossus (rare privilege!) or extract
One casual, tight-lipped nod from Veiento the
    honours-broker[69]?
X will be having his beard trimmed, Y just offering up
His boy-friend's kiss-curls: the whole house swarms with
    barbers,
Each of them on the make. You might as well swallow
Your bile, and face the fact that we hangers-on   220
Have to bribe our way, swell some sleek menial's savings.
    "What countryman ever bargained, besides, for his
      house collapsing
About his ears? Such things are unheard-of in cool
Praeneste, or rural Gabii, or Tivoli perched on its hillside,
Or Volsinii,[70] nestling amid its woodland ridges. But here
We live in a city shored up, for the most part, with
    gimcrack
Stays and props: that's how our landlords arrest
The collapse of their property, papering over great cracks
In the ramshackle fabric, reassuring the tenants
They can sleep secure, when all the time the building   230
Is poised like a house of cards. I prefer to live where
Fires and midnight panics are not quite such common
    events.
By the time the smoke's got up to your third-floor
    apartment
(And you still asleep) your downstairs neighbour is
    roaring
For water, and shifting his bits and pieces to safety.
If the alarm goes at ground-level, the last to fry
Will be the attic tenant, way up among the nesting
Pigeons, with nothing but tiles between himself and the
    weather.
What did friend Cordus own? One truckle bed, too short
For even a midget nympho; one marble-topped sideboard   240
On which stood six little mugs; beneath it, a pitcher
And an up-ended bust of Chiron,[71] one ancient settle

Crammed with Greek books (though by now
    analphabetic mice
Had gnawed their way well into his texts of the great
    poets).
Cordus could hardly be called a property-owner, and yet
What little the poor man had, he lost. Today the final
Straw on his load of woe (clothes worn to tatters, reduced
To begging for crusts) is that no one will offer him
    lodging
Or shelter, not even stand him a decent meal. But if
Some millionaire's mansion is gutted, women rend their   250
    garments,
Top people put on mourning, the courts go into recess:
Then you hear endless complaints about the hazards
Of city life, these deplorable outbreaks of fire;
Then contributions pour in while the shell is still ash-hot—
Construction materials, marble, fresh-gleaming
    sculptured nudes.
Up come A with bronzes (genuine antique works
By a real Old Master) acquired, as part of his booty,
From their hallowed niche in some Asiatic temple;
B provides bookshelves, books, and a study bust of
    Minerva;
C a sackful of silver. So it goes on, until   260
This dandified bachelor's losses are all recouped—
And more than recouped—with even rarer possessions,
And a rumour (well-founded) begins to circulate
That he fired the place himself, a deliberate piece of
    arson.
"If you can face the prospect of no more public games
Purchase a freehold house in the country. What it will
    cost you
Is no more than you pay in annual rent for some shabby
And ill-lit garret here. A garden plot's thrown in
With the house itself, and a well with a shallow basin—
No rope-and-bucket work when your seedlings need   270
    some water!
Learn to enjoy hoeing, work and plant your allotment
Till a hundred vegetarians could feast off its produce.
It's quite an achievement, even out in the backwoods,
To have made yourself master of—well, say one lizard,
    even.
    "Insomnia causes more deaths amongst Roman invalids
Than any other factor (the most common *complaints*, of
    course,
Are heartburn and ulcers, brought on by over-eating).
How much sleep, I ask you, can one get in lodgings here?
Unbroken nights—and this is the root of the trouble—
Are a rich man's privilege. The waggons thundering past   280
Through those narrow twisting streets, the oaths of
    draymen
Caught in a traffic-jam—these alone would suffice
To jolt the doziest sea-cow of an Emperor[72] into

---

[69] **Cossus and Veiento** The original Cossus was a highly honored aristocrat. This Cossus and Veiento were unsavory characters. Veiento conducted many shady deals but kept in favor with several emperors.

[70] **Praeneste, Gabii, Tivoli, Volsinii** Quiet rural towns or retreats not far from Rome.

[71] **Chiron** The wise and just centaur who was taught by the Greek gods and later instructed some Greek heroes, including Achilles and Jason.

---

[72] **sea-cow of an Emperor** The sea-cow, or seal, was believed to have curious sleeping patterns. The emperor is Claudius, who often fell asleep in public. Also, Claudius supposedly spoke in a barklike voice. Thus, the references have double meaning. Some translations use *or* rather than *of*, which probably makes more sense.

Permanent wakefulness. If a business appointment
Summons the tycoon, *he* gets there fast, by litter,
Tacking above the crowd. There's plenty of room inside:
He can read, or take notes, or snooze as he jogs along—
Those drawn blinds are most soporific. Even so
He outstrips us: however fast we pedestrians hurry
We're blocked by the crowds ahead, while those behind us   290
Tread on our heels. Sharp elbows buffet my ribs,
Poles poke into me; one lout swings a crossbeam
Down on my skull, another scores with a barrel.
My legs are mud-encrusted, big feet kick me, a hobnailed
Soldier's boot lands squarely on my toes. Do you see
All that steam and bustle? The great man's hangers-on
Are getting their free dinner, each with his own
Kitchen-boy in attendance. Those outsize dixies,[73]
And all the rest of the gear one poor little slave
Must balance on his head, while he trots along   300
To keep the charcoal glowing, would tax the strength
Of a musclebound general. Recently-patched tunics
Are ripped to shreds. Here's the great trunk of a fir-tree
Swaying along on its waggon, and look, another dray
Behind it, stacked high with pine-logs, a nodding threat
Over the heads of the crowd. If that axle snapped, and a
Cartload of marble avalanched down on them, what
Would be left of their bodies? Who could identify bits
Of ownerless flesh and bone? The poor man's flattened
    corpse
Would vanish along with his soul. And meanwhile, all   310
    unwitting,
The folk at home are busily scouring dishes,
Blowing the fire to a glow, clattering over greasy
Flesh-scrapers, filling up oil-flasks, laying out clean
    towels.
But all the time, as his houseboys hasten about their
    chores,
Himself is already sitting—the latest arrival—
By the bank of the Styx, and gawping in holy terror
At its filthy old ferryman. No chance of a passage over
That mud-thick channel for him, poor devil, without so
    much
As a copper stuck in his mouth to pay for the ride.[74]
"There are other nocturnal perils, of various sorts,   320
Which you should consider. It's a long way up to the
    rooftops,
And a falling tile can brain you—not to mention all
Those cracked or leaky pots that people toss out through
    windows.
Look at the way they smash, the weight of them, the
    damage
They do to the pavement! You'll be thought most
    improvident,
A catastrophe-happy fool, if you don't make your will
    before

Venturing out to dinner. Each open upper casement
Along your route at night may prove a death-trap:
So pray and hope (poor you!) that the local housewives
Drop nothing worse on your head than a pailful of slops.   330
    "Then there's the drunken bully, in an agonized state
For lack of a victim, who lies there tossing and turning
The whole night through, like Achilles after the death
Of his boy-friend Patroclus.[75] [This lout is doomed to
    insomnia
Unless he gets a fight.] Yet however flown with wine
Our young hothead may be, he carefully keeps his
    distance
From the man in a scarlet cloak, the man surrounded
By torches and big brass lamps and a numerous
    bodyguard.
But for me, a lonely pedestrian, trudging home by
    moonlight
Or with hand cupped round the wick of one poor   340
    guttering candle,
He has no respect whatever. This is the way the wretched
Brawl comes about (if you can term it a brawl
When you do the fighting and I'm just cast as punchbag).
He blocks my way. "Stop," he says. I have no option
But to obey—what else can one do when attacked
By a huge tough, twice one's size and fighting-mad as
    well?
"Where have *you* sprung from?" he shouts. "Ugh, what a
    stench
Of beans and sour wine! I know your sort, you've been
    round
With some cobbler-crony, scoffing a boiled sheep's head
And a dish of spring leeks. What? Nothing to say for   350
    yourself?
Speak up, or I'll kick your teeth in! Tell me, where's your
    pitch?
What synagogue do you doss in?" It makes not a jot of
    difference
Whether you try to answer, or back away from him
Without saying a word, you get beaten up just the same—
And then your irate "victim" takes *you* to court on a
    charge
Of assault and battery. Such is the poor man's "freedom":
After being slugged to a pulp, he may beg, as a special
Favour, to be left with his last few remaining teeth.
"Nor is this the sum of your terrors: when every house
Is shut up for the night, when shops stand silent, when   360
    bolts
Are shot, and doors on the chain, there are still burglars
Lurking around, or maybe some street-apache will settle
Your hash with a knife, the quick way. (Whenever armed
    detachments
Are patrolling the swamps and forests,[76] Rome becomes

---

[73] **dixies** Large cooking pots.
[74] **Styx, ferryman, copper** These terms refer to what happens when a dead person, or shade, arrives at the Styx River to be ferried over to the other side to Hades by Charon, the ferryman, who must be paid a coin. Thus, a coin would be stuck in the dead person's mouth.

---

[75] **Achilles and Patroclus** Achilles, the Greek warrior and a leader in the Trojan War, mourned the death of his close companion, Patroclus, who was killed in a battle during the siege of Troy.
[76] **swamps and forests** Swamps and forests near Rome were ideal hideouts for thieves and robbers, who would be flushed out of their dens and would head to Rome when the soldiers patrolled these areas.

A warren for this sort of scum.) Our furnaces glow, our
    anvils
Groan everywhere under their output of chains and
    fetters:
That's where most of our iron goes nowadays: one wonders
Whether ploughshares, hoes and mattocks may not soon
    be obsolete.
How fortunate they were (you well may think) those early
Forebears of ours, how happy the good old days   370
Of Kings and Tribunes, when Rome made do with one
    prison only!

"There are many other arguments I could adduce: but
    the sun
Slants down, my cattle are lowing, I must be on my way—
The muleteer has been signalling me with his whip
For some while now. So goodbye, and don't forget me—
Whenever you go back home for a break from the City,
    invite
Me over too, to share your fields and coverts,
Your country festivals: I'll put on my thickest boots
And make the trip to those chilly uplands—and listen
To your *Satires*, if I am reckoned worthy of that honour."   380

Questions for Critical Thinking

1. What did Juvenal mean by a "Greek-struck Rome," and what are some examples of Rome's being influenced by the Greeks?

2. Describe life in Rome in Juvenal's time—noting how its citizens lived and worked. In what ways are these descriptions similar to life in urban America today?

TACITUS
Selections from the *Annals*

Histories, as well as essays, odes, satires, lyrical poems, and epics, are part of Rome's rich and varied literary heritage. In the waning days of the Roman Republic, several historians, including Polybius [poe-LIB-ah-us] (ca. 198–117 BCE) and Livy (59 BCE–17 CE), made Rome their historical subject, attributing its rise to greatness to its republican government, citizen armies, and wars of conquest. Under the early empire, a new generation of historians arose, who chronicled the triumphs of the burgeoning empire. Among the imperial historians, the most productive, observant, and insightful was Gaius Cornelius Tacitus.

Tacitus [TASS-et-us] (ca. 56–ca. 120 CE) was probably born in southern Gaul (southeastern France) to a provincial family that was apparently financially and politically well established. He received an education corresponding to his family's high rank in Roman society, which involved studying literature and philosophy, especially the Greek thinkers, and training in rhetoric or public speaking—the academic training needed for careers in law, politics, and public service. Tacitus rose rapidly in the ranks of the military and civilian services. In 97 CE, after years in Rome and in the provinces holding varied offices, he was appointed as consul, the highest-ranking office in the Roman state, under Emperor Nerva (r. 96–98 CE). Later, under Emperor Trajan (r. 98–117 CE), Tacitus was appointed proconsul of Asia (most of Asia Minor) in 112 CE, the most prestigious provincial governorship in the empire.

Throughout his long and productive political and administrative years at home and abroad, Tacitus wrote several books that established his reputation as a trained professional historian, a keen observer of current events and his contemporaries, a shrewd student of human behavior, and a superb prose writer of the Latin language. Two of his works appeared in 98 CE, *Agricola* and *Germania*. *Agricola* was the biography of his father-in-law, Gnaeus Julius Agricola (40–93 CE), a general and government official who conquered and pacified much of

Britain. *Germania* was a detailed and accurate ethnological survey and analysis of the German tribes, then menacing Rome's borders, whom Tacitus depicted as exemplary models of upright behavior and contrasted them to what he perceived to be a Roman populace in decline during the reigns of the emperors who succeeded Augustus (63 BCE–14 CE).

Tacitus's fame as a historian rests on two books on Roman history: the *Historiae* and the *Annals*. Written first, the *Historiae* recorded events from 69 to 96 CE, known as the Flavian period, and the *Annals* covered the earlier period from 14 to 68 CE, known as the Julio-Claudian period. In the *Historiae,* Tacitus documented his own times, which were essentially the last thirty years of the first century CE, and in the *Annals,* he examined the early years of the empire, from the death of Caesar Augustus to the end of Nero's reign.

In the *Annals,* Tacitus relied on oral history, written sources including Senate records and decrees, official journals and reports, personal memoirs, inscriptions on monuments and in public places, and the writings of other historians or annalists—those who recorded the events of the year on an annual basis. Like many of his predecessors, Tacitus wrote in a grand style and used history to teach a moral lesson. Political freedom, as he understood it, was disappearing, and he wanted to explain why this was happening. Tacitus believed that talented men who had risen to power through the Senate and as government administrators during the republic had now been replaced by those who were passive, took a middle course, or blindly followed the emperor. His survey of the emperors and their policies and actions proved his argument, but his works overall are not free of personal bias in his accounts of the historical periods.

Reading the Selections

The first selection is the opening paragraphs of the *Annals* in which Tacitus provides a factual and concise assessment of the rise of Caesar Augustus, his reforms, and his reign. Tacitus's descriptions of individuals and events move the narrative along quickly, ending with Tiberius (r. 14–37 CE) as emperor. In the second selection, Tacitus turns his attention to foreign affairs, wars, and politics among the generals and provincial administrators. His case study is an uprising in Britain of the Icenians, a barbarian tribe, who were led by a woman warrior, Boudicca, also called Boadicea (d. 60 CE). About eighteen centuries later, Boudicca became one of the female national symbols adopted during the rise of British nationalism.

∞

Chapter I, Introduction and Brief History

When Rome was first a city, its rulers were kings. Then Lucius Junius Brutus created the consulate and free Republican institutions in general. Dictatorships were assumed in emergencies. A Council of Ten did not last more than two years; and then there was a short-lived arrangement by which senior army officers—the commanders of contingents provided by the tribes[77]—possessed consular authority. Subsequently Cinna and Sulla set up autocracies, but they too were brief. Soon Pompey and Crassus acquired predominant positions, but rapidly lost them to Caesar. Next, the military strength which Lepidus and Antony had built up was absorbed by Augustus. He found the whole state exhausted by internal dissensions, and established over it a personal regime known as the Principate.[78]

___

[77] **tribes** The Roman people were divided into "tribes" that conformed to ancient territorial areas and were the units, by the time of Tacitus, the government used to collect taxes and to recruit troops.

[78] **Principate** The imperial regime, as in contrast to the Republic. In this paragraph Tacitus refers to the following events: 753 BCE, legendary date of the foundation of Rome; 510 BCE, kings supposedly expelled by Lucius Junius Brutus; 451–449 BCE, constitution suspended in favour of two successive annual Councils of Ten to prepare codes of laws; 444–367 BCE (at intervals), commanders of tribal contingents granted consular powers; 87–84 BCE, four consulates of Lucius Cornelius Cinna; 82–79 BCE, Sulla's dictatorship; 60/59–53 BCE, informal "First Triumvirate" of Pompey, Marcus Licinius Crassus, and Julius Caesar; 49–44 BCE, Julius Caesar's dictatorships; 43 BCE, Second Triumvirate of Antony, Octavian (the future Augustus), and Marcus Aemilius Lepidus (III); 43 BCE, deaths of Brutus and Cassius; 36 BCE, Sextus Pompeius defeated and Lepidus dropped; 30 BCE, suicide of Antony (translator's footnote).

Famous writers have recorded Rome's early glories and disasters. The Augustan Age, too, had its distinguished historians. But then the rising tide of flattery exercised a deterrent effect. The reigns of Tiberius, Gaius, Claudius, and Nero[79] were described during their lifetimes in fictitious terms, for fear of the consequences; whereas the accounts written after their deaths were influenced by still raging animosities. So I have decided to say a little about Augustus, with special attention to his last period, and then go on to the reign of Tiberius and what followed. I shall write without indignation or partisanship: in my case the customary incentives to these are lacking.

The violent deaths of Brutus and Cassius left no Republican forces in the field. Defeat came to Sextus Pompeius in Sicily, Lepidus was dropped, Antony killed. So even the Caesarian party had no leader left except the "Caesar" himself, Octavian.[80] He gave up the title of Triumvir, emphasizing instead his position as consul; and the powers of a tribune,[81] he proclaimed, were good enough for him—powers for the protection of ordinary people.

He seduced the army with bonuses, and his cheap food policy was successful bait for civilians. Indeed, he attracted everybody's goodwill by the enjoyable gift of peace. Then he gradually pushed ahead and absorbed the functions of the senate, the officials, and even the law. Opposition did not exist. War or judicial murder had disposed of all men of spirit. Upper-class survivors found that slavish obedience was the way to succeed, both politically and financially. They had profited from the revolution, and so now they liked the security of the existing arrangement better than the dangerous uncertainties of the old regime. Besides, the new order was popular in the provinces. There, government by Senate and People was looked upon sceptically as a matter of sparring dignitaries and extortionate officials. The legal system had provided no remedy against these, since it was wholly incapacitated by violence, favouritism, and—most of all—bribery.

To safeguard his domination Augustus made his sister's son Marcellus a priest and a curule aedile[82]—in spite of his extreme youth—and singled out Marcus Agrippa, a commoner but a first-rate soldier who had helped to win his victories, by the award of two consecutive consulships; after the death of Marcellus, Agrippa was chosen by Augustus as his son-in-law. Next the emperor had his stepsons Tiberius and Nero Drusus hailed publicly as victorious generals. When he did this, however, there was no lack of heirs of his own blood: there were Agrippa's sons

Gaius Caesar and Lucius Caesar. Augustus had adopted them into the imperial family. He had also, despite pretended reluctance, been passionately eager that, even as minors, they should be entitled Princes of Youth and have consulships reserved for them. After Agrippa had died, first Lucius Caesar and then Gaius Casear met with premature natural deaths—unless their stepmother Livia had a secret hand in them. Lucius died on his way to the armies in Spain, Gaius while returning from Armenia incapacitated by a wound.

Nero Drusus was long dead. Tiberius was the only surviving stepson; and everything pointed in his direction. He was adopted as the emperor's son and as partner in his powers (with civil and military authority and the powers of a tribune) and displayed to all the armies. No longer was this due to his mother's secret machinations, as previously. This time she requested it openly. Livia had the aged Augustus firmly under control—so much so that he exiled his only surviving grandson to the island of Planasia. That was the young, physically tough, indeed brutish, Agrippa Postumus. Though devoid of every good quality, he had been involved in no scandal. Nevertheless, it was not he but Germanicus the son of Nero Drusus, whom the emperor placed in command of the eight divisions on the Rhine—and, although Tiberius had a grown son of his own, he ordered him to adopt Germanicus. For Augustus wanted to have another iron in the fire.

At this time there was no longer any fighting—except a war against the Germans; and that was designed less to extend the empire's frontiers, or achieve any lucrative purpose, than to avenge the disgrace of the army lost with Publius Quinctilius Varus.[83] In the capital the situation was calm. The titles of officials remained the same. Actium[84] had been won before the younger men were born. Even most of the older generation had come into a world of civil wars. Practically no one had ever seen truly Republican government. The country had been transformed, and there was nothing left of the fine old Roman character. Political equality was a thing of the past; all eyes watched for imperial commands.

Nobody had any immediate worries as long as Augustus retained his physical powers, and kept himself going, and his House, and the peace of the empire. But when old age incapacitated him, his approaching end brought hopes of change. A few people started idly talking of the blessings of freedom. Some, more numerous, feared civil war; others wanted it. The great majority, however, exchanged critical gossip about candidates for the succession. First, Agrippa Postumus—a savage without either the years or the training needed for imperial responsibilities. Tiberius, on the other hand, had the seniority and the military reputation. But he also possessed the ancient,

5

---

[79] **Tiberius, Gaius, Claudius, and Nero** The four Emperors of the Julio-Claudian line who ruled from 14 to 68 CE.
[80] **Octavian** Augustus's original name, which he used until he took the title Caesar Augustus.
[81] **Triumvir, consul, tribune** The title Triumvir refers to the triumvirate of Lepidus, Antony, and Octavian, which ruled Rome 43–33 BCE. A consul was the highest elected office in the Republic, and Augustus took this office and title as well as the powers of tribune, the official who was responsible for protecting the rights of the plebeian classes, or "ordinary people."
[82] **curule aedile** An office of rank that had responsibilities dealing with the city of Rome. The word *curule* refers to the official seat or chair in which the person with the title, such as aedile, sat.

[83] **Publius Quinctilius Varus** A former consul, then the general of a Roman army in Germany that suffered one of the worst defeats in Roman history in 9 CE.
[84] **Actium** Site of the naval battle, off the west coast of Greece, where, in 31 BCE, Octavian defeated the fleet of Antony and Cleopatra, paving the way for Octavian to become the sole ruler of the Roman government.

ingrained arrogance of the Claudian family; and signs of a cruel disposition kept breaking out, repress them as he might. Besides, it was argued, he had been brought up from earliest youth in an imperial household, had accumulated early consulships and Triumphs, and even during the years at Rhodes[85]—which looked like banishment but were called retirement—his thoughts had been solely occupied with resentment, deception, and secret sensuality. And then there was that feminine bully, his mother. "So we have got to be slaves to a woman," people were saying, "and to the two half-grown boys Germanicus and Drusus. First they will be a burden to the State—then they will tear it in two!"

Amid this sort of conversation the health of Augustus deteriorated. Some suspected his wife of foul play. For rumour had it that a few months earlier, with the knowledge of his immediate circle but accompanied only by Paullus Fabius Maximus, he had gone to Planasia to visit Agrippa Postumus; and that there had been such a

tearful display of affection on both sides that the young man seemed very likely to be received back into the home of his grandfather. Maximus, it was further said, had told his wife, Marcia, of this, and she had warned Livia—but the emperor had discovered the leakage, and when Maximus died shortly afterwards (perhaps by his own hand) his widow had been heard at the funeral moaning and blaming herself for her husband's death. Whatever the true facts about this, Tiberius was recalled from his post in Illyricum[86] (immediately after his arrival there) by an urgent letter from his mother. When he arrived at Nola,[87] it is unknown whether he found Augustus alive or dead. For the house and neighbouring streets were carefully sealed by Livia's guards. At intervals, hopeful reports were published—until the steps demanded by the situation had been taken. Then two pieces of news became known simultaneously: Augustus was dead, and Tiberius was in control.

---

[85] **Rhodes** An island in the Aegean Sea where Tiberius lived, 6 BCE to 2 CE.

[86] **Illyricum** The Roman province covering the vast area east of the Adriatic Sea.
[87] **Nola** In southern Italy, near Naples.

Chapter XIV, Uprising in Britain

The following year, when the consuls were Lucius Caesennius Paetus and Publius Petronius Turpilianus, witnessed a serious disaster in Britain.[88] The imperial governor Aulus Didius Gallus had, as I have said, merely held his own. His successor Quintus Veranius (II) had only conducted minor raids against the Silures[89] when death terminated his operations. His life had been famous for its austerity. But his testamentary last words were glaringly self-seeking, for they grossly flattered Nero and added that Veranius, if he had lived two years longer, would have presented him with the whole province.

The new imperial governor of Britain was Gaius Suetonius Paulinus. Corbulo's rival in military science, as in popular talk—which makes everybody compete—he was ambitious to achieve victories as glorious as the reconquest of Armenia. So Suetonius planned to attack the island of Mona,[90] which although thickly populated had also given sanctuary to many refugees.

Flat-bottomed boats were built to contend with the shifting shallows, and these took the infantry across. Then came the cavalry; some utilized fords, but in deeper water the men swam beside their horses. The enemy lined the shore in a dense armed mass. Among them were black-robed women with dishevelled hair like Furies,

brandishing torches. Close by stood Druids, raising their hands to heaven and screaming dreadful curses.

This weird spectacle awed the Roman soldiers into a sort of paralysis. They stood still—and presented themselves as a target. But then they urged each other (and were urged by the general) not to fear a horde of fanatical women. Onward pressed their standards and they bore down their opponents, enveloping them in the flames of their own torches. Suetonius garrisoned the conquered island. The groves devoted to Mona's barbarous superstitions he demolished. For it was their religion to drench their altars in the blood of prisoners and consult their gods by means of human entrails.

While Suetonius was thus occupied, he learnt of a sudden rebellion in the province. Prasutagus, king of the Iceni,[91] after a life of long and renowned prosperity, had made the emperor co-heir with his own two daughters. Prasutagus hoped by this submissiveness to preserve his kingdom and household from attack. But it turned out otherwise. Kingdom and household alike were plundered like prizes of war, the one by Roman officers, the other by Roman slaves. As a beginning, his widow Boudicca was flogged and their daughters raped. The Icenian chiefs were deprived of their hereditary estates as if the Romans had been given the whole country. The king's own relatives were treated like slaves.

---

[88] **in Britain** Tacitus identified the year by who were the consuls. This is the year 60 CE.
[89] **Silures** A tribe in southern Wales.
[90] **Mona** An island off northwest Wales, now Anglesey.

[91] **Iceni** A tribe located around modern-day Norfolk and Suffolk, England.

And the humiliated Iceni feared still worse, now that they had been reduced to provincial status. So they rebelled. With them rose the Trinobantes[92] and others. Servitude had not broken them, and they had secretly plotted together to become free again. They particularly hated the Roman ex-soldiers who had recently established a settlement at Camulodunum.[93] The settlers drove the Trinobantes from their homes and land, and called them prisoners and slaves. The troops encouraged the settlers' outrages, since their own way of behaving was the same and they looked forward to similar licence for themselves. Moreover, the temple created to the divine Claudius was a blatant stronghold of alien rule, and its observances were a pretext to make the natives appointed as its priests drain the whole country dry.

It seemed easy to destroy the settlement; for it had no walls. That was a matter which Roman commanders, thinking of amenities rather than needs, had neglected. At this juncture, for no visible reason, the statue of Victory at Camulodunum fell down—with its back turned as though it were fleeing the enemy. Delirious women chanted of destruction at hand. They cried that in the local senate-house outlandish yells had been heard; the theatre had echoed with shrieks; at the mouth of the Thames a phantom settlement had been seen in ruins. A blood-red colour in the sea, too, and shapes like human corpses left by the ebb tide, were interpreted hopefully by the Britons—and with terror by the settlers.

Suetonius, however, was far away. So they appealed for help to the imperial agent Catus Decianus. He sent them barely two hundred men, incompletely armed. There was also a small garrison on the spot. Reliance was placed on the temple's protection. Misled by secret pro-rebels, who hampered their plans, they dispensed with rampart or trench. They omitted also to evacuate old people and women and thus leave only fighting men behind. Their precautions were appropriate to a time of unbroken peace.

Then a native horde surrounded them. When all else had been ravaged or burnt, the garrison concentrated itself in the temple. After two days' siege, it fell by storm. The ninth Roman division, commanded by Quintus Petilius Cerialis Caesius Rufus, attempted to relieve the town, but was stopped by the victorious Britons and routed. Its entire infantry force was massacred, while the commander escaped to his camp with his cavalry and sheltered behind its defences. The imperial agent Catus Decianus, horrified by the catastrophe and by his unpopularity, withdrew to Gaul. It was his rapacity which had driven the province to war.

But Suetonius, undismayed, marched through disaffected territory to Londinium.[94] This town did not rank as a Roman settlement, but was an important centre for business-men and merchandise. At first, he hesitated whether to stand and fight there. Eventually, his numerical

inferiority—and the price only too clearly paid by the divisional commander's rashness—decided him to sacrifice the single city of Londinium to save the province as a whole. Unmoved by lamentations and appeals, Suetonius gave the signal for departure. The inhabitants were allowed to accompany him. But those who stayed because they were women, or old, or attached to the place, were slaughtered by the enemy. Verulamium[95] suffered the same fate.

The natives enjoyed plundering and thought of nothing else. Bypassing forts and garrisons, they made for where loot was richest and protection weakest. Roman and provincial deaths at the places mentioned are estimated at seventy thousand. For the British did not take or sell prisoners, or practise other war-time exchanges. They could not wait to cut throats, hang, burn, and crucify—as though avenging, in advance, the retribution that was on its way.

Suetonius collected the fourteenth brigade and detachments of the twentieth, together with the nearest available auxiliaries—amounting to nearly ten thousand armed men—and decided to attack without further delay. He chose a position in a defile with a wood behind him. There could be no enemy, he knew, except at his front, where there was open country without cover for ambushes. Suetonius drew up his regular troops in close order, with the light-armed auxiliaries at their flanks, and the cavalry massed on the wings. On the British side, cavalry and infantry bands seethed over a wide area in unprecedented numbers. Their confidence was such that they brought their wives with them to see the victory, installing them in carts stationed at the edge of the battlefield.

Boudicca drove round all the tribes in a chariot with her daughters in front of her. "We British are used to woman commanders in war," she cried. "I am descended from mighty men! But now I am not fighting for my kingdom and wealth. I am fighting as an ordinary person for my lost freedom, my bruised body, and my outraged daughters. Nowadays Roman rapacity does not even spare our bodies. Old people are killed, virgins raped. But the gods will grant us the vengeance we deserve! The Roman division which dared to fight is annihilated. The others cower in their camps, or watch for a chance to escape. They will never face even the din and roar of all our thousands, much less the shock of our onslaught. Consider how many of you are fighting—and why. Then you will win this battle, or perish. That is what I, a woman, plan to do!—let the men live in slavery if they will."

Suetonius trusted his men's bravery. Yet he too, at this critical moment, offered encouragements and appeals. "Disregard the clamours and empty threats of the natives!" he said. "In their ranks, there are more women than fighting men. Unwarlike, unarmed, when they see the arms and courage of the conquerors who have routed them so often, they will break immediately. Even when a force contains many divisions, few among them win the battles—what special glory for your small numbers to win the renown of a whole army! Just keep in close order.

---

[92] **Trinobantes** Another close-by tribe around Essex, England.
[93] **Camulodunum** Modern-day Colchester in southeast England.
[94] **Londinium** Roman town on the river Thames; now London.

[95] **Verulamium** Modern-day St. Albans, north of London.

Throw your javelins, and then carry on: use shield-bosses to fell them, swords to kill them. Do not think of plunder. When you have won, you will have everything."

The general's words were enthusiastically received: the old battle-experienced soldiers longed to hurl their javelins. So Suetonius confidently gave the signal for battle. At first the regular troops stood their ground. Keeping to the defile as a natural defense, they launched their javelins accurately at the approaching enemy. Then, in wedge formation, they burst forward. So did the auxiliary infantry. The cavalry, too, with lances extended, demolished all serious resistance. The remaining Britons fled with difficulty since their ring of wagons blocked the outlets. The Romans did not spare even the women. Baggage animals too, transfixed with weapons, added to the heaps of dead.

It was a glorious victory, comparable with bygone triumphs. According to one report almost eighty thousand Britons fell. Our own casualties were about four hundred dead and slightly larger number of wounded. Boudicca poisoned herself. Poenius Postumus, chief-of-staff of the second division which had not joined Suetonius, learning of the success of the other two formations, stabbed himself to death because he had cheated his formation of its share in the victory and broken regulations by disobeying his commander's orders.

The whole army was now united. Suetonius kept it under canvas to finish the war. The emperor raised its numbers by transferring from Germany two thousand regular troops, which brought the ninth division to full strength, also eight auxiliary infantry battalions and a thousand cavalry. These were stationed together in new winter quarters, and hostile or wavering tribes were ravaged with fire and sword. But the enemy's worst affliction was famine. For they had neglected to sow their fields and brought everyone available into the army, intending to seize our supplies. Still, the savage British tribesmen were disinclined for peace, especially as the newly arrived imperial agent Gaius Julius Alpinus Classicianus, successor to Catus Decianus, was on bad terms with Suetonius, and allowed his personal animosities to damage the national interests. For he passed round advice to wait for a new governor who would be kind to those who surrendered, without an enemy's bitterness or a conqueror's arrogance. Classicianus also reported to Rome that there was no prospect of ending the war unless a successor was appointed to Suetonius, whose failures he attributed to perversity—and his successes to luck.

So a former imperial slave, Polyclitus, was sent to investigate the British situation. Nero was very hopeful that Polyclitus' influence would both reconcile the governor and agent and pacify native rebelliousness. With his enormous escort, Polyclitus was a trial to Italy and Gaul. Then he crossed the Channel and succeeded in intimidating even the Roman army. But the enemy laughed at him. For them, freedom still lived, and the power of ex-slaves was still unfamiliar. The British marvelled that a general and an army who had completed such a mighty war should obey a slave.

But all this was toned down in Polyclitus' reports to the emperor. Retained as governor, Suetonius lost a few ships and their crews on the shore, and was then superseded for not terminating the war. His successor, the recent consul Publius Petronius Turpilianus, neither provoking the enemy nor provoked, called this ignoble inactivity peace with honour.

Questions for Critical Thinking

1. In what ways did Octavian or Augustus secure his power? What was the major crisis confronting the Roman government at the end of Augustus's life and how was it resolved?

2. How did the Romans react to the uprising in Britain? How did their reaction illustrate Rome's foreign policy and treatment of its conquered territories? Do you think this is a viable policy? Why or why not?

MARCUS AURELIUS
Selections from *Meditations*

The Roman emperor Marcus Aurelius (121–180 CE), who ruled from 161 to 180, has been remembered as the "philosopher-king" because he possessed some of the attributes of Plato's ideal leader (see Plato's *The Republic* in Chapter 3). In his youth he embraced Stoicism, the Greek philosophy, and he left an account of how he tried to apply the tenets of Stoicism to his public and private life. The *Meditations,* written in the 170s, toward the end of his reign and during a long military campaign, voiced his opinions on human behavior, provided him guidance and solace, and summarized his philosophy of life. Since the rediscovery of the *Meditations* in the sixteenth century, generations of political leaders, intellectuals, writers, and ordinary people have found his ruminations, confessions, and advice helpful and comforting when they, too, have faced life's uncertainties and disappointments.

Marcus Aurelius came from a wealthy and distinguished Roman family who had been active in politics and governance for several decades. His education, typical for an upper-class Roman, was steeped in Greek and Roman literature and rhetoric to prepare him for a political career. The new Roman emperor, Antoninus Pius (r. 81–161 CE), who was married to Marcus Aurelius's aunt, chose Marcus Aurelius, at age sixteen, to be his successor, along with another young man, Lucius Verus. Both youths furthered their education in rhetoric and oratory skills while Marcus Aurelius began his study of Greek philosophy, in particular the writings of the former slave Epictetus, who was one of the leading exponents of Stoicism. Marcus Aurelius was a consul twice before he was thirty and, in 145 CE, married Antoninus Pius's daughter—an event that further solidified his position as one of the two heirs apparent to the emperor.

Little is known of his life from 145 to 161 CE when, upon the death of Antoninus Pius, Marcus Aurelius and his adopted brother, Lucius Verus, ascended to power. The serenity identified with the *Pax Romana* (Roman Peace) and Antoninus Pius's reign faded quickly. Within a short time the co-emperors faced the Parthians, a strong enemy in the East, who were finally defeated in the mid-160s. However, the returning army brought back the plague, which devastated the empire for several decades. Floods, followed by invasions from across the Danube, bred more troubles. In the late 160s the Romans temporarily defeated the German tribes, but the wars dragged on for another six years before the Romans pushed the Germans back across the Danube. During this extended expedition, Marcus Aurelius, who was alone and without close friends or family, fighting the enemy and governing the empire from the frontiers, composed his *Meditations*.

Many upper-class Romans, like Marcus Aurelius, were attracted to Stoicism as it had evolved from its Greek origins and been reinterpreted by Greco-Roman philosophers, writers, and practitioners by the second century CE. In contrast to earlier Greek Stoicism, which was concerned with the hypothetical or theoretical aspects of knowing and understanding, Roman Stoicism offered a practical and pragmatic approach to life. More a code to live by than a speculative discourse on the meaning of life, Roman Stoicism stressed manliness, rationality, fortitude, and self-discipline, which appealed to dedicated Romans who felt responsible for governing a sprawling empire of many races and ethnic groups. However, like Greek Stoicism, Roman Stoicism believed in a supreme being that went by many names—reason, *logos*, Nature, God. The deity also resided in each human, thus giving that person reason, a connection to the divine, and a common bond with other humans who shared these same characteristics. This implied a brotherhood of all humans who could be joined together by appealing to a universal reason or Nature or God found in each individual.

Marcus Aurelius, while believing in and practicing Roman Stoicism, was more concerned with its ethical aspects than its explanations of the physical world or its theories of how knowledge is obtained. He struggled to answer the fundamental questions that all humans ask: Why are we here? What will happen to us at death? What is right and what is wrong? How do we confront life's disappointments and our failures? How do we deal with other humans? What is happiness and can it be achieved? How should we live our lives? Although his answers, which are scattered throughout the *Meditations,* cannot be easily summarized, they shared certain basic assumptions regarding the human condition. For example, humans can control some circumstances in their lives; others, like health, wealth, and death, they cannot. Humans, therefore, must be able to distinguish between what they can control and cannot control, and they must accept whatever falls their way. Likewise, people should not pass judgment on what they see or experience as being good or evil but remain indifferent, which will, consequently, keep them detached, unharmed, and protected from making errors.

Because the *Meditations* are actually the musings and inner thoughts of one person jotted down at various times in his life, the work has no beginning and end, nor is it an analysis of life's problems with ready-made remedies. An earlier title of the book, *To Himself,* comes closer to defining what Marcus Aurelius intended his work to be—personal observations and how to survive each day. The *Meditations* contain no original philosophical theses or arguments and have no story line of a person's journey through life. Therefore, the work should be read in bits and pieces and as the mood strikes the reader.

Reading the Selections

Twelve books make up the *Meditations.* Book I, "Debts and Lessons," names individuals who influenced Marcus Aurelius and to whom he was indebted for various reasons in the course of his life. Book II is titled "Written among the Quadi on the River Gran," which refers to a river in present-day central Slovakia, known as the Hron, that flows into the Danube. The Quadi were a tribe later defeated by Marcus Aurelius in the early 170s. The other books have no title or heading. Except for the similar format and entries in Book I, the other books contain a variety of structures and writing styles: short essays, commands or imperatives, aphorisms, quotations, analogies, and lists of what should be done.

Book I, "Debts and Lessons." The only autobiographical section in the *Meditations,* Book I has seventeen entries, beginning with the shortest first—thanking his grandparents and parents in the early entries and his adopted father, Antoninus Pius, and the gods in the final passages. Others he refers to are persons who aided him in life. Rusticus was a mentor who served as consul of Rome; Apollonius and Sextus were Stoic philosophers who instructed Marcus Aurelius; Fronto was one of his most influential teachers.

Book II, "Written among the Quadi on the River Gran." Marcus Aurelius advises the reader on human behavior and how to work with others. He also notes the transitory nature of life and concludes that only philosophy can be one's guide.

Book V.1. An admonition to get out of bed and be on with the day and a reminder to like and enjoy your job.

Book VI.16. "What is it in ourselves that we should prize?" The author attempts to answer this question.

Book X.1–2, 8. "To my soul" is a plea to accept one's situation in life and make the best of it. The second passage is a list of epithets and how they will assist the reader in confronting life.

Book XII.3. Marcus Aurelius claims that peace and tranquillity will come if the mind is kept under control.

∞

Book I, Debts and Lessons

7. From Rusticus:[96] to get an impression of need for reform and treatment of character; not to run off into zeal
for rhetoric, writing on speculative themes, discoursing
on edifying texts, exhibiting in fanciful colours the ascetic
or the philanthropist. To avoid oratory, poetry, and preci-
osity; not to parade at home in ceremonial costume or to
do things of that kind; to write letters in the simple style,
like his own from Sinuessa to my mother. To be easily recalled to myself and easily reconciled with those who provoke and offend, as soon as they are willing to meet me.
To read books accurately and not be satisfied with superficial thinking about things or agree hurriedly with those
who talk round a subject. To have made the acquaintance
of the *Discourses* of Epictetus, of which he allowed me to
share a copy of his own.

8. From Apollonius:[97] moral freedom, not to expose oneself to the insecurity of fortune; to look to nothing else,
even for a little while, except to reason. To be always the
same, in sharp attacks of pain, in the loss of a child, in long
illnesses. To see clearly in a living example that a man can
be at once very much in earnest and yet able to relax.

Not to be censorious in exposition; and to see a man
who plainly considered technical knowledge and ease
in communicating general truths as the least of his good
gifts. The lesson how one ought to receive from friends
what are esteemed favours, neither lowering oneself on
their account, nor returning them tactlessly.

9. From Sextus:[98] graciousness, and the pattern of a
household governed by its head, and the notion of life according to Nature. Dignity without pretence, solicitious
consideration for friends, tolerance of amateurs and of
those whose opinions have no ground in science.

A happy accommodation to every man, so that not
only was his conversation more agreeable than any flattery, but he excited the greatest reverence at that very time
in the very persons about him. Certainty of grasp, and
method in the discovery and arrangement of the principles necessary to human life.

Never to give the impression of anger or of any other
passion, but to be at once entirely passionless and yet full
of natural affection. To praise without noise, to be widely
learned without display.

11. From Fronto:[99] to observe how vile a thing is the malice
and caprice and hypocrisy of absolutism; and generally

speaking that those whom we entitle "Patricians" are
somehow rather wanting in the natural affections.

16. From my father[100] (by adoption): gentleness and un-
shaken resolution in judgements taken after full examina-
tion; no vainglory about external honours; love of work
and perseverance; readiness to hear those who had anything to contribute to the public advantage; the desire to
award to every man according to desert without partial-
ity; the experience that knew where to tighten the rein,
where to relax. Prohibition of unnatural practices, social
tact and permission to his suite not invariably to be present at his banquets nor to attend his progress from Rome,
as a matter of obligation, and always to be found the same
by those who had failed to attend him through engage-
ments. Exact scrutiny in council and patience; not that he
was avoiding investigation, satisfied with first impressions. An inclination to keep his friends, and nowhere
fastidious or the victim of manias but his own master
is everything, and his outward mien cheerful. His long
foresight and ordering of the merest trifle without making scenes. The check in his reign put upon organized applause and every form of lip-service; his unceasing watch
over the needs of the empire and his stewardship of its
resources; his patience under criticism by individuals of
such conduct. No superstitious fear of divine powers or
with man any courting of the public or obsequiousness or
cultivation of popular favour, but temperance in all things
and firmness; nowhere want of taste or search for novelty.

In the things which contribute to life's comfort, where
Fortune was lavish to him, use without display and at the
same time without apology, so as to take them when they
were there quite simply and not to require them when
they were absent. The fact that no one would have said
that he was a sophist, an impostor, or a pedant, but a ripe
man, an entire man, above flattery, able to preside over his
own and his subjects' business.

Beside all this the inclination to respect genuine followers of philosophy, but towards the other sort no tendency to reproach nor on the other hand to be hoodwinked
by them; affability, too, and humour, but not to excess. Care
of his health in moderation, not as one in love with living
nor with an eye to personal appearance nor on the other
hand neglecting it, but so far as by attention to self to need
doctoring or medicine and external applications for very
few ailments.

A very strong point, to give way without jealousy to
those who had some particular gift like literary expression or knowledge of the Civil Law or customs or other
matters, even sharing their enthusiasm that each might

---

[96] **Rusticus** Quintus Junius Rusticus, city official in Rome who
influenced Marcus Aurelius.
[97] **Apollonius** Apollonius of Chalcedon, Stoic philosopher and
one of Marcus Aurelius's teachers.
[98] **Sextus** Sextus of Chaeronea, Stoic philosher and one of
Marcus Aurelius's teachers.
[99] **Fronto** Marcus Cornelius Fronto, rhetorician from North
Africa who helped educate Marcus Aurelius.

---

[100] **father** Antoninus Pius, Roman emperor (r. 138–161 CE) who
adopted Marcus Aurelius as one of his two sons and apparent
heirs to become emperor.

get the reputation due to his individual excellence. Acting always according to the tradition of our forefathers, yet not endeavouring that this regard for tradition should be noticed. No tendency, moreover, to chop and change, but a settled course in the same places and the same practices. After acute attacks of headache, fresh and vigorous at once for his accustomed duties; and not to have many secrets, only very few and by way of exception, and those solely because of matters of State. Discretion and moderation alike in the provision of shows, in carrying out public works, in donations to the populace, and so on; the behaviour in fact of one who has an eye precisely to what it is his duty to do, not to the reputation which attends the doing.

He was not one who bathed at odd hours, not fond of building, no connoisseur of the table, of the stuff and colour of his dress, of the beauty of his slaves. His costume was brought to Rome from his country house at Lorium; his manner of life at Lanovium; the way he treated the tax-collector who apologized at Tusculum, and all his behaviour of that sort. Nowhere harsh, merciless, or blustering, nor so that you might ever say "to fever heat," but everything nicely calculated and divided into its times, as by a leisured man; no bustle, complete order, strength, consistency. What is recorded of Socrates[101] would exactly fit him: he could equally be abstinent from or enjoy what many are too weak to abstain from and too self-indulgent in enjoying. To be strong, to endure, and in either case to be sober belong to the man of perfect and invincible spirit, like the spirit of Maximus[102] in his illness.

17. From the gods: to have had good grandparents, good parents, a good sister, good masters, good intimates, kinsfolk, friends, almost everything; and that in regard to not one of them did I stumble into offence, although I had the kind of disposition which might in some circumstances have led me to behave thus; but it was the goodness of the gods that no conjunction of events came about which was likely to expose my weakness. That I was not brought up longer than I was with my grandfather's second wife, that I preserved the flower of my youth and did not play the man before my time, but even delayed a little longer. That my station in life was under a governor and a father who was to strip off all my pride and to lead me to see that it is possible to live in a palace and yet not to need a bodyguard or embroidered uniforms or candelabra and statues bearing lamps and the like accompaniments of pomp, but that one is able to contract very nearly to a private station and not on that account to lose dignity or be more remiss in the duties that a prince must perform on behalf of the public. That I met with so good a brother, able by his character not only to rouse me to care of myself but at the same time to hearten me by respect and natural affection; that my children were not deficient in mind nor deformed in body; that I made no further progress in eloquence and poetry and those other pursuits wherein, had I seen myself progressing along an easy road, I should perhaps have become absorbed. That I made haste to advance my masters to the honours which they appeared to covet and did not put them off with hopes that, as they were still young, I should do it later on. To have got to know Apollonius, Rusticus, Maximus. To have pictured to myself clearly and repeatedly what life in obedience to Nature really is, so that, so far as concerns the gods and communications from the other world, and aids and inspirations, nothing hinders my living at once in obedience to Nature, though I still come somewhat short of this by my own fault and by not observing the reminders and almost the instructions of the gods. That my body has held out so well in a life like mine; that I did not touch Benedicta or Theodotus,[103] but that even in later years when I experienced the passion of love I was cured; that though I was often angry with Rusticus I never went to extremes for which I should have been sorry; that though my mother was fated to die young, she still spent her last years with me. That whenever I wanted to help anyone in poverty or some other necessity I was never told that I could not afford it, and that I did not myself fall into the same necessity so as to take help from another; that my wife is what she is, so obedient, so affectionate, and so simple; that I was well provided with suitable tutors for my children. That I was granted assistance in dreams, especially how to avoid spitting blood and fits of giddiness, and the answer of the oracle at Caieta:[104] "Even as thou shalt employ thyself"; and that, although in love with philosophy, I did not meet with any sophist or retire to disentangle literary works or syllogisms[105] or busy myself with problems "in the clouds." For all these things require "the gods to help and Fortune's[106] hand."

---

[101] **Socrates** Greek philosopher of fifth century BCE who helped lay the foundations of Western thought. Immortalized by his pupil, Plato.
[102] **Maximus** Claudius Maximus was a Roman consul and later governor of North Africa.
[103] **Benedicta or Theodotus** Unknown but probably household slaves.
[104] **Caieta** Seaport on the west coast of Italy. Reference to an "oracle" is uncertain.
[105] **sophist or . . . syllogisms** References to two of the more arcane characteristics of philosophy. The Sophist argued and debated using clever and often complicated reasoning. Syllogisms are used in deductive reasoning. Marcus Aurelius was not interested in those aspects of philosophy.
[106] **Fortune** In this sense, the Roman belief—probably coming from Hellenistic religions and certainly popular among Romans—of a force or power immune to human control that could determine events.

∞

Book II, Written among the Quadi on the River Gran

1. Say to yourself in the early morning: I shall meet to-day inquisitive, ungrateful, violent, treacherous, envious, uncharitable men. All these things have come upon them through ignorance of real good and ill. But I, because I have seen that the nature of good is the right, and of ill the wrong, and that the nature of man himself who does wrong is akin to my own (not for the same blood and seed, but partaking with me in mind, that is in a portion of divinity), I can neither be harmed by any of them, for no man will involve me in wrong, nor can I be angry with my kinsman or hate him; for we have come into the world to work together, like feet, like hands, like eyelids, like the rows of upper and lower teeth. To work against one another therefore is to oppose Nature, and to be vexed with another or to turn away from him is to tend to antagonism.

2. This whatever it is that I am, is flesh and vital spirit and the governing self. Disdain the flesh: blood and bones and network, a twisted skein of nerves, veins, arteries. Consider also what the vital spirit is: a current of air, not even continuously the same, but every hour being expelled and sucked in again. There is then a third part, the governing self. Put away your books, be distracted no longer, they are not your portion. Rather, as if on the point of death, reflect like this: "you are an old man, suffer this governing part of you no longer to be in bondage, no longer to be a puppet pulled by selfish impulse, no longer to be indignant with what is allotted in the present or to suspect what is allotted in the future."

17. Of man's life, his time is a point, his existence a flux, his sensation clouded, his body's entire composition corruptible, his vital spirit an eddy of breath, his fortune hard to predict, his fame uncertain. Briefly, all the things of the body, a river; all the things of the spirit, dream and delirium; his life a warfare and a sojourn in a strange land, his after-fame oblivion. What then can be his escort through life? One thing and one thing only: Philosophy. And this is to keep the spirit within him unwronged and unscathed, master of pains and pleasures, doing nothing at random, nothing falsely and with pretence; needing no other to do aught or to leave aught undone; and moreover accepting what befalls it, that is, what is assigned to it, as coming from the other world from which it came itself. And in all things awaiting death, with a mind that is satisfied, counting it nothing else than a release of the elements from which each living creature is composed. Now if there is no hurt to the elements themselves in their ceaseless changing each into other, why should a man apprehend anxiously the change and dissolution of them all? For this is according to Nature; and no evil is according to Nature.

∞

Book V

1. At dawn of day, when you dislike being called, have this thought ready: "I am called to man's labour; why then do I make a difficulty if I am going out to do what I was born to do and what I was brought into the world for? Is it for this that I am fashioned, to lie in bedclothes and keep myself warm?" "But this is more pleasant." "Were you born then to please yourself; in fact for feeling, not for action? Can't you see the plants, the birds, the ants, the spiders, the bees each doing his own work, helping for their part to adjust a world? And then you refuse to do a man's office and don't make haste to do what is according to your own nature." "But a man needs rest as well." I agree, he does, yet Nature assigns limits to rest, as well as to eating and drinking, and you nevertheless go beyond her limits, beyond what is sufficient; in your actions only this is no longer so, there you keep inside what is in your power. The explanation is that you do not love your own self, else surely you would love both your nature and *her* purpose. But other men who love their own crafts wear themselves out in labours upon them, unwashed and unfed; while you hold your own nature in less honour than the smith his metal work, the dancer his art, the miser his coin, the lover of vainglory his fame. Yet they, when the passion is on them, refuse either to eat or to sleep sooner than refuse to advance the objects they care about, whereas you imagine acts of fellowship to bring a smaller return and to be deserving of less pains.

∞

Book VI

16. To transpire like plants or to breathe like cattle or wild beasts is not a thing to value, nor to be stamped by sense impression or drawn by the strings of impulse, nor to live in herds or to take in nourishment—this last is on a level with relieving the body of the dregs of that nourishment. What, then, should be valued? The clapping of hands? Surely not; and so not even the clapping of tongues, for the applause of multitudes is a clapping of tongues. Therefore you have put mere glory away. What is left to be valued? To my thinking to move and to be held back according to man's proper constitution, the end to which both rustic industries and the arts give the lead. (For every art aims at this, that what it fashions should be suited to the purpose for which it has been fashioned. This is the aim of the gardener and of the vinedresser, of the breaker of colts and the trainer of dogs.) And to what end do children's training and teaching labour? Here, then, is what is of true value, and if this be well, you will not endeavour to obtain for yourself any one of the rest. Will you not cease to value many other things besides? Then you will not be free or self-contained or passionless; for you will be obliged to entertain envy and rivalry, to regard with suspicion those who are able to take away those things, to plot against those who have what is valued by you. To sum up, he who feels the want of any one of those things must be sullied thereby and besides must often blame the gods. But to reverence and value your own understanding will make you acceptable to yourself, harmonious with your fellows, and in concord with the gods; that is, praising whatsoever they assign and have ordained.

∞

Book X

1. Wilt thou one day, my soul, be good, simple, single, naked, plainer to see than the body surrounding thee? Wilt thou one day taste a loving and devoted disposition? Wilt thou one day be filled and without want, craving nothing and desiring nothing, animate or inanimate, for indulgence in pleasures; not time wherein longer to indulge thyself, nor happy situation of place or room or breezes nor harmony of men? Wilt thou rather be satisfied with present circumstance and pleased with all the present, and convince thyself that all is present for thee from the gods and all is well for thee and will be well whatsoever is dear to them to give and whatsoever they purpose to bestow for the sustenance of the perfect living creature, the good and just and beautiful, which begets, sustains, includes, and embraces all things that are being resolved into the generation of others like themselves? Wilt thou one day be such as to dwell in the society of gods and men so as neither to find fault at all with them nor to be condemned by them?

2. Observe what your nature requires in so far as you are governed by mere physical nature; then do that and accept that, if only your nature as part of the animal world will not be rendered worse. Next you are to observe what your nature as part of the animal world requires and to take it all, if only your nature as a reasonable being will not be rendered worse. But what is reasonable is consequently also social. Make use then of these rules and do not be troubled about anything besides.

8. After giving yourself these titles: good, self-respecting, true, sane, conforming, high-minded, take care not to get others in their place; and, if you do lose these titles, be quick to return to them. Remember, further, that "sanity" was intended to denote apprehensive attention to individual objects and the reverse of negligence; "conformity" glad acceptance of the assignments of Universal Nature; and "high-mindedness" elevation of the thinking part above the smooth or interrupted movements of the flesh, above petty reputation and death and all indifferent things.

Therefore, if you continue to preserve yourself in these titles, not aspiring to be called them by others, you will be a changed man and will enter upon a changed life. For still to be such as you have been up to the present, to be torn and polluted in such a way of life, is to be utterly brutalized, to cling to mere life like half-devoured combatants in the arena, a mass of wounds and dusty blood, yet imploring to be kept alive until the morrow, only to be exposed in that state to the same teeth and claws.

Adventure yourself then upon these few titles, and if you are able to abide in them, abide like a man translated to Islands of the Blest; but if you perceive that you are falling away and losing control, go bravely away into some corner, there to recover control, or even depart altogether from life, not angrily, but simply and freely and with self-respect, having done at least this one thing in life, to have made your exit thus.

To remember the titles, however, it will be a great help to you to remember the gods, and that they at least do not wish to be the objects of servility, but for all rational beings to be made into their likeness, and that the fig-tree should be what does the work of a fig-tree, the dog of a dog, the bee of a bee, and the man the work of a man.

∞

Book XII

3. There are three things of which you are compounded: body, vital spirit, mind. Two of these are your own in so far as you must take care of them, but only the third is in the strict sense your own. So, if you separate from yourself, namely from your mind, all that others do or say, all that you yourself did or said, all that troubles you in the future, all that as part of the bodily envelope or natural spirit attaches to you without your will, and all that the external circumfluent vortex whirls round, so that your mind power, freed from the chain of necessity, lives purified and released by itself—doing what is just, willing what comes to pass, and speaking what is true; if you separate, I say, from this governing self what is attached to it by sensibility, and what of time is hereafter or has gone by, and make yourself like the sphere of Empedocles,[107] "rounded, rejoicing in the solitude which is about it," and practise only to live the life you are living, that is the present, then you will have it in your power at least to live out the time that is left until you die, untroubled and with kindness and reconciled with your own good Spirit.

---

[107] **Empedocles** Fifth-century BCE Greek philosopher and poet.

∞

Questions for Critical Thinking

1. Who are some of the individuals who influenced Marcus Aurelius, and what did they do to aid him in his life?

2. What advice does Marcus Aurelius give us in Books VI and X? Do you think his advice is helpful for someone living in the early twenty-first century? Why or why not?

6

JUDAISM AND THE RISE OF CHRISTIANITY

Selections from *The Holy Scriptures* (The Jewish Bible)

The Jewish Bible (from the Greek *biblia*, "books") is a set of sacred writings for the Jewish faithful, containing thirty-nine books, dating from the tenth to the first centuries BCE and arranged into three categories: the Torah, the Prophets, and the Writings. Originally written in Hebrew, this book collection became more accessible in the third century BCE when, as the Septuagint, it was translated into the period's international language, Greek. Later, around 100 CE, Jewish scholars declared this collection to be the Word of God, hence its title *The Holy Scriptures*, in Hebrew, *Tanakh*.

The most authoritative parts of *The Holy Scriptures* for Jewish readers are the Torah, or Law, which provides rules and instructions for everyday life, and the Prophets, which represents the sayings or writings of seers who were understood to be the voices of God. The Writings, while lacking the force of the Torah and the Prophets, nevertheless contain beautiful prose and poetic works, replete with words of comfort and moral advice, such as the book of Psalms, the book of Job, and the book of Ecclesiastes.

Genesis, the first book of the Torah, opens with the stories of creation, followed by accounts of Noah, his family, and the flood; then begins the historical narrative of Terah, the father of Abraham, from whom descend the leaders of the Hebrew people. These patriarchal tribal rulers—such as Abraham, Jacob, and Moses—make agreements (covenants) with Yahweh, their deity, to worship him and obey the rules of conduct he has given them. However, throughout their history, the Hebrews do not always live by the covenant; that is, they commit sin, and as a result, Yahweh punishes them.

After their return from exile in Egypt to their former homeland, Palestine, around 1150 BCE, the Hebrews slowly conquer the local tribes and begin to prosper. Their good fortune causes them to forget Yahweh and his moral decrees and to turn more and more away from him and the covenant. At this stage of Hebrew history, God chooses certain persons as prophets to deliver his messages of repentance or consequential destruction. Two of his prophets are Isaiah and Amos. Despite falling away from God, many Hebrews continue to honor Yahweh with songs of praise, as recorded in the book of Psalms. Yet, other Hebrews question their faith and suffering, as revealed in the book of Job—a poignant account of the torment experienced by a man who was blameworthy.

Reading the Selections

On the surface, the selections—Genesis, Exodus, Amos, Psalms, Job, and Ecclesiastes—seem quite different, but all deal with similar and profound issues, such as the nature of God's existence and power, the relationship of God to humans, and the role God plays in the lives of humans and in history. The first three chapters of Genesis offer two accounts of the creation story. In the first, God, as the source of all, creates the universe, the celestial bodies, the earth, and all living things. The second account focuses on God's relationship with his first two human creatures, Adam and Eve. The original covenant—that God will provide for humans if they obey him and not eat of the forbidden fruit—is broken. Both are cast out of the Garden of Eden; ever since, humans have been trying to reenter this paradise by attempting to create utopias on earth.

Genesis 4 records the rivalry between the two sons of Adam and Eve, Cain and Abel. Chapter 5 lists the descendants of Adam and Eve down to Noah. Chapters 6–8 is the story of Noah, his family, and the flood. Again, the themes of humans disobeying God, his punishing them for their waywardness and sins, their worshiping and sacrificing to him, and his forgiveness are repeated. However, the themes of the Hebrews' emerging monotheistic faith are woven into the story of the flood. Accounts of floods and their destructive power are found in several sources of ancient literature (see *The Epic of Gilgamesh* in Chapter 1).

At some point in history, a portion of the Hebrew tribe moved to Egypt, where they were cast into slavery. Eventually, under the leadership of Moses, they slipped their bondage and were guided to freedom through the desert by God. During years of wandering, they formed the central core of their covenant with God: a set of moral rules, of which the first ten are the Ten Commandments, laid down by Yahweh and to be obeyed by the Hebrew people. Besides the Ten Commandments, these rules included many other guidelines by which the Hebrew people were to regulate their lives as individuals and as a tribe. Later, Christians made the Ten Commandments, along with Christ's teachings, the basis of their moral code.

The excerpt from Amos illustrates how a prophet, as the voice of God, spoke to the Hebrews, warning them to change their sinful ways or suffer punishment. In his prophecy, Amos predicts the destruction of the kingdom of Israel (it was destroyed by Assyria in 722 BCE) if the populace does not give social justice to the poor. Amos's prophecy, with its rich imagery, was a favorite of the civil rights leader Martin Luther King, Jr. (see *Letter from a Birmingham Jail* in Chapter 22, Volume II).

The book of Psalms, with its prayers, laments, and wisdom, has inspired and comforted both Jews and Christians down through the ages. Psalm 22 is a lament, uttered by the speaker, who, after confessing a sense of having been betrayed by God, resolves to once again trust in the Lord. Its first two lines were spoken by Jesus on the cross. Psalm 23, among the most comforting messages in the Bible, is often recited at funerals or turned to in times of trouble. Psalm 104, in its praise of God, echoes an Egyptian poem (see *The Great Hymn to the Aten* in Chapter 1).

The book of Job concentrates on a single theological topic: the question of suffering. In prose form, the Prologue tells of the disasters that befall the blameless Job, the conversation between God and Satan about testing Job's faith, and Job's meeting with friends who offer advice on his plight. Shifting into poetic form, the book sets forth Job's complaint to God, God's magisterial response, and Job's final reply. The Epilogue, reverting to prose, shows God richly rewarding Job for not renouncing him. The book of Job steadfastly refuses to answer the bewildering question of why humans suffer, and this silence is part of the work's grandeur.

The name *Ecclesiastes* is the pseudonym of the author of this biblical work. It is the Greek word used to translate the Hebrew word *Koheleth*, meaning "the Assembler," that is, one who gathers or teaches before an assembly. The book of Ecclesiastes is part of the Megillot, five scrolls that are read at various festivals of the Jewish religious year. In literary terms, this book belongs to the tradition of Hebrew wisdom literature, yet its rationalistic point of view calls into question the doctrine of retributive justice associated with wisdom theology. Retributive justice means that rewards and punishments, respectively, are directly linked to good and evil deeds. In contrast, the author of Ecclesiastes asserts "that [it] is a sad thing about all that goes on under the sun: that the same fate is in store for all. (Not only that, but men's hearts are full of sadness, and their minds of madness, while they live; and then—to the dead!)" (9:3). Human fate is unknowable, according to the author, because it is strictly in God's hands: "He brings everything to pass precisely at his time" (3:11). Faced with such moral uncertainty, the wise person gratefully accepts the small pleasures God gives each day. Chapter 3, a famous passage, is sometimes read at funerals and has become well known as the text of a popular folk song.

∞

Genesis

1–3

1

When God began to create heaven and earth—the earth being unformed and void, with darkness over the surface of the deep and a wind from God sweeping over the water—God said, "Let there be light"; and there was light. God saw that the light was good, and God separated the light from the darkness. God called the light Day, and the darkness He called Night. And there was evening and there was morning, a first day.

God said, "Let there be an expanse in the midst of the water, that it may separate water from water." God made the expanse, and it separated the water which was below the expanse from the water which was above the expanse. And it was so. God called the expanse Sky. And there was evening and there was morning, a second day.

God said, "Let the water below the sky be gathered into one area, that the dry land may appear." And it was so. God called the dry land Earth, and the gathering of waters He called Seas. And God saw that this was good. And God said, "Let the earth sprout vegetation: seed-bearing plants, fruit trees of every kind on earth that bear fruit with the seed in it." And it was so. The earth brought forth vegetation: seed-bearing plants of every kind, and trees of every kind bearing fruit with the seed in it. And God saw that this was good. And there was evening and there was morning, a third day.

God said, "Let there be lights in the expanse of the sky to separate day from night; they shall serve as signs for the set times—the days and the years; and they shall serve as lights in the expanse of the sky to shine upon the earth." And it was so. God made the two great lights, the greater light to dominate the day and the lesser light to dominate the night, and the stars. And God set them in the expanse of the sky to shine upon the earth, to dominate the day and the night, and to separate light from darkness. And God saw that this was good. And there was evening and there was morning, a fourth day.

God said, "Let the waters bring forth swarms of living creatures, and birds that fly above the earth across the expanse of the sky." God created the great sea monsters, and all the living creatures of every kind that creep, which the waters brought forth in swarms, and all the winged birds of every kind. And God saw that this was good. God blessed them, saying, "Be fertile and increase, fill the waters in the seas, and let the birds increase on the earth." And there was evening and there was morning, a fifth day.

God said, "Let the earth bring forth every kind of living creature: cattle, creeping things, and wild beasts of every kind." And it was so. God made wild beasts of every kind and cattle of every kind, and all kinds of creeping things of the earth. And God saw that this was good. And God said, "Let us make man in our image, after our likeness. They shall rule the fish of the sea, the birds of the sky, the cattle, the whole earth, and all the creeping things that creep on earth." And God created man in His image, in the image of God He created him; male and female He created them. God blessed them and God said to them, "Be fertile and increase, fill the earth and master it; and rule the fish of the sea, the birds of the sky, and all the living things that creep on earth."

God said, "See, I give you every seed-bearing plant that is upon all the earth, and every tree that has seed-bearing fruit; they shall be yours for food. And to all the animals on land, to all the birds of the sky, and to everything that creeps on earth, in which there is the breath of life, [I give] all the green plants for food. And it was so. And God saw all that He had made, and found it very good. And there was evening and there was morning, the sixth day.

2

The heaven and the earth were finished, and all their array. On the seventh day God finished the work that He had been doing, and He ceased on the seventh day from all the work that He had done. And God blessed the seventh day and declared it holy, because on it God ceased from all the work of creation that He had done. Such is the story of heaven and earth when they were created.

When the LORD God made earth and heaven—when no shrub of the field was yet one earth and no grasses of the field had yet sprouted, because the LORD God had not sent rain upon the earth and there was no man to till the soil, but a flow would well up from the ground and water the whole surface of the earth—the LORD God formed man from the dust of the earth. He blew into his nostrils the breath of life, and man became a living being.

The Lord God planted a garden in Eden, in the east, and placed there the man whom He had formed. And from the ground the Lord God caused to grow every tree that was pleasing to the sight and good for food, with the tree of life in the middle of the garden, and the tree of knowledge of good and bad.

A river issues from Eden to water the garden, and it then divides and becomes four branches. The name of the first is Pishon, the one that winds through the whole land of Havilah, where the gold is. The gold of that land is good; bdellium is there, and lapis lazuli. The name of the second river is Gihon, the one that winds through the whole land of Cush. The name of the third river is Tigris, the one that flows east of Asshur. And the fourth river is the Euphrates.

The Lord God took the man and placed him in the garden of Eden, to till it and tend it. And the Lord God commanded the man, saying, "Of every tree of the garden you are free to eat; but as for the tree of knowledge of good and bad, you must not eat of it; for as soon as you eat of it, you shall die."

The Lord God said, "It is not good for man to be alone; I will make a fitting helper for him." And the Lord God formed out of the earth all the wild beasts and all the birds of the sky, and brought them to the man to see what he would call them; and whatever the man called each living creature, that would be its name. And the man gave names to all the cattle and to the birds of the sky and to all the wild beasts; but for Adam no fitting helper was found. So the Lord God cast a deep sleep upon the man; and, while he slept, He took one of his ribs and closed up the flesh at that spot. And the Lord God fashioned the rib that He had taken from the man into a woman; and He brought her to the man. Then the man said,

"This one at last
Is bone of my bones
And flesh of my flesh.
This one shall be called Woman,
For from man was she taken."

Hence a man leaves his father and mother and clings to his wife, so that they become one flesh.

The two of them were naked, the man and his wife, yet they felt no shame.

3

Now the serpent was the shrewdest of all the wild beasts that the Lord God had made. He said to the woman, "Did God really say: You shall not eat of any tree of the garden?" The woman replied to the serpent, "We may eat of the fruit of the other trees of the garden. It is only about fruit of the tree in the middle of the garden that God said: 'You shall not eat of it or touch it, lest you die.'" And the serpent said to the woman, "You are not going to die, but

God knows that as soon as you eat of it your eyes will be opened and you will be like divine beings who know good and bad." When the woman saw that the tree was good for eating and a delight to the eyes, and that the tree was desirable as a source of wisdom, she took of its fruit and ate. She also gave some to her husband, and he ate. Then the eyes of both of them were opened and they perceived that they were naked; and they sewed together fig leaves and made themselves loincloths.

They heard the sound of the Lord God moving about in the garden at the breezy time of day; and the man and his wife hid from the Lord God among the trees of the garden. The Lord God called out to the man and said to him, "Where are you?" He replied, "I heard the sound of You in the garden, and I was afraid because I was naked, so I hid." Then He asked, "Who told you that you were naked? Did you eat of the tree from which I had forbidden you to eat?" The man said, "The woman You put at my side—she gave me of the tree, and I ate." And the Lord God said to the woman, "What is this you have done!" The woman replied, "The serpent duped me, and I ate." Then the Lord God said to the serpent,

"Because you did this,
More cursed shall you be
Than all cattle
And all the wild beasts:
On your belly shall you crawl
And dirt shall you eat
All the days of your life.
I will put enmity
Between you and the woman,
And between your offspring and hers;
They shall strike at your head,
And you shall strike at their heel."

And to the woman He said,

"I will make most severe
Your pangs in childbearing;
In pain shall you bear children.
Yet your urge shall be for your husband,
And he shall rule over you."

To Adam He said, "Because you did as your wife said and ate of the tree about which I commanded you, 'You shall not eat of it,'

Cursed be the ground because of you;
By toil shall you eat of it
All the days of your life:
Thorns and thistles shall it sprout for you.
But your food shall be the grasses of the field;
By the sweat of your brow
Shall you get bread to eat,
Until you return to the ground—
For from it you were taken.
For dust you are,
And to dust you shall return."

The man named his wife Eve, because she was the mother of all the living. And the Lord God made garments of skins for Adam and his wife, and clothed them.

And the Lord God said, "Now that the man has become like one of us, knowing good and bad, what if he should stretch out his hand and take also from the tree of life and eat, and live forever!" So the Lord God banished him from the garden of Eden, to till the soil from which he was taken. He drove the man out, and stationed east of the garden of Eden the cherubim and the fiery ever-turning sword, to guard the way to the tree of life.

6–8

6

And it came to pass, when men began to multiply on the face of the earth, and daughters were born unto them, that the sons of God saw the daughters of men that they were fair; and they took them wives, whomsoever they chose. And the Lord said: "My spirit shall not abide in man for ever, for that he also is flesh; therefore shall his days be a hundred and twenty years." The Nephilim[1] were in the earth in those days, and also after that, when the sons of God came in unto the daughters of men, and they bore children to them; the same were the mighty men that were of old, the men of renown.

And the Lord saw that the wickedness of man was great in the earth, and that every imagination of the thoughts of his heart was only evil continually. And it repented the Lord that He had made man on the earth, and it grieved Him at His heart. And the Lord said: "I will blot out man whom I have created from the face of the earth; both man, and beast, and creeping thing, and fowl of the air; for it repenteth Me that I have made them." But Noah found grace in the eyes of the Lord.

These are the generations of Noah. Noah was in his generations a man righteous and whole-hearted; Noah walked with God. And Noah begot three sons, Shem, Ham, and Japheth. And the earth was corrupt before God, and the earth was filled with violence. And God saw the earth, and, behold, it was corrupt; for all flesh had corrupted their way upon the earth.

And God said unto Noah: "The end of all flesh is come before Me; for the earth is filled with violence through them; and, behold, I will destroy them with the earth. Make thee an ark of gopher wood; with rooms shalt thou make the ark, and shalt pitch it within and without with pitch. And this is how thou shalt make it: the length of the ark three hundred cubits, the breadth of it fifty cubits, and the height of it thirty cubits. A light shalt thou make to the ark, and to a cubit shalt thou finish it upward; and the door of the ark shalt thou set in the side thereof; with lower, second, and third stories shalt thou make it. And I, behold, I do bring the flood of waters upon the earth, to destroy all flesh, wherein is the breath of life, from under heaven; every thing that is in the earth shall perish. But I will establish My covenant with thee; and thou shalt come into the ark, thou, and thy sons, and thy wife, and thy sons' wives with thee. And of every living thing of all flesh, two of every sort shalt thou bring into the ark, to keep them alive with thee; they shall be male and female. Of the fowl after their kind, and of the cattle after their kind, of every creeping thing of the ground after its kind, two of every sort shall come unto thee, to keep them alive. And take thou unto thee of all food that is eaten, and gather it to thee; and it shall be for food for thee, and for them." Thus did Noah; according to all that God commanded him, so did he.

7

And the Lord said unto Noah: "Come thou and all thy house into the ark; for thee have I seen righteous before Me in this generation. Of every clean beast thou shalt take to thee seven and seven, each with his mate; and of the beasts that are not clean two [and two], each with his mate; of the fowl also of the air, seven and seven, male and female; to keep seed alive upon the face of all the earth. For yet seven days, and I will cause it to rain upon the earth forty days and forty nights; and every living substance that I have made will I blot out from off the face of the earth." And Noah did according unto all that the Lord commanded him.

And Noah was six hundred years old when the flood of waters was upon the earth. And Noah went in, and his sons, and his wife, and his sons' wives with him, into the ark, because of the waters of the flood. Of clean beasts, and of beasts that are not clean, and of fowls, and of every thing that creepeth upon the ground, there went in two and two unto Noah into the ark, male and female, as God commanded Noah. And it came to pass after the seven days, that the waters of the flood were upon the earth. In the six hundredth year of Noah's life, in the second month, on the seventeenth day of the month, on the same day were all the fountains of the great deep broken up, and the windows of heaven were opened. And the rain was upon the earth forty days and forty nights.

In the selfsame day entered Noah, and Shem, and Ham, and Japheth, the sons of Noah, and Noah's wife,

---

[1] **Nephilim** The word, in Hebrew, means "to fall"; thus, probably, the fallen ones. Who they were is not certain. They are mentioned twice in the Holy Scriptures, and their fate seemed to be to die in some catastrophic manner.

and the three wives of his sons with them, into the ark; they, and every beast after its kind, and all the cattle after their kind, and every creeping thing that creepeth upon the earth after its kind, and every fowl after its kind, every bird of every sort. And they went in unto Noah into the ark two and two of all flesh wherein is the breath of life. And they that went in, went in male and female of all flesh, as God commanded him; and the LORD shut him in. And the flood was forty days upon the earth; and the waters increased, and bore up the ark, and it was lifted up above the earth. And the waters prevailed, and increased greatly upon the earth; and the ark went upon the face of the waters. And the waters prevailed exceedingly upon the earth; and all the high mountains that were under the whole heaven were covered. Fifteen cubits upward did the waters prevail; and the mountains were covered. And all flesh perished that moved upon the earth, both fowl, and cattle, and beast, and every swarming thing that swarmeth upon the earth, and every man; all in whose nostrils was the breath of the spirit of life, whatsoever was in the dry land, died. And He blotted out every living substance which was upon the face of the ground, both man, and cattle, and creeping thing, and fowl of the heaven; and they were blotted out from the earth; and Noah only was left, and they that were with him in the ark. And the waters prevailed upon the earth a hundred and fifty days.

8

And God remembered Noah, and every living thing, and ₁ all the cattle that were with him in the ark; and God made a wind to pass over the earth, and the waters assuaged; the fountains also of the deep and the windows of heaven were stopped, and the rain from heaven was restrained. And the waters returned from off the earth continually; and after the end of a hundred and fifty days the waters decreased. And the ark rested in the seventh month, on the seventeenth day of the month, upon the mountains of Ararat. And the waters decreased continually until the tenth month; in the tenth month, on the first day of the month, were the tops of the mountains seen.

And it came to pass at the end of forty days, that Noah opened the window of the ark which he had made. And he sent forth a raven, and it went forth to and fro, until the waters were dried up from off the earth. And he sent forth a dove from him, to see if the waters were abated from off the face of the ground. But the dove found no rest for the sole of her foot, and she returned unto him to the ark, for the waters were on the face of the whole earth; and he put forth his hand, and took her, and brought her in unto him into the ark. And he stayed yet other seven days; and again he sent forth the dove out of the ark. And the dove came in to him at eventide; and lo in her mouth an olive-leaf freshly plucked; so Noah knew that the waters were abated from off the earth. And he stayed yet other seven days; and sent forth the dove; and she returned not again unto him any more.

And it came to pass in the six hundred and first year, in the first month, the first day of the month, the waters were dried up from off the earth; and Noah removed the covering of the ark, and looked, and, behold, the face of the ground was dried. And in the second month, on the seven and twentieth day of the month, was the earth dry.

And God spoke unto Noah, saying: "Go forth from the ark, thou, and thy wife, and thy sons, and thy sons' wives with thee. Bring forth with thee every living thing that is with thee of all flesh, both fowl, and cattle, and every creeping thing that creepeth upon the earth; that they may swarm in the earth, and be fruitful, and multiply upon the earth." And Noah went forth, and his sons, and his wife, and his sons' wives with him; every beast, every creeping thing, and every fowl, whatsoever moveth upon the earth, after their families, went forth out of the ark.

And Noah builded an altar unto the LORD; and took ₅ of every clean beast, and of every clean fowl, and offered burnt-offerings on the altar. And the LORD smelled the sweet savour; and the LORD said in His heart; "I will not again curse the ground any more for man's sake; for the imagination of man's heart is evil from his youth; neither will I again smite any more every thing living, as I have done. While the earth remaineth, seedtime and harvest, and cold and heat, and summer and winter, and day and night shall not cease."

∽

Exodus
20

God spoke all these words, saying: ₁
I the LORD am your God who brought you out of the land of Egypt, the house of bondage: You shall have no other gods besides Me.
You shall not make for yourself a sculptured image, or any likeness of what is in the heavens above, or on the earth below, or in the waters under the earth. You shall not bow down to them or serve them. For I the LORD your

God am an impassioned God, visiting the guilt of the parents upon the children, upon the third and upon the fourth generations of those who reject Me, but showing kindness to the thousandth generation of those who love Me and keep My commandments.

You shall not swear falsely by the name of the LORD your God; for the LORD will not clear one who swears falsely by His name.

Remember the sabbath day and keep it holy. Six days 5 you shall labor and do all your work, but the seventh day is a sabbath of the Lord your God: you shall not do any work—you, your son or daughter, your male or female slave, or your cattle, or the stranger who is within your settlements. For in six days the Lord made heaven and earth and sea, and all that is in them, and He rested on the seventh day; therefore the Lord blessed the sabbath day and hallowed it.

Honor your father and your mother, that you may long endure on the land that the Lord your God is assigning to you.

You shall not murder.

You shall not commit adultery.

You shall not steal.

You shall not bear false witness against your neighbor. 10

You shall not covet your neighbor's house: you shall not covet your neighbor's wife, or his male or female slave, or his ox or his ass, or anything that is your neighbor's.

All the people witnessed the thunder and lightning, the blare of the horn and the mountain smoking; and when the people saw it, they fell back and stood at a distance. "You speak to us," they said to Moses, "and we will obey; but let not God speak to us, lest we die." Moses answered the people, "Be not afraid; for God has come only in order to test you, and in order that the fear of Him may be ever with you, so that you do not go astray." So the people remained at a distance, while Moses approached the thick cloud where God was.

The Lord said to Moses:

Thus shall you say to the Israelites: You yourselves saw that I spoke to you from the very heavens: With Me, therefore, you shall not make any gods of silver, nor shall you make for yourselves any gods of gold. Make for Me an altar of earth and sacrifice on it your burnt offerings and your sacrifices of well-being, your sheep and your oxen; in every place where I cause My name to be mentioned I will come to you and bless you. And if you make for Me an altar of stones, do not build it of hewn stones; for by wielding your tool upon them you have profaned them. Do not ascend My altar by steps, that your nakedness may not be exposed upon it.

∞

Amos

5

Hear this word which I intone   1
As a dirge over you, O House of Israel:
Fallen, not to rise again,
Is Maiden Israel;
Abandoned on her soil
With none to lift her up.
For thus said my Lord God
About the House of Israel:
The town that marches out a thousand strong
Shall have a hundred left,   10
And the one that marches out a hundred strong
Shall have but ten left.

Thus said the Lord
To the House of Israel:
Seek Me, and you will live.
Do not seek Bethel,
Nor go to Gilgal,
Nor cross over to Beer-sheba²;
For Gilgal shall go into exile,
And Bethel shall become a delusion.   20
Seek the Lord, and you will live,
Else He will rush like fire upon the House of Joseph³
And consume Bethel with none to quench it.

[Ah,] you who turn justice into wormwood
And hurl righteousness to the ground!
[Seek the Lord,]
Who made the Pleiades and Orion,⁴
Who turns deep darkness into dawn
And darkens day into night,
Who summons the waters of the sea   30
And pours them out upon the earth—
His name is the Lord!
It is He who hurls destruction upon strongholds,
So that ruin comes upon fortresses!

They hate the arbiter in the gate,
And detest him whose plea is just.
Assuredly,
Because you impose a tax on the poor
And exact from him a levy of grain,
You have built houses of hewn stone,   40
But you shall not live in them;
You have planted delightful vineyards,
But shall not drink their wine.
For I have noted how many are your crimes,
And how countless your sins—
You enemies of the righteous,
You takers of bribes,

---

² **Bethel, Gilgal, Beer-sheba** Places of worship or towns in Israel.
³ **House of Joseph** The descendants of Joseph through his "house" or line who now lived in Israel.

---

⁴ **Pleiades and Orion** Two constellations.

You who subvert in the gate
The cause of the needy!
Assuredly,   50
At such a time the prudent man keeps silent,
For it is an evil time.

Seek good and not evil,
That you may live,
And that the LORD, the God of Hosts,
May truly be with you,
As you think.
Hate evil and love good,
And establish justice in the gate;
Perhaps the LORD, the God of Hosts,   60
Will be gracious to the remnant of Joseph.
Assuredly,

Thus said the LORD,
My Lord, the God of Hosts:
In every square there shall be lamenting,
In every street cries of "Ah, woe!"
And the farm hand shall be
Called to mourn,
And those skilled in wailing
To lament;   70
For there shall be lamenting
In every vineyard, too,
When I pass through your midst
                              —said the LORD.

Ah, you who wish
For the day of the LORD!
Why should you want
The day of the LORD?
It shall be darkness, not light!

—As if a man should run from a lion   80
And be attacked by a bear;
Or if he got indoors,
Should lean his hand on the wall
And be bitten by a snake!
Surely the day of the LORD shall be
Not light, but darkness,
Blackest night without a glimmer.

I loathe, I spurn your festivals,
If you offer Me burnt offerings—or your meal offerings—   90
I will not accept them;
I will pay no heed
To your gifts of fatlings.
Spare Me the sound of your hymns,
And let Me not hear the music of your lutes.
But let justice well up like water,
Righteousness like an unfailing stream.
Did you offer sacrifice and oblation to Me
Those forty years in the wilderness,
O House of Israel?   100

And you shall carry off your "king"—
Sikkuth and Kiyyun,[5]
The images you have made for yourselves
Of your astral deity—
As I drive you into exile beyond Damascus[6]
—Said the LORD, whose name is God of Hosts.

_____

[5] **Sikkuth and Kiyyun** A king and a star god, both which have been made into images or idols.
[6] **Damascus** The powerful city to the northeast of Israel that was often at war with the Hebrews and, in Amos's time, a threat. The Lord, says Amos, will drive the Israelites into exile even beyond Damascus—thus, far from their homeland.

Psalms
22

My God, my God,   1
  why have You abandoned me;
  why so far from delivering me
  and from my anguished roaring?
My God,
  I cry by day—You answer not;
  by night, and have no respite.

But You are the Holy One,
  enthroned,
  the Praise of Israel.   10
In You our fathers trusted;
  they trusted, and You rescued them.
To You they cried out
  and they escaped;
  in You they trusted
  and were not disappointed.

But I am a worm, less than human;
  scorned by men, despised by people.
All who see me mock me;
  they curl their lips,   20
  they shake their heads.
"Let him commit himself to the LORD;
  let Him rescue him,
  let Him save him,
  for He is pleased with him."
You drew me from the womb,
  made me secure at my mother's breast.
I became Your charge at birth;
  from my mother's womb You have been my God.
Do not be far from me,   30
  for trouble is near,
  and there is none to help.
Many bulls surround me,
  mighty ones of Bashan encircle me.
They open their mouths at me
  like tearing, roaring lions.
My life ebbs away:
  all my bones are disjointed;
  my heart is like wax,
  melting within me;   40
  my vigor dries up like a shard;
  my tongue cleaves to my palate;
  You commit me to the dust of death.
Dogs surround me;
  a pack of evil ones closes in on me,
  like lions [they maul] my hands and feet.
I take the count of all my bones
  while they look on and gloat.
They divide my clothes among themselves,
  casting lots for my garments.   50

But You, O LORD, be not far off;
  my strength, hasten to my aid.
Save my life from the sword,
  my precious life from the clutches of a dog.
Deliver me from a lion's mouth;
  from the horns of wild oxen rescue me.
Then will I proclaim Your fame to my brethren,
  praise You in the congregation.
You who fear the LORD, praise Him!
All you offspring of Jacob, honor Him!   60
Be in dread of Him, all you offspring of Israel!
For He did not scorn, He did not spurn
  the plea of the lowly;
  He did not hide His face from him;
  when he cried out to Him, He listened.
  Because of You I offer praise in the great congregation;
  I pay my vows in the presence of His worshipers.
Let the lowly eat and be satisfied;
  let all who seek the LORD praise Him.
Always be of good cheer!   70
Let all the ends of the earth pay heed and turn to the LORD,
  and the peoples of all nations prostrate themselves
    before You;
  for kingship is the LORD's
  and He rules the nations.
All those in full vigor shall eat and prostrate themselves;
  all those at death's door, whose spirits flag,
  shall bend the knee before Him.
Offspring shall serve Him;
  the LORD's fame shall be proclaimed to the generation
    to come;
  they shall tell of His beneficence   80
  to people yet to be born,
  for He has acted.

23

The LORD is my shepherd;   1
  I lack nothing.
He makes me lie down in green pastures;
  He leads me to water in places of repose;
  He renews my life;
  He guides me in right paths
  as befits His name.

Though I walk through a valley of deepest darkness,
  I fear no harm, for You are with me;
  Your rod and Your staff—they comfort me.   10
You spread a table for me in full view of my enemies;
  You anoint my head with oil;
  my drink is abundant.
Only goodness and steadfast love shall pursue me
  all the days of my life,
  and I shall dwell in the house of the LORD
  for many long years.

104

Bless the Lord, O my soul;   1
O Lord, my God, You are very great;
  You are clothed in glory and majesty,
  wrapped in a robe of light;
  You spread the heavens like a tent cloth.
He sets the rafters of His lofts in the waters,
  makes the clouds His chariot,
  moves on the wings of the wind.
He makes the winds His messengers,
  fiery flames His servants.   10
He established the earth on its foundations,
  so that it shall never totter.
You made the deep cover it as a garment;
  the waters stood above the mountains.
They fled at Your blast,
  rushed away at the sound of Your thunder,
  —mountains rising, valleys sinking—
  to the place You established for them.
You set bounds they must not pass
  so that they never again cover the earth.   20

You make springs gush forth in torrents;
  they make their way between the hills,
  giving drink to all the wild beasts;
  the wild asses slake their thirst.
The birds of the sky dwell beside them
  and sing among the foliage.
You water the mountains from Your lofts;
  the earth is sated from the fruit of Your work.
You make the grass grow for the cattle,
  and herbage for man's labor   30
  that he may get food out of the earth—
  wine that cheers the hearts of men
  oil that make the face shine,
  and bread that sustains man's life.
The trees of the Lord drink their fill,
  the cedars of Lebanon, His own planting,
  where birds make their nests;
  the stork has her home in the junipers.
The high mountains are for wild goats;
  the crags are a refuge for rock-badgers.   40

He made the moon to mark the seasons;
  the sun knows when to set.
You bring on darkness and it is night,
  when all the beasts of the forests stir.
The lions roar for prey,
  seeking their food from God.
When the sun rises, they come home
  and couch in their dens.
Man then goes out to his work,
  to his labor until the evening.   50

How many are the things You have made, O Lord;
  You have made them all with wisdom;
  the earth is full of Your creations.
There is the sea, vast and wide,
  with its creatures beyond number,
  living things, small and great.
There go the ships,
  and Leviathan that You formed to sport with.
All of them look to You
  to give them their food when it is due.   60
Give it to them, they gather it up;
  open Your hand, they are well satisfied;
  hide Your face, they are terrified;
  take away their breath, they perish
  and turn again into dust;
  send back Your breath, they are created,
  and You renew the face of the earth.
May the glory of the Lord endure forever;
  may the Lord rejoice in His works!
He looks at the earth and it trembles;   70
  He touches the mountains and they smoke.
I will sing to the Lord as long as I live;
  all my life I will chant hymns to my God.
May my prayer be pleasing to Him;
  I will rejoice in the Lord,
May sinners disappear from the earth,
  and the wicked be no more.
Bless the Lord, O my soul.
  Hallelujah.

∽

Job

1–3

1

There was a man in the land of Uz named Job. That man   1
was blameless and upright; he feared God and shunned
evil. Seven sons and three daughters were born to him; his
possessions were seven thousand sheep, three thousand
camels, five hundred yoke of oxen and five hundred she-
asses, and a very large household. That man was wealth-
ier than anyone in the East.

    It was the custom of his sons to hold feasts, each on
his set day in his own home. They would invite their
three sisters to eat and drink with them. When a round

of feast days was over, Job would send word to them to sanctify themselves, and, rising early in the morning, he would make burnt offerings, one for each of them; for Job thought, "Perhaps my children have sinned and blasphemed God in their thoughts." This is what Job always used to do.

One day the divine beings presented themselves before the LORD, and the Adversary[7] came along with them. The LORD said to the Adversary, "Where have you been?" The Adversary answered the LORD, "I have been roaming all over the earth." The LORD said to the Adversary, "Have you noticed My servant Job? There is no one like him on earth, a blameless and upright man who fears God and shuns evil!" The Adversary answered the LORD, "Does Job not have good reason to fear God? Why, it is You who have fenced him round, him and his household and all that he has. You have blessed his efforts so that his possessions spread out in the land. But lay Your hand upon all that he has and he will surely blaspheme You to Your face." The LORD replied to the Adversary, "See, all that he has is in your power; only do not lay a hand on him." The Adversary departed from the presence of the LORD.

One day, as his sons and daughters were eating and drinking wine in the house of their eldest brother, a messenger came to Job and said, "The oxen were plowing and the she-asses were grazing alongside them when Sabeans[8] attacked them and carried them off, and put the boys to the sword; I alone have escaped to tell you." This one was still speaking when another came and said, "God's fire fell from heaven, took hold of the sheep and the boys, and burned them up; I alone have escaped to tell you." This one was still speaking when another came and said, "A Chaldean[9] formation of three columns made a raid on the camels and carried them off and put the boys to the sword; I alone have escaped to tell you." This one was still speaking when another came and said, "Your sons and daughters were eating and drinking wine in the house of their eldest brother when suddenly a mighty wind came from the wilderness. It struck the four corners of the house so that it collapsed upon the young people and they died; I alone have escaped to tell you."

Then Job arose, tore his robe, cut off his hair, and 5 threw himself on the ground and worshiped. He said, "Naked came I out of my mother's womb, and naked shall I return there; the LORD has given, and the LORD has taken away; blessed be the name of the LORD."

For all that, Job did not sin nor did he cast reproach on God.

---

[7] **Adversary** The Lord's opponent or enemy; translated in the Christian Holy Bible as Satan.
[8] **Sabeans** Inhabitants of Sheba, a kingdom in southwest Arabia. It was known for its wealth. Job, an Israelite, supposedly lived not in Israel but in north Arabia, which makes a raid by the Sabeans more plausible.
[9] **Chaldean** The Chaldeans lived along the Euphrates River in Mesopotamia. They could have been on a raiding party into Job's homeland.

2

One day the divine beings presented themselves before 1 the LORD. The Adversary came along with them to present himself before the LORD. The LORD said to the Adversary, "Where have you been?" The Adversary answered the LORD, "I have been roaming all over the earth." The LORD said to the Adversary, "Have you noticed My servant Job? There is no one like him on earth, a blameless and upright man who fears God and shuns evil. He still keeps his integrity; so you have incited Me against him to destroy him for no good reason." The Adversary answered the LORD, "Skin for skin—all that a man has he will give up for his life. But lay a hand on his bones and his flesh, and he will surely blaspheme You to Your face." So the LORD said to the Adversary, "See, he is in your power; only spare his life." The Adversary departed from the presence of the LORD and inflicted a severe inflammation on Job from the sole of his foot to the crown of his head. He took a potsherd to scratch himself as he sat in ashes. His wife said to him, "You still keep your integrity! Blaspheme God and die!" But he said to her, "You talk as any shameless woman might talk! Should we accept only good from God and not accept evil?" For all that, Job said nothing sinful.

When Job's three friends heard about all these calamities that had befallen him, each came from his home— Eliphaz the Temanite, Bildad the Shuhite, and Zophar the Naamathite. They met together to go and console and comfort him. When they saw him from a distance, they could not recognize him, and they broke into loud weeping; each one tore his robe and threw dust into the air onto his head. They sat with him on the ground seven days and seven nights. None spoke a word to him for they saw how very great was his suffering.

3

Afterward, Job began to speak and cursed the day of his 1 birth. Job spoke up and said:

> Perish the day on which I was born,
> And the night it was announced,
> "A male has been conceived!"
> May that day be darkness;
> May God above have no concern for it;
> May light not shine on it;
> May darkness and deep gloom reclaim it;
> May a pall lie over it;
> May what blackens the day terrify it. 10
> May obscurity carry off that night;
> May it not be counted among the days of the year;
> May it not appear in any of its months;
> May that night be desolate;
> May no sound of joy be heard in it;
> May those who cast spells upon the day damn it,
> Those prepared to disable Leviathan;
> May its twilight stars remain dark;
> May it hope for light and have none;
> May it not see the glimmerings of the dawn— 20

Because it did not block my mother's womb,
And hide trouble from my eyes.
Why did I not die at birth,
Expire as I came forth from the womb?
Why were there knees to receive me,
Or breasts for me to suck?
For now would I be lying in repose, asleep and at rest,
With the world's kings and counselors who rebuild
    ruins for themselves,
Or with nobles who possess gold and who fill their
    houses with silver.
Or why was I not like a buried stillbirth,   30
Like babies who never saw the light?
There the wicked cease from troubling;
There rest those whose strength is spent.
Prisoners are wholly at ease;
They do not hear the taskmaster's voice.

Small and great alike are there,
And the slave is free of his master.

Why does He give light to the sufferer
And life to the bitter in spirit;
To those who wait for death but it does not come,   40
Who search for it more than for treasure,
Who rejoice to exultation,
And are glad to reach the grave;
To the man who has lost his way,
Whom God has hedged about?
My groaning serves as my bread;
My roaring pours forth as water.
For what I feared has overtaken me;
What I dreaded has come upon me.
I had no repose, no quiet, no rest,   50
And trouble came.

19

Job said in reply: 1

How long will you grieve my spirit,
And crush me with words?
Time and again you humiliate me,
And are not ashamed to abuse me.
If indeed I have erred,
My error remains with me.
Though you are overbearing toward me,
Reproaching me with my disgrace,
Yet know that God has wronged me;   10
He has thrown up siege works around me.
I cry, "Violence!" but am not answered;
I shout, but can get no justice.
He has barred my way; I cannot pass;
He has laid darkness upon my path.
He has stripped me of my glory,
Removed the crown from my head.
He tears down every part of me; I perish;
He uproots my hope like a tree.
He kindles His anger against me;   20
He regards me as one of His foes.
His troops advance together;
They build their road toward me
And encamp around my tent.
He alienated my kin from me;
My acquaintances disown me.
My relatives are gone;
My friends have forgotten me.
My dependents and maidservants regard me as a
    stranger;
I am an outsider to them.   30

I summon my servant but he does not respond;
I must myself entreat him.
My odor is repulsive to my wife;
I am loathsome to my children.
Even youngsters disdain me;
When I rise, they speak against me.
All my bosom friends detest me;
Those I love have turned against me.
My bones stick to my skin and flesh;
I escape with the skin of my teeth.   40

Pity me, pity me! You are my friends;
For the hand of God has struck me!
Why do you pursue me like God,
Maligning me insatiably?
O that my words were written down;
Would they were inscribed in a record,
Incised on a rock forever
With iron stylus and lead!
But I know that my Vindicator lives;
In the end He will testify on earth—   50
This, after my skin will have been peeled off.
But I would behold God while still in my flesh,
I myself, not another, would behold Him;
Would see with my own eyes:
My heart pines within me.
You say, "How do we persecute him?
The root of the matter is in him."
Be in fear of the sword,
For [your] fury is iniquity worthy of the sword;
Know there is a judgment!   60

38–42

38

Then the LORD replied to Job out of the tempest and said: 1

Who is this who darkens counsel,
Speaking without knowledge?
Gird your loins like a man;
I will ask and you will inform Me.

Where were you when I laid the earth's foundations?
Speak if you have understanding.
Do you know who fixed its dimensions
Or who measured it with a line?
Onto what were its bases sunk?   10
Who set its cornerstone
When the morning stars sang together
And all the divine beings shouted for joy?

Who closed the sea behind doors
When it gushed forth out of the womb,
When I clothed it in clouds,
Swaddled it in dense clouds,
When I made breakers My limit for it,
And set up its bar and doors,
And said, "You may come so far and no farther;   20
Here your surging waves will stop"?

Have you ever commanded the day to break,
Assigned the dawn its place,
So that it seizes the corners of the earth
And shakes the wicked out of it?
It changes like clay under the seal
Till [its hues] are fixed like those of a garment.
Their light is withheld from the wicked,
And the upraised arm is broken.

Have you penetrated to the sources of the sea,   30
Or walked in the recesses of the deep?
Have the gates of death been disclosed to you?
Have you seen the gates of deep darkness?
Have you surveyed the expanses of the earth?
If you know of these—tell Me.

Which path leads to where light dwells,
And where is the place of darkness,
That you may take it to its domain
And know the way to its home?
Surely you know, for you were born then,   40
And the number of your years is many!

Have you penetrated the vaults of snow,
Seen the vaults of hail,
Which I have put aside for a time of adversity,
For a day of war and battle?
By what path is the west wind dispersed,
The east wind scattered over the earth?

Who cut a channel for the torrents
And a path for the thunderstorms,
To rain down on uninhabited land,   50
On the wilderness where no man is,
To saturate the desolate wasteland,
And make the crop of grass sprout forth?
Does the rain have a father?
Who begot the dewdrops?
From whose belly came forth the ice?
Who gave birth to the frost of heaven?
Water congeals like stone,
And the surface of the deep compacts.

Can you tie cords to Pleiades   60
Or undo the reins of Orion?
Can you lead out Mazzaroth in its season,
Conduct the Bear with her sons[10]?
Do you know the laws of heaven
Or impose its authority on earth?
Can you send up an order to the clouds
For an abundance of water to cover you?
Can you dispatch the lightning on a mission
And have it answer you, "I am ready"?
Who put wisdom in the hidden parts?   70
Who gave understanding to the mind?
Who is wise enough to give an account of the
    heavens?
Who can tilt the bottles of the sky,
Whereupon the earth melts into a mass,
And its clods stick together?

Can you hunt prey for the lion,
And satisfy the appetite of the king of beasts?
They crouch in their dens,
Lie in ambush in their lairs.
Who provides food for the raven   80
When his young cry out to God
And wander about without food?

39

Do you know the season when the mountain goats   1
    give birth?
Can you mark the time when the hinds calve?
Can you count the months they must complete?
Do you know the season they give birth,
When they couch to bring forth their offspring,
To deliver their young?
Their young are healthy; they grow up in the open;
They leave and return no more.

---

[10] **Pleiades, Orion, Mazzaroth, Bear with her sons** All are references to constellations or images in the sky. Pleiades, Orion, and the Bear and her sons (Ursa Major and Ursa Minor) are constellations. *Mazzaroth* is the Hebrew word for the Zodiac.

Who sets the wild ass free?
Who loosens the bonds of the onager, 10
Whose home I have made the wilderness,
The salt land his dwelling-place?
He scoffs at the tumult of the city,
Does not hear the shouts of the driver.
He roams the hills for his pasture;
He searches for any green thing.

Would the wild ox agree to serve you?
Would he spend the night at your crib?
Can you hold the wild ox by ropes to the furrow?
Would he plow up the valleys behind you? 20
Would you rely on his great strength
And leave your toil to him?
Would you trust him to bring in the seed
And gather it in from your threshing floor?

The wing of the ostrich beats joyously;
Are her pinions and plumage like the stork's?
She leaves her eggs on the ground,
Letting them warm in the dirt,
Forgetting they may be crushed underfoot,
Or trampled by a wild beast. 30
Her young are cruelly abandoned as if they were
    not hers;
Her labor is in vain for lack of concern.
For God deprived her of wisdom,
Gave her no share of understanding,
Else she would soar on high,
Scoffing at the horse and its rider.

Do you give the horse his strength?
Do you clothe his neck with a mane?
Do you make him quiver like locusts,
His majestic snorting [spreading] terror? 40
He paws with force, he runs with vigor,
Charging into battle.
He scoffs at fear; he cannot be frightened;
He does not recoil from the sword.
A quiverful of arrows whizzes by him,
And the flashing spear and the javelin.
Trembling with excitement, he swallows the land;
He does not turn aside at the blast of the trumpet.
As the trumpet sounds, he says, "Aha!"
From afar he smells the battle, 50
The roaring and shouting of the officers.

Is it by your wisdom that the hawk grows pinions,
Spreads his wings to the south?
Does the eagle soar at your command,
Building his nest high,
Dwelling in the rock,
Lodging upon the fastness of a jutting rock?
From there he spies out his food;
From afar his eyes see it.
His young gulp blood; 60
Where the slain are, there is he.

40

The LORD said in reply to Job. 1

Shall one who should be disciplined complain
against Shaddai?
He who arraigns God must respond.

Job said in reply to the LORD:

See, I am of small worth; what can I answer You?
I clap my hand to my mouth.
I have spoken once, and will not reply;
Twice, and will do so no more.

Then the LORD replied to Job out of the tempest and said: 10

Gird your loins like a man;
I will ask, and you will inform Me.
Would you impugn My justice?
Would you condemn Me that you may be right?
Have you an arm like God's?
Can you thunder with a voice like His?
Deck yourself now with grandeur and eminence;
Clothe yourself in glory and majesty.
Scatter wide your raging anger
See every proud man and bring him low. 20
See every proud man and humble him,
And bring them down where they stand.
Bury them all in the earth;
Hide their faces in obscurity.
Then even I would praise you
For the triumph your right hand won you.

Take now behemoth,[11] whom I made as I did you;
He eats grass, like the cattle.
His strength is in his loins,
His might in the muscles of his belly. 30
He makes his tail stand up like a cedar;
The sinews of his thighs are knit together.
His bones are like tubes of bronze,
His limbs like iron rods.
He is the first of God's works;
Only his Maker can draw the sword against him.
The mountains yield him produce,
Where all the beasts of the field play.
He lies down beneath the lotuses,
In the cover of the swamp reeds. 40
The lotuses embower him with shade;
The willows of the brook surround him.
He can restrain the river from its rushing;
He is confident the stream will gush at his
    command.
Can he be taken by his eyes?

————————
[11] **behemoth** A monstrous-sized animal. In this context, it is
probably the hippopotamus.

Can his nose be pierced by hooks?
Can you draw out Leviathan by a fishhook?
Can you press down his tongue by a rope?
Can you put a ring through his nose,
Or pierce his jaw with a barb?   50
Will he plead with you at length?
Will he speak soft words to you?
Will he make an agreement with you
To be taken as your lifelong slave?
Will you play with him like a bird,
And tie him down for your girls?
Shall traders traffic in him?
Will he be divided up among merchants?
Can you fill his skin with darts
Or his head with fish-spears?   60
Lay a hand on him,
And you will never think of battle again.

41

See, any hope [of capturing] him must be   1
     disappointed;
One is prostrated by the very sight of him.
There is no one so fierce as to rouse him;
Who then can stand up to Me?
Whoever confronts Me I will requite,
For everything under the heavens is Mine.
I will not be silent concerning him
Or the praise of his martial exploits.
Who can uncover his outer garment?
Who can penetrate the folds of his jowls?   10
Who can pry open the doors of his face?
His bared teeth strike terror.
His protective scales are his pride,
Locked with a binding seal.
One scale touches the other;
Not even a breath can enter between them.
Each clings to each;
They are interlocked so they cannot be parted.
His sneezings flash lightning,
And his eyes are like the glimmerings of dawn.   20
Firebrands stream from his mouth;
Fiery sparks escape.
Out of his nostrils comes smoke
As from a steaming, boiling cauldron.
His breath ignites coals;
Flames blaze from his mouth.
Strength resides in his neck;
Power leaps before him.
The layers of his flesh stick together;
He is as though cast hard; he does not totter.   30
His heart is cast hard as a stone,
Hard as the nether millstone.
Divine beings are in dread as he rears up;
As he crashes down, they cringe.
No sword that overtakes him can prevail,
Nor spear, nor missile, nor lance.

He regards iron as straw,
Bronze, as rotted wood.
No arrow can put him to flight;
Slingstones turn into stubble for him.   40
Clubs are regarded as stubble;
He scoffs at the quivering javelin.
His underpart is jagged shards;
It spreads a threshing-sledge on the mud.
He makes the depths seethe like a cauldron;
He makes the sea [boil] like an ointment-pot.
His wake is a luminous path;
He makes the deep seem white-haired.
There is no one on land who can dominate him,
Made as he is without fear.   50
He sees all that is haughty;
He is king over all proud beasts.

42

Job said in reply to the Lord: 1

I know that You can do everything,
That nothing you propose is impossible for You.
Who is this who obscures counsel without
     knowledge?
Indeed, I spoke without understanding
Of things beyond me, which I did not know.
Hear now, and I will speak;
I will ask, and You will inform me.
I had heard You with my ears,
But now I see You with my eyes;   10
Therefore, I recant and relent,
Being but dust and ashes.

After the Lord had spoken these words to Job, the Lord said to Eliphaz the Temanite, "I am incensed at you and your two friends, for you have not spoken the truth about Me as did My servant Job. Now take seven bulls and seven rams and go to My servant Job and sacrifice a burnt offering for yourselves. And let Job, My servant, pray for you; for to him I will show favor and not treat you vilely, since you have not spoken the truth about Me as did My servant Job." Eliphaz the Temanite and Bildad the Shuhite and Zophar the Naamathite[12] went and did as the Lord had told them, and the Lord showed favor to Job. The Lord restored Job's fortunes when he prayed on behalf of his friends, and the Lord gave Job twice what he had before.

All his brothers and sisters and all his former friends came to him and had a meal with him in his house. They consoled and comforted him for all the misfortune that the

---

[12] **Eliphaz the Temanite, Bildad the Shuhite, and Zophar the Naamathite** Job's three friends who came to counsel him and offer him their advice. Their speeches and Job's responses explore many issues regarding relationships between humans and God.

Lord had brought upon him. Each gave him one *kesitah* and each one gold ring. Thus the Lord blessed the latter years of Job's life more than the former. He had fourteen thousand sheep, six thousand camels, one thousand yoke of oxen, and one thousand she-asses. He also had seven sons and three daughters. The first he named Jemimah,

the second Keziah, and the third Keren-happuch. Nowhere in the land were women as beautiful as Job's daughters to be found. Their father gave them estates together with their brothers. Afterward, Job lived one hundred and forty years to see four generations of sons and grandsons. So Job died old and contented.

∞

Ecclesiastes

3

A season is set for everything, a time for every experience under heaven: 1
A time for being born and a time for dying,
A time for planting and a time for uprooting the planted;
A time for slaying and a time for healing,
A time for tearing down and a time for building up;
A time for weeping and a time for laughing,
A time for wailing and a time for dancing;
A time for throwing stones and a time for gather- ing stones,
A time for embracing and a time for shunning embraces;
A time for seeking and a time for losing, 10
A time for keeping and a time for discarding;
A time for ripping and a time for sewing,
A time for silence and a time for speaking;
A time for loving and a time for hating;
A time for war and a time for peace.

What value, then, can the man of affairs get from what he earns? I have observed the business that God gave man to be concerned with: He brings everything to pass precisely at its time; He also puts eternity in their mind, but without man ever guessing, from first to last, all the things that God brings to pass. Thus I realized that the only worthwhile thing there is for them is to enjoy themselves and do what is good in their lifetime; also, that

whenever a man does eat and drink and get enjoyment out of all his wealth, it is a gift of God.

I realized, too, that whatever God has brought to pass will recur evermore:
Nothing can be added to it
And nothing taken from it—
and God has brought to pass that men revere Him
What is occurring occurred long since, 20
And what is to occur occurred long since: and God seeks the pursued. And, indeed, I have observed under the sun:
Alongside justice there is wickedness,
Alongside righteousness there is wickedness. I mused: "God will doom both righteous and wicked, for there is a time for every experience and for every happening." So I decided, as regards men, to dissociate them [from] the divine beings and to face the fact that they are beasts. For in respect of the fate of man and the fate of beast, they have one and the same fate; as the one dies so dies the other, and both have the same lifebreath; man has no superiority over beast, since both amount to nothing. Both go to the same place; both came from dust and both return to dust. Who knows if a man's lifebreath does rise upward and if a beast's breath does sink down into the earth?

I saw that there is nothing better for man than to enjoy his possessions, since that is his portion. For who can enable him to see what will happen afterward?

∞

Questions for Critical Thinking

1. Discuss and give examples of how God plays a role in the lives of humans regarding Adam and Eve, Noah, and Job.

2. In what ways do humans not obey God, and how does he punish those who do not obey him as recorded in *The Holy Scriptures*? Does such behavior indicate that all humans are incapable of upholding their moral code and will always "sin"?

Selections from *The Revised Standard Version of the Holy Bible*

Christians adopted the Jewish Bible, *The Holy Scriptures,* renaming it the Old Testament and rearranging its thirty-nine books into the Pentateuch, the Historical Books, the Wisdom Books, and the Prophetical Books. Christians also developed the New Testament—twenty-seven books about Jesus, grouped into the Gospels, the Acts of the Apostles, Epistles, and Apocalypse. The Christian Bible thus numbers sixty-six books. The books in the New Testament, written between 50 and 100 CE, were brought together around 150 CE as the sacred text for the new religion of Christianity. Greek, the New Testament's language, enabled it to circulate freely in Rome's Greek-speaking eastern provinces. When Christianity triumphed in Rome around 400 CE, the saintly Jerome rewrote the entire Bible into the ordinary, or common, Latin of that era; thereafter, his work was known as the Vulgate version (from Latin *vulgatus,* "common"). Since then, the Vulgate has been the church's official text, although the Protestants composed vernacular versions after 1500.

From the fall of Rome until recent times, the Holy Bible has been the West's most significant book, touching the lives of everyone in all walks of life. This privileged status rose not simply because the Bible contained God's holy words for Christian and Jewish believers, but most important, because it was the all-encompassing glue that bound the culture together. It influenced every aspect of culture, most notably in the arts, language, and personal behavior. The Bible offered an alternative body of writing to that of Greece and Rome and, as such, inspired artists, writers, and musicians. Its words and rhetoric enriched spoken and written language, and its parables and poems served as a handbook for moral guidance. Even in today's secular world, biblical knowledge is still indispensable for interpreting Western culture and history.

Reading the Selections

The selections from Matthew's Gospel include key scenes from the life of Jesus, including the virgin birth, the baptism by John the Baptist, the temptation by the devil, and the Sermon on the Mount. Most notably, the Sermon on the Mount presents Jesus's moral teachings. He begins this sermon with the beatitudes—a list of blessings on those who often are at odds with earthly society, such as the poor and the downtrodden. He next reinterprets the Jewish law. Jesus expresses his law of love in what Christians later call the Golden Rule: "So whatever you wish that men would do to you, do so to them . . ." (Matthew 7:12). He also describes the correct way to worship God, giving the Lord's Prayer as the best model. Jesus concludes with a caution against false prophets—those who call on the Lord but refuse to obey his will.

The final selection is from the Epistles—the letters written by early Christian leaders to new congregations needing further knowledge of Christ and his teachings, advice on church organization, and help with understanding the rituals and beliefs of the emerging religion. The letters of Paul, the first Christian missionary, make up the largest number of the Epistles—fourteen out of twenty-one. Chapter 13 from Paul's First Letter to the Corinthians (the church in Corinth, Greece) is an exemplary summary of Christian love, which forgives others and asks nothing in return.

∞

The Gospel According to Matthew
1:18–25; 2–4
The Coming of Christ

Now the birth of Jesus Christ took place in this way. When his mother Mary had been betrothed to Joseph, before they came together she was found to be with child of the Holy Spirit; and her husband Joseph, being a just man and unwilling to put her to shame, resolved to divorce her quietly. But as he considered this, behold, an angel of the Lord appeared to him in a dream, saying, "Joseph, son of David, do not fear to take Mary your wife, for that which is conceived in her is of the Holy Spirit; she will bear a son, and you shall call his name Jesus, for he will save his people from their sins." All this took place to fulfill what the Lord had spoken by the prophet:

"Behold, a virgin shall conceive and bear a son,
and his name shall be called Emman'u-el"
(which means, God with us).

When Joseph woke from sleep, he did as the angel of the Lord commanded him; he took his wife, but knew her not until she had borne a son; and he called his name Jesus.

2

Now when Jesus was born in Bethlehem of Judea in the days of Herod the king, behold, wise men from the East came to Jerusalem, saying, "Where is he who has been born king of the Jews? For we have seen his star in the East, and have come to worship him." When Herod the king heard this, he was troubled, and all Jerusalem with him; and assembling all the chief priests and scribes of the people, he inquired of them where the Christ was to be born. They told him, "In Bethlehem of Judea; for so it is written by the prophet:

'And you, O Bethlehem, in the land of Judah,
are by no means least among the rulers of Judah;
for from you shall come a ruler
who will govern my people Israel.'"

Then Herod summoned the wise men secretly and ascertained from them what time the star appeared; and he sent them to Bethlehem, saying, "Go and search diligently for the child, and when you have found him bring me word, that I too may come and worship him." When they had heard the king they went their way; and lo, the star which they had seen in the East went before them, till it came to rest over the place where the child was. When they saw the star, they rejoiced exceedingly with great joy; and going into the house they saw the child with Mary his mother, and they fell down and worshiped him. Then, opening their treasures, they offered him gifts, gold and frankincense and myrrh. And being warned in a dream not to return to Herod, they departed to their own country by another way.

Now when they had departed, behold, an angel of the Lord appeared to Joseph in a dream and said, "Rise, take the child and his mother, and flee to Egypt, and remain there till I tell you; for Herod is about to search for the child, to destroy him." And he rose and took the child and his mother by night, and departed to Egypt, and remained there until the death of Herod. This was to fulfil what the Lord had spoken by the prophet, "Out of Egypt have I called my son."

Then Herod, when he saw that he had been tricked by the wise men, was in a furious rage, and he sent and killed all the male children in Bethlehem and in all that region who were two years old or under, according to the time which he had ascertained from the wise men. Then was fulfilled what was spoken by the prophet Jeremiah:

"A voice was heard in Ramah,
wailing and loud lamentation,
Rachel weeping for her children;
she refused to be consoled,
because they were no more."

But when Herod died, behold, an angel of the Lord appeared in a dream to Joseph in Egypt, saying, "Rise, take the child and his mother, and go to the land of Israel, for those who sought the child's life are dead." And he rose and took the child and his mother, and went to the land of Israel. But when he heard that Archela'us reigned over Judea in place of his father Herod, he was afraid to go there, and being warned in a dream he withdrew to the district of Galilee. And he went and dwelt in a city called Nazareth, that what was spoken by the prophets might be fulfilled, "He shall be called a Nazarene."

3

In those days came John the Baptist, preaching in the wilderness of Judea, "Repent, for the kingdom of heaven is at hand." For this is he who was spoken of by the prophet Isaiah when he said,

"The voice of one crying in the wilderness:
Prepare the way of the Lord,
make his paths straight."

Now John wore a garment of camel's hair, and a leather girdle around his waist; and his food was locusts and wild honey. Then went out to him Jerusalem and all Judea and all the region about the Jordan, and they were baptized by him in the river Jordan, confessing their sins.

But when he saw many of the Pharisees and Sad'ducees[13] coming for baptism, he said to them, "You brood of vipers! Who warned you to flee from the wrath to come? Bear fruit that befits repentance, and do not presume to say to yourselves, 'We have Abraham as our father'; for I tell you, God is able from these stones to raise up children to Abraham. Even now the ax is laid to the root of the trees; every tree therefore that does not bear good fruit is cut down and thrown into the fire.

"I baptize you with water for repentance, but he who is coming after me is mightier than I, whose sandals I am not worthy to carry; he will baptize you with the Holy Spirit and with fire. His winnowing fork is in his hand, and he will clear his threshing floor and gather his wheat into the granary, but the chaff he will burn with unquenchable fire."

Then Jesus came from Galilee to the Jordan to John, to be baptized by him. John would have prevented him, saying, "I need to be baptized by you, and do you come to me?" But Jesus answered him, "Let it be so now; for thus it is fitting for us to fulfil all righteousness." Then he consented. And when Jesus was baptized, he went up immediately from the water, and behold, the heavens were opened and he saw the Spirit of God descending like a dove, and alighting on him; and lo, a voice from heaven, saying, "This is my beloved Son, with whom I am well pleased."

4

Then Jesus was led up by the Spirit into the wilderness to be tempted by the devil. And he fasted forty days and forty nights, and afterward he was hungry. And the tempter came and said to him, "If you are the Son of God, command these stones to become loaves of bread." But he answered, "It is written,

> 'Man shall not live by bread alone,
>   but by every word that proceeds from the mouth
>   of God.'"

Then the devil took him to the holy city, and set him on the pinnacle of the temple, and said to him, "If you are the Son of God, throw yourself down; for it is written,

> 'He will give his angels charge you,'

and

> 'On their hands they will bear you up,
>   lest you strike your foot against a stone.'"

Jesus said to him, "Again it is written, 'You shall not tempt the Lord your God.'" Again, the devil took him to a very high mountain, and showed him all the kingdoms of the world and the glory of them; and he said to him, "All these I will give you, if you will fall down and worship me." Then Jesus said to him, "Begone, Satan! for it is written,

> 'You shall worship the Lord your God
>   and him only shall you serve.'"

Then the devil left him, and behold, angels came and ministered to him.

Now when he heard that John had been arrested, he withdrew into Galilee; and leaving Nazareth he went and dwelt in Caper'na-um by the sea, in the territory of Zeb'ulun and Naph'tali, that what was spoken by the prophet Isaiah might be fulfilled:

> "The land of Zeb'ulun and the land of Naph'tali,
>   toward the sea, across the Jordan,
>   Galilee of the Gentiles—
>   the people who sat in darkness
>   have seen a great light,
>   and for those who sat in the region and shadow of
>   death
>   light has dawned."

From that time Jesus began to preach, saying, "Repent, for the kingdom of heaven is at hand."

As he walked by the Sea of Galilee, he saw two brothers, Simon who is called Peter and Andrew his brother, casting a net into the sea; for they were fishermen. And he said to them, "Follow me, and I will make you fishers of men." Immediately they left their nets and followed him. And going on from there he saw two other brothers, James the son of Zeb'edee and John his brother, in the boat with Zeb'edee their father, mending their nets, and he called them. Immediately they left the boat and their father, and followed him.

And he went about all Galilee, teaching in their synagogues and preaching the gospel of the kingdom and healing every disease and every infirmity among the people. So his fame spread throughout all Syria, and they brought him all the sick, those afflicted with various diseases and pains, demoniacs, epileptics, and paralytics, and he healed them. And great crowds followed him from Galilee and the Decap'olis and Jerusalem and Judea and from beyond the Jordan.

---

[13] **Pharisees and Sad'ducees** Two factions or parties in Israel who often held opposing views on many Jewish beliefs and practices. Both groups questioned Jesus and never supported him or his followers. The early Christians saw the Pharisees and the Sad'ducees as their major critics and opponents.

∞

5–7

Sermon on the Mount

5

Seeing the crowds, he went up on the mountain, and when ₁ he sat down his disciples came to him. And he opened his mouth and taught them, saying:

"Blessed are the poor in spirit, for theirs is the kingdom of heaven.

"Blessed are those who mourn, for they shall be comforted.

"Blessed are the meek, for they shall inherit the earth.

"Blessed are those who hunger and thirst for righ- ₅ teousness, for they shall be satisfied.

"Blessed are the merciful, for they shall obtain mercy.

"Blessed are the pure in heart, for they shall see God.

"Blessed are the peacemakers, for they shall be called sons of God.

"Blessed are those who are persecuted for righteousness' sake, for theirs is the kingdom of heaven.

"Blessed are you when men revile you and persecute ₁₀ you and utter all kinds of evil against you falsely on my account. Rejoice and be glad, for your reward is great in heaven, for so men persecuted the prophets who were before you.

"You are the salt of the earth; but if salt has lost its taste, how shall its saltness be restored? It is no longer good for anything except to be thrown out and trodden under foot by men.

"You are the light of the world. A city set on a hill cannot be hid. Nor do men light a lamp and put it under a bushel, but on a stand, and it gives light to all in the house. Let your light so shine before men, that they may see your good works and give glory to your Father who is in heaven.

"Think not that I have come to abolish the law and the prophets; I have come not to abolish them but to fulfil them. For truly, I say to you, till heaven and earth pass away, not an iota, not a dot, will pass from the law until all is accomplished. Whoever then relaxes one of the least of these commandments and teaches men so, shall be called least in the kingdom of heaven; but he who does them and teaches them shall be called great in the kingdom of heaven. For I tell you, unless your righteousness exceeds that of the scribes and Pharisees, you will never enter the kingdom of heaven.

"You have heard that it was said to the men of old, 'You shall not kill; and whoever kills shall be liable to judgment.' But I say to you that every one who is angry with his brother shall be liable to judgment; whoever insults his brother shall be liable to the council, and whoever says, 'You fool!' shall be liable to the hell of fire. So if you are offering your gift at the altar, and there remember that your brother has something against you, leave your gift there before the altar and go; first be reconciled to your brother,

and then come and offer your gift. Make friends quickly with your accuser, while you are going with him to court, lest your accuser hand you over to the judge, and the judge to the guard, and you be put in prison; truly, I say to you, you will never get out till you have paid the last penny.

"You have heard that it was said, 'You shall not com- ₁₅ mit adultery.' But I say to you that every one who looks at a woman lustfully has already committed adultery with her in his heart. If your right eye causes you to sin, pluck it out and throw it away; it is better that you lose one of your members than that your whole body be thrown into hell. And if your right hand causes you to sin, cut it off and throw it away; it is better that you lose one of your members than that your whole body go into hell.

"It was also said, 'Whoever divorces his wife, let him give her a certificate of divorce.' But I say to you that every one who divorces his wife, except on the ground of unchastity, makes her an adulteress; and whoever marries a divorced woman commits adultery.

"Again you have heard that it was said to the men of old, 'You shall not swear falsely, but shall perform to the Lord what you have sworn.' But I say to you, Do not swear at all, either by heaven, for it is the throne of God, or by the earth, for it is his footstool, or by Jerusalem, for it is the city of the great King. And do not swear by your head, for you cannot make one hair white or black. Let what you say be simply 'Yes' or 'No'; anything more than this comes from evil.

"You have heard that it was said, 'An eye for an eye and a tooth for a tooth.' But I say to you, Do not resist one who is evil. But if any one strikes you on the right cheek, turn to him the other also; and if any one would sue you and take your coat, let him have your cloak as well; and if any one forces you to go one mile, go with him two miles. Give to him who begs from you, and do not refuse him who would borrow from you.

"You have heard that it was said, 'You shall love your neighbor and hate your enemy.' But I say to you, Love your enemies and pray for those who persecute you, so that you may be sons of your Father who is in heaven; for he makes his sun rise on the evil and on the good, and sends rain on the just and on the unjust. For if you love those who love you, what reward have you? Do not even the tax collectors do the same? And if you salute only your brethren, what more are you doing than others? Do not even the Gentiles do the same? You, therefore, must be perfect, as your heavenly Father is perfect.

6

"Beware of practicing your piety before men in order to be ₁ seen by them; for then you will have no reward from your Father who is in heaven.

"Thus, when you give alms, sound no trumpet before you, as the hypocrites do in the synagogues and in the streets, that they may be praised by men. Truly, I say to you, they have their reward. But when you give alms, do not let your left hand know what your right hand is doing, so that your alms may be in secret; and your Father who sees in secret will reward you.

"And when you pray, you must not be like the hypocrites; for they love to stand and pray in the synagogues and at the street corners, that they may be seen by men. Truly, I say to you, they have their reward. But when you pray, go into your room and shut the door and pray to your Father who is in secret; and your Father who sees in secret will reward you.

"And in praying do not heap up empty phrases as the Gentiles do; for they think that they will be heard for their many words. Do not be like them, for your Father knows what you need before you ask him. Pray then like this:

> Our Father who art in heaven,
> Hallowed be thy name.
> Thy kingdom come,
> Thy will be done,
>   On earth as it is in heaven.
> Give us this day our daily bread;
> And forgive us our debts,
>   As we also have forgiven our debtors;
> And lead us not into temptation
>   But deliver us from evil.

For if you forgive men their trespasses, your heavenly Father also will forgive you; but if you do not forgive men their trespasses, neither will your Father forgive your trespasses.

"And when you fast, do not look dismal, like the 5 hypocrites, for they disfigure their faces that their fasting may be seen by men. Truly, I say to you, they have their reward. But when you fast, anoint your head and wash your face, that your fasting may not be seen by men but by your Father who is in secret; and your Father who sees in secret will reward you.

"Do not lay up for yourselves treasures on earth, where moth and rust consume and where thieves break in and steal, but lay up for yourselves treasures in heaven, where neither moth nor rust consumes and where thieves do not break in and steal. For where your treasure is, there will your heart be also.

"The eye is the lamp of the body. So, if your eye is sound, your whole body will be full of light; but if your eye is not sound, your whole body will be full of darkness. If then the light in you is darkness, how great is the darkness!

"No one can serve two masters; for either he will hate the one and love the other, or he will be devoted to the one and despise the other. You cannot serve God and mammon.

"Therefore I tell you, do not be anxious about your life, what you shall eat or what you shall drink, nor about your body, what you shall put on. Is not life more than food, and the body more than clothing? Look at the birds of the air: they neither sow nor reap nor gather into barns, and yet your heavenly Father feeds them. Are you not of more value than they? And which of you by being anxious can add one cubit to his span of life? And why are you anxious about clothing? Consider the lilies of the field, how they grow; they neither toil nor spin; yet I tell you, even Solomon in all his glory was not arrayed like one of these. But if God so clothes the grass of the field, which today is alive and tomorrow is thrown into the oven, will he not much more clothe you, O men of little faith? Therefore do not be anxious, saying, 'What shall we eat?' or 'What shall we drink?' or 'What shall we wear?' For the Gentiles seek all these things; and your heavenly Father knows that you need them all. But seek first his kingdom and his righteousness, and all these things shall be yours as well.

"Therefore do not be anxious about tomorrow, for to- 10 morrow will be anxious for itself. Let the day's own trouble be sufficient for the day.

7

"Judge not, that you be not judged. For with the judgment 1 you pronounce you will be judged, and the measure you give will be the measure you get. Why do you see the speck that is in your brother's eye, but do not notice the log that is in your own eye? Or how can you say to your brother, 'Let me take the speck out of your eye,' when there is the log in your own eye? You hypocrite, first take the log out of your own eye, and then you will see clearly to take the speck out of your brother's eye.

"Do not give dogs what is holy; and do not throw your pearls before swine, lest they trample them underfoot and turn to attack you.

"Ask, and it will be given you; seek and you will find; knock, and it will be opened to you. For every one who asks receives, and he who seeks finds, and to him who knocks it will be opened. Or what man of you, if his son asks him for a loaf, will give him a stone? Or if he asks for a fish, will give him a serpent? If you then, who are evil, know how to give good gifts to your children, how much more will your Father who is in heaven give good things to those who ask him? So whatever you wish that men would do to you, do so to them; for this is the law and the prophets.

"Enter by the narrow gate; for the gate is wide and the way is easy, that leads to destruction, and those who enter by it are many. For the gate is narrow and the way is hard, that leads to life, and those who find it are few.

"Beware of false prophets, who come to you in sheep's 5 clothing but inwardly are ravenous wolves. You will know them by their fruits. Are grapes gathered from thorns, or figs from thistles? So, every sound tree bears good fruit, but the bad tree bears evil fruit. A sound tree cannot bear evil fruit, nor can a bad tree bear good fruit. Every tree that does not bear good fruit is cut down and thrown into the fire. Thus you will know them by their fruits.

"Not every one who says to me, 'Lord, Lord,' shall enter the kingdom of heaven, but he who does the will of my Father who is in heaven. On that day many will say to me, 'Lord, Lord, did we not prophesy in your name, and cast out demons in your name, and do many mighty works in your name?' And then will I declare to them, 'I never knew you; depart from me, you evildoers.'

"Every one then who hears these words of mine and does them will be like a wise man who built his house upon the rock; and the rain fell, and the floods came, and the winds blew and beat upon that house, but it did not fall, because it had been founded on the rock. And every one who hears these words of mine and does not do them will be like a foolish man who built his house upon the sand; and the rain fell, and the floods came, and the winds blew and beat against that house, and it fell; and great was the fall of it."

And when Jesus finished these sayings, the crowds were astonished at his teaching, for he taught them as one who had authority, and not as their scribes.

∞

1 Corinthians

13

If I speak in the tongues of men and of angels, but have not love, I am a noisy gong or a clanging cymbal. And if I have prophetic powers, and understand all mysteries and all knowledge, and if I have all faith, so as to remove mountains, but have not love, I am nothing. If I give away all I have, and if I deliver my body to be burned, but have not love, I gain nothing.

Love is patient and kind; love is not jealous or boastful; it is not arrogant or rude. Love does not insist on its own way; it is not irritable or resentful; it does not rejoice at wrong, but rejoices in the right. Love bears all things, believes all things, hopes all things, endures all things.

Love never ends; as for prophecy, it will pass away; as for tongues, they will cease; as for knowledge, it will pass away. For our knowledge is imperfect and our prophecy is imperfect; but when the perfect comes, the imperfect will pass away. When I was a child, I spoke like a child, I thought like a child, I reasoned like a child; when I became a man, I gave up childish ways. For now we see in a mirror dimly, but then face to face. Now I know in part; then I shall understand fully, even as I have been fully understood. So faith, hope, love abide, these three; but the greatest of these is love.

∞

Questions for Critical Thinking

1. What are the temptations that the devil offers Jesus? Are they similar to the "temptations" humans confront in their lives today?

2. Compare and contrast the Jewish set of laws with Jesus's interpretation of these laws. In the Sermon on the Mount, does Jesus ask too much from humans to live up to the standards he sets for them?

∞

TERTULLIAN
Selections from *The Apparel of Women*

Tertullian (ca. 160 CE–ca. 230 CE) was one of the most influential figures of the early Christian church. He received a classical education that aided him in relating his Christian faith to the era's dominant Greco-Roman thought. However, any attempts to bridge the gap between these conflicting views ultimately failed because once Tertullian converted to Christianity, he became a "true believer," with strict fundamentalist views. Nevertheless, Tertullian helped formulate the new religion's beliefs within the broader pagan humanistic traditions and learning.

Scant evidence allows us to piece together Tertullian's life. Apparently, he was born into a pagan family living in Carthage, one of the major intellectual hubs of the empire outside of Rome. He studied literature, philosophy, and law before going to Rome, where he probably pursued a career in law and was first exposed to Christianity. He returned to Carthage and converted to the new faith, which was winning many followers as a result of its dedicated leaders and zealous supporters. He quickly became a strong voice in the North African church as a teacher and a writer. Some years later, Tertullian joined a splinter Christian group, Montanism. He was attracted to the movement's rigorous moral code. However, finding Montanism to be too lax for his high standards, he established his own group, which removed him even further from the Christian community. He apparently died an embittered and disappointed old man who demanded a level of perfection unattainable by his followers.

Tertullian's works, written in Latin, defined many early beliefs and practices that later became part of the Christian tradition. Tertullian not only explained his faith and railed against pagan culture, but he also wrote on moral and practical choices that early Christians faced daily, such as whether to serve in Rome's armies and how to respond to religious persecution. Most provocatively, he addressed the matter of personal conduct, offering strict guidelines on sex, personal habits, leisure activities, proper dress, and public behavior. Overall, he was more a propagandist than a theologian, as he attacked his enemies and called for strict adherence to Christian morals. The bedrock of his faith was the call for Christians never to give in to the alien cultures that he saw as threats to their religion. When he famously asked, "What has Athens to do with Jerusalem?" Tertullian was merely reconfirming his Christian conviction that the old must give way to the new, that the classical world must yield to the Age of Faith. After his death, Terullian's writings were ignored until the fifth century CE, when Christian scholars mined many ideas from his works. Because of his Montanist beliefs, however, the church has never seen fit to canonize him.

Reading the Selections

The Apparel of Women, written as two separate books, is addressed to women who were new converts to Christianity. Echoing the central thesis of his other works, these two books called for true Christians to renounce the pagan world and surrender to the teachings of Christ—as he, Tertullian, understood them. His moral gaze didn't spare men, as he also cautioned the male sex about the evils of vanity.

Tertullian's moral teachings reflect his basic belief in original sin—a belief shaped by Adam and Eve's expulsion from the Garden of Eden. He makes his position clear in the first selection—Chapter 1 of Book One. There, he blames Eve for all of humanity's subsequent sins, quoting Genesis 3 to support his argument: "In sorrow and anxiety, you will bring forth, O woman, and you are subject to your husband, and he is your master." In the second selection— five chapters from Book II—Tertullian sets forth his detailed, puritanical views about how women should dress and adorn their bodies.

❧

Book One

Chapter 1

If there existed upon earth a faith in proportion to the reward that faith will receive in heaven, no one of you, my beloved sisters, from the time when you came to know the living God and recognized your own state, that is, the condition of being a woman, would have desired a too attractive garb, and much less anything that seemed too ostentatious. I think, rather, that you would have dressed in mourning garments and even neglected your exterior, acting the part of mourning and repentant Eve in order to expiate more fully by all sorts of penitential garb that which woman derives from Eve—the ignominy, I mean, of original sin and the odium of being the cause of the fall of the human race. "In sorrow and anxiety, you will bring forth, O woman, and you are subject to your husband, and he is your master." Do you not believe that you are (each) an Eve?

The sentence of God on this sex of yours lives on even in our times and so it is necessary that the guilt should live on, also. You are the one who opened the door to the Devil, you are the one who first plucked the fruit of the forbidden tree, you are the first who deserted the divine law; you are the one who persuaded him whom the Devil was not strong enough to attack. All too easily you destroyed the image of God, man. Because of your desert, that is, death, even the Son of God had to die. And you still think of putting adornments over the skins of animals that cover you?

Well, now—if, in the very beginning of the world, the Milesians[14] had invented wool by shearing sheep, and if the Chinese had woven the strands of silk, and the Tyrians

had invented dye and the Phrygians embroidery and the Babylonians weaving, if pearls had gleamed and rubies flashed with light, if gold itself had already been brought forth from the bowels of earth by man's greed, and finally, if a mirror had already been capable of giving forth its lying image, do you think that Eve, after she had been expelled from Paradise and was already dead, would have longed for all of these fineries? She would not. Therefore, she ought not to crave them or even to know them now, if she desires to be restored to life again. Those things which she did not have or know when she lived in God, all those things are the trappings appropriate to a woman who was condemned and is dead, arrayed as if to lend splendor to her funeral.

---

[14] **Milesians** Tertullian shows his anticonsumerist bias in this list of prized consumer goods to be avoided: Milesian wool from the Greek city-state of Miletus, in Asia Minor; Chinese silk; the famed purple dye from Tyre in Phoenecia; embroidery from Phrygia, in Anatolia; and weavings from Mesopotamia (modern Iraq).

Book Two

Chapter 4

Holy women, let none of you, if she is naturally beautiful, be an occasion of sin; certainly, if even she be so, she must not increase beauty, but try to subdue it. If I were speaking to Gentiles,[15] I would give you a Gentile precept and one that is common to all: you are bound to please no one except your own husbands. And, you will please your husbands in the proportion that you take no pains to please anyone else. Be unconcerned, blessed sisters: no wife is really ugly to her own husband. She was certainly pleasing to him when he chose to marry her, whether it was for her beauty or for her character. Let none of you think that she will necessarily incur the hatred and aversion of her husband if she spends less time in the adornment of her person.

Every husband demands that his wife be chaste; but beauty a Christian husband certainly does not demand, because we Christians are not fascinated by the same things that the Gentiles think to be good. If, on the other hand, the husband be an infidel, he will be suspicious of beauty precisely because of the unfavorable opinion the Gentiles have of us. For whose sake, then, are you cultivating your beauty? If for a Christian, he does not demand it, and if for an infidel, he does not believe it unless it is artless. Why, then, are you so eager to please either one who is suspicious or one who does not desire it?

---

[15] **Gentiles** Non-Christians. Tertullian has appropriated the Jewish term and applied it to non-believers.

Chapter 6

I see some women dye their hair blonde by using saffron. They are even ashamed of their country, sorry that they were not born in Germany or in Gaul! Thus, as far as their hair is concerned, they give up their country. It is hardly a good omen for them that they wish their hair to be flame-colored and mistake for beauty something which merely stains them.

As a matter of fact, the strength of these bleaches really does harm to the hair, and the constant application of even any natural moist substance will bring ruin to the head itself, just as the warmth of the sun, while desirable for giving life and dryness to the hair, if overdone is hurtful. How can they achieve beauty when they are doing themselves harm; how can they make something attractive by means of filth? Shall a Christian woman heap saffron on her hair as upon an altar? For, surely, anything that is normally burned in honor of an unclean spirit, may be considered as a sacrifice to idols, unless it is applied for honest and necessary and wholesome uses for which all of God's creatures were provided.

But the Lord has said: "Which of you can make a white hair black or out of a black a white?" Thus do they refute the word of the Lord. "Behold," they say, "out of white or black we make it blonde, which is surely more attractive." Why, you will even find people who are ashamed of having lived to old age and try to make their hair black when it is white. Are you not ashamed of such folly? Trying to keep it a secret that you have reached that age for which you longed and prayed, sighing for youth which was a time of sin, missing the chance to show some true maturity! I hope that the daughters of Wisdom will avoid such foolishness. The harder we work to conceal our age the more we reveal it.

Or does your eternal life depend on the youthful appearance of your hair? Is that the incorruptibility which we have to put on for the reign that is to come—the incorruptibility promised by the kingdom that will be free from sin? Well, indeed, you speed toward the Lord, well you make haste to be free from this most wicked world, you who find it unpleasant to approach your own end!

Chapter 8

Of course, I am now merely talking as a man and, jealous 1 of women, I try to deprive them of what is their own! But are there not certain things that are forbidden to us, too, out of regard for the sobriety we should maintain out of fear we owe to God?

Now, since, by a defect of nature, there is inborn in men because of women (just as in women because of men) the desire to please, the male sex also has its own peculiar trickeries for enhancing their appearance: for instance, cutting the beard a bit too sharply, trimming it too neatly, shaving around the mouth, arranging and dyeing our hair, darkening the first signs of gray hair, disguising the down on the whole body with some female ointments, smoothing off the rest of the body by means of some gritty powder, then always taking occasion to look in a mirror, gazing anxiously into it. Are not all of these things quite idle and hostile to modesty once we have known God, have put aside the desire to please others and forsworn all lasciviousness?

For, where God is there is modesty, where modesty is there is dignity, its assistant and companion. How shall we ever practice modesty if we do not make use of its normal means, that is, dignity? How shall we ever be able to make use of dignity in practicing modesty unless we bear a certain seriousness in our countenance, in our dress, and in the appearance of the entire man?

Chapter 10

Of course, it was God who taught men how to dye wool 1 with the juice of herbs and the slime of shells; it had escaped Him, when He bade all things to come into existence, to issue a command for the production of purple and scarlet sheep! It was God, too, who devised the manufacture of those very garments which, light and thin in themselves, are heavy only in their price; God it was who produced such a great amount of gold for the careful setting and fitting of jewels; and it was God, too, to be sure, who caused the puncturing of ears and was so interested in tormenting his own creatures as to order suffering to infants with their first breath; and this, in order that from these scars on the body—it seems as if the latter was born to be cut—there might hang some sort of precious stones which, as is well known, the Parthians insert in their shoes in place of studs!

As a matter of fact, this gold whose glitter you find so attractive is used by some nations for chains, as pagan literature tells us. And so, it is not because of intrinsic value that these things are good, but merely because they happen to be rare. After artistic skills, however, had been introduced by the fallen angels, who had also discovered the materials themselves, elaborate workmanship, combined with the rareness of these things, brought about the idea of their being precious and stimulated the desire on the part of the women to possess them because of their precious character.

Now, if these very angels who discovered the material substances of this kind as well as their charms—I mean gold and precious stones—and passed on the techniques of working them and taught, among other things, the use of eyelid-powder and the dyeing of cloth, if these angels, I say, condemned by God, as Henoch tells us, how are we ever going to please God by taking pleasure in things developed by those who because of those acts provoked the wrath and punishment of God?

I will grant you that God foresaw all these things and that He has permitted them, and that Isaias does not object to any purple garments, permits the wearing of an ornament shaped like a bunch of grapes in the hair, and finds no fault with crescent-shaped necklaces. Still, let us not flatter ourselves, as the pagans are accustomed to do, that God is merely the Creator of the world and thereafter pays no attention to the works He has created.

Could we not be acting much more usefully and cau- 5 tiously if we were to presume that all these things have been provided by God at the beginning and placed in the world in order that they should now be means of testing the moral strength of His servants, so that, in being permitted to use things, we might have the opportunity of showing our self-restraint? Do not wise masters purposely offer and permit some things to their servants in order to try them and to see whether and how they make use of things thus permitted, whether they will do so with moderation and honesty?

However, is not that servant deserving more praise who abstains totally, thus manifesting a reverential fear of the kindness of his master? Therefore the Apostle concludes: "All things are lawful, but not all things are expedient." It will be much easier for one to dread what is forbidden who has a reverential fear of what is permitted.

Chapter 13

Some women may say: "I do not need the approval of 1 men. For I do not ask for the testimony of men: it is God who sees my heart." We all know that, to be sure, but let us recall what the Lord said through the Apostle: "Let your modesty appear before men." Why would he have said that unless we should be an example and a witness to those who are evil? Or, what did Christ mean by "let your works shine before men"? Why did the Lord call us "the light of the world"? Why did He compare us to a city set on a mountain if we were not to shine in (the midst of) darkness and stand out among those who are sunk down?

"If you hide your light under the measure," you will necessarily be lost in darkness and run down by many people. It is our good works that make us to be the lights of the world. Moreover, what is good, provided it be true and full, does not love the darkness; it rejoices to be seen and exults in being pointed out by others.

It is not enough for Christian modesty merely to be so, but to seem so, too. So great and abundant ought to be your modesty that it may flow out from the mind to the garb, and burst forth from the conscience to the outer appearance, so that even from the outside it may examine, as it were, its own–furniture—a furniture that is suited to retain the faith forever. We must, therefore, get rid of such delicacies as tend by their softness and effeminacy to weaken the strength of our faith.

Otherwise, I am not so sure that the wrist which is always surrounded by a bracelet will be able to bear the hardness of chains with resignation; I have some doubts that the leg which now rejoices to wear an anklet will be able to bear the tight squeeze of an ankle chain; and I sometimes fear that the neck which is now laden with strings of pearls and emeralds will give no room to the executioner's sword.

Therefore, my blessed sisters, let us think of the hardships to come, and we will not feel them. Let us abandon luxuries and we will never miss them. Let us stand ready to endure every violence, having nothing which we would be afraid to leave behind. For, these things are really the bonds that hold down the wings of our hope. Let us cast away the ornaments of this world if we truly desire those of heaven.

Do not love gold—that substance which caused the very first sins of the people of Israel to be branded with infamy. You should hate that which ruined your fathers, that gold which they adored when they abandoned God, for even then gold was food for the fire.

But the lives of Christians are never spent in gold, and now less than ever, but in iron. The stoles of martyrdom are being prepared, and the angels who are to carry us (to heaven) are being awaited.

Go forth to meet those angels, adorned with the cosmetics and ornaments of the Prophets and Apostles. Let your whiteness flow from simplicity, let modesty be the cause of your rosy complexion; paint your eyes with demureness, your mouth with silence; hang on your ears the words of God, bind on your neck the yoke of Christ; bow your heads to your husbands—and that will be ornament enough for you. Keep your hands busy with spinning and stay at home—and you will be more pleasing than if you were adorned in gold. Dress yourselves in the silk of probity, the fine linen of holiness, and the purple of chastity. Decked out in this manner, you will have God Himself for your lover.

Questions for Critical Thinking

1. What role did the concept of original sin play in Tertullian's teachings? What impact did the concept of original sin have on early Christian culture?

2. How does Tertullian reconcile Christian values with Greco-Roman culture?

7

LATE ANTIQUITY
The Transformation of the Roman Empire and the Triumph of Christianity

ST. AUGUSTINE
Selections from *Confessions* and *The City of God*

St. Augustine (354–430 CE) is one of the West's pivotal figures who appear at disjunctures in time and whose mission seems to be to culminate one phase of civilization and point history on a new path. St. Augustine, who lived in the final days of the western Roman Empire (476 CE is the traditional date of its fall), functioned as a bridge between the dying classical era and the embryonic Christian world. Born in North Africa to a Christian mother (Monica) and pagan father, he was a pagan himself until he joined Christianity at age thirty-three. Later, he became Bishop of Hippo, an ancient city near his birthplace; from that post, through his vast writings, he dominated the Roman world for almost thirty-five years. Fusing his knowledge of Greco-Roman philosophy, especially Platonism (see Plato, *The Republic* and *Phaedo*, in Chapter 3) and Neoplatonism, with his understanding of Christian beliefs, he developed a theology now called Augustinianism. This theology provided a justification for a religious-centered world—the intellectual framework in which the Christian church operated until about 1300. A controversialist who wrote on every major Christian topic of his day, including original sin, salvation, and God and history, he became an authoritative voice whose influence is still active in Catholic theology.

St. Augustine was possessed of a ferocious vision that saw life on earth as a vale of tears through which humanity must travel. Within this vale of tears, St. Augustine did not sit idly on the sidelines; he actively engaged in the intellectual wars that consumed this age. Reflecting his self-ascribed natural combativeness, he had, before turning Christian, subscribed for nine years to Manichaeanism, a religion that viewed the world as locked in a gigantic struggle between the forces of good and the forces of evil. He relished acrimonious quarrels, notably with fellow churchmen who differed from him on difficult points in theology. A prolific author, he wrote many pamphlets, letters, and essays that belong to Christian theology, as well as two classics of world literature: *Confessions* (ca. 390s), his personal memoirs; and *The City of God* (ca. 420s), his Christian-inspired philosophy of history.

Reading the Selection from Confessions

Prior to Book VIII of *Confessions*, St. Augustine recounted his youth, education, and above all, his search for a final truth, whether philosophical or religious. What fueled his personal search was his longing to feel moral, to gain relief from the guilt that had dogged him since youth, stemming from such sins as stealing pears and, in the main, consorting with mistresses. He often found solutions to his quest in, for example, the writings of Cicero (see *On the Republic* in Chapter 5) or the dualistic religion of the Manichaeans; however, none of these could finally quench his restless spirit.

Book VIII of *Confessions* concludes Augustine's quest with his conversion to Christianity. The heart of his conversion story occurs in Chapter 12. While reading a passage from the Bible, St. Augustine feels flooded with light, and his earlier darkness falls away. Now, as a Christian convert, he hurries to tell his mother, who is overjoyed to learn that God has answered her prayers.

Reading the Selections from **The City of God**

In 410 CE the Visigoths, a tribe of German invaders, sacked Rome, a calamity that had happened only once before (400 BCE) in the city's eleven-hundred-year history. Pagans blamed this most recent calamity on the weak Christian God. To counter this pagan charge, Augustine wrote *The City of God* and, in the process, formulated a philosophy of history that was highly influential throughout the Middle Ages.

The City of God numbers about a thousand pages, divided into twenty-two books. Books I–X recount Rome's history and summarize pagan philosophical and religious arguments against Christian beliefs. In Books XI–XXII, Augustine sets forth his main theme about the City of Man and the City of God, which constitutes a belief in predestination: The citizens of the City of Man are doomed to hell, and the citizens of the City of God are destined for heaven. In Book XIV, he asserts that the two cities may be distinguished from one another by their origins. In Chapter 17 of Book XIX, he points out that the two cities may coexist, except in regard to religious laws. Here, Augustine laid down the principle of separation of church and state, an issue that became a battleground in medieval Europe and about which skirmishes are still being fought.

∾

Confessions
Book VIII

10

There are many abroad[1] *who talk of their own fantasies and lead men's minds astray.* They assert that because they have observed that there are two wills at odds with each other when we try to reach a decision, we must therefore have two minds of different natures, one good, the other evil. *Let them vanish at God's presence as the smoke vanishes.* As long as they hold these evil beliefs they are evil themselves, but even they will be good if they see the truth and accept it, so that your apostle may say to them *Once you*

were all darkness; now, in the Lord you are all daylight. These people want to be light, not in the Lord, but in themselves, because they think that the nature of the soul is the same as God. In this way their darkness becomes denser still, because in their abominable arrogance they have separated themselves still further from you, who are *the true Light which enlightens every soul born into the world.* I say to them, "Take care what you say, and blush for shame. Enter God's presence, and find their enlightenment; *here is no room for downcast looks.*"

When I was trying to reach a decision about serving the Lord my God, as I had long intended to do, it was I who willed to take this course and again it was I who willed not to take it. It was I and I alone. But I neither willed to do it nor refused to do it with my full will. So I was at odds with myself. I was throwing myself into confusion. All this happened to me although I did not want it, but it did not prove that there was some second mind in me besides my own. It only meant that my mind was being punished. *My action*

---

[1] **many abroad** The Manichaeans, followers of Manichaeanism, a dualistic religion, based on the beliefs that matter is evil and the soul is good. They taught that salvation came from knowledge of the soul's oneness with God; ethically, they abstained from the things of the flesh; founded in Persia by the prophet Mani (d. 274/277 CE). Augustine, before becoming Christian, was a Manichaean.

did not come from me, but from the sinful principle that dwells in me.[2] It was part of the punishment of a sin freely committed by Adam, my first father.

If there were as many different natures in us as there are conflicting wills, we should have a great many more natures than merely two. Suppose that someone is trying to decide whether to go to the theatre or to the Manichees' meetinghouse. The Manichees will say, "Clearly he has two natures, the good one bringing him here to us and the bad one leading him away. Otherwise, how can you explain this dilemma of two opposing wills?" I say that the will to attend their meetings is just as bad as the will to go off to the theatre,[3] but in their opinion it can only be a good will that leads a man to come to them. Suppose then that one of us is wavering between two conflicting wills and cannot make up his mind whether to go to the theatre or to our church. Will not the Manichees be embarrassed to know what to say? Either they must admit—which they will not do—that it is a good will which brings a man to our church, just as in their opinion it is a good will which brings their own communicants and adherents to their church; or they must presume that there are two evil natures and two evil minds in conflict in one man. If they think this, they will disprove their own theory that there is one good and one evil will in man. The only alternative is for them to be converted to the truth and to cease to deny that when a man tries to make a decision, he has one soul which is torn between conflicting wills.

So let us hear no more of their assertion, when they observe two wills in conflict in one man, that there are two opposing minds in him, one good and the other bad, and that they are in conflict because they spring from two opposing substances and two opposing principles. For you, O God of truth, prove that they are utterly wrong. You demolish their arguments and confound them completely. It may be that both the wills are bad. For instance, a man may be trying to decide whether to commit murder by poison or by stabbing; whether he should swindle another man out of one part of his property or another, that is, if he cannot obtain both; whether he should spend his money extravagantly on pleasure or hoard it like a miser; or whether he should go to the games in the circus or to the theatre, when there is a performance at both places on the same day. In this case there may be a third possibility, that he should go and rob another person's house, if he has the chance. There may even be a fourth choice open to him, because he may wonder whether to go and commit adultery, if the occasion arises at the same time. These possibilities may all occur at the same moment and all may seem equally desirable. The man cannot do all these things at once, and his mind is torn between four wills which cannot be reconciled—perhaps more than four, because there are a great many things that he might wish to do. But the Manichees do not claim that there are as many different substances in us as this.

It is just the same when the wills are good. If I question the Manichees whether it is good to find pleasure in reading Paul's Epistles or in the tranquil enjoyment of a Psalm or in a discussion of the Gospel, they will reply in each case that it is good. Supposing, then, that a man finds all these things equally attractive and the chance to do all of them occurs at the same time, is it not true that as long as he cannot make up his mind which of them he most wants to do his heart is torn between several different desires? All these different desires are good, yet they are in conflict with each other until he chooses a single course to which the will may apply itself as a single whole, so that it is no longer split into several different wills.

The same is true when the higher part of our nature aspires after eternal bliss while our lower self is held back by the love of temporal pleasure. It is the same soul that wills both, but it wills neither of them with the full force of the will. So it is wrenched in two and suffers great trials, because while truth teaches it to prefer one course, habit prevents it from relinquishing the other.

11

This was the nature of my sickness. I was in torment, reproaching myself more bitterly than ever as I twisted and turned in my chain. I hoped that my chain might be broken once and for all, because it was only a small thing that held me now. All the same it held me. And you, O Lord, never ceased to watch over my secret heart. In your stern mercy you lashed me with the twin scourge of fear and shame in case I should give way once more and the worn and slender remnant of my chain should not be broken but gain new strength and bind me all the faster. In my heart I kept saying "Let it be now, let it be now!", and merely by saying this I was on the point of making the resolution. I was on the point of making it, but I did not succeed. Yet I did not fall back into my old state. I stood on the brink of resolution, waiting to take fresh breath. I tried again and came a little nearer to my goal, and then a little nearer still, so that I could almost reach out and grasp it. But I did not reach it. I could not reach out to it or grasp it, because I held back from the step by which I should die to death and become alive to life. My lower instincts, which had taken firm hold of me, were stronger than the higher, which were untried. And the closer I came to the moment which was to mark the great change in me, the more I shrank from its horror. But it did not drive me back or turn me from my purpose: it merely left me hanging in suspense.

I was held back by mere trifles, the most paltry inanities, all my old attachments. They plucked at my garment of flesh and whispered, "Are you going to dismiss us? From this moment we shall never be with you again, for ever and ever. From this moment you will never again be allowed to do this thing or that, for evermore." What was it, my God, that they meant when they whispered "this thing or that"? Things so sordid and so shameful that I beg you in your mercy to keep the soul of your servant free from them! These voices, as I heard them, seemed less than half as loud as they had been before. They no

---

[2] *My action . . . dwells in me.* Romans 7:17.
[3] **the theatre** The early Christian Church considered the theatre to be evil.

longer barred my way, blatantly contradictory, but their mutterings seemed to reach me from behind, as though they were stealthily plucking at my back, trying to make me turn my head when I wanted to go forward. Yet, in my state of indecision, they kept me from tearing myself away, from shaking myself free of them and leaping across the barrier to the other side, where you were calling me. Habit was too strong for me when it asked "Do you think you can live without these things?"

But by now the voice of habit was very faint. I had turned my eyes elsewhere, and while I stood trembling at the barrier, on the other side I could see the chaste beauty of Continence[4] in all her serene, unsullied joy, as she modestly beckoned me to cross over and to hesitate no more. She stretched out loving hands to welcome and embrace me, holding up a host of good examples to my sight. With her were countless boys and girls, great numbers of the young and people of all ages, staid widows and women still virgins in old age. And in their midst was Continence herself, not barren but a fruitful mother of children, of joys born of you, O Lord, her Spouse. She smiled at me to give me courage, as though she were saying, "Can you not do what these men and these women do? Do you think they find the strength to do it in themselves and not in the Lord their God? It was the Lord their God who gave me to them. Why do you try to stand in your own strength and fail? Cast yourself upon God and have no fear. He will not shrink away and let you fall. Cast yourself upon him without fear, for he will welcome you and cure you of your ills." I was overcome with shame, because I was still listening to the futile mutterings of my lower self and I was still hanging in suspense. And again Continence seemed to say, "Close your eyes to the unclean whispers of your body, so that it may be mortified. It tells you of things that delight you, but not such things as the law of the Lord your God has to tell."

In this way I wrangled with myself, in my own heart, about my own self. And all the while Alypius[5] stayed at my side, silently awaiting the outcome of this agitation that was new in me.

12

I probed the hidden depths of my soul and wrung its pitiful secrets from it, and when I mustered them all before the eyes of my heart, a great storm broke within me, bringing with it a great deluge of tears. I stood up and left Alypius so that I might weep and cry to my heart's content, for it occurred to me that tears were best shed in solitude. I moved away far enough to avoid being embarrassed even by his presence. He must have realized what my feelings were, for I suppose I had said something and he had known from the sound of my voice that I was ready to burst into tears. So I stood up and left him where we had been sitting, utterly bewildered. Somehow I flung

myself down beneath a fig tree and gave way to the tears which now streamed from my eyes, the sacrifice that is acceptable to you. I had much to say to you, my God, not in these very words but in this strain: *Lord, will you never be content? Must we always taste your vengeance? Forget the long record of our sins.* For I felt that I was still the captive of my sins, and in my misery I kept crying "How long shall I go on saying 'tomorrow, tomorrow'? Why not now? Why not make an end of my ugly sins at this moment?"

I was asking myself these questions, weeping all the while with the most bitter sorrow in my heart, when all at once I heard the sing-song voice of a child in a nearby house. Whether it was the voice of a boy or a girl I cannot say, but again and again it repeated the refrain "Take it and read, take it and read." At this I looked up, thinking hard whether there was any kind of game in which children used to chant words like these, but I could not remember ever hearing them before. I stemmed my flood of tears and stood up, telling myself that this could only be a divine command to open my book of Scripture and read the first passage on which my eyes should fall. For I had heard the story of Antony,[6] and I remembered how he had happened to go into a church while the Gospel was being read and had taken it as a counsel addressed to himself when he heard the words *Go home and sell all that belongs to you. Give it to the poor, and so the treasure you have shall be in heaven; then come back and follow me.*[7] By this divine pronouncement he had at once been converted to you.

So I hurried back to the place where Alypius was sitting, for when I stood up to move away I had put down the book containing Paul's Epistles. I seized it and opened it, and in silence I read the first passage on which my eyes fell: *Not in revelling and drunkenness, not in lust and wantonness, not in quarrels and rivalries. Rather, arm yourselves with the Lord Jesus Christ; spend no more thought on nature and nature's appetites.*[8] I had no wish to read more and no need to do so. For in an instant, as I came to the end of the sentence, it was as though the light of confidence flooded into my heart and all the darkness of doubt was dispelled.

I marked the place with my finger or by some other sign and closed the book. My looks now were quite calm as I told Alypius what had happened to me. He too told me what he had been feeling, which of course I did not know. He asked to see what I had read. I showed it to him and he read on beyond the text which I had read. I did not know what followed, but it was this: *Find room among you for a man of over-delicate conscience.*[9] Alypius applied this to himself and told me so. This admonition was enough to give him strength, and without suffering the distress of hesitation he made his resolution and took this good purpose to himself. And it very well suited his moral character, which had long been far, far better than my own.

Then we went in and told my mother,[10] who was overjoyed. And when we went on to describe how it had all

---

[4] **Continence** Self-restraint, especially the ability to control bodily desires.
[5] **Alypius** A friend of Augustine.

[6] **Antony** St. Antony of Egypt (d. 356), patron saint of monks.
[7] *Go home . . . and follow me.* Matthew 19:21.
[8] *Not in revelling . . . nature's appetites.* Romans 13:13–14.
[9] *Find room . . . over-delicate conscience.* Romans 14:1.
[10] **mother** Monica (333–387), later St. Monica; born in Tagaste (modern Souk-Ahras, Algeria).

happened, she was jubilant with triumph and glorified you, *who are powerful enough, and more than powerful enough, to carry out your purpose beyond all our hopes and dreams.* For she saw that you had granted her far more than she used to ask in her tearful prayers and plaintive lamentations. You converted me to yourself, so that I no longer desired a wife or placed any hope in this world but stood firmly upon the rule of faith, where you had shown me to her in a dream so many years before. And you *turned her sadness into rejoicing,* into joy far fuller than her dearest wish, far sweeter and more chaste than any she had hoped to find in children begotten of my flesh.

∞

The City of God
Book XIV

Chapter 28
The Character of the Two Cities

We see then that the two cities were created by two kinds of love: the earthly city was created by self-love reaching the point of contempt for God, the Heavenly City by the love of God carried as far as contempt of self. In fact, the earthly city glories in itself, the Heavenly City glories in the Lord. The former looks for glory from men, the latter finds its highest glory in God, the witness of a good conscience. The earthly lifts up its head in its own glory, the Heavenly City says to its God: "My glory; you lift up my head."[11] In the former, the lust for domination lords it over its princes as over the nations it subjugates; in the other both those put in authority and those subject to them serve one another in love, the rulers by their counsel, the subjects by obedience. The one city loves its own strength shown in its powerful leaders; the other says to its God, "I will love you, my Lord, my strength."[12]

Consequently, in the earthly city its wise men who live by men's standards have pursued the goods of the body or of their own mind, or of both. Or those of them who were able to know God "did not honour him as God, nor did they give thanks to him, but they dwindled into futility in their thoughts, and their senseless heart was darkened: in asserting their wisdom"—that is, exalting themselves in their wisdom, under the domination of pride—"they became foolish, and changed the glory of the imperishable God into an image representing a perishable man, or birds or beasts or reptiles"—for in the adoration of idols of this kind they were either leaders or followers of the general public—"and they worshipped and served created things instead of the Creator, who is blessed for ever."[13] In the Heavenly City, on the other hand, man's only wisdom is the devotion which rightly worships the true God, and looks for its reward in the fellowship of the saints, not only holy men but also holy angels, "so that God may be all in all."[14]

[11] **"My glory . . . my head."** Psalm 3:3.
[12] **"I will . . . my strength."** Psalm 18:1.

[13] **"did not honour . . . who is blessed for ever."** Romans 1:21ff.
[14] **"so that God may be all in all."** 1 Corinthians 15:29.

Book XV

Chapter 4
Conflict and Peace in the Earthly City

The earthly city will not be everlasting; for when it is condemned to the final punishment it will no longer be a city. It has its good in this world, and rejoices to participate in it with such gladness as can be derived from things of such a kind. And since this is not the kind of good that causes no frustrations to those enamoured of it, the earthly city is generally divided against itself by litigation, by wars, by battles, by the pursuit of victories that bring death with them or at best are doomed to death. For if any section of that city has risen up in war against another part, it seeks to be victorious over other nations, though it is itself the slave of base passions; and if, when victorious, it is exalted in its arrogance, that victory brings death in its train. Whereas if it considers the human condition and the changes and chances common to mankind, and is more tormented by possible misfortunes than puffed up by its present success, then its victory is only doomed to death. For it will not be able to lord it permanently over those whom it has been able to subdue victoriously.

However, it would be incorrect to say that the goods which this city desires are not goods, since even that city is better, in its own human way, by their possession. For example, that city desires an earthly peace, for the sake of the lowest goods; and it is that peace which it longs to attain by making war. For if it wins the war and no one survives to resist, then there will be peace, which the warring sections did not enjoy when they contended in their unhappy poverty for the things which they could not both possess at the same time. This peace is the aim of wars, with all their hardships; it is this peace that glorious victory (so called) achieves.

Now when the victory goes to those who were fighting for the juster cause, can anyone doubt that the victory is a matter for rejoicing and the resulting peace is something to be desired? These things are goods and undoubtedly they are gifts of God. But if the higher goods are neglected, which belong to the City on high, where victory will be serene in the enjoyment of eternal and perfect peace—if these goods are neglected and those other goods are so desired as to be considered the only goods, or are loved more than the goods which are believed to be higher, the inevitable consequence is fresh misery, and an increase of the wretchedness already there.

Book XIX

Chapter 17
The Origin of Peace between the Heavenly Society and the Earthly City, and of Discord between Them

But a household of human beings whose life is not based on faith is in pursuit of an earthly peace based on the things belonging to this temporal life, and on its advantages, whereas a household of human beings whose life is based on faith looks forward to the blessings which are promised as eternal in the future, making use of earthly and temporal things like a pilgrim in a foreign land, who does not let himself be taken in by them or distracted from his course towards God, but rather treats them as supports which help him more easily to bear the burdens of "the corruptible body which weighs heavy on the soul"[15]; they must on no account be allowed to increase the load. Thus both kinds of men and both kinds of households alike make use of the things essential for this mortal life; but each has its own very different end in making use of them. So also the earthly city, whose life is not based on faith, aims at an earthly peace, and it limits the harmonious agreement of citizens concerning the giving and obeying of orders to the establishment of a kind of compromise between human wills about the things relevant to mortal life. In contrast, the Heavenly City—or rather that part of it which is on pilgrimage in this condition of mortality, and which lives on the basis of faith—must needs make use of this peace also, until this mortal state, for which this kind of peace is essential, passes away. And therefore, it leads what we may call a life of captivity in this earthly city as in a foreign land, although it has already received the promise of redemption, and the gift of the Spirit as a kind of pledge of it; and yet it does not hesitate to obey the laws of the earthly city by which those things which are designed for the support of this mortal life are regulated; and the purpose of this obedience is that, since this mortal condition is shared by both cities, a harmony may be preserved between them in things that are relevant to this condition.

But this earthly city has had some philosophers belonging to it whose theories are rejected by the teaching inspired by God. Either led astray by their own speculation or deluded by demons, these thinkers reached the belief that there are many gods who must be won over to serve human ends, and also that they have, as it were, different departments with different responsibilities attached. Thus the body is the department of one god, the mind that of another; and within the body itself, one god is in charge of the head, another of the neck and so on with each of the separate members. Similarly, within the mind, one is responsible for natural ability, another for learning, another for anger, another for lust; and in the accessories of life there are separate gods over the departments of flocks, grain, wine, oil, forests, coinage, navigation, war and victory, marriage, birth, fertility, and so on. The Heavenly City, in contrast, knows only one God as the object of worship, and decrees, with faithful devotion, that he only is to be served with that service which the Greeks call *latreia*,[16] which is due to God alone. And the result of this difference has been that the Heavenly City could not have laws of religion common with the earthly city, and in defence of her religious laws she was bound to dissent from those who thought differently and to prove a burdensome nuisance to them. Thus she had to endure their anger and hatred, and the assaults of persecution; until at length that City shattered the morale of her adversaries by the terror inspired by her numbers, and by the help she continually received from God.

While this Heavenly City, therefore, is on pilgrimage in this world, she calls out citizens from all nations and so collects a society of aliens, speaking all languages. She takes on account of any difference in customs, laws, and institutions, by which earthly peace is achieved and preserved—not that she annuls or abolishes any of those, rather, she maintains them and follows them (for whatever divergences there are among the diverse nations, those institutions have one single aim—earthly peace), provided that no hindrance is presented thereby to the religion which teaches that the one supreme and true God is to be worshipped. Thus even the Heavenly City in her pilgrimage here on earth makes use of the earthly peace and defends and seeks the compromise between human wills in respect of the provisions relevant to the mortal nature of man, so far as may be permitted without detriment to true religion and piety. In fact, that City relates the earthly peace to the heavenly peace, which is so truly peaceful that it should be regarded as the only peace deserving the

---

[15] **"the corruptible body . . . the soul"** Wisdom 9:15.

[16] *latreia* Latria, in Greek, means "the state of a hired servant"; used here by Augustine to refer to divine service to God.

name, at least in respect of the rational creation; for this peace is the perfectly ordered and completely harmonious fellowship in the enjoyment of God, and of each other in God. When we arrive at that state of peace, there will be no longer a life that ends in death, but a life that is life in sure and sober truth; there will be no animal body to "weigh down the soul" in its process of corruption; there will be a spiritual body with no cravings, a body subdued in every part to the will. This peace the Heavenly City possesses in faith while on its pilgrimage, and it lives a life of righteousness, based on this faith, having the attainment of that peace in view in every good action it performs in relation to God, and in relation to a neighbour, since the life of a city is inevitably a social life.

Questions for Critical Thinking

1. In the *Confessions,* how does St. Augustine describe the Manichaeans, and what does he think of them?
2. Describe the scene of St. Augustine's conversion in *Confessions.* What single event led him to read the Bible, and what was the message of the passage he read?
3. In *The City of God,* what are the origins of the Two Cities and their basic characteristics?
4. Discuss the "discord" that exists between the Heavenly Society and the Earthly City in *The City of God.* Can this discord be resolved? Why or why not?

EUSEBIUS
Selections from *The History of the Church*

Eusebius of Caesarea (ca. 260–340) wrote a history of the Christian church that covered events from its founding by Christ to the time of Constantine (r. 306–337), the first Christian Roman emperor. Since Eusebius believed that God operated in human affairs and that the future belonged to the Christians, he concluded that a history of the spread of Christianity would disseminate these beliefs to a wider audience. He intended this didactic book for fellow Christians, but he also had in mind Rome's educated elite, most of whom were pagan when he wrote. Recognized today as the "founder of ecclesiastical history," Eusebius set the standard for church history until the Renaissance, when modern research methods, with their human-centered outlook and concern for scientific accuracy, rendered his pious type of history obsolete. Still, his account remains a classic, for it is one of the main sources for events and historical figures in the first years of Christianity.

Eusebius was probably born in Caesarea, in Palestine, an early Christian center under Roman rule. As a young man, he was mentored by Pamphilius, a devout and classically trained Christian whose school awakened Eusebius to the challenge of reconciling Christian thought with Greco-Roman learning. With Pamphilius, he wrote several books—all since lost—on Christian themes. Because of his beliefs, Eusebius was imprisoned in 309 and 311 in Rome's empire-wide assault on Christianity and its leaders. But in 314 he was made Bishop of Caesarea, a step that reflected Rome's changed policy toward Christians coincident with Constantine's conversion in 312. As Bishop of Caesarea, Eusebius himself baptized the pagan emperor into the new faith. Favored by Constantine, Eusebius grew in reputation to become one of the era's outstanding Christians, playing important roles at the historic Council of Nicaea and other church gatherings.

The History of the Church, arranged in ten books, was written over a sixteen-year period, a time frame based on internal evidence, such as mentions of historic events datable from other sources. Begun during the Great Persecution in 309, this history was completed in 325, when

Constantine was presiding over a Christianized imperial court and Eusebius was one of its ornaments. Eusebius's plan for the book embraced a wide range of topics—namely, tracing the "lines of succession" of the first apostles, telling the stories of early Christian leaders, exposing heretics, detailing the calamities suffered by the Jews because of their treatment of Jesus, setting forth Rome's final assault on the Christian faith, and paying homage to the martyrs whose blood was "the seed of the church," in the words of another early Christian writer, Tertullian (see Chapter 6).

Reading the Selections

These passages from Eusebius's work show his method of writing God-centered history. Focusing on a person or event as a framing device, he creates a historical snapshot and at the same time stresses his belief in God's presence everywhere. For example, the treatment of the executions of Peter and Paul dwells on both their martyrdom and the folly of Emperor Nero, "the first to be heralded as a conspicuous fighter against God." Just so, the narratives of the Great Persecution blend details of Roman atrocities with a moving account of Christians willingly facing martyrdom. Finally, Constantine's triumph is described, although Eusebius makes it clear that the result was because of God, "in his fulfillment of His purpose."

❧

The Neronian Persecutions, in Which Peter and Paul Died

When Nero's[17] power was now firmly established he gave 1 himself up to unholy practices and took up arms against the God of the universe. To describe the monster of depravity that he became lies outside the scope of the present work. Many writers have recorded the facts about him in minute detail, enabling anyone who wishes to get a complete picture of this perverse and extraordinary madness, which led him to the senseless destruction of innumerable lives, and drove him in the end to such a lust for blood that he did not spare even his nearest and dearest but employed a variety of methods to do away with mother, brothers, and wife alike, to say nothing of countless other members of his family, as if they were personal and public enemies. All this left one crime still to be added to his account— he was the first of the emperors to be the declared enemy of the worship of Almighty God. To this the Roman Tertullian[18] refers in the following terms:

Study your records: there you will find that Nero was the first to persecute this teaching when, after subjecting the entire East, in Rome especially he treated everyone with savagery. That such a man was author of our chastisement fills us with pride. For anyone who knows him can understand that anything not supremely good would never have been condemned by Nero.

So it came about that this man, he first to be heralded as a conspicuous fighter against God, was led on to murder the apostles. It is recorded that in his reign Paul was beheaded in Rome itself, and that Peter was likewise crucified, and the record is confirmed that the cemeteries there are still called by the names of Peter and Paul, and equally so by a churchman named Gaius[19] who was living while Zephyrinus[20] was Bishop of Rome. In his published Dialogue with Proclus,[21] the leader of the Phrygian heretics, Gaius has this to say about the places where the mortal remains of the two apostles have been reverently laid:

I can point out the monuments of the victorious apostles. If you will go as far as the Vatican or the Ostian Way, you will find the monuments of those who founded this church.

That they were both martyred at the same time Bishop 5 Dionysius of Corinth[22] informs us in a letter written to the Romans:

---

[17] **Nero** Cruel and immoral Roman emperor (54–68) who led a dissipated private life and murdered members of his family and political rivals.
[18] **Tertullian** (ca. 160–ca. 230) Early church writer who defended the Christian faith and defined many of its practices and traditions.

[19] **Gaius** Also known as Caius. Early-third-century Christian writer.
[20] **Zephyrinus** Bishop of Rome 199–217.
[21] **Proclus** During the persecutions of Christians by Emperor Severus (193–211) Proclus, a Christian, was tortured and later became a heretic. The Phrygian heretics were so named because they originated in Phrygia, a Roman province in Asia Minor. The Phrygians believed in the power of the Holy Spirit and lived a highly ethical life.
[22] **Bishop Dionysius of Corinth** One of his letters, cited by Eusebius and now lost, refers to the martyrdom of Peter and Paul. Dionysius of Corinth lived in the late second century.

In this way by your impressive admonition you have bound together all that has grown from the seed which Peter and Paul sowed in Romans and Corinthians alike. For both of them sowed in our Corinth and taught us jointly: in Italy too they taught jointly in the same city, and were martyred at the same time.

These evidences make the truth of my account still more certain.

The Destruction of the Churches

Everything indeed has been fulfilled in my time; I saw 1 with my own eyes the places of worship thrown down from top to bottom, to the very foundations, the inspired holy Scriptures committed to the flames in the middle of the public squares, and the pastors of the churches hiding disgracefully in one place or another, while others suffered the indignity of being held up to ridicule by their enemies—a reminder of another prophetic saying: for contempt was poured on rulers, and He made them wander in a trackless land where there was no road. But it is not for me to describe their wretched misfortunes in the event: nor is it my business to leave on record their quarrels and inhumanity to each other before the persecutions, so I have made up my mind to relate no more about them than enough to justify the divine judgment. I am determined therefore to say nothing even about those who have been tempted by the persecution or have made complete shipwreck of their salvation and of their own accord flung themselves into the depths of the stormy sea; I shall include in my overall account only those things by which first we ourselves, then later generations, may benefit. Let me therefore proceed from this point to describe in outline the hallowed ordeals of the martyrs of God's word.

It was the nineteenth year of Diocletian's[23] reign and the month Dystrus, called March by the Romans, and the festival of the Saviour's Passion[24] was approaching, when an imperial decree was published everywhere, ordering the churches to be razed to the ground and the Scriptures destroyed by fire and giving notice that those in places of honour would lose their places, and domestic staff, if they continued to profess Christianity, would be deprived of their liberty. Such was the first edict against us. Soon afterwards other decrees arrived in rapid succession, ordering that the presidents of the churches in every place should all be first committed to prison and then coerced by every possible means into offering sacrifice.

----

[23] **Diocletian** Roman emperor (284–305) Chief of the four rulers of the Roman Empire who reformed and centralized the government, reorganized and enlarged the army, and, in 303, issued an edict against the Christians, thus initiating a decade of persecutions (303–313).

[24] **Saviour's Passion** The days of the trial and execution of Jesus Christ.

Ordeals Endured in the Persecution: God's Glorious Martyrs

Then, then it was that many rulers of the churches bore 1 up heroically under horrible torments, an object lesson in the endurance of fearful ordeals; while countless others, their souls already numbed with cowardice, promptly succumbed to the first onslaught. Of the rest, each was subjected to a series of different tortures, one flogged unmercifully with the whip, another racked and scraped beyond endurance, so that the lives of some came to a most miserable end. But different people came through the ordeal very differently: one man would be forcibly propelled by others and brought to the disgusting, unholy sacrifices, and dismissed as if he had sacrificed, even if he had done no such thing; another, who had not even approached any abomination, much less touched it, but was said by others to have sacrificed, would go away without attempting to repudiate the baseless charge. Another would be picked up half dead, and thrown away as if already a corpse; and again a man lying on the ground might be dragged a long way by his feet, though included among the willing sacrifices. One man would announce at the top of his voice his determination not to sacrifice, another would shout that he was a Christian, exulting in the confession of the Saviour's Name, while yet another insisted that he had never sacrificed and never would. These were struck on the mouth and silenced by a formidable body of soldiers lined up for the purpose: their faces and cheeks were battered and they were forcibly removed. It was the one object in life of the enemies of true religion to gain credit for having finished the job.

But no such methods could enable them to dispose of the holy martyrs. What could I say that would do full justice to them? I could tell of thousands who showed magnificent enthusiasm for the worship of the God of the universe, not only from the beginning of the general persecution, but much earlier when peace was still secure. For at long last the one who had received the authority was as it were awaking from the deepest sleep, after making attempts—as yet secret and surreptitious—against the churches, in the interval that followed Decius and Valerian.[25] He did not make his preparations all at once for the war against us, but for the time being took action only against members of the legions. In this way he thought that the rest would easily be mastered if he joined battle with these and emerged victorious. Now could be seen large numbers of serving soldiers most happy to embrace civil life, in order to avoid having to repudiate their loyalty

---

[25] **Decius and Valerian** The Roman emperors Decius (249–251) and Valerian (253–260) had similar careers as soldiers and persecutors of Christians.

to the Architect of the universe. The commander-in-chief, whoever he was, was now first setting about persecuting the soldiery, classifying and sorting those serving in the legions, and allowing them to choose either to obey orders and retain their present rank, or alternatively to be stripped of it if they disobeyed the enactment. But a great many soldiers of Christ's kingdom without hesitation or question chose to confess Him rather than cling to the outward glory and prosperity they enjoyed. Already here and there one or two of them were suffering not only loss of position but even death as the reward of their unshakable devotion: for the time being the man behind the plot was acting cautiously and going as far as bloodshed in a few cases only; he was apparently afraid of the number of believers, and shrank from launching out into war with them all at once. But when he stripped more thoroughly for battle, words are inadequate to depict the host of God's noble martyrs whom the people of every city and every region were privileged to see with their own eyes.

Victory of Constantine; the Benefits He Conferred on His Subjects

When Licinius[26] had rushed headlong to the limits of madness, this seemed no longer endurable to the emperor,[27] God's friend who—reasoning along sound lines and tempering the rigidity of justice with humanity—determined to rescue the tyrant's victims, and by putting a few destroyers out of the way made haste to save the bulk of the human race. He had treated Licinius with nothing but kindness hitherto, and had shown mercy where no sympathy deserved. But Licinius grew no better: his wickedness continued unabated, and he raged more and more madly against his subject peoples; while for his victims there remained no hope of escape, with a wild beast tyrannizing over them.

And so, his love of goodness blended with a hatred of evil, the champion of the good set out with his son Crispus,[28] that most humane emperor by his side, holding

---

[26] **Licinius** The Roman emperor Valerius Licinianus Licinius (308–324) was the sole emperor in the Eastern Empire. He won many battles in the Eastern Empire, was the ally of Constantine the Great until they became enemies, and was defeated by Constantine in 324 and executed.
[27] **the emperor** Constantine the Great (307–337), who emerged as sole emperor of the Western Empire after several battles. Christians believe that at this last triumphant battle a divine sign appeared in the sky: a cross and the words (translated into English) "by this sign thou shalt conquer." Seeing the sign, Constantine converted to Christianity and issued the Edict of Milan (313), which extended rights and toleration to Christians. Constantine ruled as sole emperor after defeating Licinius in 324. He took an active role in church disputes and helped shape church policies and doctrines. The city of Byzantium was renamed renamed Constantinople in his honor.
[28] **Crispus** Son of Constantine, a soldier and a victor in a naval battle against Licinius. Executed by Constantine on the charge of high treason in 326.

out a saving hand to all who were perishing. Then, taking God the Universal King, and God's Son the Saviour of all, as Guide and Ally, father and son together divided their battle array against God's enemies on every side, and easily carried off the victory: every detail of the encounter was made easy for them by God, in fulfillment of His purpose. Suddenly in less time than it takes to say it, those who a day or two before had been breathing death and threats were no more, and even their name was forgotten; their portraits and tributes were swept into merited oblivion; and the very things that Licinius with his own eyes had seen befall the wicked tyrants who preceded him he underwent himself, because he did not allow himself to be disciplined or learn wisdom from the blows that fell on his neighbours; and having pursued the same path of wickedness as they, he deservedly toppled over the identical cliff.

His adversary thus finally thrown down, the mighty victor Constantine, pre-eminent in every virtue that true religion can confer, with his son Crispus, an emperor most dear to god and in every way resembling his father, won back their own eastern lands and reunited the Roman Empire into a single whole, bringing it all under their peaceful sway, in a wide circle embracing north and south alike from east to the farthest west. Men had now lost all fear of their former oppressors; day after day they kept dazzling festival; light was everywhere, and men who once dared not look up greeted each other with smiling face and shining eyes. They danced and sang in city and country alike, giving honour first of all to God our Sovereign Lord, as they had been instructed, and then to the pious emperor with his sons, so dear to God. Old troubles were forgotten, and all irreligion passed into oblivion;

good things present were enjoyed, those yet to come eagerly awaited. In every city the victorious emperor published decrees full of humanity and laws that gave proof of munificence and true piety. Thus all tyranny had been purged away, and the kingdom that was theirs was preserved securely and without question for Constantine

and his sons alone. They, having made it their first task to wipe the world clean from the hatred of God, rejoiced in the blessings that He had conferred upon them, and, by the things they did for all men to see, displayed love of virtue and love of God, devotion and thankfulness to the Almighty.

∞

Questions for Critical Thinking

1. What inspired Eusebius to write a history of the early Christian church using the language he did?

2. Compare Eusebius and a historian today, focusing on writing style, point of view, and how each explains historical change.

8

THE HEIRS TO THE ROMAN EMPIRE: BYZANTIUM AND THE WEST IN THE EARLY MIDDLE AGES

Selection from *Beowulf*

Beowulf is the first great poem in the English tradition. Its language was Anglo-Saxon, or Old English. It was composed orally, probably in England in the eighth century, and is preserved, presumably in complete form, in a single manuscript dating from about 1000. Like *The Epic of Gilgamesh* (see Chapter 1) and Homer's *Iliad* (see Chapter 2), it is an epic, meant originally to be recited rather than read. Composed anonymously, *Beowulf* gives voice to the creative Anglo-Saxon imagination as it peopled the dark with primordial monsters.

The poem focuses on Beowulf, prince of the Geats (a tribe in Sweden). In the first part, Beowulf sails to Denmark to rescue King Hrothgar from Grendel and Grendel's mother, two monsters. Swamp-dwellers, the monsters have been attacking Hrothgar's great hall by night and devouring his people. Beowulf kills the monsters. Back home, he is made king of the Geats and reigns for fifty years. In the second half of the poem, Beowulf faces a dragon. With his comrade Wiglaf's help, Beowulf defeats the dragon, only to die of his wounds.

Woven into *Beowulf* is a chilling theme: the never-ceasing battle of good against evil. The poem shows that evil never sleeps and comes in many forms, demonic and human, and that good, however vigilant, does not always win. Like Greek drama (see Sophocles' *Oedipus the King* in Chapter 3), it offers the gloomy message that life is tragic and nothing is guaranteed.

Beowulf was written in alliterative verse, a rhymeless verse characterized by the repetition of consonant sounds, usually at the beginning of words, as in this example from a modern translation:

> *Down off the moorlands' misting fells came*
> *Grendel stalking; God's brand was on him.*
> *The spoiler meant to snatch away*
> *From the high hall some of human race.*

Alliterative verse was typical of Anglo-Saxon poetry and remained an essential feature of English poetry until the late Middle Ages.

The setting in which Beowulf fights Grendel may be primitive and chaotic, but the society that spawned the poem was not. Modern scholars describe eighth-century England as Christian, law-abiding, and aristocratic. The Anglo-Saxons of the period were civilized, much altered from their pagan ancestors who settled England on the heels of the Roman withdrawal in about 400 CE.

Reading the Selection

This brief selection from *Beowulf* deals with the defeat of the half-human Grendel. Among other things, it offers some insight into the poet's religious faith. The poet's world is decidedly Christian. Yet the older, primitive world of Anglo-Saxon myth keeps breaking through, in Beowulf's savagery and later in the primordial, nonhuman dragon. This seeming contradiction may be resolved by recognizing that the poem was composed when the Anglo-Saxon conversion to Christianity was only about one century old.

Beowulf's love of fame, or glory, also comes from the pre-Christian, Anglo-Saxon world. Not Christian salvation but desire for glory was his prime motive for living. "To Beowulf the glory of this fight was granted." At the epic's end (not included here), his epitaph reads: "The gentlest and most gracious of men, the kindest to his people and the most desirous of renown."

. . .

Gliding through the shadows came 1
the walker in the night; the warriors slept
whose task was to hold the horned building,
all except one. It was well-known to men
that the demon could not drag them to the shades
without God's willing it; yet the one man kept
unblinking watch. He awaited, heart swelling
with anger against his foe, the ordeal of battle.
Down off the moorlands' misting fells came
Grendel stalking; God's brand was on him.   10
The spoiler meant to snatch away
from the high hall some of human race.
He came on under the clouds, clearly saw at last
the gold-hall of men, the mead-drinking place
nailed with gold plates. That was not the first visit
he had paid to the hall of Hrothgar the Dane:[1]
he never before and never after
harder luck nor hall-guards found.

Walking to the hall came this warlike creature
condemned to agony. The door gave way,   20
toughened with iron, at the touch of those hands.
Rage-inflamed, wreckage-bent, he ripped open
the jaws of the hall. Hastening on,
the foe then stepped onto the unstained floor,
angrily advanced: out of his eyes stood
an unlovely light like that of fire.
He saw then in the hall a host of young soldiers,
a company of kinsmen caught away in sleep,
a whole warrior-band. In his heart he laughed then,
horrible monster, his hopes swelling   30
to a gluttonous meal. He meant to wrench
the life from each body that lay in the place
before night was done. It was not to be;
he was no longer to feast on the flesh of mankind
after that night.

Narrowly the powerful
kinsman of Hygelac[2] kept watch how the ravager
set to work with his sudden catches;
nor did the monster mean to hang back.
As a first step he set his hands on   40
a sleeping soldier, savagely tore at him,
gnashed at his bone-joints, bolted huge gobbets,
sucked at his veins, and had soon eaten
all of the dead man, even down to his
hands and feet.
        Forward he stepped,
stretched out his hands to seize the warrior
calmly at rest there, reached out for him with his
unfriendly fingers: but the faster man
forestalling, sat up, sent back his arm.   50
The upholder of evils at once knew
he had not met, on middle earth's
extremest acres, with any man
of harder hand-grip: his heart panicked.
He was quit of the place no more quickly for that.

Eager to be away, he ailed for his darkness
and the company of devils; the dealings he had there
were like nothing he had come across in his lifetime.
Then Hygelac's brave kinsman called to mind
that evening's utterance, upright he stood,   60
fastened his hold till fingers were bursting.
The monster strained away: the man stepped closer.
The monster's desire was for darkness between them,
direction regardless, to get out and run
for his fen-bordered lair; he felt his grip's strength
crushed by his enemy. It was an ill journey
the rough marauder had made to Heorot.[3]

---

[1] **Hrothgar the Dane** King of the Danish people.

[2] **Hygelac** King of the Geats and uncle to Beowulf; Beowulf is not named in this passage, but he is described as the "powerful kinsman," the "brave kinsman," and the "great-hearted kinsman" of Hygelac.

[3] **Heorot** The mead hall, or gathering place, for the Danes.

The crash in the banqueting-hall came to the Danes,
the men of the guard that remained in the building,
with the taste of death. The deepening rage 70
of the claimants to Heorot caused it to resound.
It was indeed wonderful that the wine-supper-hall
withstood the wrestling pair, that the world's palace
fell not to the ground. But it was girt firmly,
both inside and out, by iron braces
of skilled manufacture. Many a figured
gold-worked wine-bench, as we heard it,
started from the floor at the struggles of that pair.
The men of the Danes had not imagined that
any of mankind by what method soever 80
might undo that intricate, antlered hall,
sunder it by strength—unless it were swallowed up in
the embraces of fire.
                    Fear entered into
the listening North Danes, as that noise rose up again
strange and strident. It shrilled terror
to the ears that heard it through the hall's side-wall,
the grisly plaint of God's enemy,
his song of ill-success, the sobs of the damned one
bewailing his pain. He was pinioned there 90
by the man of all mankind living
in this world's estate the strongest of his hands.

Not for anything would the earls' guardian
let his deadly guest go living:
he did not count his continued existence
of the least use to anyone. The earls ran
to defend the person of their famous prince;
they drew their ancestral swords to bring
what aid they could to their captain, Beowulf.
They were ignorant of this, when they entered the fight, 100
boldly-intentioned battle-friends,
to hew at Grendel, hunt his life
on every side—that no sword on earth,
not the truest steel, could touch their assailant;
for by a spell he had dispossessed all
blades of their bite on him.
                    A bitter parting
from life was that day destined for him;
the eldritch spirit was sent off on his
far faring into the fiends' domain. 110

It was then that this monster, who, moved by spite
against human kind, had caused so much harm

—so feuding with God—found at last
that flesh and bone were to fail him in the end;
for Hygelac's great-hearted kinsman
had him by the hand; and hateful to each
was the breath of the other.
                    A breach in the giant
flesh-frame showed then, shoulder-muscles
sprang apart, there was a snapping of tendons, 120
bone-locks burst. To Beowulf the glory
of this fight was granted; Grendel's lot
to flee the slopes fen-ward with flagging heart,
to a den where he knew there could be no relief,
no refuge for a life at its very last stage,
whose surrender-day had dawned. The Danish hopes
in this fatal fight had found their answer.

He had cleansed Heorot. He who had come from afar,
deep-minded, strong-hearted, had saved the hall
from persecution. He was pleased with his night's work, 130
the deed he had done. Before the Danish people
the Great captain had made good his boast,
had taken away all their unhappiness,
the evil menace under which they had lived,
enduring it by dire constraint,
no slight affliction. As a signal to all
the hero hung up the hand, the arm
and torn-off shoulder, the entire limb,
Grendel's whole grip, below the gable of the roof.

There was, as I heard it, at hall next morning 140
a great gathering in the gift-hall yard
to see the wonder. Along the wide highroads
the chiefs of the clans came from near and far
to see the foe's footprints. It may fairly be said
that his parting from life aroused no pity in any
who tracked the spoor-blood of his blind flight
for the monster's mere-pool; with mood flagging
and strength crushed, he had staggered onwards;
each step evidenced his ebbing life's blood.
The tarn was troubled; a terrible wave-thrash 150
brimmed it, bubbling; black-mingled,
the warm wound-blood welled upwards.
He had dived to his doom, he had died miserably;
here in his fen-lair he had laid aside
his heathen soul. Hell welcomed it.

Questions for Critical Thinking

1. Discuss and give some examples of the imagery used to describe Grendel in his appearance and his character.

2. How does Beowulf kill Grendel, what proof does he offer of Grendel's death, and what does the fight between Beowulf and Grendel symbolize?

...

BENEDICT OF NURSIA
Selections from *The Rule of St. Benedict*

Western monasticism (from the Greek *monos*, "to live alone") originated in the early years of the Christian church. From its birth, the church existed outside the Roman law, as an underground faith, its members the target of persecution by the Roman state. In this turbulent setting, some men and a few women withdrew from the world to follow their faith in isolated, single-sex communities. After Christianity became the official religion of Rome (ca. 400), monasticism came into its own. Until the Protestant Reformation began (1517), it played a central role in European life and culture, by

- raising the moral level of society (monks and nuns took strict religious vows);
- contributing to the feudal economy (monasteries owned vast tracts of farmlands);
- helping define the era's art and architecture (monastic complexes, comprising several buildings, were filled with various forms of religious art);
- strengthening intellectual life (monasteries founded schools, where the Greek and Latin classics were copied and taught); and
- meeting social needs (monasteries functioned as hospitals and retirement homes).

The monastic impulse sprang from many sources, especially from the Christian scriptures' call for a new covenant (Hebrews 8:8–12) with God. Lacking an authoritative guide, the early monks and nuns would sometimes engage in excessive practices to demonstrate their religious faith, such as fasting until death or scourging and even mutilating their bodies. To rein in unbridled religious zeal, the Italian monk Benedict of Nursia (480–543) founded a monastery on Monte Cassino, in central Italy (ca. 529), where the monks' lives were regulated by an abbot (from Greek and Aramaic *abba*, "my father"). *The Rule of St. Benedict* is the work he wrote for the guidance of the abbot. Monte Cassino's success soon spawned a network of Benedictine abbeys across Europe. Later monastic orders adapted the Benedictine model to their own ends. Thus, St. Benedict can truly be hailed as "the father of Western monasticism."

St. Benedict envisioned a community ruled by a judicious, yet compassionate abbot. *The Rule* was to function as a constitution for the group of monks, and the abbot himself was not above the monastic "laws." Both he and the monks were held to the same high moral standard: to make lifelong vows of poverty, chastity, and obedience; for the monks, the latter meant obedience to the abbot. Membership in the monastery required a year of probation—a tactic designed to weed out the uncertain and the unstable.

The Rule allowed no personal time for the monks. They ate and prayed together but, otherwise, stayed busy except for the Sabbath and holy days. Six days a week, they engaged in physical labor (tilling the fields or working in the shops—a monastic complex was economically self-sufficient) or spiritual exercises (study, prayer, or mediation). At night, the monks slept alone in sparsely furnished cells, or rooms. By joining physical and spiritual labors in the Benedictine *Rule*, a monastery offered hope of salvation for many and, at the same time, was a valuable cog in the feudal economy.

Reading the Selections

These fourteen selections from St. Benedict's *Rule* range over many matters, from "the qualities necessary for an abbot," through "obedience" and "humility" to "the daily labor of the monks" and "monks should not have personal property." Although the classic monastic vows are in the forefront, it is also clear that many other issues are in play, including knowing when to speak and when to keep silent; restraining pride in thought and speech; training the monks equally, regardless of social background; and setting forth the proper ritual admission to the monastic order.

∞

The qualities necessary for an abbot.—The abbot who is worthy to rule over a monastery ought always to bear in mind by what name he is called and to justify by his life his title of superior. For he represents Christ in the monastery, receiving his name from the saying of the apostle:[4] "Ye have received the Spirit of adoption, whereby we cry, Abba, Father" [Rom. 8:15]. Therefore the abbot should not teach or command anything contrary to the precepts of the Lord, but his commands and his teaching should be in accord with divine justice. He should always bear in mind that both his teaching and the obedience of his disciples will be inquired into on the dread day of judgment. For the abbot should know that the shepherd will have to bear the blame if the Master finds anything wrong with the flock. Only in case the shepherd has displayed all diligence and care in correcting the fault of a restive and disobedient flock will he be freed from blame at the judgment of God, and be able to say to the Lord in the words of the prophet: "I have not hid thy righteousness within my heart; I have declared thy faithfulness and thy salvation" [Ps. 40:10]; but "they despising have scorned me" [Ezek. 20:27]. Then shall the punishment fall upon the flock who scorned his care and it shall be the punishment of death. The abbot ought to follow two methods in governing his disciples: teaching the commandments of the Lord to the apt disciples by his words, and to the obdurate and the simple by his deeds. And when he teaches his disciples that certain things are wrong, he should demonstrate in his own life not doing those things, lest when he has preached to others he himself should be a castaway [1 Cor. 9:27], and lest God should sometime say to him, a sinner: "What has thou to do to declare my statues, or that thou shouldest take my covenant in thy mouth? Seeing that thou hatest instruction, and castest my words behind thee" [Ps. 50:16, 17], or "Why beholdest thou the mote that is in thy brother's eye, but considerest not the beam that is in thine own eye?" [Matt. 7:3]. Let there be no respect of persons in the monastery. Let the abbot not love one more than another, unless it be one who excels in good works and in obedience. The freeman is not to be preferred to the one who comes into the monastery out of servitude, unless there be some other good reason. But if it seems right and fitting to the abbot, let him show preference to anyone of any rank whatsoever; otherwise let them keep their own places. For whether slave or free, we are all one in Christ [Gal. 3:28] and bear the same yoke of servitude to the one Lord, for there is no respect of persons with God [Rom. 2:11]. For we have special favor in His sight only in so far as we excel others in all good works and in humility. Therefore, the abbot should have the same love toward all and should subject all to the same discipline according to their respective merits. In his discipline the abbot should follow the rule of the apostle who says: "Reprove, rebuke, exhort" [2 Tim. 4:2].

That is, he should suit his methods to the occasion, using either threats or compliments, showing himself either a hard master or a loving father, according to the needs of the case. Thus he should reprove harshly the obdurate and disobedient, but the obedient, the meek, and the gentle he should exhort to grow in grace. We advise also that he rebuke and punish those who neglect and scorn his teaching. He should not disregard the transgressions of sinners, but should strive to root them out as soon as they appear, remembering the peril of Eli, the priest of Siloam.[5] Let him correct the more worthy and intelligent with words for the first or second time, but the wicked and hardened and scornful and disobedient he should punish with blows in the very beginning of their fault, as it is written: "A fool is not bettered by words" [cf. Prov. 17:10]; and again "Thou shalt beat him with the rod, and shalt deliver his soul from hell" [Prov. 23:14].

The abbot should always remember his office and his title, and should realize that as much is intrusted to him, so also much will be required from him. Let him realize how difficult and arduous a task he has undertaken, to rule the hearts and care for the morals of many persons, who require, one encouragements, another threats, and another persuasion. Let him so adapt his methods to the disposition and intelligence of each one that he may not only preserve the flock committed to him entire and free from harm, but may even rejoice in its increase. . . .

. . .

Obedience.—The first grade of humility is obedience without delay, which is becoming to those who hold nothing dearer than Christ. So, when one of the monks receives a command from a superior, he should obey it immediately, as if it came from God himself, being impelled thereto by the holy service he has professed and by the fear of hell and the desire of eternal life. Of such the Lord says: "As soon as he heard of me, he obeyed me" [Ps. 17:44]; and again to the apostles, "He that heareth you, heareth me" [Luke 10:16]. Such disciples, when they are commanded, immediately abandon their own business and their own plans, leaving undone what they were at work upon. With ready hands and willing feet they hasten to obey the commands of their superior, their act following on the heels of his command, and both the order and the fulfillment occurring, as it were, in the same moment of time—such promptness does the fear of the Lord inspire.

Good disciples who are inspired by the desire for eternal life gladly take up that narrow way of which the Lord said: "Narrow is the way which leadeth unto life" [Matt. 7:14]. They have no wish to control their own lives or to obey their own will and desires, but prefer to be ruled by an abbot, and to live in a monastery, accepting

---

[4] **the Apostle** St. Paul. In medieval times, the saint is commonly called the Apostle.

[5] **Eli . . . Siloam** I Samuel, chs. 1–4. Eli, high priest and a judge of Israel, was punished by God for failing to correct his sinful sons, who also were priests. Siloam is another name for Shiloh.

the guidance and control of another. Surely such disciples follow the example of the Lord who said: "I came not to do mine own will, but the will of him that sent me" [John 6:38]. But this obedience will be acceptable to God and pleasing to men only if it be not given fearfully, or halfheartedly, or slowly, or with grumbling and protests. For the obedience which is given to a superior is given to God, as he himself has said: "Who heareth you, heareth me" [Luke 10:16]. Disciples ought to obey with glad hearts, "for the Lord loveth a cheerful giver" [2 Cor. 9:7]. If the disciple obeys grudgingly and complains even within his own heart, his obedience will not be accepted by God, who sees his unwilling heart; he will gain no favor for works done in that spirit, but, unless he does penance and mends his ways, he will rather receive the punishment of those that murmur against the Lord's commands.

. . .

Humility.—Now the first step of humility is this, to escape destruction by keeping ever before one's eyes the fear of the Lord, to remember always the commands of the Lord, for they who scorn him are in danger of hell-fire, and to think of the eternal life that is prepared for them that fear him. So a man should keep himself in every hour from the sins of the heart, of the tongue, of the eyes, of the hands, and of the feet. He should cast aside his own will and the desires of the flesh; he should think that God is looking down on him from heaven all the time, and that his acts are seen by God and reported to him hourly by his angels. For the prophet shows that the Lord is ever present in the midst of our thoughts, when he says: "God trieth the hearts and the reins" [Ps. 7:9], and again, "The Lord knoweth the thoughts of men" [Ps. 94:11], and again he says, "Thou hast known my thoughts from afar" [Ps. 139:2], and "The thoughts of a man are known to thee" [Ps. 76:11]. So a zealous brother will strive to keep himself from perverse thoughts by saying to himself: "Then only shall I be guiltless in his sight, if I have kept me from mine iniquity" [Ps. 18:23]. And the holy Scriptures teach us in divers places that we should not do our own will; as where it says: "Turn from thine own will" [Ecclesiasticus 18:30]; and where we ask in the Lord's Prayer that his will be done in us; and where it warns us: "There is a way that seemeth right unto a man, but the end thereof are the ways of death" [Prov. 14:12]; and again, concerning the disobedient: "They are corrupt and abominable in their desires" [Ps. 14:1]. And we should always remember God is aware of our fleshly desires; as the prophet says, speaking to the Lord: "All my desire is before thee" [Ps. 38:9]. Therefore, we should shun evil desires, for death lieth in the way of the lusts; as the Scripture shows, saying: "Go not after thy lusts" [Ecclesiasticus 18:30]. Therefore since the eyes of the Lord are upon the good and the wicked, and since "the Lord looked down from heaven upon the children of men to see if there were any that did understand and seek God" [Ps. 14:2], and since our deeds are daily reported to him by the angels whom he assigns to each one of us; then, surely, brethren, we should be on our guard every hour, lest at any time, as the prophet says in the Psalms, the Lord should look down upon us as we are

falling into sin, and should spare us for a space, because he is merciful and desires our conversion, but should say at the last: "These things hast thou done and I kept silence" [Ps. 50:21].

The second step of humility is this, that a man should not delight in doing his own will and desires, but should imitate the Lord who said: "I came not to do mine own will, but the will of him that sent me" [John 6:38]. And again the Scripture saith: "Lust hath its punishment, but hardship winneth a crown."

The third step of humility is this, that a man be subject to his superior in all obedience for the love of God, imitating the Lord, of whom the apostle says: "He became obedient unto death" [Phil. 2:8].

The fourth step of humility is this, that a man endure all the hard and unpleasant things and even undeserved injuries that come in the course of his service, without wearying or withdrawing his neck from the yoke, for the Scripture saith: "He that endureth to the end shall be saved" [Matt. 10:22], and again: "Comfort thy heart and endure the Lord" [Ps. 27:14]. And yet again the Scripture, showing that the faithful should endure all unpleasant things for the Lord, saith, speaking in the person of those that suffer: "Yea, for thy sake are we killed all the day long; we are counted as sheep for the slaughter" [Ps. 44:22]; and again, rejoicing in the sure hope of divine reward: "In all things, we are more than conquerors through him that loved us" [Rom. 8:37]; and again in another place: "For thou, O God, hast proved us; thou hast tried us as silver is tried; thou broughtest us into the net, thou laidst affliction upon our loins" [Ps. 66:10 f]; and again to show that we should be subject to a superior: "Thou hast placed men over our heads" [Ps 66:12]. Moreover, the Lord bids us suffer injuries patiently, saying: "Whosoever shall smite thee on the right cheek, turn to him the other also. And if any man will sue thee at the law, and take away thy coat, let him have thy cloak also. And whosoever shall compel thee to go a mile, go with him twain" [Matt. 5:39–41]. And with the apostle Paul we should suffer with false brethren, and endure persecution, and bless them that curse us.

The fifth step of humility is this, that a man should not hide the evil thoughts that arise in his heart or the sins which he has committed in secret, but should humbly confess them to his abbot; as the Scripture exhorteth us, saying "Commit thy way unto the Lord, trust also in him" [Ps. 37:5]; and again: "O, give thanks unto the Lord, for he is good; for his mercy endureth forever" [Ps. 106:1]; and yet again the prophet saith: "I have acknowledged my sin unto thee, and mine iniquity have I not hid. I said, I will confess my transgressions unto the Lord; and thou forgavest the iniquity of my sin" [Ps. 32:5].

The sixth step of humility is this, that the monk should be contented with any lowly or hard condition in which he may be placed, and should always look upon himself as an unworthy laborer, not fitted to do what is intrusted to him; saying to himself in the words of the prophet: "I was reduced to nothing and was ignorant; I was as a beast before thee and I am always with thee" [Ps. 73:22 f].

The seventh step of humility is this, that he should not only say, but should really believe in his heart that he is the lowest and most worthless of all men, humbling himself and saying with the prophet: "I am a worm and no man; a reproach of men, and despised of all people" [Ps. 22:6]; and "I that was exhalted am humbled and confounded" [Ps. 88:15]; and again: "It is good for me that I have been afflicted, that I might learn thy statues" [Ps. 119:71].

. . .

The order of divine worship during the day.—The prophet says: "Seven times a day do I praise thee" [Ps. 119:164]; and we observe this sacred number in the seven services of the day; that is, matins, prime, terce, sext, nones, vespers, and completorium; for the hours of the daytime are plainly intended here, since the same prophet provides for the nocturnal vigils, when he says in another place: "At midnight I will rise to give thanks unto thee" [Ps. 119:62]. We should therefore praise the Creator for his righteous judgments at the aforesaid times: matins, prime, terce, sext, nones, vespers, and completorium; and at night we should rise to give thanks unto Him.[6]

. . .

The daily labor of the monks.—Idleness is the great enemy of the soul, therefore the monks should always be occupied, either in manual labor or in holy reading. The hours for these occupations should be arranged according to the seasons, as follows: From Easter to the first of October, the monks shall go to work at the first hour and labor until the fourth hour, and the time from the fourth to the sixth hour shall be spent in reading. After dinner, which comes at the sixth hour, they shall lie down and rest in silence; but anyone who wishes may read, if he does it so as not to disturb anyone else. Nones shall be observed a little earlier, about the middle of the eighth hour, and the monks shall go back to work, laboring until vespers. But if the conditions of the locality or the needs of the monastery, such as may occur at harvest time, should make it necessary to labor longer hours, they shall not feel themselves ill-used, for true monks should live by the labor of their own hands, as did the apostles and the holy fathers. But the weakness of human nature must be taken into account in making these arrangements. From the first of October to the beginning of Lent, the monks shall have until the full second hour for reading, at which hour the service of terce shall be held. After terce, they shall work at their respective tasks until the ninth hour. When the ninth hour

sounds they shall cease from labor and be ready for the service at the second bell. After dinner they shall spend the time in reading the lessons and the psalms. During Lent the time from daybreak to the third hour shall be devoted to reading, and then they shall work at their appointed tasks until the tenth hour. At the beginning of Lent each of the monks shall be given a book from the library of the monastery which he shall read entirely through. One or two of the older monks shall be appointed to go about through the monastery during the hours set apart for reading, to see that none of the monks are idling away the time, instead of reading, and so not only wasting their own time but perhaps disturbing others as well. Anyone found doing this shall be rebuked for the first or second offence, and after that he shall be severely punished, that he may serve as a warning and an example to others. Moreover, the brothers are not to meet together at unseasonable hours. Sunday is to be spent by all the brothers in holy reading, except by such as have regular duties assigned to them for that day. And if any brother is negligent or lazy, refusing or being unable profitably to read or meditate at the time assigned for that, let him be made to work, so that he shall at any rate not be idle. The abbot shall have consideration for the weak and the sick, giving them tasks suited to their strength, so that they may neither be idle not yet be distressed by too heavy labor.

Monks should not have personal property.—The sin of owning private property should be entirely eradicated from the monastery. No one shall presume to give or receive anything except by the order of the abbot; no one shall possess anything of his own, books, paper, pens, or anything else; for monks are not to own even their own bodies and wills to be used at their own desire, but are to look to the father [abbot] of the monastery for everything. So they shall have nothing that has not been given or allowed to them by the abbot; all things are to be had in common according to the command of the Scriptures, and no one shall consider anything as his own property. If anyone has been found guilty of this most grievous sin, he shall be admonished for the first and second offence, and then if he does not mend his ways he shall be punished.

All the brothers are to be treated equally.—It is written: "Distribution was made unto every man as he had need" [Acts 4:35]. This does not mean that there should be respect of persons, but rather consideration for infirmities. The one who has less need should give thanks to God and not be envious; the one who has greater need should be humbled because of his infirmity, and not puffed up by the greater consideration shown him. Thus all members of the congregation shall dwell together in peace. Above all let there be no complaint about anything, either in word or manner, and if anyone is guilty of this let him be strictly disciplined.

. . .

Silence is to be kept after completorium.—The monks should observe the rule of silence at all times, but especially during the hours of the night. This rule shall be observed both on fast-days and on other days, as follows: on

---

[6] **seven services . . . Him** One of the first records of the Divine Office, part of the Catholic liturgy. A Divine Office is a duty performed for God. The Divine Office was organized according to medieval custom, which divided the day into twelve hours, followed by twelve hours of night. The length of the hours varied by the season. Benedict, in this passage, sets forth the prayer services to be held by the monks: matins, at daybreak; prime, the first part of day; terce, the third part of the day; sext, the sixth part of the day; nones, the ninth part of the day; vespers, early evening; and completorium, or compline, at bedtime. One nocturnal service, vigils, was held about midnight.

other than fast-days, as soon as the brothers rise from the table they shall sit down together, while one of them reads from the Collations or the lives of the fathers or other holy works. But the reading at this time shall not be from the Heptateuch or from the books of the Kings, which are not suitable for weak intellects to hear at this hour and may be read at other times. On fast-days the brethren shall assemble a little while after vespers, and listen to readings from the Collations. All shall be present at this reading except those who have been given other duties to be done at this time, and after the reading of four or five pages, or as much as shall occupy an hour's time, the whole congregation shall meet for completorium. After completorium no one shall be allowed to speak to another, unless some unforeseen occasion arises, as that of caring for guests, or unless the abbot has to give a command to some one; and in these cases such speaking as is necessary shall be done quietly and gravely. If anyone breaks this rule of silence he shall be severely disciplined.

. . .

Monks are not to receive letters or anything.—No monk shall receive letters or gifts or anything from his family or from any persons on the outside, nor shall he send anything, except by the command of the abbot. And if anything has been sent to the monastery for him he shall not receive it unless he has first shown it to the abbot and received his permission. And if the abbot orders such a thing to be received, he may yet bestow it upon anyone whom he chooses, and the brother to whom it was sent shall acquiesce without ill-will, lest he give occasion to the evil one by his discontent. If anyone breaks this rule, he shall be severely disciplined.

The vestiarius [one who has charge of the clothing] and the calciarius [one who has charge of the footwear].—The brothers are to be provided clothes suited to the locality and the temperature, for those in colder regions require warmer clothing than those in warmer climates. The abbot shall decide such matters. The following garments should be enough for those who live in moderate climates: A cowl and a robe apiece (the cowl to be of wool in winter and in summer light or old); a rough garment for work; and shoes and boots for the feet. The monks shall not be fastidious about the color and texture of these clothes, which are to be made of the stuff commonly used in the region where they dwell, or of the cheapest material. The abbot shall also see that the garments are of suitable length and not too short. When new garments are given out the old ones should be returned, to be kept in the wardrobe for the poor. Each monk may have two cowls and two robes to allow for change at night and for washing; anything more than this is superfluous and should be dispensed with as being a form of luxury. The old boots and shoes are also to be returned when new ones are given out. Those who are sent out on the road shall be provided with trousers, which shall be washed and restored to the vestiary when they return. There shall also be cowls and robes of slightly better material for the use of those who are sent on journeys, which also shall be given back when they return. A mattress, a blanket, a sheet, and a pillow shall be

sufficient bedding. The beds are to be inspected by the abbot frequently, to see that no monk has hidden away anything of his own in them, and if anything is found there which has not been granted to that monk by the abbot, he shall be punished very severely. To avoid giving occasion to this vice, the abbot shall see that the monks are provided with everything that is necessary: cowl, robe, shoes, boots, girdle,[7] knife, pen, needle, handkerchief, tablets, etc. For he should remember how the fathers did in this matter, as it is related in the Acts of the Apostles: "There was given unto each man according to his need" [Acts 2:45]. He should be guided in this by the requirements of the needy, rather than by the complaints of the discontented, remembering always that he shall have to give an account of all his decisions to God on the day of judgment.

The table of the abbot.—The table of the abbot shall always be for the use of guests and pilgrims, and when there are no guests the abbot may invite some of the brothers to eat with him. But in that case, he should see that one or two of the older brothers are always left at the common table to preserve the discipline of the meal.

Artisans of the monastery.—If there are any skilled artisans in the monastery, the abbot may permit them to work at their chosen trade, if they will do so humbly. But if any one of them is made proud by his skill in his particular trade or by his value to the monastery, he shall be made to give up that work and shall not go back to it until he has convinced the abbot of his humility. And if the products of any of these trades are sold, those who conduct the sales shall see that no fraud is perpetrated upon the monastery. For those who have any part in defrauding the monastery are in danger of spiritual destruction, just as Ananias and Sapphira[8] for this sin suffered physical death. Above all, avarice is to be avoided in these transactions; rather the prices asked should be a little lower than those current in the neighborhood, that God may be glorified in all things.

The way in which new members are to be received.—Entrance into the monastery should not be made too easy, for the apostle says: "Try the spirits, whether they are of God" [1 John 4:1]. So when anyone applies at the monastery, asking to be accepted as a monk, he should first be proved by every test. He shall be made to wait outside four or five days, continually knocking at the door and begging to be admitted; and then he shall be taken in as a guest and allowed to stay in the guest chamber a few days. If he satisfies these preliminary tests, he shall be made to serve a novitiate[9] of at least one year, during which he shall be placed under the charge of one of the older and wiser brothers, who shall examine him and prove, by every possible means, his sincerity, his zeal, his obedience, and his ability to endure shame. And he shall be told in the plainest manner all the hardships and difficulties of

20

---

[7] **girdle** A belt.
[8] **Ananias and Sapphira** A husband and wife (Acts 4, 5) in the early church, who told lies to God and promptly dropped dead on the spot. In folk culture, Ananias became a common epithet bestowed on liars.
[9] **novitiate** In the Catholic religion, the period of being a novice, that is, a probationary member of a religious order.

the life which he has chosen. If he promises never to leave the monastery [*stabilitas loci*] the rule shall be read to him after the first two months of his novitiate, and again at the end of six more months, and finally, four months later, at the end of his year. Each time he shall be told that this is the guide which he must follow as a monk, the reader saying to him at the end of the reading: "This is the law under which you have expressed a desire to live; if you are able to obey it, enter; if not, depart in peace." Thus he shall have been given every chance for mature deliberation and every opportunity to refuse the yoke of service. But if he still persists in asserting his eagerness to enter and his willingness to obey the rule and the commands of his superiors, he shall then be received into the congregation, with the understanding that from that day forth he shall never be permitted to draw back from the service or to leave the monastery. The ceremony of receiving a new brother into the monastery shall be as follows: first he shall give a solemn pledge, in the name of God and his holy saints, of constancy, conversion of life, and obedience (*stabilitas loci, conversio morum, obedientia*);[10] this promise shall be in writing drawn up by his own hand (or, if he cannot write, it may be drawn up by another at his request, and signed with his own mark), and shall be placed by him upon the altar in the presence of the abbot, in the name of the saints whose relics are in the monastery. Then he shall say: "Receive me, O Lord, according to thy word, and I shall live; let me not be cast down from mine expectation" [Ps. 119:116]; which shall be repeated by the whole congregation three times, ending with the "Gloria Patri." Then he shall prostrate himself at the feet

of all the brothers in turn, begging them to pray for him, and therewith he becomes a member of the congregation. If he has any property he shall either sell it all and give to the poor before he enters the monastery, or else he shall turn it over to the monastery in due form, reserving nothing at all for himself; for from that day forth he owns nothing, not even his own body and will. Then he shall take off his own garments there in the oratory, and put on the garments provided by the monastery. And those garments which he [took] off shall be stored away in the vestiary, so that if he should ever yield to the promptings of the devil and leave the monastery, he shall be made to put off the garments of a monk, and to put on his own worldly clothes, in which he shall be cast forth. But the written promise which the abbot took from the altar where he placed it shall not be given back to him, but shall be preserved in the monastery.

The presentation of children.—If persons of noble rank wish to dedicate their son to the service of God in the monastery, they shall make the promise for him, according to the following form: they shall bind his hand and the written promise along with the consecrated host in the altarcloth and thus offer him to God. And in that document they shall promise under oath that their son shall never receive any of the family property, from them or any other person in any way whatsoever. If they are unwilling to do this, and desire to make some offering to the monastery for charity and the salvation of their souls, they may make a donation from that property, reserving to themselves the usufruct during their lives, if they wish. This shall all be done so clearly that the boy shall never have any expectations that might lead him astray, as we know to have happened. Poor people shall do the same when they offer their sons; and if they have no property at all they shall simply make the promise for their son and present him to the monastery with the host before witnesses.

---

[10] ***stabilitas loci, conversio morum, obedientia*** The Latin for "constancy, conversion of life, and obedience." This language offers in summary fashion the lifelong vows taken by the monks.

∞

Questions for Critical Thinking

1. St. Benedict's *Rule* has been described as encouraging an abbot to be judicious and compassionate while dealing with his monks. Identify evidence in *The Rule* to support this characterization.

2. Explain the appeal of the Benedictine monasticism in medieval life. Would you want to follow this lifestyle today? Explain.

BEDE

Selection from *A History of the English Church and People*

The English poet and monk known as the Venerable Bede (673–735) spent nearly all his life in the church. At age seven his parents placed him under the care of an abbot (the head of a monastery); at nine he was moved to the new monastery at Jarrow, in northern England, where he remained for the rest of his life. At nineteen he became a deacon, a sign of his worthiness in the eyes of his ecclesiastical superiors, since by law, one was not to be made a deacon until age twenty-five. He was ordained a priest at thirty. According to his own account, Bede devoted much of his life to scholarship, writing books on the scriptures, lives of saints and abbots, hymns and epigrams, and above all, *A History of the English Church and People*—his masterpiece. Completed just before his death, this history reflected the recent triumph of Roman Catholicism over Celtic (Irish) Christianity, whose supporters clashed over the right to dominate England in the early eighth century. Indeed, some aspects of Celtic Christianity are apparent in Bede's own life, such as his extreme asceticism and love of learning. Still, he was a devout servant of the Pope and supporter of Roman theology.

A History of the English Church and People, consisting of five books, surveys the almost eight-hundred-year history of Britain from the mid–first century BCE to events in Bede's day. Book I covers the period from the founding of Roman Britain, under Julius Caesar, to 596 CE, when St. Augustine (not to be confused with the earlier saint of the same name who wrote *Confessions)* introduced Roman Catholicism into southeastern England. As the first Bishop of Canterbury, St. Augustine converted the king of Kent, ruler of one of the Anglo-Saxon kingdoms into which the land of England was then divided. Books II through V focus on church history, recounting the process by which the north-country Anglo-Saxons, as well as the Scots, were brought into the Christian fold.

More than a chronicler of events, Bede was a careful historian who consulted primary sources and took pains to get the dates right. If he has a flaw, it is that he was overly credulous concerning miracles, perhaps reflecting his years in a monastery. Bede believed that miracles did happen and were part of everyday life; as a historian, he simply documented their reported occurrence. Today's readers can thus learn from Bede's account about one of the fundamental ways in which eighth-century and twenty-first-century worldviews differ.

Reading the Selection

This selection from Bede's *History* is famous for being the only existing record of the first English poet, Caedmon, who was also a monk. Caedmon's story, including his call to be a poet and his death, appears in Book IV, Chapter 24, where Bede continues his account of the spread of Christianity among the English people. Caedmon is depicted as a simple man blessed with a genius for poetry, which Bede thinks is a gift from God. In his brief narrative, Bede inserts a few lines of Caedmon's lyrics translated into Latin (Bede's original work was in Latin). These lines constitute all that remains of Caedmon's poetry. Bede's interest in vernacular English poetry is highly unusual during this period, because all of his writings were in Latin, the language of the educated throughout medieval times.

Book IV

Chapter 24
A Brother of the Monastery Is Found to Possess God's Gift of Poetry (680 CE)

In this monastery of Streanaeshalch[11] lived a brother singularly gifted by God's grace. So skilful was he in composing religious and devotional songs that, when any passage of Scripture was explained to him by interpreters, he could quickly turn it into delightful and moving poetry in his own English tongue. These verses of his have stirred the hearts of many folk to despise the world and aspire to heavenly things. Others after him tried to compose religious poems in English, but none could compare with him; for he did not acquire the art of poetry from men or through any human teacher but received it as a free gift from God. For this reason he could never compose any frivolous or profane verses; but only such as had a religious theme fell fittingly from his devout lips. He had followed a secular occupation[12] until well advanced in years without ever learning anything about poetry. Indeed it sometimes happened at a feast that all the guests in turn would be invited to sing and entertain the company; then, when he saw the harp coming his way, he would get up from table and go home.

On one such occasion he had left the house in which the entertainment was being held and went out to the stable, where it was his duty that night to look after the beasts. There when the time came he settled down to sleep. Suddenly in a dream he saw a man standing beside him who called him by name, 'Caedmon,' he said, 'sing me a song.' 'I don't know how to sing,' he replied. 'It is because I cannot sing that I left the feast and came here.' The man who addressed him then said, 'But you shall sing to me.' 'What should I sing about?' he replied. 'Sing about the Creation of all things,' the other answered. And Caedmon immediately began to sing verses in praise of God the Creator that he had never heard before, and their theme ran thus:

> *Praise we the Fashioner now of Heaven's fabric,*
> *The majesty of his might and his mind's wisdom,*
> *Work of the world-warden, worker of all wonders,*
> *How he the Lord of Glory everlasting,*
> *Wrought first for the race of men Heaven as a rooftree,*
> *Then made he Middle Earth to be their mansion.*

This is the general sense, but not the actual words that Caedmon sang in his dream; for verses, however masterly, cannot be translated literally from one language into another without losing much of their beauty and dignity. When Caedmon awoke, he remembered everything that he had sung in his dream, and soon added more verses in the same style to a song truly worthy of God.

Early in the morning he went to his superior the reeve,[13] and told him about this gift. All of them agreed that Caedmon's gift had been given him by our Lord. And they explained to him a passage of scriptural history or doctrine and asked him to render it into verse if he could. He promised to do this, and returned next morning with excellent verses as they had ordered him. The abbess[14] was delighted that God had given such grace to the man, and advised him to abandon secular life and adopt the monastic state. And when she had admitted him into the Community as a brother, she ordered him to be instructed in the events of sacred history. So Caedmon stored up in his memory all that he learned, and like one of the clean animals chewing the cud, turned it into such melodious verse that his delightful renderings turned his instructors into auditors. He sang of the creation of the world,[15] the origin of the human race, and the whole story of Genesis. He sang of Israel's exodus from Egypt, the entry into the Promised Land, and many other events of scriptural history. He sang of the Lord's Incarnation, Passion, Resurrection, and Ascension into heaven, the coming of the Holy Spirit, and the teaching of the Apostles. He also made many poems on the terrors of the Last Judgement, the horrible pains of Hell, and the joys of the Kingdom of Heaven. In addition to these, he composed several others on the blessings and judgements of God, by which he sought to turn his hearers from delight in wickedness and to inspire them to love and do good. For Caedmon was a deeply religious man, who humbly submitted to regular discipline and hotly rebuked all who tried to follow another course. And so he crowned his life with a happy end.

For, when the time of his death drew near, he felt the onset of physical weakness for fourteen days, but not seriously enough to prevent his walking or talking the whole time. Close by there was a house to which all who were sick or likely to die were taken. Towards nightfall on the day when he was to depart this life, Caedmon asked his attendant to prepare a resting-place for him in this house. The attendant was surprised at this request from a man who did not appear likely to die yet; nevertheless, he did as he was asked. So Caedmon went to the house, and conversed and jested cheerfully with those who were already there; and when it was past midnight, he asked, 'Is the Eucharist[16] in the house?' 'Why do you want the Eucharist?'

---

[11] **Streanaeshalch** Port in North Yorkshire, England, near Whitby, the monastery home of Caedmon.
[12] **occupation** Caedmon was a cowherd before becoming a monk.

---

[13] **reeve** The manager of an estate; in this case, the manager of Whitby monastery lands.
[14] **abbess** St. Hilda (ca. 614–680), the founding abbess of the double monastery of Whitby.
[15] **creation of the world . . . Judgments of God** The key points of biblical scripture for Christians.
[16] **Eucharist** Also called Holy Communion, the bread and wine of the Christian sacrament.

they enquired; 'you are not likely to die yet, when you are talking so cheerfully to us and seem to be in perfect health.' 'Nevertheless,' he said, 'bring me the Eucharist.' And taking it in his hands, Caedmon asked whether they were all charitably disposed towards him, and whether they had any complaint or ill-feeling against him. They replied that they were all most kindly disposed towards him, and free from all bitterness. Then in turn they asked him to clear his heart of bitterness towards them. At once he answered: 'Dear sons, my heart is at peace with all the servants of God.' Then, when he had fortified himself with the heavenly Viaticum,[17] he prepared to enter the other life, and asked how long it would be before the brothers were roused to sing God's praises in the Night Office.[18] 'Not long,' they replied. 'Good, then let us wait until then,' he answered, and signing himself with the holy Cross, he laid his head on the pillow and passed away quietly in his sleep. So, having served God with a simple and pure mind, and with tranquil devotion, he left the world and departed to his presence by a tranquil death. His tongue, which had sung so many inspiring verses in praise of his Maker, uttered its last words in his praise as he signed himself with the Cross and commended his soul into his hands. For, as I have already said, Caedmon seems to have had a premonition of his death.

---

[17] **Viaticum** In Roman Catholicism, the administering of the **Eucharist** to a sick or dying person.

[18] **Night Office** In a monastery, the prayer session performed after midnight.

Questions for Critical Thinking

1. Describe early English poetry, as reflected in the life of the poet Caedmon.

2. How would you describe English secular life in the early middle ages, as reflected in Bede's *History*?

ANNA COMNENA
Selections from *The Alexiad*

The Alexiad, as the first known history written by a woman, is a milestone in world literature. The author was Anna Comnena (1083–1153), the daughter of the Byzantine emperor Alexius I, whose reign (1081–1118) is covered in her book. Ignored by the Byzantines, *The Alexiad* was absorbed into Western culture after being discovered by Renaissance scholars, who translated it from Greek into European languages. Today it is accepted as a valuable historical source, partly as an eyewitness account of Alexius's reign and, equally important, as a sound work of scholarship.

Alexius Comnenus, the subject of *The Alexiad*, ruled Byzantium during a crucial time in its history. His career began as the empire, racked by internal chaos, faced probable extinction from all sides: Seljuk Turks were on the move through Asia Minor, Normans advanced against Adriatic outposts, and varied tribes from the north menaced Constantinople, the capital. A gifted general and master of intrigue, Alexius seized the throne and, as Alexius I, gave the empire a new lease on life. He conducted winning campaigns against both Turks and Normans and weathered the First Crusade. His political and army reforms allowed the empire to endure until 1204, when soldiers of the Fourth Crusade conquered Constantinople and divided up its lands among themselves.

Anna Comnena's account of Alexius's reign uses the methods of the Greek historian Thucydides (see *History of the Peloponnesian War* in Chapter 3). Like him, she writes contemporary history based on personal knowledge, memories of credible witnesses, and archival documents and treaties. Unlike him, she concentrates on wars and uprisings, a narrow focus that undoubtedly reflects her troubled age. Told from an insider's point of view and instilled with Christian and classical learning, hers is a highly readable, persuasive account of Alexius's reign.

The Alexiad is not without flaws. Foremost among these are Anna's biases: She glorifies her father and ignores her brother, John, probably because John succeeded Alexius to the throne (r. 1118–1143), thus ending her hopes of being empress. She was also a religious zealot, gloating over the deaths of heretics. Her love of country led her to overdramatize events ("They descended on their enemies like lions."). But overall, the book's virtues outweigh these flaws.

Reading the Selections

Anna Comnena, writing in the Preface to The Alexiad, echoes Thucydides when she asserts that history is a "bulwark against the stream of Time," thus allowing humans to salvage what is important from "the depths of Oblivion." From this high-minded ideal, she descends to the reality of her subject, Alexius's empire as it is simultaneously invaded by Turks and soldiers of the First Crusade (1097–1104), known variously as Franks, Latins, or Kelts. The selection taken from Book XIV, the next to last chapter, offers a uniquely non-Western view of the crusaders, both as individuals and as a group. The selection ends with Anna digressing about her critics.

∞

Preface

The stream of Time, irresistible, ever moving, carries off and bears away all things that come to birth and plunges them into utter darkness, both deeds of no account and deeds which are mighty and worthy of commemoration; as the playwright[19] says, it "brings to light that which was unseen and shrouds from us that which was manifest." Nevertheless, the science of History is a great bulwark against this stream of Time; in a way it checks this irresistible flood, it holds in a tight grasp whatever it can seize floating on the surface and will not allow it to slip away into the depths of Oblivion.

I, Anna, daughter of the Emperor Alexius[20] and the Empress Irene,[21] born and bred in the Purple,[22] not without some acquaintance with literature—having devoted the most earnest study to the Greek language, in fact, and being not unpractised in Rhetoric[23] and having read thoroughly the treatises of Aristotle and the dialogues of Plato, and having fortified my mind with the Quadrivium of sciences[24] (these things must be divulged, and it is not

self-advertisement to recall what Nature[25] and my own zeal for knowledge have given me, nor what God has apportioned to me from above and what has been contributed by Opportunity); I, having realized the effects wrought by Time, desire now by means of my writings to give an account of my father's deeds, which do not deserve to be consigned to Forgetfulness nor to be swept away on the flood of Time into an ocean of Non-Remembrance; I wish to recall everything, the achievements before his elevation to the throne and his actions in the service of others before his coronation.

I approach the task with no intention of flaunting my skill as a writer; my concern is rather that a career so brilliant should not go unrecorded in the future, since even the greatest exploits, unless by some chance their memory is preserved and guarded in history, vanish in silent darkness. My father's actions themselves prove his ability as a ruler and show, too, that he was prepared to submit to authority, within just limits.

Now that I have decided to write the story of his life, I am fearful of an underlying suspicion: someone might conclude that in composing the history of my father I am glorifying myself; the history, wherever I express admiration for any act of his, may seem wholly false and mere panegyric.[26] On the other hand, if he himself should ever lead me, under the compulsion of events, to criticize some action taken by him, not because of what he decided but because of the circumstances, here again I fear the cavillers: in their all-embracing jealousy and refusal to accept what is right, because they are malicious and full of envy,

---

[19] **the playwright** Sophocles.
[20] **Alexius** Reign name, Alexius I Comnenus. Byzantine emperor (r. 1081–1118); founded Comnenian dynasty.
[21] **Irene** Full name **Irene Ducas** (about 1066–1120). Byzantine empress; wife of **Alexius I Comnenus,** Byzantine emperor. Retired to a monastery in 1118.
[22] **bred in the Purple** Greek, *Porphyra.* The Purple was the imperial nursery, where the ruler's offspring were born. The children were called *porphyrogeniti,* prince or princess. In Byzantium, the color purple was reserved for imperial or high rank.
[23] **Rhetoric** The art of speaking and writing effectively. Together with grammar and logic, it comprises the trivium, or arts portion of the seven liberal arts.
[24] **Quadrivium of sciences** Four areas of study—arithmetic, music, geometry, and astronomy—that comprise the science portion of the seven liberal arts.

---

[25] **Nature** The natural gift of intellect.
[26] **panegyric** A formal declaration of praise.

they may cast in my teeth the story of Noah's son Ham[27] and, as Homer says, "blame the guiltless."[28]

---

[27] **Noah's son Ham** Genesis 9:21–27 describes a drunken Noah, after the flood, being seen naked by his son Ham, who tells his brothers, Shem and Japheth. Shem and Japheth cover Noah's nakedness, while averting their gaze. When Noah awakens, he blesses Shem and Japheth and curses Ham's son Canaan. (Why Ham is not cursed is not explained.) The episode is often interpreted as an allegory: The descendants of Shem are the Semitic people; the descendants of Japheth are the Gentiles; and the descendants of Ham, through Canaan, are slaves. Also, the curse on the descendants of Canaan offers a justification for the Hebrews' later conquest of the land of Canaan (Palestine).

[28] **"blame the guiltless"** From *Odyssey*, Book 20.

Whenever one assumes the role of historian, friendship and enmities have to be forgotten; often one has to bestow on adversaries the highest commendation (where their deeds merit it); often, too, one's nearest relatives, if their pursuits are in error and suggest the desirability of reproach, have to be censured. The historian, therefore, must shirk neither remonstrance with his friends, nor praise of his enemies. For my part, I hope to satisfy both parties, both those who are offended by us and those who accept us, by appealing to the evidence of the actual events and of eye-witnesses. The fathers and grandfathers of some men living today saw these things.

Book XIV

One day he was exercising at polo, his partner being the Taticius I have often mentioned. Taticius[29] was carried away by his horse and fell on the emperor, whose kneecap was injured by the impact (Taticius was a heavy man). The pain affected the whole of his foot and although he did not show that he was in distress—he was used to bearing pain—he did receive some minor treatment. Little by little the trouble wore off and disappeared, so that his normal habits were resumed. That was the prime origin of his gout, for the painful areas attracted rheumatism. There was a second, more obvious cause of all this illness. Everyone knows that countless multitudes of Kelts[30] came to the imperial city, having migrated from their own lands and hurried from all directions to us. It was then that the emperor was plunged into a vast ocean of worries. He had long been aware of their dream of Empire; he was aware too of their overwhelming numbers—more than the grains of sand on the sea-shore or all the stars of heaven; the sum total of Roman[31] forces would equal not one tiny part of their multitudes, even if they were concentrated in one place—much less when they were dissipated over wide areas, for some were on guard in the valleys of Serbia and in Dalmatia,[32] others keeping watch near the Danube against Cuman[33] and Dacian[34] incursions, and many had been entrusted with the task of saving Dyrrachium[35] from a second Keltic victory. Under the circumstances he

---

[29] **Taticius** One of the emperor's generals.

[30] **Kelts** Another name for the European Crusaders.

[31] **Roman** Byzantine. With Byzantium as the successor to the old Eastern Roman Empire, the Byzantine rulers considered themselves and their people to be Romans.

[32] **Dalmatia** The area along the Adriatic coast, of modern Yugoslavia, Bosnia and Herzegovina, and Croatia.

[33] **Cuman** Turkic people from the steppe zone, ranging from the Ukraine to Central Eurasia, from the eleventh to the fourteenth centuries.

[34] **Dacian** The people of Dacia, modern Romania.

[35] **Dyrrachium** Modern Durres, Albania; a seaport on the Adriatic Sea.

devoted his whole attention now to these Kelts and all else was considered of secondary importance. The barbarian world on our borders, which was restless but had not yet broken out into open hostility, he kept in check by granting honours and presents, while the ambition of the Kelts was confined by all possible means. The rebellious spirit of his own subjects caused no less trouble—in fact he suspected them even more and hastened to protect himself as best he could. Their plots were skilfully averted. But no one could adequately describe the ferment of troubles which descended on him at this period. It compelled him to become all things to all men, to accommodate himself as far as he could to circumstances. Like a trained physician (following the rules of his craft) he had to apply himself to the most pressing need. At daybreak, as soon as the sun leapt up over the eastern horizon, he took his seat on the imperial throne and every day on his orders all Kelts were freely admitted to his presence. The purpose of this was twofold: he liked them to make their own requests, and he strove by various arguments to reconcile them to his wishes. The Keltic counts are brazen-faced, violent men, money-grubbers and where their personal desires are concerned quite immoderate. These are natural characteristics of the race. They also surpass all other nations in loquacity. So when they came to the palace they did so in an undisciplined fashion, every count bringing with him as many comrades as he wished; after him, without interruption, came another and then a third—an endless queue. Once there they did not limit the conversation by the waterclock, like the orators of ancient times, but each, whoever he was, enjoyed as much time as he wanted for the interview with the emperor. Men of such character, talkers so exuberant, had neither respect for his feelings nor thought for the passing of time nor any idea of the by-standers' wrath; instead of giving way to those coming behind them, they talked on and on with an incessant stream of petitions. Every student of human customs will be acquainted with Frankish verbosity and their pettifogging love of detail; but the audience on these occasions learnt the lesson more thoroughly—from actual experience. When evening came, after remaining without food all through the day, the emperor would rise from his throne and retire to his private apartment, but even then he was not free from the importunities of the Kelts. They came one after another, not only those who had failed to obtain a hearing during the day, but those who had already been heard returned as well, putting forward this or that excuse for more talk. In the midst of them, calmly enduring their endless chatter stood the emperor. One could see them there, all asking questions, and him, alone and unchanging, giving them prompt replies. But there was no limit to their foolish babbling, and if a court official did try to cut them short, he was himself interrupted by Alexius. He knew the traditional pugnacity of the Franks and feared that from some trivial pretext a mighty blaze of trouble might spring up, resulting in serious harm to the prestige of Rome. It was really a most extraordinary sight. Like a statue wrought by the hammer, made perhaps of bronze or cold-forged iron, the emperor would sit through the night, often from evening till midnight, often till third cock-crow, sometimes almost until the sun was shining clearly. The attendants were all worn out, but by frequently retiring had a rest and then came back again—in bad humour. Thus not one of them would stay motionless as long as he did; all in one way or another kept changing position: one would sit down, another turned his head away and rested it on something, another propped himself against a wall. Only one man, the emperor, faced this tremendous task without weakening. His endurance was truly remarkable. Hundreds of people were talking, each one prattling on at length, "brawling away unbridled of tongue"[36] as Homer says. As one stood aside he passed the conversation on to another, and he to the next, and so on and on. They stood only in these intervals but he all the time, up to first or even second cock-crow. After a brief rest, when the sun rose he was again seated on his throne and once more fresh labours and twofold troubles succeeded those of the night. It was for this reason, then, that the emperor was attacked by the pain in his feet. From that time to the end of his life the rheumatism came on at regular intervals and caused him dreadful pain. Despite this he bore it so well that not once did he murmur in complaint; all he said was, "I deserve to suffer. This happens to me justly because of the multitude of my sins." And if by chance a cross word did escape his lips he immediately made the sign of the Cross against the assault of the evil demon. "Flee from me, wicked one," he would say. "A curse on you and your tempting of Christians!" I will say no more now about the pain that afflicted him. Maybe there was someone who contributed to this malady of his and increased the sufferings he bore (and surely his cup of bitterness was already full). I will give a brief outline of the story, not the full details. The empress smeared the rim of the cup with honey, as it were, and

contrived that he should avoid most of his troubles, for she unceasingly watched over him.

·   ·   ·

At this stage of my history the reader perhaps will say that I am naturally biased. My answer is this: I swear by the perils the emperor endured for the well-being of the Roman people, by his sorrows and the travails he suffered on behalf of the Christians, that I am not favouring him when I say or write such things. On the contrary, where I perceive that he was wrong I deliberately transgress the law of nature and stick to the truth. I regard him as dear, but truth as dearer still. As one of the philosophers somewhere remarked, "Both are dear, but it is best to honour truth more highly." I have followed the actual course of events, without additions of my own, without suppression, and so I speak and write. And the proof of this is near to hand. I am not writing the history of things that happened 10,000 years ago, but there are men still alive today who knew my father and tell me of his deeds. They have in fact made a not inconsiderable contribution to the history, for one reported or recalled to the best of his ability one fact, while another told me something else—but there was no discrepancy in their accounts. Most of the time, moreover, we were ourselves present, for we accompanied our father and mother. Our lives by no means revolved round the home; we did not live a sheltered, pampered existence. From my very cradle—I swear it by God and His Mother—troubles, afflictions, continual misfortunes were my lot, some from without, some from within. As to my physical characteristics, I will not speak of them—the attendants in the gynaeconitis[37] can describe and talk of them. But if I write of the evils that befell me from without, the troubles I encountered even before I had completed my eighth year and the enemies raised up against me by the wickedness of men, I would need the Siren[38] of Isocrates,[39] the grandiloquence of Pindar,[40] Polemo's[41] vivacity, the Calliope[42] of Homer, Sappho's[43] lyre or some other power greater still. For no danger, great or small from near or far away, failed to attack us at once. I was truly overwhelmed by the flood and ever since, right up to the present time, even to this moment when I write these words, the sea of misfortunes advances upon me, wave after wave. But I must stop—I have inadvertently drifted away into my own troubles.

---

[36] **"brawling away unbridled of tongue"** From *Iliad*, Book 2.

[37] **gynaeconitis** From Greek, the place set aside for the exclusive use of women.
[38] **Siren** A Siren, half-woman, half-bird, cast a spell of enchantment with her song.
[39] **Isocrates** (436–338 BCE) Athenian orator and founder of a school of rhetoric.
[40] **Pindar** (ca. 522–ca. 438 BCE) Greek lyric poet from Thebes.
[41] **Polemo** (ca. 88–145 CE) Greek orator from Laodicea.
[42] **Calliope** The muse of epic poetry; one of the nine muses of Greek culture.
[43] **Sappho** (ca. 600 BCE) Greek lyric poet from Lesbos.

Questions for Critical Thinking

1. Describe how Anna Comnena explains why and how she wants to write the history of her father's reign, and note what she thinks to be the role of the historian.

2. Discuss Anna Comnena's views and opinions of the crusaders and what she observed about their behavior. What was the effect of their being in Constantinople on her father?

BOETHIUS
Selection from *The Consolation of Philosophy*

Boethius (ca. 480–524), like St. Augustine (see *Confessions* in Chapter 7), was a transitional figure who bridged the classical and Christian worlds. Privileged as an aristocrat and traditionally educated in liberal studies, Boethius, at an early age, came to the attention of Theodoric, the Ostrogoth (German) general who had conquered Italy before 493 and made himself its king. With the king's favor, Boethius rose through the ranks at the royal court, finally becoming, in effect, prime minister.

Despite his administrative duties, Boethius still found time for his studies, writing books on arithmetic, astronomy, and music, and translating the works of Aristotle and other Greek scholars into Latin. His translations of Aristotle laid the foundation for Scholasticism and systematized late classical/Christian philosophy—two of his major contributions to thought during the Middle Ages.

Even though Boethius received royal favor, the king had him arrested as the result of palace intrigue that was part of a conflict between Theodoric and the Byzantine emperor over political and religious issues. While awaiting death, Boethius composed one of the masterpieces of Western thought, *The Consolation of Philosophy*, which reflected his classical education. He was executed in 524.

Reading the Selection

Boethius's *The Consolation of Philosophy* is a hybrid work that alternates prose and poetry. The author's mouthpiece in the first three chapters is Dame Philosophy, a personification technique that influenced later medieval writers (see Christine de Pizan's *The Book of the City of Ladies* in Chapter 11). Dame Philosophy addresses Boethius and, by extension, the reader, in the ways that philosophy can help mortals face terrible misfortunes. Overall, her advice seems to be one of Stoic resignation to the unaccountable whims of Fortune, an ancient idea of the randomness at work in the world. Dame Philosophy herself does not oppose Fortune. She points out to Boethius that Fortune has been good to him. But he must learn to accept life's bitterness with the sweet.

In Book III, Dame Philosophy introduces a new note when she says that there is no true happiness except in union with God. She pledges that she (that is, philosophy) will guide Boethius (the reader) to true happiness, though he must seek help from God.

God, as defined and addressed in this work, is a philosophical concept. It suggests the influence of Plato (see *The Republic* and *Phaedo* in Chapter 3) and Aristotle (see *Poetics* in Chapter 3). Thus, as Boethius, one of the last Romans but also one of the first medieval Christians, faced death, he expressed no hope in the Christian belief of personal immortality but placed his trust in the truths of Greek philosophy.

This selection's mode of reasoning relies on quotations from famous authors and the Bible (appeals to authority), definitions of terms, and summary of all sides to an argument. Because the work was one of the few that was continuously read after the fall of the Western Roman Empire, the reasoning methods employed by Boethius were widely imitated until about 1500.

∞

Book III

Chapter IX

. . .

"Even a blind man could see it," I[44] said, "and you[45] revealed it just now when you were trying to show the causes of false happiness. For unless I'm mistaken, true and perfect happiness is that which makes a man self-sufficient, strong, worthy of respect, glorious and joyful. And to show you that I have more than a superficial understanding, without a shadow of doubt I can see that happiness to be true happiness which, since they are all the same thing, can truly bestow any one of them."

"You are blessed in this belief, my child, provided you add one thing."

"What is that?"

"Do you think there is anything among these mortal and degenerate things which could confer such a state?"

"No, I don't, and you have proved it as well as anyone could wish." [5]

"Clearly, therefore, these things offer man only shadows of the true good,[46] or imperfect blessings, and cannot confer true and perfect good."

"Yes."

"Since then you have realized the nature of true happiness and seen its false imitations, what remains now is that you should see where to find this true happiness."

"Which is the very thing I have long and eagerly been waiting for."

"But since in the *Timaeus*[47] my servant Plato was pleased to ask for divine help even over small matters, what do you think we ought to do now in order to be worthy of discovering the source of that supreme good?" [10]

"We ought to pray to the Father of all things. To omit to do so would not be laying a proper foundation."

"Right," she said, and immediately began the following hymn.

"O Thou who dost by everlasting reason rule,
Creator of the planets and the sky, who time

From timelessness didst bring, unchanging Mover,
No cause drove Thee to mould unstable matter, but
The form benign of highest good within Thee set.
All things Thou bringest forth from Thy high archetype:
Thou, height of beauty, in Thy mind the beauteous world
Dost bear, and in that ideal likeness shaping it,
Dost order perfect parts a perfect whole to frame.
The elements[48] by harmony Thou dost constrain,
That hot to cold and wet to dry[49] are equal made,
That fire grow not too light, or earth too fraught with
*   weight.*
The bridge of threefold nature madest Thou soul, which
*   spreads*
Through nature's limbs harmonious and all things moves.
The soul once cut, in circles two its motion joins,
Goes round and to itself returns encircling mind,
And turns in pattern similar the firmament.
From causes like Thou bringst forth souls and lesser lives,
Which from above in chariots swift Thou dost disperse
Through sky and earth, and by Thy law benign they turn
And back to Thee they come through fire that brings them
*   home.*
Grant, Father, that our minds Thy august seat may scan,
Grant us the sight of true good's source, and grant us light
That we may fix on Thee our mind's unblinded eye.
Disperse the clouds of earthly matter's cloying weight;
Shine out in all Thy glory; for Thou art rest and peace
To those who worship Thee; to see Thee is our end,
Who art our source and maker, lord and path and goal."

Chapter X

"Since, then, you have seen the form both of imperfect and of perfect good, I think we now have to show where this perfect happiness is to be found. [1]

"The first question to ask is, I think, whether any good of the kind I defined a moment ago can exist in the natural world. This will prevent our being led astray from

---

[44] **I** The narrator, Boethius himself.
[45] **you** Dame Philosophy.
[46] **shadows of the true good** An echo of Plato's argument in "The Allegory of the Cave."
[47] ***Timaeus*** Plato's book on cosmology, physics, and biology.

[48] **elements** Earth, air, fire, and water.
[49] **hot . . . cold . . . wet . . . dry** Qualities derived from the four **elements:** hot (fire); cold (earth); wet (water); and dry (air).

the truth of the matter before us by false and ill-founded reasoning. But the existence of this good and its function as a kind of fountain-head of all good things cannot be denied; for everything that is said to be imperfect is held to be so by the absence of perfection. So that if a certain imperfection is visible in any class of things, it follows that there is also a proportion of perfection in it. For if you do away with perfection, it is impossible to imagine how that which is held to be imperfect could exist. The natural world did not take its origin from that which was impaired and incomplete, but issues from that which is unimpaired and perfect and then degenerates into this fallen and worn out condition. But we showed just now that there is a certain imperfect happiness in perishable good, so that there can be no doubt that a true and perfect happiness exists."

"Which is a very sound and true conclusion," I said.

"As to where it is to be found, then, you should think as follows. It is the universal understanding of the human mind that God, the author of all things, is good. Since nothing can be conceived better than God, everyone agrees that that which has no superior is good. Reason shows that God is so good that we are convinced that His goodness is perfect. Otherwise He couldn't be the author of creation. There would have to be something else possessing perfect goodness over and above God, which would seem to be superior to Him and of greater antiquity. For all perfect things are obviously superior to those that are imperfect. Therefore, to avoid an unending argument, it must be admitted that the supreme God is to the highest degree filled with supreme and perfect goodness. But we have agreed that perfect good is true happiness; so that it follows that true happiness is to be found in the supreme God."

"I accept that. There is nothing in any way open to contradiction."   5

"But," she said, "I must ask you to make sure that your approval of our statement that the supreme God is to the highest degree filled with supreme good is unqualified and final."

"How do you mean?" I asked.

"By avoiding the assumption that this Father of creation has received this supreme good with which He is said to be filled from outside Himself, or that He possesses it by nature but in such a way as would lead you to suppose that the substance of God the possessor was a separate thing from the substance of the happiness He possesses. If you thought that He received it from outside Himself, you would be able to count the giver superior to the receiver. But we are in agreement that it is right to consider God the most excellent of things.

"On the other hand, if goodness is a natural property of God, but something logically distinct from Him, whenever we speak of God as the author of creation, an able mind might be able to imagine the existence of a power responsible for bringing together the two that were separate.

"Finally, if one thing is distinct from another, it cannot be the thing from which it is perceived to be distinct. So that which by its own nature is something distinct   10

from supreme good, cannot be supreme good; but this is something we may not hold about Him to whom we agree there is nothing superior. It is impossible for anything to be by nature better than that from which it is derived. I would therefore conclude with perfect logic that that which is the origin of all things is in its own substance supreme good."

"Perfectly right."

"But we have agreed that supreme good is the same as happiness."

"Yes."

"So that we have to agree that God is the essence of happiness."

"Your premises are incontestable and I see that this inference follows upon them."   15

"Then consider whether this, too, can be firmly accepted: that it is impossible for two supreme goods to exist separate from one another. For it is clear that if the two goods are separate, the one cannot be the other, so that neither could be perfect when each is lacking to the other. But that which is not perfect is obviously not supreme. It is therefore impossible for there to be two separate supreme goods. However, we deduced that both happiness and God are supreme goodness, so that it follows that supreme happiness is identical with supreme divinity."

"There could scarcely be a conclusion more true to reality, or more sure in its reasoning, or more worthy of God."

"I will add something to it. Just as in geometry some additional inference may be drawn from a theorem that has been proved, called in technical language, in Greek a *porisma* and in Latin a corollary, I too will give you a kind of corollary. Since it is through the possession of happiness that people become happy, and since happiness is in fact divinity, it is clear that it is through the possession of divinity that they become happy. But by the same logic as men become just through the possession of justice, or wise through the possession of wisdom, so those who possess divinity necessarily become divine. Each happy individual is therefore divine. While only God is so by nature, as many as you like may become so by participation."

"What you say is beautiful and valuable, whether you give it the Greek or the Latin name."

"But the most beautiful thing is what logic leads us to add to all this."   20

"What is that?"

"Are all the many things we see included under the word happiness like parts combining to form a single body, yet separate in their variety, or is there any one of them which can fully supply the essence of happiness and under which the others may be classed?"

"Could you clarify the question by being more specific?"

"Well, we consider happiness something good, don't we?"

"Yes, the supreme good."   25

"You could say the same of all of them. Absolute sufficiency is judged to be the same as happiness, and so too are power, reverence, glory and pleasure. Well, the question is this, all these things—sufficiency, power and the others—are they good as if happiness were a body of which they were members, or is goodness a kind of heading to which they belong?"

"I understand the question which you are proposing we should ask, but I should like to hear what your answer would be."

"This is how I would resolve it. If all these were related to happiness like limbs to a body, they would differ from one another, because it is the nature of parts that the body is one, but the parts that make it up are diverse. But all these things have been proved to be identical. So that they are not like limbs. Moreover it would appear that happiness was a body made up of a single limb, which is impossible."

"There is no doubt of that; but I am eager for what is to come."

"It is clear that the other properties are classed un-   30
der good. It is just because sufficiency is judged a good that people want it, and it is just because it too is believed to be a good that power is sought after. And exactly the same conclusion may be reached about reverence, glory and pleasure.

"The chief point and reason, therefore, for seeking all things is goodness. For it is quite impossible for that which contains no good in itself whether real or apparent, to be an object of desire. On the other hand, things which are not good by nature are sought after if they nevertheless seem as if they were truly good.

"The result is, therefore, that there is justice in the belief that goodness is the chief point upon which the pursuit of everything hinges and by which it is motivated. What seems most to be desired is the thing that motivates the pursuit of something, as, for example, if a man wants to go riding for the sake of health; it is not so much the motion of horse-riding he desires as the resultant good health. Since, therefore, all things are desired for the sake of the good in them, no one desires them as much as the

good itself. But we are agreed that the reason for desiring things is happiness. So that it is patently obvious that the good itself and happiness are identical."

"I can see no reason for anyone to disagree."

"But we have shown that God and happiness are one and the same thing."

"Yes."   35

"We may safely conclude, then, that God is to be found in goodness itself and nowhere else.

"Come hither now all you who captive are,
Whom false desire enchains in wicked bonds,
Desire that makes her home in earthly minds;
Here will you find release from grievous toil,
Here find a haven blessed with peaceful calm,
An ever open refuge from distress.
Not all the gold that Tagus'[50] *sands bestow,*
That Hermus[51] *from his glittering banks casts up,*
Or Indus,[52] *on whose torrid shores are strewn*
Green emeralds intermixed with dazzling pearls,
May sharpen and make bright the intellect,
But wealth in its own darkness clouds the thoughts.
For all that thus excites and charms the mind
Dim earth has fostered in her caverns deep;
While that bright light which rules and animates
The sky, will shun such dark and ruined souls:
Whoever once shall see this shining light
Will say the sun's own rays are not so bright."

----

[50] **Tagus** A river in Spain that flows from central Spain to the Atlantic Ocean; longest river in the Iberian peninsula.
[51] **Hermus** Also Gediz. A river in modern western Turkey, emptying into the Gulf of Izmir.
[52] **Indus** An Asian river running from Tibet, through China, Kashmir, and Pakistan, to the Arabian Sea.

Questions for Critical Thinking

1. Give examples from Dame Philosophy's hymn about true happiness that shows the influence of Greek thought.

2. How does Dame Philosophy describe God and argue that God and happiness are one and the same?

EINHARD
Selection from *The Life of Charlemagne*

The Life of Charlemagne is a precious relic from one of Western civilization's most unenlightened periods, when the fate of culture itself was in doubt. It dates from the early Middle Ages (500–1000), as Europe, phoenix-like, struggled to rise from the ashes of Rome. Rome's empire in the West had disappeared, its regime wrecked by Germanic invaders, leaving people to either huddle in wooden huts beside armed fortresses or flee to monasteries. For such a masterly work to appear at this time was a sign that Europe's dark night was almost over.

This book is a brief and simple biography of Charlemagne (French, "Charles the Great") (r. 768–814), the ruler of the Germanic Franks; he originated the idea of Europe in his vast multiethnic empire, the first since Rome. In style, the book breaks no new ground but illustrates that this was a timid age, still in the shadow of Rome. Written in Latin and divided into five books, it is modeled on the Roman writer Suetonius's *Lives of the Twelve Caesars*, in terms of length and order of material. Passages are even taken from Suetonius and applied to Charlemagne.

The author, Einhard (ca. 770–840), was a noble-born Frank educated at the monastic school of Fulda, near Frankfurt. From 791 to 814, he served Charlemagne at the Palace School near the imperial court at Aachen, in modern Germany; here he helped train gifted boys of all social ranks for careers in public life. He was among a handful of scholars who made this school the driving force of the Carolingian Renaissance, which blended classical learning and Christian ideals. Einhard became the ruler's trusted adviser, a position that gave him intimate knowledge of the man whose biography he later wrote.

Written between 829 and 836, this biography is essentially a work of praise. He indeed achieves this goal, but when the topic touches on dangerous subjects, the text is either silent or veiled. For instance, he writes shyly of scandals involving the imperial daughters: "[Charlemagne] shut his eyes to all that happened, as if no suspicion of any immoral conduct had ever reached him, or as if the rumour was without foundation."

The lasting value of Einhard's work is that it is the fullest eyewitness account of Charlemagne. More than eighty copies of this work survive, attesting to its popularity. Even though Charlemagne's empire fell to pieces after a generation (843), his dream lived on. Today the European Union is a realization of his vision.

Reading the Selection

Book III of Einhard's biography is concerned with Charlemagne's private life, though of necessity it touches on affairs of state in this age when power was so personal and immediate. The most astonishing fact to be gleaned from this life is that Charlemagne was illiterate. He nevertheless was awed by the written word, as his liberal patronage of scholars proves. His own tongue was Frankish, an early form of French. In this chaotic age, literacy was for monastic scholars, such as Einhard; everyone else, like Charlemagne, was illiterate.

∞

Book III, The Emperor's Private Life

. . .

§19. Charlemagne was determined to give his children, his daughters just as much as his sons, a proper training in the liberal arts[53] which had formed the subject of his own studies. As soon as they were old enough he had his sons taught to ride in the Frankish fashion, to use arms and to hunt. He made his daughters learn to spin and weave wool, use the distaff[54] and spindle,[55] and acquire every womanly accomplishment, rather than fritter away their time in sheer idleness. . . .

When the death of Hadrian, the Pope of Rome[56] and his close friend, was announced to him, he wept as if he had lost a brother or a dearly loved son. He was firm and steady in his human relationships, developing friendship easily, keeping it up with care and doing everything he possibly could for anyone whom he had admitted to this degree of intimacy.

He paid such attention to the upbringing of his sons and daughters that he never sat down to table without them when he was at home, and never set out on a journey without taking them with him. His sons rode at his side and his daughters followed along behind. Handpicked guards watched over them as they closed the line of march. These girls were extraordinarily beautiful and greatly loved by their father. It is a remarkable fact that, as a result of this, he kept them with him in his household until the very day of his death, instead of giving them in marriage to his own men or to foreigners, maintaining that he could not live without them. The consequence was that he had a number of unfortunate experiences,[57] he who had been so lucky in all else that he undertook. However, he shut his eyes to all that happened, as if no suspicion of any immoral conduct had ever reached him, or as if the rumour was without foundation.

§20. I did not mention with the others a son called Pepin[58] who was born to Charlemagne by a concubine.[59] He was handsome enough, but a hunchback. At a moment when his father was wintering in Bavaria, soon after the beginning of his campaign against the Huns,[60] this Pepin pretended to be ill and conspired with certain of the Frankish leaders who had won him over to their cause by pretending to offer him the kingship.[61] The plot was discovered and the conspirators were duly punished. Pepin was tonsured[62] and permitted to take up, in the monastery of Prüm,[63] the life of a religious[64] for which he had already expressed a vocation.

Earlier on there had been another dangerous conspiracy against Charlemagne in Germany.[65] All the plotters were exiled, some having their eyes put out first, but the others were not maltreated physically. Only three of them were killed. These resisted arrest, drew their swords and started to defend themselves. They slaughtered a few men in the process and had to be destroyed themselves, as there was no other way of dealing with them.

The cruelty of Queen Fastrada[66] is thought to have been the cause of both these conspiracies, since it was under her influence that Charlemagne seemed to have taken actions which were fundamentally opposed to his normal kindliness and good nature. Throughout the remainder of his life he so won the love and favour of all his fellow human beings, both at home and abroad, that no one ever levelled against him the slightest charge of cruelty or injustice.

§21. He loved foreigners and took great pains to make them welcome. So many visited him as a result that they were rightly held to be a burden not only to the palace, but to the entire realm. In his magnanimity he took no notice at all of this criticism, for he considered that his reputation for hospitality and the advantage of the good name which he acquired more than compensated for the great nuisance of their being there.

§22. The Emperor was strong and well built. He was tall in stature, but not excessively so, for his height was just seven times the length of his own feet. The top of his head was round, and his eyes were piercing and unusually large. His nose was slightly longer than normal, he had a fine head of white hair and his expression was gay and good-humoured. As a result, whether he was seated or standing, he always appeared masterful and dignified. His neck was short and rather thick, and his stomach a trifle too heavy, but the proportions of the rest of his body prevented one from noticing these blemishes. His step was firm and he was manly in all his movements. He spoke distinctly, but his voice was thin for a man of

---

[53] **liberal arts** Greek educational ideal comprised of the arts (grammar, rhetoric, logic) and the sciences (arithmetic, music, astronomy, and geometry).

[54] **distaff** Staff for holding the flax, tow, or wool for spinning; ancient term for "women's work."

[55] **spindle** Round stick with tapered ends used to form and twist yarn in hand spinning.

[56] **Hadrian, the Pope of Rome** Hadrian I (r. 772–795).

[57] **unfortunate experiences** Charlemagne's daughter Rotrude gave birth to the illegitimate Lewis, who became Abbot of Saint Denis; another daughter, Bertha, had several illegitimate children, including the historian Nithard.

[58] **Pepin** Illegitimate son of Charlemagne.

[59] **concubine** Himiltrude.

[60] **the Huns** The Avars, an indeterminate people, perhaps Slavic nomads, who established an empire in eastern Europe, centered in Pannonia (modern Hungary), in the 550s; they fought periodic wars with Charlemagne until conquered by him in 805.

[61] **the kingship** In 792.

[62] **tonsured** The clipping or shaving of the crown of the head; a medieval ritual for admission to a Roman Catholic monastic vocation.

[63] **Prüm** A Benedictine abbey, near Trier, in modern Germany; founded in 720.

[64] **a religious** A member of a Roman Catholic order.

[65] **in Germany** The conspiracy of Hadrad, in 785–786.

[66] **Queen Fastrada** The third wife of Charlemagne, the mother of two of his daughters.

his physique. His health was good, except that he suffered from frequent attacks of fever during the last four years of his life, and towards the end he was lame in one foot. Even then he continued to do exactly as he wished, instead of following the advice of his doctors, whom he came positively to dislike after they advised him to stop eating the roast meat to which he was accustomed and to live on stewed dishes.

He spent much of his time on horseback and out hunting, which came naturally to him, for it would be difficult to find another race on earth who could equal the Franks in this activity. He took delight in steam-baths at the thermal springs, and loved to exercise himself in the water whenever he could. He was an extremely strong swimmer and in this sport no one could surpass him. It was for this reason that he built his palace at Aachen[67] and remained continuously in residence there during the last years of his life and indeed until the moment of his death. He would invite not only his sons to bathe with him, but his nobles and friends as well, and occasionally even a crowd of his attendants and bodyguards, so that sometimes a hundred men or more would be in the water together.

§23. He wore the national dress of the Franks. Next to his skin he had a linen shirt and linen drawers; and then long hose and a tunic edged with silk. He wore shoes on his feet and bands of cloth wound round his legs. In winter he protected his chest and shoulders with a jerkin[68] made of otter skins or ermine. He wrapped himself in a blue cloak and always had a sword strapped to his side, with a hilt and belt of gold or silver. Sometimes he would use a jewelled sword, but this was only on great feast days or when ambassadors came from foreign peoples. He hated the clothes of other countries, no matter how becoming they might be, and he would never consent to wear them. The only exception to this was one day in Rome when Pope Hadrian entreated him to put on a long tunic and a Greek mantle, and to wear shoes made in the Roman fashion; and then a second time, when Leo,[69] Hadrian's successor, persuaded him to do the same thing. On feast days he walked in procession in a suit of cloth of gold, with jewelled shoes, his cloak fastened with a golden brooch and with a crown of gold and precious stones on his head. On ordinary days his dress differed hardly at all from that of the common people.

§24. He was moderate in his eating and drinking, and especially so in drinking; for he hated to see drunkenness in any man, and even more so in himself and his friends. All the same, he could not go long without food, and he often used to complain that fasting made him feel ill. He rarely gave banquets and these only on high feast days, but then he would invite a great number of guests. His main meal of the day was served in four courses, in addition to the roast meat which his hunters used to bring in on spits and which he enjoyed more than any other food. During his meal he would listen to a public reading or some other entertainment. Stories would be recited for him, or the doings of the ancients told again. He took great pleasure in the books of Saint Augustine[70] and especially in those which are called *The City of God*. . . .

§25. He spoke easily and fluently, and could express with great clarity whatever he had to say. He was not content with his own mother tongue, but took the trouble to learn foreign languages. He learnt Latin so well that he spoke it as fluently as his own tongue; but he understood Greek better than he could speak it. He was eloquent to the point of sometimes seeming almost garrulous.

He paid the greatest attention to the liberal arts; and he had great respect for men who taught them, bestowing high honours upon them. When he was learning the rules of grammar he received tuition from Peter the Deacon of Pisa,[71] who by then was an old man, but for all other subjects he was taught by Alcuin,[72] surnamed Albinus, another Deacon, a man of the Saxon[73] race who came from Britain and was the most learned man anywhere to be found. Under him the Emperor spent much time and effort in studying rhetoric, dialectic and especially astrology. He applied himself to mathematics and traced the course of the stars with great attention and care. He also tried to learn to write. With this object in view he used to keep writing-tablets and notebooks under the pillows on his bed, so that he could try his hand at forming letters during his leisure moments; but, although he tried very hard, he had begun too late in life and he made little progress. . . .

§29. Now that he was Emperor, he discovered that there were many defects in the legal system of his own people, for the Franks have two separate codes of law which differ from each other in many points. He gave much thought to how he could best fill the gaps, reconcile the discrepancies, correct the errors and rewrite the laws which were ill-expressed. None of this was ever finished; he added a few sections, but even these remained incomplete. What he did do was to have collected together and committed to writing the laws of all the nations under his jurisdiction which still remained unrecorded.

At the same time he directed that the age-old narrative poems, barbarous enough, it is true, in which were celebrated the warlike deeds of the kings of ancient times, should be written out and so preserved. He also began a grammar of his native tongue. . . .

---

[67] **Aachen** French, Aix-la-Chapelle. Capital of Charlemagne; site of Roman baths.
[68] **jerkin** Sleeveless, knee-length jacket.
[69] **Leo** Pope Leo III (795–816). Crowned Charlemagne emperor of the West, in 800.

[70] **Saint Augustine** (354–430 CE). One of the fathers of the church (see *The City of God* in Chapter 7).
[71] **Peter the Deacon of Pisa** A scholar attached to Charlemagne's palace school; taught grammar to Charlemagne.
[72] **Alcuin** Also called Albinus; **Saxon** scholar, head of the cathedral school at York, England; at Charlemagne's invitation, he became head of the palace school at **Aachen** in 781.
[73] **Saxon** A member of a Germanic people, who invaded England with the Angles and Jutes in the fifth century CE, merging with them to become the Anglo-Saxons.

Questions for Critical Thinking

1. How did Charlemagne rear his children, and what did he do when one of them nearly betrayed him? Do you think his treatment of his son to be fair? Why or why not?

2. Describe the day-to-day life of Charlemagne as to his dress, his activities, his education, and his interests.

HROTSVITHA
Selection from *Abraham*

Hrotsvitha (ca. 935–1000), spelled variously as Hrosvitha, Hrotsvit, and Roswitha, is the first known German woman writer. She lived during the Old High German period, the first phase of German literature, which lasted from 800 to 1050. German literature was still in its infancy, and most writers were clerics who composed in Latin rather than the German tongue. Hrotsvitha was thus typical of the period's writers, for she was a nun writing exclusively in Latin.

As a woman writer, however, Hrotsvitha was anything but typical, because most women then had few educational opportunities. What educational opportunity existed was mainly for women from culturally privileged social positions, such as Hrotsvitha. A member of the nobly born class of religious women, she was encouraged to study the classical liberal arts. At an early age, she entered the Benedictine abbey at Gandersheim, a convent catering to aristocratic women, which was under the patronage of the counts of Saxony, vassals of the Holy Roman emperor. This imperial abbey, founded in 852, was renowned as a center of service and learning with a library rich in classical and medieval manuscripts. As a novice nun, she mastered Christian and classical learning, especially the poets of pagan Rome, and learned to write fluent Latin. This training, coupled with her own gifts, enabled Hrotsvitha to leave a legacy of eight verse legends, six plays, two epics, and a short poem.

Of Hrotsvitha's works, the plays, all composed in rhymed, rhythmic prose, are considered her finest creations. In the preface to the plays, she describes her literary style as imitating that of the Roman playwright Terence, but she dissociates herself from what she deems his indecent focus on the "shameless acts of lascivious women." Offering a Christian alternative to Terence's pagan indecency, Hrotsvitha's plays tend to emphasize assaults against women, especially virginal women, who strive to protect their virtue from any stain and, with God's grace, thereby to earn eternal life in heaven. Her sources belong to the hagiography, or lives of the Christian saints, that circulated in Europe and the Byzantine Empire.

From the perspective of the history of Western theater, these works should be viewed as a postscript to Roman drama, not as a harbinger of a new tradition. The plays were probably never performed but were intended as edifying reading for the Gandersheim sisters. When modern drama developed, it began not out of the imitations of Terence but from the mystery plays of the church, blended with the spectacles of jugglers and mimes.

Hrotsvitha's reputation has fluctuated over the centuries. After her death, her name and her works soon lapsed into obscurity. In the Renaissance, her plays, discovered in an early-eleventh-century manuscript, were printed in book form (1501). In the Gothic Revival (1800s), she became a source of interest to scholars exploring the Germanic heritage. Today, Hrotsvitha has become a feminist icon, especially in her identification of the female body as a battle zone in the ongoing war between the sexes.

Reading the Selection

Abraham, the best known of Hrotsvitha's dramas, is concerned with the themes of fall and redemption. The plot is based on a Christian legend preserved by a Byzantine author. Abraham, a Christian monk, leaves his ascetic life to become the spiritual father of his orphaned niece, Mary. Ignoring Abraham's moral warnings, Mary elopes with a monk who seduces her. Quickly abandoned, she becomes a prostitute in a brothel where Abraham rescues her three years later. This selection from *Abraham*, the so-called recognition scene, is greatly admired by scholars for its drama and emotional impact.

∞

ABRAHAM: Greetings, good host!   1

INNKEEPER: Who calls? Greetings!

ABR.: Do you have a nice place for a traveler to stay overnight?

INN.: Indeed we do; our hospitality extends to all who alight.

ABR.: Good!

INN.: Come in, so that dinner can be prepared for you.

ABR.: I owe you much for this merry welcome, but I ask for even more from you.

INN.: Tell me what you desire, so that I may fulfill it.

ABR.: Here, take this little gold for the deal;
and arrange for the most beautiful girl who, as I hear,   10
stays with you, to share our meal.

INN.: Why do you wish to see her?

ABR.: I would delight in getting to know her whose beauty I have heard praised by so many and so often.

INN.: Whoever praised her beauty did not tell a lie, for in the loveliness of her face she outshines all other women.

ABR.: That is why I yearn for her love.

INN.: I wonder that in your old age you desire the love of a young woman.

ABR.: For sure, I come for no other purpose but to see her.

INN.: Come, Mary, come along. Show your beauty to our newcomer.

MARY: Here I am.

ABR.: What boldness, what constancy of mind I must muster as I see her whom I raised in my hidden hermitage[74] decked out in a harlot's garb.
But this is not the time to show in my face what is in   20
my heart;
I must be on guard:
I will bravely suppress my tears gushing forth, like a man. With feigned cheerfulness of countenance I will veil the bitterness of my internal grief.

INN.: Lucky Mary, be merry,
because now not only men your age flock hither, as before, but even men of ripe old age seek your favors. It is you whom they querry.

MARY: I will not only give you a taste of sweet kisses   1
but will caress your ancient neck with close embraces.

ABR.: That is what I am after.

MARY: What is it I feel? What is this spell?
What is this rare and wonderful odor I smell?
Oh, the smell of this fragrance reminds me of the   30
fragrance of chastity I once practiced!

ABR.: Now, now I must pretend, now I must persist, now I must be lustful in the manner of lewd young men and play the game
so that I am not recognized by my seriousness or else she might leave and hide for shame.

MARY: Woe is me, wretched woman! How I sank, how I fell into perdition's pit!

ABR.: This is not a fit place for complaints, where jolly guests sit.

INN.: Lady Mary, why do you sigh? Why do you cry? In the two years you have lived here, I never heard such grieving, not even a trace.

MARY: Oh, I wish I could have died three years ago!
Then I would not have sunk into such disgrace!

ABR.: I didn't come all this way
to join you in lamenting your sins, but to be joined to   40
you making love and being gay.

MARY: I was moved by a slight regret to utter such words;
but let us now dine and be merry
because, as you admonished me,
this is certainly not the time to bewail one's sins.

ABR.: Abundantly we have wined,
abundantly we have dined,
and are now tipsy, good host, with generous portions you served. Give us now leave to rise from the table
so that I might be able   50
to lay down and refresh my weary body by sweet rest.

INN.: I'll do as you request.

MARY: Rise, my lord, rise up. I shall accompany you to your bedroom.

ABR.: That pleases me. In fact, I could not have been forced to go, were I not going with you.

---

[74] **hermitage** Monastery.

. . .

MARY: Here is a bedroom for us to stay in. Here is the bed,
    decked with rich and lovely coverlets. Sit down, so
    that I may take off your shoes and then you won't   60
    have to tire yourself removing them.

ABR.: First, lock the door so that no one may enter.

MARY: Don't worry on that account. I will make sure
    that the bolt is secure,
    and that no one finds easy access to disturb us.

ABR.: Now the time has come to remove my hat and
    reveal who I am. Oh my adoptive daughter, oh part of
    my soul, Mary,
    don't you recognize me,
    the old man who raised you like a father and who   70
    pledged you with a ring
    to the only begotten Son of the Heavenly King?

MARY: Woe is me! It is my father and teacher Abraham
    who speaks!

ABR.: What happened to you, my daughter Mary?

MARY: Tremendous misery.

ABR.: Who deceived you?
    Who seduced you?

MARY: He who overthrew our first parents too.[75]

ABR.: Where is that angelic life that already here on earth   80
    you led?

MARY: Destroyed, it fled.

ABR.: Where is the modesty of your virginity? Where
    your admirable countenance?

MARY: Lost and gone from hence.

ABR.: What reward for the efforts of your fasting,
    prayers, and vigils can you hope for unless you
    return to your senses, you who fell
    from the height of Heaven and have sunk into the
    depths of Hell?   90

MARY: Woe is me, alas!

ABR.: Why did you disdain me?
    Why did you desert me?
    Why did you not tell me of your wretched sin, so that
    I and my beloved friend Effrem could perform worthy
    penance for you?

MARY: After I first sinned, and sank into perfidy,
    I did not dare, polluted as I was, to even approach your
    sanctity.

ABR.: Who ever has lived free from sin except for the   100
    Virgin's Son?

MARY: No one.

ABR.: It is human to err but evil to persist in sin; he who
    fell suddenly is not the one to be blamed,
    only he who fails to rise promptly again.

MARY: Woe is me, wretched woman.

ABR.: Why do you fall down?
    Why do you stay immobile lying on the ground?
    Arise and hear what I have to say!

MARY: I fell, shaken with fear, because I could not bear   110
    the force of your fatherly admonitions' sway.

ABR.: Consider my love for you and put aside your fears.

MARY: I cannot; I cannot cease my tears.

ABR.: Did I not relinquish my accustomed hermitage on
    your behalf, and did I not leave aside all observance
    of our regular rule,[76]
    so much so, that I who am an old hermit, have turned
    into a pleasure-seeking lewd fool,
    and I, who for so long practiced silence, made jokes
    and spoke merry words so that I wouldn't be rec-
    ognized? Why do you still stare at the ground with   120
    lowered face? Why do you refuse to speak with me?

MARY: I am troubled by my grave offense;
    this is why I don't dare to presume to lift my eyes to
    Heaven or have the confidence
    to speak with you.

ABR.: Don't lose faith, my daughter, but abandon the
    abyss of dejection and place your hope in God.

MARY: The enormity of my sins has cast me into the
    depths of despair.

ABR.: Your sins are grave, I admit,   130
    but heavenly pity is greater than any sin we may
    commit.
    Therefore cast off your despair and beware of leaving
    unused this short time given to you for penitence.
    Know that Divine Grace abounds even where the
    abomination of sins prevails.

MARY: If I had any hope of receiving forgiveness, my
    eagerness to do penance would burst forth.

ABR.: Have mercy on my exhaustion, which I incurred on
    your account, cast off this dangerous and sinful de-   140
    spair, which we know to be a graver offense than all
    other sins. For whoever despairs, thinking that God
    would not come to the aid of sinners, that person sins
    irremediably. Because just as the spark from a flint
    stone one cannot set the sea on fire,
    so the bitter taste of our sins cannot likewise aspire
    to alter the sweetness of Divine goodwill.

MARY: It is not the magnificence of Heavenly Grace which
    I doubt, but when I consider the enormity of my own
    sin, then I fear that the performance of even a worthy   150
    penance will not suffice.

ABR.: I take your sins upon myself; only come back to the
    place which you deserted
    and take up again the life which you subverted.

MARY: I will never go against any of your wishes but will
    embrace obediently all your commandments.

ABR.: Now, I believe that you are my child, whom I
    raised; now I feel that you are the one to be loved
    above all others.

MARY: I possess some clothes and a little gold;   160
    I wait to be told
    how to dispose of them.

---

[75] **He who overthrew our first parents too.** Satan, who coerced Adam and Eve to eat the forbidden fruit, thereby provoking God to exile them from the Garden of Eden.

[76] **regular rule** From Latin *regula*, "rule." Regular clergy follow an ascetic rule, such as the Rule of Benedict, which typically requires vows of poverty, chastity, and obedience.

ABR.: What you acquired through sin
must be cast off together with the sins.
MARY: I thought, perhaps, they could be offered to the
sacred altar or be given to the poor.
ABR.: It is neither sanctioned nor acceptable that gifts be
given to God which were acquired through sin and are
impure.
MARY: Beyond this, I have no concern.   170
ABR.: Dawn arrives; the day breaks. Let us return!
MARY: You, beloved father, must lead the way
as the good shepherd leads the sheep gone astray;
and I, advancing in your footsteps, will follow your
lead.
ABR.: Not so; I will proceed on foot but you will ride on
my horse so that the sharp rocks of the road will not
hurt your tender little feet.
MARY: What shall I say? How shall I ever repay your kindness? You do not force me, miserable wretch, with   180
threats, but exhort me to do penance with kindness.
ABR.: I ask nothing of you, except that you remain
intent upon spending the rest of your life in God's
service.
MARY: Out of my own free will I shall remain contrite,
I shall persist in my penance with all my might,
and even if I lose the ability to perform the act,
the will to do it shall never lack.
ABR.: It is important that you serve the Divine will as
eagerly as you served worldly vanities.   190

MARY: The will of the Lord be done in me, because of
your merits.
ABR.: Let us return and hurry on our way.
MARY: Let us hurry, I am weary of delay.

. . .

MARY: With what speed we have traveled over this
difficult and rugged road!
ABR.: Whatever is done with devotion is accomplished
with ease. Behold, here is your deserted abode.
MARY: Woe is me, this cell is witness to my sin; therefore I
fear to enter.   200
ABR.: That's understandable. Any place where the ancient
enemy has won a triumph is to be avoided forever.
MARY: And where to you intend me to stay and perform
my penance?
ABR.: Go into the small interior room[77] so that the ancient
serpent will not find another opportunity to deceive
you.
MARY: I will not contradict you but embrace eagerly what
you command.
ABR.: I shall go to Effrem, my friend, so that he, who   210
alone mourned with me over your loss, may rejoice
with me over your return.
MARY: A worthy concern!

---

[77] **the small interior room** A cloistered room, or cell, within the
monastery.

Questions for Critical Thinking

1. How does Abraham gain entrance to see Mary, his daughter, and what is her reaction in their initial encounter?

2. Discuss the conversation between Abraham and Mary. What does Mary decide to do at the end of their conversation? How is this scene a lesson in Christian morality?

9

THE RISE OF ISLAM
622–1520

Selections from the Qur'an

The Qur'an (from Arabic, "recitation," "reading," or "discourse") is the sacred book of Islam, the religion founded by Muhammad (ca. 570–632) in the early seventh century. The Qur'an is the heart and soul of Islamic culture. Its pages record Muhammad's words, which were dictated to secretaries and preserved as fragments on leaves and stones and in his followers' memories. After his death, Muhammad's words were compiled into a book. Islamic tradition holds that every word in the Qur'an is divinely inspired, being a direct revelation from God to his prophet, and is inimitable; that is, it cannot be imitated. Muhammad's work is the supreme manifestation of Islam's two central beliefs: There is but one God (Allah), and Muhammad is his prophet.

The work consists of 114 *suras* (chapters) arranged not in order of their original composition, which was unknown to its compilers, but in order of their descending length. The shorter and more poetic suras, which are the earliest words of the Prophet, appear at the end of the Qur'an. These suras, known as the Meccan suras since they are believed to have been revealed to Muhammad before he fled to Medina, focus on personal issues and speak more directly to the individual than do the other suras. Muslims quote and recite these prophetic and revelatory passages because they offer guidance and advice on how to live a just and rewarding life. The so-called later Meccan suras, also revealed to Muhammad while still in Mecca, trace the origins and history of the prophets, including the biblical prophets, from Adam, the first prophet in Islam, to Muhammad. The Medinan suras concentrate on legal, historical, and religious issues, often in a polemic tone. Their content reflects the challenges facing Muhammad in Medina after he had established his religion, controlled the city, and confronted secular political, social, and economic issues.

As a book, the Qur'an has no narrative or chronological structure, nor does it tell stories in a linear format. For example, the lives of the other prophets, such as Abraham, Moses, and Jesus, are scattered through the Meccan suras. Like other religious writings, the Qur'an utilizes metaphors, similes, and illustrations. Its lyrical character and repetitive words and phrases enhance the Qur'an's poetic sense and makes the public reciting of the suras both inspiring and appealing.

The Qur'an grew out of the experiences and traditions of the Arab world, but its ideas owed much to Judaism and somewhat less to Christianity. Recognizing Jews and Christians as "People of the Book," it claimed to replace their "books" with God's final word. Like the Jewish and Christian Bibles, the Qur'an teaches monotheism, God's total power and knowledge; his divine mercy and forgiveness; human weaknesses and sins (but not original sin); and faith.

Like the Talmud—Jewish writings on the Bible—it stresses the last judgment, resurrection, heaven, and hell. Like the New Testament, the Qur'an accepts Jesus as a prophet, though denies that he is the son of God.

The Qur'an must be approached and understood on its own terms. Its meaning or structure cannot be grasped in a total sense. Each sura stands alone, and many are a particular response to a specific problem or historic situation or event. Nearly all take the form of discourse by Allah or the angel Gabriel to Muhammad, his followers, or his enemies. The discourses typically announce a doctrine, tell a story, call for Holy War *(jihad),* urge charitable giving, regulate trade and finance, or prescribe rituals. Because of its organization, the Qur'an should not be read from start to finish but should be sampled and browsed in order to appreciate and enjoy the richness of its diversity.

Reading the Selections

The following suras are arranged by topic, not by their appearance in the Qur'an. This arrangement introduces a number of topics and themes that might otherwise be difficult to understand if they were reprinted in the order they appear in the Qur'an.

The first selection is the first sura in the Qur'an. Known as the *Fatihah,* which means "The Opening," this passage has been described as the Qur'an in brief because of its profound truths, its summative affirmations, and its invocation to commune with God. Allah is described as being both compassionate—that is, the provider and giver of everything humans need—and merciful—that is, the guide humans need to lead righteous lives and to do good deeds. Like all suras, it begins with the prayer "In the Name of God, the Compassionate, the Merciful."

Sura 96, titled "Clots of Blood" or "The Embryo," is believed to be the first revelation from Allah to Muhammad. The passage's first line is interpreted to be Allah's original command to Muhammad for him to recite what he, Allah, will now reveal to Muhammad, his chosen Prophet. The second line, which contains the title of the sura, probably refers to the origins of humans—from a clot of blood or an embryo. The pen reference, found in another sura, may be a metaphor for Allah's divine intellect. The next part of the sura warns humans to behave or suffer the consequences—a visit from the "guards of hell." The last lines admonish the reader not to follow the individual who disobeys Allah and tells him to prostrate himself in prayer, which is one of the five pillars of faith.

Sura 5 ("The Table"), verses 42–50, addresses the historical roles and importance of the Torah and its messages and of Jesus and the gospel. The Qur'an is the final word, the "Book with the truth" that confirms what is in the earlier books. God has, in his wisdom, formed not one but three communities that compete with one another to do good works, and, in the end, he will resolve their differences. Be warned, however, notes the sura, that one should not be misled by other believers who, since they do not follow the Islamic faith, will be punished for their sins.

Sura 21 ("The Prophets") is a discourse by Allah, speaking as the divine "We." This is only one of the many ways the Qur'an refers to Allah. By referring to him in different persons, such as "I," "him," or "your Lord," Allah does not take on anthropomorphic qualities—unlike the Jewish and Christian deity. To those who question the last judgment ("the day of Reckoning"), God says he will indeed punish doubters of his word ("blasphemers"), as he has done in the past. To show that he is merciful and not vengeful, he offers a line of prophets (Jews, Christians, and Arabs) who prospered because they submitted to him. One who has submitted, is, of course, a *muslim*— a person who has accepted submission, or islam.

Sura 24 ("Light"), verses 35–46, defines God's nature, linking his essence to light, as in "His light is found in temples which God has sanctioned." The theme—God is light—derives from ancient sun worship (see *The Great Hymn to the Aten* in Chapter 1) and was a prominent idea in early Christianity. This sura recognizes that such metaphors—as calling God "Light"—are proper for symbolizing Allah. As a result, Islamic mosques were outfitted with ritual lamps. Concerning religious paintings and statues, however, the Qur'an, like the Jewish *Holy Scriptures,* condemned such objects as idolatrous.

∞

The Opening (The Exordium)

In the Name of God, the Compassionate, the Merciful

Praise be to God, Lord of the Universe,   1
The Compassionate, the Merciful,
Sovereign of the Day of Judgement!
You alone we worship, and to You alone
we turn for help.   5

Guide us to the straight path,
The path of those whom You have favoured,
Not of those who have incurred Your wrath,
Nor of those who have gone astray.

∞

Clots of Blood

In the Name of God, the Compassionate, the Merciful

Recite in the name of your Lord who created—created   1
man from clots of blood.

Recite! Your Lord is the Most Bountiful One, who by
the pen taught man what he did not know.

Indeed, man transgresses in thinking himself his
own master: for to your Lord all things return.

Observe the man who rebukes Our servant when he
prays. Think: does he follow the right guidance or enjoin
true piety?

Think: if he denies the Truth and pays no heed, does   5
he not realize that God observes all?

No. Let him desist, or We will drag him by the forelock, his lying, sinful forelock.

Then let him call his helpmates. We will call the
guards of Hell.

No, never obey him! Prostrate yourself and come
nearer.

∞

The Table

In the Name of God, the Compassionate, the Merciful

They listen to falsehoods and practise what is unlawful.   1
If they come to you, give them your judgement or avoid
them. If you avoid them, they can in no way harm you; but
if you do act as their judge, judge them with fairness. God
loves those that deal justly.

But how will they come to you for judgement when
they already have the Torah which enshrines God's own
judgement? Soon after, they will turn their backs: they are
no true believers.

We have revealed the Torah, in which there is guidance and light. By it the prophets who submitted to God
judged the Jews, and so did the rabbis and the divines, according to God's Book which had been committed to their
keeping and to which they themselves were witnesses.

Have no fear of man; fear Me, and do not sell My revelations for a paltry sum. Unbelievers are those who do
not judge according to God's revelations.

We decreed for them a life for a life, an eye for an   5
eye, a nose for a nose, an ear for an ear, a tooth for a tooth,
and a wound for a wound. But if a man charitably for-
bears from retaliation, his remission shall atone for him.

Transgressors are those that do not judge according to
God's revelations.

After them We sent forth Jesus son of Mary, confirm-
ing the Torah already revealed, and gave him the Gospel,
in which there is guidance and light, corroborating what
was revealed before it in the Torah: a guide and an admonition to the righteous. Therefore let those who follow the
Gospel judge according to what God has revealed therein.
Evil-doers are those that do not judge according to God's
revelations.

And to you We have revealed the Book with the truth.
It confirms the Scriptures which came before it and stands
as a guardian over them. Therefore give judgement among
men according to God's revelations, and do not yield to
their whims or swerve from the truth made known to you.

We have ordained a law and assigned a path for each
of you. Had God pleased, He could have made of you one
community: but it is His wish to prove you by that which
He has bestowed upon you. Vie with each other in good
works, for to God shall you all return and He will resolve
your differences for you.

Pronounce judgement among them according to God's revelations and do not be led by their desires. Take heed lest they turn you away from a part of that which God has revealed to you. If they reject your judgement, know that it is God's wish to scourge them for their sins. A great many of mankind are evil-doers.

Is it pagan laws that they wish to be judged by? Who 10 is a better judge than God for men whose faith is firm?

The Prophets

In the Name of God, the Compassionate, the Merciful

The day of Reckoning for mankind is drawing near, yet 1 they blithely persist in unbelief. They listen with ridicule to each fresh warning that their Lord gives them: their hearts are set on pleasure.

In private the wrongdoers say to each other: "Is this man not a mortal like yourselves? Would you follow witchcraft with your eyes open?"

Say: "My Lord has knowledge of whatever is said in heaven and earth. He hears all and knows all."

Some say: "It[1] is but a medley of dreams." Others: "He has invented it himself." And yet others: "He is a poet: let him show us some sign, as did the apostles in days gone by."

[Yet though We showed them signs,] the communities 5 whom We destroyed before them did not believe either. Will *they* believe?

The apostles We sent before you were but men whom We inspired. Ask the People of the Book if you do not know this. The bodies We gave them could not dispense with food, nor were they immortal. Then We fulfilled Our promise: We delivered them and those We willed, and utterly destroyed the transgressors.

And now We have revealed a Book for your admonishment. Will you not understand?

We have destroyed many a sinful nation and replaced them by other men. And when they felt Our might they took to their heels and fled. They were told: "Do not run away. Return to your comforts and to your dwellings. You shall be questioned all."

"Woe betide us, we have done wrong!" was their reply. And this they kept repeating until We mowed them down and put out their light.

It was not in sport that We created that heaven and 10 the earth and all that lies between them. Had it been Our will to find a diversion, We could have found one near at hand.

Indeed, We will hurl Truth at Falsehood, until Truth shall triumph and Falsehood be no more. Woe betide you, for all the falsehoods you have uttered.

His are all who dwell in the heavens and on earth. Those who stand in His presence do not disdain to worship Him, nor are they ever wearied. They praise Him night and day, tirelessly.

Have they chosen earthly deities? And can these deities restore the dead to life? Were there other gods in heaven or earth besides God, both heaven and earth would be ruined. Exalted be God, Lord of the Throne, above their falsehoods!

None shall question Him about His works, but they shall be questioned. Have they chosen other gods besides Him?

Say: "Show us your proof. Here are the Scriptures of 15 today and those of long ago." But most of them know not the Truth, and this is why they pay no heed.

We inspired all the apostles We sent before you, saying: "There is no god but Me. Therefore serve Me."

They say: "The Merciful has begotten children," God forbid! They are but His honoured servants. They do not speak till He has spoken: they act by His command. He knows what is before them and behind them. They intercede for none save those whom He accepts, and tremble in awe of Him. Whoever of them declares: "I am a god besides Him," We shall requite with Hell. Thus shall We reward the wrongdoers.

Are the disbelievers unaware that the heavens and the earth were but one solid mass which We tore asunder, and that We made every living thing from water? Will they not have faith?

We set firm mountains upon the earth lest it should move away with them, and hewed out highways in the rock so that they might be rightly guided.

We spread the heaven like a canopy and provided it 20 with strong support: yet of its signs they are heedless.

It was He who created the night and the day, and the sun and the moon: each moves swiftly in an orbit of its own.

No man before you[2] have We made immortal. If you yourself are doomed to die, will they live on for ever?

Every soul shall taste death. We will prove you all with evil and good. To Us shall you return.

When the unbelievers see you, they only mock you, saying: "Is this the man who fulminates against your gods?" And they deny all mention of the Merciful.

Impatience is the very stuff man is made of. I shall 25 show you My signs: do not ask Me to hurry them on.

They say: "When will this promise be fulfilled, if what you say be true?"

---

[1] **The Qur'an.**

[2] **Muhammad.**

If only the unbelievers knew the day when they shall strive in vain to shield their faces and their backs from the fire of Hell; the day when none shall help them! Indeed, it will overtake them unawares and stupefy them. They shall have no power to ward it off, nor shall they be reprieved.

Other apostles have been mocked before you; but those who derided them were felled by the very scourge they mocked.

Say: "Who will protect you, by night and by day, from the Lord of Mercy?" Yet are they unmindful of their Lord's remembrance.

Have they other gods to defend them? Their idols shall be powerless over their own salvation, nor shall they be protected from Our scourge.   30

Yet have We indulged them and their fathers, so that they have lived too long. Can they not see how We invade their land and diminish its borders? Is it they who will triumph?

Say: "I warn you only by inspiration." But the deaf can hear no plea when they are warned.

Yet if the lightest whiff from the vengeance of your Lord touched them, they would say: "Woe betide us: we have done wrong!"

We shall set up just scales on the Day of Resurrection, so that no man shall in the least be wronged. Actions as small as a grain of mustard seed shall be weighed out. Our reckoning shall suffice.

We showed Moses and Aaron the distinction between right and wrong, and gave them a light and an admonition for righteous men: those who truly fear their Lord, although unseen, and dread the terrors of the final hour.   35

And this[3] is a blessed admonition We have sent down. Will you then reject it?

We formerly bestowed guidance on Abraham, for We knew him well. He said to his father and to his people: "What are these images to which you are so devoted?"

They replied: "They are the gods our fathers worshipped."

He said: "Then you and your fathers have surely been in evident error."

"Is it the truth that you are preaching," they asked, "or is this but a jest?"   40

"Indeed," he answered, "your Lord is the Lord of the heavens and the earth. It was He that made them: to this I bear witness. By the Lord, I will overthrow your idols as soon as you have turned your backs."

He broke them all in pieces, except their supreme god, so that they might return to him.

"Who has done this to our deities?" asked some. "He must surely be: a wicked man."

Others replied: "We have heard a youth called Abraham speak of them."

They said: "Then bring him here in sight of all the people, that they may act as witnesses."   45

"Abraham," they said, "was it you who did this to our deities?"

---

[3] **The Qur'an.**

"No," he replied. "It was their chief who smote them. Ask *them,* if they can speak."

Thereupon they turned their thoughts upon themselves and said to each other: "Surely you are the ones who have done wrong."

Crest-fallen as they were, [they said to Abraham:] "You know they cannot speak."

He answered: "Would you then worship that, instead of God, which can neither help nor harm you? Shame on you and on your idols! Have you no sense?"   50

They cried: "Burn him and avenge your gods, if you must punish him!"

"Fire," We said, "be cool to Abraham and keep him safe."

They sought to lay a snare for him, but it was they whom We ruined. We delivered him and Lot, and brought them to the land which We had blessed for all mankind.

We gave him Isaac, and then Jacob for a grandson; and We made each a righteous man. We ordained them leaders to give guidance at Our behest, and enjoined on them charity, prayer and almsgiving. They served none but Ourself.

To Lot We gave wisdom and knowledge and delivered him from the city that had committed deeds of abomination; surely they were men of iniquity and evil. We admitted him to Our mercy: he was a righteous man.   55

Before him Noah invoked Us, and We answered his prayer. We saved him and all his kinsfolk from the great calamity, and delivered him from those who had denied Our revelations. Evil were they; We drowned them all.

And tell of David and Solomon: how they passed judgement regarding the cornfield in which strayed lambs had grazed by night. We gave Solomon insight into the case and bore witness to their judgement.

We bestowed on both of them wisdom and knowledge, and caused the mountains and the birds to join with David in Our praise. All this We did.

We taught him the armourer's craft, so that you might have protection in your wars. Will you then give thanks?

To Solomon We subjected the raging wind: it sped at his bidding to the land which We had blessed. We had knowledge of all things.   60

We assigned him devils who dived for him into the sea and who performed other tasks besides. Over them We kept a watchful eye.

And tell of Job: how he called on his Lord, saying: "I am sorely afflicted: but of all those that show mercy You are the most merciful."

We answered his prayer and relieved his affliction. We restored to him his family and as many more with them a blessing from Ourself and an admonition to the devout.

And you shall also tell of Ishmael, Idrīs, and Dhūl-Kifl,[4] who all endured with patience. To Our mercy We admitted them, for they were upright men.

---

[4] **Ishmael, Idrīs, and Dhūl-Kifl** Ishmael was the son of Abraham and Hagar. By tradition, Muslims trace their origins back to Abraham through Ishmael. Idīs is Enoch, an early legendary figure in the *Holy Scriptures* and a favorite of God. Dhūl-Kifl is probably the prophet Ezekiel.

And of Dhūl-Nūn:[5] how he went away in anger, 65 thinking We had no power over him. But in the darkness he cried: "There is no god but You. Glory be to You! I have done wrong."

We answered his prayer and delivered him from distress. Thus shall We save the true believers.

And of Zacharias, who invoked his Lord, saying: "Lord, let me not remain childless, though of all heirs You are the best."

We answered his prayer and gave him John, curing his wife of sterility. They vied with each other in good works and called on Us with piety, fear, and submission.

And of the woman who kept her chastity. We breathed into her of Our spirit, and made her and her son a sign to all mankind.

Your community is but one community, and I am 70 Your only Lord. Therefore serve Me. Men have divided themselves into factions, but to Us shall they all return. He that does good works in the fullness of his faith, his endeavours shall not be lost: We record them all.

It is ordained that no community We have destroyed shall ever rise again. But when Gog and Magog[6] are let loose and rush headlong down every hill; when the true promise nears its fulfilment; the unbelievers shall stare in amazement, crying: "Woe betide us! Of this we have been heedless. We have assuredly done wrong."

You and your idols shall be the fuel of Hell; therein shall you all go down. Were they true gods, your idols would not go there: but there shall they abide for ever. They shall groan with anguish and be bereft of hearing.

But those to whom We have long since shown Our favour shall be far removed from Hell. They shall not hear its roar, but shall delight for ever in what their souls desire.

The Supreme Terror shall not grieve them, and the angels will receive them, saying: "This is the day you have been promised."

On that day We shall roll up the heaven like a scroll 75 of parchment. Just as We brought the First Creation into being, so will We restore it. This is a promise We shall assuredly fulfil.

We wrote in the Psalms[7] after the Torah was revealed: "The righteous among My servants shall inherit the earth." That is an admonition to those who serve Us.

We have sent you forth but as a blessing to mankind. Say: "It is revealed to me that your God is one God. Will you submit to Him?"

If they pay no heed, say: "I have warned you all alike though I cannot tell whether the scourge you are promised is imminent or far off. He knows your spoken words and hidden thoughts. For all I know, this may be a test for you and a short reprieve."

Say: "Lord, judge with fairness Our Lord is the Merciful, whose help We seek against your blasphemies."

---

[5] **Dhūl-Nūn** Dhūl-Nūn is Jonah, a prophet who at first resisted the call of God.
[6] **Gog and Magog** In the *Holy Scriptures*, enemies of Israel whom God lets loose on the Israelites but then destroys before they can conquer Israel. In the *Holy Bible* they are connected to some type of Satanic invasion after the thousand-year reign of the Messiah.

---

[7] **Psalms** 37:29 "The righteous shall inherit the land, and dwell therein for ever."

Light

In the Name of God, the Compassionate, the Merciful

God is the light of the heavens and the earth. His light 1 may be compared to a niche that enshrines a lamp, the lamp within a crystal of star-like brilliance. It is lit from a blessed olive tree neither eastern nor western. Its very oil would almost shine forth, though no fire touched it. Light upon light; God guides to His light whom He will.

God speaks in parables to mankind. God has knowledge of all things.

His light is found in temples which God has sanctioned to be built for the remembrance of His name. In them, morning and evening, His praise is sung by men whom neither trade nor profit can divert from remembering God, from offering prayers, or from giving alms; who dread the day when men's hearts and eyes shall writhe with anguish; who hope that God will requite them for their noblest deeds and lavish His grace upon them. God gives without reckoning to whom He will.

As for the unbelievers, their works are like a mirage in a desert. The thirsty traveller thinks it is water, but when he comes near he finds that it is nothing. He finds God there, who pays him back in full. Swift is God's reckoning.

Or like darkness on a bottomless ocean spread with 5 clashing billows and overcast with clouds: darkness upon darkness. If he stretches out his hand he can scarcely see it. Indeed the man from whom God withholds His light shall find no light at all.

Do you not see how God is praised by those in the heavens and those on earth? The very birds praise Him as they wing their way. He notes the prayers and praises of all His creatures; God has knowledge of all their actions.

It is God who has sovereignty over the heavens and the earth. To God shall all return.

Do you not see how God drives the clouds, then gathers and piles them up in masses which pour down torrents of rain? From heaven's mountains He sends down the hail, pelting with it whom He will and turning it away from whom He pleases. The flash of His lightning almost snatches out men's eyes.

God makes the night succeed the day: surely in this there is a lesson for clear-sighted men.

God created every beast from water. Some creep upon their bellies, others walk on two legs, and others yet on four. God creates what He pleases. God has power over all things.

We have sent down revelations demonstrating the Truth. God guides whom He will to a straight path.

Questions for Critical Thinking

1. In what ways is the Qur'an similar to and different from the Holy Bible? Give examples from each work to illustrate their similarities and differences.

2. Discuss some types of imagery used in the Qur'an. How effective do you think they are in delivering the messages in the Qur'an?

IBN KHALDUN
Selections from the *Muqaddimah*

Ibn Khaldun (1332–1406), statesman, jurist, and scholar, wrote the most famous historical work in Islamic literature. Today's scholars consider his multivolume *Universal History* and the *Muqaddimah* or *Prolegomena* to be pioneering studies in history and sociology. Although his *Universal History* provides valuable information on the Muslim world, in particular North Africa, his *Muqaddimah* or *Prolegomena*—an introductory essay or discussion to explain and interpret a longer work—is more often read. The *Muqaddimah* ranges over many topics, including the theories, principles, and techniques of writing history (historiography), explanations of how and why civilizations rise and fall, and descriptions and analyses of the socioeconomic structures of societies.

Ibn Khaldun witnessed and participated in some of the most tumultuous events in Islamic history. His ancestors had served the Moorish (Muslim) rulers in Spain before the Christians started to conquer southern Spain. The family fled to Tunis, in North Africa, where Ibn Khaldun was born. His education, for a young man from the upper class, consisted of studies of the Qur'an, which he memorized, grammar, poetry, philosophy, and jurisprudence. At age twenty he entered government service in Tunis but soon left for Fez, another North African city. A victim of political turmoils and intrigues, Ibn Khaldun escaped to Spain in 1362. In 1365 he returned to North Africa and again found himself caught in power struggles among the regional rulers. He survived by his wits and bravery, often changing sides and, on one occasion, raising an army of desert Arabs for a local sultan. Ibn Khaldun and his family, in 1375, under the protection of a tribal chief, found refuge in a rural retreat. During this time he worked on his *Universal History* and *Muqaddimah*. However, he eventually became bored and, three years later, was back in Tunis.

Ibn Khaldun's life took another turn in 1382 when, on his way to Mecca, he stopped in Cairo. The Mameluke Sultan of Egypt brought him into his court, and Ibn Khaldun quickly rose to be chief justice of the judicial system that he proceeded to reform. While combating those unhappy with his changes, he suffered a shattering personal loss when his family was drowned in a shipwreck. Crushed by this tragedy, he resigned his office and made a pilgrimage to Mecca. Upon his return to Egypt, he held some academic posts and resumed his judgeship position, which continued to be an unsettling experience. In 1400 he met and negotiated with Tamerlane (1336–1405), the Tatar warrior and conqueror of much of the Middle East, over the siege of Damascus. Tamerlane eventually sacked Damascus, but Ibn Khaldun successfully saved some of its leading citizens. Ibn Khaldun returned to Cairo and resumed his judgeship until his death in 1406.

The *Muqaddimah* or *Prolegomena* includes the author's original Preface and Book I of his *Universal History*. After noting the wrong and right ways to study history, Ibn Khaldun defines the nature of civilization and notes what is necessary to create a civilization, the types of government identified with civilizations, and the economic structure and social systems found in a civilized society. In the concluding chapters, he surveys the various fields of learning and discusses the uniqueness and importance of the human thinking process.

Ibn Khaldun, influenced by earlier Muslim scholars who had read the Greek philosophers, and, in particular, Aristotle, recognized that individuals could survive only in some form of a social organization—be it a city-state, a desert tribe, or an urban complex. From this sense of belonging sprang the desires not only to form a civilization but also to conquer others. And from such conquests and strife came larger civilizations—and dynasties. The sense of cooperation, however, was subject to change, and as the dynasty lost its sense of "solidarity," the society started to decay. Ultimately, a more vigorous civilization, characterized by a strong "solidarity," would rise and conquer the weakened civilization, thus explaining the cyclical nature of history. Although the focus of his works is clearly on humans and their ways of living together or being engaged in conflict, the author never forgets that Allah is responsible for all and that he must be praised for what he has bestowed on humans.

Reading the Selections

These selections from the *Muqaddimah* represent the breadth of Ibn Khaldun's learning and interest. They range across many topics he discusses in his work: his understanding of the historical process, his definition of civilization, his recognition of how nature and humans are related, his insight into political power and leadership, his grasp of economic relationships, and his respect for the human intellect. These topics, however, constitute only a fraction of the total number of issues and subjects Ibn Khaldun examines in his historical study.

The first selections set the tone and provide the framework for the discussions that follow. Ibn Khaldun devotes much of his writing to describing civilizations and comments on their origins, characteristics, and fate, because he believes that this is the highest form of human endeavor. As he dissects the workings of a civilization, he reveals his knowledge of how societies function, and he shares his wisdom on why humans behave the way they do in a social setting. Finally, he notes what separates humans from other animals and asserts that humans should develop their minds to the highest levels they can achieve.

❧

The Introduction

The Excellence of Historiography. An Appreciation of the Various Approaches to History. A Glimpse of the Different Kinds of Errors to Which Historians Are Liable. Why These Errors Occur.

It should be known that history is a discipline that has a great number of approaches. Its useful aspects are very many. Its goal is distinguished.

History makes us acquainted with the conditions of past nations as they are reflected in their national character. It makes us acquainted with the biographies of the prophets and with the dynasties and policies of rulers. Whoever so desires may thus achieve the useful result of being able to imitate historical examples in religious and worldly matters.

The (writing of history) requires numerous sources and much varied knowledge. It also requires a good speculative mind and thoroughness, which lead the historian to the truth and keep him from slips and errors. If he trusts historical information in its plain transmitted form and has no clear knowledge of the principles resulting from custom, the fundamental facts of politics, the nature of civilization, or the conditions governing human social organization, and if, furthermore, he does not evaluate remote or ancient material through comparison with near or contemporary material, he often cannot avoid stumbling and slipping and deviating from the path of truth. Historians, Qur'ân commentators and leading transmitters have committed frequent errors in the stories and events they reported. They accepted them in the plain transmitted form, without regard for its value. They did not check them with the principles underlying such historical situations, nor did they compare them with similar material. Also, they did not probe with the yardstick of philosophy, with the help of knowledge of the nature of things, or with the help of speculation and historical insight. Therefore, they strayed from the truth and found themselves lost in the desert of baseless assumptions and errors.

This is especially the case with figures, either of sums of money or of soldiers, whenever they occur in stories. They offer a good opportunity for false information and constitute a vehicle for nonsensical statements. They must be controlled and checked with the help of known fundamental facts. . . .

There are many such stories. They are always crop- ping up in the works of the historians. The incentive for inventing and reporting them shows a tendency to forbidden pleasures and for smearing the reputation of others. People justify their own subservience to pleasure by citing the supposed doings of men and women of the past. Therefore, they often appear very eager for such information and are alert to find it when they go through the pages of published works.

I once criticized a royal prince for being so eager to learn to sing and play the strings. I told him it was not a matter that should concern him and that it did not befit his position. He referred me to Ibrâhîm b. al-Mahdî[8] who was the leading musician and best singer of his time. I replied: "For heaven's sake, why do you not rather follow the example of his father or his brother? Do you not see how that pursuit prevented Ibrâhîm from attaining their position?" The prince, however, was deaf to my criticism and turned away.

Further silly information is accepted by many historians. They do not care to consider the factual proofs and circumstantial evidence that require us to recognize that the contrary is true. . . .

Dynasty and government serve as the world's marketplace, attracting to it the products of scholarship and craftsmanship alike. Wayward wisdom and forgotten lore turn up there. In this market stories are told and items of historical information are delivered. Whatever is in demand on this market is in general demand everywhere

else. Now, whenever the established dynasty avoids injustice, prejudice, weakness, and double-dealing, with determination keeping to the right path and never swerving from it, the wares on its market are as pure silver and fine gold. However, when it is influenced by selfish interests and rivalries, or swayed by vendors of tyranny and dishonesty, the wares of its market-place become as dross and debased metals. The intelligent critic must judge for himself as he looks around, examining this, admiring that, and choosing the other. . . .

Lengthy discussion of these mistakes has taken us rather far from the purpose of this work. However, many competent persons and expert historians slipped in connection with such stories and assertions, and they stuck in their minds. Many weak-minded and uncritical men learned these things from them, and even (competent historians) accepted them without critical investigation, and thus (strange stories) crept into their material. In consequence, historiography became nonsensical and confused, and its students fumbled around. Historiography came to be considered a domain of the common people. Therefore, today, the scholar in this field needs to know the principles of politics, the nature of things, and the differences among nations, places, and periods with regard to ways of life, character qualities, customs, sects, schools, and everything else. He further needs a comprehensive knowledge of present conditions in all these respects. He must compare similarities or differences between present and past conditions. He must know the causes of the similarities in certain cases and of the differences in others. He must be aware of the differing origins and beginnings of dynasties and religious groups, as well as of the reasons and incentives that brought them into being and the circumstances and history of the persons who supported them. His goal must be to have complete knowledge of the reasons for every happening, and to be acquainted with the origin of every event. Then, he must check transmitted information with the basic principles he knows. If it fulfils their requirements, it is sound. Otherwise, the historian must consider it as spurious and dispense with it. It was for this reason alone that historiography was highly esteemed by the ancients, so much so that at-Ṭabarî, al-Bukhârî, and, before them, Ibn Isḥâq and other Muslim religious scholars, chose to occupy themselves with it. Most scholars, however, forgot this, the secret of historiography, with the result that it became a stupid occupation. Ordinary people as well as scholars who had no firm foundation of knowledge, considered it a simple matter to study and know history, to delve into it and sponge on it. Strays got into the flock, bits of shell were mixed with the nut, truth was adulterated with lies.

"The final outcome of things is up to God."[9]

A hidden pitfall in historiography is disregard for the fact that conditions within nations and races change with the change of periods and the passage of time. This is a sore affliction and is deeply hidden, becoming noticeable only after a long time, so that rarely do more than a few individuals become aware of it.

[8] **Ibrâhîm b. al-Mahdî** The son of the caliph al-Mahdî, whom some considered, for a short time, to be the caliph. He lived 162–224 (Muslim calendar), or 779–839 CE.

[9] **Qur'an** Sura 31.22.

This is as follows. The condition of the world and of nations, their customs and sects, does not persist in the same form or in a constant manner. There are differences according to days and periods, and changes from one condition to another. Such is the case with individuals, times, and cities, and it likewise happens in connection with regions and districts, periods and dynasties.

The old Persian nations, the Syrians, the Nabataeans, the Tubba's, the Israelites, and the Copts, all once existed. They all had their own particular institutions in respect of dynastic and territorial arrangements, their own politics, crafts, languages, technical terminologies, as well as their own ways of dealing with their fellow men and handling their cultural institutions. Their historical relics testify to that. They were succeeded by the later Persians, the Byzantines, and the Arabs. The old institutions changed and former customs were transformed, either into something very similar, or into something distinct and altogether different. Then, there came Islam. Again, all institutions underwent another change, and for the most part assumed the forms that are still familiar at the present time as the result of their transmission from one generation to the next.

Then, the days of Arab rule were over. The early generations who had cemented Arab might and founded the realm of the Arabs were gone. Power was seized by others, by non-Arabs like the Turks in the east, the Berbers in the west, and the European Christians in the north. With their passing, entire nations ceased to exist, and institutions and customs changed. Their glory was forgotten, and their power no longer heeded.

The widely accepted reason for changes in institu- 15 tions and customs is the fact that the customs of each race depend on the customs of its ruler. As the proverb says: "The common people follow the religion of the ruler."[10]

---

[10] **religion of the ruler** The word for religion, *din,* is used here in the sense of the "way of doing things."

Chapter 1

Human Civilization in General

First Prefatory Discussion

Human social organization is something necessary. The 1 philosophers expressed this fact by saying: "Man is 'political' by nature." That is, he cannot do without the social organization for which the philosophers use the technical term "town" (*polis*).

This is what civilization means. (The necessary character of human social organization or civilization) is explained by the fact that God created and fashioned man in a form that can live and subsist only with the help of food. He guided man to a natural desire for food and instilled in him the power that enables him to obtain it.

However, the power of the individual human being is not sufficient for him to obtain (the food) he needs, and does not provide him with as much food as he requires to live. Even if we assume an absolute minimum of food—that is, food enough for one day, (a little) wheat, for instance—that amount of food could be obtained only after much preparation such as grinding, kneading, and baking. Each of these three operations requires utensils and tools that can be provided only with the help of several crafts, such as the crafts of the blacksmith, the carpenter, and the potter. Assuming that a man could eat unprepared grain, an even greater number of operations would be necessary in order to obtain the grain: sowing and reaping, and threshing to separate it from the husks of the ear. Each of these operations requires a number of tools and many more crafts than those just mentioned. It is beyond the power of one man alone to do all that, or part of it, by himself. Thus, he cannot do without a combination of many powers from among his fellow beings, if he is to obtain food for himself and for them. Through cooperation, the needs of a number of persons, many times greater than their own number, can be satisfied.

Likewise, each individual needs the help of his fellow beings for his defence. When God fashioned the natures of all living beings and divided the various powers among them, many dumb animals were given more perfect powers than God gave to man. The power of a horse, for instance, is much greater than the power of a man, and so is the power of a donkey or an ox. The power of a lion or an elephant is many times greater than the power of man.

Aggressiveness is natural in living beings. Therefore, 5 God gave each of them a special limb for defence against aggression. To man, instead, He gave the ability to think, and the hand. With the help of the ability to think, the hand is able to prepare the ground for the crafts. The crafts, in turn, procure for man the instruments that serve him instead of limbs, which other animals possess for their de-fence. Lances, for instance, take the place of horns for goring, swords the place of claws to inflict wounds, shields the place of thick skins, and so on. There are other such things. They were all mentioned by Galen in *De usu partium.*[11]

The power of one individual human being cannot withstand the power of any one dumb animal, especially the power of the predatory animals. Man is generally unable to defend himself against them by himself. Nor is his unaided power sufficient to make use of the existing instruments of defence, because there are so many of

---

[11] *De usu partium* Translated as "At the Beginning of the Work."

them and they require so many crafts and things. It is absolutely necessary for man to have the co-operation of his fellow men. As long as there is no such co-operation, he cannot obtain any food or nourishment, and life cannot materialize for him, because God fashioned him so that he must have food if he is to live. Nor, lacking weapons, can he defend himself. Thus, he falls prey to animals and dies much before his time. Under such circumstances, the human species would vanish. When, however, mutual cooperation exists, man obtains food for his nourishment and weapons for his defence. God's wise plan that mankind should subsist and the human species be preserved will be fulfilled.

Consequently, social organization is necessary to the human species. Without it, the existence of human beings would be incomplete. God's desire to settle the world with human beings and to leave them as His representatives on earth[12] would not materialize. This is the meaning of civilization, the object of the science under discussion.

The aforementioned remarks have been in the nature of establishing the existence of the object in this particular field. A scholar in a particular discipline is not obliged to do this, since it is accepted in logic that a scholar in a particular science does not have to establish the existence of the object in that science.[13] . . .

(THE REAL MEANING OF PROPHECY)

This world with all the created things in it has a certain order and solid construction. It shows nexuses between causes and things caused, combinations of some parts of creation with others, and transformations of some existent things into others, in a pattern that is both remarkable and endless. Beginning with the world of the body and sensual perception, and therein first with the world of the visible elements, one notices how these elements are arranged gradually and continually in an ascending order, from earth to water, to air, and to fire. Each one of the elements is prepared to be transformed into the next higher or lower one, and sometimes is transformed. The higher one is always finer than the one preceding it. Eventually, the world of the spheres is reached. They are finer than anything else. They are in layers which are interconnected, in a shape which the senses are able to perceive only through the existence of motions. These motions provide some people with knowledge of the measurements and positions of the spheres, and also with knowledge of the existence of the essences beyond, the influence of which is noticeable in the spheres through the fact that they have motion.

One should then look at the world of creation. It started out from the minerals and progressed, in an ingenious, gradual manner, to plants and animals. The last stage of

minerals is connected with the first stage of plants, such as herbs and seedless plants. The last stage of plants, such as palms and vines, is connected with the first stage of animals, such as snails and shellfish which have only the power of touch. The word "connection" with regard to these created things means that the last stage of each group is fully prepared to become the first stage of the next group.

The animal world then widens, its species become numerous, and, in a gradual process of creation, it finally leads to man, who is able to think and to reflect. The higher stage of man is reached from the world of the monkeys, in which both sagacity and perception are found, but which has not reached the stage of actual reflection and thinking. At this point we come to the first stage of man. This is as far as our (physical) observation extends.

Human Civilization Requires Political Leadership for Its Organization

We have mentioned before in more than one place that human social organization is something necessary. It is the thing that is meant by "the civilization" which we have been discussing. (People) in any social organization must have someone who exercises a restraining influence and rules them and to whom recourse may be had. His rule over them is sometimes based upon a divinely revealed religious law. They are obliged to submit to it in view of their belief in reward and punishment in the other world. Sometimes, (his rule is based) upon rational politics. People are obliged to submit to it in view of the reward they expect from the ruler after he has become acquainted with what is good for them.

The first (type of rule) is useful for this world and for the other world, because the lawgiver knows the ultimate interest of the people and is concerned with the salvation of man in the other world. The second is useful only for this world.

We do not mean here that which is known as "political utopianism." By that, the philosophers mean the disposition of soul and character which each member of a social organization must have, if, eventually, people are completely to dispense with rulers. They call the social organization that fulfills these requirements the "ideal city." The norms observed in this connection are called "political utopias." They do not mean the kind of politics that the members of a social organization are led to adopt through laws for the common interest. That is something different. The "ideal city" (of the philosophers) is something rare and remote. They discuss it as a hypothesis.

Now, the aforementioned rational politics may be of two types. The first type of rational politics may concern itself with the general interest, and with the ruler's interest in connection with the administration of his realm, in particular. This was the politics of the Persians. It is something related to philosophy. God made this type of politics superfluous for us in Islam at the time of the caliphate. The religious laws take its place in connection with both general and (particular) interests, for they also include the maxims (of the philosophers) and the rules of royal authority.

The second type (of rational politics) is the one con- 5 cerned with the interest of the ruler and how he can maintain his rule through the forceful use of power. The general interest is, here, secondary. This is the type of politics practised by all rulers, whether they are Muslims or unbelievers. Muslim rulers, however, practise this type of politics in accordance with the requirements of the Muslim religious law, as much as they are able to. Therefore, the political norms here are a mixture of religious laws and ethical rules, norms that are natural in social organization together with a certain necessary concern for strength and group feeling. . . .

With Regard to the Amount of Prosperity and Business Activity in Them, Cities and Towns Differ in Accordance with the Different Size of Their Population

The reason for this is that the individual human being 1 cannot by himself obtain all the necessities of life. All human beings must co-operate to that end in their civilization. But what is obtained through the co-operation of a group of human beings satisfies the need of a number many times greater than themselves. For instance, no one, by himself, can obtain the share of the wheat he needs for food. But when six or ten persons, including a smith and a carpenter to make the tools, and others who are in charge of the oxen, the ploughing of the soil, the harvesting of the ripe grain, and all the other agricultural activities, undertake to obtain their food and work toward that purpose either separately or collectively and thus obtain through their labour a certain amount of food, (that amount) will be food for a number of people many times their own. The combined labour produces more than the needs and necessities of the workers.

If the labour of the inhabitants of a town or city is distributed in accordance with the necessities and needs of those inhabitants, a minimum of that labour will suffice. The labour (available) is more than is needed. Consequently, it is spent to provide the conditions and customs of luxury and to satisfy the needs of the inhabitants of other cities. They import (the things they need) from (people who have a surplus) through exchange or purchase. Thus, the (people who have a surplus) get a good deal of wealth.

It will become clear in the fifth chapter, which deals with profit and sustenance, that profit is the value realized from labour. When there is more labour, the value realized from it increases among the (people). Thus, their profit of necessity increases. The prosperity and wealth they enjoy leads them to luxury and the things that go with it, such as splendid houses and clothes, fine vessels and utensils, and the use of servants and mounts. All these involve activities that require their price and skillful people must be chosen to do them and be in charge of them. As a consequence, industry and the crafts thrive. The income and the expenditure of the city increase. Affluence comes to those who work and produce these things by their labour.

When population increases, the available labour again increases. In turn, luxury again increases in correspondence with the increasing profit, and the customs and needs of luxury increase. Crafts are created to obtain (luxury products). The value realized from them increases, and, as a result, profits are again multiplied in the town. Production there is thriving even more than before. And so it goes with the second and third increases. All the additional labour serves luxury and wealth, in contrast to the original labour that served (the necessities of) life. The city that is superior to another in (population) becomes superior to it also by its increased profit and prosperity and by its customs of luxury which are not found in the other city. The more numerous and the more abundant the population in a city, the more luxurious is the life of its inhabitants. This applies equally to all levels of the population. . . .

∞

Chapter 6
The Various Kinds of Sciences. The Methods of Instruction.
The Conditions That Obtain in These Connections

Prefatory Discussion

On man's ability to think, which distinguishes human beings from animals and which enables them to obtain their livelihood, to co-operate to this end with their fellow men, and to study the Master whom they worship, and the revelations that the Messengers transmitted from Him. God thus caused all animals to obey man and to be in the grasp of his power. Through his ability to think, God gave man superiority over many of His creatures.

I MAN'S ABILITY TO THINK

God distinguished man from all the other animals by an 1 ability to think which He made the beginning of human perfection and the end of man's noble superiority over existing things.

This comes about as follows. Perception—that is, consciousness on the part of the person who perceives—is something peculiar to living beings to the exclusion of all other possible and existent things. Living beings may obtain consciousness of things that are outside their essence through the external senses God has given them, that is, the senses of hearing, vision, smell, taste, and touch. Man has this advantage over other beings: he can perceive things outside his essence through his ability to think, which is something beyond his senses. It is the result of (special) powers placed in the cavities of his brain. With the help of these powers, man takes the pictures of the *sensibilia*, applies his mind to them, and thus abstracts from them other pictures. The ability to think is the occupation with pictures that are beyond sense perception, and the application of the mind to them for analysis and synthesis.

The ability to think has several degrees. The first degree is man's intellectual understanding of the things that exist in the outside world in a natural or arbitrary order, so that he may try to arrange them with the help of his own power. This kind of thinking mostly consists of perceptions. It is the discerning intellect, with the help of which man obtains the things that are useful for him and his livelihood, and repels the things that are harmful to him.

The second degree is the ability to think which provides man with the ideas and the behaviour needed in dealing with his fellow men and in leading them. It mostly conveys apperceptions, which are obtained one by one through experience, until they have become really useful. This is called the experimental intellect.

The third degree is the ability to think which provides the knowledge, or hypothetical knowledge, of an object beyond sense perception without any practical activity (going with it). This is the speculative intellect. It consists of both perceptions and apperceptions. They are arranged according to a special order, following special conditions, and thus provide some other knowledge of the same kind, that is, either perceptive or apperceptive. Then, they are again combined with something else, and again provide some other knowledge. The end of the process is to be provided with the perception of existence as it is, with its various genera, differences, reasons and causes. By thinking about these things, man achieves perfection in his reality and becomes pure intellect and perceptive soul. This is the meaning of human reality.

Questions for Critical Thinking

1. What is Ibn Khaldun's definition of civilization, how does the individual fit into a civilization, and what are the interactions between the individual and civilization?

2. Compare and contrast Ibn Khaldun, as a historian, with Herodotus, Thucydides, and St. Augustine, noting their views of history and how and why events occur.

Selections from *The Arabian Nights*

The Arabian Nights is the most famous literary work produced by Islamic culture. Europeans first became acquainted with it through a French translation in the early 1700s, and later versions, rendered into most of the world's languages, made it a classic of world literature. Starting in the 1900s, with the rise of the mass media, the audience for *The Arabian Nights* expanded greatly, when many of the book's stories and characters, such as Ali Baba and the Forty Thieves and Aladdin and his Magic Lamp, became staples of popular culture, featured in comic strips, animated cartoons, and feature-length films.

Ironically, the world of Islam has been slow to appreciate the book's literary value. Only recently, in 1984, did there appear a definitive edition, by a Muslim scholar, of the fourteenth-century Syrian manuscript of *The Arabian Nights* in the Bibliothèque Nationale de France, which is one of the oldest versions and thus is thought to be close to the original form of the work. In the past, Islam's literary elite, although finding the work entertaining, disdained its colloquial language and grammatical errors and thought it suitable only for unsophisticated readers. Most important, Islam has a strong didactic element, so that literature, as all other elements of serious culture, is expected to serve a religious end, which is clearly not the case with the lighthearted stories in *The Arabian Nights.*

The stories in *The Arabian Nights* began circulating orally in the Muslim world, starting in the Golden Age, 800–1300, especially under the influence of Persian culture. Islam had initially been hostile to the story genre, because it was an offense against the religion's aesthetic code. A story "represented" reality and, thus, not being real, had no claim to truth. As Persians took leading roles in politics and society, they introduced elements of their tradition, such as the story form, into the fabric of Islamic life.

The earliest fragment from *The Arabian Nights* dates from the ninth century. The first reference to *The Arabian Nights* occurred in a tenth-century Arabic history, in a discussion of an Arabic work titled *The Thousand Tales* or *The Thousand Nights*, which was a translation of a Persian work called *Hazar Afsana* ("A Thousand Legends"). Neither work has survived, but the *Hazar Afsana* inspired the alternative title, *A Thousand and One Nights,* by which *The Arabian Nights* is known. *Hazar Afsana* also supplied the framing tale, imported from an Indian source, which tells of the woman, Shahrazad, who develops a storytelling plan to keep King Shahrayar from his crazed plan of murdering a new wife each day, after their wedding night, because of an earlier wife's infidelity. At first, fewer than a thousand tales existed, but over time, new ones were added to make the number exact.

The sources for the tales reflect Islam's ethnic diversity, including mainly Indian, Persian, and Arabic origins, but a few come from Iraq, Egypt, and Turkey. Many genres are represented: fairy tales, romances, legends, fables, parables, anecdotes, and realistic adventures. The stories, though often ancient, were modified when they were written down to bring them into harmony with the conditions of Islamic society and culture.

The literary style is typical of Islamic writing, which has been compared to the intricate weaving of a hand-loomed carpet: highly colored, filled with details, scenes, and figures, both animal and human, each interesting in its own way but not readily related to one another, yet with an allover pattern that gives a general coherence. Especially appealing is the style's bold blend of the colloquial and the lofty, the tragic and the comic, the supernatural and the natural.

Reading the Selections

The book's setting is imaginary: the court of King (Caliph) Shahrayar, ruler of India and Indochina. Betrayed by a wife, he kills her and vows to kill a new wife each day, after their wedding night. The vizier, the highest official serving the king, has the unhappy duty of putting the women to death. As the selection begins, Shahrazad, the vizier's daughter, has devised a strategy both to save her life and end the senseless killings.

Divided into nights, the book develops two plot lines simultaneously, one telling a portion of a tale each night, often ending with a cliff-hanging incident, the other consisting of bits of dialogue among the King, Shahrazad, and Dinarzad, Shahrazad's sister. The work is made more intricate by the periodic insertion of poetic passages, either borrowed from existing collections or supplied by the anonymous author—a reflection of the deep respect given to poetry in the Muslim world.

The selection contains eight nights, during which Shahrazad tells three stories: "The Story of the Merchant and the Demon," "The First Old Man's Tale," and "The Second Old Man's Tale." Each tale is a parable, offering a moral lesson that echoes the book's overall message: Victims can overcome their demon and human enemies if they keep their wits about them and rely on their storytelling gifts.

❧

. . .

Tired and exhausted, the vizier went to King Shahrayar and, kissing the ground before him, told him about his daughter, adding that he would give her to him that very night. The king was astonished and said to him, "Vizier, how is it that you have found it possible to give me your daughter, knowing that I will, by God, the Creator of heaven, ask you to put her to death the next morning and that if you refuse, I will have you put to death too?" He replied, "My King and Lord, I have told her everything and explained all this to her, but she refuses and insists on being with you tonight." The king was delighted and said, "Go to her, prepare her, and bring her to me early in the evening."

The vizier went down, repeated the king's message to his daughter, and said, "May God not deprive me of you." She was very happy and, after preparing herself and packing what she needed, went to her younger sister, Dinarzad, and said, "Sister, listen well to what I am telling you. When I go to the king, I will send for you, and when you come and see that the king has finished with me, say,

'Sister, if you are not sleepy, tell us a story.' Then I will begin to tell a story, and it will cause the king to stop his practice, save myself, and deliver the people." Dinarzad replied, "Very well."

At nightfall the vizier took Shahrazad and went with her to the great King Shahrayar. But when Shahrayar took her to bed and began to fondle her, she wept, and when he asked her, "Why are you crying?" she replied, "I have a sister, and I wish to bid her good-bye before daybreak." Then the king sent for the sister, who came and went to sleep under the bed. When the night wore on, she woke up and waited until the king had satisfied himself with her sister Shahrazad and they were by now all fully awake. Then Dinarzad cleared her throat and said, "Sister, if you are not sleepy, tell us one of your lovely little tales to while away the night, before I bid you good-bye at daybreak, for I don't know what will happen to you tomorrow." Shahrazad turned to King Shahrayar and said, "May I have your permission to tell a story?" He replied, "Yes," and Shahrazad was very happy and said, "Listen":

∞

The First Night

The Story of the Merchant and the Demon

It is said, O wise and happy King, that once there was a prosperous merchant who had abundant wealth and investments and commitments in every country. He had many women and children and kept many servants and slaves. One day, having resolved to visit another country, he took provisions, filling his saddlebag with loaves of bread and with dates, mounted his horse, and set out on his journey. For many days and nights, he journeyed under God's care until he reached his destination. When he finished his business, he turned back to his home and family. He journeyed for three days, and on the fourth day, chancing to come to an orchard, went in to avoid the heat and shade himself from the sun of the open country. He came to a spring under a walnut tree and, tying his horse, sat by the spring, pulled out from the saddlebag some loaves of bread and a handful of dates, and began to eat, throwing the date pits right and left until he had had enough. Then he got up, performed his ablutions,[14] and performed his prayers.

But hardly had he finished when he saw an old demon, with sword in hand, standing with his feet on the ground and his head in the clouds. The demon approached until he stood before him and screamed, saying, "Get up, so that

I may kill you with this sword, just as you have killed my son." When the merchant saw and heard the demon, he was terrified and awestricken. He asked, "Master, for what crime do you wish to kill me?" The demon replied, "I wish to kill you because you have killed my son." The merchant asked, "Who has killed your son?" The demon replied, "You have killed my son." The merchant said, "By God, I did not kill your son. When and how could that have been?" The demon said, "Didn't you sit down, take out some dates from your saddlebag, and eat, throwing the pits right and left?" The merchant replied, "Yes, I did." The demon said, "You killed my son, for as you were throwing the stones right and left, my son happened to be walking by and was struck and killed by one of them, and I must now kill you." The merchant said, "O my lord, please don't kill me." The demon replied, "I must kill you as you killed him—blood for blood." The merchant said, "To God we belong and to God we return. There is no power or strength, save in God the Almighty, the Magnificent. If I killed him, I did it by mistake. Please forgive me." The demon replied, "By God, I must kill you, as you killed my son." Then he seized him and, throwing him to the ground, raised the sword to strike him. The merchant began to weep and mourn his family and his wife and children. Again, the demon raised his sword to strike, while the merchant cried until he was drenched with tears, saying, "There is no power or strength, save in God the Almighty, the Magnificent." Then he began to recite the following verses:

---

[14] **ablutions** Ritual washing.

Life has two days: one peace, one wariness,
And has two sides: worry and happiness.
Ask him who taunts us with adversity,
"Does fate, save those worthy of note, oppress?
Don't you see that the blowing, raging storms
Only the tallest of the trees beset,
And of earth's many green and barren lots,
Only the ones with fruits with stones are hit,
And of the countless stars in heaven's vault
None is eclipsed except the moon and sun?
You thought well of the days, when they were good,
Oblivious to the ills destined for one.
You were deluded by the peaceful nights,
Yet in the peace of night does sorrow stun.

When the merchant finished and stopped weeping, the demon said, "By God, I must kill you, as you killed my son, even if you weep blood." The merchant asked, "Must you?" The demon replied, "I must," and raised his sword to strike.

But morning overtook Shahrazad, and she lapsed into silence, leaving King Shahrayar burning with curiosity to hear the rest of the story. Then Dinarzad said to her sister Shahrazad, "What a strange and lovely story!" Shahrazad replied, "What is this compared with what I shall tell you tomorrow night if the king spares me and lets me live? It will be even better and more entertaining." The king thought to himself, "I will spare her until I hear the rest of the story; then I will have her put to death the next day." When morning broke, the day dawned, and the sun rose; the king left to attend to the affairs of the kingdom, and the vizier, Shahrazad's father, was amazed and delighted. King Shahrayar governed all day and returned home at night to his quarters and got into bed with Shahrazad. Then Dinarzad said to her sister Shahrazad, "Please, sister, if you are not sleepy, tell us one of your lovely little tales to while away the night." The king added, "Let it be the conclusion of the story of the demon and the merchant, for I would like to hear it." Shahrazad replied, "With the greatest pleasure, dear, happy King":

The Second Night

It is related, O wise and happy King, that when the demon raised his sword, the merchant asked the demon again, "Must you kill me?" and the demon replied, "Yes." Then the merchant said, "Please give me time to say good-bye to my family and my wife and children, divide my property among them, and appoint guardians. Then I shall come back, so that you may kill me." The demon replied, "I am afraid that if I release you and grant you time, you will go and do what you wish, but will not come back." The merchant said, "I swear to keep my pledge to come back, as the God of Heaven and earth is my witness." The demon asked, "How much time do you need?" The merchant replied, "One year, so that I may see enough of my children, bid my wife good-bye, discharge my obligations to people, and come back on New Year's Day."[15] The demon asked, "Do you swear to God that if I let you go, you will come back on New Year's Day?" The merchant replied, "Yes, I swear to God."

After the merchant swore, the demon released him, and he mounted his horse sadly and went on his way. He journeyed until he reached his home and came to his wife and children. When he saw them, he wept bitterly, and when his family saw his sorrow and grief, they began to reproach him for his behavior, and his wife said, "Husband, what is the matter with you? Why do you mourn, when we are happy, celebrating your return?" He replied, "Why not mourn when I have only one year to live?" Then

he told her of his encounter with the demon and informed her that he had sworn to return on New Year's Day, so that the demon might kill him.

When they heard what he said, everyone began to cry. His wife struck her face in lamentation and cut her hair, his daughters wailed, and his little children cried. It was a day of mourning, as all the children gathered around their father to weep and exchange good-byes. The next day he wrote his will, dividing his property, discharged his obligations to people, left bequests and gifts, distributed alms, and engaged reciters to read portions of the *Qur'an* in his house. Then he summoned legal witnesses and in their presence freed his slaves and slave-girls, divided among his elder children their shares of the property, appointed guardians for his little ones, and gave his wife her share, according to her marriage contract. He spent the rest of the time with his family, and when the year came to an end, save for the time needed for the journey, he performed his ablutions, performed his prayers, and, carrying his burial shroud, began to bid his family good-bye. His sons hung around his neck, his daughters wept, and his wife wailed. Their mourning scared him, and he began to weep, as he embraced and kissed his children good-bye. He said to them, "Children, this is God's will and decree, for man was created to die." Then he turned away and, mounting his horse, journeyed day and night until he reached the orchard on New Year's Day.

He sat at the place where he had eaten the dates, waiting for the demon, with a heavy heart and tearful eyes. As he waited, an old man, leading a deer on a leash, approached and greeted him, and he returned the greeting. The old man inquired, "Friend, why do you sit here in this place of demons and devils? For in this haunted orchard

---

[15] **New Year's Day** In the Arabic calendar, the first day of *Muharram,* which commemorates the *Hijra,* Muhammad's flight from Mecca to Medina; the actual day varies with the lunar calendar.

none come to good." The merchant replied by telling him what had happened to him and the demon, from beginning to end. The old man was amazed at the merchant's fidelity and said, "Yours is a magnificent pledge," adding, "By God, I shall not leave until I see what will happen to you with the demon." Then he sat down beside him and chatted with him. As they talked. . . .

But morning overtook Shahrazad, and she lapsed into silence. 5 *As the day dawned, and it was light, her sister Dinarzad said, "What a strange and wonderful story!" Shahrazad replied, "Tomorrow night I shall tell something even stranger and more wonderful than this."*

❧

The Third Night

When it was night and Shahrazad was in bed with the king, 1 *Dinarzad said to her sister Shahrazad, "Please, if you are not sleepy, tell us one of your lovely little tales to while away the night." The king added, "Let it be the conclusion of the merchant's story." Shahrazad replied, "As you wish":*

I heard, O happy King, that as the merchant and the man with the deer sat talking, another old man approached, with two black hounds, and when he reached them, he greeted them, and they returned his greeting. Then he asked them about themselves, and the man with the deer told him the story of the merchant and the demon, how the merchant had sworn to return on New Year's Day, and how the demon was waiting to kill him. He added that when he himself heard the story, he swore never to leave until he saw what would happen between the merchant and the demon. When the man with the two dogs heard the story, he was amazed, and he too swore never to leave them until he saw what would happen between them. Then he questioned the merchant, and the merchant repeated to him what had happened to him with the demon.

While they were engaged in conversation, a third old man approached and greeted them, and they returned his greeting. He asked, "Why do I see the two of you sitting here, with this merchant between you, looking abject, sad, and dejected?" They told him the merchant's story and explained that they were sitting and waiting to see what would happen to him with the demon. When he

heard the story, he sat down with them, saying, "By God, I too like you will not leave, until I see what happens to this man with the demon." As they sat, conversing with one another, they suddenly saw the dust rising from the open country, and when it cleared, they saw the demon approaching, with a drawn steel sword in his hand. He stood before them without greeting them, yanked the merchant with his left hand, and, holding him fast before him, said, "Get ready to die." The merchant and the three old men began to weep and wail.

But dawn broke and morning overtook Shahrazad, and she lapsed into silence. Then Dinarzad said, "Sister, what a lovely story!" Shahrazad replied, "What is this compared with what I shall tell you tomorrow night? It will be even better; it will be more wonderful, delightful, entertaining, and delectable if the king spares me and lets me live." The king was all curiosity to hear the rest of the story and said to himself, "By God, I will not have her put to death until I hear the rest of the story and find out what happened to the merchant with the demon. Then I will have her put to death the next morning, as I did with the others." Then he went out to attend to the affairs of his kingdom, and when he saw Shahrazad's father, he treated him kindly and showed him favors, and the vizier was amazed. When night came, the king went home, and when he was in bed with Shahrazad, Dinarzad said, "Sister, if you are not sleepy, tell us one of your lovely little tales to while away the night." Shahrazad replied, "With the greatest pleasure":

❧

The Fourth Night

It is related, O happy King, that the first old man with the 1 deer approached the demon and, kissing his hands and feet, said, "Fiend and King of the demon kings, if I tell you what happened to me and that deer, and you find it strange and amazing, indeed stranger and more amazing than what happened to you and the merchant, will you grant me a third of your claim on him for his crime and guilt?" The demon replied, "I will." The old man said:

The First Old Man's Tale

Demon, this deer is my cousin, my flesh and blood. I married her when I was very young, and she a girl of twelve, who reached womanhood only afterward. For thirty years we lived together, but I was not blessed with children, for she bore neither boy nor girl. Yet I continued to be kind to her, to care for her, and to treat her generously. Then I took a mistress, and she bore me a son, who grew up to look like a slice of the moon. Meanwhile, my wife grew jealous of my mistress and my son. One day, when he was ten, I had to go on a journey. I entrusted my wife, this one here, with my mistress and son, bade her take good care of them, and was gone for a whole year. In my absence my wife, this cousin of mine, learned soothsaying and magic and cast a spell on my son and turned him into a young bull. Then she summoned my shepherd, gave my son to him, and said, "Tend this bull with the rest of the cattle." The shepherd took him and tended him for a while. Then she cast a spell on the mother, turning her into a cow, and gave her also to the shepherd.

When I came back, after all this was done, and inquired about my mistress and my son, she answered, "Your mistress died, and your son ran away two months ago, and I have had no news from him ever since." When I heard her, I grieved for my mistress, and with an anguished heart I mourned for my son for nearly a year. When the Great Feast of the Immolation[16] drew near, I summoned the shepherd and ordered him to bring me a fat cow for the sacrifice. The cow he brought me was in reality my enchanted mistress. When I bound her and pressed against her to cut her throat, she wept and cried, as if saying, "My son, my son," and her tears coursed down her cheeks. Astonished and seized with pity, I turned away and asked the shepherd to bring me a different cow. But my wife shouted, "Go on. Butcher her, for he has none better or fatter. Let us enjoy her meat at feast

---

[16] **Immolation** A Muslim festival, celebrated over four days, with the slaughter of sheep and cattle as offerings to Allah, that commemorates the pilgrimage to Mecca.

time." I approached the cow to cut her throat, and again she cried, as if saying, "My son, my son." Then I turned away from her and said to the shepherd, "Butcher her for me." The shepherd butchered her, and when he skinned her, he found neither meat nor fat but only skin and bone. I regretted having her butchered and said to the shepherd, "Take her all for yourself, or give her as alms to whomever you wish, and find me a fat young bull from among the flock." The shepherd took her away and disappeared, and I never knew what he did with her.

Then he brought me my son, my heartblood, in the guise of a fat young bull. When my son saw me, he shook his head loose from the rope, ran toward me, and, throwing himself at my feet, kept rubbing his head against me. I was astonished and touched with sympathy, pity, and mercy, for the blood hearkened to the blood and the divine bond, and my heart throbbed within me when I saw the tears coursing over the cheeks of my son the young bull, as he dug the earth with his hoofs. I turned away and said to the shepherd, "Let him go with the rest of the flock, and be kind to him, for I have decided to spare him. Bring me another one instead of him." My wife, this very deer, shouted, "You shall sacrifice none but this bull." I got angry and replied, "I listened to you and butchered the cow uselessly. I will not listen to you and kill this bull, for I have decided to spare him." But she pressed me, saying, "You must butcher this bull," and I bound him and took the knife. . . .

But dawn broke, and morning overtook Shahrazad, and she lapsed into silence, leaving the king all curiosity for the rest of the story. Then her sister Dinarzad said, "What an entertaining story!" Shahrazad replied, "Tomorrow night I shall tell you something even stranger, more wonderful, and more entertaining if the king spares me and lets me live."

∞

The Fifth Night

The following night, Dinarzad said to her sister Shahrazad, "Please, sister, if you are not sleepy, tell us one of your little tales." Shahrazad replied, "With the greatest pleasure":

I heard, dear King, that the old man with the deer said to the demon and to his companions:

I took the knife and as I turned to slaughter my son, he wept, bellowed, rolled at my feet, and motioned toward me with his tongue. I suspected something, began to waver with trepidation and pity, and finally released him, saying to my wife, "I have decided to spare him, and I commit him to your care." Then I tried to appease and please my wife, this very deer, by slaughtering another bull, promising her to slaughter this one next season. We slept that night, and when God's dawn broke, the shepherd came to me without letting my wife know, and said, "Give me credit for bringing you good news." I replied, "Tell me, and the credit is

yours." He said, "Master, I have a daughter who is fond of soothsaying and magic and who is adept at the art of oaths and spells. Yesterday I took home with me the bull you had spared, to let him graze with the cattle, and when my daughter saw him, she laughed and cried at the same time. When I asked her why she laughed and cried, she answered that she laughed because the bull was in reality the son of our master the cattle owner, put under a spell by his stepmother, and that she cried because his father had slaughtered the son's mother. I could hardly wait till daybreak to bring you the good news about your son."

Demon, when I heard that, I uttered a cry and fainted, and when I came to myself, I accompanied the shepherd to his home, went to my son, and threw myself at him, kissing him and crying. He turned his head toward me, his tears coursing over his cheeks, and dangled his tongue, as if to say, "Look at my plight." Then I turned to the shepherd's daughter and asked, "Can you release him from the spell? If you do, I will give you all my cattle and all my possessions." She smiled and replied, "Master, I have no desire for your wealth, cattle, or possessions. I will deliver him, but on two conditions: first, that you let me marry him; second, that you let me cast a spell on her who had cast a spell on him, in order to control her and guard against her evil power." I replied, "Do whatever you wish and more. My possessions are for you and my son. As for my wife, who has done this to my son and made me slaughter his mother, her life is forfeit to you." She said, "No, but I will let her taste what she has inflicted on others." Then the shepherd's daughter filled a bowl with water, uttered an incantation and an oath, and said to my son, "Bull, if you have been created in this image by the All-Conquering, Almighty Lord, stay as you are, but if you have been treacherously put under a spell, change back to your human form, by the will of God, Creator of the wide world." Then she sprinkled him with the water, and he shook himself and changed from a bull back to his human form.

As I rushed to him, I fainted, and when I came to myself, he told me what my wife, this very deer, had done to him and to his mother. I said to him, "Son, God has sent us someone who will pay her back for what you and your mother and I have suffered at her hands." Then, O demon, I gave my son in marriage to the shepherd's daughter, who turned my wife into this very deer, saying to me, "To me this is a pretty form, for she will be with us day and night, and it is better to turn her into a pretty deer than to suffer her sinister looks." Thus she stayed with us, while the days and nights followed one another, and the months and years went by. Then one day the shepherd's daughter died, and my son went to the country of this very man with whom you have had your encounter. Some time later I took my wife, this very deer, with me, set out to find out what had happened to my son, and chanced to stop here. This is my story, my strange and amazing story.

The demon assented, saying, "I grant you one-third of this man's life."

Then, O King Shahrayar, the second old man with the two black dogs approached the demon and said, "I too shall tell you what happened to me and to these two dogs, and if I tell it to you and you find it stranger and more amazing than this man's story will you grant me one-third of this man's life?" The demon replied, "I will." Then the old man began to tell his story, saying . . .

But dawn broke, and morning overtook Shahrazad, and she lapsed into silence. Then Dinarzad said, "This is an amazing story," and Shahrazad replied, "What is this compared with what I shall tell you tomorrow night if the king spares me and lets me live!" The king said to himself, "By God, I will not have her put to death until I find out what happened to the man with the two black dogs. Then I will have her put to death, God the Almighty willing."

∞

The Sixth Night

When the following night arrived and Shahrazad was in bed with King Shahrayar, her sister Dinarzad said, "Sister, if you are not sleepy, tell us a little tale. Finish the one you started." Shahrazad replied, "With the greatest pleasure":

I heard, O happy King, that the second old man with the two dogs said:

The Second Old Man's Tale

Demon, as for my story, these are the details. These two dogs are my brothers. When our father died, he left behind three sons, and left us three thousand dinars,[17] with which each of us opened a shop and became a shop keeper. Soon my older brother, one of these very dogs, went and sold the contents of his shop for a thousand dinars, bought trading goods, and, having prepared himself for his trading trip, left us. A full year went by, when one day, as I sat in my shop, a beggar stopped by to beg. When I refused him, he tearfully asked, "Don't you recognize me?" and when

I looked at him closely, I recognized my brother. I embraced him and took him into the shop, and when I asked him about his plight, he replied, "The money is gone, and the situation is bad." Then I took him to the public bath, clothed him in one of my robes, and took him home with me. Then I examined my books and checked my balance, and found out that I had made a thousand dinars and that my net worth was two thousand dinars. I divided the amount between my brother and myself, and said to him, "Think as if you have never been away." He gladly took the money and opened another shop.

Soon afterward my second brother, this other dog, went and sold his merchandise and collected his money, intending to go on a trading trip. We tried to dissuade him, but he did not listen. Instead, he bought merchandise and trading goods, joined a group of travelers, and was gone for a full year. Then he came back, just like his older brother. I said to him, "Brother, didn't I advise you not to go?" He replied tearfully, "Brother, it was foreordained. Now I am poor and penniless, without even a shirt on my back." Demon, I took him to the public bath, clothed him in one of my new robes, and took him back to the shop. After we had something to eat, I said to him, "Brother, I shall do my business accounts, calculate my

---

[17] **dinars** Gold coins; the basic form of Muslim money.

net worth for the year, and after subtracting the capital, whatever the profit happens to be, I shall divide it equally between you and myself. When I examined my books and subtracted the capital, I found out that my profit was two thousand dinars, and I thanked God and felt very happy. Then I divided the money, giving him a thousand dinars and keeping a thousand for myself. With that money he opened another shop, and the three of us stayed together for a while. Then my two brothers asked me to go on a trading journey with them, but I refused, saying, "What did you gain from your ventures that I can gain?"

They dropped the matter, and for six years we worked in our stores, buying and selling. Yet every year they asked me to go on a trading journey with them, but I refused, until I finally gave in. I said, "Brothers, I am ready to go with you. How much money do you have?" I found out that they had eaten and drunk and squandered everything they had, but I said nothing to them and did not reproach them. Then I took inventory, gathered all I had together, and sold everything. I was pleased to discover that the

5

sale netted six thousand dinars. Then I divided the money into two parts, and said to my brothers, "The sum of three thousand dinars is for you and myself to use on our trading journey. The other three thousand I shall bury in the ground, in case what happened to you happens to me, so that when we return, we will find three thousand dinars to reopen our shops." They replied, "This is an excellent idea." Then, demon, I divided my money and buried three thousand dinars. Of the remaining three I gave each of my brothers a thousand and kept a thousand for myself. After I closed my shop, we bought merchandise and trading goods, rented a large seafaring boat, and after loading it with our goods and provisions, sailed day and night, for a month.

But morning overtook Shahrazad, and she lapsed into silence. Then her sister Dinarzad said, "Sister, what a lovely story!" Shahrazad replied, "Tomorrow night I shall tell you something even lovelier, stranger, and more wonderful if I live, the Almighty God willing."

∞

The Seventh Night

The following night Dinarzad said to her sister Shahrazad, "For God's sake, sister, if you are not sleepy, tell us a little tale." The king added, "Let it be the completion of the story of the merchant and the demon." Shahrazad replied, "With the greatest pleasure":

1

I heard, O happy King, that the second old man said to the demon:

For a month my brothers, these very dogs, and I sailed the salty sea, until we came to a port city. We entered the city and sold our goods, earning ten dinars for every dinar. Then we bought other goods, and when we got to the seashore to embark, I met a girl who was dressed in tatters. She kissed my hands and said, "O my lord, be charitable and do me a favor, and I believe that I shall be able to reward you for it." I replied, "I am willing to do you a favor regardless of any reward." She said, "O my lord, marry me, clothe me, and take me home with you on this boat, as your wife, for I wish to give myself to you. I, in turn, will reward you for your kindness and charity, the Almighty God willing. Don't be misled by my poverty and present condition." When I heard her words, I felt pity for her, and guided by what God the Most High had intended for me, I consented. I clothed her with an expensive dress and married her. Then I took her to the boat, spread the bed for her, and consummated our marriage. We sailed many days and nights, and I, feeling love for her, stayed with her day and night, neglecting my brothers. In the meantime they, these very dogs, grew jealous of me, envied me for my increasing merchandise and wealth, and coveted all our possessions. At last they decided to betray me and, tempted by the Devil, plotted to kill me.

One night they waited until I was asleep beside my wife; then they carried the two of us and threw us into the sea.

When we awoke, my wife turned into a she-demon and carried me out of the sea to an island. When it was morning, she said, "Husband, I have rewarded you by saving you from drowning, for I am one of the demons who believe in God. When I saw you by the seashore, I felt love for you and came to you in the guise in which you saw me, and when I expressed my love for you, you accepted me. Now I must kill your brothers." When I heard what she said, I was amazed and I thanked her and said, "As for destroying my brothers, this I do not wish, for I will not behave like them." Then I related to her what had happened to me and them, from beginning to end. When she heard my story, she got very angry at them, and said, "I shall fly to them now, drown their boat, and let them all perish." I entreated her, saying, "For God's sake, don't. The proverb advises 'Be kind to those who hurt you.' No matter what, they are my brothers after all." In this manner, I entreated her and pacified her. Afterward, she took me and flew away with me until she brought me home and put me down on the roof of my house. I climbed down, threw the doors open, and dug up the money I had buried. Then I went out and, greeting the people in the market, reopened my shop. When I came home in the evening, I found these two dogs tied up, and when they saw me, they came to me, wept, and rubbed themselves against me. I started, when I suddenly heard my wife say, "O my lord, these are your brothers." I asked, "Who has done this to them?" She replied, "I sent to my sister and asked her to do it. They will stay in this condition for ten years, after which they may be delivered." Then she told me where to find her and departed. The ten years have passed, and I was with my brothers on my way to her to have the spell lifted, when I met this man, together with this old man with the deer. When I asked him about himself, he told me about his encounter with you, and I resolved not to leave until I found out what would happen between you and him. This is my story. Isn't it amazing?

The demon replied, "By God, it is strange and amazing. ₅ I grant you one-third of my claim on him for his crime."

Then the third old man said, "Demon, don't disappoint me. If I told you a story that is stranger and more amazing than the first two would you grant me one-third of your claim on him for his crime?" The demon replied, "I will." Then the old man said, "Demon, listen":

But morning overtook Shahrazad, and she lapsed into silence. Then her sister said, "What an amazing story!" Shahrazad replied, "The rest is even more amazing." The king said to himself, "I will not have her put to death until I hear what happened to the old man and the demon; then I will have her put to death, as is my custom with the others."

∞

The Eighth Night

The following night Dinarzad said to her sister Shahrazad, "For ₁ *God's sake, sister, if you are not sleepy, tell us one of your lovely little tales to while away the night." Shahrazad replied, "With the greatest pleasure":*

I heard, O happy King, that the third old man told the demon a story that was even stranger and more amazing than the first two. The demon was very much amazed and, swaying with delight, said, "I grant you one-third of my claim on him for his crime." Then the demon released the merchant and departed. The merchant turned to the

three old men and thanked them, and they congratulated him on his deliverance and bade him good-bye. Then they separated, and each of them went on his way. The merchant himself went back home to his family, his wife, and his children, and he lived with them until the day he died. But this story is not as strange or as amazing as the story of the fisherman.

Dinarzad asked, "Please, sister, what is the story of the fisherman?"

· · ·

∞

Questions for Critical Thinking

1. Discuss some of the images and techniques used in "The Story of the Merchant and the Demon." What is the moral lesson of this story?

2. What does "The First Old Man's Tale" reveal about families and human behavior? What is the moral lesson within this tale?

——————————— ∞ ———————————

RUMI

Selections from the *Masnavi*

Rumi (1207–1273), a Persian poet and Sufi mystic, was one of the most original figures in medieval Islam. His life and poetry helped define Sufism, the mystical tradition that played a creative role in Muslim society, by educating the masses, stressing spiritual values rather than the strict legalism of orthodox religious leaders, and inspiring missionary efforts around the globe. The greatest Persian poet, Rumi created two major works that had a profound impact on Muslim mysticism and literature: the *Diwan-e Shams*, lyrical verses, and the *Masnavi-ye Ma'navi* ("Spiritual Couplets"), a compendium of mystical thought. After his death, disciples in Anatolia (modern Turkey) founded a Sufi ascetic order, the Whirling Dervishes (in Persian, the Sufis were known as *darvish*, "the poor"), who used singing, chanting, and a whirling dance to achieve union with God. Rumi's *Masnavi* has been widely translated, with many commentaries written on it; Persian-speaking Sufis consider it second only to the Qur'an as a spiritual guide.

The son of an eminent mystic, writer, and thinker, Rumi readily followed in his father's footsteps. Born in the Persian Empire, in the city of Balkh (in modern Afghanistan), where he was called Jalal ad-Din Balkhi, he and the rest of his family fled from invading Mongols in 1218. After wandering the Middle East, the family settled in Anatolia, known as Rum, meaning "Roman Anatolia," which then enjoyed peace under a Seljuk Turkish dynasty. There, living in Konya, the capital, he became known as *Rumi*, that is, "the one from the country of Rum." On his father's death, in 1231, Rumi replaced him as a prominent teacher in the local religious schools, or *madrasas*.

Having become a fixture in the civic life of Konya, Rumi had his quiet existence shattered by a meeting, in 1244, with the wandering dervish, Shams ad-Din ("Sun of Religion"), formerly of Tabriz (in modern Iran), an encounter that forever transformed Rumi's life. Instantly finding Shams's simple faith persuasive, Rumi made the dervish his lifelong passion in a Platonic friendship. The two friends grew inseparable, spending days together in mystic conversation. Through friendship the men deepened their sense of communion with God, but it provoked turmoil in Rumi's family and among his students, who felt neglected. Seeking to avoid conflict, Shams abruptly disappeared, fleeing to Damascus, only to be discovered and summoned back to Konya. After another dramatic meeting, the pair renewed their friendship, with Shams's moving into Rumi's house and marrying a young girl of the household. This arrangement once again caused murmuring among Rumi's family and students. In 1248, Shams disappeared again, perhaps murdered by one of Rumi's sons—according to rumors of the period.

In response to his lost friend, Rumi composed the *Diwan-e Shams* ("The Poetry of Shams"), which he wrote in an ecstatic state, after listening to music, singing, and whirling about hour after hour. Using the themes of love and loss, Rumi speaks through the voice of Shams, thus symbolizing their union, a model of the Sufi goal of union with God. The operative word here is *fana*, Persian for "annihilation in God." In later years, Rumi developed similar friendships, as part of the Sufi search for mystical union with God.

Rumi's friendship with his student Husam ad-Din Chelebi sparked the poet's last work, the *Masnavi-ye Ma'navi*, a monumental collection of about 26,000 couplets, or poetic units of two successive rhyming lines. Dictated by Rumi as he went about his daily tasks and recorded by Husam, this work teaches the Sufi way, by indirection, using vivid and folksy examples, drawn from stories, anecdotes, proverbs, fables, and folktales.

Reading the Selections

The seven poems are from the *Masnavi*, in a free verse version by an American poet, who manages to capture the liveliness, earthiness, and surprise of the original poems. In several poems, the lover converses with or about the beloved, a symbol of the soul's ongoing love affair with God. Each piece teaches a similar moral lesson, usually involving the annihilation of the self (*fana*), so that the soul may be united with God.

The sources for four of the poems are proverbs: "The Food Sack," "The Grasses," "Zikr (Remembering)," and "The Core of Masculinity." In these poems, many short, pithy expressions embodying folk wisdom are used, as, for example, in "The Food Sack," "A nursing baby does not know the taste of roasted meat," and in "The Grasses," "Never brag of being strong." Two poems are meditations based on conversations, one called "I Have Five Things to Say" and the other called "A Man and a Woman Arguing." In the last poem, "Put This Design in Your Carpet," the poet interprets "spiritual experience" as a dense tapestry woven from everyday life—in many ways, a summary of Rumi's teachings about ultimate reality.

∞

I Have Five Things to Say

The wakened lover speaks directly to the beloved,   1
"You are the sky my spirit circles in,
the love inside love, the resurrection-place.

Let this window be your ear.
I have lost consciousness many times
with longing for your listening silence,
and your life-quickening smile.

You give attention to the smallest matters,
my suspicious doubts, and to the greatest.

You know my coins are counterfeit,   10
but you accept them anyway,
my impudence and my pretending!

I have five things to say,
five fingers to give
into your grace.

First, when I was apart from you,
this world did not exist,
nor any other.

Second, whatever I was looking for
was always you.   20

Third, why did I ever learn to count to three?

Fourth, my cornfield is burning!

Fifth, this finger stands for Rabia,[18]
and this is for someone else.
Is there a difference?

Are these words or tears?
Is weeping speech?
What shall I do, my love?"

So he speaks, and everyone around
begins to cry with him, laughing crazily,   30
moaning in the spreading union
of lover and beloved.

This is the true religion. All others
are thrown-away bandages beside it.

This is the sema[19] of slavery and mastery
dancing together. This is not-being.

Neither words, nor any natural fact
can express this.

I know these dancers.
Day and night I sing their songs   40
in this phenomenal cage.

My soul, don't try to answer now!
Find a friend, and hide.

But what can stay hidden?
Love's secret is always lifting its head
out from under the covers,
"Here I am!"

---

[18] **Rabia** (d. 801) An Islamic woman mystic from Basra.

[19] *sema* The whirling dance of the Sufis.

∞

The Food Sack

One day a sufi sees an empty food sack hanging on a nail.   1
He begins to turn[20] and tear his shirt, saying,
Food for what needs no food!
A cure for hunger!

His burning grows and others join him,
shouting and moaning in the love-fire.

An idle passerby comments, "It's only an empty sack."
The sufi says, *Leave. You want what we do not want.*
You are not a lover.

A lover's food is the love of bread,   10
not the bread. No one who really loves,
loves existence.

Lovers have nothing to do with existence.
They collect the interest without the capital.

---

[20] **turn** Whirl, the characteristic dance of the Whirling Dervishes.

No wings, yet they fly all over the world. No hands,
but they carry the polo ball from the field.

That dervish got a sniff of reality.
Now he weaves baskets of pure vision.

Lovers pitch tents on a field of nowhere.
They are all one color like that field.   20

A nursing baby does not know the taste of roasted meat.
To a spirit the foodless scent is food.

To an Egyptian, the Nile looks bloody.
To an Israelite, clear.
What is a highway to one is disaster to the other.

The Grasses

The same wind that uproots trees   1
makes the grasses shine.

The lordly wind loves the weakness
and the lowness of grasses.
Never brag of being strong.

The axe doesn't worry how thick the branches are.
It cuts them to pieces. But not the leaves.
It leaves the leaves alone.

A flame doesn't consider the size of the woodpile.
A butcher doesn't run from a flock of sheep.   10

What is form in the presence of reality?
Very feeble. Reality keeps the sky turned over
like a cup above us, revolving. Who turns
the sky wheel? The universal intelligence.

And the motion of the body comes
from the spirit like a waterwheel
that's held in a stream.

The inhaling-exhaling is from spirit,
now angry, now peaceful.

Wind destroys, and wind protects.   20

There is no reality but God,
says the completely surrendered sheikh,[21]
who is an ocean for all beings.

The levels of creation are straws in that ocean.
The movement of the straws comes from an agitation
in the water. When the ocean wants the straws calm,
it sends them close to shore. When it wants them
back in the deep surge, it does with them
as the wind does with the grasses.
                                  This never ends.[22]   30

---

[21] **sheikh** In Sufism, a religious leader held in deep respect.
[22] **This never ends.** A metaphor, like the whirling dance of the Sufis, for the universal motion in Nature and the cosmos. Only God doesn't move.

A Man and a Woman Arguing

One night in the desert   1
a poor Bedouin woman has this to say
to her husband,
                "Everyone is happy
and prosperous, except us! We have no bread.
We have no spices. We have no water jug.
We barely have any clothes. No blankets

for the night. We fantasize that the full moon
is a cake. We reach for it! We're an embarrassment
even to the beggars. Everyone avoids us.   10

Arab men are supposed to be generous warriors,
but look at you, stumbling around! If some guest
were to come to us, we'd steal his rags

when he fell asleep. Who is your guide
that leads you to this? We can't even get
a handful of lentils! Ten years' worth
of nothing, that's what we are!"
                                  She went on and on.
"If God is abundant, we must be following
an imposter. Who's leading us? Some fake,   20
that always says, *Tomorrow, illumination
will bring you treasure, tomorrow.*

As everyone knows, that never comes.
Though I guess, it happens very rarely, sometimes,
that a disciple following an imposter can somehow
surpass the pretender. But still I want to know
what this deprivation says about us."

The husband replied, finally,
                    "How long will you complain
about money and our prospects for money? The torrent   30
of our life has mostly gone by. Don't worry about
transient things. Think how the animals live.

The dove on the branch giving thanks.
The glorious singing of the nightingale.
The gnat. The elephant. Every living thing
trusts in God for its nourishment.

These pains that you feel are messengers.
Listen to them. Turn them to sweetness. The night
is almost over. You were young once, and content.
Now you think about money all the time.   40

You used to *be* that money. You were a healthy vine.
Now you're a rotten fruit. You ought to be growing
sweeter and sweeter, but you've gone bad.
As my wife, you should be equal to me.
Like a pair of boots, if one is too tight,
the pair is of no use.

Like two folding doors, we can't be mismatched.
A lion does not mate with a wolf."

So this man who was happily poor
scolded his wife until daybreak,   50
when she responded,
                    "Don't talk to me
about your high station! Look how you act!
Spiritual arrogance is the ugliest of all things.
It's like a day that's cold and snowy,
and your clothes are wet too!

It's too much to bear!
And don't call me your mate, you fraud!
You scramble after scraps of bone
with the dogs.   60

You're not as satisfied as you pretend!
You're the snake and the snake charmer
at the same time, but you don't know it.
You're charming a snake for money,
and the snake is charming you.

You talk about God a lot, and you make me feel guilty
by using that word. You better watch out!
That word will poison you, if you use it
to have power over me."

So the rough volume of her talking   70
fell on the husband, and he fought back,
                    "Woman,
this poverty is my deepest joy.
This bare way of life is honest and beautiful.
We can hide nothing when we're like this.
You say I'm really arrogant and greedy,
and you say I'm a snake charmer and a snake,
but those nicknames are for you.

In your anger and your wantings
you see those qualities in me.   80
I want nothing from this world.

You're like a child that has turned round and round,
and now you think the house is turning.

It's your eyes that see wrong. Be patient,
and you'll see the blessings and the lord's light
in how we live."
                    This argument continued[23]
throughout the day, and even longer.

---

[23] **This argument continued** A metaphor, like the whirling dance of the Sufis, for the universal motion in Nature and the cosmos. Only God doesn't move.

∞

Zikr[24]

A naked man jumps in the river, hornets swarming   1
above him. The water is the *zikr*, remembering,
There is no reality but God. There is only God.

The hornets are his sexual remembering, this woman,
that woman. Or if a woman, this man, that.
The head comes up. They sting.

Breathe water. Become river head to foot.
Hornets leave you alone then. Even if you're far
from the river, they pay no attention.

No one looks for stars when the sun's out.   10
A person blended into God does not disappear.
   He, or she,
is just completely soaked in God's qualities.
Do you need a quote from the *Qur'an*?

All shall be brought into our Presence.

---

[24] **Zikr** Persian, "remembering."

Join those travelers. The lamps we burn go out,
some quickly. Some last till daybreak.
Some are dim, some intense, all fed with fuel.

If a light goes out in one house, that doesn't affect
the next house. This is the story of the animal soul,
not the divine soul. The sun shines on every house.   20
When it goes down, all houses get dark.

Light is the image of your teacher. Your enemies
love the dark. A spider weaves a web over a light,
out of himself, or herself, makes a veil.

Don't try to control a wild horse by grabbing its leg.
Take hold the neck. Use a bridle. Be sensible.
Then ride! There is a need for self-denial.

Don't be contemptuous of old obediences. They help.

∞

The Core of Masculinity

The core of masculinity   1
does not derive from being male,
nor friendliness from those who console.

Your old grandmother says, "Maybe you shouldn't
go to school. You look a little pale."

Run when you hear that.
A father's stern slaps are better.

Your bodily soul wants comforting.
The severe father wants spiritual clarity.

He scolds but eventually   10
leads you into the open.

Pray for a tough instructor
to hear and act and stay within you.

We have been busy accumulating solace.
Make us afraid of how we were.

∞

Put This Design in Your Carpet

Spiritual experience is a modest woman
who looks lovingly at only one man.

It's a great river where ducks
live happily, and crows drown.

The visible bowl of form contains food
that is both nourishing and a source of heartburn.

There is an unseen presence we honor
that gives the gifts.

You're water. We're the millstone.
You're wind. We're dust blown up into shapes.   10
You're spirit. We're the opening and closing
of our hands. You're the clarity.
We're this language that tries to say it.
You're joy. We're all the different kinds of laughing.

Any movement or sound is a profession of faith,
as the millstone grinding is explaining how it believes

in the river! No metaphor can say this,   1
but I can't stop pointing
to the beauty.

Every moment and place says,   20
"Put this design in your carpet!"

Like the shepherd . . .
who wanted to pick the lice off God's robe,
and stitch up God's shoes, I want to be
in such a passionate adoration
that my tent gets pitched against the sky!

Let the beloved come
and sit like a guard dog
in front of the tent.

When the ocean surges,   30
don't let me just hear it.
Let it splash inside my chest!

∞

Questions for Critical Thinking

1. Compare and contrast the conversations in "I Have Five Things to Say" and "A Man and a Woman Arguing." What are the themes in the two poems?

2. What are some of the themes in the five remaining poems? Which of them is your favorite and why? Do you think Rumi is writing about issues that are important for us? Explain.

10

THE HIGH MIDDLE AGES
1000–1300

Selections from *Song of Roland*

The anonymous poem *Song of Roland* belongs to the literary genre known as *chanson de geste* (from French, "song of deeds"), which dominated medieval literature in the first half of the twelfth century. Based on historical events, it tells of Count Roland, a vassal and knight of Charlemagne, the king of the Franks who ruled the then largest and most centralized state since the fall of Rome. According to medieval records, Roland governed the Breton march (modern Brittany) in the name of Charlemagne and died fighting in Spain in 778. Einhard (see *The Life of Charlemagne* in Chapter 8) names Roland as a leader of Charlemagne's rear guard, who was killed by Christian Basques in an ambush in northern Spain while protecting the king and his forward army.

Only a distant echo of these actual events survives in *Song of Roland,* which glorifies the knight and his sacrificial death. The poem was written down in about 1100, having circulated orally in songs performed by bards (singing poets) for several centuries. By the time it received its final form, what had been a minor skirmish had been transformed by poetic art into a battle of vast proportions. Roland, who was only one of the many "brave knights" sung about in the Middle Ages, became the central figure in a rousing tale of bravery, treachery, and pride.

The world described in *Song of Roland* reflects more the time it was finally set in writing (the twelfth century) than the period when Roland lived (the eighth century). Medieval Europe had launched the Crusades (the first began in 1095) against the Muslim world; hence, in the poem, Charlemagne's enemies are changed from Christian Basques to Spanish Saracens (Muslims). France was also in the early stages of becoming a unified state; thus, in the poem, the far-flung Frankish kingdom is transformed into France—a sign of embryonic nationalism that French kings wanted to nurture. Finally, the twelfth-century church was more powerful than in Charlemagne's day, and in the poem, this increased power is expressed in the pivotal role played by the warrior Archbishop Turpin.

Song of Roland is typical of *chansons de geste* in that it celebrates a defeat. In an elaborately complicated story set at Charlemagne's court, Roland instigates a possibly deadly mission for his rival, Ganelon. But he suddenly finds the tables turned and himself a victim when Ganelon plots an ambush with the Spanish Saracens.

Reading the Selections

These thirteen verses *(laisses)*, 79–87 and 129–132, depict the doomed Franks as they fall into the trap laid by the Saracens. The turning point of the poem, these verses also set forth the work's theme and moral. Roland, in verse 79, gives voice to the anonymous author's chivalric and self-consciously literary theme:

> *We know our duty: to stand here for our King . . .*
> *let them not sing a bad song about us!*

∞

79.

They arm themselves in Saracen hauberks,[1]   1
all but a few are lined with triple mail;
they lace on their good helms[2] of Saragossa,
gird on their swords, the steel forged in Vienne;
they have rich shields, spears of Valencia,
and gonfanons[3] of white and blue and red.
They leave the mules and riding horses now,
mount their war horses and ride in close array.
The day was fair, the sun was shining bright,
all their armor was aflame with the light;   10
a thousand trumpets blow: that was to make it finer.
That made a great noise, and the men of France heard.
Said Oliver: "Companion, I believe
we may yet have a battle with the pagans."
Roland replies: "Now may God grant us that.
We know our duty: to stand here for our King.
A man must bear some hardships for his lord,
stand everything, the great heat, the great cold,
lose the hide and hair on him for his good lord.
Now let each man make sure to strike hard here: 20
let them not sing a bad song about us!
Pagans are wrong and Christians are right!
They'll make no bad example of me this day!"

80.

Oliver climbs to the top of a hill,
looks to his right, across a grassy vale,
sees the pagan army on its way there;
and called down to Roland, his companion:
"That way, toward Spain: the uproar I see coming!
All their hauberks, all blazing, helmets like flames!
It will be a bitter thing for our French.   30
Ganelon knew, that criminal, that traitor,
when he marked us out before the Emperor."

"Be still, Oliver," Roland the Count replies.
"He is my stepfather—my stepfather.
I won't have you speak one word against him."

81.

Oliver has gone up upon a hill,
sees clearly now: the kingdom of Spain,
and the Saracens assembled in such numbers:
helmets blazing, bedecked with gems in gold,
those shields of theirs, those hauberks sewn with brass,   40
and all their spears, the gonfanons affixed;
cannot begin to count their battle corps,
there are too many, he cannot take their number.
And he is deeply troubled by what he sees.
He made his way quickly down from the hill,
came to the French, told them all he had seen.

82.

Said Oliver: "I saw the Saracens,
no man on earth ever saw more of them—
one hundred thousand, with their shields, up in front,
helmets laced on, hauberks blazing on them,   50
the shafts straight up, the iron heads[4] like flames—
you'll get a battle, nothing like it before.
My lords, my French, may God give you the strength.
Hold your ground now! Let them not defeat us!"
And the French say: "God hate the man who runs!
We may die here, but no man will fail you."

83.

Said Oliver: "The pagan force is great;
from what I see, our French here are too few.
Roland, my companion, sound your horn then,
Charles will hear it, the army will come back."   60
Roland replies: "I'd be a fool to do it.
I would lose my good name all through sweet France.

---

[1] **hauberks** Coats of mail or tunics of chained mail to cover the body.
[2] **helms** Helmets.
[3] **gonfanons** Standards or battle flags, often decorated with pendants or small flags.

[4] **iron heads** Wooden shafts with iron spikes or heads on them.

I will strike now, I'll strike with Durendal,[5]
the blade will be bloody to the gold from striking!
These pagan traitors came to these passes doomed!
I promise you, they are marked men, they'll die."

84.

"Roland, Companion, now sound the olifant,[6]
Charles will hear it, he will bring the army back,
the King will come with all his barons to help us."
Roland replies: "May it never please God   70
that my kin should be shamed because of me,
or that sweet France should fall into disgrace.
Never! Never! I'll strike with Durendal,
I'll strike with this good sword strapped to my side,
you'll see this blade running its whole length with blood.
These pagan traitors have gathered here to die.
I promise you, they are all bound for death."

85.

"Roland, Companion, sound your olifant now,
Charles will hear it, marching through those passes.
I promise you, the Franks will come at once."   80
Roland replies: "May it never please God
that any man alive should come to say
that pagans—pagans!—once made me sound this horn:
no kin of mine will ever bear that shame.
Once I enter this great battle coming
and strike my thousand seven hundred blows,
you'll see the bloody steel of Durendal.
These French are good—they will strike like brave men.
Nothing can save the men of Spain from death."

86.

Said Oliver: "I see no blame in it—   90
I watched the Saracens coming from Spain,
the valleys and mountains covered with them,
every hillside and every plain all covered,
hosts and hosts everywhere of those strange men—
and here we have a little company."
Roland replies: "That whets my appetite.
May it not please God and his angels and saints
to let France lose its glory because of me—
let me not end in shame, let me die first.
The Emperor loves us when we fight well."   100

87.

Roland is good, and Oliver is wise,
both these vassals men of amazing courage:
once they are armed and mounted on their horses,
they will not run, though they die for it, from battle.

———————
[5] **Durendal** Roland's sword.
[6] **olifant** Roland's ivory horn.

Good men, these Counts, and their words full of spirit.
Traitor pagans are riding up in fury.
Said Oliver: "Roland, look—the first one,
on top of us—and Charles is far away.
You did not think it right to sound your olifant:
if the King were here, we'd come out without losses.   110
Now look up there, toward the passes of Aspre—
you can see the rear-guard: it will suffer.
No man in that detail will be in another."
Roland replies: "Don't speak such foolishness—
shame on the heart gone coward in the chest.
We'll hold our ground, we'll stand firm—we're the ones!
We'll fight with spears, we'll fight them hand to hand!"

. . .

129.

And Roland said: "I'll sound the olifant,
Charles will hear it, drawing through the passes,
I promise you, the Franks will return at once."   120
Said Oliver: "That would be a great disgrace,
a dishonor and reproach to all your kin,
the shame of it would last them all their lives.
When I urged it, you would not hear of it;
you will not do it now with my consent.
It is not acting bravely to sound it now—
look at your arms, they are covered with blood."
The Count replies: "I've fought here like a lord."

130.

And Roland says: "We are in a rough battle.
I'll sound the olifant, Charles will hear it."   130
Said Oliver: "No good vassal would do it.
When I urged it, friend, you did not think it right.
If Charles were here, we'd come out with no losses.
Those men down there—no blame can fall on them."
Oliver said: "Now by this beard of mine,
If I can see my noble sister, Aude,
once more, you will never lie in her arms!"

131.

And Roland said: "Why are you angry at me?"
Oliver answers: "Companion, it is your doing.
I will tell you what makes a vassal good: 140
   it is judgment, it is never madness;
restraint is worth more than the raw nerve of a fool.
Frenchmen are dead because of your wildness.
And what service will Charles ever have from us?
If you had trusted me, my lord would be here,
we would have fought this battle through to the end,
Marsilion would be dead, or our prisoner.
Roland, your prowess—had we never seen it!
   And now, dear friend, we've seen the last of it.
No more aid from us now for Charlemagne,   150
a man without equal till Judgment Day,
you will die here, and your death will shame France.

We kept faith, you and I, we were companions;
and everything we were will end today.
We part before evening, and it will be hard."

132.

Turpin the Archbishop hears their bitter words,
digs hard into his horse with golden spurs
and rides to them; begins to set them right:
"You, Lord Roland, and you, Lord Oliver,
I beg you in God's name do not quarrel.   160

To sound the horn could not help us now, true,
but still it is far better that you do it:
let the King come, he can avenge us then—
these men of Spain must not go home exulting!
Our French will come, they'll get down on their feet,
and find us here—we'll be dead, cut to pieces.
They will lift us into coffins on the backs of mules,
and weep for us, in rage and pain and grief,
and bury us in the courts of churches;
and we will not be eaten by wolves or pigs or dogs."   170
Roland replies, "Lord, you have spoken well."

. . .

Questions for Critical Thinking

1. Why is Oliver described as wise in the *Song of Roland*? Give incidents in the poem to support his attributes.

2. What is the fatal flaw in Roland's character, how is this manifested in the poem, and what are the consequences of his major weakness?

CHRÉTIEN DE TROYES
Selection from *Arthurian Romances*

Lancelot belongs to the legendary world of King Arthur and his knights, which gripped the imagination of writers and public alike in the twelfth and thirteenth centuries. Chrétien de Troyes' *Lancelot, or the Knight of the Cart*, was one of the works that enhanced this tradition. The tradition has lived on in the popular consciousness for centuries, as evidenced by modern films and fiction on Arthurian themes.

The Arthurian legends sprang from the history of the Celts, ancient peoples (Gauls and Britons) who dominated western and central Europe until Germanic invaders pushed them to the continent's fringes of Ireland, Scotland, Wales, and Brittany. The historic Arthur ruled probably in sixth-century Wales, where his wars against both Romans and Germans made him a figure larger than life. Over the next six hundred years, the historic Arthur gave way to the Arthur of legend; in 1125 a writer could comment on the "idle fictions" and "wild tales" then circulating about the Welsh king. Little remains of these works, which were recited by wandering storytellers; but they form the background for Chrétien's writing.

Chrétien places the spotlight not on Arthur but on the court and the knights. The Arthurian court is depicted as the epitome of civilization. To be received there is joy; banishment is misery. The stories of the knights express the ideals of courtly love, the code that made duty to women a higher good than personal honor.

Chrétien de Troyes (fl. 1170) composed works for the feudal courts of northern France. Chrétien credits one patron, Countess Marie of Champagne, as inspiring *Lancelot*. Written in French, these poems are long narratives of fantastic adventures of knights and ladies. They are the first romances, the genre that replaced the *chansons de geste* (see *Song of Roland*) in popularity after 1150. The romances, with their ideal of love as an ennobling passion, helped raise women's status, especially among the feudal elite.

Reading the Selection

The plot of *Lancelot* is typical of Chrétien's romances. It is organized around a quest—Lancelot's search for Guinevere, Arthur's queen, who is abducted by the evil Meleagant, Prince of Gorre. The plot is complicated by Lancelot's initial and almost unforgivable sin: he hesitates for two steps to mount into the shameful cart. Lancelot's "sin" against the courtly code is that he chose even for an instant personal honor before love.

To redeem himself, Lancelot goes through a series of tests meant to teach him to serve women unhesitatingly. Only in the poem's climax (not included here) does Lancelot reach the courtly ideal: he obeys the queen's every whim, even shaming himself in public. The final meaning of the two lovers' passion is hotly debated today. Was it meant to glorify adultery, or was it a traitorous love to be condemned by a courtly audience?

∞

Lancelot

· · ·

Late in the afternoon they arrive at a town, which, you must know, was very rich and beautiful. All three entered through the gate; the people are greatly amazed to see the knight borne upon the cart, and they take no pains to conceal their feelings, but small and great and old and young shout taunts at him in the streets, so that the knight hears many vile and scornful words at his expense. They all inquire: "To what punishment is this knight to be consigned? Is he to be flayed, or hanged, or drowned, or burned upon a fire of thorns? Tell us, thou dwarf, who art driving him, in what crime was he caught? Is he convicted of robbery? Is he a murderer, or a criminal?" And to all this the dwarf made no response, vouchsafing to them no reply. He conducts the knight to a lodging-place; and Gawain[7] follows the dwarf closely to a tower, which stood on the same level over against the town. Beyond there stretched a meadow, and the tower was built close by, upon a lofty eminence of rock, whose face formed a sharp precipice. Following the horse and cart, Gawain entered the tower. In the hall they met a damsel elegantly attired, than whom there was none fairer in the land, and with her they saw coming two fair and charming maidens. As soon as they saw my lord Gawain, they received him joyously and saluted him, and then asked news about the other knight: "Dwarf, of what crime is this knight guilty, whom thou dost drive like a lame man?" He would not answer her question, but he made the knight get out of the cart, and then he withdrew, without their knowing whither he went. Then my lord Gawain dismounts, and valets come forward to relieve

the two knights of their armour. The damsel ordered two green mantles to be brought, which they put on. When the hour for supper came, a sumptuous repast was set. The damsel sat at table beside my lord Gawain. They would not have changed their lodging-place to seek any other, for all that evening the damsel showed them great honour, and provided them with fair and pleasant company.

Vv. 463–538—When they had sat up long enough, two long, high beds were prepared in the middle of the hall; and there was another bed alongside, fairer and more splendid than the rest; for, as the story testifies, it possessed all the excellence that one could think of in a bed. When the time came to retire, the damsel took both the guests to whom she had offered her hospitality; she shows them the two fine, long, wide beds, and says: "These two beds are set up here for the accommodation of your bodies; but in that one yonder no one ever lay who did not merit it: it was not set up to be used by you." The knight who came riding on the cart replies at once: "Tell me," he says, "for what cause this bed is inaccessible." Being thoroughly informed of this, she answers unhesitatingly: "It is not your place to ask or make such an inquiry. Any knight is disgraced in the land after being in a cart, and it is not fitting that he should concern himself with the matter upon which you have questioned me; and most of all it is not right that he should lie upon the bed, for he would soon pay dearly for his act. So rich a couch has not been prepared for you, and you would pay dearly for ever harbouring such a thought." He replies: "You will see about that presently." . . . "Am I to see it?" . . . "Yes." . . . "It will soon appear." . . . "By my head," the knight replies, "I know not who is to pay the penalty. But whoever may object or disapprove, I intend to lie upon this bed and

―――――――
[7] **Gawain** A knight in the service of King Arthur.

repose there at my ease." Then he at once disrobed in the bed, which was long and raised half an ell above the other two, and was covered with a yellow cloth of silk and a coverlet with gilded stars. The furs were not of skinned vair but of sable; the covering he had on him would have been fitting for a king. The mattress was not made of straw or rushes or of old mats. At midnight there descended from the rafters suddenly a lance, as with the intention of pinning the knight through the flanks to the coverlet and the white sheets where he lay. To the lance there was attached a pennon all ablaze. The coverlet, the bedclothes, and the bed itself all caught fire at once. And the tip of the lance passed so close to the knight's side that it cut the skin a little, without seriously wounding him. Then the knight got up, put out the fire and, taking the lance, swung it in the middle of the hall, all this without leaving his bed; rather did he lie down again and slept as securely as at first.

Vv. 539–982—In the morning, at daybreak, the damsel of the tower had Mass celebrated on their account, and had them rise and dress. When Mass had been celebrated for them, the knight who had ridden in the cart sat down pensively at a window, which looked out upon the meadow, and he gazed upon the fields below. The damsel came to another window close by, and there my lord Gawain conversed with her privately for a while about something, I know not what. I do not know what words were uttered, but while they were leaning on the window-sill they saw carried along the river through the fields a bier, upon which there lay a knight, and alongside three damsels walked, mourning bitterly. Behind the bier they saw a crowd approaching, with a tall knight in front, leading a fair lady by the horse's rein. The knight at the window knew that it was the Queen. He continued to gaze at her attentively and with delight as long as she was visible. And when he could no longer see her, he was minded to throw himself out and break his body down below. And he would have let himself fall out had not my lord Gawain seen him, and drawn him back, saying: "I beg you, sire, be quiet now. For God's sake, never think again of committing such a mad deed. It is wrong for you to despise your life." "He is perfectly right," the damsel says; "for will not the news of his disgrace be known everywhere? Since he has been upon the cart, he has good reason to wish to die, for he would be better dead than alive. His life henceforth is sure to be one of shame, vexation, and unhappiness." Then the knights asked for their armour, and armed themselves, the damsel treating them courteously, with distinction and generosity; for when she had joked with the knight and ridiculed him enough, she presented him with a horse and lance as a token of her goodwill. The knights then courteously and politely took leave of the damsel, first saluting her, and then going off in the direction taken by the crowd they had seen. Thus they rode out from the town without addressing them. They proceeded quickly in the direction they had seen taken by the Queen, but they did not overtake the procession, which had advanced rapidly. After leaving the fields, the knights enter an enclosed place, and find a beaten road. They advanced through the woods until it might be six o'clock, and then at a crossroads they met a damsel, whom they both saluted,

each asking and requesting her to tell them, if she knows, whither the Queen has been taken. Replying intelligently, she said to them: "If you would pledge me your word, I could set you on the right road and path, and I would tell you the name of the country and of the knight who is conducting her; but whoever would essay to enter that country must endure sore trials, for before he could reach there he must suffer much." Then my lord Gawain replies: "Damsel, so help me God, I promise to place all my strength at your disposal and service, whenever you please, if you will tell me now the truth." And he who had been on the cart did not say that he would pledge her all his strength; but he proclaims, like one whom love makes rich, powerful and bold for any enterprise, that at once and without hesitation he will promise her anything she desires, and he puts himself altogether at her disposal. "Then I will tell you the truth," says she. Then the damsel relates to them the following story: "In truth, my lords, Meleagant, a tall and powerful knight, son of the King of Gorre, has taken her off into the kingdom whence no foreigner returns, but where he must perforce remain in servitude and banishment." Then they ask her: "Damsel, where is this country? Where can we find the way thither?" She replies: "That you shall quickly learn; but you may be sure that you will meet with many obstacles and difficult passages, for it is not easy to enter there except with the permission of the king, whose name is Bademagu; however, it is possible to enter by two very perilous paths and by two very difficult passage-ways. One is called 'the water-bridge,' because the bridge is under water, and there is the same amount of water beneath it as above it, so that the bridge is exactly in the middle; and it is only a foot and a half in width and in thickness. This choice is certainly to be avoided, and yet it is the less dangerous of the two. In addition there are a number of other obstacles of which I will say nothing. The other bridge is still more impracticable and much more perilous, never having been crossed by man. It is just like a sharp sword, and therefore all the people call it 'the sword-bridge.' Now I have told you all the truth I know." But they ask of her once again: "Damsel, deign to show us these two passages." To which the damsel makes reply: "This road here is the most direct to the water-bridge, and that one yonder leads straight to the sword-bridge." Then the knight, who had been on the cart, says: "Sire, I am ready to share with you without prejudice: take one of these two routes, and leave the other one to me; take whichever you prefer." "In truth," my lord Gawain replies, "both of them are hard and dangerous: I am not skilled in making such a choice, and hardly know which of them to take; but it is not right for me to hesitate when you have left the choice to me: I will choose the water-bridge." The other answers: "Then I must go uncomplainingly to the sword-bridge, which I agree to do." Thereupon, they all three part, each one commending the others very courteously to God. And when she sees them departing, she says: "Each one of you owes me a favour of my choosing, whenever I may choose to ask it. Take care not to forget that." "We shall surely not forget it, sweet friend," both the knights call out. Then each one goes his own way, and he of the cart is occupied with deep reflections, like one who has no strength or defence against love which holds him in its sway. His thoughts are such that he totally forgets himself, and he knows not whether he is alive or dead, forgetting even his own name, not knowing whether he is armed or not, or whither he is going or whence he came. Only one creature he has in mind, and for her his thought is so occupied that he neither sees nor hears aught else. And his horse bears him along rapidly, following no crooked road, but the best and the most direct; and thus proceeding unguided, he brings him into an open plain. In this plain there was a ford, on the other side of which a knight stood armed, who guarded it, and in his company there was a damsel who had come on a palfrey.[8] By this time the afternoon was well advanced, and yet the knight, unchanged and unwearied, pursued his thoughts. The horse, being very thirsty, sees clearly the ford, and as soon as he sees it, hastens toward it. Then he on the other side cries out: "Knight, I am guarding the ford, and forbid you to cross." He neither gives him heed, nor hears his words, being still deep in thought. In the meantime, his horse advanced rapidly toward the water. The knight calls out to him that he will do wisely to keep at a distance from the ford, for there is no passage that way; and he swears by the heart within his breast that he will smite him if he enters the water. But his threats are not heard, and he calls out to him a third time: "Knight, do not enter the ford against my will and prohibition; for, by my head, I shall strike you as soon as I see you in the ford." But he is so deep in thought that he does not hear him. And the horse, quickly leaving the bank, leaps into the ford and greedily begins to drink. And the knight says he shall pay for this, that his shield and the hauberk he wears upon his back shall afford him no protection. First, he puts his horse at a gallop, and from a gallop he urges him to a run, and he strikes the knight so hard that he knocks him down flat in the ford which he had forbidden him to cross. His lance flew from his hand and the shield from his neck. When he feels the water, he shivers, and though stunned, he jumps to his feet, like one aroused from sleep, listening and looking about him with astonishment, to see who it can be who has struck him. Then face to face with the other knight, he said: "Vassal, tell me why you have struck me, when I was not aware of your presence, and when I had done you no harm." "Upon my word, you had wronged me," the other says; "did you not treat me disdainfully when I forbade you three times to cross the ford, shouting at you as loudly as I could? You surely heard me challenge you at least two or three times, and you entered in spite of me, though I told you I should strike you as soon as I saw you in the ford." Then the knight replies to him: "Whoever heard you or saw you, let him be damned, so far as I am concerned. I was probably deep in thought when you forbade me to cross the ford. But be assured that I would make you regret it, if I could just lay one of my hands on your bridle." And the other replies: "Why, what of that? If you dare, you may seize my bridle here and now. I do not esteem your proud threats so much as a handful of ashes." And he replies: "That suits me perfectly. However

the affair may turn out, I should like to lay my hands on you." Then the other knight advances to the middle of the ford, where the other lays his left hand upon his bridle, and his right hand upon his leg, pulling, dragging and pressing him so roughly that he remonstrates, thinking that he would pull his leg out of his body. Then he begs him to let go, saying: "Knight, if it please thee to fight me on even terms, take thy shield and horse and lance, and joust with me." He answers: "That will I not do, upon my word; for I suppose thou wouldst run away as soon as thou hadst escaped my grip." Hearing this, he was much ashamed, and said: "Knight, mount thy horse, in confidence for I will pledge thee loyally my word that I shall not flinch or run away." Then once again he answers him: "First, thou wilt have to swear to that, and I insist upon receiving thy oath that thou wilt neither run away nor flinch, nor touch me, nor come near me until thou shalt see me on my horse; I shall be treating thee very generously, if, when thou art in my hands, I let thee go." He can do nothing but give his oath; and when the other hears him swear, he gathers up his shield and lance which were floating in the ford and by this time had drifted well down-stream; then he returns and takes his horse. After catching and mounting him, he seizes the shield by the shoulder-straps and lays his lance in rest. Then each spurs toward the other as fast as their horses can carry them. And he who had to defend the ford first attacks the other, striking him so hard that his lance is completely splintered. The other strikes him in return so that he throws him prostrate into the ford, and the water closes over him. Having accomplished that, he draws back and dismounts, thinking he could drive and chase away a hundred such. While he draws from the scabbard his sword of steel, the other jumps up and draws his excellent flashing blade. Then they clash again, advancing and covering themselves with the shields which gleam with gold. Ceaselessly and without repose they wield their swords; they have the courage to deal so many blows that the battle finally is so protracted that the Knight of the Cart is greatly ashamed in his heart, thinking that he is making a sorry start in the way he has undertaken, when he has spent so much time in defeating a single knight. If he had met yesterday a hundred such, he does not think or believe that they could have withstood him; so now he is much grieved and wroth to be in such an exhausted state that he is missing his strokes and losing time. Then he runs at him and presses him so hard that the other knight gives way and flees. However reluctant he may be, he leaves the ford and crossing free. But the other follows him in pursuit until he falls forward upon his hands; then he of the cart runs up to him, swearing by all he sees that he shall rue the day when he upset him in the ford and disturbed his revery. The damsel, whom the knight had with him, upon hearing the threats, is in great fear, and begs him for her sake to forbear from killing him; but he tells her that he must do so, and can show him no mercy for her sake, in view of the shameful wrong that he has done him. Then, with sword drawn, he approaches the knight who cries in sore dismay: "For God's sake and for my own, show me the mercy I ask of you." And he replies: "As God may save me, no one ever

---

[8] **palfrey** A small saddle horse suited for a woman to ride.

sinned so against me that I would not show him mercy once, for God's sake as is right, if he asked it of me in God's name. And so on thee I will have mercy; for I ought not to refuse thee when thou hast besought me. But first, thou shalt give me thy word to constitute thyself my prisoner whenever I may wish to summon thee." Though it was hard to do so, he promised him. At once the damsel said: "O knight, since thou hast granted the mercy he asked of thee, if ever thou hast broken any bonds, for my sake now be merciful and release this prisoner from his parole. Set him free at my request, upon condition that when the time comes, I shall do my utmost to repay thee in any way that thou shalt choose." Then he declares himself satisfied with the promise she has made, and sets the knight at liberty. Then she is ashamed and anxious, thinking that he will recognise her, which she did not wish. But he goes away at once, the knight and the damsel commending him to God, and taking leave of him. He grants them leave to go, while he himself pursues his way, until late in the afternoon he met a damsel coming, who was very fair and charming, well attired and richly dressed. The damsel greets him prudently and courteously, and he replies: "Damsel, God grant you health and happiness." Then the damsel said to him: "Sire, my house is prepared for you, if you will accept my hospitality; but you shall find shelter there only on condition that you will lie with me; upon these terms I propose and make the offer." Not a few there are who would have thanked her five hundred times for such a gift; but he is much displeased, and made a very different answer: "Damsel, I thank you for the offer of your house, and esteem it highly; but, if you please, I should be very sorry to lie with you." "By my eyes," the damsel says, "then I retract my offer." And he, since it is unavoidable, lets her have her way, though his heart grieves to give consent. He feels only reluctance now; but greater distress will be his when it is time to go to bed. The damsel, too, who leads him away, will pass through sorrow and heaviness. For it is possible that she will love him so that she will not wish to part with him. As soon as he had granted her wish and desire, she escorts him to a fortified place, than which there was none fairer in Thessaly; for it was entirely enclosed by a high wall and a deep moat, and there was no man within except him whom she brought with her.

Vv. 983–1042—Here she had constructed for her residence a quantity of handsome rooms, and a large and roomy hall. Riding along a river bank, they approached their lodging-place, and a drawbridge was lowered to allow them to pass. Crossing the bridge, they entered in, and found the hall open with its roof of tiles. Through the open door they pass, and see a table laid with a broad white cloth, upon which the dishes were set, and the candles burning in their stands, and the gilded silver drinking-cups, and two pots of wine, one red and one white. Standing beside the table, at the end of a bench, they found two basins of warm water in which to wash their hands, with a richly embroidered towel, all white and clean, with which to dry their hands. No valets, servants, or squires were to be found or seen. The knight, removing his shield from about his neck, hangs it upon a hook, and, taking his lance, lays it

above upon a rack. Then he dismounts from his horse, as does the damsel from hers. The knight, for his part, was pleased that she did not care to wait for him to help her to dismount. Having dismounted, she runs directly to a room and brings him a short mantle of scarlet cloth which she puts on him. The hall was by no means dark; for beside the light from the stars, there were many large twisted candles lighted there, so that the illumination was very bright. When she had thrown the mantle about his shoulders, she said to him: "Friend, here is the water and the towel; there is no one to present or offer it to you except me whom you see. Wash your hands, and then sit down, when you feel like doing so. The hour and the meal, as you can see, demand that you should do so." He washes, and then gladly and readily takes his seat, and she sits down beside him, and they eat and drink together, until the time comes to leave the table.

Vv. 1043–1206—When they had risen from the table, the damsel said to the knight: "Sire, if you do not object, go outside and amuse yourself; but, if you please, do not stay after you think I must be in bed. Feel no concern or embarrassment; for then you may come to me at once, if you will keep the promise you have made." And he replies: "I will keep my word, and will return when I think the time has come." Then he went out, and stayed in the courtyard until he thought it was time to return and keep the promise he had made. Going back into the hall, he sees nothing of her who would be his mistress; for she was not there. Not finding or seeing her, he said: "Wherever she may be, I shall look for her until I find her." He makes no delay in his search, being bound by the promise he had made her. Entering one of the rooms, he hears a damsel cry aloud, and it was the very one with whom he was about to lie. At the same time, he sees the door of another room standing open, and stepping toward it, he sees right before his eyes a knight who had thrown her down, and was holding her naked and prostrate upon the bed. She, thinking that he had come of course to help her, cried aloud: "Help, help, thou knight, who art my guest. If thou dost not take this man away from me, I shall find no one to do so; if thou dost not succour me speedily, he will wrong me before thy eyes. Thou art the one to lie with me, in accordance with thy promise; and shall this man by force accomplish his wish before thy eyes? Gentle knight, exert thyself, and make haste to bear me aid." He sees that the other man held the damsel brutally uncovered to the waist, and he is ashamed and angered to see him assault her so; yet it is not jealousy he feels, nor will he be made a cuckold by him. At the door there stood as guards two knights completely armed and with swords drawn. Behind them there stood four men-at-arms, each armed with an axe—the sort with which you could split a cow down the back as easily as a root of juniper or broom. The knight hesitated at the door, and thought: "God, what can I do? I am engaged in no less an affair than the quest of Queen Guinevere. I ought not to have the heart of a hare, when for her sake I have engaged in such a quest. If cowardice puts its heart in me, and if I follow its dictates, I shall never attain what I seek. I am disgraced, if I stand here; indeed, I am ashamed even to have thought of holding back. My heart is very sad and oppressed: now I am so ashamed and distressed that I would gladly die for having hesitated here so long. I say it not in pride: but may God have mercy on me if I do not prefer to die honourably rather than live a life of shame! If my path were unobstructed, and if these men gave me leave to pass through without restraint, what honour would I gain? Truly, in that case the greatest coward alive would pass through; and all the while I hear this poor creature calling for help constantly, and reminding me of my promise, and reproaching me with bitter taunts." Then he steps to the door, thrusting in his head and shoulders; glancing up, he sees two swords descending. He draws back, and the knights could not check their strokes: they had wielded them with such force that the swords struck the floor, and both were broken in pieces. When he sees that the swords are broken, he pays less attention to the axes, fearing and dreading them much less. Rushing in among them, he strikes first one guard in the side and then another. The two who are nearest him he jostles and thrusts aside, throwing them both down flat; the third missed his stroke at him, but the fourth, who attacked him, strikes him so that he cuts his mantle and shirt, and slices the white flesh on his shoulder so that the blood trickles down from the wound. But he, without delay, and without complaining of his wound, presses on more rapidly, until he strikes between the temples him who was assaulting his hostess. Before he departs, he will try to keep his pledge to her. He makes him stand up reluctantly. Meanwhile, he who had missed striking him comes at him as fast as he can, and, raising his arm again, expects to split his head to the teeth with the axe. But the other, alert to defend himself, thrusts the knight toward him in such a way that he receives the axe just where the shoulder joins the neck, so that they are cleaved apart. Then the knight seizes the axe, wresting it quickly from him who holds it; then he lets go the knight whom he still held, and looks to his own defence; for the knights from the door, and the three men with axes are all attacking him fiercely. So he leaped quickly between the bed and the wall, and called to them: "Come on now, all of you. If there were thirty-seven of you, you would have all the fight you wish, with me so favourably placed; I shall never be overcome by you." And the damsel watching him, exclaimed: "By my eyes, you need have no thought of that henceforth where I am." Then at once she dismisses the knights and the men-at-arms, who retire from there at once, without delay or objection. And the damsel continues: "Sire you have well defended me against the men of my household. Come now, and I'll lead you on." . . .

Questions for Critical Thinking

1. Describe the four episodes or series of tests Lancelot endures to serve women.

2. What are some of the examples of chivalry manifested in this story? Do you think chivalry is relevant and useful to men and women in the twenty-first century? Why or why not?

MARIE DE FRANCE
Lanval

After 1150, Marie de France originated the narrative lay, a short poem telling a story and meant to be sung to the accompaniment of a musical instrument, such as a harp. (Lyrical lays were begun somewhat later [early thirteenth century] by a French poet and have a history different from that of narrative lays.) Like the romance (see Chrétien de Troyes' *Arthurian Romances*), with which it was contemporary, the narrative lay tells a courtly love tale based on Celtic sources. The narrative lay had a short life and vanished around 1300. After 1600, the term "lay" came to denote any simple song or narrative of adventure. The lay genre enjoyed a brief comeback in the Neogothic revival of the 1800s.

Marie de France wrote in Old French; she was part of the so-called twelfth-century renaissance, centered in France, which produced Scholastic philosophy (Abelard), the Gothic church (Suger), the universities (Bologna and Paris), polyphonic music, liturgical drama, and most especially, vernacular literature, including the *chansons de geste*, Arthurian romances, and love lyrics. Marie contributed to this movement by being the first known European woman to write successfully in the vernacular.

Of Marie de France (fl. 1160–1190), very little is known for certain. She was probably French, working as a professional writer at the English royal court. It was only after 1880 that scholars firmly linked de France with these lays. Even so, one expert claims her name is used "since [it is] convenient and attractive."

The mystery surrounding Marie extends to her works. Her lays are preserved in five manuscripts, the earliest dating from about fifty years after she wrote. Each of these contains several lays in varied groupings, with a few appearing in only one manuscript and most found in two or more, such as *Lanval*.

The general Prologue (not included here) to the manuscript containing *Lanval* offers insight into Marie's literary habits. In it she speaks of not being bullied into giving up her work because of gossip and threats. Whatever provoked these remarks, it seems that Marie valued her reputation and literary gifts. She dedicated these short tales to a "noble king," probably Henry II (1133–1189), the husband of Eleanor of Aquitaine (ca. 1122–1204), herself reputedly the founder of courtly love.

Reading the Selection

Lanval, probably the most admired of Marie de France's lays, is set in Brittany, a setting that points to its origin perhaps in one of the French courts. Typical of her lays, it offers a moral message along with being a love story with a happy ending.

The hero Lanval, the son of a foreign king, joins Arthur's Round Table for the express purpose of advancing his career. As the lay opens, Lanval sees all of his hopes dashed. Lanval, in despair, goes off alone and, for the first time, experiences true love with a woman, perhaps a figment of his imagination but certainly an allegorical figure, who gives him everything that his heart desired. The sole condition for her love is that he must keep their relationship secret from the world.

Lanval, rejuvenated in spirit and purse, thanks to the magical powers of his unearthly love, returns to Arthur's court, where he is welcomed with open arms. Things soon fall apart. However, events are sorted out with the unexpected arrival of Lanval's true love, who reveals herself to all. Lanval leaves Arthur's court and joins his true love in Avalun, an allegorical land where pure love is sufficient unto itself.

∞

Lanval

I shall tell you the adventure of another *lai*,
just as it happened:
it was composed about a very noble vassal;
in Breton, they call him Lanval.
Arthur, the brave and the courtly king,
was staying at Cardoel,[9]
because the Scots and the Picts

were destroying the land.
They invaded Logres[10]
and laid it waste.
At Pentecost,[11] in summer,
the king stayed there.

---

[9] **Cardoel** Also known as "Carlion," the legendary place where King Arthur was crowned and held court. Modern-day Caerleon is in southeast Wales.

[10] **Logres** England.
[11] **Pentecost** A Christian feast or celebration on the seventh Sunday after Easter, commemorating the Holy Spirit descending on the Apostles. Before the advent of numerical yearly calendars, dating was kept by events Christians believed were associated with Christ.

He gave out many rich gifts:
to counts and barons,
members of the Round Table—
such a company had no equal in all the world—
he distributed wives and lands,
to all but one who had served him.
That was Lanval; Arthur forgot him,
and none of his men favored him either.   20
For his valor, for his generosity,
his beauty and his bravery,
most men envied him;
some feigned the appearance of love
who, if something unpleasant happened to him,
would not have been at all disturbed.
He was the son of a king of high degree
but he was far from his heritage.
He was of the king's household
but he had spent all his wealth,   30
for the king gave him nothing
nor did Lanval ask.
Now Lanval was in difficulty,
depressed and very worried.
My lords, don't be surprised:
a strange man, without friends,
is very sad in another land,
when he doesn't know where to look for help.
The knight of whom I speak,
who had served the king so long,   40
one day mounted his horse
and went off to amuse himself.
He left the city
and came, all alone, to a field;
he dismounted by a running stream
but his horse trembled badly.
He removed the saddle and went off,
leaving the horse to roll around in the meadow.
He folded his cloak beneath his head
and lay down.   50
He worried about his difficulty,
he could see nothing that pleased him.
As he lay there
he looked down along the bank
and saw two girls approaching;
he had never seen any lovelier.
They were richly dressed,
tightly laced,
in tunics of dark purple;
their faces were very lovely.   60
The older one carried basins,
golden, well made, and fine;
I shall tell you the truth about it, without fail.
The other carried a towel.
They went straight
to where the knight was lying.
Lanval, who was very well bred,
got up to meet them.
They greeted him first
and gave him their message: 70
"Sir Lanval, my lady,
who is worthy and wise and beautiful,

sent us for you.
Come with us now.
We shall guide you there safely.
See, her pavilion is nearby!"
The knight went with them;
giving no thought to his horse
who was feeding before him in the meadow.
They led him up to the tent,   80
which was quite beautiful and well placed.
Queen Semiramis,[12]
however much more wealth,
power, or knowledge she had,
or the emperor Octavian[13]
could not have paid for one of the flaps.
There was a golden eagle on top of it,
whose value I could not tell,
nor could I judge the value of the cords or the poles
that held up the sides of the tent;   90
there is no king on earth who could buy it,
no matter what wealth he offered.
The girl was inside the tent:
the lily and the young rose
when they appear in the summer
are surpassed by her beauty.
She lay on a beautiful bed—
the bedclothes were worth a castle—
dressed only in her shift.
Her body was well shaped and elegant;   100
for the heat, she had thrown over herself,
a precious cloak of white ermine,
covered with purple alexandrine,[14]
but her whole side was uncovered,
her face, her neck and her bosom;
she was whiter than the hawthorn flower.
The knight went forward
and the girl addressed him.
He sat before the bed.
"Lanval," she said, "sweet love,   110
because of you I have come from my land;
I came to seek you from far away.
If you are brave and courtly,
no emperor or count or king
will ever have known such joy or good;
for I love you more than anything."
He looked at her and saw that she was beautiful;
Love stung him with a spark
that burned and set fire to his heart.
He answered her in a suitable way.   120
"Lovely one," he said, "if it pleased you,
if such joy might be mine
that you would love me,
there is nothing you might command,
within my power, that I would not do,
whether foolish or wise.

---

[12] **Queen Semiramis** Legendary queen who was very wealthy and powerful and was reputed to have built Babylon.
[13] **Octavian** Caesar Augustus, first emperor of the Roman Empire (31 BCE–14 CE).
[14] **alexandrine** A type of semiprecious stone.

I shall obey your command;
for you, I shall abandon everyone.
I want never to leave you.
That is what I most desire."   130
When the girl heard the words
of the man who could love her so,
she granted him her love and her body.
Now Lanval was on the right road!
Afterward, she gave him a gift:
he would never again want anything,
he would receive as he desired;
however generously he might give and spend,
she would provide what he needed.
Now Lanval is well cared for.   140
The more lavishly he spends,
the more gold and silver he will have.
"Love," she said, "I admonish you now,
I command and beg you,
do not let any man know about this.
I shall tell you why:
you would lose me for good
if this love were known;
you would never see me again
or possess my body."   150
He answered that he would do
exactly as she commanded.
He lay beside her on the bed;
now Lanval is well cared for.
He remained with her
that afternoon, until evening
and would have stayed longer, if he could,
and if his love had consented.
"Love," she said, "get up.
You cannot stay any longer.   160
Go away now; I shall remain
but I will tell you one thing:
when you want to talk to me
there is no place you can think of
where a man might have his mistress
without reproach or shame,
that I shall not be there with you
to satisfy all your desires.
No man but you will see me
or hear my words."   170
When he heard her, he was very happy,
he kissed her, and then got up.
The girls who had brought him to the tent
dressed him in rich clothes;
when he was dressed anew,
there wasn't a more handsome youth in all the world;
he was no fool, no boor.
They gave him water for his hands
and a towel to dry them,
and they brought him food.   180
He took supper with his love;
it was not to be refused.
He was served with great courtesy,
he received it with great joy.
There was an entrement
that vastly pleased the knight

for he kissed his lady often
and held her close.
When they finished dinner,
his horse was brought to him.   190
The horse had been well saddled;
Lanval was very richly served.
The knight took his leave, mounted,
and rode toward the city,
often looking behind him.
Lanval was very disturbed;
he wondered about his adventure
and was doubtful in his heart;
he was amazed, not knowing what to believe;
he didn't expect ever to see her again.   200
He came to his lodging
and found his men well dressed.
That night, his accommodations were rich
but no one knew where it came from.
There was no knight in the city
who really needed a place to stay
whom he didn't invite to join him
to be well and richly served.
Lanval gave rich gifts,
Lanval released prisoners,   210
Lanval dressed jongleurs [performers],
Lanval offered great honors.
There was no stranger or friend
to whom Lanval didn't give.
Lanval's joy and pleasure were intense;
in the daytime or at night,
he could see his love often;
she was completely at his command.

In that same year, it seems to me,
after the feast of St. John,[15]   220
about thirty knights
were amusing themselves
in an orchard beneath the tower
where the queen was staying.
Gawain was with them
and his cousin, the handsome Yvain;
Gawain, the noble, the brave,
who was so loved by all, said:
"By God, my lords, we wronged
our companion Lanval,   230
who is so generous and courtly,
and whose father is a rich king,
when we didn't bring him with us."
They immediately turned back,
went to his lodging
and prevailed on Lanval to come along with them.
At a sculpted window
the queen was looking out;
she had three ladies with her.
She saw the king's retinue,   240

---

[15] **feast of St. John** Christian feast honoring John the Baptist; June 24 by modern calendars and close to the date of midsummer festivals.

recognized Lanval and looked at him.
Then she told one of her ladies
to send for her maidens,
the loveliest and the most refined;
together they went to amuse themselves
in the orchard where the others were.
She brought thirty or more with her;
they descended the steps.
The knights came to meet them,
because they were delighted to see them.   250
The knights took them by the hand;
their conversation was in no way vulgar.
Lanval went off to one side,
far from the others; he was impatient
to hold his love,
to kiss and embrace and touch her;
he thought little of others' joys
if he could not have his pleasure.
When the queen saw him alone,
she went straight to the knight.   260
She sat beside him and spoke,
revealing her whole heart:
"Lanval, I have shown you much honor,
I have cherished you, and loved you.
You may have all my love;
just tell me your desire.
I promise you my affection.
You should be very happy with me."
"My lady." he said, "let me be!
I have no desire to love you.   270
I've served the king a long time;
I don't want to betray my faith to him.
Never, for you or for your love,
will I do anything to harm my lord."
The queen got angry;
in her wrath, she insulted him:
"Lanval," she said, "I am sure
you don't care for such pleasure;
people have often told me
that you have no interest in women.   280
You have fine-looking boys
with whom you enjoy yourself.
Base coward, lousy cripple,
my lord made a bad mistake
when he let you stay with him.
For all I know, he'll lose God because of it."
When Lanval heard her, he was quite disturbed;
he was not slow to answer.
He said something out of spite
that he would later regret.   290
"Lady," he said, "of that activity
I know nothing,
but I love and I am loved
by one who should have the prize
over all the women I know.
And I shall tell you one thing;
you might as well know all:
any one of those who serve her,
the poorest girl of all,
is better than you, my lady queen,   300

in body, face, and beauty,
in breeding and in goodness."
The queen left him
and went, weeping, to her chamber.
She was upset and angry
because he had insulted her.
She went to bed sick;
never, she said, would she get up
unless the king gave her satisfaction
for the offense against her.   310
The king returned from the woods,
he'd had a very good day.
He entered the queen's chambers.
When she saw him, she began to complain.
She fell at his feet, asked his mercy,
saying that Lanval had dishonored her;
he had asked for her love,
and because she refused him
he insulted and offended her:
he boasted of a love   320
who was so refined and noble and proud
that her chambermaid,
the poorest one who served her,
was better than the queen.
The king got very angry;
he swore an oath:
if Lanval could not defend himself in court
he would have him burned or hanged.
The king left her chamber
and called for three of his barons;   330
he sent them for Lanval
who was feeling great sorrow and distress.
He had come back to his dwelling,
knowing very well
that he'd lost his love,
he had betrayed their affair.
He was all alone in a room,
disturbed and troubled;
he called on his love, again and again,
but it did him no good.   340
He complained and sighed,
from time to time he fainted;
then he cried a hundred times for her to have mercy
and speak to her love.
He cursed his heart and his mouth;
it's a wonder he didn't kill himself.
No matter how much he cried and shouted,
ranted and raged,
she would not have mercy on him,
not even let him see her.   350
How will he ever contain himself?
The men the king sent
arrived and told him
to appear in court without delay:
the king had summoned him
because the queen had accused him.
Lanval went with his great sorrow;
they could have killed him, for all he cared.
He came before the king;
he was very sad, thoughtful, silent;   360

his face revealed great suffering.
In anger the king told him:
"Vassal, you have done me a great wrong!
This was a base undertaking,
to shame and disgrace me
and to insult the queen.
You have made a foolish boast:
your love is much too noble
if her maid is more beautiful,
more worthy, than the queen."   370
Lanval denied that he'd dishonored
or shamed his lord,
word for word, as the king spoke:
he had not made advances to the queen;
but of what he had said,
he acknowledged the truth,
about the love he had boasted of,
that now made him sad because he'd lost her.
About that he said he would do
whatever the court decided.   380
The king was very angry with him;
he sent for all his men
to determine exactly what he ought to do
so that no one could find fault with his decision.
They did as he commanded,
whether they liked it or not.
They assembled,
judged, and decided,
that Lanval should have his day;
but he must find pledges for his lord   390
to guarantee that he would await the judgment,
return, and be present at it.
Then the court would be increased,
for now there were none but the king's household.
The barons came back to the king
and announced their decision.
The king demanded pledges.
Lanval was alone and forlorn,
he had no relative, no friend.
Gawain went and pledged himself for him,   400
and all his companions followed.
The king addressed them: "I release him to you
on forfeit of whatever you hold from me,
lands and fiefs, each one for himself."
When Lanval was pledged, there was nothing else to do.
He returned to his lodging.
The knights accompanied him,
they reproached and admonished him
that he give up his great sorrow;
they cursed his foolish love.   410
Each day they went to see him,
because they wanted to know
whether he was drinking and eating;
they were afraid that he'd kill himself.
On the day that they had named,
the barons assembled.
The king and queen were there
and the pledges brought Lanval back.
They were all very sad for him:
I think there were a hundred   420

who would have done all they could
to set him free without a trial
where he would be wrongly accused.
The king demanded a verdict
according to the charge and rebuttal.
Now it all fell to the barons.
They went to the judgment,
worried and distressed
for the noble man from another land
who'd gotten into such trouble in their midst.   430
Many wanted to condemn him
in order to satisfy their lord.
The Duke of Cornwall said:
"No one can blame us;
whether it makes you weep or sing
justice must be carried out.
The king spoke against his vassal
whom I have heard named Lanval;
he accused him of felony,
charged him with a misdeed—   440
a love that he had boasted of,
which made the queen angry.
No one but the king accused him:
by the faith I owe you,
if one were to speak the truth,
there should have been no need for defense,
except that a man owes his lord honor
in every circumstance.
He will be bound by his oath,
and the king will forgive us our pledges   450
if he can produce proof;
if his love would come forward,
if what he said,
what upset the queen, is true,
then he will be acquitted,
because he did not say it out of malice.
But if he cannot get his proof,
we must make it clear to him
that he will forfeit his service to the king;
he must take his leave."   460
They sent to the knight,
told and announced to him
that he should have his love come
to defend and stand surety for him.
He told them that he could not do it:
he would never receive help from her.
They went back to the judges,
not expecting any help from Lanval.
The king pressed them hard
because of the queen who was waiting.   470
When they were ready to give their verdict
they saw two girls approaching,
riding handsome palfreys.[16]
They were very attractive,
dressed in purple taffeta,
over their bare skin.
The men looked at them with pleasure.

---

[16] **palfreys** Saddle horses for young women.

Gawain, taking three knights with him,
went to Lanval and told him;
he pointed out the two girls. 480
Gawain was extremely happy, and begged him
to tell if his love were one of them.
Lanval said he didn't know who they were,
where they came from or where they were going.
The girls proceeded
still on horseback;
they dismounted before the high table
at which Arthur, the king, sat.
They were of great beauty,
and spoke in a courtly manner: 490
"King, clear your chambers,
have them hung with silk
where my lady may dismount;
she wishes to take shelter with you."
He promised it willingly
and called two knights
to guide them up to the chambers.
On that subject no more was said.
The king asked his barons
for their judgment and decision; 500
he said they had angered him very much
with their long delay.
"Sire," they said, "we have decided.
Because of the ladies we have just seen
we have made no judgment.
Let us reconvene the trial."
Then they assembled, everyone was worried;
there was much noise and strife.
While they were in that confusion,
two girls in noble array, 510
dressed in Phrygian silks[17]
and riding Spanish mules,
were seen coming down the street.
This gave the vassals great joy;
to each other they said that now
Lanval, the brave and bold, was saved.
Gawain went up to him,
bringing his companions along.
"Sire," he said, "take heart.
For the love of God, speak to us. 520
Here come two maidens,
well adorned and very beautiful;
one must certainly be your love."
Lanval answered quickly
that he did not recognize them,
he didn't know them or love them.
Meanwhile they'd arrived,
and dismounted before the king.
Most of those who saw them praised them
for their bodies, their faces, their coloring; 530
each was more impressive
than the queen had ever been.
The older one was courtly and wise,

she spoke her message fittingly:
"King, have chambers prepared for us
to lodge my lady according to her need
she is coming here to speak with you."
He ordered them to be taken
to the others who had preceded them.
There was no problem with the mules. 540
When he had seen to the girls,
he summoned all his barons
to render their judgment;
it had already dragged out too much.
The queen was getting angry
because she had fasted so long.
They were about to give their judgment
when through the city came riding
a girl on horseback:
there was none more beautiful in the world. 550
She rode a white palfrey,
who carried her handsomely and smoothly:
he was well apportioned in the neck and head,
no finer beast in the world.
The palfrey's trappings were rich;
under heaven there was no count or king
who could have afforded them all
without selling or mortgaging lands.
She was dressed in this fashion:
in a white linen shift 560
that revealed both her sides
since the lacing was along the side.
Her body was elegant, her hips slim,
her neck whiter than snow on a branch,
her eyes bright, her face white,
a beautiful mouth, a well-set nose,
dark eyebrows and an elegant forehead,
her hair curly and rather blond;
golden wire does not shine
like her hair in the light. 570
Her cloak, which she had wrapped around her,
was dark purple.
On her wrist she held a sparrow hawk,
a greyhound followed her.
In the town, no one, small or big,
old man or child,
failed to come look.
As they watched her pass,
there was no joking about her beauty.
She proceeded at a slow pace. 580
The judges who saw her
marveled at the sight;
no one who looked at her
was not warmed with joy.
Those who loved the knight
came to him and told him
of the girl who was approaching,
if God pleased, to rescue him.
"Sir companion, here comes one
neither tawny nor dark; 590
this is, of all who exist,
the most beautiful woman in the world."
Lanval heard them and lifted his head;

---

[17] **Phrygian silks** Reference to the far-off land of Phrygia in Asia Minor; hence expensive clothes from an exotic place.

he recognized her and sighed.
The blood rose to his face;
he was quick to speak.
"By my faith," he said, "that is my love.
Now I don't care if I am killed,
if only she forgives me.
For I am restored, now that I see her."   600
The lady entered the palace;
no one so beautiful had ever been there.
She dismounted before the king
so that she was well seen by all.
And she let her cloak fall
so they could see her better.
The king, who was well bred,
rose and went to meet her;
all the others honored her
and offered to serve her.   610
When they had looked at her well,
when they had greatly praised her beauty,
she spoke in this way,
she didn't want to wait:
"I have loved one of your vassals:
you see him before you—Lanval.
He has been accused in your court—
I don't want him to suffer
for what he said; you should know
that the queen was in the wrong.   620
He never made advances to her.
And for the boast that he made,

if he can be acquitted through me,
let him be set free by your barons."
Whatever the barons judged by law
the king promised would prevail.
To the last man they agreed
that Lanval had successfully answered the charge.
He was set free by their decision
and the girl departed.   630
The king could not detain her,
though there were enough people to serve her.
Outside the hall stood
a great stone of dark marble
where heavy men mounted
when they left the king's court;
Lanval climbed on it.
When the girl came through the gate
Lanval leapt, in one bound,
onto the palfrey, behind her.   640
With her he went to Avalun,[18]
so the Bretons tell us,
to a very beautiful island;
there the youth was carried off.
No man heard of him again,
and I have no more to tell.

_____

[18] **Avalun** Also spelled Avalon. The paradise place in Arthurian legends; where King Arthur went upon his death.

Questions for Critical Thinking

1. How does Lanval suffer at King Arthur's court, and what happens to him upon his return?

2. Describe Lanval's character. Do you find him a sympathetic person? Why or why not? Compare him to one of your film or literary heroes.

ST. THOMAS AQUINAS
Selection from *Summa theologica*

Thomas Aquinas's (1226–1274) theology, called Thomism, is the climax of the key intellectual trend that characterized the High Middle Ages (1000–1300). Thomism uniquely embodies the age's spirit, which tried to harmonize the opposing domains of philosophy and theology, reason and faith. Thomas performed this feat with two vast *summas* (from Latin, a comprehensive treatise), namely the *Summa theologica* and the *Summa contra gentiles*. In these works, he founded a rational theology that aligned Aristotle's thought with Christian principles. Some of Thomas's ideas (on the Trinity) were called into question after his death, but his reputation steadily grew; in 1874 the papacy declared Thomism to be the official basis of Roman Catholic beliefs.

In order to develop a rational theology along the lines laid down by Aristotle, Thomas had to come to terms with the pessimistic thought of Augustine (see *Confessions* in Chapter 7), which had dominated Christian discourse since the fifth century. To Augustine, reason is helpless because it cannot operate apart from the human will, which has lost its freedom because of original sin. In reply, Thomas held that the will is free, and reason, while spoiled by sin, is yet able to discover much about the world; reason, even if limited, must be obeyed as far as it goes. Augustine further claimed that true knowledge can arise only if God implants it in the mind, either slowly or all at once. In contrast, Thomas was more hopeful, saying that all knowledge begins in the senses, even of things that lie beyond the senses. Finally, Augustine thought that not only was human nature impaired, but so was the world of nature. Thomas's opposing view was that the natural world, though necessarily incomplete because it is created, is nonetheless good since it reflects God as its creator. Thus, Thomism ranged widely over human concerns, covering topics such as justice, fair prices, usury, and good government.

Reading the Selection

This selection from the *Summa theologica* deals with faith, or belief. Faith, to Thomas, is one of the three theological virtues—the others are hope and charity—which have God as their object and bring eternal life to those who obey them. In discussing the theological, or spiritual, virtues, Thomas was inspired by the Greek thinker Aristotle, who had identified the four cardinal virtues of secular life: wisdom, courage, justice, and temperance. Thomist thought eventually embraced both the theological and the cardinal virtues, maintaining that both were essential to a Christian.

The Fifth Article from the *Summa theologica* deals with the question "Should matters of faith be tested by the rules of science?" Thomas's argument is typical of the medieval style of reasoning, which included a question, discussion, and resolution. The opening question is followed by a series of arguments, pro and con. Thomas gives the resolution in the first person ("I answer that"), though his presence is ever felt, shaping the argument as he replies to both the pro and con sides of the debate. Because of its give-and-take format, this method is believed to have begun in the classroom practices of schools and universities, hence the name *Scholasticism*.

∞

Fifth Article

Whether Those Things That Are of Faith Can Be an Object of Science?

We proceed thus to the Fifth Article:—Objection 1. It would seem that those things that are of faith can be an object of science. For where science is lacking there is ignorance, since ignorance is the opposite of science. Now we are not in ignorance of those things we have to believe, since ignorance of such things savors of unbelief, according to 1 Tim. i. 13: *I did it ignorantly in unbelief.* Therefore things that are of faith can be an object of science.

Obj. 2. Further, science is acquired by reasons. Now sacred writers employ reasons to inculcate things that are of faith. Therefore such things can be an object of science.

Obj. 3. Further, things which are demonstrated are an object of science, since a *demonstration is a syllogism that produces science.* Now certain matters of faith have been demonstrated by the philosophers, such as the Existence and Unity of God, and so forth. Therefore things that are of faith can be an object of science.

Obj. 4. Further, opinion is further from science than faith is, since faith is said to stand between opinion and science. Now opinion and science can, in a way, be about the same object, as stated in *Poster.* i. Therefore faith and science can be about the same object also.

On the contrary, Gregory[19] says (*Hom.* xxvi *in Ev.*) that ₅ *when a thing is manifest, it is the object, not of faith, but of perception.* Therefore things that are of faith are not the object of perception, whereas what is an object of science is the object of perception. Therefore there can be no faith about things which are an object of science.

I answer that, All science is derived from self-evident and therefore *seen* principles; wherefore all objects of science must needs be, in a fashion, seen.

Now as stated above (A. 4) it is impossible that one and the same thing should be believed and seen by the same person. Hence it is equally impossible for one and the same thing to be an object of science and of belief for the same person. It may happen, however, that a thing which is an object of vision or science for one, is believed by another: since we hope to see some day what we now believe about the Trinity, according to 1 Cor. xiii. 12: *We see now through a glass in a dark manner; but then face to face:* which vision the angels possess already; so that what we believe, they see. In like manner it may happen that what is an object of vision or scientific knowledge for one man, even in the state of a wayfarer, is, for another man, an object of faith, because he does not know it by demonstration.

Nevertheless, that which is proposed to be believed equally by all, is equally unknown by all as an object of science: such are the things which are of faith simply. Consequently faith and science are not about the same things.

Reply Obj. 1. Unbelievers are in ignorance of things that are of faith, for neither do they see or know them in themselves, nor do they know them to be credible. The faithful, on the other hand, know them, not as by demonstration, but by the light of faith which makes them see that they ought to believe them, as stated above (A. 4, *ad* 2, 3).

Reply Obj. 2. The reasons employed by holy men to prove ₁₀ things that are of faith, are not demonstrations; they are either persuasive arguments showing that what is proposed to our faith is not impossible, or else they are proofs drawn from the principles of faith, i.e. from the authority of Holy Writ, as Dionysius[20] declares (*Div. Nom.* ii). Whatever is based on these principles is as well proved in the eyes of the faithful, as a conclusion drawn from self-evident principles is in the eyes of all. Hence again, theology is a science, as we stated at the outset of this work (P. I, Q. 1, A. 2).

Reply Obj. 3. Things which can be proved by demonstration are reckoned among the articles of faith, not because they are believed simply by all, but because they are a necessary presupposition to matters of faith, so that those who do not know them by demonstration must know them first of all by faith.

Reply Obj. 4. As the Philosopher[21] says *(loc. cit.), science and opinion about the same object can certainly be in different men,* as we have stated above about science and faith; yet it is possible for one and the same man to have science and faith about the same thing relatively, i.e. in relation to the object, but not in the same respect. For it is possible for the same person, about one and the same object, to know one thing and to think another: and, in like manner, one may know by demonstration the unity of the Godhead, and, by faith, the Trinity. On the other hand, in one and the same man, about the same object, and in the same respect, science is incompatible with either opinion or faith, yet for different reasons. Because science is incompatible with opinion about the same object simply, for the reason that science demands that its object should be deemed impossible to be otherwise, whereas it is essential to opinion, that its object should be deemed possible to be otherwise. Yet that which is the object of faith, on account of the certainty of faith, is also deemed impossible to be otherwise: and the reason why science and faith cannot be about the same object and in the same respect is because the object of science is something seen, whereas the object of faith is the unseen, as stated above.

---

[19] **Gregory** St. Gregory, or Gregory the Great, pope (590–604) who expanded the church, wrote many theological works, and supposedly arranged the Gregorian chant.

[20] **Dionysius** Known as Dionysius the Areopagite, lived around 500 CE and was probably from Syria. Wrote many mystical and theological books that influenced medieval thinkers.
[21] **the Philosopher** Aristotle, the famous Greek thinker who lived in the fourth century BCE.

∞

Questions for Critical Thinking

1. Discuss and cite specific examples to show how Thomas uses both Christian and classical sources to prove his argument.

2. Explain the framework and steps of the Scholastic argument process. What is Thomas's conclusion about mingling faith and reason?

DANTE ALIGHIERI
Selections from *The Divine Comedy*

(The introduction to the cantos and footnotes accompanying *The Divine Comedy* written by John Ciardi.)

Few writers of any time have had such an impact on Western culture as the medieval writer Dante Alighieri (1265–1321) of Florence. So great were his gifts that the world was not the same after he wrote. His works in Italian had such broad appeal that the geographic focus of Europe's culture shifted from France to Italy, where it stayed until about 1600. His poetry affected all of Europe and changed the terms in which poets wrote. Dante, for example, composed lyrics celebrating his undying love for the beautiful Beatrice; later poets, enchanted by these poems, followed his lead, with Petrarch writing verses to Laura (see *Canzoniere* in Chapter 11), Shakespeare to the Dark Lady, and so on. Scholars often link Dante to the Renaissance, but this surely is an exaggeration, given his religious views. He is better understood as the culmination of the medieval spirit, as he balances the secular and the spiritual, the ancient and the new.

Of Dante's works, *The Divine Comedy* (about 1314) is his enduring masterpiece. In form, this long narrative poem belongs to the epic genre with its hero of superhuman caliber, dangerous journey, misadventures, divine dimension, digressions, long speeches, vivid descriptions, and general lofty tone (see *The Epic of Gilgamesh* in Chapter 1, Homer's *Iliad* and *Odyssey* in Chapter 2, and Virgil's *Aeneid* in Chapter 5). But *The Divine Comedy* is *much* more than an epic, because Dante worked into the poem anything he felt like including. It is an allegory of great complexity, meant by Dante to be interpreted on many levels, such as depicting the way to God or the way of the artist. It is a hymn to the Middle Ages, including scholastic reasoning, mysticism, numerology, Thomism (see *Summa theologica*), Aristotelianism, and Italian history. Above all, it is a vision of Christianity and classicism reconciled.

The elaborate framework is built over a fairly simple plot. The hero, Dante himself, goes on a journey of self-discovery through hell, purgatory, and heaven, led first by Virgil, the Latin poet, and later by Beatrice, his human muse. The time is Easter 1300. The perennial appeal of this plot is that Dante becomes a stand-in for readers, virtually all of whom have been prey to self-doubts similar to those driving this hero on his life-or-death voyage.

Reading the Selections

The selections include four cantos (chapters) from the *Inferno* portion of *The Divine Comedy*. The Inferno, or hell, is the realm of sinners who suffer not because of predestined fate but because of their own bad choices. Here are found those who rejected spiritual values and yielded to animal appetites or violence, or perverted their human reason to fraud or malice against other human beings.

Canto I introduces Dante, who is tortured by self-doubts: "I went astray . . . and woke to find myself alone in a dark wood." He learns that two guides will lead him back to "the straight road."

Dante and Virgil enter hell in Canto III and are instantly greeted by the cries of the Opportunists, those sinners who chose to sit on the fence rather than side with evil or good. Dante begins to understand that God's justice reigns even in hell, as the Opportunists are punished in a manner appropriate to their sin. In Canto V, Dante and Virgil encounter the Carnal, those who succumbed to lust. The *Inferno*'s last canto, XXXIV, describes the center of hell, where a mindless Satan (called Dis)—a three-faced fallen angel, representative of the anti-Trinity and characterized by impotence, ignorance, and hatred—sits enthroned in ice. Dis's three mouths chew eternally on those ultimate rebels who betrayed church and state.

∞

Inferno, Canto I

The Dark Wood of Error

Midway in his allotted threescore years and ten, Dante comes to himself with a start and realizes that he has strayed from the True Way into the Dark Wood of Error (Worldliness). As soon as he has realized his loss, Dante lifts his eyes and sees the first light of the sunrise (the Sun is the Symbol of Divine Illumination) lighting the shoulders of a little hill (The Mount of Joy). It is the Easter Season, the time of resurrection, and the sun is in its equinoctial rebirth. This juxtaposition of joyous symbols fills Dante with hope and he sets out at once to climb directly up the Mount of Joy, but almost immediately his way is blocked by the Three Beasts of Worldliness: THE LEOPARD OF MALICE AND FRAUD, THE LION OF VIOLENCE AND AMBITION, and THE SHE-WOLF OF INCONTINENCE. These beasts, and especially the She-Wolf, drive him back despairing into the darkness of error. But just as all seems lost, a figure appears to him. It is the shade of VIRGIL, Dante's symbol of HUMAN REASON.

Virgil explains that he has been sent to lead Dante from error. There can, however, be no direct ascent past the beasts: the man who would escape them must go a longer and harder way. First he must descend through Hell (The Recognition of Sin), then he must ascend through Purgatory (The Renunciation of Sin), and only then may he reach the pinnacle of joy and come to the Light of God. Virgil offers to guide Dante, but only as far as Human Reason can go. Another guide (BEATRICE, symbol of DIVINE LOVE) must take over for the final ascent, for Human Reason is self-limited. Dante submits himself joyously to Virgil's guidance and they move off.

Midway in our life's journey,[22] I went astray   1
   from the straight road and woke to find myself
   alone in a dark wood. How shall I say

what wood that was! I never saw so drear,
   so rank, so arduous a wilderness!
   Its very memory gives a shape to fear.

Death could scarce be more bitter than that place!
   But since it came to good, I will recount
   all that I found revealed there by God's grace.

How I came to it I cannot rightly say,   10
   so drugged and loose with sleep had I become
   when I first wandered there from the True Way.

But at the far end of that valley of evil
   whose maze had sapped my very heart with fear!
   I found myself before a little hill

and lifted up my eyes. Its shoulders glowed
   already with the sweet rays of that planet[23]
   whose virtue leads men straight on every road,

and the shining strengthened me against the fright
   whose agony had wracked the lake of my heart   20
   through all the terrors of that piteous night.

Just as a swimmer, who with his last breath
   flounders ashore from perilous seas, might turn
   to memorize the wide water of his death—

so did I turn, my soul still fugitive
   from death's surviving image, to stare down
   that pass that none had ever left alive.

And there I lay to rest from my heart's race
   till calm and breath returned to me. Then rose
   and pushed up that dead slope at such a pace   30

each footfall rose above the last.[24] And lo!
   almost at the beginning of the rise
   I faced a spotted Leopard, all tremor and flow

and gaudy pelt. And it would not pass, but stood
   so blocking my every turn that time and again
   I was on the verge of turning back to the wood.

This fell at the first widening of the dawn
   as the sun was climbing Aries with those stars
   that rode with him to light the new creation.[25]

---

[22] **Midway in our life's journey** The biblical life span is three-score years and ten. The action opens in Dante's thirty-fifth year, i.e., 1300.

[23] **that planet** The sun. Ptolemaic astronomers considered it a planet. It is also symbolic of God as He who lights man's way.

---

[24] **each footfall rose above the last** The literal rendering would be "So that the fixed foot was ever the lower." "Fixed" has often been translated "right" and an ingenious reasoning can support that reading, but a simpler explanation offers itself and seems more competent: Dante is saying that he climbed with such zeal and haste that every footfall carried him above the last despite the steepness of the climb. At a slow pace, on the other hand, the rear foot might be brought up only as far as the forward foot. This device of selecting a minute but exactly-centered detail to convey the whole of a larger action is one of the central characteristics of Dante's style.

THE THREE BEASTS: Leopard, Lion, and She-Wolf. These three beasts undoubtedly are taken from Jeremiah v, 6. Many additional and incidental interpretations have been advanced for them, but the central interpretation must remain as noted. They foreshadow the three divisions of Hell (incontinence, violence, and fraud), which Virgil explains at length in Canto XI, 16–111.

[25] **Aries . . . that rode with him to light the new creation** The medieval tradition had it that the sun was in Aries at the time of the Creation. The significance of the astronomical and religious conjunction is an important part of Dante's intended allegory. It is just before dawn of Good Friday 1300 when he awakens in the Dark Wood. Thus his new life begins under Aries, the sign of creation, at dawn (rebirth) and in the Easter season (resurrection). Moreover, the moon is full and the sun is in the equinox, conditions that did not fall together on any Friday of 1300. Dante is obviously constructing poetically the perfect Easter as a symbol of his new awakening.

Thus the holy hour and the sweet season   40
  of commemoration did much to arm my fear
  of that bright murderous beast with their good omen.

Yet not so much but what I shook with dread
  at sight of a great Lion that broke upon me
  raging with hunger, its enormous head

held high as if to strike a mortal terror
  into the very air. And down his track,
  a She-Wolf drove upon me, a starved horror

ravening and wasted beyond all belief.
  She seemed a rack for avarice, gaunt and craving.   50
  Oh many the souls she has brought to endless grief!

She brought such heaviness upon my spirit
  at sight of her savagery and desperation,
  I died from every hope of that high summit.

And like a miser—eager in acquisition
  but desperate in self-reproach when Fortune's wheel
  turns to the hour of his loss—all tears and attrition

I wavered back; and still the beast pursued,
  forcing herself against me bit by bit
  till I slid back into the sunless wood.   60

And as I fell to my soul's ruin, a presence
  gathered before me on the discolored air,
  the figure of one who seemed hoarse from long
    silence.

At sight of him in that friendless waste I cried:
  "Have pity on me, whatever thing you are,
  whether shade or living man." And it replied:

"Not man, though man I once was, and my blood
  was Lombard, both my parents Mantuan.
  I was born, though late, *sub Julio*,[26] and bred

in Rome under Augustus in the noon   70
  of the false and lying gods. I was a poet
  and sang of old Anchises' noble son

who came to Rome after the burning of Troy.
  But you—why do *you* return to these distresses
  instead of climbing that shining Mount of Joy.

which is the seat and first cause of man's bliss?"
  "And are you then that Vergil and that fountain
  of purest speech?" My voice grew tremulous:

"Glory and light of poets! now may that zeal
  and love's apprenticeship that I poured out   80
  on your heroic verses serve me well!

For you are my true master and first author,
  the sole maker from whom I drew the breath
  of that sweet style whose measures have brought me
    honor.

See there, immortal sage, the beast I flee.
  For my soul's salvation, I beg you, guard me from her,
  for she has struck a mortal tremor through me."

And he replied, seeing my soul in tears:
  "He must go by another way who would escape
  this wilderness, for that mad beast that fleers   90

before you there, suffers no man to pass.
  She tracks down all, kills all, and knows no glut,
  but, feeding, she grows hungrier than she was.

She mates with any beast and will mate with more
  before the Greyhound becomes to hunt her down.
  He will not feed on lands nor loot, but honor

and love and wisdom will make straight his way.
  He will rise between Feltro and Feltro,[27] and in him
  shall be the resurrection and new day

of that sad Italy for which Nisus died,   100
  and Turnus, and Euryalus, and the maid Camilla.[28]
  He shall hunt her through every nation of sick pride

till she is driven back forever to Hell
  whence Envy first released her on the world.
  Therefore, for your own good, I think it well

you follow me and I will be your guide
  and lead you forth through an eternal place.
  There you shall see the ancient spirits tried

in endless pain, and hear their lamentation
  as each bemoans the second death[29] of souls   110
  Next you shall see upon a burning mountain

souls in fire and yet content in fire,
  knowing that whensoever it may be
  they yet will mount into the blessed choir.

---

[27] **the Greyhound . . . Feltro and Feltro** Almost certainly refers to Can Grande della Scala (1290–1329), great Italian leader born in Verona, which lies between the towns of Feltre and Montefeltro.
[28] **Nisus, Turnus, Euryalus, Camilla** All were killed in the war between the Trojans and the Latians when, according to legend, Aeneas led the survivors of Troy into Italy. Nisus and Euryalus (*Aeneid IX*) were Trojan comrades-in-arms who died together. Camilla (*Aeneid XI*) was the daughter of the Latian king and one of the warrior women. She was killed in a horse charge against the Trojans after displaying great gallantry. Turnus (*Aeneid XII*) was killed by Aeneas in a duel.
[29] **the second death** Damnation. "This is the second death, even the lake of fire" (*Revelation* xx, 14).

---

[26] *sub Julio* In the reign of Julius Caesar.

To which, if it is still your wish to climb,
  a worthier spirit shall be sent to guide you.
  With her shall I leave you, for the King of Time,

who reigns on high, forbids me to come there
  since, living, I rebelled against his law.[30]
  He rules the waters and the land and air   120

and there holds court, his city and his throne.
  Oh blessed are they he chooses!" And I to him:
  "Poet, by that God to you unknown,

---

[30] **forbids me to come there since, living, . . . law** Salvation is only through Christ in Dante's theology. Virgil lived and died before the establishment of Christ's teachings in Rome, and cannot therefore enter Heaven.

lead me this way. Beyond this present ill
  and worse to dread, lead me to Peter's gate[31]
  and be my guide through the sad halls of Hell."

And he then: "Follow." And he moved ahead
  in silence, and I followed where he led.

---

[31] **Peter's gate** The gate of Purgatory. (See *Purgatorio* IX, 76 ff.) The gate is guarded by an angel with a gleaming sword. The angel is Peter's vicar (Peter, the first Pope, symbolized all Popes; i.e., Christ's vicar on earth) and is entrusted with the two great keys.

Some commentators argue that this is the gate of Paradise, but Dante mentions no gate beyond this one in his ascent to Heaven. It should be remembered, too, that those who pass the gate of Purgatory have effectively entered Heaven.

The three great gates that figure in the entire journey are the gate of Hell (Canto III, 1–11), the gate of Dis (Canto VIII, 79–113, and Canto IX, 86–87), and the gate of Purgatory, as above.

∞

Inferno, Canto III

The Vestibule of Hell

THE OPPORTUNISTS

The Poets pass the Gate of Hell and are immediately assailed by cries of anguish. Dante sees the first of the souls in torment. They are THE OPPORTUNISTS, those souls who in life were neither for good nor evil but only for themselves. Mixed with them are those outcasts who took no sides in the Rebellion of the Angels. They are neither in Hell nor out of it. Eternally unclassified, they race round and round pursuing a wavering banner that runs forever before them through the dirty air; and as they run they are pursued by swarms of wasps and hornets, who sting them and produce a constant flow of blood and putrid matter which trickles down the bodies of the sinners and is feasted upon by loathsome worms and maggots who coat the ground.

The law of Dante's Hell is the law of symbolic retribution. As they sinned so are they punished. They took no sides, therefore they are given no place. As they pursued the ever-shifting illusion of their own advantage, changing their courses with every changing wind, so they pursue eternally an elusive, ever-shifting banner. As their sin was a darkness, so they move in darkness. As their own guilty conscience pursued them, so they are pursued by swarms of wasps and hornets. And as their actions were a moral filth, so they run eternally through the filth of worms and maggots which they themselves feed.

Dante recognizes several, among them POPE CELESTINE V, but without delaying to speak to any of these souls, the Poets move on to ACHERON, the first of the rivers of Hell. Here the newly arrived souls of the damned gather and wait for monstrous CHARON to ferry them over to punishment. Charon recognizes Dante as a living man and angrily refuses him passage. Virgil forces Charon to serve them, but Dante swoons with terror, and does not reawaken until he is on the other side.

I AM THE WAY INTO THE CITY OF WOE.   1
I AM THE WAY TO A FORSAKEN PEOPLE.

I AM THE WAY INTO ETERNAL SORROW.
SACRED JUSTICE MOVED MY ARCHITECT.
I WAS RAISED HERE BY DIVINE OMNIPOTENCE,
PRIMORDIAL LOVE AND ULTIMATE INTELLECT.

ONLY THOSE ELEMENTS TIME CANNOT WEAR[32]
WERE MADE BEFORE ME, AND BEYOND TIME I
    STAND.[33]
ABANDON ALL HOPE YE WHO ENTER HERE.[34]

---

[32] **Only those elements time cannot wear** The Angels, the Empyrean, and the First Matter are the elements time cannot wear, for they will last to all time. Man, however, in his mortal state, is not eternal. The Gate of Hell, therefore, was created before man. The theological point is worth attention. The doctrine of Original Sin is, of course, one familiar to many creeds. Here, however, it would seem that the preparation for damnation predates Original Sin. True, in one interpretation, Hell was created for the punishment of the Rebellious Angels and not for man. Had man not sinned, he would never have known Hell. But on the other hand, Dante's God was one who knew all, and knew therefore that man would indeed sin. The theological problem is an extremely delicate one.

It is significant, however, that having sinned, man lives out his days on the rind of Hell, and that damnation is forever below his feet. This central concept of man's sinfulness, and, opposed to it, the doctrine of Christ's ever-abounding mercy, are central to all of Dante's theology. Only as man surrenders himself to Divine Love may he hope for salvation, and salvation is open to all who will surrender themselves.

[33] **and beyond time I stand** So odious is sin to God that there can be no end to its just punishment.

[34] **Abandon all hope ye who enter here.** The admonition, of course, is to the damned and not to those who come on Heaven-sent errands. The Harrowing of Hell (see Canto IV, note to 1. 53) provided the only exemption from this decree, and that only through the direct intercession of Christ.

These mysteries I read cut into stone   10
   above a gate. And turning I said: "Master,
   what is the meaning of this harsh inscription?"

And he then as initiate to novice:
   "Here must you put by all division of spirit
   and gather your soul against all cowardice.

This is the place I told you to expect.
   Here you shall pass among the fallen people,
   souls who have lost the good of intellect."

So saying, he put forth his hand to me,
   and with a gentle and encouraging smile   20
   he led me through the gate of mystery.

Here sighs and cries and wails coiled and recoiled
   on the starless air, spilling my soul to tears.
   A confusion of tongues and monstrous accents toiled

in pain and anger. Voices hoarse and shrill
   and sounds of blows, all intermingled, raised
   tumult and pandemonium that still

whirls on the air forever dirty with it
   as if a whirlwind sucked at sand. And I,
   holding my head in horror, cried: "Sweet Spirit,   30

what souls are these who run through this black haze?"
   And he to me: "These are the nearly soulless
   whose lives concluded neither blame nor praise.

They are mixed here with that despicable corps
   of angels who were neither for God nor Satan,
   but only for themselves. The High Creator

scourged them from Heaven for its perfect beauty,
   and Hell will not receive them since the wicked
   might feel some glory over them." And I:

"Master, what gnaws at them so hideously   40
   their lamentation stuns the very air?"
   "They have no hope of death," he answered me,

"and in their blind and unattaining state
   their miserable lives have sunk so low
   that they must envy every other fate.

No word of them survives their living season.
   Mercy and Justice deny them even a name.
   Let us not speak of them: look, and pass on."

I saw a banner there upon the mist.
   Circling and circling, it seemed to scorn all pause.   50
   So it ran on, and still behind it pressed

a never-ending rout of souls in pain.
   I had not thought death had undone so many
   as passed before me in that mournful train.

And some I knew among them; last of all
   I recognized the shadow of that soul
   who, in his cowardice, made the Great Denial.[35]

At once I understood for certain: these
   were of that retrograde and faithless crew
   hateful to God and to His enemies.   60

These wretches never born and never dead
   ran naked in a swarm of wasps and hornets
   that goaded them the more they fled,

and made their faces stream with bloody gouts
   of pus and tears that dribbled to their feet
   to be swallowed there by loathsome worms and
      maggots.

Then looking onward I made out a throng
   assembled on the beach of a wide river,
   whereupon I turned to him: "Master, I long

to know what souls these are, and what strange usage   70
   makes them as eager to cross as they seem to be
   in this infected light." At which the Sage:

"All this shall be made known to you when we stand
   on the joyless beach of Acheron." And I
   cast down my eyes, sensing a reprimand

in what he said, and so walked at his side
   in silence and ashamed until we came
   through the dead cavern to that sunless tide.

There, steering toward us in an ancient ferry
   came an old man[36] with a white bush of hair,   80
   bellowing: "Woe to you depraved souls! Bury

here and forever all hope of Paradise:
   I come to lead you to the other shore,
   into eternal dark, into fire and ice.

---

[35] **who, in his cowardice, made the Great Denial** This is almost certainly intended to be Celestine V, who became pope in 1294. He was a man of saintly life, but allowed himself to be convinced by a priest named Benedetto that his soul was in danger since no man could live in the world without being damned. In fear for his soul he withdrew from all worldly affairs and renounced the papacy. Benedetto promptly assumed the mantle himself and became Boniface VIII, a pope who became for Dante a symbol of all the worst corruptions of the church. Dante also blamed Boniface and his intrigues for many of the evils that befell Florence. We shall learn in Canto XIX that the fires of Hell are waiting for Boniface in the pit of the Simoniacs, and we shall be given further evidence of his corruption in Canto XXVII. Celestine's great guilt is that his cowardice (in selfish terror for his own welfare) served as the door through which so much evil entered the church.

[36] **an old man** Charon. He is the ferryman of dead souls across the Acheron in all classical mythology.

And you who are living yet, I say begone
  from these who are dead." But when he saw me stand
  against his violence he began again:

"By other windings[37] and by other steerage
  shall you cross to that other shore. Not here! Not here!
  A lighter craft than mine must give you passage."   90

And my Guide to him: "Charon, bite back your spleen:
  this has been willed where what is willed must be,
  and is not yours to ask what it may mean."

The steersman of that marsh of ruined souls,
  who wore a wheel of flame around each eye,
  stifled the rage that shook his woolly jowls.

But those unmanned and naked spirits there
  turned pale with fear and their teeth began to chatter
  at sound of his crude bellow. In despair

they blasphemed God,[38] their parents, their time on   100
    earth,
  the race of Adam, and the day and the hour
  and the place and the seed and the womb that gave
    them birth.

But all together they drew to that grim shore
  where all must come who lose the fear of God.
  Weeping and cursing they come for evermore,

and demon Charon with eyes like burning coals
  herds them in, and with a whistling oar
  flails on the stragglers to his wake of souls.

As leaves in autumn loosen and stream down
  until the branch stands bare above its tatters   110
  spread on the rustling ground, so one by one

the evil seed of Adam in its Fall
  cast themselves, at his signal, from the shore
  and streamed away like birds who hear their call.

So they are gone over that shadowy water,
  and always before they reach the other shore
  a new noise stirs on this, and new throngs gather.

"My son," the courteous Master said to me,
  "all who die in the shadow of God's wrath
  converge to this from every clime and country.   120

And all pass over eagerly, for here
  Divine Justice transforms and spurs them so
  their dread turns wish: they yearn for what they fear.[39]

No soul in Grace comes ever to this crossing;
  therefore if Charon rages at your presence
  you will understand the reason for his cursing."

When he had spoken, all the twilight country
  shook so violently, the terror of it
  bathes me with sweat even in memory:

the tear-soaked ground gave out a sigh of wind   130
  that spewed itself in flame on a red sky,
  and all my shattered senses left me. Blind,

like one whom sleep comes over in a swoon,[40]
I stumbled into darkness and went down.

---

[37] **By other windings** Charon recognizes Dante not only as a living man but also as a soul in grace, and knows, therefore, that the Infernal Ferry was not intended for him. He is probably referring to the fact that souls destined for Purgatory and Heaven assemble not at his ferry point, but on the banks of the Tiber, from which they are transported by an Angel.

[38] **they blasphemed God** The souls of the damned are not permitted to repent, for repentance is a divine grace.

[39] **they yearn for what they fear** Hell (allegorically Sin) is what the souls of the damned really wish for. Hell is their actual and deliberate choice, for divine grace is denied to none who wish for it in their hearts. The damned must, in fact, deliberately harden their hearts to God in order to become damned. Christ's grace is sufficient to save all who wish for it.

[40] **Dante's swoon** This device (repeated at the end of Canto V) serves a double purpose. The first is technical: Dante uses it to cover a transition. We are never told how he crossed Acheron, for that would involve certain narrative matters he can better deal with when he crosses Styx in Canto VII. The second is to provide a point of departure for a theme that is carried through the entire descent: the theme of Dante's emotional reaction to Hell. These two swoons early in the descent show him most susceptible to the grief about him. As he descends, pity leaves him, and he even goes so far as to add to the torments of one sinner. The allegory is clear: we must harden ourselves against every sympathy for sin.

∞

Inferno, Canto V

Circle Two

THE CARNAL

The Poets leave Limbo and enter the SECOND CIRCLE. Here begin the torments of Hell proper, and here, blocking the way, sits MINOS, the dread and semibestial judge of the damned who assigns to

each soul its eternal torment. He orders the Poets back; but Virgil silences him as he earlier silenced Charon, and the Poets move on.

    They find themselves on a dark ledge swept by a great whirlwind, which spins within it the souls of the CARNAL, those who betrayed reason to their appetites. Their sin was to abandon themselves to the tempest of their passions: so they are swept forever

in the tempest of Hell, forever denied the light of reason and of
God. Virgil identifies many among them. SEMIRAMIS *is there, and*
DIDO, CLEOPATRA, HELEN, ACHILLES, PARIS, *and* TRISTAN. *Dante sees*
PAOLO *and* FRANCESCA *swept together, and in the name of love he*
calls to them to tell their sad story. They pause from their eternal
flight to come to him, and Francesca tells their history while Paolo
weeps at her side. Dante is so stricken by compassion at their
tragic tale that he swoons once again.

So we went down to the second ledge alone;   1
  a smaller circle[41] of so much greater pain
  the voice of the damned rose in a bestial moan.

There Minos[42] sits, grinning, grotesque, and hale.
  He examines each lost soul as it arrives
  and delivers his verdict with his coiling tail.

That is to say, when the ill-fated soul
  appears before him it confesses all,[43]
  and that grim sorter of the dark and foul

decides which place in Hell shall be its end,   10
  then wraps his twitching tail about himself
  one coil for each degree it must descend.

The soul descends and others take its place:
  each crowds in its turn to judgment, each confesses,
  each hears its doom and falls away through space.

"O you who come into this camp of woe,"
  cried Minos when he saw me turn away
  without awaiting his judgment, "watch where you go

once you have entered here, and to whom you turn!
  Do not be misled by that wide and easy passage!"   20
  And my Guide to him: "That is not your concern;

it is his fate to enter every door.
  This has been willed where what is willed must be,
  and is not yours to question. Say no more."

Now the choir of anguish, like a wound,
  strikes through the tortured air. Now I have come
  to Hell's full lamentation,[44] sound beyond sound.

I came to a place stripped bare of every light
  and roaring on the naked dark like seas
  wracked by a war of winds. Their hellish flight   30

of storm and counterstorm through time foregone,
  sweeps the souls of the damned before its charge.
  Whirling and battering it drives them on,

and when they pass the ruined gap of Hell[45]
  through which we had come, their shrieks begin anew.
  There they blaspheme the power of God eternal.

And this, I learned, was the never ending flight
  of those who sinned in the flesh, the carnal and lusty
  who betrayed reason to their appetite.

As the wings of wintering starlings bear them on   40
  in their great wheeling flights, just so the blast
  wherries these evil souls through time foregone.

Here, there, up, down, they whirl and, whirling, strain
  with never a hope of hope to comfort them,
  not of release, but even of less pain.

As cranes go over sounding their harsh cry,
  leaving the long streak of their flight in air,
  so come these spirits, wailing as they fly.

And watching their shadows lashed by wind, I cried:
  "Master, what souls are these the very air   50
  lashes with its black whips from side to side?"

"The first of these whose history you would know,"
  he answered me, "was Empress of many tongues.[46]
  Mad sensuality corrupted her so

---

[41] **a smaller circle** The pit of Hell tapers like a funnel. The
circles of ledges accordingly grow smaller as they descend.
[42] **Minos** Like all the monsters Dante assigns to the various
offices of Hell, Minos is drawn from classical mythology. He
was the son of Europa and of Zeus, who descended to her in the
form of a bull. Minos became a mythological king of Crete, so
famous for his wisdom and justice that after death his soul was
made judge of the dead. Virgil presents him fulfilling the same
office at Aeneas's descent to the underworld. Dante, however,
transforms him into an irate and hideous monster with a tail.
The transformation may have been suggested by the form Zeus
assumed for the rape of Europa—the monster is certainly bull-
ish enough here—but the obvious purpose of the brutalization
is to present a figure symbolic of the guilty conscience of the
wretches who come before it to make their confessions. Dante
freely reshapes his materials to his own purposes.
[43] **it confesses all** Just as the souls appeared eager to cross
Acheron, so they are eager to confess even while they dread.
Dante is once again making the point that sinners elect their
Hell by an act of their own will.

[44] **Hell's full lamentation** It is with the second circle that the
real tortures of Hell begin.
[45] **the ruined gap of Hell** See note to Canto II, 53. At the time of
the Harrowing of Hell, a great earthquake shook the underworld
shattering rocks and cliffs. Ruins resulting from the same shock
are noted in Canto XII, 34, and Canto XXI, 112 ff. At the beginning of Canto XXIV, the Poets leave the *bolgia* of the Hypocrites
by climbing the ruined slabs of a bridge that was shattered by
this earthquake.
THE SINNERS OF THE SECOND CIRCLE (THE CARNAL):
Here begin the punishments for the various sins of Incontinence
(the sins of the She-Wolf). In the second circle are punished
those who sinned by excess of sexual passion. Since this is the
most natural sin and the sin most nearly associated with love, its
punishment is the lightest of all to be found in Hell proper. The
Carnal are whirled and buffeted endlessly through the murky
air (symbolic of the beclouding of their reason by passion) by a
great gale (symbolic of their lust).
[46] **Empress of many tongues** Semiramis, a legendary queen of
Assyria who assumed full power at the death of her husband,
Ninus.

that to hide the guilt of her debauchery
  she licensed all depravity alike,
  and lust and law were one in her decree.

She is Semiramis of whom the tale is told
  how she married Ninus and succeeded him
  to the throne of that wide land the Sultans hold.   60

The other is Dido[47]; faithless to the ashes
  of Sichaeus, she killed herself for love.
  The next whom the eternal tempest lashes

is sense-drugged Cleopatra. See Helen there,
  from whom such ill arose. And great Achilles,[48]
  who fought at last with love in the house of prayer.

And Paris. And Tristan." As they whirled above
  he pointed out more than a thousand shades
  of those torn from the mortal life by love.

I stood there while my Teacher one by one   70
  named the great knights and ladies of dim time;
  and I was swept by pity and confusion.

At last I spoke: "Poet, I should be glad
  to speak a word with those two swept together[49]
  so lightly on the wind and still so sad."

And he to me: "Watch them. When next they pass,
  call to them in the name of love that drives
  and damns them here. In that name they will pause."

Thus, as soon as the wind in its wild course
  brought them around, I called: "O wearied souls!   80
  if none forbid it, pause and speak to us."

As mating doves that love calls to their nest
  glide through the air with motionless raised wings,
  borne by the sweet desire that fills each breast—

Just so those spirits turned on the torn sky
  from the band where Dido whirls across the air;
  such was the power of pity in my cry.

"O living creature, gracious, kind, and good,
  going this pilgrimage through the sick night,
  visiting us who stained the earth with blood,   90

were the King of Time our friend, we would pray His
    peace
  on you who have pitied us. As long as the wind
  will let us pause, ask of us what you please.

The town where I was born lies by the shore
  where the Po descends into its ocean rest
  with its attendant streams in one long murmur.

Love, which in gentlest hearts will soonest bloom
  seized my lover with passion for that sweet body
  from which I was torn unshriven to my doom.

Love, which permits no loved one not to love,   100
  took me so strongly with delight in him
  that we are one in Hell, as we were above.[50]

Love led us to one death. In the depths of Hell
  Caïna waits for him[51] who took our lives."
  This was the piteous tale they stopped to tell.

And when I had heard those world-offended lovers
  I bowed my head. At last the Poet spoke:
  "What painful thoughts are these your lowered brow
    covers?"

When at length I answered, I began: "Alas!
  What sweetest thoughts, what green and young desire   110
  led these two lovers to this sorry pass."

---

[47] **Dido** Queen and founder of Carthage. She had vowed to re-main faithful to her husband, Sichaeus, but she fell in love with Aeneas. When Aeneas abandoned her, she stabbed herself on a funeral pyre she had had prepared.

  According to Dante's own system of punishments, she should be in the Seventh Circle (Canto XIII) with the suicides. The only clue Dante gives to the tempering of her punishment is his statement that "she killed herself for love." Dante always seems readiest to forgive in that name.

[48] **Achilles** He is placed among this company because of his passion for Polyxena, the daughter of Priam. For love of her, he agreed to desert the Greeks and to join the Trojans, but when he went to the temple for the wedding (according to the legend Dante has followed), he was killed by Paris.

[49] **those two swept together** Paolo and Francesca [PAH-oe-loe and Frahn-CHAY-ska]. Dante's treatment of these two lovers is certainly the tenderest and most sympathetic accorded any of the sinners in Hell, and legends immediately began to grow about this pair.

  The facts are these. In 1275 Giovanni Malatesta [Djoe-VAH-nee Mahl-ah-TEH-stah] of Rimini, called Giovanni the Lame, a some-what deformed but brave and powerful warrior, made a politi-cal marriage with Francesca, daughter of Guido da Polenta of Ravenna. Francesca came to Rimini and there an amour grew be-tween her and Giovanni's younger brother Paolo. Despite the fact that Paolo had married in 1269 and had become the father of two daughters by 1275, his affair with Francesca continued for many years. It was sometime between 1283 and 1286 that Giovanni sur-prised them in Francesca's bedroom and killed both of them.

  Around these facts the legend has grown that Paolo was sent by Giovanni as his proxy to the marriage, that Francesca thought he was her real bridegroom and accordingly gave him her heart irrevocably at first sight. The legend obviously increases the pathos, but nothing in Dante gives it support.

[50] **that we are one in Hell, as we were above** At many points of *The Inferno*, Dante makes clear the principle that the souls of the damned are locked so blindly into their own guilt that none can feel sympathy for another, or find any pleasure in the pres-ence of another. The temptation of many readers is to interpret this line romantically: i.e., that the love of Paolo and Francesca survives Hell itself. The more Dantean interpretation, however, is that they add to one another's anguish (a) as mutual remind-ers of their sin, and (b) as insubstantial shades of the bodies for which they once felt such great passion.

[51] **Caïna waits for him** Giovanni Malatesta was still alive at the writing. His fate is already decided, however, and upon his death, his soul will fall to Caïna, the first ring of the last circle (Canto XXXII), where lie those who performed acts of treachery against their kin.

Then turning to those spirits once again,
  I said: "Francesca, what you suffer here
  melts me to tears of pity and of pain.

But tell me: in the time of your sweet sighs
  by what appearances found love the way
  to lure you to his perilous paradise?"

And she: "The double grief of a lost bliss
  is to recall its happy hour in pain.
  Your Guide and Teacher knows the truth of this.   120

But if there is indeed a soul in Hell
  to ask of the beginning of our love
  out of his pity, I will weep and tell:

On a day for dalliance we read the rhyme
  of Lancelot,[52] how love had mastered him.
  We were alone with innocence and dim time.[53]

Pause after pause that high old story drew
  our eyes together while we blushed and paled;
  but it was one soft passage overthrew

our caution and our hearts. For when we read   130
  how her fond smile was kissed by such a lover,
  he who is one with me alive and dead

breathed on my lips the tremor of his kiss.
  That book, and he who wrote it, was a pander.[54]
  That day we read no further." As she said this,

the other spirit, who stood by her, wept
  so piteously, I felt my senses reel
  and faint away with anguish. I was swept

by such a swoon as death is, and I fell,
  as a corpse might fall, to the dead floor of Hell.   140

---

[52] **the rhyme of Lancelot** The story exists in many forms. The details Dante makes use of are from an Old French version.
[53] **dim time** The original simply reads "We were alone, suspecting nothing." "Dim time" is rhyme-forced, but not wholly outside the legitimate implications of the original, I hope. The old courtly romance may well be thought of as happening in the dim ancient days. The apology, of course, comes after the fact: one does the possible, then argues for justification, and there probably is none.

[54] **That book, and he who wrote it, was a pander.** *Galeotto*, the Italian word for "pander," is also the Italian rendering of the name of Gallehault, who is the French romance Dante refers to here, urged Lancelot and Guinevere on to love.

∞

Inferno, Canto XXXIV

NINTH CIRCLE: *Cocytus*
ROUND FOUR: *Judecca*
THE CENTER

Compound Fraud
The Treacherous to Their Masters
Satan

"On march the banners of the King," Virgil begins as the Poets face the last depth. He is quoting a medieval hymn, and to it he adds the distortion and perversion of all that lies about him. "On march the banners of the King—of Hell." And there before them, in an infernal parody of Godhead, they see Satan in the distance, his great wings beating like a windmill. It is their beating that is the source of the icy wind of Cocytus, the exhalation of all evil.

All about him in the ice are strewn the sinners of the last round, JUDECCA, named for Judas Iscariot. These are the TREACHEROUS TO THEIR MASTERS. They lie completely sealed in the ice, twisted and distorted into every conceivable posture. It is impossible to speak to them, and the Poets move on to observe Satan.

He is fixed into the ice at the center to which flow all the rivers of guilt; and as he beats his great wings as if to escape, their icy wind only freezes him more surely into the polluted ice. In a grotesque parody of the Trinity, he has three faces, each a different color, and in each mouth he clamps a sinner whom he rips eternally with his teeth. JUDAS ISCARIOT is in the central mouth: BRUTUS and CASSIUS in the mouths on either side.

Having seen all, the Poets now climb through the center, grappling hand over hand down the hairy flank of Satan himself— a last supremely symbolic action—and at last, when they have

passed the center of all gravity, they emerge from Hell. A long climb from the earth's center to the Mount of Purgatory awaits them, and they push on without rest, ascending along the sides of the river Lethe, till they emerge once more to see the stars of Heaven, just before dawn on Easter Sunday.

"On march the banners of the King[55] of Hell,"   1
  my Master said. "Toward us. Look straight ahead:
  can you make him out at the core of the frozen shell?"

Like a whirling windmill seen afar at twilight,
  or when a mist has risen from the ground—
  just such an engine rose upon my sight

stirring up such a wild and bitter wind
  I cowered for shelter at my Master's back,
  there being no other windbreak I could find.

---

[55] **On march the banners of the King** The hymn (*Vexilla regis prodeunt*) was written in the sixth century by Venantius Fortunatus, Bishop of Poitiers. The original celebrates the Holy Cross and is part of the service for Good Friday to be sung at the moment of uncovering the cross.

I stood now where the souls of the last class   10
  (with fear my verses tell it) were covered wholly;
  they shone below the ice like straws in glass.

Some lie stretched out; others are fixed in place
  upright, some on their heads, some on their soles;
  another, like a bow, bends foot to face.

When we had gone so far across the ice
  that it pleased my Guide to show me the foul creature[56]
  which once had worn the grace of Paradise,

he made me stop, and, stepping aside, he said:
  "Now see the face of Dis! This is the place   20
  where you must arm your soul against all dread."

Do not ask, Reader, how my blood ran cold
  and my voice choked up with fear. I cannot write it:
  this is a terror that cannot be told.

I did not die, and yet I lost life's breath:
  imagine for yourself what I became,
  deprived at once of both my life and death.

The Emperor of the Universe of Pain
  jutted his upper chest above the ice;
  and I am closer in size to the great mountain   30

the Titans make around the central pit,
  than they to his arms. Now, starting from this part,
  imagine the whole that corresponds to it!

If he was once as beautiful as now
  he is hideous, and still turned on his Maker,
  well may he be the source of every woe!

With what a sense of awe I saw his head
  towering above me! for it had three faces:[57]
  one was in front, and it was fiery red;

the other two, as weirdly wonderful,   40
  merged with it from the middle of each shoulder
  to the point where all converged at the top of the skull;

the right was something between white and bile;
  the left was about the color that one finds
  on those who live along the banks of the Nile.

Under each head two wings rose terribly,
  their span proportioned to so gross a bird:
  I never saw such sails upon the sea.

They were not feathers—their texture and their form
  were like a bat's wings—and he beat them so   50
  that three winds blew from him in one great storm:

it is these winds that freeze all Cocytus.
  He wept from his six eyes, and down three chins
  the tears ran mixed with bloody froth and pus.[58]

In every mouth he worked a broken sinner
  between his rake-like teeth. Thus he kept three
  in eternal pain at his eternal dinner.

For the one in front the biting seemed to play
  no part at all compared to the ripping: at times
  the whole skin of his back was flayed away.   60

"That soul that suffers most," explained my Guide,
  "is Judas[59] Iscariot, he who kicks his legs on the fiery
  chin and has his head inside.

Of the other two, who have their heads thrust forward,
  the one who dangles down from the black face
  is Brutus: note how he writhes without a word.

And there, with the huge and sinewy arms,[60] is the soul
  of Cassius.—But the night is coming on[61]
  and we must go, for we have seen the whole."

Then, as he bade, I clasped his neck, and he,
  watching for a moment when the wings   70
  were opened wide, reached over dexterously

and seized the shaggy coat of the king demon;
  then grappling matted hair and frozen crusts
  from one tuft to another, clambered down.

When we had reached the joint where the great thigh
  merges into the swelling of the haunch,
  my Guide and Master, straining terribly,

turned his head to where his feet had been
  and began to grip the hair as if he were climbing;
  so that I thought we moved toward Hell again.   80

"Hold fast!" my Guide said, and his breath came shrill[62]
  with labor and exhaustion. "There is no way
  but by such stairs to rise above such evil."

At last he climbed out through an opening
  in the central rock, and he seated me on the rim;
  then joined me with a nimble backward spring.

---

[56] **the foul creature** Satan.
[57] **three faces** Numerous interpretations of these three faces exist. What is essential to all explanation is that they be seen as perversions of the qualities of the Trinity.
[58] **bloody froth and pus** The gore of the sinners he chews, which is mixed with his slaver.
[59] **Judas** Note how closely his punishment is patterned on that of the Simoniacs (Canto XIX).
[60] **huge and sinewy arms** The Cassius who betrayed Caesar was more generally described in terms of Shakespeare's "lean and hungry look." Another Cassius is described by Cicero (*Catiline* III) as huge and sinewy. Dante probably confused the two.
[61] **the night is coming on** It is now Saturday evening.
[62] **his breath came shrill** Cf. Canto XXIII, 85, where the fact that Dante breathes indicates to the Hypocrites that he is alive. Virgil's breathing is certainly a contradiction.

I looked up, thinking to see Lucifer
   as I had left him, and I saw instead
   his legs projecting high into the air.

Now let all those whose dull minds are still vexed   90
   by failure to understand what point it was
   I had passed through, judge if I was perplexed.

"Get up. Up on your feet," my Master said.
   "The sun already mounts to middle tierce,[63]
   and a long road and hard climbing lie ahead."

It was no hall of state we had found there,
   but a natural animal pit hollowed from rock
   with a broken floor and a close and sunless air.

"Before I tear myself from the Abyss,"
   I said when I had risen, "O my Master,   100
   explain to me my error in all this:

where is the ice? and Lucifer—how has he
   been turned from top to bottom: and how can the sun
   have gone from night to day so suddenly?"

And he to me: "You imagine you are still
   on the other side of the center where I grasped
   the shaggy flank of the Great Worm of Evil

which bores through the world—you *were* while I
   climbed down,
   but when I turned myself about, you passed
   the point to which all gravities are drawn.   110

You are under the other hemisphere where you stand;
   the sky above us is the half opposed
   to that which canopies the great dry land.

Under the mid-point of that other sky
   the Man who was born sinless and who lived
   beyond all blemish, came to suffer and die.

You have your feet upon a little sphere
   which forms the other face of the Judecca.
   There it is evening when it is morning here.

And this gross Fiend and Image of all Evil   120
   who made a stairway for us with his hide
   is pinched and prisoned in the ice-pack still.

On this side he plunged down from heaven's height,
   and the land that spread here once hid in the sea
   and fled North to our hemisphere for fright;

and it may be that moved by that same fear,
   the one peak[64] that still rises on this side
   fled upward leaving this great cavern[65] here.

Down there, beginning at the further bound
   of Beelzebub's dim tomb, there is a space   130
   not known by sight, but only by the sound

of a little stream[66] descending through the hollow
   it has eroded from the massive stone
   in its endlessly entwining lazy flow."

My Guide and I crossed over and began
   to mount that little known and lightless road
   to ascend into the shining world again.

He first, I second, without thought of rest
   we climbed the dark until we reached the point
   where a round opening brought in sight the blest   140

and beauteous shining of the Heavenly cars.
   And we walked out once more beneath the Stars.[67]

---

[63] **middle tierce** In the canonical day, tierce is the period from about six to nine A.M. Middle tierce, therefore, is seven-thirty. In going through the center point, they have gone from night to day. They have moved ahead twelve hours.

---

[64] **the one peak** The Mount of Purgatory.
[65] **this great cavern** The natural animal pit of line 97. It is also "Beelzebub's dim tomb," line 130.
[66] **a little stream** Lethe. In classical mythology, the river of forgetfulness, from which souls drank before being born. In Dante's symbolism it flows down from the top of Purgatory, where it washes away the memory of sin from the souls that have achieved purity. That memory it delivers to Hell, which draws all sin to itself.
[67] **Stars** As part of his total symbolism, Dante ends each of the three divisions of the *Commedia* with this word. Every conclusion of the upward soul is toward the stars, God's shining symbols of hope and virtue. It is just before dawn of Easter Sunday that the Poets emerge—a further symbolism.

∞

Questions for Critical Thinking

1. What is Dante's rationale for the punishments meted out to sinners? Discuss some of the types of sins and their punishments.

2. Discuss and provide examples of how Dante includes some of the most important themes and ideas of the High Middle Ages. What would be some of the most important themes and ideas of today you would include in your "Divine Comedy"?

∽

HILDEGARD OF BINGEN
Selections from *Scivias (Know the Ways of the Lord)*

Hildegard of Bingen (1098–1179) is a rare female voice from the Middle Ages. Indeed, in an era defined by a hierarchical male-dominated political, religious, and cultural system, she stands out as a remarkable individual. In particular, she expressed her most intimate feelings in books and participated in the period's major debates through public discourses and correspondence with leading figures. Today, as her reputation is on the rise, she has become a protean figure viewed from myriad angles, some contradictory, but all of them pioneering. Some admirers claim her as the first in a long line of visionary women who offers guidance to souls in distress. Others place her in the tradition of Christian thinkers who focus on Divine Wisdom, as evidenced by her stress on creation and redemption. Modern feminists salute her as a role model, for her managerial skills and willingness to confront patriarchal power. Traditionalists also admire her for her strong papalist politics, as a supporter of the church's hierarchy and the conservative reforms of Pope Gregory VII. Musicians and musicologists are now beginning to recognize her as an innovative composer of hymns and sacred songs. Historians study her letters for clues to the personalities of the period and for insight into medieval problems. Historians of science believe she broke new ground with her works on nature and medicine, especially regarding diagnosis and treatment of diseases. Finally, literary scholars identify her as a master of medieval prose with her prodigious and varied writings; they also marvel at the secret language she created, composed of nearly nine hundred words, to disguise her most confidential writing.

From the age of five to her last days, Hildegard experienced visions of God, in which she claimed she was directed to write down the details of her encounters as an aid to others. At first skeptical of her mystical writings, the church investigated but ultimately was satisfied and thereafter encouraged her in this path. Over the course of her life, she wrote three visionary books that are still considered classics of this genre. The first book dealt with religious beliefs, the second was concerned with virtue and vice, and the third summarized her theological ideas.

Scito vias Domini or *Know the Ways of the Lord*, better known by its shortened title, *Scivias,* was the first of Hildegard's three visionary and prophetic books. She worked on the book for ten years, from 1141 to 1151. Divided into three sections, it comprises a series of twenty-six visions, each accompanied by a commentary and an interpretation of the vision. Book One is on God the creator and what he has created; Book Two is on God the redeemer and his power of redemption; Book Three is a history of salvation as symbolized as a building with its towers, walls, and pillars representing various aspects of Christian salvation.

Hildegard explains each of the twenty-six visions by first describing the vision. She then interprets the vision with the aid of biblical texts and often in allegorical terms. Throughout, she continually asks what is the meaning of each vision and concludes each vision with an admonition to the reader. By way of her visions, Hildegard addresses many topics of medieval Christian thought and doctrine, such as the power of God, the story of the Creation, the various ways humans have fallen from grace, the Trinity, the role of the church, the devil, and the Day of Judgment.

Reading the Selections

The first selection is the "Declaration," which sets the pattern and tone for the remaining visions in *Scivias.* Hildegard describes her encounter with a "voice from heaven." Her final words recall the voice from heaven telling her that she must write about her visions.

"Confirmation," Vision Four in Book Two, begins, as do all the visions, with Hildegard's description of her vision or visual experience, followed by an explanation of the vision. In paragraph 1, she connects the first baptism with the power of confirmation for all Christians. Paragraphs 2, 3, and 4 offer further explanations of her vision. In paragraph 5, Hildegard turns to the scriptures to reinforce her argument, a device she often employed. In paragraph 6, Hildegard notes how the power of the bishop in the baptismal ceremony enhances those he has baptized. In paragraph 14, the concluding passage, she quotes the prophet Ezekiel to underscore her argument.

∞

Declaration
These Are True Visions Flowing from God

And behold! In the forty-third year of my earthly course, as I was gazing with great fear and trembling attention at a heavenly vision, I saw a great splendor in which resounded a voice from Heaven, saying to me,

"O fragile human, ashes of ashes, and filth of filth! Say and write what you see and hear. But since you are timid in speaking, and simple in expounding, and untaught in writing, speak and write these things not by a human mouth, and not by the understanding of human invention, and not by the requirements of human composition, but as you see and hear them on high in the heavenly places in the wonders of God. Explain these things in such a way that the hearer, receiving the words of his instructor, may expound them in those words, according to that will, vision and instruction. Thus therefore, O human, speak these things that you see and hear. And write them not by yourself or any other human being, but by the will of Him Who knows, sees and disposes all things in the secrets of His mysteries."

And again I heard the voice from Heaven saying to me, "Speak therefore of these wonders, and, being so taught, write them and speak."

It happened that, in the eleven hundred and forty-first year of the Incarnation of the Son of God, Jesus Christ, when I was forty-two years and seven months old, Heaven was opened and a fiery light of exceeding brilliance came and permeated my whole brain, and inflamed my whole heart and my whole breast, not like a burning but like a warming flame, as the sun warms anything its rays touch. And immediately I knew the meaning of the exposition of the Scriptures, namely the Psalter, the Gospel and the other catholic volumes of both the Old and the New Testaments, though I did not have the interpretation of the words of their texts or the division of the syllables or the knowledge of cases or tenses. But I had sensed in myself wonderfully the power and mystery of secret and admirable visions from my childhood—that is, from the age of five—up to that time, as I do now. This, however, I showed to no one except a few religious persons who were living in the same manner as I; but meanwhile, until the time when God by His grace wished it to be manifested, I concealed it in quiet silence. But the visions I saw

I did not perceive in dreams, or sleep, or delirium, or by the eyes of the body, or by the ears of the outer self, or in hidden places; but I received them while awake and seeing with a pure mind and the eyes and ears of the inner self, in open places, as God willed it. How this might be is hard for mortal flesh to understand.

But when I had passed out of childhood and had reached the age of full maturity mentioned above, I heard a voice from Heaven saying, "I am the Living Light, Who illuminates the darkness. The person [Hildegard] whom I have chosen and whom I have miraculously stricken as I willed, I have placed among great wonders, beyond the measure of the ancient people who saw in Me many secrets; but I have laid her low on the earth, that she might not set herself up in arrogance of mind. The world has had in her no joy or lewdness or use in worldly things, for I have withdrawn her from impudent boldness, and she feels fear and is timid in her works. For she suffers in her inmost being and in the veins of her flesh; she is distressed in mind and sense and endures great pain of body, because no security has dwelt in her, but in all her undertakings she has judged herself guilty. For I have closed up the cracks in her heart that her mind may not exalt itself in pride or vainglory, but may feel fear and grief rather than joy and wantonness. Hence in My love she searched in her mind as to where she could find someone who would run in the path of salvation. And she found such a one and loved him [the monk Volmar of Disibodenberg], knowing that he was a faithful man, working like herself on another part of the work that leads to Me. And, holding fast to him, she worked with him in great zeal so that My hidden miracles might be revealed. And she did not seek to exalt herself above herself but with many sighs bowed to him whom she found in the ascent of humility and the intention of good will.

"O human, who receives these things meant to manifest what is hidden not in the disquiet of deception but in the purity of simplicity, write, therefore, the things you see and hear."

But I, though I saw and heard these things, refused to write for a long time through doubt and bad opinion and the diversity of human words, not with stubbornness but in the exercise of humility, until, laid low by the scourge of God, I fell upon a bed of sickness; then, compelled at last by many illnesses, and by the witness of a certain noble maiden of good conduct [the nun Richardis of Stade] and of that man whom I had secretly sought and found, as mentioned above, I set my hand to the writing. While I was doing it, I sensed, as I mentioned before, the deep profundity of scriptural exposition; and, raising myself from illness by the strength I received, I brought this work to a close—though just barely—in ten years.

These visions took place and these words were written in the days of Henry, Archbishop of Mainz, and of Conrad, King of the Romans, and of Cuno, Abbot of Disibodenberg, under Pope Eugenius.

And I spoke and wrote these things not by the invention of my heart or that of any other person, but as by the secret mysteries of God I heard and received them in the heavenly places.

And again I heard a voice from Heaven saying to me, 10 "Cry out therefore, and write thus!"

∞

Vision Four
Confirmation

And then I saw the image of an immense round tower, all made 1 *of a single white stone, with three windows in its summit from which shone so much brilliance that even the roof of the tower, which was constructed like a cone, showed very clearly in its light. These windows were adorned all round with beautiful emeralds. And the tower stood directly in back of the image of the woman described in the previous vision, just as a tower is placed in the wall of a city, so that because of its strength the image could not fall.*

And I saw those children who, as mentioned before, had passed through the womb of that image, shining with great brightness; some of them were adorned with gold color from their foreheads to their feet, but others lacked that color and had only the brightness. And some of these children were looking at a pure and brilliant splendor, but the rest at a turbulent red flash located in the East. Of those who were meditating on the pure and brilliant splendor, some had clear eyes and strong feet and were marching forward vigorously in the womb of the image; but others had weak eyes and crippled feet and were blown here and there by the wind. These, however, had a staff in their hands, and they flew in front of the image and touched it at times, though languidly. Still others had calm eyes but weak feet, and they moved back and forth in the air before the image; and others had weak eyes and strong feet, but they walked before the image languidly. But of the ones who were contemplating the turbulent red flash, some were well-ornamented and advanced into the image with vigor; but others tore themselves away from her and attacked her and broke her established rules. Among these, some by the fruit of penitence humbly returned to her, but others by obstinacy and neglect remained in the elation of the way of death. And again I heard the voice from Heaven saying to me:

1 Each Baptized Person Should Be Anointed and Confirmed by a Bishop

After the illumination of baptism, which rose with the Sun of Justice Who sanctified the world by His own washing, the new Bride of the Lamb was adorned and confirmed in the fire of the ardor of the Holy Spirit for the perfection of her beauty. So also each of the faithful who is regenerated by the Spirit and water should be decorated and confirmed by a bishop's anointing, so that he will be strengthened in all his members toward achieving beatitude and find himself most perfectly adorned with the full fruits of highest justice.

Therefore, *this tower that you see* represents the flaming forth of the gifts of the Holy Spirit, which the Father sent into the world for love of His Son, to enkindle the hearts of His disciples with fiery tongues and make them stronger in the name of the Holy and True Trinity. Before the coming upon them of the Holy Spirit in fire, they were sitting shut up in their house, protecting their bodies, for they were timid about speaking of God's justice and feeble in facing their enemies' persecutions. Because they had seen My Son in the flesh, their inner vision was unopened and they loved Him in the flesh, and thus did not yet see the bright teaching that afterward, when they were made strong in the Holy Spirit, they spread abroad in the world. But by Its coming they were so confirmed that they did not shrink from any penalty, but bravely endured it. And this is the strength of that tower, which strengthened the Church so much that the insane fury of the Devil can never overcome it.

2 Confirmation Confers the Immense Sweetness of the Holy Spirit

You see the tower as immense and round, all made of a single 5 *white stone.* This means that the sweetness of the Holy Spirit is boundless and swift to encompass all creatures in grace, and no corruption can take away the fullness of its just integrity. Its path is a torrent, and streams of sanctity flow from it in its bright power, with never a stain of dirt in them; for the Holy Spirit Itself is a burning and shining serenity, which cannot be nullified, and which enkindles ardent virtue so as to put all darkness to flight.

3 In Confirmation the Trinity Manifests Itself by Verdant Virtues

It has three windows in its summit from which shine so much brilliance that even the roof of the tower, which is constructed like a cone, shows very clearly in its light; for the ineffable Trinity is manifested in the outpouring of the gifts of the power of the Holy Spirit. And from the blessed Trinity so much clarity of justice emanates through the teaching of the apostles that in it the great power of Divinity, which in the height of its omnipotent majesty is incomprehensible, is shown more clearly to mortal creatures, that is, humans. But it can be grasped only as much as possible for the faith of a believing and faithful person.

Hence these windows are adorned all round with beautiful emeralds; for the Trinity is declared openly throughout the world by the verdant virtues and tribulations of the apostles, which are never greeted with arid apathy. How? Because it is known how ravening wolves sought to tear apart the apostles for their faith in the truth, and these various calamities strengthened them for the struggle, so that by fighting they constructed the Church and strengthened her with strong virtues to build up the faith and adorned her with many brilliancies. And because the Church, through the inspiration of the Holy Spirit, has been so strengthened by them, she desires and asks that her children also be adorned in this anointing by the Holy Spirit, Which penetrated the hearts of the faithful in that high and mystical mercy when by the will of God the Father It came into the world in fiery tongues. Therefore, the person who was baptized with the baptism of salvation must also be confirmed by the anointing of that excellent Teacher, as the Church is confirmed on the firm rock.

4 How the Church, Fortified by the Holy Spirit, Can Never Fall into Error

Hence the tower stands directly in back of the image of the woman described in the previous vision, just as a tower is placed in the wall of a city, so that because of its strength the image cannot fall. For the Holy Spirit has worked marvels in the exceeding strength of Him Who is the true Bridegroom of the Church, and It shows the Church to be so strong in her defenses that, because of the fortitude she derives from Its fiery gift, she can never be thrown down by any error of wickedness. Under heavenly protection she will always rejoice, without spot or wrinkle, in the love of her Bridegroom, because My Only-Begotten was conceived nobly by the Holy Spirit and born without stain of the Virgin, as I said to Moses:

5 Words of Moses on This Subject

"Behold, He said, there is a place with Me, and you shall stand upon the rock. And when My glory shall pass by, I will set you in a hole of the rock and protect you with My right hand, until I pass. And I will take away My hand, and you shall see My back parts" [Exodus 33:21–23]. What does this mean? The miracle is at hand that will be fulfilled in My will. But first you will fight with harsh legal precepts whose force is in their outward significance and where you will not find the sweetness and gentleness that will be revealed in My Son. And this harshness of the Law, which by My command you will write down, will stand in hard and stony hearts until you and your followers have shown all the glory that is to be rendered to Me until the coming of My Son. And when this is fulfilled in the Law you are writing, I will be glorified, and I will place you inside the pierced rock. How? I will place you in the hardness of the Law, appointing you to be over it as master of the old times, which will be pierced by My Son, when I send Him into the world at the right time and He expounds it farther than you have in His mystical words. So His strength will protect you, for He will bring words more acute than yours; and He will open the Law's commands that are now closed until He returns to Me. What does this mean?

He, taking on a body from the Virgin, will in that body give words of salvation to the world until in it He passes through death. Then I will take away My hand, when I lift Him up to Me above the stars and lay bare all His mysteries through the Holy Spirit; and thus you will see His Incarnation as a person is seen from the back and not the front, seeing Him when incarnate but not grasping His Divinity. For your children will see him when he returns to Me, more than they understood Him when He lived visibly among them.

6 The Baptized Are Adorned When They Are Anointed by the Bishop

And you see those children who, as mentioned before, had passed through the womb of that image, shining with great brightness. These are they who in the innocence of a clean and pure heart have gained a mother, the Church, in the font of regeneration, as was shown to you before, and are children of light, for their sins are washed away. *Some of them are adorned with gold color from their foreheads to their feet;* for from their beginning in good works to their end in sanctity, they are adorned with the shining gifts of the Holy Spirit by their anointing with chrism in the true faith at the hand of the bishop. How? Just as gold is adorned by having precious stones set into it, so baptism is adorned with the chrism given to those baptized in faith by the hand of the bishop, as it is written. . . .

14 Words of Ezekiel

"The King shall mourn, and the prince shall be clothed with sorrow, and the hands of the people of the land shall be troubled. I will do to them according to their way, and I will judge them according to their judgments, and they shall know that I am the Lord" [Ezekiel 7:27]. What does this mean? The soul in which Reason is king, feeling the pleasure of sin at hand, assents to it mournfully because it knows the evil of it. How? Because its reason, wisdom and knowledge are inspired by God; and thus, though the body consents, it finds the evil shameful, knowing that it is not good.

Therefore, when it is polluted with many crimes by the acts of the flesh, it heaves deep sighs and yearns for God. And when in the breath of pride the sinful deed is done, the body is clothed with confusion like an unworthy prince, having exercised its sovereignty in uncleanness; for as a person grieves when clothed in vile garments, so also he is sad when a shameful reputation originates, to his confusion, in himself. Therefore the bad deeds of those prostrate in their evils on the ground will be confounded by heavenly commands, for such do not have the garments of salvation, which is beatitude with God; and

evil confusion will possess those who lack this happiness. And so I will deal with them in the road of iniquity in which they stand, honoring the path of sin and putting no justice into their hearts though warned by the Holy Spirit; I will grant them no mercy, because they do not know the good or fear Me, but disdain Me, the Creator of all, with raging wickedness, and do whatever they like.

Therefore I will judge them according to their own judgments, which are the works they desire and do; I will give them no rewards of happiness, but set the punishment of damnation in their way, since they show Me no honor; and they shall know that no one can free them from it except Me, the Lord of all.

But let the one who sees with watchful eyes and 15 hears with attentive ears welcome with a kiss My mystical words, which proceed from Me Who am life.

Questions for Critical Thinking

1. What does the "voice from heaven" tell Hildegard to do, and how does she go about obeying its commands?

2. How do baptism and confirmation aid Christians? What is ultimately necessary, beyond the sacraments, for salvation? Do you think Hildegard of Bingen deserves the attention and admiration now accorded her?

11

THE LATE MIDDLE AGES
Crisis and Recovery
1300–1500

PETRARCH
Selections from *Canzoniere* and "Letter to Posterity"

Francesco Petrarch (in Italian, "Petrarca") (1304–1374) is another of the West's great bridge figures (see St. Augustine's *Confessions* in Chapter 7), whose careers straddle historical periods with opposing cultural tendencies. He lived in the late Middle Ages, a period dominated by Gothic forms and ideals; yet, he was a founder of the Renaissance, for he was the first author to make his writing task the recovery and updating of the classical literary tradition. He is particularly noted for his reintroduction of lost or neglected texts from antiquity into European culture. Inspired by classicism, he placed the natural before the supernatural, thus reversing the judgment of his age; and he was the first European writer to defend secular culture and earthly fame. Despite his modern outlook, he saw some merit in the medieval view, as in the dialogue *Secretum* (or *My Secret*), in which he gives St. Augustine some of the best lines.

Despite being born in Italy and residing there, notably in Rome and Florence, for much of his life, Petrarch was a true European. Widely traveled, in part because of his studies and in part because his patrons required that he act as a diplomat, he spent months in France, Flanders, and the Rhineland. During these travels, he searched for and found old manuscripts (for example, some letters of Cicero), revised earlier works, and began new tasks. His most famous visit was to Avignon, a papal territory, where the worldliness of the papal court led him to coin the famous phrase "the Babylonian Captivity of the Papacy" to denote the seventy-year period when the popes lived in Avignon instead of Rome. His works, regardless of where written, reflect his impressions of daily life and his drive for self-understanding.

Reading the Selections

Besides being devoted to classicism and Latin literature, Petrarch was equally famed as a master of Italian poetry, as shown in *Canzoniere* (*Songbook* or *Rhymes*), his masterpiece in his native tongue. Drawing on classical models and the ethos of the troubadour poets of southern France, these poems were inspired by the living woman he called Laura, whom he first saw in Avignon in 1327. Though she was married to someone else and completely uninterested in the poet's attentions, Laura personified beauty and truth for Petrarch. Nevertheless, in private life he wooed other women and fathered two children. When Laura was carried off by the Black Death in 1348, Petrarch turned to God, struggling with his sense of sin and the fate of his soul.

Three of the 366 poems in the *Canzoniere* are presented here. All were composed in the form of sonnets, the fourteen-line verse form that Petrarch inherited from Italian predecessors and brought to perfection. The Petrarchan sonnet is divided into two parts: the first eight lines usually rhyme *abbaabba;* the following six lines usually rhyme *cdecde.* This verse form was imported into England in the sixteenth century, where it enjoyed great vogue.

The three poems in the category of *in vita* ("on life") recall Petrarch's introduction to Laura, who ignored him. They dwell on the pain of unrequited love.

Petrarch organized and edited most of the 550 letters he wrote during his lifetime. Some scholars believe that his letters provide the most accurate portrait of the man, as they reveal his personality and private thoughts and are less concerned with contemporary political and religious issues, which dominated much of his writing. His "Letter to Posterity" is usually considered to be quite different from his other letters. He probably meant it to be his autobiography, but it records his life only up to 1351, twenty-three years before his death in 1374. During that period Petrarch wrote many works, traveled on several diplomatic missions, and lived in Milan and Prague before settling in Padua and then Arquà, a small village outside Padua, where he spent his last years.

In this edited version of his Letter, Petrarch deprecates himself while, at the same time, implying that he has enjoyed his fame and reputation. His heart belonged to literature, and he dedicated the rest of his life to writing poems, essays, epics, histories, and his letters. Petrarch cherished friendships, one of the genuine pleasures of life, over material comforts; and he preferred small towns to large cities, which made Vaucluse, and later Arquà, so attractive to him.

3

It was the day the sun's ray had turned pale
with pity for the suffering of his Maker
when I was caught, and I put up no fight,
my lady, for your lovely eyes had bound me.

It seemed no time to be on guard against
Love's blows; therefore, I went my way
secure and fearless—so, all my misfortunes
began in midst of universal woe.

Love found me all disarmed and found the way
was clear to reach my heart down through the eyes
which have become the halls and doors of tears.

It seems to me it did him little honour
to wound me with his arrow in my state
and to you, armed, not show his bow at all.

132

If it's not love, then what is it I feel?
But if it's love, by God, what is this thing?
If good, why then the bitter mortal sting?
If bad, then why is every torment sweet?

If I burn willingly, why weep and grieve?
And if against my will, what good lamenting?
O living death, O pleasurable harm,
how can you rule me if I not consent?

And if I do consent, it's wrong to grieve.
Caught in contrasting winds in a frail boat
on the high seas I am without a helm,

so light of wisdom, so laden of error,
that I myself do not know what I want,
and shiver in midsummer, burn in winter.

∞

134

I find no peace, and I am not at war,
I fear and hope, and burn and I am ice;
I fly above the heavens, and lie on earth,
and I grasp nothing and embrace the world.

One keeps me jailed who neither locks nor opens,
nor keeps me for her own nor frees the noose;
Love does not kill, nor does he loose my chains;
he wants me lifeless but won't loosen me.

I see with no eyes, shout without a tongue;
I yearn to perish, and I beg for help;
I hate myself and love somebody else.

I thrive on pain and laugh with all my tears;
I dislike death as much as I do life:
because of you, lady, I am this way.

∞

"Letter to Posterity"

To Posterity, an Account of His Background, Conduct, and the Development of His Character and Studies.

Francis Petrarch to posterity, greetings. Perhaps you will have heard something about me, although this too is doubtful, whether a petty, obscure name would reach far into either space or time. And perhaps you will wish to know what sort of man I was, or what were the results of my labors, especially of those whose fame has reached you or whose bare titles you have heard. On the first point men's opinions will vary. For almost everyone speaks as his pleasure, not the truth, impels, and there are no standards for either praise or blame. But I was one of your troop, a poor mortal man, neither of too great nor of base origin, but of an ancient family, as Augustus Caesar[1] says of himself; by nature, anyhow, I was of neither foul nor shameless temperament, had the habits caught from others not harmed it. Adolescence misled me, youth swept me away, but old age set me right, and taught me by experience that truth I had read long before: that adolescence and pleasure are vain; or rather, it was the Creator of all ages and times who set me right. He sometimes allows wretched mortals, puffed up with nothing, to go astray so that, being aware of their sins, however late, they may know themselves. In my youth my body was not very strong, but quite supple. I do not boast of being especially handsome, but enough to be pleasing in my greener years—with a clear complexion, between light and dark, lively eyes, and for a long time very keen vision, which unexpectedly abandoned me after the sixtieth year, so that, to my disgust I had to resort to glasses. Old age invaded my body, which had been very

healthy in every age, and surrounded it with the usual array of ills.

I was born in exile in Arezzo in the year 1304 of this last age, which began with Christ, at dawn on a Monday, July [20], of honorable parents, Florentine in origin, of modest fortune, and, to tell the truth, verging on poverty, but driven from their homeland. I am a confirmed despiser of riches, not because I would not wish for them, but because I hated toil and worry, the inseparable companions of wealth—not that access to a fancy dinner requires such worry! I have led a happier life with plain living and ordinary fare than all the followers of Apicius,[2] with their elaborate feasts. What are called banquets, since they are revels, injurious to decency and good manners I have always disliked. I considered it irksome and useless to invite others for that purpose, and no less so to be invited by others. But dining with friends is so delightful that I have thought nothing more welcome than their unexpected arrival, nor have I ever willingly taken a meal without a companion. Nothing has displeased me more than pomp, not only because it is evil and contrary to humility, but because it is troublesome and distracting. I struggled in my adolescence with the most intense but constant and honorable love, and would have struggled even longer, had not a premature but expedient death extinguished the flame that was already cooling. I wish, of course, I could say I was utterly free of lust, but, if I did, I would be lying. This I shall say with confidence, that, though carried away by the fervor of that age and of my temperament, I have always cursed such vileness in my heart. But as soon as I was approaching my fortieth year,

---

[1] **Augustus Caesar** First Roman emperor (31 BCE–14 CE). Julius Caesar was his great-uncle and adopted him as his son.

[2] **Apicius** Marcus Gavius Apicius, first-century CE Roman who supposedly spent much of his money to satisfy his desire for rare foods and delicacies.

while I still had plenty of ardor and strength, I so completely threw off not only that obscene act, but the very recollection of it, that it seemed I had never looked at a woman. I count this among my greatest blessings, thanks be to God who freed me, while still sound and vigorous, from so vile and hateful a slavery.

But I turn to other matters. I have perceived pride in others, not in myself; and unimportant though I have been, in my own judgment I have always been even less important. My anger has very often hurt me, but never others. I have been a most eager and faithful devotee of honorable friendships. Fearlessly, because I know I speak the truth, I boast of being hot-tempered, but very forgetful of wrongs and ever mindful of kindnesses. I was fortunate to the point of envy in my associations with princes and kings, and in my friendships with nobles. But this is the penalty for growing old: to weep ever so often over the deaths of your dear ones. The greatest rulers of this age have loved and courted me; but I know not why—let them explain it. And I stayed with some of them in a way that they were, so to speak, my guests, so that I derived many advantages and no annoyances from their eminence. I fled, however, from many of those whom I loved a great deal; such love for freedom was implanted in me that I studiously avoided anyone whose very name seemed incompatible with it.

I had a well-balanced rather than a keen intellect, fit for all kinds of good and wholesome study, but especially inclined to moral philosophy and poetry. Yet in the course of time I abandoned the latter, when I found delight in sacred letters, in which I felt the hidden sweetness I once despised; for I limit poetry to embellishment only. I have dwelt single-mindedly on learning about antiquity, among other things because this age has always displeased me, so that, unless love for my dear ones pulled me the other way, I always wished to have been born in any other age whatever, and to forget this one, seeming always to graft myself in my mind onto other ages. I have therefore been charmed by the historians, though I was no less offended by their disagreements; and, when in doubt, I followed the version toward which either the verisimilitude of the content or the authority of the writers pulled me. My style, as some have said, was clear and powerful, but it seemed to me weak and obscure. In ordinary conversation with friends or relatives I have no concern for eloquence, and I marvel that Augustus Caesar did take such pains. But when the subject itself or the place or the listener seemed to demand otherwise, I have exerted myself a little, how successfully I do not know; let them judge in whose presence I spoke. As long as I lived well, I would care little how I had spoken; to seek fame merely from verbal elegance is but empty glory.

Either luck or my will has up to now divided my time in this fashion. The first year of my life I spent partially in Arezzo, where nature had brought me to light: the six following years in my father's country home in Incisa, fourteen miles above Florence, after my mother had been recalled from exile; my eighth year in Pisa, the ninth and thereafter in Transalpine Gaul, on the left bank of the

Rhone in the city called Avignon, where the Roman Pontiff holds, and has long held, the Church of Christ in shameful exile, although a few years ago Urban V[3] seemed to have led her back to her own See. But it came to nothing, as is obvious; and what I bear all the harder, it was even while he was alive, as if he repented of his good work. Had he lived a little longer, he would doubtless have learned how I felt about his retreat. My pen was already in hand, but that unhappy man abruptly deserted that glorious undertaking along with his life. How happily he could have died before the altar of Peter and in his own home! For had his successors remained in their See, he would have been the author of that fine achievement; or had they left, his virtue would have been all the nobler, the more obvious their fault. But this complaint is too long and not to the point.

There, then, on the bank of that very windy river, I spent my boyhood under my parents, and then my whole adolescence under my follies, but not without long absences. During this time I spent four whole years in the small city of Carpentras, a little to the east of Avignon; and in these two cities I learned as much of grammar, logic, and rhetoric as my age could, or rather, as is usually learned in school; and you, dear reader, know how little that is. Then I set out for Montpellier for the study of law, staying another four years there; then to Bologna where I spent three years and heard lectures on the whole body of civil law, and would have been a young man with a great future, as many thought, had I concentrated on the project. But I abandoned that subject altogether as soon as my parents abandoned me [because of their death]. Not that I did not like the dignity of the law, which is doubtless great and replete with Roman antiquity which delights me, but that practicing it is perverted by men's wickedness. It therefore irked me to master something I did not want to use dishonestly, and could scarcely use honestly; and had I wanted to, my good intentions would have been ascribed to inexperience.

So at the age of twenty-two I returned home. I call home that place of exile, Avignon, where I had been since my later childhood, for habit is like second nature. I already had begun to be known there, and my friendship sought by great men. Just why, I confess I do not now know, and marvel at it, though I did not marvel then, being of an age when I thought myself most worthy of every honor. I was sought primarily by the distinguished and generous Colonna family, which then frequented the Roman Curia, or rather, gave it luster. They summoned me and held me in great esteem which, however it may be now, I certainly did not deserve then; and that illustrious and incomparable man, Giacomo Colonna, then Bishop of Lombez, whose peer I know not whether I have ever seen or shall see, who took me to Gascony, where I spent a nearly heavenly summer in the foothills of the Pyrenees;

---

[3] **Urban V** Pope (1378–1389) who tried to return the papacy to Rome between 1367 and 1370. He failed, and the church remained in Avignon until 1377. Petrarch was a bitter critic of the Avignon exile.

my master and his retinue were so charming that I always sigh as I remember that time. Returning from there, for many years I was under his brother, Giovanni Cardinal Colonna, not as under a master but under a father, or rather, not even that, but with a most loving brother or with myself in my own home.

At that time a youthful craving drove me to travel through France and Germany; and although I invented other reasons to have my elders approve my journey, the real reason was my ardor and curiosity to see many things. On that journey I saw Paris for the first time and was delighted to inquire what was true and what was mythical in the stories told about that city. On my return, I went to Rome, which I had ardently longed to see since childhood. There I so waited upon Stefano Colonna, the noble head of the family, a man equal to any of the ancients, and I was so well received that you would say there was no distinction between me and any of his sons. The love and affection of that excellent man for me always remained constant until the last day of his life; and even now it lives in me, and will never end, unless I come to an end first.

When I again returned from there, since I cannot bear the nausea and hate for all cities implanted in my heart by nature, and above all for that most disgusting city [Avignon]. I sought some refuge as though it were a haven; and I discovered a tiny valley, secluded and delightful, called Vaucluse, about fifteen miles from Avignon, where the king of all springs, the Sorgue, rises. Taken by the charm of the place, I moved my books and myself there. It will be a long story if I go on to describe what I did there over many, many years. To be brief, almost all of the works I have let fall from my pen were either completed or begun or conceived there. . . .

Later on, the blazon of fame won me the good will 10 of a fine man; I do not know whether among the lords of his time there has been anyone like him, or rather I know there has been none—I mean Giacomo da Carrara the Younger, through whose messengers and letters I was wearied with such earnest entreaties beyond the Alps when I was there, and wherever I was throughout Italy for many years. I was so urged into friendship with him that, though I hoped for nothing from the well-to-do, I decided at last to go to him and see what this insistence on the part of a great man, unknown to me, meant. Thus, I came, though late, to Padua, where I was received by that man of illustrious memory, not just kindly, but as the blessed souls are greeted in heaven, with such joy and such inestimable love and fondness, that, since I cannot hope to equal it with words, it is better to cover it with silence. Among many things, knowing that I had led a clerical life since childhood, he made me a canon of Padua in order to bind me more tightly not only to himself but to his city. In short, had his life been longer, it would have been the end of all my wandering and journeys. But alas, among mortals nothing is enduring; and if anything sweet appears, it soon ends in bitterness. In not quite two years, God, who had sent him to me, to his fatherland, and to the world, took him away; neither I nor his fatherland nor the world—I am not blinded by love—was worthy of him. And although he was succeeded by his son, a most prudent and eminent man who, following in his father's footsteps, always loved and honored me, still, after the loss of the one with whom I had been better matched, especially in age. I again returned to France, incapable of staying still, and not so much with a yearning to see again what I had seen a thousand times, as with an effort to cope with stiffness—as sick people do—by a shift of position.

Questions for Critical Thinking

1. Define "unrequited love" and give examples of how Petrarch expresses his pain of unrequited love. How do persons express themselves of unrequited love in the modern world?

2. Discuss the phases of Petrarch's life, and note how these phases tell us about his personality and ambitions.

GIOVANNI BOCCACCIO
Selections from *The Decameron*

The Decameron is one of the most important works of European literature. It was written by Giovanni Boccaccio (1313–1375), the contemporary of his fellow humanist and friend, Petrarch (see *Canzoniere* and "Letter to Posterity"), in turbulent fourteenth-century Italy. Like Petrarch, he was devoted to classicism, especially to reading and translating the great works of Latin literature. Boccaccio, too, was attracted to the world's delights, recognizing that life was to be experienced and, for the most part, enjoyed. He also suffered the pangs of guilt for his sins and, in his old age, expressed regrets about his earlier life.

The illegitimate son of a successful Florentine financier, Boccaccio prepared for a banking career and studied law before turning to a life of letters. Awakened to the possibility of a literary career while attached to the court of the well-educated king of Naples, Robert the Wise (r. 1309–1343), he became enamored of a court lady whom he christened Fiammetta (Little Flame) and wrote sonnets to her in the style of Petrarch. Removed to Florence, where his literary fame and fortune soared, he lived an active life engaged in diplomatic missions that took him up and down the Italian peninsula. In Florence, he survived the devastation of the Black Death, which, by one estimate, killed nearly half the Florentine population in 1348.

Boccaccio's classical scholarship, medieval romances in both poetry and prose, and Italian love lyrics would have ensured him an honored place in Western letters; however, *The Decameron* has made him one of the literary immortals. Composed between 1349 and 1353, *The Decameron* presents this chaotic age in microcosm, showing the good and evil therein. It contains a rich collection of folktales, parables, romances, and stories from Italian, French, Near Eastern, classical, and biblical sources. The work's realism, secular spirit, and frank probing of the human heart had an immediate impact on European fiction, leading ultimately to the modern novel. In later years, Boccaccio expressed regret about his most famous work, deploring its lighthearted style.

Reading the Selections

The Decameron (from the Greek for "ten") is a tale within a tale, an old genre most famously realized in *The Arabian Nights* (see Chapter 9). In Boccaccio's work, this structure unfolds as ten young Florentines—seven ladies and three gentlemen—escape the plague that is ravaging their city and take refuge in a country palace. There, they pass the time, each telling a story a day for ten days, hence one hundred tales total.

The first selection, taken from the author's introduction to *The Decameron*, opens with Boccaccio addressing female readers, the audience for vernacular literature in the Middle Ages because male readers supposedly were interested only in works in Latin. He advises these "fairest ladies" not to give up too soon on his book, though he knows that the details of the plague, which of necessity he must include in his story, may be unappetizing to them. After this warning, he describes the plague, showing how it disrupted Florentine life at every level—one of the most valuable aspects of this work for modern scholars.

The second selection (from First Day, Third Story) contains the philosophical tale known as "the legend of the three rings." In it, Melchisedech, a Jew, escapes a trap set by Saladin, a Muslim warrior whose deeds made him a hero to medieval Europeans even though his reputation came from fighting Christians during the Crusades. Saladin, needing money, invites the rich Melchisedech to dinner and asks which of the three faiths—Christianity, Judaism, or Islam—is best. Aware that this is a trick question, Melchisedech replies with an allegorical fable that artfully avoids calling one religion the best. Saladin, recognizing Melchisedech's wisdom, adopts him as a close friend. Such a tale suggests that Boccaccio was freer of religious bigotry than most Europeans of the time.

∞

Introduction

. . .

Whenever, fairest ladies, I pause to consider how com- 1 passionate you all are by nature, I invariably become aware that the present work will seem to you to possess an irksome and ponderous opening. For it carries at its head the painful memory of the deadly havoc wrought by the recent plague, which brought so much heartache and misery to those who witnessed, or had experience of it. But I do not want you to be deterred, for this reason, from reading any further, on the assumption that you are to be subjected, as you read, to an endless torrent of tears and sobbing. You will be affected no differently by this grim beginning than walkers confronted by a steep and rugged hill, beyond which there lies a beautiful and delectable plain. The degree of pleasure they derive from the latter will correspond directly to the difficulty of the climb and the descent. And just as the end of mirth is heaviness, so sorrows are dispersed by the advent of joy.

This brief unpleasantness (I call it brief, inasmuch as it is contained within few words) is quickly followed by the sweetness and the pleasure which I have already promised you, and which, unless you were told in advance, you would not perhaps be expecting to find after such a beginning as this. Believe me, if I could decently have taken you whither I desire by some other route, rather than along a path so difficult as this, I would gladly have done so. But since it is impossible without this memoir to show the origin of the events you will read about later, I really have no alternative but to address myself to its composition.

I say, then, that the sum of thirteen hundred and forty-eight years had elapsed since the fruitful Incarnation of the Son of God, when the noble city of Florence, which for its great beauty excels all others in Italy, was visited by the deadly pestilence. Some say that it descended upon the human race through the influence of the heavenly bodies, others that it was a punishment signifying God's righteous anger at our iniquitous way of life. But whatever its cause, it had originated some years earlier in the East, where it had claimed countless lives before it unhappily spread westward, growing in strength as it swept relentlessly on from one place to the next.

In the face of its onrush, all the wisdom and ingenuity of man were unavailing. Large quantities of refuse were cleared out of the city by officials specially appointed for the purpose, all sick persons were forbidden entry, and numerous instructions were issued for safeguarding the people's health, but all to no avail. Nor were the countless petitions humbly directed to God by the pious, whether by means of formal processions or in any other guise, any less ineffectual. For in the early spring of the year we have mentioned, the plague began, in a terrifying and extraordinary manner, to make its disastrous effects apparent. It did not take the form it had assumed in the East, where if anyone bled from the nose it was an obvious portent of certain death. On the contrary, its earliest symptom, in men and women alike, was the appearance of certain swellings in the groin or the armpit, some of which were egg-shaped whilst others were roughly the size of the common apple. Sometimes the swellings were large, sometimes not so large, and they were referred to by the populace as *gavòccioli*. From the two areas already mentioned, this deadly *gavòcciolo* would begin to spread, and within a short time it would appear at random all over the body. Later on, the symptoms of the disease changed, and many people began to find dark blotches and bruises on their arms, thighs, and other parts of the body, sometimes large and few in number, at other times tiny and closely spaced. These, to anyone unfortunate enough to contract them, were just as infallible a sign that he would die as the *gavòcciolo* had been earlier, and as indeed it still was.

Against these maladies, it seemed that all the advice 5 of physicians and all the power of medicine were profitless and unavailing. Perhaps the nature of the illness was such that it allowed no remedy: or perhaps those people who were treating the illness (whose numbers had increased enormously because the ranks of the qualified were invaded by people, both men and women, who had never received any training in medicine), being ignorant of its causes, were not prescribing the appropriate cure. At all events, few of those who caught it ever recovered, and in most cases death occurred within three days from the appearance of the symptoms we have described, some people dying more rapidly than others, the majority without any fever or other complications.

But what made this pestilence even more severe was that whenever those suffering from it mixed with people who were still unaffected, it would rush upon these with the speed of a fire racing through dry or oily substances that happened to be placed within its reach. Nor was this the full extent of its evil, for not only did it infect healthy persons who conversed or had any dealings with the sick, making them ill or visiting an equally horrible death upon them, but it also seemed to transfer the sickness to anyone touching the clothes or other objects which had been handled or used by its victims.

It is a remarkable story that I have to relate. And were it not for the fact that I am one of many people who saw it with their own eyes, I would scarcely dare to believe it, let alone commit it to paper, even though I had heard it from a person whose word I could trust. The plague I have been describing was of so contagious a nature that very often it visibly did more than simply pass from one person to another. In other words, whenever an animal other than a human being touched anything belonging to a person who had been stricken or exterminated by the disease, it not only caught the sickness, but died from it almost at once. To all of this, as I have just said, my own eyes bore witness on more than one occasion. One day, for instance, the rags of a pauper who had died from the disease were thrown into the street, where they attracted the attention of two pigs. In their wonted fashion, the pigs first of all gave the rags a thorough mauling with their snouts after which they took them between their teeth and shook them against their cheeks. And within a short time they began to writhe as though they had been poisoned, then they both dropped dead to the ground, spreadeagled upon the rags that had brought about their undoing.

These things, and many others of a similar or even worse nature, caused various fears and fantasies to take root in the minds of those who were still alive and well. And almost without exception, they took a single and very inhuman precaution, namely to avoid or run away from the sick and their belongings, by which means they all thought that their own health would be preserved.

Some people were of the opinion that a sober and abstemious mode of living considerably reduced the risk of infection. They therefore formed themselves into groups and lived in isolation from everyone else. Having withdrawn to a comfortable abode where there were no sick persons, they locked themselves in and settled down to a peaceable existence, consuming modest quantities of delicate foods and precious wines and avoiding all excesses. They refrained from speaking to outsiders, refused to receive news of the dead or the sick, and entertained themselves with music and whatever other amusements they were able to devise.

Others took the opposite view, and maintained that 10 an infallible way of warding off this appalling evil was to drink heavily, enjoy life to the full, go round singing and merrymaking, gratify all of one's cravings whenever the opportunity offered, and shrug the whole thing off as one enormous joke. Moreover, they practised what they preached to the best of their ability, for they would visit one tavern after another, drinking all day and night to immoderate excess; or alternatively (and this was their more frequent custom), they would do their drinking in various private houses, but only in the ones where the conversation was restricted to subjects that were pleasant or entertaining. Such places were easy to find, for people behaved as though their days were numbered, and treated their belongings and their own persons with equal abandon. Hence most houses had become common property, and any passing stranger could make himself at home as naturally as though he were the rightful owner. But for all their riotous manner of living, these people always took good care to avoid any contact with the sick.

In the face of so much affliction and misery, all respect for the laws of God and man had virtually broken down and been extinguished in our city. For like everybody else, those ministers and executors of the laws who were not either dead or ill were left with so few subordinates that they were unable to discharge any of their duties. Hence everyone was free to behave as he pleased.

There were many other people who steered a middle course between the two already mentioned, neither restricting their diet to the same degree as the first group, nor indulging so freely as the second in drinking and other forms of wantonness, but simply doing no more than satisfy their appetite. Instead of incarcerating themselves,

these people moved about freely, holding in their hands a posy of flowers, or fragrant herbs, or one of a wide range of spices, which they applied at frequent intervals to their nostrils, thinking it an excellent idea to fortify the brain with smells of that particular sort; for the stench of dead bodies, sickness, and medicines seemed to fill and pollute the whole of the atmosphere.

Some people, pursuing what was possibly the safer alternative, callously maintained that there was no better or more efficacious remedy against a plague than to run away from it. Swayed by this argument, and sparing no thought for anyone but themselves, large numbers of men and women abandoned their city, their homes, their relatives, their estates and their belongings, and headed for the countryside, either in Florentine territory or, better still, abroad. It was as though they imagined that the wrath of God would not unleash this plague against men for their iniquities irrespective of where they happened to be, but would only be aroused against those who found themselves within the city walls; or possibly they assumed that the whole of the population would be exterminated and that the city's last hour had come.

Of the people who held these various opinions, not all of them died. Nor, however, did they all survive. On the contrary, many of each different persuasion fell ill here, there, and everywhere, and having themselves, when they were fit and well, set an example to those who were as yet unaffected, they languished away with virtually no one to nurse them. It was not merely a question of one citizen avoiding another, and of people almost invariably neglecting their neighbours and rarely or never visiting their relatives, addressing them only from a distance; this scourge had implanted so great a terror in the hearts of men and women that brothers abandoned brothers, uncles their nephews, sisters their brothers, and in many cases wives deserted their husbands. But even worse, and almost incredible, was the fact that fathers and mothers refused to nurse and assist their own children, as though they did not belong to them.

Hence the countless numbers of people who fell ill, 15 both male and female, were entirely dependent upon either the charity of friends (who were few and far between) or the greed of servants, who remained in short supply despite the attraction of high wages out of all proportion to the services they performed. Furthermore, these latter were men and women of coarse intellect and the majority were unused to such duties, and they did little more than hand things to the invalid when asked to do so and watch over him when he was dying. And in performing this kind of service, they frequently lost their lives as well as their earnings.

As a result of this wholesale desertion of the sick by neighbours, relatives and friends, and in view of the scarcity of servants, there grew up a practice almost never previously heard of, whereby when a woman fell ill, no matter how gracious or beautiful or gently bred she might be, she raised no objection to being attended by a male servant, whether he was young or not. Nor did she have any scruples about showing him every part of her body as freely as she would have displayed it to a woman, provided that the nature of her infirmity required her to do so; and this explains why those women who recovered were possibly less chaste in the period that followed.

Moreover a great many people died who would perhaps have survived had they received some assistance. And hence, what with the lack of appropriate means for tending the sick, and the virulence of the plague, the number of deaths reported in the city whether by day or night was so enormous that it astonished all who heard tell of it, to say nothing of the people who actually witnessed the carnage. And it was perhaps inevitable that among the citizens who survived there arose certain customs that were quite contrary to established tradition.

It had once been customary, as it is again nowadays, for the women relatives and neighbours of a dead man to assemble in his house in order to mourn in the company of the women who had been closest to him; moreover his kinfolk would forgather in front of his house along with his neighbours and various other citizens, and there would be a contingent of priests, whose numbers varied according to the quality of the deceased; his body would be taken thence to the church in which he had wanted to be buried, being borne on the shoulders of his peers amidst the funeral pomp of candles and dirges. But as the ferocity of the plague began to mount, this practice all but disappeared entirely and was replaced by different customs. For not only did people die without having many women about them, but a great number departed this life without anyone at all to witness their going. Few indeed were those to whom the lamentations and bitter tears of their relatives were accorded; on the contrary, more often than not bereavement was the signal for laughter and witticisms and general jollification—the art of which the women, having for the most part suppressed their feminine concern for the salvation of the souls of the dead, had learned to perfection. Moreover it was rare for the bodies of the dead to be accompanied by more than ten or twelve neighbours to the church, nor were they borne on the shoulders of worthy and honest citizens, but by a kind of grave digging fraternity, newly come into being and drawn from the lower orders of society. These people assumed the title of sexton, and demanded a fat fee for their services, which consisted in taking up the coffin and hauling it swiftly away, not to the church specified by the dead man in his will, but usually to the nearest at hand. They would be preceded by a group of four or six clerics, who between them carried one or two candles at most, and sometimes none at all. Nor did the priests go to the trouble of pronouncing solemn and lengthy funeral rites, but, with the aid of these so-called sextons, they hastily lowered the body into the nearest empty grave they could find.

As for the common people and a large proportion of the bourgeoisie, they presented a much more pathetic spectacle, for the majority of them were constrained, either by their poverty or the hope of survival, to remain in their houses. Being confined to their own parts of the city, they fell ill daily in their thousands, and since they had no one to assist them or attend to their needs, they inevitably perished almost without exception. Many dropped dead in the open streets, both by day and by night, whilst a great many others, though dying in their own houses, drew their neighbours' attention to the fact more by the smell of their rotting corpses than by any other means. And what with these, and the others who were dying all over the city, bodies were here, there and everywhere.

Whenever people died, their neighbours nearly always followed a single, set routine, prompted as much by their fear of being contaminated by the decaying corpse as by any charitable feelings they may have entertained towards the deceased. Either on their own, or with the assistance of bearers whenever these were to be had, they extracted the bodies of the dead from their houses and left them lying outside their front doors, where anyone going about the streets, especially in the early morning, could have observed countless numbers of them. Funeral biers would then be sent for, upon which the dead were taken away, though there were some who, for lack of biers, were carried off on plain boards. It was by no means rare for more than one of these biers to be seen with two or three bodies upon it at a time; on the contrary, many were seen to contain a husband and wife, two or three brothers and sisters, a father and son, or some other pair of close relatives. And times without number it happened that two priests would be on their way to bury someone, holding a cross before them, only to find that bearers carrying three or four additional biers would fall in behind them; so that whereas the priests had thought they had only one burial to attend to, they in fact had six or seven, and sometimes more. Even in these circumstances, however, there were no tears or candles or mourners to honour the dead; in fact, no more respect was accorded to dead people than would nowadays be shown towards dead goats. For it was quite apparent that the one thing which, in normal times, no wise man had ever learned to accept with patient resignation (even though it struck so seldom and unobtrusively), had now been brought home to the feeble-minded as well, but the scale of the calamity caused them to regard it with indifference.

Such was the multitude of corpses (of which further consignments were arriving every day and almost by the hour at each of the churches), that there was not sufficient consecrated ground for them to be buried in, especially if each was to have its own plot in accordance with long-established custom. So when all the graves were full, huge trenches were excavated in the churchyards, into which new arrivals were placed in their hundreds, stowed tier upon tier like ships' cargo, each layer of corpses being covered over with a thin layer of soil till the trench was filled to the top.

But rather than describe in elaborate detail the calamities . . . experienced in the city at that time, I must mention that, whilst an ill wind was blowing through Florence itself, the surrounding region was no less badly affected. In the fortified towns, conditions were similar to those in the city itself on a minor scale; but in the scattered hamlets and the countryside proper, the poor unfortunate peasants and their families had no physicians or servants whatever to assist them, and collapsed by the wayside, in their fields, and in their cottages at all hours of the day and night, dying more like animals than human beings. Like the townspeople, they too grew apathetic in their ways, disregarded their affairs, and neglected their possessions. Moreover they all behaved as though each day was to be their last, and far from making provision for the future by tilling their lands, tending their flocks, and adding to their previous labors, they tried in every way they could think of to squander the assets already in their possession. Thus it came about that oxen, asses, sheep, goats, pigs, chickens, and even dogs (for all their deep fidelity to man) were driven away and allowed to roam freely through the fields, where the crops lay abandoned and had not even been reaped, let alone gathered in. And after a whole day's feasting, many of these animals, as though possessing the power of reason, would return glutted in the evening to their own quarters, without any shepherd to guide them.

But let us leave the countryside and return to the city. What more remains to be said, except that the cruelty of heaven (and possibly, in some measure, also that of man) was so immense and so devastating that between March and July of the year in question, what with the fury of the pestilence and the fact that so many of the sick were inadequately cared for or abandoned in their hour of need because the healthy were too terrified to approach them, it is reliably thought that over a hundred thousand human lives were extinguished within the walls of the city of Florence? Yet before this lethal catastrophe fell upon the city, it is doubtful whether anyone would have guessed it contained so many inhabitants.

Ah, how great a number of splendid palaces, fine houses, and noble dwellings, once filled with retainers, with lords and with ladies, were bereft of all who had lived there, down to the tiniest child! How numerous were the famous families, the vast estates, the notable fortunes, that were seen to be left without a rightful successor! How many gallant gentlemen, fair ladies, and sprightly youths, who would have been judged hale and hearty by Galen, Hippocrates and Aesculapius[4] (to say nothing of others), having breakfasted in the morning with their kinsfolk, acquaintances and friends, supped that same evening with their ancestors in the next world! . . .

---

[4] **Galen, Hippocrates and Aesculapius** Galen and Hippocrates were famous Greek physicians well known in the Middle Ages. Aesculapius was the Greek god of healing, who was also worshiped by the Romans.

∞

First Day, Third Story

Melchisedech, a Jew, by means of a short story about three rings, escapes from a trap set for him by Saladin.

Neifile's tale was praised by all, and when she had finished talking, at the queen's command, Filament began to speak in this fashion.

The tale that Neifile told brings back to my memory a dangerous incident that once happened to a Jew; and since God and the truth of our faith have already been well dealt with by us, we should not be forbidden to descend to the acts of men from now on. Now, I shall tell you this story and when you have heard it, perhaps you will become more cautious when you reply to questions put to you.

You should know, my dear companions, that just as stupidity can often remove one from a state of happiness and place him in the greatest misery, so, too, intelligence can rescue the wise man from the gravest of dangers and restore him to his secure state. The fact that stupidity leads one from a state of happiness to one of misery is shown by many examples which, at present, I do not intend to relate, since thousands of clear illustrations of this appear every day; but, as I promised, I shall demonstrate briefly in a little story how intelligence may be the cause of some consolation.

Saladin, whose worth was such that from humble beginnings he became Sultan of Babylon and won many victories over Christian and Saracen kings, discovered one day that he had consumed, in his various wars and his displays of grandiose magnificence, all his treasury, while the occasion arose in which he needed a large amount of money. Not being able to envision a means of obtaining what he needed in a short time, he happened to recall a rich Jew, whose name was Melchisedech, who loaned money at usurious rates in Alexandria, and he thought that this man might be able to assist him, if only he would agree to. But this Jew was so avaricious that he would not do so of his own free will, and the Sultan did not wish to have recourse to force; therefore, as his need was pressing, he thought of nothing but finding a means of getting the Jew to help him, and he decided to use some colorful pretext to accomplish this. He had him summoned, and after welcoming him in a friendly manner, he had him sit beside him and said to him:

"Worthy man, I have heard from many people that you are very wise and most versed in the affairs of God; because of this, I should like to know from you which of the three Laws you believe to be the true one: the Jewish, the Saracen,[5] or the Christian."

---

[5] **Saracen** Islam.

GIOVANNI BOCCACCIO | Selections from *The Decameron* 285

The Jew, who really was a wise man, realized too well that Saladin was trying to catch him with his words in order to accuse him of something, and he understood that he could not praise any of the three Laws more than the other without Saladin achieving his goal; therefore, he sharpened his wits, like one who seems to need an answer in order not to be entrapped, and knew well what he had to say before he had to, and said:

"My Lord, the question which you have put to me is a good one, and in order to give you an answer, I shall have to tell you a little story which you shall now hear. If I am not mistaken, I remember having heard many times that there once was a great and wealthy man who had a most beautiful and precious ring among the many precious jewels in his treasury. Because of its worth and its beauty, he wanted to honor it by bequeathing it to his descendants forever, and he ordered that whichever of his sons would be found in possession of this ring, which he would have left him, should be honored and revered as his true heir and head of the family by all the others. The man to whom he left the ring did the same as his predecessor had, having left behind the same instructions to his descendants; in short, this ring went from hand to hand through many generations, and finally it came into the hands of a man who had three handsome and virtuous sons, all of whom were obedient to their father, and for this reason, all three were equally loved by him. Since the father was growing old and they knew about the tradition of the ring, each of the three men was anxious to be the most honored among his sons, and each one, as best he knew how, begged the father to leave the ring to him when he died. The worthy man, who loved them all equally, did not know himself which of the three he would choose to leave the ring, and since he had promised it to each of them, he decided to try and satisfy all three: he had a good jeweler secretly make two more rings which were so much like the first one that he himself, who had had them made, hardly could tell which was the real one. When the father was dying, he gave a ring to each of his sons in secret, and after he died each son claimed the inheritance and position and one son denied the claims of the other, each bringing forth his ring to prove his case; when they discovered the rings were so much alike that they could not recognize the true one, they put aside the question of who the true heir was and left it undecided as it is to this day.

"And let me say the same thing to you, my lord, concerning the three Laws given the three peoples by God our Father which are the subject of the question you posed to me: each believes itself to be the true heir, to possess the true Law, and to follow the true commandments, but whoever is right, just as in the case of the rings, is still undecided."

Saladin realized how the man had most cleverly avoided the trap which he had set to snare him, and for that reason he decided to make his needs known openly to him and to see if he might wish to help him; and he did so, revealing to him what he had in mind to do if the Jew had not replied to his question as discreetly as he had. The Jew willingly gave Saladin as much money as he desired, and Saladin later repaid him in full; in fact, he more than repaid him: he gave him great gifts and always esteemed him as his friend and kept him near at court in a grand and honorable fashion.

Questions for Critical Thinking

1. How did Boccaccio describe the conditions under which people died or survived the plague and the ways they responded to the plague? Do you think their responses are typical of humans under those conditions, and how would you respond to such a situation?

2. Discuss the allegorical fable Melchisedech tells Saladin. What does the relationship between Melchisedech and Saladin reveal about Jews living in the Muslim world?

GEOFFREY CHAUCER
Selections from *The Canterbury Tales*

The Canterbury Tales, by Geoffrey Chaucer (ca. 1340–1400), is generally recognized as the earliest masterpiece in English. Its popularity helped ensure the triumph of the native tongue over Anglo-Norman, the French spoken in England after the Norman conquest (1066). Recited perhaps as court entertainment and circulated privately in manuscript, it quickly established Chaucer as a master storyteller and a melodious poet, a judgment shared by generations of readers. Today, it is among the best-loved works in English; its lively tales are enjoyed by children and adults alike, and its unique characters are a part of popular culture. For scholars, the poem is a treasure trove for the social attitudes of its day.

The literary form of *The Canterbury Tales* (ca. 1385–1400) is beautifully simple, a tale within a tale, a genre inspired by Boccaccio's *The Decameron.* For plot, Chaucer introduces himself as a traveler who joins a motley band of English men and women at the Tabard Inn in Southwark (South London); he rides horseback with them on their partly religious, partly diverting pilgrimage to the shrine of St. Thomas à Becket at Canterbury. On the journey, he put into their mouths the tales and learning that he had acquired during his lifetime. For reasons unknown, Chaucer left the work unfinished; he completed only twenty-three tales of the more than 120 projected.

For the modern reader, much of the interest of this work lies in the full-blooded description of the pilgrims. Together, the thirty-one pilgrims constitute a cross section of late-medieval English society. Especially in the "end-bits" linking the tales, Chaucer presents the pilgrims in their own words, as they joke, quarrel, and philosophize. The frank, sometimes obscene language spoken by a few lower-class characters (e.g., the Miller) reflects the open speech of England before the advent of Puritanism in the late 1500s.

Reading the Selections

The Prologue—the opening section of the poem—introduces each pilgrim with a pithy description full of telling detail. Chaucer's method is to blend random data of physical traits, personal and work habits, clothing features, and speech patterns in order to create memorable characters. The unforgettable portrait of the Wife of Bath is one such character—a talented weaver in her native town, with her wide-spaced teeth, large hips, even larger hat, vulgar taste for red clothes, roving eye, and skill at "wandering by the way." His insight into personality proves he was a keen psychologist, perhaps the finest in European letters prior to Machiavelli.

The Wife of Bath's Tale is typical of Chaucer's comical-moral tales. Originating the literary device that each tale should morally suit its teller, he presents the domineering Wife of Bath as she recounts a tale whose theme is that happy wives need henpecked husbands. The tale is a reworking of a common folk story ("The Loathly Lady"), which Chaucer embellishes with magnificently irrelevant references to Ovid (see *Metamorphoses* in Chapter 5), Dante (see *The Divine Comedy* in Chapter 10), Boethius (see *The Consolation of Philosophy* in Chapter 8), and Juvenal (see *Satire III* in Chapter 5). Beneath the sexual politics, however, Chaucer offers a revolutionary moral: gentility comes from God alone, not from social breeding.

To illustrate Chaucer's language, the first thirty-four lines of the General Prologue are reprinted in the original Middle English. Modern English equivalents are provided in the right margin for certain words. Note especially variations in spelling and verb forms, and the frequency of the final *e,* which was pronounced with the "schwa" sound, as in sof*a* and *a*bout. Final *e* was not pronounced when it occurred before words beginning with vowels or weakly pronounced *h*s.

The General Prologue
(in Middle English)

Whan that Aprill with his shoures sote°	*sweet showers* 1
The droghte° of Marche hath perced to	
the rote,°	*dryness / root*
And bathed every veyne° in swich	
licour,°	*vein / such moisture*
Of which vertu° engendred is the	
flour;	*By power of which*
Whan Zephirus° eek with his swete	
breeth	*the west wind*
Inspired° hath in every holt°	
and heeth°	*Breathed into / wood / heath*
The tendre croppes,° and the yonge sonne	*sprouts*
Hath in the Ram his halfe cours y-ronne;	
And smale fowles° maken melodye,	*birds*
That slepen al the night with open yë°—	*eye(s)* 10
So priketh hem Nature in hir corages—	
Than longen° folk to goon° on pilgrimages,	*Then long / go*
And palmeres for to seken straunge strondes,	
To ferne halwes,° couthe° in sondry	
londes;	*far-off shires / known*
And specially, from every shires ende	
Of Engelond to Caunterbury they wende,	

The holy blisful martir for to seke,°	*seek*
That hem hath holpen,° whan that they	
were seke.°	*helped / sick*
Bifel° that, in that seson on a day,	*It befell*
In Southwerk at the Tabard° as I lay°	*(an inn) / lodged* 20
Redy to wenden° on my pilgrimage	*depart*
To Caunterbury with ful devout corage,°	*heart*
At night was come into that hostelrye°	*inn*
Wel nyne and twenty in a companye	
Of sondry folk, by aventure° y-falle°	*chance / fallen*
In felawshipe, and pilgrims were they alle,	
That toward Caunterbury wolden° ryde.	*wished to*
The chambres° and the stables	
weren wyde,°	*bedrooms / spacious*
And wel we weren esed°	
atte beste.°	*made comfortable / in the best (ways)*
And shortly, whan the sonne was to° reste,	*at* 30
So hadde I spoken with hem	
everichon°	*each and every one*
That I was of hir felawshipe anon,	
And made forward° erly for to ryse,	*agreement*
To take oure wey, ther as I yow devyse.°	*(will) tell*

The Prologue

When in April the sweet showers fall 1
And pierce the drought of March to the root, and all
The veins are bathed in liquor of such power
As brings about the engendering of the flower,
When also Zephyrus with his sweet breath
Exhales an air in every grove and heath
Upon the tender shoots, and the young sun
His half-course in the sign of the *Ram* has run,[6]
And the small fowl are making melody
That sleep away the night with open eye 10
(So nature pricks them and their heart engages)
Then people long to go on pilgrimages
And palmers[7] long to seek the stranger strands
Of far-off saints, hallowed in sundry lands,
And specially, from every shire's end
Of England, down to Canterbury they wend

To seek the holy blissful martyr,[8] quick
To give his help to them when they were sick.
  It happened in that season that one day
In Southwark, at *The Tabard*, as I lay 20
Ready to go on pilgrimage and start
For Canterbury, most devout at heart,
At night there came into that hostelry
Some nine and twenty in a company
Of sundry folk happening then to fall
In fellowship, and they were pilgrims all
That towards Canterbury meant to ride.
The rooms and stables of the inn were wide;
They made us easy, all was of the best.
And, briefly, when the sun had gone to rest, 30
I'd spoken to them all upon the trip
And was soon one with them in fellowship,

---

[6] **His half-course in the sign of the *Ram* has run** The Ram, or Aries in the Zodiac, is the time between March 21 and April 20; thus it is early April.
[7] **palmers** Pilgrims who displayed crossed palm leaves as a sign that they were going to the Holy Land.

---

[8] **the holy blissful martyr** Thomas à Becket, the martyred Archbishop of Canterbury, murdered in the cathedral by men loyal to King Henry II of England, had become a saint by Chaucer's time. Becket supposedly had healing powers to help the sick.

Pledged to rise early and to take the way
To Canterbury, as you heard me say.
   But none the less, while I have time and space,
Before my story takes a further pace,
It seems a reasonable thing to say
What their condition was, the full array
Of each of them, as it appeared to me,
According to profession and degree,   40
And what apparel they were riding in;
And at a Knight I therefore will begin.
There was a *Knight,* a most distinguished man,
Who from the day on which he first began
To ride abroad had followed chivalry,
Truth, honour, generousness and courtesy.
He had done nobly in his sovereign's war
And ridden into battle, no man more,
As well in Christian as in heathen places,
And ever honoured for his noble graces.   50
   When we took Alexandria, he was there.
He often sat at table in the chair
Of honour, above all nations, when in Prussia.
In Lithuania he had ridden, and Russia,
No Christian man so often, of his rank.
When, in Granada, Algeciras sank
Under assault, he had been there, and in
North Africa, raiding Benamarin;
In Anatolia he had been as well
And fought when Ayas and Attalia fell,   60
For all along the Mediterranean coast
He had embarked with many a noble host.
In fifteen mortal battles he had been
And jousted for our faith at Tramissene
Thrice in the lists, and always killed his man.
This same distinguished knight had led the van
Once with the Bey of Balat, doing work
For him against another heathen Turk;
He was of sovereign value in all eyes.
And though so much distinguished, he was wise   70
And in his bearing modest as a maid.
He never yet a boorish thing had said
In all his life to any, come what might;
He was a true, a perfect gentle-knight.
   Speaking of his equipment, he possessed
Fine horses, but he was not gaily dressed.
He wore a fustian tunic stained and dark
With smudges where his armour had left mark;
Just home from service, he had joined our ranks
To do his pilgrimage and render thanks.   80
He had his son with him, a fine young *Squire,*
A lover and cadet, a lad of fire
With locks as curly as if they had been pressed.
He was some twenty years of age, I guessed.
In stature he was of a moderate length,
With wonderful agility and strength.
He'd seen some service with the cavalry
In Flanders and Artois and Picardy
And had done valiantly in little space
Of time, in hope to win his lady's grace.   90
He was embroidered like a meadow bright

And full of freshest flowers, red and white.
Singing he was, or fluting all the day;
He was as fresh as is the month of May.
Short was his gown, the sleeves were long and wide;
He knew the way to sit a horse and ride.
He could make songs and poems and recite,
Knew how to joust and dance, to draw and write.
He loved so hotly that till dawn grew pale
He slept as little as a nightingale.   100
Courteous he was, lowly and serviceable,
And carved to serve his father at the table.
   There was a *Yeoman*[9] with him at his side,
No other servant; so he chose to ride.
This Yeoman wore a coat and hood of green,
And peacock-feathered arrows, bright and keen
And neatly sheathed, hung at his belt the while
—For he could dress his gear in yeoman style,
His arrows never dropped their feathers low—
And in his hand he bore a mighty bow.   110
His head was like a nut, his face was brown.
He knew the whole of woodcraft up and down.
A saucy brace was on his arm to ward
It from the bow-string, and a shield and sword
Hung at one side, and at the other slipped
A jaunty dirk,[10] spear-sharp and well-equipped.
A medal of St Christopher he wore
Of shining silver on his breast, and bore
A hunting-horn, well slung and burnished clean,
That dangled from a baldrick of bright green.   120
He was a proper forester, I guess.
   There also was a *Nun,* a Prioress,
Her way of smiling very simple and coy.
Her greatest oath was only "By St Loy!"
And she was known as Madam Eglantyne.
And well she sang a service, with a fine
Intoning through her nose, as was most seemly,
And she spoke daintily in French, extremely,
After the school of Stratford-atte-Bowe;
French in the Paris style she did not know.   130
At meat her manners were well taught withal;
No morsel from her lips did she let fall,
Nor dipped her fingers in the sauce too deep;
But she could carry a morsel up and keep
The smallest drop from falling on her breast.
For courtliness she had a special zest,
And she would wipe her upper lip so clean
That not a trace of grease was to be seen
Upon the cup when she had drunk; to eat,
She reached a hand sedately for the meat.   140
She certainly was very entertaining,
Pleasant and friendly in her ways, and straining
To counterfeit a courtly kind of grace,
A stately bearing fitting to her place,

---

[9] *Yeoman* Can be an independent landholder who owns a small
amount of land, or an attendant to a member of a noble or royal
household. In this case, he seems to be both.
[10] **dirk** A long straight-bladed knife.

And to seem dignified in all her dealings.
As for her sympathies and tender feelings,
She was so charitably solicitous
She used to weep if she but saw a mouse
Caught in a trap, if it were dead or bleeding.
And she had little dogs she would be feeding   150
With roasted flesh, or milk, or fine white bread.
And bitterly she wept if one were dead
Or someone took a stick and made it smart[11];
She was all sentiment and tender heart.
Her veil was gathered in a seemly way,
Her nose was elegant, her eyes glass-grey;
Her mouth was very small, but soft and red,
Her forehead, certainly, was fair of spread,
Almost a span across the brows, I own[12];
She was indeed by no means undergrown.   160
Her cloak, I noticed, had a graceful charm.
She wore a coral trinket on her arm,
A set of beads, the gaudies tricked in green,
Whence hung a golden brooch of brightest sheen
On which there first was graven a crowned A,
And lower, *Amor vincit omnia.*[13]
Another *Nun,* the secretary at her cell,
Was riding with her, and *three Priests* as well.
    A *Monk* there was, one of the finest sort
Who rode the country; hunting was his sport.   170
A manly man, to be an Abbot able;
Many a dainty horse he had in stable.
His bridle, when he rode, a man might hear
Jingling in a whistling wind as clear,
Aye, and as loud as does the chapel bell
Where my lord Monk was Prior of the cell.
The Rule of good St Benet or St Maur[14]
As old and strict he tended to ignore;
He let go by the things of yesterday
And took the modern world's more spacious way.   180
He did not rate that text at a plucked hen
Which says that hunters are not holy men
And that a monk uncloistered is a mere
Fish out of water, flapping on the pier,
That is to say a monk out of his cloister.
That was a text he held not worth an oyster;
And I agreed and said his views were sound;
Was he to study till his head went round
Poring over books in cloisters? Must he toil
As Austin[15] bade and till the very soil?   190
Was he to leave the world upon the shelf?

Let Austin have his labour to himself.
    This Monk was therefore a good man to horse;
Greyhounds he had, as swift as birds, to course.
Hunting a hare or riding at a fence
Was all his fun, he spared for no expense.
I saw his sleeves were garnished at the hand
With fine grey fur, the finest in the land,
And on his hood, to fasten it at his chin
He had a wrought-gold cunningly fashioned pin;   200
Into a lover's knot it seemed to pass.
His head was bald and shone like looking-glass;
So did his face, as if it had been greased.
He was a fat and personable priest;
His prominent eyeballs never seemed to settle.
They glittered like the flames beneath a kettle;
Supple his boots, his horse in fine condition.
He was a prelate[16] fit for exhibition,
He was not pale like a tormented soul.
He liked a fat swan best, and roasted whole.   210
His palfrey was as brown as is a berry.
    There was a *Friar,* a wanton one and merry,
A Limiter,[17] a very festive fellow.
In all Four Orders there was none so mellow,
So glib with gallant phrase and well-turned speech.
He'd fixed up many a marriage, giving each
Of his young women what he could afford her.[18]
He was a noble pillar to his Order.
Highly beloved and intimate was he
With County folk within his boundary,   220
And city dames of honour and possessions;
For he was qualified to hear confessions,
Or so he said, with more than priestly scope;
He had a special licence from the Pope.
Sweetly he heard his penitents at shrift
With pleasant absolution, for a gift.
He was an easy man in penance-giving
Where he could hope to make a decent living;
It's a sure sign whenever gifts are given
To a poor Order that a man's well shriven,[19]   230
And should he give enough he knew in verity
The penitent repented in sincerity.
For many a fellow is so hard of heart
He cannot weep, for all his inward smart.
Therefore instead of weeping and of prayer
One should give silver for a poor Friar's care.
He kept his tippet stuffed with pins for curls,
And pocket-knives, to give to pretty girls.
And certainly his voice was gay and sturdy,
For he sang well and played the hurdy-gurdy.   240
At sing-songs he was champion of the hour.

---

[11] **smart** Sharp or pointed.
[12] **own** To acknowledge or to claim to be true.
[13] *Amor vincit omnia.* Latin; in English, "Love conquers all."
[14] **St Benet or St Maur** Both saints wrote rules and regulations for monastic orders. St. Benedict founded the Benedictine order in the sixth century, which was the first of many monastic orders.
[15] **Austin** St. Augustine, one of the early church fathers, who, after his conversion to Christianity, spent his life working for the church, wrote many books on Christian thought, and described how a holy man should live. He lived in the late fourth and early fifth centuries.

---

[16] **prelate** An official in the hierarchy of the church. Obviously, Chaucer is giving the monk a title above his ranking to make the point that the monk, in his dress and tastes, lives like a prelate.
[17] **A Limiter** A member of an order who travels about begging for contributions to his order.
[18] **He'd fixed up many . . . afford her.** The reference is not to his officiating at weddings but to his impregnating young women.
[19] **shriven** To be free from guilt after having confessed one's sins.

His neck was whiter than a lily-flower
But strong enough to butt a bruiser down.
He knew the taverns well in every town
And every innkeeper and barmaid too
Better than lepers, beggars and that crew,
For in so eminent a man as he
It was not fitting with the dignity
Of his position, dealing with a scum
Of wretched lepers; nothing good can come   250
Of commerce with such slum-and-gutter dwellers,
But only with the rich and victual-sellers.
But anywhere a profit might accrue
Courteous he was and lowly of service too.
Natural gifts like his were hard to match.
He was the finest beggar of his batch,
And, for his begging-district, paid a rent;
His brethren did no poaching where he went.
For though a widow mightn't have a shoe,
So pleasant was his holy how-d'ye-do   260
He got his farthing from her just the same
Before he left, and so his income came
To more than he laid out. And how he romped,
Just like a puppy! He was ever prompt
To arbitrate disputes on settling days
(For a small fee) in many helpful ways,
Not then appearing as your cloistered scholar
With threadbare habit hardly worth a dollar,
But much more like a Doctor or a Pope.
Of double-worsted was the semi-cope   270
Upon his shoulders, and the swelling fold
About him, like a bell about its mould
When it is casting, rounded out his dress.
He lisped a little out of wantonness
To make his English sweet upon his tongue.
When he had played his harp, or having sung,
His eyes would twinkle in his head as bright
As any star upon a frosty night.
This worthy's name was Hubert, it appeared.
    There was a *Merchant* with a forking beard   280
And motley dress; high on his horse he sat,
Upon his head a Flemish beaver hat
And on his feet daintily buckled boots.
He told of his opinions and pursuits
In solemn tones, he harped on his increase
Of capital; there should be sea-police
(He thought) upon the Harwich-Holland ranges[20];
He was expert at dabbling in exchanges.
This estimable Merchant so had set
His wits to work, none knew he was in debt,   290
He was so stately in administration,
In loans and bargains and negotiation.
He was an excellent fellow all the same;
To tell the truth I do not know his name.
    An *Oxford Cleric*, still a student though,
One who had taken logic long ago,

Was there; his horse was thinner than a rake,
And he was not too fat, I undertake,
But had a hollow look, a sober stare;
The thread upon his overcoat was bare.   300
He had found no preferment in the church
And he was too unworldly to make search
For secular employment. By his bed
He preferred having twenty books in red
And black, of Aristotle's philosophy,
Than costly clothes, fiddle or psaltery.
Though a philosopher, as I have told,
He had not found the stone for making gold.
Whatever money from his friends he took
He spent on learning or another book   310
And prayed for them most earnestly, returning
Thanks to them thus for paying for his learning.
His only care was study, and indeed
He never spoke a word more than was need,
Formal at that, respectful in the extreme,
Short, to the point, and lofty in his theme.
A tone of moral virtue filled his speech
And gladly would he learn, and gladly teach.
    A *Serjeant at the Law*[21] who paid his calls,
Wary and wise, for clients at St Paul's   320
There also was, of noted excellence.
Discreet he was, a man to reverence,
Or so he seemed, his sayings were so wise.
He often had been Justice of Assize[22]
By letters patent, and in full commission.
His fame and learning and his high position
Had won him many a robe and many a fee.
There was no such conveyancer as he;
All was fee-simple to his strong digestion,
Not one conveyance could be called in question.   330
Though there was nowhere one so busy as he,
He was less busy than he seemed to be.
He knew of every judgment, case and crime
Ever recorded since King William's time.[23]
He could dictate defences or draft deeds;
No one could pinch a comma from his screeds[24]
And he knew every statute off by rote.
He wore a homely parti-coloured coat,
Girt with a silken belt of pin-stripe stuff;
Of his appearance I have said enough.   340
    There was a *Franklin*[25] with him, it appeared;
White as a daisy-petal was his beard.
A sanguine man, high-coloured and benign,
He loved a morning sop of cake in wine.
He lived for pleasure and had always done,

---

[20] **the Harwich-Holland ranges** The sea route between Harwich, an English port, and Holland.

[21] *Serjeant at the Law* Today, a special ranking for a barrister (one who practices before the bar or in a court in England) in the sovereign's court system. Chaucer describes him as a regular lawyer.
[22] **Justice of Assize** The district civil court.
[23] **King William's time** William the Conqueror (r. 1066–1087).
[24] **screeds** A lengthy discourse or argument.
[25] *Franklin* A country landowner who was free or not indentured but not of noble birth.

For he was Epicurus' very son,[26]
In whose opinion sensual delight
Was the one true felicity in sight.
As noted as St Julian[27] as for bounty
He made his household free to all the County.   350
His bread, his ale were finest of the fine
And no one had a better stock of wine.
His house was never short of bake-meat pies,
Of fish and flesh, and these in such supplies
It positively snowed with meat and drink
And all the dainties that a man could think.
According to the seasons of the year
Changes of dish were ordered to appear.
He kept fat partridges in coops, beyond,
Many a bream and pike were in his pond.   360
Woe to the cook unless the sauce was hot
And sharp, or if he wasn't on the spot!
And in his hall a table stood arrayed
And ready all day long, with places laid.
As Justice at the Sessions none stood higher;
He often had been Member for the Shire.[28]
A dagger and a little purse of silk
Hung at his girdle, white as morning milk.
As Sheriff he checked audit, every entry.
He was a model among landed gentry.   370
    A *Haberdasher*, a *Dyer*, a *Carpenter*,
A *Weaver* and a *Carpet-maker* were
Among our ranks, all in the livery
Of one impressive guild-fraternity.[29]
They were so trim and fresh their gear would pass
For new. Their knives were not tricked out with brass
But wrought with purest silver, which avouches
A like display on girdles and on pouches.
Each seemed a worthy burgess, fit to grace
A guild-hall with a seat upon the dais.   380
Their wisdom would have justified a plan
To make each one of them an alderman;
They had the capital and revenue,
Besides their wives declared it was their due.
And if they did not think so, then they ought;
To be called *"Madam"* is a glorious thought,
And so is going to church and being seen
Having your mantle carried, like a queen.
    They had a *Cook* with them who stood alone
For boiling chicken with a marrow-bone,   390
Sharp flavouring-powder and a spice for savour.
He could distinguish London ale by flavour,
And he could roast and seethe and broil and fry,
Make good thick soup and bake a tasty pie.

But what a pity—so it seemed to me,
That he should have an ulcer on his knee.
As for blancmange, he made it with the best.
    There was a *Skipper* hailing from far west;
He came from Dartmouth, so I understood.
He rode a farmer's horse as best he could,   400
In a woollen gown that reached his knee.
A dagger on a lanyard falling free
Hung from his neck under his arm and down.
The summer heat had tanned his colour brown,
And certainly he was an excellent fellow.
Many a draught of vintage, red and yellow,
He'd drawn at Bordeaux, while the trader snored.
The nicer rules of conscience he ignored.[30]
If, when he fought, the enemy vessel sank,
He sent his prisoners home; they walked the plank.   410
As for his skill in reckoning his tides,
Currents and many another risk besides,
Moons, harbours, pilots, he had such dispatch
That none from Hull to Carthage was his match.
Hardy he was, prudent in undertaking;
His beard in many a tempest had its shaking,
And he knew all the heavens as they were
From Gottland to the Cape of Finisterre,
And every creek in Brittany and Spain;
The barge he owned was called *The Maudelayne*.   420
    A *Doctor* too emerged as we proceeded;
No one alive could talk as well as he did
On points of medicine and of surgery,
For, being grounded in astronomy,
He watched his patient closely for the hours
When, by his horoscope, he knew the powers
Of favourable planets, then ascendent,
Worked on the images for his dependent.
The cause of every malady you'd got
He knew, and whether dry, cold, moist or hot;   430
He knew their seat, their humour and condition.
He was a perfect practising physician.
These causes being known for what they were,
He gave the man his medicine then and there.
All his apothecaries in a tribe
Were ready with the drugs he would prescribe
And each made money from the other's guile;
They had been friendly for a goodish while.
He was well-versed in Aesculapius too
And what Hippocrates and Rufus knew   440
And Dioscorides, now dead and gone,
Galen and Rhazes, Hali, Serapion,
Averroes, Avicenna, Constantine,
Scotch Bernard, John of Gaddesden, Gilbertine.[31]

---

[26] **Epicurus' very son** The Franklin thought that Epicurus, the Greek philosopher, advocated a life of bodily pleasures, which was not what the thinker really believed.
[27] **St Julian** The patron saint of hospitality.
[28] **Member for the Shire** Representative of his district to Parliament.
[29] **guild-fraternity** The five pilgrims mentioned were members of their respective guilds and dressed in their livery or identifying clothing.

---

[30] **The nicer rules of conscience he ignored.** The "skipper" is really a pirate.
[31] **Aesculapius, Hippocrates, Rufus, Dioscorides, Galen, Rhazes, Hali, Serapion, Averroes, Avicenna, Constantine, Scotch Bernard, John of Gaddesden, Gilbertine** List of legendary, ancient, medieval, Muslim, and contemporary men of medicine. Many wrote medical books that would have been read and used by the doctor.

In his own diet he observed some measure;
There were no superfluities for pleasure,
Only digestives, nutritives and such.
He did not read the Bible very much.
In blood-red garments, slashed with bluish grey
And lined with taffeta, he rode his way; 450
Yet he was rather close as to expenses
And kept the gold he won in pestilences.
Gold stimulates the heart, or so we're told.
He therefore had a special love of gold.
    A worthy *woman* from beside *Bath* city
Was with us, somewhat deaf, which was a pity.
In making cloth she showed so great a bent
She bettered those of Ypres and of Ghent.
In all the parish not a dame dared stir
Towards the altar steps in front of her, 460
And if indeed they did, so wrath was she
As to be quite put out of charity.
Her kerchiefs were of finely woven ground;
I dared have sworn they weighed a good ten pound,
The ones she wore on Sunday, on her head.
Her hose were of the finest scarlet red
And gartered tight; her shoes were soft and new.
Bold was her face, handsome, and red in hue.
A worthy woman all her life, what's more
She'd had five husbands, all at the church door, 470
Apart from other company in youth;
No need just now to speak of that, forsooth.
And she had thrice been to Jerusalem,
Seen many strange rivers and passed over them;
She'd been to Rome and also to Boulogne,
St James of Compostella and Cologne,
And she was skilled in wandering by the way.
She had gap-teeth, set widely, truth to say.
Easily on an ambling horse she sat
Well wimpled up,[32] and on her head a hat 480
As broad as is a buckler or a shield;
She had a flowing mantle that concealed
Large hips, her heels spurred sharply under that.
In company she liked to laugh and chat
And knew the remedies for love's mischances,
An art in which she knew the oldest dances.
    A holy-minded man of good renown
There was, and poor, the *Parson* to a town,
Yet he was rich in holy thought and work.
He also was a learned man, a clerk, 490
Who truly knew Christ's gospel and would preach it
Devoutly to parishioners, and teach it.
Benign and wonderfully diligent,
And patient when adversity was sent
(For so he proved in much adversity)
He hated cursing to extort a fee,[33]
Nay rather he preferred beyond a doubt

Giving to poor parishioners round about
Both from church offerings and his property;
He could in little find sufficiency. 500
Wide was his parish, with houses far asunder,
Yet he neglected not in rain or thunder,
In sickness or in grief, to pay a call
On the remotest, whether great or small,
Upon his feet, and in his hand a stave.
This noble example to his sheep he gave
That first he wrought, and afterwards he taught;
And it was from the Gospel he had caught
Those words, and he would add this figure too,
That if gold rust, what then will iron do? 510
For if a priest be foul in whom we trust
No wonder that a common man should rust;
And shame it is to see—let priests take stock—
A shitten shepherd and a snowy flock.
The true example that a priest should give
Is one of cleanness, how the sheep should live.[34]
He did not set his benefice to hire[35]
And leave his sheep encumbered in the mire
Or run to London to earn easy bread
By singing masses for the wealthy dead, 520
Or find some Brotherhood and get enrolled.
He stayed at home and watched over his fold
So that no wolf should make the sheep miscarry.
He was a shepherd and no mercenary.
Holy and virtuous he was, but then
Never contemptuous of sinful men,
Never disdainful, never too proud or fine,
But was discreet in teaching and benign.
His business was to show a fair behaviour
And draw men thus to Heaven and their Saviour, 530
Unless indeed a man were obstinate;
And such, whether of high or low estate,
He put to sharp rebuke, to say the least.
I think there never was a better priest.
He sought no pomp or glory in his dealings,
No scrupulosity had spiced his feelings.
Christ and His Twelve Apostles and their lore
He taught, but followed it himself before.
    There was a *Plowman*[36] with him there, his brother;
Many a load of dung one time or other 540
He must have carted through the morning dew.
He was an honest worker, good and true,
Living in peace and perfect charity,
And, as the gospel bade him, so did he,
Loving God best with all his heart and mind
And then his neighbour as himself, repined
At no misfortune, slacked for no content,
For steadily about his work he went

---

[32] **Well wimpled up** Her head covered with a veil or a wimple, a cloth worn outdoors to cover the head, neck, and chin.
[33] **He hated cursing to extort a fee** The Parson refused to curse or to excommunicate a person who did not tithe or contribute a tenth of his income to the church, which was supposed to be the normal pattern of giving.

---

[34] **And shame it is to see . . . how the sheep should live.** The priest, like the shepherd, should not be dirty (shitten), but be clean and live an exemplary life in order to lead his flock.
[35] **He did not set his benefice to hire** Some priests would deliberately (set) hire or sell their benefice to other priests to make money. A *benefice* was an ecclesiastical office with a source of revenue—thus, a steady income.
[36] **Plowman** A peasant farmer or farm laborer.

To thrash his corn, to dig or to manure
Or make a ditch; and he would help the poor   550
For love of Christ and never take a penny
If he could help it, and, as prompt as any,
He paid his tithes in full when they were due
On what he owned, and on his earnings too.
He wore a tabard smock and rode a mare.
    There was a *Reeve*, also a *Miller*, there,
A College *Manciple* from the Inns of Court,
A papal *Pardoner* and, in close consort,
A Church-Court *Summoner*, riding at a trot,[37]
And finally myself—that was the lot.   560
    The *Miller* was a chap of sixteen stone,
A great stout fellow big in brawn and bone.
He did well out of them, for he could go
And win the ram at any wrestling show.
Broad, knotty and short-shouldered, he would boast
He could heave any door off hinge and post,
Or take a run and break it with his head.
His beard, like any sow or fox, was red
And broad as well, as though it were a spade;
And, at its very tip, his nose displayed   570
A wart on which there stood a tuft of hair
Red as the bristles in an old sow's ear.
His nostrils were as black as they were wide.
He had a sword and buckler at his side,
His mighty mouth was like a furnace door.
A wrangler and buffoon, he had a store
Of tavern stories, filthy in the main.
His was a master-hand at stealing grain.
He felt it with his thumb and thus he knew
Its quality and took three times his due—   580
A thumb of gold, by God, to gauge an oat!
He wore a hood of blue and a white coat.
He liked to play his bagpipes up and down
And that was how he brought us out of town.
    The *Manciple* came from the Inner Temple;
All caterers might follow his example
In buying victuals; he was never rash
Whether he bought on credit or paid cash.
He used to watch the market most precisely
And got in first, and so he did quite nicely.   590
Now isn't it a marvel of God's grace
That an illiterate fellow can outpace
The wisdom of a heap of learned men?
His masters—he had more than thirty then—
All versed in the abstrusest legal knowledge,

Could have produced a dozen from their College
Fit to be stewards in land and rents and game
To any Peer in England you could name,
And show him how to live on what he had
Debt-free (unless of course the Peer were mad)   600
Or be as frugal as he might desire,
And make them fit to help about the Shire
In any legal case there was to try;
And yet this Manciple could wipe their eye.
    The *Reeve* was old and choleric and thin;
His beard was shaven closely to the skin,
His shorn hair came abruptly to a stop
Above his ears, and he was docked on top
Just like a priest in front; his legs were lean,
Like sticks they were, no calf was to be seen.   610
He kept his bins and garners[38] very trim;
No auditor could gain a point on him.
And he could judge by watching drought and rain
The yield he might expect from seed and grain.
His master's sheep, his animals and hens,
Pigs, horses, dairies, stores and cattle-pens
Were wholly trusted to his government.
He had been under contract to present
The accounts, right from his master's earliest years.
No one had ever caught him in arrears.   620
No bailiff, serf or herdsman dared to kick,
He knew their dodges, knew their every trick;
Feared like the plague he was, by those beneath.
He had a lovely dwelling on a heath,
Shadowed in green by trees above the sward.
A better hand at bargains than his lord,
He had grown rich and had a store of treasure
Well tucked away, yet out it came to pleasure
His lord with subtle loans or gifts of goods,
To earn his thanks and even coats and hoods.   630
When young he'd learnt a useful trade and still
He was a carpenter of first-rate skill.
The stallion-cob he rode at a slow trot
Was dapple-grey and bore the name of Scot.
He wore an overcoat of bluish shade
And rather long; he had a rusty blade
Slung at his side. He came, as I heard tell,
From Norfolk, near a place called Baldeswell.
His coat was tucked under his belt and splayed.
He rode the hindmost of our cavalcade.   640
    There was a *Summoner* with us at that Inn,
His face on fire, like a cherubin,
For he had carbuncles. His eyes were narrow,
He was as hot and lecherous as a sparrow.
Black scabby brows he had, and a thin beard.
Children were afraid when he appeared.
No quicksilver, lead ointment, tartar creams,
No brimstone, no boracic, so it seems,
Could make a salve that had the power to bite,
Clean up or cure his whelks of knobby white   650
Or purge the pimples sitting on his cheeks.
Garlic he loved, and onions too, and leeks,

---

[37] *Reeve, Miller, Manciple, Pardoner, Summoner* All five are reprehensible characters—petty white-collar thieves who cheat their customers, take bribes, steal from their superiors, or play upon the fears of credulous Christians. A reeve was a manager or overseer of an estate. A miller, of course, was one who would grind grain or corn. A manciple was the financial manager of an educational institution. A summoner summoned people to a court that tried offenses against the church, similar to a process-server today. A pardoner sold holy relics and also pardons to those who confessed their sins and sought forgiveness—thus putting a cash price on a spiritual act or sacrament. By Chaucer's time, such practices were scandalous ways for unscrupulous churchmen to make money.

---

[38] **garners** Granary or grain bins.

And drinking strong red wine till all was hazy.
Then he would shout and jabber as if crazy,
And wouldn't speak a word except in Latin
When he was drunk, such tags[39] as he was pat in;
He had only a few, say two or three,
That he had mugged up out of some decree;
No wonder, for he heard them every day.
And, as you know, a man can teach a jay   660
To call out "Walter" better than the Pope.
But had you tried to test his wits and grope
For more, you'd have found nothing in the bag.
Then *"Questio quid juris"*[40] was his tag.
He was a noble varlet[41] and a kind one,
You'd meet none better if you went to find one.
Why, he'd allow—just for a quart of wine—
Any good lad to keep a concubine
A twelvemonth and dispense him altogether!
And he had finches of his own to feather:[42]   670
And if he found some rascal with a maid
He would instruct him not to be afraid
In such a case of the Archdeacon's curse
(Unless the rascal's soul were in his purse)
For in his purse the punishment should be.
"Purse is the good Archdeacon's Hell," said he.
But well I know he lied in what he said;
A curse should put a guilty man in dread,
For curses kill, as shriving brings, salvation.
We should beware of excommunication.   680
Thus, as he pleased, the man could bring duress
On any young fellow in the diocese.
He knew their secrets, they did what he said.
He wore a garland set upon his head
Large as the holly-bush upon a stake
Outside an ale-house, and he had a cake,
A round one, which it was his joke to wield
As if it were intended for a shield.
      He and a gentle *Pardoner* rode together,
A bird from Charing Cross of the same feather,   690
Just back from visiting the Court of Rome.
He loudly sang *"Come hither, love, come home!"*
The Summoner sang deep seconds to this song,
No trumpet ever sounded half so strong.
This Pardoner had hair as yellow as wax,
Hanging down smoothly like a hank of flax.
In driblets fell his locks behind his head
Down to his shoulders which they overspread;
Thinly they fell, like rat-tails, one by one.
He wore no hood upon his head, for fun;   700
The hood inside his wallet had been stowed,
He aimed at riding in the latest mode;

But for a little cap his head was bare
And he had bulging eye-balls, like a hare.
He'd sewed a holy relic on his cap;
His wallet lay before him on his lap,
Brimful of pardons come from Rome, all hot.
He had the same small voice a goat has got.
His chin no beard had harboured, nor would harbour,
Smoother than ever chin was left by barber.   710
I judge he was a gelding, or a mare.
As to his trade, from Berwick down to Ware[43]
There was no pardoner of equal grace,
For in his trunk he had a pillow-case
Which he asserted was Our Lady's veil.
He said he had a gobbet[44] of the sail
Saint Peter had the time when he made bold
To walk the waves, till Jesu Christ took hold.
He had a cross of metal set with stones
And, in a glass, a rubble of pigs' bones.   720
And with these relics, any time he found
Some poor up-country parson to astound,
In one short day, in money down, he drew
More than the parson in a month or two,
And by his flatteries and prevarication
Made monkeys of the priest and congregation.
But still to do him justice first and last
In church he was a noble ecclesiast.[45]
How well he read a lesson or told a story!
But best of all he sang an Offertory,   730
For well he knew that when that song was sung
He'd have to preach and tune his honey-tongue
And (well he could) win silver from the crowd.
That's why he sang so merrily and loud.
Now I have told you shortly, in a clause,
The rank, the array, the number and the cause
Of our assembly in this company
In Southwark, at that high-class hostelry
Known as *The Tabard,* close beside *The Bell.*
And now the time has come for me to tell   740
How we behaved that evening; I'll begin
After we had alighted at the Inn,
Then I'll report our journey, stage by stage,
All the remainder of our pilgrimage.
But first I beg of you, in courtesy,
Not to condemn me as unmannerly
If I speak plainly and with no concealings
And give account of all their words and dealings,
Using their very phrases as they fell.
For certainly, as you all know so well,   750
He who repeats a tale after a man
Is bound to say, as nearly as he can,

---

[39] **tags** Verbal expressions, sayings, or quotations.
[40] *"Questio quid juris"* "What portion of the law applies in this case?" was a phrase the summoner would sometimes repeat in the court.
[41] **varlet** An unprincipled person.
[42] **And he had finches of his own to feather** The summoner had to make certain that he got his own share or reward. Similar to a saying of our times: "To feather one's nest."

[43] **Berwick, Ware** Berwick-upon-Tweed and Ware are two towns in England some distance apart; thus Chaucer is emphasizing the large territory over which the pardoner sells his relics.
[44] **gobbet** A small piece.
[45] **a noble ecclesiast** A very effective and talented preacher who could spellbind a congregation, sing the Offertory, and sell his relics.

Each single word, if he remembers it,
However rudely spoken or unfit,
Or else the tale he tells will be untrue,
The things pretended and the phrases new.
He may not flinch although it were his brother,
He may as well say one word as another.
And Christ Himself spoke broad in Holy Writ,

Yet there is no scurrility in it, 760
And Plato says, for those with power to read,
"The word should be as cousin to the deed."
Further I beg you to forgive it me
If I neglect the order and degree
And what is due to rank in what I've planned.
I'm short of wit as you will understand. . . .

The Wife of Bath's Tale

When good King Arthur ruled in ancient days, 1
(A king that every Briton loves to praise.)
This was a land brim-full of fairy folk.
The Elf-Queen and her courtiers joined and broke
Their elfin dance on many a green mead,[46]
Or so was the opinion once, I read,
Hundreds of years ago, in days of yore.
But no one now sees fairies any more,
For now the saintly charity and prayer
Of holy friars seem to have purged the air; 10
They search the countryside through field and stream
As thick as motes that speckle a sun-beam,
Blessing the halls, the chambers, kitchens, bowers,
Cities and boroughs, castles, courts and towers,
Thorpes,[47] barns and stables, outhouses and dairies,
And that's the reason why there are no fairies.
Wherever there was wont to walk an elf
To-day there walks the holy friar himself
As evening falls or when the daylight springs,
Saying his mattins and his holy things, 20
Walking his limit round from town to town.
Women can now go safely up and down.
By every bush or under every tree;
There is no other incubus[48] but he,
So there is really no one else to hurt you
And he will do no more than take your virtue.
    Now it so happened, I began to say,
Long, long ago in good King Arthur's day,
There was a knight who was a lusty liver.
One day as he came riding from the river 30
He saw a maiden walking all forlorn
Ahead of him, alone as she was born.
And of that maiden, spite of all she said.
By very force he took her maidenhead.[49]
    This act of violence made such a stir,
So much petitioning of the king for her,
That he condemned the knight to lose his head
By course of law. He was as good as dead

(It seems that then the statues took that view)
But that the queen, and other ladies too, 40
Implored the king to exercise his grace
So ceaselessly, he gave the queen the case
And granted her his life, and she could choose
Whether to show him mercy or refuse.
    The queen returned him thanks with all her might,
And then she sent a summons to the knight
At her convenience, and expressed her will:
"You stand, for such is the position still,
In no way certain of your life," said she,
"Yet you shall live if you can answer me: 50
What is the thing that women most desire?
Beware the axe and say as I require.
    "If you can't answer on the moment, though,
I will concede you this: you are to go
A twelvemonth and a day to seek and learn
Sufficient answer then you shall return.
I shall take gages[50] from you to extort
Surrender of your body to the court."
    Sad was the knight and sorrowfully sighed,
But there! All other choices were denied, 60
And in the end he chose to go away
And to return after a year and day
Armed with such answer as there might be sent
To him by God. He took his leave and went.
    He knocked at every house, searched every place,
Yes, anywhere that offered hope of grace.
What could it be that women wanted most?
But all the same he never touched a coast,
Country or town in which there seemed to be
Any two people willing to agree. 70
    Some said that women wanted wealth and treasure,
"Honour," said some, some "Jollity and pleasure,"
Some "Gorgeous clothes" and others "Fun in bed,"
"To be oft widowed and remarried," said
Others again, and some that what most mattered
Was that we should be cossetted and flattered.
That's very near the truth, it seems to me;
A man can win us best with flattery.
To dance attendance on us, make a fuss,

---

[46] **mead** Meadow.
[47] **Thorpes** Villages.
[48] **incubus** Evil spirit.
[49] **took her maidenhead** The knight raped the maiden.

---

[50] **gages** Pledges.

Ensnares us all, the best and worst of us.　80
Some say the things we most desire are these:
Freedom to do exactly as we please,
With no one to reprove our faults and lies,
Rather to have one call us good and wise.
Truly there's not a woman in ten score
Who has a fault, and someone rubs the sore,
But she will kick if what he says is true;
You try it out and you will find so too.
However vicious we may be within
We like to be thought wise and void of sin.　90
Others assert we women find it sweet
When we are thought dependable, discreet
And secret, firm of purpose and controlled,
Never betraying things that we are told.
But that's not worth the handle of a rake;
Women conceal a thing? For Heaven's sake!
Remember Midas? Will you hear the tale?

　Among some other little things, now stale,
Ovid[51] relates that under his long hair
The unhappy Midas grew a splendid pair　100
Of ass's ears; as subtly as he might,
He kept his foul deformity from sight;
Save for his wife, there was not one that knew.
He loved her best, and trusted in her too.
He begged her not to tell a living creature
That he possessed so horrible a feature.
And she—she swore, were all the world to win,
She would not do such villainy and sin
As saddle her husband with so foul a name;
Besides to speak would be to share the shame.　110
Nevertheless she thought she would have died
Keeping this secret bottled up inside;
It seemed to swell her heart and she, no doubt,
Thought it was on the point of bursting out.

　Fearing to speak of it to woman or man,
Down to a reedy marsh she quickly ran
And reached the sedge.[52] Her heart was all on fire
And, as a bittern bumbles in the mire,[53]
She whispered to the water, near the ground,
"Betray me not, O water, with thy sound!　120
To thee alone I tell it: it appears
My husband has a pair of ass's ears!
Ah! My heart's well again, the secret's out!
I could no longer keep it, not a doubt."
And so you see, although we may hold fast
A little while, it must come out at last,
We can't keep secrets; as for Midas, well,
Read Ovid for his story; he will tell.

　This knight that I am telling you about
Perceived at last he never would find out　130
What it could be that women loved the best.

Faint was the soul within his sorrowful breast
As home he went, he dared no longer stay;
His year was up and now it was the day.

　As he rode home in a dejected mood,
Suddenly, at the margin of a wood,
He saw a dance upon the leafy floor
Of four and twenty ladies, nay, and more.
Eagerly he approached, in hope to learn
Some words of wisdom ere he should return;　140
But lo! Before he came to where they were,
Dancers and dance all vanished into air!
There wasn't a living creature to be seen
Save one old woman crouched upon the green.
A fouler-looking creature I suppose
Could scarcely be imagined. She arose
And said, "Sir knight, there's no way on from here.
Tell me what you are looking for, my dear,
For peradventure that were best for you;
We old, old women know a thing or two."　150

　"Dear Mother," said the knight, "alack the day!
I am as good as dead if I can't say
What thing it is that women most desire;
If you could tell me I would pay your hire."
"Give me your hand," she said, "and swear to do
Whatever I shall next require of you
—If so to do should lie within your might—
And you shall know the answer before night."
"Upon my honour," he answered, "I agree."
"Then," said the crone,[54] "I dare to guarantee　160
Your life is safe; I shall make good my claim.
Upon my life the queen will say the same.
Show me the very proudest of them all
In costly cover chief or jewelled caul
That dare say no to what I have to teach.
Let us go forward without further speech."
And then she crooned her gospel in his ear
And told him to be glad and not to fear.

　They came to court. This knight, in full array,
Stood forth and said, "O Queen, I've kept my day　170
And kept my word and have my answer ready."

　There sat the noble matrons and the heady
Young girls, and widows too, that have the grace
Of wisdom, all assembled in that place,
And there the queen herself was throned to hear
And judge his answer. Then the knight drew near
And silence was commanded through the hall.

　The queen then bade the knight to tell them all
What thing it was that women wanted most.
He stood not silent like a beast or post,　180
But gave his answer with the ringing word
Of a man's voice and the assembly heard:

　"My liege and lady, in general," said he,
"A woman wants the self-same sovereignty
Over her husband as over her lover,
And master him; he must not be above her.
That is your greatest wish, whether you kill
Or spare me; please yourself. I wait your will."

---

[51] **Ovid** The Roman author who wrote the story about Midas and his ears in *Metamorphoses II*. Ovid based his story on one of the ancient myths about King Midas of Phrygia.
[52] **sedge** A type of tufted marsh plant.
[53] **And, as a bittern bumbles in the mire** The bittern is a bird that, according to popular lore, produced its cry by sticking its beak in the mud and bumbling or droning.

---

[54] **crone** Hag.

In all the court not one that shook her head
Or contradicted what the knight had said;
Maid, wife and widow cried, "He's saved his life!"   190

    And on the word up started the old wife,
The one the knight saw sitting on the green,
And cried, "Your mercy, sovereign lady queen!
Before the court disperses, do me right!
'Twas I who taught this answer to the knight,
For which he swore, and pledged his honour to it,
That the first thing I asked of him he'd do it,
So far as it should lie within his might.
Before this court I ask you then, sir knight,   200
To keep your word and take me for your wife;
For well you know that I have saved your life.
If this be false, deny it on your sword!"

    "Alas!" he said, "Old lady, by the Lord
I know indeed that such was my behest,
But for God's love think of a new request,
Take all my goods, but leave my body free."
"A curse on us," she said, "if I agree!
I may be foul, I may be poor and old,
Yet will not choose to be, for all the gold   210
That's bedded in the earth or lies above,
Less than your wife, nay, than your very love!"

    "My love?" said he. "By Heaven, my damnation!
Alas that any of my race and station
Should ever make so foul a misalliance!"
Yet in the end his pleading and defiance
All went for nothing, he was forced to wed.
He takes his ancient wife and goes to bed.

    Now peradventure some may well suspect
A lack of care in me since I neglect   220
To tell of the rejoicings and display
Made at the feast upon their wedding-day.
I have but a short answer to let fall;
I say there was no joy or feast at all,
Nothing but heaviness of heart and sorrow.
He married her in private on the morrow
And all day long stayed hidden like an owl,
It was such torture that his wife looked foul.

    Great was the anguish churning in his head
When he and she were piloted to bed;   230
He wallowed back and forth in desperate style.
His ancient wife lay smiling all the while;
At last she said "Bless us! Is this, my dear,
How knights and wives get on together here?
Are these the laws of good King Arthur's house?
Are knights of his all so contemptuous?
I am your own beloved and your wife,
And I am she, indeed, that saved your life;
And certainly I never did you wrong.
Then why, this first of nights, so sad a song?   240
You're carrying on as if you were half-witted!
Say, for God's love, what sin have I committed?
I'll put things right if you will tell me how."

    "Put right?" he cried. "That never can be now!
Nothing can ever be put right again!
You're old, and so abominably plain,
So poor to start with, so low-bred to follow;
It's little wonder if I twist and wallow!

God, that my heart would burst within my breast!"
    "Is that," said she, "the cause of your unrest?"   250
    "Yes, certainly," he said, "and can you wonder?"
    "I could set right what you suppose a blunder,
That's if I cared to, in a day or two,
If I were shown more courtesy by you.
Just now," she said, "you spoke of gentle birth,
Such as descends from ancient wealth and worth.
If that's the claim you make for gentlemen
Such arrogance is hardly worth a hen.
Whoever loves to work for virtuous ends,
Public and private, and who most intends   260
To do what deeds of gentleness he can,
Take him to be the greatest gentleman.
Christ wills we take our gentleness from Him,
Not from a wealth of ancestry long dim,
Though they bequeath their whole establishment
By which we claim to be of high descent.
Our fathers cannot make us a bequest
Of all those virtues that became them best
And earned for them the name of gentleman,
But bade us follow them as best we can.   270

    "Thus the wise poet of the Florentines,
Dante by name, has written in these lines,
For such is the opinion Dante launches:
'Seldom arises by these slender branches
Prowess of men, for it is God, no less,
Wills us to claim of Him our gentleness.'
For of our parents nothing can we claim
Save temporal things, and these may hurt and maim.

    "But everyone knows this as well as I;
For if gentility were implanted by   280
The natural course of lineage down the line,
Public or private, could it cease to shine
In doing the fair work of gentle deed?
No vice or villainy could then bear seed.

    "Take fire and carry it to the darkest house
Between this kingdom and the Caucasus,
And shut the doors on it and leave it there,
It will burn on, and it will burn as fair
As if ten thousand men were there to see,
For fire will keep its nature and degree,   290
I can assure you, sir, until it dies.

    "But gentleness, as you will recognize,
Is not annexed in nature to possessions,
Men fail in living up to their professions;
But fire never ceases to be fire.
God knows you'll often find, if you enquire,
Some lording full of villainy and shame.
If you would be esteemed for the mere name
Of having been by birth a gentleman
And stemming from some virtuous, noble clan,   300
And do not live yourself by gentle deed
Or take your father's noble code and creed,
You are no gentleman, though duke or earl.
Vice and bad manners are what make a churl.[55]

    "Gentility is only the renown

---

[55] **churl** A rude and ill-bred person.

For bounty that your fathers handed down,
Quite foreign to your person, not your own;
Gentility must come from God alone.
That we are gentle comes to us by grace
And by no means is it bequeathed with place.   310
    "Reflect how noble (says Valerius)
Was Tullius surnamed Hostilius,
Who rose from poverty to nobleness.
And read Boethius, Seneca no less,[56]
Thus they express themselves and are agreed:
'Gentle is he that does a gentle deed.'
And therefore, my dear husband, I conclude
That even if my ancestors were rude,
Yet God on high—and so I hope He will—
Can grant me grace to live in virtue still,   320
A gentlewoman only when beginning
To live in virtue and to shrink from sinning.
    "As for my poverty which you reprove,
Almighty God Himself in whom we move,
Believe and have our being, chose a life
Of poverty, and every man or wife
Nay, every child can see our Heavenly King
Would never stoop to choose a shameful thing.
No shame in poverty if the heart is gay,
As Seneca and all the learned say.   330
He who accepts his poverty unhurt
I'd say is rich although he lacked a shirt.
But truly poor are they who whine and fret
And covet what they cannot hope to get.
And he that, having nothing, covets not,
Is rich, though you may think he is a sot.
    "True poverty can find a song to sing.
Juvenal[57] says a pleasant little thing:
'The poor can dance and sing in the relief
Of having nothing that will tempt a thief.'   340
Though it be hateful, poverty is good,
A great incentive to a livelihood,
And a great help to our capacity
For wisdom, if accepted patiently.
Poverty is, though wanting in estate,
A kind of wealth that none calumniate.
Poverty often, when the heart is lowly,
Brings one to God and teaches what is holy,
Gives knowledge of oneself and even lends
A glass by which to see one's truest friends.   350
And since it's no offence, let me be plain;
Do not rebuke my poverty again.
    "Lastly you taxed me, sir, with being old.
Yet even if you never had been told
By ancient books, you gentlemen engage
Yourselves in honour to respect old age.

To call an old man 'father' shows good breeding,
And this could be supported from my reading.
    "You say I'm old and fouler than a fen.[58]
You need not fear to be a cuckold, then.   360
Filth and old age, I'm sure you will agree,
Are powerful wardens upon chastity.
Nevertheless, well knowing your delights,
I shall fulfil your worldly appetites.
"You have two choices; which one will you try?
To have me old and ugly till I die,
But still a loyal, true and humble wife
That never will displease you all her life,
Or would you rather I were young and pretty
And chance your arm what happens in a city   370
Where friends will visit you because of me,
Yes, and in other places too, maybe.
Which would you have? The choice is all your own."
    The knight thought long, and with a piteous groan
At last he said, with all the care in life,
"My lady and my love, my dearest wife,
I leave the matter to your wise decision.
You make the choice yourself, for the provision
Of what may be agreeable and rich
In honour to us both, I don't care which;   380
Whatever pleases you suffices me."
    "And have I won the mastery?" said she,
"Since I'm to choose and rule as I think fit?"
"Certainly, wife," he answered her, "that's it."
"Kiss me," she cried. "No quarrels! On my oath
And word of honour, you shall find me both,
That is, both fair and faithful as a wife;
May I go howling mad and take my life
Unless I prove to be as good and true
As ever wife was since the world was new!   390
And if to-morrow when the sun's above
I seem less fair than any lady-love,
Than any queen or empress east or west,
Do with my life and death as you think best.
Cast up the curtain, husband. Look at me!"
    And when indeed the knight had looked to see,
Lo, she was young and lovely, rich in charms.
In ecstasy he caught her in his arms,
His heart went bathing in a bath of blisses
And melted in a hundred thousand kisses,   400
And she responded in the fullest measure
With all that could delight or give him pleasure.
    So they lived ever after to the end
In perfect bliss; and may Christ Jesus send
Us husbands meek and young and fresh in bed,
And grace to overbid them when we wed.
And—Jesu hear my prayer!—cut short the lives
Of those who won't be governed by their wives;
And all old, angry niggards of their pence,
God send them soon a very pestilence!   410

---

[56] **Valerius, Tullius Hostilius, Boethius, Seneca** Valerius Maximus, a Roman author, wrote about Tullius Hostilius, a legendary king of Rome. Boethius was an early Christian philosopher, and Seneca was a Roman writer and playwright. The three authors wrote on the nature of human character and values.
[57] **Juvenal** Roman poet and satirist.

---

[58] **fen** A marshy land or boggy area.

Questions for Critical Thinking

1. Cite three pilgrims from the Prologue, describe their work and personality, and note how they characterize human traits common to all of us.

2. What did the knight do to get himself into trouble, and how does he get himself out of trouble and win his true love? Given what the knight did, do you think the outcome of the tale is just and fair?

CHRISTINE DE PIZAN
Selections from *The Book of the City of Ladies*

History pretty much overlooked Christine de Pizan's *The Book of the City of Ladies* (1405) for almost 550 years, until the upsurge of feminism after World War II. Although the author was recognized as a minor poet, this book, existing in four manuscript copies, remained almost unknown. Recently, because of its topical theme—the problem of female authority—feminists have rescued the book from oblivion. Today, it is accepted as one of the earliest feminist texts, and its author is hailed as the first to identify the "woman question"—a central concern in the West's ongoing intellectual debate.

Christine's *City of Ladies* was a late medieval salvo fired in the perennial battle of the sexes. It was meant to counter the misogyny (hatred of women) of men who claimed that women were innately inferior because female frailty descended from Eve, the first mother. It avoided the thorny debate over Eve and, forecasting a modern view, assumed woman's basic morality and goodness. Although medieval in its reasoning style and antidemocratic ideas, this book is a seminal work of Western literature.

In form, the *City of Ladies* is an allegorical debate modeled on Boethius's *Consolation of Philosophy* (see Chapter 8). The debate members are Christine herself and the three Virtues who appear in a waking dream. Dressed as goddesses, the Virtues are Lady Reason, carrying a mirror, who shows viewers their true images; Lady Rectitude, carrying a ruler, who divides good from evil; and Lady Justice, holding a measuring cup, who sets limits to earthly things. They offer Christine moral guidance as she frames an ideal city where women will be safe for all time from misogynist attack.

The Book of the City of Ladies consists of three "books," or chapters. Lady Reason dominates the first book, praising women who founded cities and cultural institutions. Lady Rectitude holds forth in the second book, telling stories of female seers and offering insight into mother-child and husband-wife relations. The third book features Lady Justice's tales of saints' lives, mainly of martyrs.

Christine de Pizan's (1364–ca. 1430) sensitivity to women's issues sprang from her marginal status as an Italian at the French court. She was moved there by her Venetian father, who served as court astrologer, and she later wed a court secretary. Marginalized even more by her husband's death in 1389, she supported her family through writing, with patronage from the French kings and the dukes of Burgundy. She was France's first professional woman of letters.

Reading the Selections

These selections are taken from Books I and II of *City of Ladies*. In section I.1, Christine explains her book's purpose: to reject the misogynist's view that "women [are] inclined to and full of every vice." In section I.27, Lady Reason advances the radical notion that women and men, though unequal physically, are equal mentally, if given equal access to education and public careers. In section II.36, Dame Rectitude argues that the sexes should have the same education, especially in morality.

∽

Book I

1. Here Begins the Book of the City of Ladies, Whose First Chapter Tells Why and for What Purpose This Book Was Written.

One day as I was sitting alone in my study surrounded by books on all kinds of subjects, devoting myself to literary studies, my usual habit, my mind dwelt at length on the weighty opinions of various authors whom I had studied for a long time. I looked up from my book, having decided to leave such subtle questions in peace and to relax by reading some light poetry. With this in mind, I searched for some small book. By chance a strange volume came into my hands, not one of my own, but one which had been given to me along with some others. When I held it open and saw from its title page that it was by Mathéolus,[59] I smiled, for though I had never seen it before, I had often heard that like other books it discussed respect for women. I thought I would browse through it to amuse myself. I had not been reading for very long when my good mother called me to refresh myself with some supper, for it was evening. Intending to look at it the next day, I put it down. The next morning, again seated in my study as was my habit, I remembered wanting to examine this book by Mathéolus. I started to read it and went on for a little while. Because the subject seemed to me not very pleasant for people who do not enjoy lies, and of no use in developing virtue or manners, given its lack of integrity in diction and theme, and after browsing here and there and reading the end, I put it down in order to turn my attention to more elevated and useful study. But just the sight of this book, even though it was of no authority, made me wonder how it happened that so many different men—and learned men among them—have been and are so inclined to express both in speaking and in

their treatises and writings so many wicked insults about women and their behavior. Not only one or two and not even just this Mathéolus (for this book had a bad name anyway and was intended as a satire) but, more generally, judging from the treatises of all philosophers and poets and from all the orators—it would take too long to mention their names—it seems that they all speak from one and the same mouth. They all concur in one conclusion: that the behavior of women is inclined to and full of every vice. Thinking deeply about these matters, I began to examine my character and conduct as a natural woman and, similarly, I considered other women whose company I frequently kept, princesses, great ladies, women of the middle and lower classes, who had graciously told me of their most private and intimate thoughts, hoping that I could judge impartially and in good conscience whether the testimony of so many notable men could be true. To the best of my knowledge, no matter how long I confronted or dissected the problem, I could not see or realize how their claims could be true when compared to the natural behavior and character of women. Yet I still argued vehemently against women, saying that it would be impossible that so many famous men—such solemn scholars, possessed of such deep and great understanding, so clear-sighted in all things, as it seemed—could have spoken falsely on so many occasions that I could hardly find a book on morals where, even before I had read it in its entirety, I did not find several chapters or certain sections attacking women, no matter who the author was. This reason alone, in short, made me conclude that, although my intellect did not perceive my own great faults and, likewise, those of other women because of its simpleness and ignorance, it was however truly fitting that such was the case. And so I relied more on the judgment of others than on what I myself felt and knew. I was so transfixed in this line of thinking for such a long time that it seemed as if I were in a stupor. Like a gushing fountain, a series of authorities, whom I recalled one after another, came to mind, along with their opinions on this topic. And I finally decided that God formed a vile creature when He made woman, and I wondered how such a worthy artisan could have deigned to make such an abominable work which, from

---

[59] **Mathéolus** Mathieu of Boulogne, or Mathéolus, was the author of *The Lamentations of Mathéolus,* written about 1295. Mathéolus, a confirmed misogynist, or woman hater, advised his readers on all the ills and evils of women. Christine de Pizan uses his work as a foil to begin her defense and admiration for women.

what they say, is the vessel as well as the refuge and abode of every evil and vice. As I was thinking this, a great unhappiness and sadness welled up in my heart, for I detested myself and the entire feminine sex, as though we were monstrosities in nature. And in my lament I spoke these words:

"Oh, God, how can this be? For unless I stray from my faith, I must never doubt that Your infinite wisdom and most perfect goodness ever created anything which was not good. Did You yourself not create woman in a very special way and since that time did You not give her all those inclinations which it pleased You for her to have? And how could it be that You could go wrong in anything? Yet look at all these accusations which have been judged, decided, and concluded against women. I do not know how to understand this repugnance. If it is so, fair Lord God, that in fact so many abominations abound in the female sex, for You Yourself say that the testimony of two or three witnesses lends credence, why shall I not doubt that this is true? Alas, God, why did You not let me be born in the world as a man, so that all my inclinations would be to serve You better, and so that I would not stray in anything and would be as perfect as a man is said to be? But since Your kindness has not been extended to me, then forgive my negligence in Your service, most fair Lord God, and may it not displease You, for the servant who receives fewer gifts from his lord is less obliged in his service." I spoke these words to God in my lament and a great deal more for a very long time in sad reflection, and in my folly I considered myself most unfortunate because God had made me inhabit a female body in this world. . . .

27. Christine Asks Reason Whether God Has Ever Wished to Ennoble the Mind of Woman with the Loftiness of the Sciences; and Reason's Answer.

After hearing these things, I replied to the lady who spoke infallibly: "My lady, truly has God revealed great wonders in the strength of these women whom you describe. But please enlighten me again, whether it has ever pleased this God, who has bestowed so many favors on women, to honor the feminine sex with the privilege of the virtue of high understanding and great learning, and whether women ever have a clever enough mind for this. I wish very much to know this because men maintain that the mind of women can learn only a little."

She answered, "My daughter, since I told you before, you know quite well that the opposite of their opinion is true, and to show you this even more clearly, I will give you proof through examples. I tell you again—and don't doubt the contrary—if it were customary to send daughters to school like sons, and if they were then taught the natural sciences, they would learn as thoroughly and understand the subtleties of all the arts and sciences as well as sons. And by chance there happen to be such women, for, as I touched on before, just as women have

more delicate bodies than men, weaker and less able to perform many tasks, so do they have minds that are freer and sharper whenever they apply themselves."

"My lady, what are you saying? With all due respect, could you dwell longer on this point, please. Certainly men would never admit this answer is true, unless it is explained more plainly, for they believe that one normally sees that men know more than women do."

She answered, "Do you know why women know less?"

"Not unless you tell me, my lady."

"Without the slightest doubt, it is because they are not involved in many different things, but stay at home, where it is enough for them to run the household, and there is nothing which so instructs a reasonable creature as the exercise and experience of many different things."

"My lady, since they have minds skilled in conceptualizing and learning, just like men, why don't women learn more?"

She replied, "Because, my daughter, the public does not require them to get involved in the affairs which men are commissioned to execute, just as I told you before. It is enough for women to perform the usual duties to which they are ordained. As for judging from experience, since one sees that women usually know less than men, that therefore their capacity for understanding is less, look at men who farm the flatlands or who live in the mountains. You will find that in many countries they seem completely savage because they are so simple-minded. All the same, there is no doubt that Nature provided them with the qualities of body and mind found in the wisest and most learned men. All of this stems from a failure to learn, though, just as I told you, among men and women, some possess better minds than others. Let me tell you about women who have possessed great learning and profound understanding and treat the question of the similarity of women's minds to men's."

30. Here She Speaks of Sappho, That Most Subtle Woman, Poet, and Philosopher.

"The wise Sappho, who was from the city of Mytilene, was no less learned than Proba. This Sappho had a beautiful body and face and was agreeable and pleasant in appearance, conduct, and speech. But the charm of her profound understanding surpassed all the other charms with which she was endowed, for she was expert and learned in several arts and sciences, and she was not only well-educated in the works and writings composed by others but also discovered many new things herself and wrote many books and poems. Concerning her, Boccaccio[60] has offered these fair words couched in the sweetness of poetic language: 'Sappho, possessed of sharp wit and burning desire for

---

[60] **Boccaccio** The renowned fourteenth-century Italian poet and author who wrote *On Famous Women,* in which he planned to extol the virtues of many women. He finished chapters on only four women.

constant study in the midst of bestial and ignorant men, frequented the heights of Mount Parnassus, that is, of perfect study. Thanks to her fortunate boldness and daring, she kept company with the Muses, that is, the arts and sciences, without being turned away. She entered the forest of laurel trees filled with may boughs, greenery, and different colored flowers, soft fragrances and various aromatic spices, where Grammar, Logic, noble Rhetoric, Geometry, and Arithmetic live and take their leisure. She went on her way until she came to the deep grotto of Apollo, god of learning, and found the brook and conduit of the fountain of Castalia, and took up the plectrum and quill of the harp and played sweet melodies, with the nymphs all the while leading the dance, that is, following the rules of harmony and musical accord.' From what Boccaccio says about her, it should be inferred that the profundity of both her understanding and of her learned books could only be known and understood by men of great perception and learning, according to the testimony of the ancients. Her writings and poems have survived to this day, most remarkably constructed and composed, and they serve as illumination and models of consummate poetic craft and composition to those who have come afterward. She invented different genres of lyric and poetry, short narratives, tearful laments and strange lamentations about love and other emotions, and these were so well made and so well ordered that they were named 'Sapphic' after her. Horace recounts, concerning her poems, that when Plato, the great philosopher who was Aristotle's teacher, died, a book of Sappho's poems was found under his pillow.

"In brief this lady was so outstanding in learning that in the city where she resided a statue of bronze in her image was dedicated in her name and erected in a prominent place so that she would be honored by all and be remembered forever. This lady was placed and counted among the greatest and most famous poets, and according to Boccaccio, the honors of the diadems and crowns of kings and the miters of bishops are not any greater, nor are the crowns of laurel and victor's palm.

"I could tell you a great deal about women of great learning. Leontium was a Greek woman and also such a great philosopher that she dared, for impartial and serious reasons, to correct and attack the philosopher Theophrastus,[61] who was quite famous in her time."

34. Here She Speaks of Minerva, Who Invented Many Sciences and the Technique of Making Armor from Iron and Steel.

"Minerva, just as you have written elsewhere, was a maiden of Greece and surnamed Pallas. This maiden was of such excellence of mind that the foolish people of that time, because they did not know who her parents were and saw her doing things which had never been done

---

[61] **Theophrastus** Greek philosopher and scientist, a disciple of Aristotle and his successor. Lived in fourth and third centuries BCE.

before, said she was a goddess descended from Heaven; for the less they knew about her ancestry, the more marvelous her great knowledge seemed to them, when compared to that of the women of her time. She had a subtle mind, of profound understanding, not only in one subject but also generally, in every subject. Through her ingenuity she invented a shorthand Greek script in which a long written narrative could be transcribed with far fewer letters, and which is still used by the Greeks today, a fine invention whose discovery demanded great subtlety. She invented numbers and a means of quickly counting and adding sums. Her mind was so enlightened with general knowledge that she devised various skills and designs which had never before been discovered. She developed the entire technique of gathering wool and making cloth and was the first who ever thought to shear sheep of their wool and then to pick, comb, and card it with iron spindles and finally to spin it with a distaff, and then she invented the tools needed to make the cloth and also the method by which the wool should finally be woven.

"Similarly she initiated the custom of extracting oil from different fruits of the earth, also from olives, and of squeezing and pressing juice from other fruits. At the same time she discovered how to make wagons and carts to transport things easily from one place to another.

"This lady, in a similar manner, did even more, and it seems all the more remarkable because it is far removed from a woman's nature to conceive of such things; for she invented the art and technique of making harnesses and armor from iron and steel, which knights and armed soldiers employ in battle and with which they cover their bodies, and which she first gave to the Athenians whom she taught how to deploy an army and battalions and how to fight in organized ranks.

"Similarly she was the first to invent flutes and fifes, trumpets and wind instruments. With her considerable force of mind, this lady remained a virgin her entire life. Because of her outstanding chastity, the poets claimed in their fictions that Vulcan, the god of fire, wrestled with her for a long time and that finally she won and overcame him, which is to say that she overcame the ardor and lusts of the flesh which so strongly assail the young. The Athenians held this maiden in such high reverence that they worshiped her as a goddess and called her the goddess of arms and chivalry because she was the first to devise their use, and they also called her the goddess of knowledge because of her learnedness.

"After her death they erected a temple in Athens dedicated to her, and there they placed a statue of her, portraying a maiden, as a representation of wisdom and chivalry. This statue had terrible and cruel eyes because chivalry has been instituted to carry out rigorous justice; they also signified that one seldom knows toward what end the meditation of the wise man tends. She wore a helmet on her head which signified that a knight must have strength, endurance, and constant courage in the deeds of arms, and further signified that the counsels of the wise are concealed, secret, and hidden. She was dressed in a coat of mail which stood for the power of the estate of chivalry and also taught that the wise man is always armed against the whims of Fortune, whether good or bad. She held some kind of spear or very long lance, which meant that the knight must be the rod of justice and also signified that the wise man casts his spears from great distances. A buckler or shield of crystal hung at her neck, which meant that the knight must always be alert and oversee everywhere the defense of his country and people and further signified that things are open and evident to the wise man. She had portrayed in the middle of this shield the head of a serpent called Gorgon, which teaches that the knight must always be wary and watchful over his enemies like the serpent, and furthermore, that the wise man is aware of all the malice which can hurt him. Next to this image they also placed a bird that flies by night, named the owl, as if to watch over her, which signified that the knight must be ready by night as well as by day for civil defense, when necessary, and also that the wise man should take care at all times to do what is profitable and fitting for him. For a long time this lady was held in such high regard and her great fame spread so far that in many places temples were founded to praise her. Even long afterward, when the Romans were at the height of their power, they included her image among their gods."

Book II

36. Against Those Men Who Claim It Is Not Good for Women to Be Educated.

Following these remarks, I, Christine, spoke, "My lady, I realize that women have accomplished many good things and that even if evil women have done evil, it seems to me, nevertheless, that the benefits accrued and still accruing because of good women—particularly the wise and literary ones and those educated in the natural sciences whom I mentioned above—outweigh the evil. Therefore, I am amazed by the opinion of some men who claim that they do not want their daughters, wives, or kinswomen to be educated because their mores would be ruined as a result."

She responded, "Here you can clearly see that not all opinions of men are based on reason and that these men are wrong. For it must not be presumed that mores necessarily grow worse from knowing the moral sciences, which teach the virtues, indeed, there is not the slightest doubt that moral education amends and ennobles them. How could anyone think or believe that whoever follows good teaching or doctrine is the worse for it? Such an opinion cannot be expressed or maintained. I do not mean that it would be good for a man or a woman to study the art of divination or those fields of learning which are forbidden—for the holy Church did not remove them from common use without good reason—but it should not be believed that women are the worse for knowing what is good.

"Quintus Hortensius, a great rhetorician and consummately skilled orator in Rome, did not share this opinion. He had a daughter, named Hortensia, whom he greatly loved for the subtlety of her wit. He had her learn letters and study the science of rhetoric, which she mastered so thoroughly that she resembled her father Hortensius not only in wit and lively memory but also in her excellent delivery and order of speech—in fact, he surpassed her in nothing. As for the subject discussed above, concerning the good which comes about through women, the benefits realized by this woman and her learning were, among others, exceptionally remarkable. That is, during the time when Rome was governed by three men, this Hortensia began to support the cause of women and to undertake what no man dared to undertake. There was a question whether certain taxes should be levied on women and on their jewelry during a needy period in Rome. This woman's eloquence was so compelling that she was listened to, no less readily than her father would have been, and she won her case.

"Similarly, to speak of more recent times, without searching for examples in ancient history, Giovanni Andrea, a solemn law professor in Bologna not quite sixty years ago, was not of the opinion that it was bad for women to be educated. He had a fair and good daughter, named Novella, who was educated in the law to such an advanced degree that when he was occupied by some task and not at leisure to present his lectures to his students, he would send Novella, his daughter, in his place to lecture to the students from his chair. And to prevent her beauty from distracting the concentration of her audience, she had a little curtain drawn in front of her. In this manner she could on occasion supplement and lighten her father's occupation. He loved her so much that, to commemorate her name, he wrote a book of remarkable lectures on the law which he entitled *Novella super Decretalium*, after his daughter's name.

"Thus, not all men (and especially the wisest) share the opinion that it is bad for women to be educated. But it is very true that many foolish men have claimed this because it displeased them that women knew more than they did. Your father, who was a great scientist and philosopher, did not believe that women were worth less by knowing science; rather, as you know, he took great pleasure from seeing your inclination to learning. The feminine opinion of your mother, however, who wished to keep you busy with spinning and silly girlishness, following the common custom of women, was the major obstacle to your being more involved in the sciences. But just as the proverb already mentioned above says, 'No one can take away what Nature has given,' your mother could not hinder in you the feeling for the sciences which you, through natural inclination, had nevertheless gathered together in little droplets. I am sure that, on account of these things, you do not think you are worth less but rather that you consider it a great treasure for yourself; and you doubtless have reason to."

And I, Christine, replied to all of this, "Indeed, my lady, what you say is as true as the Lord's Prayer."

Questions for Critical Thinking

1. How does Christine de Pizan set up her argument and then begin to answer her critic?

2. Discuss Dame Rectitude's argument that both men and women should have the same education. Do you agree with her reasons? Would they apply to education today?

12

THE EARLY RENAISSANCE
Return to Classical Roots
1400–1494

GIOVANNI PICO DELLA MIRANDOLA
Selections from *On the Dignity of Man*

The Latin oration *On the Dignity of Man* is a tour de force by Pico (1463–1494), a son of the noble house of Mirandola (Italy). Written when Pico was twenty-four, the oration is a mixture of Aristotelian, Hebraic, Arabic, Persian, and Aramaic notions held together by Neoplatonism— a blend of Plato's ideas and Christian beliefs. Its central Neoplatonic motif is that love is the divine glue unifying the universe. Christian in structure, this synthesis of ideas breaks free of its frame to become a nonsectarian philosophy.

Pico's oration embodies the Renaissance spirit. In its appeal to wide-ranging sources, it expresses Renaissance zeal for the classic texts of Greece and Rome as well as hitherto ignored ancient sources. Its theme is the Renaissance belief that the findings of reason and the truths of the Bible share a basic unity that is reflected in the history of thought. Most of all, its view that human nature has no limits is the prototype of the Renaissance idea of unlimited possibility. Today this idea, with its corollary of free expression, is a defining trait of Western culture.

The oration was composed to introduce a debate Pico scheduled for Rome in 1487. In this debate, Pico proposed to defend nine hundred theses gleaned from his vast readings; he even offered to pay his potential opponents' travel expenses. The debate, however, did not take place because Pope Innocent VIII (pope 1484–1492) forbade it. The pope also appointed a commission to examine the debate topics, with the result that seven theses were condemned as heretical and six more were suspect. Threatened by church officials, Pico subsequently settled in Florence, where he was caught up in the anti-Renaissance crusade of the monk Savonarola. Pico's plan to wander as an evangelist was cut short in 1494, when he died suddenly at age thirty-one.

Reading the Selections

The first selection from the oration *On the Dignity of Man* begins with a greeting—"Most venerable fathers"—thus establishing that the work was meant to be recited orally, ostensibly before a group of clergy. The major insights to be gained from this selection are Pico's concept of human nature and his style of reasoning.

Pico's concept of human nature is his major contribution to Western thought. For him, human nature is not fixed, and the will is perfectly free. In a burst of lyricism, he claimed that human beings are shape-shifting creatures who may be vegetative, bestial, rational, divine, or even co-equal with God: When humanity's quest ends, "We shall . . . not be ourselves, but He himself who made us." Brushing aside medieval ideas, Pico expresses the radiant faith of Renaissance humanism, that human beings are not flawed by original sin but are capable of becoming godlike.

Pico's style of reasoning reflects the Renaissance trend of treating old problems in new ways. To deal with the question of human nature, he takes the Platonic concept of the Great Chain of Being, which maintains that creation is a linked cord reaching step by step from the simplest life to God, and gives it a modern twist. Ancient thinkers had used the Great Chain of Being to argue that human potential is limited, since the place of human beings in the chain is fixed, and that change would destroy the whole creation. In contrast, Pico claimed that human beings may make of themselves anything they please, because as hybrids of the whole creation, they exist both outside and above the Great Chain of Being.

∞

Most venerable fathers, I have read in the records of the Arabians that Abdul the Saracen, on being asked what thing on, so to speak, the world's stage, he viewed as most greatly worthy of wonder, answered that he viewed nothing more wonderful than man. And Mercury's, "a great wonder, Asclepius, is man!" agrees with that opinion. On thinking over the reason for these sayings, I was not satisfied by the many assertions made by many men concerning the outstandingness of human nature: that man is the messenger between creatures, familiar with the upper and king of the lower; by the sharpsightedness of the senses, by the hunting-power of reason, and by the light of intelligence, the interpreter of nature; the part in between the standstill of eternity and the flow of time, and, as the Persians say, the bond tying the world together, nay, the nuptial bond; and, according to David,[1] "a little lower than the angels." These reasons are great but not the chief ones, that is, they are not reasons for a lawful claim to the highest wonder as to a prerogative. Why should we not wonder more at the angels themselves and at the very blessed heavenly choirs?

Finally, it seemed to me that I understood why man is the animal that is most happy, and is therefore worthy of all wonder; and lastly, what the state is that is allotted to man in the succession of things, and that is capable of arousing envy not only in the brutes but also in the stars and even in minds beyond the world. It is wonderful and beyond belief. For this is the reason why man is rightly said and thought to be a great marvel and the animal

really worthy of wonder. Now hear what it is, fathers; and with kindly ears and for the sake of your humanity, give me your close attention:

Now the highest Father, God the master-builder, had, by the laws of his secret wisdom, fabricated this house, this world which we see, a very superb temple of divinity. He had adorned the super-celestial region with minds. He had animated the celestial globes with eternal souls; he had filled with a diverse throng of animals the cast-off and residual parts of the lower world. But, with the work finished, the Artisan desired that there be someone to reckon up the reason of such a big work, to love its beauty, and to wonder at its greatness. Accordingly, now that all things had been completed, as Moses and Timaeus[2] testify, He lastly considered creating man. But there was nothing in the archetypes from which He could mold a new sprout, nor anything in His storehouses which He could bestow as a heritage upon a new son, nor was there an empty judiciary seat where this contemplator of the universe could sit. Everything was filled up; all things had been laid out in the highest, the lowest, and the middle orders. But it did not belong to the paternal power to have failed in the final parturition, as though exhausted by child-bearing; it did not belong to wisdom, in a case of necessity, to have been tossed back and forth through want of a plan; it did not belong to the loving-kindness which was going to praise divine liberality in others to be forced to condemn itself. Finally, the best of workmen decided that that to which nothing of its very own could be given should be, in composite fashion, whatsoever had belonged individually to each and every thing. Therefore He took up man, a work of indeterminate form; and, placing him at the midpoint of the world, He spoke to him as follows:

[1] **Abdul the Saracen, Mercury, Asclepius, David** Pico is including various sources to show that man is a wonder in himself and worthy of study and praise. Abdul the Saracen is probably the famous Arabian physician, Abul Kassim, who wrote a medical textbook used for more than five hundred years in Europe. Mercury is the Roman god of merchants and traders who, by the Renaissance, was seen as a symbol of the human intellect and the mediator between the human mind and divine wisdom. Asclepius was the Greek god of healing; he became a Roman god in the third century BCE after a plague. King David of the Old Testament was often referenced by writers and scholars for his wisdom as recorded in the Bible.

[2] **Moses and Timaeus** Moses, from the Old Testament, to whom God gave the Ten Commandments, and who led his people to the Promised Land, was considered a strong and wise leader. Timaeus was a Greek philosopher who was the major voice in Plato's work *Timaeus*. The dialogue refers to the creation of the world that Christians later associated with God as the creator. The Neoplatonists used Timaeus in their works against the Aristotelians and Scholasticism.

"We have given to thee, Adam, no fixed seat, no form of thy very own, no gift peculiarly thine, that thou mayest feel as thine own, have as thine own, possess as thine own the seat, the form, the gifts which thou thyself shalt desire. A limited nature in other creatures is confined within the laws written down by Us. In conformity with thy free judgment, in whose hand We have placed thee, thou art confined by no bounds; and thou wilt fix limits of nature for thyself. I have placed thee at the center of the world, that from there thou mayest more conveniently look around and see whatsoever is in the world. Neither heavenly nor earthly, neither mortal nor immortal have We made thee. Thou, like a judge appointed for being honorable, art the molder and maker of thyself; thou mayest sculpt thyself into whatever shape thou dost prefer. Thou canst grow downward into the lower natures which are brutes. Thou canst again grow upward from thy soul's reason into the higher natures which are divine."

O great liberality of God the Father! O great and wonderful happiness of man. It is given him to have that which he chooses and to be that which he wills. As soon as brutes are born, they bring with them, "from their dam's bag," as Lucilius[3] says, what they are going to possess. Highest spirits have been, either from the beginning or soon after, that which they are going to be throughout everlasting eternity. At man's birth the Father placed in him every sort of seed and sprouts of every kind of life. The seeds that each man cultivates will grow and bear their fruit in him. If he cultivates vegetable seeds, he will become a plant. If the seeds of sensation, he will grow into brute. If rational, he will come out a heavenly animal. If intellectual, he will be an angel, and a son of God. And if he is not contented with the lot of any creature but takes himself up into the center of his own unity, then, made one spirit with God and settled in the solitary darkness of the Father, who is above all things, he will stand ahead of all things. Who does not wonder at this chameleon which we are? Or who at all feels more wonder at anything else whatsoever? It was not unfittingly that Asclepius the Athenian said that man was symbolized by Prometheus in the secret rites, by reason of our nature sloughing its skin and transforming itself; hence metamorphoses were popular among the Jews and the Pythagoreans.[4] For the more secret Hebrew theology at one time reshapes holy Enoch[5] into an angel of divinity, whom they call *malach hashechina*, and at other times reshapes other men into other divinities. According to the Pythagoreans, wicked men are deformed into brutes and, if you believe Empedocles,[6] into plants too. And copying them, Maumeth [Mohammed] often had it on his lips

that he who draws back from divine law becomes a brute. And his saying so was reasonable: for it is not the rind which makes the plant, but a dull and non-sentient nature; not the hide which makes a beast of burden, but a brutal and sensual soul; not the spherical body which makes the heavens, but right reason; and not a separateness from the body but a spiritual intelligence which makes an angel. For example, if you see a man given over to his belly and crawling upon the ground, it is a bush not a man that you see. If you see anyone blinded by the illusions of his empty and Calypso-like[7] imagination, seized by the desire of scratching, and delivered over to the senses, it is a brute not a man that you see. If you come upon a philosopher winnowing out all things by right reason, he is a heavenly not an earthly animal. If you come upon a pure contemplator, ignorant of the body, banished to the innermost places of the mind, he is not an earthly, not a heavenly animal; he more superbly is a divinity clothed with human flesh.

Who is there that does not wonder at man? And it is not unreasonable that in the mosaic and Christian holy writ man is sometimes denoted by the name "all flesh" and at other times by that of "every creature"; and man fashions, fabricates, transforms himself into the shape of all flesh, into the character of every creature. Accordingly, where Evantes the Persian tells of the Chaldaean theology, he writes that man is not any inborn image of himself, but many images coming in from the outside: hence that saying of the Chaldaeans: *enosh hu shinuy vekamah tevaoth baal chayim*, that is, man is an animal of diverse, multiform, and destructible nature.

But why all this? In order for us to understand that, after having been born in this state so that we may be what we will to be, then, since we are held in honor, we ought to take particular care that no one may say against us that we do not know that we are made similar to brutes and mindless beasts of burden. But rather, as Asaph[8] the prophet says: "Ye are all gods, and sons of the most high," unless by abusing the very indulgent liberality of the Father, we make the free choice, which he gave to us, harmful to ourselves instead of helpful toward salvation. Let a certain holy ambition invade the mind, so that we may not be content with mean things but may aspire to the highest things and strive with all our forces to attain them: for if we will to, we can. Let us spurn earthly things; let us struggle toward the heavenly. Let us put in last place whatever is of the world; and let us fly beyond the chambers of the world to the chamber nearest the most lofty divinity. There, as the sacred mysteries reveal, the seraphim, cherubim, and thrones occupy the first places. Ignorant of how to yield to them and unable to endure the second places, let us compete with the angels in dignity and glory. When we have willed it, we shall be not at all below them. . . .

---

[3] **Lucilius** Roman poet, third and second century BCE, who supposedly originated the satirical form used by later Roman poets. Only fragments of his works remain.
[4] **Pythagoreans** Followers of the sixth-century BCE Greek philosopher and mathematician Pythagoras. The Pythagoreans contributed to the study of mathematics and astronomy.
[5] **Enoch** Biblical figure who, according to the book of Genesis, did not die as a mortal because "God took him."
[6] **Empedocles** Fifth-century BCE Greek philosopher who explained the physical world as composed of four elements controlled by Strife and Love.

---

[7] **Calypso-like** Calypso, the nymph who kept Odysseus on the island for seven years, was also associated with the "hidden"; thus, an illusion or one who creates illusions.
[8] **Asaph** Several Asaphs in the Old Testament. One was the Choirmaster during David's time; his name is connected to a small collection of psalms, and he is probably the one Pico is referencing in this passage.

. . .

Not only the Mosaic or Christian mysteries but also the theology of the ancients show the advantages for us and the dignity of these liberal arts about which I have come here to dispute. For what else is meant by the degrees of initiation that are customary in the secret rites of the Greeks? First, to those who had been purified by moral and dialectic arts, which we have called, as it were, purgative, befell the reception of the mysteries. And what else can this reception be but the interpretation of more hidden nature by means of philosophy? Then lastly, to those who had been thus prepared, came that ἐποπτεία, that is, a vision of divine things by means of the light of theology. Who does not seek to be initiated into such rites? Who does not set all human things at a lower value and, contemning the goods of fortune and neglecting the body, does not desire, while still continuing on earth, to become the drinking-companion of the gods; and, drunken with the nectar of eternity, to bestow the gift of immortality upon the mortal animal? Who does not wish to have breathed into him the Socratic frenzies sung by Plato in the *Phaedrus*, that by the oarlike movement of wings and feet he may quickly escape from here, that is, from this world where he is laid down as in an evil place, and be carried in speediest flight to the heavenly Jerusalem. We shall be possessed, fathers, we shall be possessed by these Socratic frenzies, which will so place us outside of our minds that they will place our mind and ourselves in God. We shall be possessed by them if we have first done what is in us to do. For if through morality the forces of the passions will have been so stretched to the [proper] measure, through due proportions, that they sound together in fixed concord, and if through dialectic, reason will have moved, keeping time in her forward march, then, aroused by the frenzy of the muses, we shall drink in the heavenly harmony of our ears. Then Bacchus the leader of the muses, in his own mysteries, that is, in the visible signs of nature, will show the invisible things of God to us as we philosophize, and will make us drunk with the abundance of the house of God. In this house, if we are faithful like Moses, holiest theology will approach, and will inspire us with a twofold frenzy. We, raised up into the loftiest watchtower of theology, from which, measuring with indivisible eternity the things that are, will be, and shall have been, and looking at their primeval beauty, shall be prophets of Phoebus,[9] his winged lovers, and finally, aroused with ineffable charity as with fire, placed outside of ourselves like burning Seraphim,[10] filled with divinity, we shall now not be ourselves, but He himself who made us.

---

[9] **Phoebus** Another name for Apollo, the Greek god of prophecy, the patron of music and poetry; also connected with the sun and, thus, the "shining one," as Phoebus is likewise called.
[10] **Seraphim** In the Hebrew tradition and Bible, they are supernatural beings associated with the presence of God. Pico is using both Phoebus and the Seraphim as images of light to lift the reader to new heights of knowledge and wisdom.

Questions for Critical Thinking

1. According to Pico, what are the ways man can exercise his free will and what can be the results of his using his free will?

2. Discuss and give examples of how Pico blends Christian and non-Christian sources to support his argument about the nature of man.

LEON BATTISTA ALBERTI
Selections from *On Painting* and *Dinner Pieces*

Leon Battista Alberti (1404–1472) was the "universal man," the beau ideal of the age, and his achievements rivaled those of the later Leonardo da Vinci. Besides painting, Alberti mastered music, mathematics, engineering, architecture, sculpture, poetry, drama, and civil and canon law and wrote books on most of these fields. A friend of Cosimo de' Medici (1389–1464), the merchant-banker who dominated Florence, Alberti was active in Cosimo's Platonic Academy, the club of artists and thinkers who studied Plato (see *Phaedo* and *The Republic* in Chapter 3).

Alberti's spirit had such force that his friends called him the complete genius, hence the authority attributed to his works.

Alberti's *On Painting* helped ensure the triumph of the new Renaissance style over older medieval art. Published in Latin (1435) and Italian (1436), this was the first modern treatise on the theory of painting. It became the era's authoritative guide for painters, both within and outside Florence, including Fra Angelico (ca. 1400–1455), Piero della Francesca (1420–1492), and perhaps Leonardo da Vinci (1452–1519). From 1600 until 1800, Alberti's treatise was invoked as an authority for painting practices approved by Europe's art academies. Today's historians still find this work invaluable, for it prepared the way for the art, the artist, and the patron of the Renaissance.

On Painting is divided into three "books," or parts. Book I presents a mathematical method for creating perspective—the illusion of depth on a flat surface. Book II deals with painterly matters, such as color, drawing, and grace and beauty in poses and movements. Book III sets forth a type of humanist painting that uses Greco-Roman themes and depicts the soul's condition through bodily gestures and facial expressions.

Alberti's *Dinner Pieces*, written between 1430 and 1440, consists of dialogues, stories, and fables. Never published during Alberti's lifetime, they remained scattered and in manuscript form until the late nineteenth century, and were finally edited and translated into English in the 1980s.

According to Alberti, his brief essays or "short books," as he labeled them, were "to be read over dinner and drinks." While many of these pieces were written to entertain readers, they also allowed the author to satirize popular subjects, ridicule his contemporaries, and initiate serious discussions.

In setting up conversations on particular topics, Alberti often spoke through two characters: Philoponius (from Greek, "lover of toil") and Lepidus (from Latin, "witty"). Lepidus is the voice out of the past, derived from Cynicism, the fourth-century BCE Hellenistic philosophy, which emphasized self-control and self-sufficiency and was later made popular during the Roman Empire by the Greek satirical writer, Lucian (ca. 120–after 180 CE). Alberti also borrowed from writers and thinkers, including Aesop, Petrarch (see "Letter to Posterity" in Chapter 11), Horace (see *Odes* in Chapter 5), Juvenal (see *Satire III* in Chapter 5), and Cicero (see *On the Republic* in Chapter 5). However, he did not mix Christian sources with classical references as did most Renaissance humanists.

Reading the Selections

The selection from Book II of *On Painting* shows Alberti as a Renaissance humanist, making the case for a radical new role for the age's painters. These painters are characterized by intellect, with the ascendancy of mind over hand visible in their art. This argument echoes the familiar rationale of humanists that studying and practicing grammar, rhetoric, logic, arithmetic, geometry, music, and astronomy—the seven liberal arts—are good exercises for the soul. What is radical in Alberti's claim is the ranking of painting with the liberal arts. During the Middle Ages, painting had ranked low, on a par with crafts (shoemaking, weaving, and such). The favorable reception of this treatise encouraged the rise of independent artists, as evidenced around 1500 in the careers of Michelangelo, Leonardo da Vinci, and Raphael.

Alberti also argued that painting should be part of the core curriculum of the schools. To prove his case, he used examples from antiquity showing that the best families required that painting be taught to their sons and daughters. By 1513, Alberti's hope was realized in the well-rounded backgrounds of the idealized lady and gentleman of Castiglione's highly influential *The Book of the Courtier*.

Finally, Alberti was a pioneer in his claim for the sovereign power of painting: "Who can doubt that painting is the master art?" A generation later Leonardo gave voice to the identical claim.

The four selections from *Dinner Pieces*—Religion, Wealth, Preface to Poggio Bracciolini, and The Clouds—summarize some of Alberti's philosophical interests, record his observations on contemporary Italian life, and showcase his satirical skills. In Religion (from Book One),

Alberti has Libripeta (from Latin, "seeker of books") and Lepidus engage in a conversation about the usefulness of worshiping in temples, the nature of the gods, and their relationships to humans. In Wealth (from Book Two), Alberti, speaking through his grandfather, defines what is of real value in life and what is worthwhile that should be left to one's heirs. This selection is also autobiographical as the Alberti family was exiled from Florence in the late fourteenth century, a few years before Leon Battista's birth. In Preface to Poggio Bracciolini (from Book Four), Alberti offers an Aesopian fable to compare himself to others as a way to explain why he is writing *Dinner Pieces*. The last selection—The Clouds (from Book Ten)—opens by raising the issue of the Italian city-states employing mercenary troops, which was one of the most contentious issues at that time. Alberti then spins another Aesopian fable—about the Clouds' petitioning the gods to be given their own king—which meanders over various topics, but eventually returns to the opening question about a state hiring foreign troops.

On Painting, Book II

Because this [process of] learning may perhaps appear a fatiguing thing to young people, I ought to prove here that painting is not unworthy of consuming all our time and study.

Painting contains a divine force which not only makes absent men present, as friendship is said to do, but moreover makes the dead seem almost alive. Even after many centuries they are recognized with great pleasure and with great admiration for the painter. Plutarch[11] says that Cassander, one of the captains of Alexander, trembled through all his body because he saw a portrait of his King. Agesilaos, the Lacedaemonian, never permitted anyone to paint him or to represent him in sculpture; his own form so displeased him that he avoided being known by those who would come after him. Thus the face of a man who is already dead certainly lives a long life through painting. Some think that painting shaped the gods who were adored by the nations. It certainly was their greatest gift to mortals, for painting is most useful to that piety which joins us to the gods, and keeps our souls full of religion. They say that Phidias[12] made in Aulis a god Jove[13] so beautiful that it considerably strengthened the religion then current.

The extent to which painting contributes to the most honourable delights of the soul and to the dignified beauty of things can be clearly seen not only from other things but especially from this: you can conceive of almost nothing so precious which is not made far richer and much more beautiful by association with painting. Ivory, gems and similar expensive things become more precious when worked by the hand of the painter. Gold worked by the art of painting outweighs an equal amount of unworked gold. If figures were made by the hand of Phidias or Praxiteles[14] from lead itself—the lowest of metals—they would be valued more highly than silver. The painter, Zeuxis,[15] began to give away his things because, as he said, they could not be bought. He did not think it possible to come to a just price which would be satisfactory to the painter, for in painting animals he set himself up almost as a god.

Therefore, painting contains within itself this virtue that any master painter who sees his works adored will feel himself considered another god. Who can doubt that painting is the master art or at least not a small ornament of things? The architect, if I am not mistaken, takes from the painter architraves, bases, capitals, columns, façades and other similar things. All the smiths, sculptors, shops and guilds are governed by the rules and art of the painter. It is scarcely possible to find any superior art which is not concerned with painting, so that whatever beauty is found can be said to be born of painting. *But also this, a dignified painting is held in high honour by many so that among all artists some smiths are named, only this is not the rule among smiths.* For this reason, I say among my friends that Narcissus who was changed into a flower, according to the poets, was the inventor of painting. Since painting is already the flower of every art, the story of Narcissus[16] is most to the point. What else can you call painting but a similar embracing with art of what is presented on the surface of the water in the fountain?

Quintilian[17] said that the ancient painters used to circumscribe shadows cast by the sun, and from this our art

---

[11] **Plutarch** Greek biographer who wrote *Parallel Lives*, which were character studies comparing famous Greeks and Romans who lived from antiquity to Plutarch's time in the first century CE.
[12] **Phidias** Regarded as the most famous of all Greek sculptors. Lived in fifth-century BCE Athens and produced many works, including sculptures for the Parthenon.
[13] **Jove** Another Latin name for Jupiter, who was the chief deity of the Roman system of gods and goddesses.

[14] **Praxiteles** Greek sculptor of the fourth century BCE; many of his works are extant.
[15] **Zeuxis** Fifth-century BCE Greek painter whose paintings were very realistic. None of his works exist today.
[16] **Narcissus** A handsome youth who fell in love with his own image reflected in a fountain pool and died of frustration from being unable to fulfill his love.
[17] **Quintilian** First-century CE Roman lawyer, orator, and author of a book on Roman education.

has grown. There are those who say that a certain Philocles, an Egyptian, and a Cleantes were among the first inventors of this art. The Egyptians affirm that painting was in use among them a good 6000 years before it was carried into Greece. They say that painting was brought to us from Greece after the victory of Marcellus[18] over Sicily. But we are not interested in knowing who was the inventor of the art or the first painter, since we are not telling stories like Pliny.[19] We are, however, building anew an art of painting about which nothing, as I see it, has been written in this age. They say that Euphranor of Isthmus wrote something about measure and about colours, that Antigonos and Xenocrates exchanged something in their letters about painting, and that Apelles wrote to Pelleus about painting. Diogenes Laertius recounts that Demetrius made commentaries on painting.[20] Since all the other arts were recommended in letters by our great men, and since painting was not neglected by our Latin writers, I believe that our ancient Tuscan [ancestors] were already most expert masters in painting.

Trismegistus,[21] an ancient writer, judged that painting and sculpture were born at the same time as religion, *for thus he answered Aesclepius: mankind portrays the gods in his own image from his memories of nature and his own origins.* Who can here deny that in all things public and private, profane and religious, painting has taken all the most honourable parts to itself so that nothing has ever been so esteemed by mortals?

The incredible prices of painted pictures have been recorded. Aristides the Theban sold a single picture for one hundred talents. They say that Rhodes was not burned by King Demetrius for fear that a painting of Protogenes' should perish. It could be said that the city of Rhodes was ransomed from the enemy by a single painting. Pliny collected many other such things in which you can see that good painters have always been greatly honoured by all. The most noble citizens, philosophers and quite a few kings not only enjoyed painted things but also painted with their own hands. Lucius Manilius, Roman citizen, and Fabius, a most noble man, were painters. Turpilius, a Roman knight, painted at Verona. Sitedius, praetor and proconsul, acquired renown as a painter. Pacuvius, tragic poet and nephew of the poet Ennius, painted Hercules in the Roman forum. Socrates, Plato, Metrodorus, Pyrrho were connoisseurs of painting. The emperors Nero, Val-

entinian, and Alexander Severus were most devoted to painting. It would be too long, however, to recount here how many princes and kings were pleased by painting. Nor does it seem necessary to me to recount all the throng of ancient painters. Their number is seen in the fact that 360 statues, part on horseback and part in chariots, were completed in four hundred days for Demetrius Phalerius,[22] son of Phanostratus. In a land in which there was such a great number of sculptors, can you believe that painters were lacking? I am certain that both these arts are related and nurtured by the same genius, painting with sculpture. But I always give higher rank to the genius of the painter because he works with more difficult things.

However, let us return to our work. Certainly the number of sculptors and painters was great in those times when princes and plebeians, learned and unlearned enjoyed painting, and when painted panels and portraits, considered the choicest booty from the provinces, were set up in the theatres. Finally L. Paulus Aemilius and not a few other Roman citizens taught their sons painting along with the fine arts and the art of living piously and well. This excellent custom was frequently observed among the Greeks who, because they wished their sons to be well educated, taught them painting along with geometry and music. It was also an honour among women to know how to paint. Martia, daughter of Varro,[23] is praised by the writers because she knew how to paint. Painting had such reputation and honour among the Greeks that laws and edicts were passed forbidding slaves to learn painting. It was certainly well that they did this, for the art of painting has always been most worthy of liberal minds and noble souls.

As for me, I certainly consider a great appreciation of painting to be the best indication of a most perfect mind, even though it happens that this art is pleasing to the uneducated as well as to the educated. It occurs rarely in any other art that what delights the experienced also moves the inexperienced. In the same way you will find that many greatly desire to be well versed in painting. Nature herself seems to delight in painting, for in the cut faces of marble she often paints centaurs and faces of bearded and curly headed kings. It is said, moreover, that in a gem from Pyrrhus all nine Muses, each with her symbol, are to be found clearly painted by nature. Add to this that in no other art does it happen that both the experienced and the inexperienced of every age apply themselves so voluntarily to the learning and exercising of it. Allow me to speak of myself here. Whenever I turn to painting for my recreation, which I frequently do when I am tired of more pressing affairs, I apply myself to it with so much pleasure that I am surprised that three or four hours have passed. Thus this art gives pleasure and praise to whoever is skilled in it; riches and perpetual fame to one who is master of it. Since these things are so, since painting is

---

[18] **Marcellus** Roman general who conquered Sicily in the third century BCE.
[19] **Pliny** Probably Pliny the Elder, not his son, the Younger. The Elder, who lived in the first century CE, wrote extensively on many topics, including an extant encyclopedia of natural science.
[20] **Euphranor of Isthmus, Antigonos, Xenocrates, Apelles, Pelleus, Diogenes Laertius, Demetrius** All these men were ancient Greek sculptors, painters, or philosophers who lived in the fourth and third centuries BCE. Many of their works are lost; most are known only by name or secondary references.
[21] **Trismegistus** Alberti is probably referring to the author of a set of ancient books who was supposed to be Thoth, the Egyptian god of wisdom, and whom the Greeks called Hermes Trismegistus. The books were reputed to include information on every possible topic.

[22] **Demetrius Phalerius** Fourth- and third-century BCE Athenian orator and statesman.
[23] **Varro** Probably Marcus Terentius Varro, second- and first-century BCE Roman scholar and author of many books on law, customs, religion, and philosophy.

the best and most ancient ornament of things, worthy of free men, pleasing to learned and unlearned, I greatly encourage our studious youth to exert themselves as much as possible in painting.

Therefore, I recommend that he who is devoted to painting should learn this art. The first great care of one who seeks to obtain eminence in painting is to acquire the fame and renown of the ancients. It is useful to remember

that avarice is always the enemy of virtue. Rarely can anyone given to acquisition of wealth acquire renown. I have seen many in the first flower of learning suddenly sink to money-making. As a result they acquire neither riches nor praise. However, if they had increased their talent with study, they would have easily soared into great renown. Then they would have acquired much riches and pleasure. . . .

Questions for Critical Thinking

1. Discuss some of the sources and references from the past that Alberti offers in proving the value of painting.

2. What advice does Alberti give to a person who wishes to become a painter? Do you think this advice would apply to someone who wants to be an artist today? Why or why not?

Dinner Pieces, Book One
Religion

LIBRIPETA:[24] This fig tree seems to me quite pious and compassionate, for from it, as from Timon's famous tree,[25] many have hanged themselves to end life's afflictions. But here comes Lepidus,[26] whom I have expected for some time now.

LEPIDUS: Greetings, Libripeta. Did the sacrifice detain me in the temple longer than you would have wished?

LIBR.: Much longer. But tell me, what business did you have with the gods that occasioned your lengthy discussions?

LEP.: What, is it shameful to worship the gods devoutly and to pray that they favor our wishes?

LIBR.: Doubtless under that roof, with its mob of lurking priests, the gods hear you quite well!

LEP.: Don't you know that everything is filled with gods?

LIBR.: Then you could properly have done beneath this fig tree exactly what, following the superstitious custom of the ignorant, you accomplished in the temple. But tell me, please, did you pray only for yourself before those painted gods, or did you act as an agent for others?

LEP.: Why do you ask?

LIBR.: Because I would find you arrogant, if you thought that the gods hold you so dear that they are more moved by your words than by those of people who truly need assistance. Besides, in my view, whoever prays to the gods asks them above all to grant and keep his goods, present and future, and to remove and avert his ills. What do you say to this?

LEP.: I'm of the same opinion.

LIBR.: O foolish ones, do you want the gods to act as your hirelings and thieves? For no goods can come to you but those snatched from others who own them. Can you show me a servant so base that you could honorably order him to commit such a crime? Is anyone so unrestrained as to order corrupt assassins to make him rich with booty taken from others?

LEP.: I see your point. Yet I did not ask that they act as thieves, but as laborers, for I asked them to see that golden cabbages grow in my garden.

LIBR.: If they are wise, the gods will detest your impudence.

LEP.: Will you deny, Libripeta, that the gods often aid mankind in adversity?

[24] **Libripeta** Alberti's name for the character who acts as a foil in this dialogue. May be a reference to Niccolò Niccoli (c. 1364–1437), the Florentine humanist, who, like Alberti, was a student of classical times and culture.
[25] **Timon's famous tree** Plutarch, in his essay on Marc Antony in *The Lives of the Noble Grecians and Romans,* includes a passage on Timon, an Athenian citizen. Timon, who disliked most people, announced before the assembled Athenians that he had a fig tree on his property on which many persons had hanged themselves, and if anyone wanted to hang himself, he should do it now before the tree was cut down. Thus, the reference is to a misanthrope—one who does not like other humans.
[26] **Lepidus** From the Latin word for "witty." Hence, the voice of Alberti in this dialogue.

LIBR.: Will you deny, Lepidus, that men are themselves   15
the cause of all the ills that vex them? Just climb this
fig tree and hang yourself from this branch; then ask
the gods to rescue you. If you didn't ruin your health
by reading in continual vigils, Lepidus, you would
hardly be so pale or so dyspeptic. Men willingly
submit to the ills they suffer. Believe me, no sailors
would know of gods to calm the storm, if they didn't
trust themselves to the surging sea. But such is their
custom: when their own senseless folly subjects them
to the gravest dangers, they turn at once to the gods.
Thus, by wishing the gods to stop what they themselves have undertaken, they seem not to pray, but to
engage in conflict and controversy. And you too, if
you avoid whatever causes your ills, will never have
need of any gods to remove them. Or if you judge that
it is men who harm other men, there is no need to invoke protecting gods, but rather to reconcile men. But
if the gods themselves are the cause of our ills, please
consider that they will scarcely depart from their
former custom because of your prayers. For ages, men
have been plagued by adversity; and if something
else—fate, or chance, or time—causes our afflictions,
without a doubt it exercises its office freely and with
the gods' assent, and will spurn your paltry supplica-
tions, O men of religion. Besides, do you think the
gods resemble us small human beings? Do they make
decisions on the spur of the moment, like imprudent
and reckless people, and then abruptly change their
former resolves? Indeed, men of learning tell me that
the gods are incomparably industrious in their great
task of administration, and that they rule the world
according to a practically eternal order. Consequently,
you rave like madmen if you think your words or
arguments will sway the gods' intent and actions
from their age-old course toward new undertakings.
Besides, the gods would be groveling slaves if they
abandoned their own resolves for your hopes and
desires. In fine, you must remember that the gods are
quite busy moving the sun, the moon, and the other
heavenly bodies through the vast heavens. Even your
men of religion assert publicly that the gods toss
mountainous waves on the sea, send down winds and
lightning bolts, and control countless such terrifying
phenomena. Engaged in such great matters, the gods
have little time to listen to the interminable, futile,
and utterly ridiculous prayers of men. And if the gods
paid attention to trivial matters, they would more
gladly listen to the pure voices of cicadas and crickets
than to the foolish entreaties of impure men. Know
then that the gods are deafened only by the prayers of
the wicked. For good men are clearly content with the
goods they have, and they yield to adversity. But the
wicked never show reason or restraint in demanding
goods or bearing ills.

LEP.: I regard your remarks, Libripeta, as made for the
sake of disputation, but shall always maintain my
own view of the gods and believe that they welcome
the prayers and vows of good men. And I remained
convinced that many of the misfortunes we deserve
are averted by the mercy of the gods, who are most
generous to meritorious men. Goodbye.

∞

Dinner Pieces, Book Two
Wealth

My grandfather, Benedetto Alberti, a Florentine knight   1
noted for his fine character and virtue, had been driven
into exile by seditious citizens, and lay on his death bed
on the island of Rhodes.[27] Urged by his friends to draw up
a will, he asked them what things they wished him to include in it. His friends replied: "Your own, Benedetto, for
no one doubts that you are the richest man in Tuscany."[28]

He said: "I assure you that there is nothing of which I
am more ignorant and unaware. As for those things which
I suppose you mean, I scarcely know now what is mine.
But in my youth, I labored many years under such an error, and imprudently deemed mine those things which
are popularly thought to belong to a person. I followed
the common usage of my fellow-citizens, and called them
my estates, *my* property, and *my* wealth, as people do."

"But weren't they yours?" his friends asked.

"No," my grandfather replied. "Even more surpris-
ingly, I have long realized that even this body which con-
fines me was never really mine. For I recall how against
my will these members were always subject to cold, to
heat, or to various pains, and how they hindered and opposed my nobler intentions and desires. I recall how this
body continually suffered hunger, thirst, and other such
harsh and savage masters. And I perceive how in a single
day fortune, mistress of our affairs, has snatched from me
all my wealth and goods and even my homeland, and has
driven me into exile. What, then, dare I call mine, either
past or present?

[27] **Rhodes** An island in the Aegean Sea, off the coast of Turkey.
Settled by Greeks around 1000 BCE and became a prosperous
island until its alliance with Rome in the second century BCE.
In Alberti's times, Rhodes was under the control of Knights of
St. John of Jerusalem, and then fell to the Turks in 1522. Thus, it
could have been where his grandfather took refuge after being
exiled from Florence.

[28] **Tuscany** The region in central Italy where Florence is located,
which was the center of the early Italian Renaissance.

"Now, wealth in human life is like a game with a ball. ₅ For it is not holding the ball in your hands a long time, but throwing it with skill and returning it accurately, that helps you win the victory. Just so, I judge that it is not the possession but the use of wealth that contributes to happiness. And as for myself, I admit that I have virtually nothing left that I may especially call mine, except the knowledge of my deeds and the recollection of what I suffered in life. I wish, therefore, to leave my heirs this sole inheritance. They may claim that, above all others in our city, I was the most devoted to my country, and the most desirous of peace, tranquillity, and freedom; that I was by no means ignorant of liberal studies, letters, and arts; and that I defended the public weal with great vigilance and faith, and was always content with my private estate. Let these deeds of mine pass to my heirs."

∞

Dinner Pieces, Book Four
Preface to Poggio Bracciolini[29]

While wallowing in the lowly swamp-grass of a muddy ₁ river bank, some heifers, they say, saw a she-goat seated on the ruins of an ancient temple which had collapsed atop a rocky crag, and admonished her in these words. "You there, wanton one, what temerity possesses you, that you spurn this verdant bank and attempt that arduous and virtually inaccessible height? Don't you see that it is better to fill yourself with sweet and juicy grass than always to graze thirstily amid jagged ruins, nourished on bitter wild figs? Take care that you don't come to regret your dangerous rambles on such precipices."

The she-goat, they say, replied to the heifers in these words: "Ha! grave, ill-humored, tender-footed beasts! Don't you know that the mouth carefully serves the stomach, and the feet the mouth? I have a goat's stomach, not a cow's. If you disdain what I graze on because you can't reach it, I spurn your swamp-grass because it is available everywhere to even the idlest cattle. And if others' peril bothers you in your sloth, you should have reproved the vultures, who search for carcasses from the highest reaches of heaven. Their fall is far more dangerous than mine."

Now, the very same thing, dear Poggio, I find happening to me as I engage in writing these *Dinner Pieces*. For many of us today seek food and sustenance in the more plentiful and pleasant fields of eloquence. And the same people censure me for delighting in difficult pursuits, rather than in those filled with the juice of commonplace eloquence and material reward. But if these critics heed the goat in the fable, I think they will find no cause to reproach me. If they blame me for choosing to spurn other lucrative arts and for following my natural abilities, then they must also blame the mathematicians and all others who devote themselves to understanding the stars and profoundly recondite subjects. Can't everyone see how ruinously they fail when they fall short of the hope that led them to contemplate the farthest realms of the heavens? Yet no one denies that they pursue a liberal goal.

For myself, I take pleasure in rare subjects which, like piquant herbs in an appetizer, should not be excluded from the lavish dinners of writers who I confess are richer than myself. Besides, if I wish to prove my diligence in this field—in which zeal furthers talent, and application zeal—whose envy can distract me from bringing forth diverse and rare inventions like these?

---

[29] **Poggio Bracciolini** Famous Renaissance humanist (1380–1459) who discovered many classical writings in monasteries. He and Alberti were at the Vatican as secretaries to the Pope. Later, in the mid-1450s, Poggio served in the Florentine government.

∞

Dinner Pieces, Book Ten
The Clouds

In the recent age of our fathers, Italians employed hired ₁ troops and foreign armies rather than conscripted citizens, as had been our ancestors' custom. They did this by prudent choice, I believe, since exposing the lives of ignoble mercenaries to the perils of battle seemed more practical than risking the lives of citizens in the fortunes in war. They may also have wished to prevent Italian troops from taking up arms only to abuse them later to the ruin of their homeland, as in fact happened. For continual invaders, led by their hope of victory and their desire of booty, ravaged the peaceful and wealthy peoples of Italy; and the youths of Italy, being of fierce and aggressive stock, gradually began to rouse themselves to martial pursuits. Soon nearly countless military commanders sprang up throughout Italy. Endowed with great courage and emboldened by the glory of their exploits, they looked beyond mere victories and triumphs, and aspired to kingdoms, disdaining any conquest which did not subject the vanquished to their personal dictates and decrees.

Since the ambition of these men was to rule, they did their utmost to seize power. But the ambition of the free cities was to serve no master, and they did their utmost to defend their freedom. As a result, such great civil wars arose that not only men, but even the gods were astonished. Hence, almighty Jupiter,[30] who has always cherished mankind's peace and tranquillity, sent the gods' envoy Mercury[31] to learn the meaning of such great and widespread preparations for war. Donning his winged sandals, the god descended to a mountain in the Alps, from which he could view both the Po Valley and Tuscany.[32] There he removed his sandals and shed his divine appearance so that he could more gracefully blend into the company of mortals. Suddenly, he was joined by the Clouds, who formed a circle around him and greeted him as an old friend, for Mercury had often used their aid in his missions.

"Your arrival is indeed timely," said Mercury. "Unless I am mistaken, you may relieve me of the task which brings me here in such incertitude. Since you float above men's cities night and day and may easily know the reason, tell me why mortals have taken up arms on all sides?"

"So that you know, Mercury," the Clouds replied, "Pluto's[33] daughter is a girl named Ambition, who is perhaps not unknown to the gods themselves. Because of her singular beauty, she is greatly desired by many young noblemen and by not a few patrician youths. Being a wanton and forward young woman, she is extremely delighted by the large number of her suitors, and promises all of them that she will try to satisfy their wishes. Inflamed with love for her, they devote all their efforts and energies to courting her, and employ any means they can to thwart and hinder their rivals. Hence arise rivalries, enmities, and altercations, and in the zeal for their factions, they have resolved to fight for her, and have deployed their troops in battle formation."

Hearing this, Mercury exclaimed: "What a plague on mortals this woman is! She is the perpetual source of quarrels, discords, dissensions, and the ruin of all things public and private." Then, making ready to return to Jupiter, he asked whether the Clouds wished to request anything of him.

The Clouds replied: "We welcome your question, Mercury. For we hope that, as you bear us affection, you will not refuse to take up our cause, which is just, righteous, and hardly troublesome, and we pray and entreat you to do so. The issue is this. You know, Mercury, that we are not ignoble. We think no one is unaware that, whether our mother was Earth or Juno,[34] we were certainly begotten by our father Phoebus.[35] As for our peaceable and modest way of life, we scarcely need to describe here something so familiar to you.

"What then? The Fires have Etna[36] as their seat, and Vulcan[37] as their king. The waters fill immense and multitudinous gulfs, and are rolled far and wide by their king Neptune.[38] And the Winds, not content with their caves or their king [Neptune], sport through all the skies, seas, mountains, and the whole earth. Isn't it unjust, then, that we, who are harmless and constant in our duty, are neither honored with a king nor protected by laws? Nay, it is our harsh lot to be driven constantly as exiles and outcasts, never allowed to abide in one place or to repose in tranquillity. Shall we forever nurture the dark earth with our tears?[39] We collect dew and sustenance which make the seeds and fruits bloom and ripen, and these feed both animals sacrificed to the gods and mortal men, who are the darlings of the gods. By contrast, the Winds strike down the flowers, the Waters flood and lay low the burgeoning fields, and the Fires devastate the full-grown crops.

"You are wise, and we know that you are in haste to return to Jupiter. So we need not detain you with prolix entreaties. But there is one thing we ask again. Plead the cause of our well-being and dignity before Jupiter—but only if you judge it honorable and consonant with your affection for us. We wish you to know, Mercury, that we could hope for nothing more than to obtain this just and easily granted favor with you as our spokesman. We wish to be honored with a king and, as if after a long exile, to be granted a homeland in which, at last in peace, we may some day worship the gods devoutly and piously. We refuse no homeland or king, as long as it is honorable. If, as we hope, Mercury, you help us to attain this, you will truly find that those you have aided are grateful and mindful of your kindness."

Mercury replied: "I desire to have your honor and interests at heart. But you must decide whether it is better for Mercury to appear before the gods as the Clouds' ambassador, or as Jupiter's counselor. In my view, you should send your own emissaries to Jupiter. I shall see that the senate of the gods convenes to receive them with honor."

The Clouds thus decided to send emissaries to accompany Mercury on his return to Jupiter. They say that, when he had heard their speech and its petitions, Jupiter

5

10

---

[30] **Jupiter**　Chief god of the Romans, equivalent to Zeus among the Greek deities.

[31] **Mercury**　Roman god of messages or herald for the deities. Hermes in the Greek system.

[32] **Po Valley and Tuscany**　Two well-known regions in Italy. Florence, the home of Alberti, is located in Tuscany. On top of the mountain in the Alps, Mercury could look south—first to the Po Valley—and beyond that, to Tuscany.

[33] **Pluto**　Ruling god of the underworld. Alberti asserts that Ambition is his daughter, but there is no evidence in Roman or Greek myths that she was his daughter.

[34] **Earth or Juno**　Earth, or Gaia, came out of primeval Chaos. Earth gave birth to the generation of Titans, who were then followed by the Olympian deities. Juno is Roman queen of the gods and goddesses and associated with Hera, the Greek goddess.

[35] **Phoebus**　Another name for Apollo, who is associated with the sun and often identified as "the shining one."

[36] **Etna**　An active volcano in Sicily.

[37] **Vulcan**　Roman god of fire and craftsmanship; the Greek god is Hephaestos.

[38] **Neptune**　Roman god of the sea, equated with Poseidon of the Greek Olympians.

[39] **our tears**　Rain.

frowned slightly. Then, after briefly relecting in silence, he dismissed them with the following reply. The gods had decided to grant the Clouds whatever king and kingdom would give them joy. Yet, in order to satisfy the Clouds' desires without creating rancor, the gods delegated to the various orders of the Clouds the task of electing a king fitting and worthy of the heavenly powers. He therefore bade them hold an election, and to rest assured that the gods would not hesitate to give their appointed king both a dwelling-place and all due honors.

Soon, little Clouds were flying across the land as bailiffs[40] to summon the bearded patrician clouds to the royal elections. The latter appeared one by one, each dressed in white and sunk in deep meditation, with brows raised haughtily, as if already engaged in administering a tyrannical regime and in drafting new laws. The Clouds were so puffed with pride that they disdained their usual steeds, and arrived mounted on strange and horrible beasts like the hydra, centaur, the Lernaean beast, and such monsters.[41] They say that the Clouds' haughty arrogance disgusted their father Phoebus, who turned away, unable to bear the sight of them. As the Clouds gathered to meet, they greeted one another with an intolerable show of dignity and majesty, lowering their deep and rumbling voices to subdued and muted tones. Yet the centuriate[42] assembly had scarcely been admitted, much less all the other orders, when the Clouds bustled throughout their ranks, canvassing for votes with a zeal which can hardly be described. You could have heard their deep and husky

---

[40] **bailiffs** Used in this context as one who is a messenger. In the U.S. judiciary system, a bailiff occupies a similar role.
[41] **the hydra, centaur, the Lernaean beast, and such monsters** A hydra is a many-headed mythological beast; the centaur was a half-man, half-horse creature; the Lernaean beast refers to the second labor of Hercules, when he killed the Lernaean hydra, or snakelike beast of nine heads that lived in Lake Lerna.
[42] **centuriate** That is, the assembly was divided into sections of hundreds. Alberti thus paints a scene of many "clouds."

voices swell until they burst into thunderous roars. Then, the fierce contention between factions erupted into violence. The furious candidates wrapped their arms in their cloaks, and they used stones and firebrands as weapons against the others' stones. The din of the battle and the rumbling of the combatants inspired incredible terror in the hearts of men and gods alike. Rivers overflowed with the blood of the Clouds, and the mountains and temples of the gods shook with fright and terror. No doubt, the gods themselves were in suspense, as if the foundations of heaven were collapsing.

Only Jupiter, they say, maintained a very placid and serene countenance, and after sighing, he smiled at the great turbulence of the Clouds. When asked why, he replied that he had not rashly decided to bid the Clouds elect their own king. For he knew well the preposterous and perverse nature of the Clouds, who were puffed up with their own superiority, and whose excessive squeamishness always led them to approve a shifting and unstable way of life. He added that he was not unfamiliar with their arrogant insolence, which was clear, among other things, from their desire for a king and a kingdom. Had they acquired these, and had they learned to direct their strength, wisdom, and energies toward their common glory, their savage and reckless nature would have carried their insolence so far that they would have attempted to seize the stars, the moon, and even the sun.

Therefore, Jupiter said, he could have found no better way to restrain and repress their aggressiveness. For those who share a common vice or virtue readily associate with each other. Hence, we see that drunkards, gluttons, paramours, dicers, thieves, brigands, assassins, and other such reprobates and criminals, induced by the urging and pleasure of their common nature, all live together sociably and intimately. Only one who is proud disdains and detests his brothers in pride, and no one is harsher to his peers than proud men. It is in the nature of the proud to vex and antagonize each other incessantly.

Questions for Critical Thinking

1. What are the main arguments put forward in *Religion* regarding the nature of the gods and their relationships with humans? Who do you think has the better argument, Libripeta or Lepidus?

2. Summarize the series of events regarding the Clouds' efforts to choose a king. What are the lessons Alberti is offering his reader in this *Dinner Piece*?

13

THE HIGH RENAISSANCE
AND EARLY MANNERISM
1494–1564

BALDASSARE CASTIGLIONE
Selections from *The Book of the Courtier*

The Book of the Courtier (*courtier* being a "gentleman") belongs to the genre of etiquette books that flourished in Renaissance Europe as a religious-based culture gave way to a more humanistic world. Books of this type were much in evidence, in response to this period's ideal that secular life in the upper levels of society should be marked by reserved grace, especially between the sexes. Court life, whether in the royal or aristocratic domain, already had well-established rules of behavior derived from the medieval chivalric code; however, courts were still dominated by a male ethos, manifested in rough speech, crude manners, and general lack of refinement between men and women. Whereas most Renaissance etiquette books were meant to correct crude behavior and speech, *The Courtier* took a broader view by offering an idealized vision of court life in which courteous ladies became the arbiters of society. Published in 1528 and translated into most Western languages by 1600, this work became the bible of politeness for Europe's upper classes, and its rules were formalized into strict expectations. This Renaissance book is the source from which modern notions of "lady" and "gentleman" descend.

The Courtier's author, Baldassare Castiglione (1478–1529), was himself a polished courtier, growing up among the Italian nobility and studying the classics at the University of Milan. Later, he was attached to various northern Italian ducal courts (Milan, Urbino, and Mantua), for whose rulers he performed military and diplomatic missions. While serving as the Duke of Mantua's ambassador to Rome, he was brought by his duties into the cultivated court of the Medici pope, Leo X (pope 1513–1521). A later pope, Clement VII (pope 1523–1534), made Castiglione the papal representative to Spain, a post he held until he died.

The Courtier, Castiglione's only publication, was his life's work. He was moved to write it during his eleven years at the ducal court of Urbino, which was the center of an accomplished circle of artists, writers, and intellectuals presided over by the old duke and his young wife, Elisabetta. This Urbino circle, with its witty talk, integrity, and grace, came to embody Castiglione's social ideal. When he wrote *The Courtier*, Castiglione tried to capture the conversational tone of this circle by making the work a dialogue, divided into four books, set during an evening in the ducal palace. In his book, as in life, Duchess Elisabetta is the playful leader of the group.

Reading the Selections

These selections from *The Book of the Courtier* are excerpts from Books I and III, dealing respectively with the qualities that define a courtier and a lady. Not based on real life, these attributes are ideals meant as a guide for correct deportment and had been gleaned from Castiglione's readings in medieval and classical literature. Of the ideal courtier, the participants agree that he should be both a soldier trained in the bearing of arms and a scholar skilled in the liberal arts and social graces; however, they are of two minds as to which role should dominate.

No such dispute divides Castiglione's participants over the ideal lady: all concur that she should be the consummate hostess—charming, witty, graceful, physically attractive, and utterly feminine. An innovative aspect of this idealized model is the insistence that a lady be educated in the liberal arts in the same way as a gentleman. This idea swept away the barrier that, since the Middle Ages, had excluded women from higher learning. However, women remained barred from universities until the nineteenth century.

∞

Book I

. . .

"But to come to specific details, I[1] judge that the first and true profession of the courtier must be that of arms; and this above everything else I wish him to pursue vigorously. Let him also stand out from the rest as enterprising, bold, and loyal to whomever he serves. And he will win a good reputation by demonstrating these qualities whenever and wherever possible, since failure to do so always incurs the gravest censure. Just as once a woman's reputation for purity has been sullied it can never be restored, so once the reputation of a gentleman-at-arms has been stained through cowardice or some other reproachful behaviour, even if only once, it always remains defiled in the eyes of the world and covered with ignominy. The more our courtier excels in this art, therefore, the more praise he will deserve, although I do not think he needs to have the professional knowledge of such things and the other qualities appropriate to a military commander. However, since the subject of what constitutes a great captain takes us into very deep waters, we shall be content, as we said, for the courtier to show complete loyalty and an undaunted spirit, and for these to be always in evidence. For men demonstrate their courage far more often in little things than in great. Very often in the face of appalling danger but where there are numerous witnesses one will find those who, though ready to drop dead with fear, driven on by shame or the presence of others, will press forward, with their eyes closed, and do their duty; and only God knows how. But in things of trifling importance, when they believe they can avoid danger without its being noticed, they are only too willing to play for safety. As for those who, even when they are sure they are not being observed or seen or recognized by anyone, are full of ardour and avoid doing anything, no matter how trivial, for which they would incur reproach, they possess the temper and quality we are looking for in our courtier. All the same, we do not wish the courtier to make a show of being so fierce that he is always blustering and bragging, declaring that he is married to his cuirass,[2] and glowering with the haughty looks that we know only too well in Berto.[3] To these may very fairly be said what a worthy lady once remarked jokingly, in polite company, to a certain man (I don't want just now to mention him by name) whom she had honoured by asking him to dance and who not only refused but would not listen to music or take part in the many other entertainments offered, protesting all the while that such frivolities were not his business. And when at length the lady asked what his business was, he answered with a scowl: "Fighting . . ."

"'Well then,' the lady retorted, 'I should think that since you aren't at war at the moment and you are not engaged in fighting, it would be a good thing if you were to have yourself well greased and stowed away in a cupboard with all your fighting equipment, so that you avoid getting rustier than you are already.'

"And of course everyone burst out laughing at the way she showed her contempt for his stupid presumption.

"Therefore," Count Lodovico went on, "the man we are seeking should be fierce, rough and always to the fore, in the presence of the enemy; but anywhere else he should

---

[1] **I** Count Lodovico da Canossa (1476–1532) is speaking. A noble from Verona, he was appointed papal ambassador to England and France by Pope Leo X (pope 1513–1521); made Bishop of Bayeux (in France) in 1520; appointed emissary to Venice by King Francis I of France; resident at Urbino at intervals after 1496. A relative of Castiglione.

[2] **cuirass** Breastplate armor covering the body from neck to waist.
[3] **Berto** Perhaps a papal buffoon, or fool, during the time of Pope Julius II (pope 1503–1513) or Leo X.

be kind, modest, reticent and anxious above all to avoid ostentation or the kind of outrageous self-glorification by which a man always arouses loathing and disgust among those who have to listen to him. . . .

"I should like our courtier to be a more than average scholar, at least in those studies which we call the humanities; and he should have a knowledge of Greek as well as Latin, because of the many different things that are so beautifully written in that language. He should be very well acquainted with the poets, and no less with the orators and historians, and also skilled at writing both verse and prose, especially in our own language; for in addition to the satisfaction this will give him personally, it will enable him to provide constant entertainment for the ladies, who are usually very fond of such things. But if because of his other activities or through lack of study he fails to achieve a commendable standard in his writing, then he should take pains to suppress his work, to avoid ridicule, and he should show it only to a friend he can trust. And the exercise of writing will be profitable for him at least to the extent that it will teach him how to judge the work of others. For it is very unusual for someone who is not a practised writer, however erudite he may be, to understand completely the demanding work done by writers, or appreciate their stylistic accomplishments and triumphs and those subtle details characteristic of the writers of the ancient world. Moreover, these studies will make our courtier well informed and eloquent and (as Aristippus[4] said to the tyrant) self-confident and assured no matter whom he is talking to. However, I should like our courtier to keep one precept firmly in mind: namely, that in what I have just discussed and in everything else he should always be diffident and reserved rather than forward, and he should be on his guard against assuming that he knows what he does not know. For we are instinctively all too greedy for praise, and there is no sound or song that comes sweeter to our ears; praise, like Sirens'[5] voices, is the kind of music that causes shipwreck to the man who does not stop his ears to its deceptive harmony. Recognizing this danger, some of the philosophers of the ancient world wrote books giving advice on how a man can tell the difference between a true friend and a flatterer. Even so, we may well ask what use is this, seeing that there are so many who realize perfectly well that they are listening to flattery, and yet love the flatterer and detest the one who tells them the truth. Indeed, very often, deciding that the one who praises them is not being fulsome enough, they lend him a hand themselves and say such things that even the most outrageous flatterer feels ashamed. Let us leave these blind fools to their errors and decide that our courtier should possess such good judgement that he will not be told that black is white or presume anything of himself unless he is certain that it is true, and especially in regard to those flaws which, if you remember, when he was

suggesting his game for the evening Cesare[6] recalled we had often used to demonstrate the particular folly of this person or another. To make no mistake at all, the courtier should, on the contrary, when he knows the praises he receives are deserved, not assent to them too openly nor let them pass without some protest. Rather he should tend to disclaim them modestly, always giving the impression that arms are, as indeed they should be, his chief profession, and that all his other fine accomplishments serve merely as adornments; and this should especially be his attitude when he is in the company of soldiers, lest he behave like those who in the world of scholarship want to be taken for warriors and among warriors want to seem men of letters. In this way, as we have said, he will avoid affectation, and even his modest achievements will appear great."

At this point, Pietro Bembo[7] interrupted: "I cannot see, my dear Count, why you wish this courtier, who is so literate and so well endowed with other worthy qualities, to regard everything as serving to adorn the profession of arms, and not arms and the rest as serving to adorn the profession of letters, which, taken by themselves, are as superior in dignity to arms as is the soul to the body, since letters are a function of the soul, just as arms are of the body."

Then the Count answered: "On the contrary, the profession of arms pertains both to the soul and to the body. But I should not want you to be the judge of this, Pietro, because by one of the parties concerned it would be assumed that you were prejudiced. And as this is a controversy that the wisest men have already thrashed out, there is no call to re-open it. As it is, I consider that it has been settled in favour of arms; and since I may form our courtier as I wish, I want him to be of the same opinion. If you think the contrary, wait until you hear of a contest in which the man who defends the cause of arms is allowed to use them, just as those who defend the cause of letters make use of letters in their defence; for if each one uses his own weapons, you will see that the men of letters will lose."

"Ah," said Pietro Bembo, "you were only too ready earlier on to damn the French for their scant appreciation of letters, and you mentioned the glory that they bring to men and the way they make a man immortal. And now you seem to have changed your mind. Do you not remember that:

> *Giunto Alessandro alla famosa tomba*
> *del fero Achille, sospirando disse:*
> *O fortunato, che sì chiara tromba*
> *trovasti, e chi di te sì alto scrisse![8]*

---

[4] **Aristippus** (ca. 435–366 BCE) Greek philosopher who founded a hedonistic school of philosophy in Cyrene, North Africa.
[5] **Sirens** In Homer's *Odyssey*, monstrous creatures, half-woman, half-bird, whose singing lured sailors onto destructive rocks at sea.

[6] **Cesare** Cesare Gonzaga (1475–1512), a famous warrior, from the illustrious Gonzaga family in Mantua; a cousin and friend of Castiglione.
[7] **Pietro Bembo** (1470–1547), a Venetian noble and Renaissance man; regarded as an authority on language, style, and Platonic love. Appointed papal secretary by Pope Leo X; made cardinal in 1539; resident at Urbino, 1506–1512.
[8] *. . . alto scrisse!* The first quatrain of a sonnet by Petrarch, literally: "When Alexander reached the famous tomb of fierce Achilles, he sighed and said: 'O happy man, who found so illustrious a trumpet, and one to write of you so nobly!'"

And if Alexander[9] was envious of Achilles[10] not because of what he had done himself but because of the way he was blessed by fortune in having his deeds celebrated by Homer, we must conclude that he put a higher value on the writings of Homer than on the arms of Achilles. What other judge do you want, or what other verdict on the relative worth of arms and letters than the one delivered by one of the greatest commanders that has ever lived?"

The Count replied: "I blame the French for believing that letters are harmful to the profession of arms, and I maintain myself that it is more fitting for a warrior to be educated than for anyone else; and I would have these two accomplishments, the one helping the other, as is most fitting, joined together in our courtier. I do not think that this means I have changed my opinion. But, as I said, I do not wish to argue which of them is more praiseworthy. Let it be enough that men of letters hardly ever choose to praise other than great men and glorious deeds, which deserve praise both on their own account and because, in addition, they provide writers with a truly noble theme. And this subject-matter embellishes what is written and, no doubt, is the reason why such writings endure, for otherwise, if they dealt not with noble deeds but with vain and trivial subjects, they would surely be read and appreciated less. And if Alexander was envious of Achilles because he was praised by Homer, it still does not necessary follow that he thought more of letters than of arms;

and if he had thought that he was as inferior to Achilles as a soldier as he believed that all those who would write about him were inferior to Homer as writers, he would, I[11] am sure, have far preferred brave exploits on his own part to brave talk from others. Therefore I believe that when he said what he did, Alexander was tacitly praising himself, and expressing a desire for what he thought he lacked, namely supreme ability as a writer, rather than for what he took for granted he already had, namely prowess as a warrior, in which he was far from acknowledging Achilles as his superior. So when he called Achilles fortunate he meant that if so far his own fame did not rival that of Achilles (which had been made bright and illustrious through so inspired a poem) this was not because his valour and merits were less notable or less deserving of the highest praise but because of the way fortune had granted Achilles a born genius to be his herald and to trumpet his deeds to the world. Moreover, perhaps Alexander wanted to encourage some gifted person to write about him, showing that his pleasure in this would be as great as his love and respect for the sacred monuments of literature. And now we have said enough about this subject."

"Indeed, far too much," remarked signor Lodovico, "for I don't think that one could discover anywhere in the world a vessel big enough to hold all the things you want to put into our courtier" . . .

---

[9] **Alexander** Alexander III, called Alexander the Great (r. 336–323 BCE). Macedonian general and founder of a great empire, stretching from his homeland to the Indus River.
[10] **Achilles** Ancient Greek hero (see Homer's *Iliad* in Chapter 2).

[11] **I** Giuliano de' Medici (1479–1516), of Florence; son of Lorenzo de' Medici and brother of Pope Leo X; during the exile of the Medici from Florence, 1494–1512, Giuliano lived in Urbino, where he was called the "Magnifico Giuliano."

∞

Book III

. . .

"Thus just as it is very fitting that a man should display a certain robust and sturdy manliness, so it is well for a woman to have a certain soft and delicate tenderness, with an air of feminine sweetness in her every movement, which, in her going and staying and whatsoever she does, always makes her appear a woman, without any resemblance to a man. If this precept be added to the rules that these gentlemen have taught the courtier, then I think that she ought to be able to make use of many of them, and adorn herself with the finest accomplishments, as signor Gaspare[12] says. For I consider that many virtues of the mind are as necessary to a woman as to a man; as it is to be of good family; to shun affectation; to be naturally graceful; to be well mannered, clever and prudent; to be

neither proud, envious or evil-tongued, nor vain, contentious or clumsy; to know how to gain and keep the favour of her mistress and of everyone else; to perform well and gracefully the sports suitable for women. It also seems to me that good looks are more important to her than to the courtier, for much is lacking to a woman who lacks beauty. She must also be more circumspect and at greater pains to avoid giving an excuse for someone to speak ill of her; she should not only be beyond reproach but also beyond even suspicion, for a woman lacks a man's resources when it comes to defending herself. And now, seeing that Count Lodovico has explained in great detail what should be the principal occupation of a courtier, namely, to his mind, the profession of arms, it seems right for me to say what I consider ought to be that of the lady at Court. And when I have done this, then I shall believe that most of my task has been carried out.

"Leaving aside, therefore, those virtues of the mind which she must have in common with the courtier, such as

---

[12] **signor Gaspare** (1486–1511), of a distinguished Lombard family; friend of Castiglione.

prudence, magnanimity, continence[13] and many others besides, and also the qualities that are common to all kinds of women, such as goodness and discretion, the ability to take good care, if she is married, of her husband's belongings and house and children, and the virtues belonging to a good mother, I say that the lady who is at Court should properly have, before all else, a certain pleasing affability whereby she will know how to entertain graciously every kind of man with charming and honest conversation, suited to the time and the place and the rank of the person with whom she is talking. And her serene and modest behaviour, and the candour that ought to inform all her actions, should be accompanied by a quick and vivacious spirit by which she shows her freedom from boorishness; but with such a virtuous manner that she makes herself thought no less chaste, prudent and benign than she is pleasing, witty and discreet. Thus she must observe a certain difficult mean,[14] composed as it were of contrasting qualities, and take care not to stray beyond certain fixed limits. . . .

"Now since signor Gaspare also asks what are the many things a lady at Court should know about, how she ought to converse, and whether her virtues should be such as to contribute to her conversation, I declare that I want her to understand what these gentlemen have said the courtier himself ought to know; and as for the activities we have said are unbecoming to her, I want her at least to have the understanding that people can have of things they do not practise themselves; and this so that she may know how to value and praise the gentlemen concerned in all fairness, according to their merits. And, to repeat in just a few words something of what has already been said, I want this lady to be knowledgeable about literature and painting, to know how to dance and play games, adding a discreet modesty and the ability to give a good impression of herself to the other principles that have been

taught the courtier. And so when she is talking or laughing, playing or jesting, no matter what, she will always be most graceful, and she will converse in a suitable manner with whomever she happens to meet, making use of agreeable witticisms and jokes. And although continence, magnanimity, temperance, fortitude of spirit, prudence and the other virtues may not appear to be relevant in her social encounters with others, I want her to be adorned with these as well, not so much for the sake of good company, though they play a part in this too, as to make her truly virtuous, and so that her virtues, shining through everything she does, make her worthy of honour."

"I am quite surprised," said signor Gaspare with a laugh, "that since you endow women with letters, continence, magnanimity and temperance, you do not want them to govern cities as well, and to make laws and lead armies, while the men stay at home to cook and spin."

The Magnifico replied, also laughing: "Perhaps that would not be so bad, either." 5

Then he added: "Do you not know that Plato, who was certainly no great friend of women, put them in charge of the city and gave all the military duties to the men[15]? Don't you think that we might find many women just as capable of governing cities and armies as men? But I have not imposed these duties on them, since I am fashioning a Court lady and not a queen. I'm fully aware that you would like by implication to repeat the slander that signor Ottaviano[16] made against women yesterday, namely, that they are most imperfect creatures, incapable of any virtuous act, worth very little and quite without dignity compared with men. But truly both you and he would be very much in error if you really thought this.". . .

---

[13] **continence** Self-restraint in matters of the flesh.
[14] **mean** An idea rooted in Aristotle's ethics.

---

[15] **Plato . . . to the men** Plato reasoned that in the ideal state both men and women philosophers should rule (see Plato, *The Republic,* in Chapter 3).
[16] **signor Ottaviano** Ottaviano Fregosa (d. 1524), a noble from Genoa; elected *doge,* or chief magistrate, of Genoa, in 1513; appointed governor of Genoa by King Francis I, of France.

∞

Questions for Critical Thinking

1. Discuss the influence of classical culture on Castiglione's ideal courtier and lady.

2. Are there any lingering influences of Castiglione's portrait of the ideal courtier and lady in the contemporary world today? Discuss.

NICCOLÒ MACHIAVELLI
Selections from *The Prince*

The Prince is a short and strikingly honest handbook on how to win power and keep it. Based on Niccolò Machiavelli's (1469–1527) personal experiences as diplomat and government employee (in the service of his beloved Florence), the book has become the foundation of modern political theory. In his other works, in particular his histories of Italy and Florence, Machiavelli drew upon his classical education and personal experiences to develop this message: Learn from the past what works and what does not. But nowhere else does Machiavelli express his thesis so boldly and succinctly as in *The Prince*: "The end justifies any means."

The Prince's harsh and amoral attitude toward politics sparked controversies when first published. Many of Machiavelli's contemporaries, who were witnessing the end of the medieval Age of Faith and experiencing the dawn of a secular time, were sharply divided over the meaning of his writings. Especially damaging to the book's reputation was its persistent low opinion of human nature. Succeeding generations have debated his analysis of human behavior and his consequent rationale for a strong government. In modern secular society, many readers have come to accept Machiavelli's view that political power, driven by personal or group interests, must be understood in utilitarian and practical terms.

The Prince, a treatise on the art of successful governing, is composed of three parts. The first part, comprising eleven chapters, categorizes and describes the various types of existing governments. The second part, which consists of fourteen chapters, offers advice and examples on winning and maintaining political power. In these fourteen chapters, Machiavelli instructs the ruler on how to raise and organize armies, how to keep subjects loyal, and how to avoid the pitfalls of overconfidence and flattery. Throughout *The Prince*, the author compares and contrasts key traits that make a ruler a success or a failure. He also addresses the issue of fortune—what is now called opportunity—and emphasizes how often it affects a ruler. In the third part—the concluding chapter—Machiavelli calls upon "the prince" to unite the Italians against foreign oppressors and drive them from Italy.

Reading the Selections

Chapters XV, XVI, and XVII appear in the second part of *The Prince*, in which Machiavelli discusses the most effective way for a ruler to govern his subjects. He points out that his discussion is rooted in practical politics, rather than based on imaginary regimes created by writers—a reference to the idealized commonwealths of Plato and medieval Christian authors. In Chapter XV, Machiavelli lists traits for which rulers are praised or blamed—such as being called stubborn or flexible, religious or skeptical—and notes that no ruler could continuously practice the best of these without damaging his ability to govern. Thus, in a crisis the ruler should not shrink from being blamed for vices if they are needed to safeguard the state, though most of the time, the prince should pretend to be what he is not in order to keep his subjects' loyalty.

In Chapter XVI, Machiavelli focuses on the traits of generosity and miserliness and shows, through ancient and current examples, the consequences for rulers who practiced one or the other of them. He concludes, given his dark view of human nature, that it is better for a ruler to be miserly than generous. In Chapter XVII, Machiavelli raises perhaps the most controversial question in the treatise: Is it better for the ruler to be loved or feared? Ideally, the ruler should be both loved and feared, but as this is nearly impossible, then the ruler should be feared. Machiavelli, realizing that fear has its limits, ends on a cautionary note: The "wise prince" must avoid being hated by his subjects, for hatred is the soil out of which rebellions grow.

Chapter XV

The Things for Which Men, and Especially Princes, Are Praised or Blamed

It now remains for us to see how a prince should govern his conduct towards his subjects or his friends. I know that this has often been written about before, and so I hope it will not be thought presumptuous for me to do so, as, especially in discussing this subject, I draw up an original set of rules. But since my intention is to say something that will prove of practical use to the inquirer, I have thought it proper to represent things as they are in real truth, rather than as they are imagined. Many have dreamed up republics and principalities which have never in truth been known to exist; the gulf between how one should live and how one does live is so wide that a man who neglects what is actually done for what should be done learns the way to self-destruction rather than self-preservation. The fact is that a man who wants to act virtuously in every way necessarily comes to grief among so many who are not virtuous. Therefore if a prince wants to maintain his rule he must learn how not to be virtuous, and to make use of this or not according to need.

So leaving aside imaginary things, and referring only to those which truly exist, I say that whenever men are discussed (and especially princes, who are more exposed to view), they are noted for various qualities which earn them either praise or condemnation. Some, for example, are held to be generous, and others miserly (I use the Tuscan[17]

word rather than the word avaricious: we call a man who is mean with what he possesses, miserly, and a man who wants to plunder others, avaricious). Some are held to be benefactors, others are called grasping; some cruel, some compassionate; one man faithless, another faithful; one man effeminate and cowardly, another fierce and courageous; one man courteous, another proud; one man lascivious, another pure; one guileless, another crafty; one stubborn, another flexible; one grave, another frivolous; one religious, another sceptical; and so forth. I know everyone will agree that it would be most laudable if a prince possessed all the qualities deemed to be good among those I have enumerated. But, human nature being what it is, princes cannot possess those qualities, or rather they cannot always exhibit them. So a prince should be so prudent that he knows how to escape the evil reputation attached to those vices which could lose him his state, and how to avoid those vices which are not so dangerous, if he possibly can; but, if he cannot, he need not worry so much about the latter. And then, he must not flinch from being blamed for vices which are necessary for safeguarding the state. This is because, taking everything into account, he will find that some of the things that appear to be virtues will, if he practises them, ruin him, and some of the things that appear to be wicked will bring him security and prosperity.

---

[17] **Tuscan** Having to do with Tuscany, the Italian region, whose capital is Florence, Machiavelli's home.

Chapter XVI

Generosity and Parsimony

So, starting with the first of the qualities I enumerated above, I say it would be splendid if one had a reputation for generosity; nonetheless if your actions are influenced by the desire for such a reputation you will come to grief. This is because if your generosity is good and sincere it may pass unnoticed and it will not save you from being reproached for its opposite. If you want to acquire a reputation for generosity, therefore, you have to be ostentatiously lavish; and a prince acting in that fashion will soon squander all his resources, only to be forced in the end, if he wants to maintain his reputation, to lay excessive burdens on the people, to impose extortionate taxes, and to do everything else he can to raise money. This will start to make his subjects hate him, and, since he will have impoverished himself, he will be generally despised. As a result, because of this generosity of his, having injured

many and rewarded few, he will be vulnerable to the first minor setback, and the first real danger he encounters will bring him to grief. When he realizes this and tries to retrace his path he will immediately be reputed a miser.

So as a prince cannot practise the virtue of generosity in such a way that he is noted for it, except to his cost, he should if he is prudent not mind being called a miser. In time he will be recognized as being essentially a generous man, seeing that because of his parsimony his existing revenues are enough for him, he can defend himself against an aggressor, and he can embark on enterprises without burdening the people. So he proves himself generous to all those from whom he takes nothing, and they are innumerable, and miserly towards all those to whom he gives nothing, and they are few. In our own times great things have been accomplished only by those who have been held miserly, and the others have met disaster. Pope Julius II[18] made use of a reputation for generosity to win the papacy, but subsequently he made no effort to maintain this reputation, because he wanted to be able to finance his wars. The present king of France[19] has been able to wage so many wars without taxing his subjects excessively only because his long-standing parsimony enabled him to meet the additional expenses involved. Were the present king of Spain[20] renowned for his generosity he would not have started and successfully concluded so many enterprises.

So if a prince does not have to rob his subjects, if he can defend himself, if he is not plunged into poverty and shame, if he is not forced to become rapacious, he ought not to worry about being called a miser. Miserliness is one of those vices which sustain his rule. Someone may object: Caesar[21] came to power by virtue of his generosity, and many others, because they practised and were known for their generosity, have risen to the very highest positions. My answer to this is as follows. Either you are already a prince, or you are on the way to becoming one. In the first case, your generosity will be to your cost; in the second, it is certainly necessary to have a reputation for generosity. Caesar was one of those who wanted to establish his

own rule over Rome; but if, after he had established it, he had remained alive and not moderated his expenditure he would have fallen from power.

Again, someone may retort: there have been many princes who have won great successes with their armies, and who have had the reputation of being extremely generous. My reply to this is: the prince gives away what is his own or his subjects', or else what belongs to others. In the first case he should be frugal; in the second, he should indulge his generosity to the full. The prince who campaigns with his armies, who lives by pillaging, sacking, and extortion, disposes of what belongs to aliens; and he must be open-handed, otherwise the soldiers would refuse to follow him. And you can be more liberal with what does not belong to you or your subjects, as Caesar, Cyrus,[22] and Alexander were. Giving away what belongs to strangers in no way affects your standing at home; rather it increases it. You hurt yourself only when you give away what is your own. There is nothing so self-defeating as generosity: in the act of practising it, you lose the ability to do so, and you become either poor and despised or, seeking to escape poverty, rapacious and hated. A prince should try to avoid, above all else, being despised and hated; and generosity results in your being both. Therefore it is wiser to incur the reputation of being a miser, which invites ignominy but not hatred, than to be forced by seeking a name for generosity to incur a reputation for rapacity, which brings you hatred as well as ignominy.

---

[18] **Pope Julius II** (pope 1503–1513).
[19] **king of France** Louis XII (r. 1498–1515).
[20] **king of Spain** Ferdinand V (r. 1474–1504), joint ruler, with Isabella, of Castile; their marriage created the modern state of Spain; served as regent of Castile for his daughter, Joanna the Mad, 1506–1516. As Ferdinand II, he ruled Aragon, 1479–1516.
[21] **Caesar** Julius Caesar (100–44 BCE). Roman general and statesman.

---

[22] **Cyrus** Cyrus II, known as the Great (ca. 585–ca. 529 BCE). King of Persia and founder of the Achaemenian dynasty and empire.

✖

Chapter XVII

Cruelty and Compassion; and Whether It Is Better to Be Loved than Feared, or the Reverse

Taking others of the qualities I enumerated above, I say that a prince should want to have a reputation for compassion rather than for cruelty: nonetheless, he should be careful that he does not make bad use of compassion. Cesare Borgia[23] was accounted cruel; nevertheless, this cruelty of his reformed the Romagna, brought it unity, and restored order and obedience. On reflection, it will be seen

that there was more compassion in Cesare than in the Florentine people, who, to escape being called cruel, allowed Pistoia to be devastated.[24] So a prince should not worry if he incurs reproach for his cruelty so long as he keeps his subjects united and loyal. By making an example or two he will prove more compassionate than those who, being too compassionate, allow disorders which lead to murder and rapine. These nearly always harm the whole community, whereas executions ordered by a prince only affect individuals. A new prince, of all rulers, finds it impossible to avoid a reputation for cruelty, because of the abundant

---

[23] **Cesare Borgia** (1475/1476–1507) Member of an illustrious Italian family of Spanish origin. Son of Pope Alexander VI (d. 1503) by the Roman woman Vannozza Cattanei; appointed bishop of Pamplona in 1491, archbishop of Valencia in 1492, and cardinal in 1493; served as papal legate in 1497 and 1498; gave up cardinal's hat in 1498. Captain general of papal army in 1499; conquered, with French aid, Romagna and the Marches, 1499–1501; made duke by his father, 1501; seized Urbino in 1501; opposed by enemies, including Pope Julius II (elected 1503); imprisoned, 1504–1506; escaped and killed.

---

[24] **Pistoia . . . devastated** Pistoia was a subject-city of Florence, which forcibly restored order there when conflict broke out between two rival factions in 1501–1502. Machiavelli was concerned with this business at first hand.

dangers inherent in a newly won state. Vergil,[25] through the mouth of Dido,[26] says:

> *Res dura, et regni novitas me talia cogunt*
> *Moliri, et late fines custode tueri.*[27]

Nonetheless, a prince should be slow to take action, and should watch that he does not come to be afraid of his own shadow; his behaviour should be tempered by humanity and prudence so that over-confidence does not make him rash or excessive distrust make him unbearable.

From this arises the following question: whether it is better to be loved than feared, or the reverse. The answer is that one would like to be both the one and the other; but because it is difficult to combine them, it is far better to be feared than loved if you cannot be both. One can make this generalization about men: they are ungrateful, fickle, liars, and deceivers, they shun danger and are greedy for profit; while you treat them well, they are yours. They would shed their blood for you, risk their property, their lives, their children, so long, as I said above, as danger is remote; but when you are in danger they turn against you. Any prince who has come to depend entirely on promises and has taken no other precautions ensures his own ruin; friendship which is bought with money and not with greatness and nobility of mind is paid for, but it does not last and it yields nothing. Men worry less about doing an injury to one who makes himself loved than to one who makes himself feared. The bond of love is one which men, wretched creatures that they are, break when it is to their advantage to do so; but fear is strengthened by a dread of punishment which is always effective.

The prince should nonetheless make himself feared in such a way that, if he is not loved, at least he escapes being hated. For fear is quite compatible with an absence of hatred; and the prince can always avoid hatred if he abstains from the property of his subjects and citizens and from their women. If, even so, it proves necessary to execute someone, this should be done only when there is proper justification and manifest reason for it. But above all a prince should abstain from the property of others; because men sooner forget the death of their father than the loss of their patrimony.[28] It is always possible to find pretexts for confiscating someone's property; and a prince who starts to live by rapine always finds pretexts for seizing what belongs to others. On the other hand, pretexts for executing someone are harder to find and they are less easily sustained.

However, when a prince is campaigning with his soldiers and is in command of a large army then he need not worry about having a reputation for cruelty; because, without such a reputation, he can never keep his army united and disciplined. Among the admirable achievements of Hannibal[29] is included this: that although he led a huge army, made up of countless different races, on foreign campaigns, there was never any dissension, either among the troops themselves or against their leader, whether things were going well or badly. For this, his inhuman cruelty was wholly responsible. It was this, along with his countless other qualities, which made him feared and respected by his soldiers. If it had not been for his cruelty, his other qualities would not have been enough. The historians, having given little thought to this, on the one hand admire what Hannibal achieved, and on the other condemn what made his achievements possible.

That his other qualities would not have been enough by themselves can be proved by looking at Scipio,[30] a man unique in his own time and through all recorded history. His armies mutinied against him in Spain, and the only reason for this was his excessive leniency, which allowed his soldiers more licence than was good for military discipline. Fabius Maximus[31] reproached him for this in the Senate and called him a corrupter of the Roman legions.[32] Again, when the Locri[33] were plundered by one of Scipio's officers, he neither gave them satisfaction nor punished his officer's insubordination; and this was all because of his having too lenient a nature. By way of excuse for him some senators argued that many men were better at not making mistakes themselves than at correcting them in others. But in time Scipio's lenient nature would have spoilt his fame and glory had he continued to indulge it during his command; when he lived under orders from the Senate, however, this fatal characteristic of his was not only concealed but even brought him glory.

So, on this question of being loved or feared, I conclude that since some men love as they please but fear when the prince pleases, a wise prince should rely on what he controls, not on what he cannot control. He should only endeavour, as I said, to escape being hated.

---

[25] **Vergil** Also spelled Virgil (70–19 BCE); Roman poet (see *The Aeneid* in Chapter 5).

[26] **Dido** Legendary Queen of Carthage. Originally a Phoenician princess from Tyre, she fled to Africa and founded Carthage. Vergil made her tragic love affair with Aeneas, the founder of ancient Rome, the unifying theme for the first four books of the *Aeneid*.

[27] ***Res . . . custode tueri.*** "Harsh necessity, and the newness of my kingdom, force me to do such things and to guard my frontiers everywhere" (*Aeneid* I, 563).

[28] **patrimony** An estate inherited from one's father.

[29] **Hannibal** (247–183 BCE) Carthaginian general. In the Second Punic War, led his troops from Spain, across the Alps, and into Italy, where he fought various battles and eventually marched on Rome, 218–211 BCE; Romans held on and waited him out; recalled to Carthage in 203, and defeated at battle of Zama in 202 BCE; headed Carthaginian government, 202–195 BCE; fled to Asia Minor; committed suicide.

[30] **Scipio** Scipio Africanus (236–184/183 BCE) Roman general. In the Second Punic War, led army in Spain, 210–206 BCE; led Roman invasion of Carthage; defeated **Hannibal** at battle of Zama in 202 BCE.

[31] **Fabius Maximus** (d. 203 BCE) Called *Cunctator*, the "Delayer." Roman general, famous for his delaying strategy against Hannibal in the Second Punic War. Fabius successfully made quick incursions against Hannibal's forces, while avoiding set battles. A group of English socialists in the late 1800s adopted the name Fabian in honor of this strategy.

[32] **legions** Roman army units, each composed of three thousand to six thousand foot soldiers with cavalry.

[33] **Locri** Ancient city founded by the Greeks, located on the eastern side of the "toe" of Italy; Locri changed sides between Rome and its enemies until it was captured by **Scipio Africanus** and made Roman, in the Second Punic War.

Questions for Critical Thinking

1. According to Machiavelli, which is more important for a prince: to be feared or to be loved? Explain.

2. *The Prince* has been charged with creating the mind-set called "Machiavellian," meaning that "the end justifies any means." Is this a valid judgment of Machiavelli's ideas? Explain.

MICHELANGELO
Poems

Michelangelo Buonarroti (1475–1564) and Leonardo da Vinci (1452–1519) are recognized today as the most influential and famous artists of the High Renaissance. Michelangelo, like Leonardo da Vinci, was a Universal Man, a person blessed and cursed with many talents. With his conflicted sense of his successes and failures, a bigger-than-life ego, a commanding physical presence, and a driving ambition, he found himself constantly at odds with his patrons and always seeking approval from his friends. Nonetheless, he was honored and admired in his own times for his contributions to the arts. Painters and sculptors have looked to him for inspiration and as their ideal ever since his death, and posterity considers him to be the personification of the Italian Renaissance.

He spent most of his career serving the powerful Medici family in Florence and the popes in Rome—a situation which, over his lifetime, intensified his troubled relationships with supporters, complicated his personal life, and channeled his creativity into nearly every art form. Despite his fluctuating moods and being overburdened with too many commissions and commitments, Michelangelo left the world some of the most lasting works in the history of art.

While his reputation and legacy rest principally on his paintings, sculpture, architecture, and urban planning, Michelangelo is also known for his literary contributions, especially his poems. He wrote over three hundred, including sonnets and madrigals, philosophical poems, and love poems. The three central themes running through his poems were love, both physical and Platonic, or spiritual; the passing of time, or the phases of life and death; and religious faith, especially the yearning for the love of God, and salvation. They also record his lifelong conflict between his admiration for classical or pagan values, which he acquired as a young artist while living in Florence, and his Christian beliefs and faith, which deepened in his later years.

Michelangelo, though considering himself to be an amateur poet, wanted his poems to be published during his lifetime. He was not a polished stylist, and literary critics do not judge his works to be "high" poetry. However, what he said in his poems—the outpouring of his inner thoughts—has endeared them to readers. His literary efforts reveal his creative talents and processes as a visual artist because, in his poems, Michelangelo broods over his works and what they mean to him and others. His sense of success and failure weaves in and out of the poems, and they leave a self-portrait of a person who was constantly in doubt about himself and life.

Reading the Selections

Poems 166 and 248 touch upon some of Michelangelo's most personal concerns and pay tribute to two individuals who had inspired and influenced him—one a female friend and the other a historical figure. Poem 166, a madrigal, was written to Vittoria Colonna (1490–1547), a woman whom he knew in Rome. She was the subject of many of his poems, in which he expressed his love and respect for her, his thoughts on religion, and the prospect of death. She seemed to be the only woman to whom he was ever closely attached, even though their relationship was clearly intellectual and spiritual. They communicated with one another for over a decade, and she became his inspiration and ideal. She was, in his life, what Beatrice was to Dante (see *The Divine Comedy* in Chapter 10) and Laura was to Petrarch (see the *Canzoniere* and "Letter to Posterity" in Chapter 11). Poem 248 is a paean, or tribute, to Dante in which Michelangelo compares his life to Dante's life and legacy.

Poem 285, one of his best-known sonnets, was written around 1552–1554 in the later years of his life, and focuses on old age. Michelangelo laments what he considers to be what was once an idol—art—and how he, now, faces his demise. In his later years, confronting his own mortality and worried about the future of the Catholic Church in its struggle with the newly unleashed Protestant Reformation movement, Michelangelo wrote several poems expressing these themes.

Poems

166

My eyes can easily see your beautiful face[34]
wherever it appears, near or far away;
but my feet, lady, are prevented from bearing
my arms or either hand to that same place.[35]

The soul, the intellect complete and sound,   1
more free and unfettered, can rise through the eyes
up to your lofty beauty; but great ardor
gives no such privilege to the human body,
which, weighed down and mortal, and still lacking
    wings,
can hardly follow the flight of a little angel;   10
so sight alone can take pride and pleasure in doing so.[36]
  If you have as much power in heaven as here among us,
make my whole body nothing but an eye:
let there be no part of me that can't enjoy you.

---

[34] **My eyes can easily see your beautiful face** The opening refers to the Neoplatonic argument that the human eyes see human or bodily beauty, but there is a higher or spiritual beauty that can be "seen" at a higher level. Thus, Michelangelo sees Vittoria Colonna's physical beauty (actually, she was rather homely), but her beauty is only a step to a higher level of beautiful, which is on a metaphysical plane.

[35] **my arms or either hand to that same place** That is, so I, Michelangelo, might be able to embrace you, Vittoria.

---

[36] **so sight alone can take pride and pleasure in doing so** This means that only the eyes can follow her.

248

He came down from heaven, and once he had seen   1
the just hell and the merciful one, he went
back up, with his body alive, to contemplate God,
in order to give us the true light of it all.[37]
  For such a shining star, who with his rays
undeservedly brightened the nest where I was born,[38]

the whole wicked world would not be enough reward;
only you,[39] who created him, could ever be that.
  I speak of Dante, for his deeds were poorly
appreciated by that ungrateful people   10
who fail to welcome only righteous men.[40]
  If only I were he! To be born to such good fortune,
to have his harsh exile along with his virtue,
I would give up the happiest state in the world.

---

[37] **He came down from heaven . . . as the true light of it all.** These four lines refer to Dante, who, born as a human, made a journey through Hell, Purgatory, and Heaven in *The Divine Comedy.*

[38] **undeservedly brightened the nest where I was born** The city of Florence, home to Dante and Michelangelo.

---

[39] **only you** God.

[40] **who fail to welcome only righteous men** Both Dante and Michelangelo were exiled from Florence.

285

The voyage of my life at last has reached,   1
across a stormy sea, in a fragile boat,[41]
the common port[42] all must pass through, to give
an accounting for every evil and pious deed.
    So now I recognize how laden with error
was the affectionate fantasy
that made art an idol and sovereign to me,
like all things men want in spite of their best interests.[43]

What will become of all my thoughts of love,
once gay and foolish, now that I'm nearing two deaths?[44]   10
I'm certain of one and the other looms over me.
    Neither painting nor sculpture will be able any longer
to calm my soul, now turned toward that divine love
that opened his arms on the cross to take us in.[45]

---

[41] **across a stormy sea, in a fragile boat** Life is like being in a stormy sea in a small, light boat.
[42] **the common port** Death.
[43] **So now I recognize . . . of their best interests.** This four-line verse is a confession from Michelangelo that he, like most men, pursued worldly goals and ambition—in this case, art—which is sinful and distracts from the true meaning of life.

---

[44] **two deaths** The death of the body, which is certain, and the fear of the death of the soul, which would be even worse.
[45] **that opened his arms on the cross to take us in** The image of Christ opening his arms to embrace sinners. Michelangelo drew such a scene and also used this image in other poems.

※

Questions for Critical Thinking

1. How does Michelangelo compare his respect and admiration for Vittoria Colonna and Dante? Which do you think is more persuasive?

2. Discuss the major themes in all three poems, and note how they are manifested in images and references.

CREDITS

LEON BATTISTA ALBERTI, From *ON PAINTING*, translated by Cecil Grayson. Copyright © 1972 by Cecil Grayson. Reprinted with the permission of the Estate of Cecil Grayson.

Excerpt from *LEON BATTISTA ALBERTI'S "DINNER PIECES"*, translated by David Marsh. MRTS Volume 45 (Binghamton, NY 1987). Copyright Arizona Board of Regents for Arizona State University. Reprinted with permission.

APPOLLONIUS OF RHODES, From *THE VOYAGE OF ARGO (THE ARGONAUTICA)*, translated by E. V. Rieu (Penguin Classics 1959, Second edition 1971). Copyright © the Estate of E. V. Rieu, 1959, 1971. Reprinted with permission of Penguin Books Ltd.

ST. THOMAS AQUINAS, "Fifth Article" from *SUMMA THEOLOGICA, VOLUME II*, translated by the Fathers of the English Dominican Province. Copyright © 1947 by Benzinger Publishing Company. Reproduced with permission of Benzinger Publishing Company.

ARISTOTLE, From *CLASSICAL LITERARY CRITICISM* translated with an introduction by T. Dorsch (Penguin Books Ltd., 1965, 1967, 1969, 1970). Copyright © T. S. Dorsch, 1965. Reproduced with permission of Penguin Books Ltd.

"Politica" translated by Jowett from Politics and Economics from *THE OXFORD TRANSLATION OF ARISTOTLE* edited by W. D. Ross (Volume 10, 1921). Reprinted by permission of Oxford University Press.

ST. AUGUSTINE, From *CONCERNING THE CITY OF GOD AGAINST THE PAGANS*, translated by Henry Bettenson, introduction by David Knowles (Pelican Books, 1972). Translation © Henry Bettenson, 1972. Introduction copyright © David Knowles. Reproduced with permission of Penguin Books Ltd.

From *CONFESSIONS* by Saint Augustine, translated with an introduction by R. S. Pine-Coffin (Penguin Classics, 1961). Copyright © R. S. Pine-Coffin, 1961. Reproduced with permission of Penguin Books Ltd.

MARCUS AURELIUS, Excerpts from *MARCUS AURELIUS: MEDITATIONS*, translated by Farquharson (1998). Used by permission of Oxford University Press.

BEDE, From *BEDE: ECCLESIASTICAL HISTORY OF THE ENGLISH PEOPLE*, translated by Leo Sherley-Price (Penguin Classics 1955, Revised edition 1968). Translation copyright © Leo Sherley-Price, 1955, 1968. Reproduced with permission from Penguin Books Ltd.

ST. BENEDICT, *"The Rule of St. Benedict"* from *A SOURCE BOOK FOR MEDIEVAL HISTORY* by Oliver Joseph Thatcher & Edgar Holmes McNeal, Copyright © 1905 Scribner.

Selections from *BEOWULF* edited with an introduction, glossary and notes by Michael Alexander (Penguin Classics, 1995). Copyright © Michael Alexander, 1995. Reproduced with permission from Penguin Books Ltd.

BIBLE, Reprinted from the *TAHAKH: THE HOLY SCRIPTURES* by permission of the University of Nebraska Press. Copyright © 1985 The Jewish Publication Society, Philadelphia.

Matthew 1:18-4:25, 5:1-7:29; Corinthians 13:1-13 from *THE REVISED STANDARD VERSION OF THE HOLY BIBLE*. Copyright © 1946, 1952, 1971 by the Division of Christian Education of the National Council of the Churches of Christ in the USA. Reprinted with permission.

GIOVANNI BOCCACCIO, "Introduction," by Giovanni Boccaccio, "First Day, Third Story", translated by Peter Bondanella & Mark Musa, from *THE DECAMERON* by Giovanni Boccaccio, translated by Peter Bondanella and Mark Musa, copyright © 1982 by Mark Musa and Peter Bondanella. Used by permission of Dutton Signet, a division of Penguin Group (USA) Inc.

BOETHIUS, From *THE CONSOLATION OF PHILOSOPHY*, translated with an introduction by V. E. Watts (Penguin, 1969). Copyright © V. E. Watts, 1969. Reproduced with permission of Penguin Books Ltd.

INDEX